THE SIMPLE ART OF
EatingWell®
COOKBOOK

Library of Congress Cataloging-in-Publication Data has been applied for.

ISBN 978-1-58157-219-3

Published by The Countryman Press, P.O. Box 748, Woodstock, VT 05091

Distributed by W.W. Norton & Company, Inc., 500 Fifth Avenue, New York, NY 10110
Printed in China by R.R. Donnelley
10 9 8 7 6 5 4 3 2 1

Photography by Ken Burris
Front cover photograph by Ian Batchelor/
StockFood Creative/Getty Images

THE SIMPLE ART OF
EatingWell®
COOKBOOK

400 EASY RECIPES, TIPS AND TECHNIQUES

FOR DELICIOUS, HEALTHY MEALS

By Jessie Price & the EATINGWELL Test Kitchen
Principal photography by Ken Burris

AUTHORS | Jessie Price & the EATINGWELL Test Kitchen

TEST KITCHEN

TEST KITCHEN MANAGER | Stacy Fraser

ASSOCIATE EDITOR: FOOD | Carolyn Malcoun

ASSISTANT EDITOR | Hilary Meyer

RECIPE DEVELOPER, TESTER | Carolyn Casner

RECIPE DEVELOPER, FOOD STYLIST | Katie Webster

FOOD STYLISTS | Patsy Jamieson, Susan Herr

TEST KITCHEN INTERN | Katelyn McCarthy

ART DIRECTOR | Michael J. Balzano

PHOTOGRAPHER | Ken Burris

DESIGNER | Amanda Coyle

MANAGING EDITOR | Wendy S. Ruopp

ASSISTANT MANAGING EDITOR | Alesia Depot

PRODUCTION MANAGER | Jennifer B. Brown

DEPUTY EDITOR: FEATURES & NUTRITION | Nicci Micco, M.S.

ASSOCIATE EDITOR: NUTRITION | Brierley Wright, M.S., R.D.

DIETITIAN & NUTRITION ADVISOR | Sylvia Geiger, M.S., R.D.

RESEARCH EDITOR | Anne Bliss

EDITORIAL INTERNS | Nicole McDermott, Samantha Merrill

INDEXER | Amy Novick, BackSpace Indexing

EATINGWELL MEDIA GROUP

CEO | Tom Witschi

EDITORIAL DIRECTOR | Lisa Gosselin

Table of Contents

Green Salad with Asparagus & Peas

The Simple Art of EatingWell

by Jessie Price

When I was a kid, my mom planted a big vegetable garden every summer. She grew enormous, deep green-blue kale with leaves that were sturdy and curly. On summer nights when it was too hot to cook, she'd wash a sinkful of that kale, pile it up in a giant wooden salad bowl and toss it raw (yes, raw, and this was not that fancy baby kale you might find in a nice mesclun mix at the farmers' market) with hard-boiled eggs, mushrooms, a little bacon and a super-tangy vinaigrette. It was her version of the classic spinach salad. My sister and I gobbled it down. Kale? Yes, we loved kale.

Unlike kids today, we *did* eat our vegetables; we loved them because Mom knew the secrets of making them taste good, like adding flavorful bits of bacon or taming the bitterness of kale with vinaigrette. That didn't mean we never ate rich foods you might think are "unhealthy." She also made amazing baked macaroni & cheese with sharp Cheddar, milk and fresh toasty breadcrumbs on top.

The truth is, in both cases, we were simply eating well. Eating natural, homemade, satisfying food. It was food that both tasted good *and* provided the nutrients our bodies needed.

After decades of consuming fast food and processed snacks, following fad diets, downing energy drinks and popping supplements, Americans are starting to turn back to the simple art of eating well. Perhaps the wake-up call is that some of the biggest killers in our country—heart disease and type 2 diabetes—could be reduced with a healthier diet. Or that nearly one in three children is overweight or obese. Everywhere there's a renewed interest in cooking and where our food comes from. We like to think that the change has come with the realization that—armed with the right tools, recipes and nutritional information—you *can* make food that is both delicious *and* healthy, quick *and* easy, satisfying *and* slimming.

At EATINGWELL, our tagline is "Where Good Taste Meets Good Health." We've been working on that concept for more than 20 years, testing recipes, vetting them nutritionally and publishing them in EATINGWELL Magazine, in EATINGWELL books and online at *eatingwell.com*.

We know the recipes are going to work reliably when you try them at home, because we taste, test, taste and then test again (on average seven times) to make sure each recipe is clearly written and easy to follow. We test each recipe on both gas and electric stoves, having both culinary-school grads and home cooks try them. The cooks in the EATINGWELL Test Kitchen spend hours in supermarkets each week shopping for ingredients and choosing ones that are readily accessible. If our readers didn't understand our recipes we'd hear from them, and thanks to reader feedback we know that carefully explaining instructions, giving advice on where to find ingredients and showing step-by-step photos of trickier techniques is essential to making cooking at home easy for cooks of every level. In this book we've included hundreds of tips and techniques, ranging from how to make your own breadcrumbs (*you can use those on top of our mac & cheese on page 232*) to how to make homemade gnocchi (*page 248*).

We know that the recipes are delicious, because we hear about that from our readers too. What makes this cookbook different is that the recipes are not just from one or two people: we work with many of the best chefs and well-known cookbook authors from around the world. Among those who have contributed to this book are Rick Bayless, Deborah Madison, Bruce Aidells and Mark Bittman.

We know the recipes in this book can also make you healthier. Each recipe has been reviewed and approved by a registered dietitian (*for our nutritional guidelines, see page 473*). We want to make it mouthwateringly easy to follow your doctors' advice: eat fish high in omega-3s twice a week, get your daily servings of fruits and vegetables, eat heart-healthy whole grains. We do this by using the same types of secrets my mom taught me—using healthy oils, limiting added sugars, swapping low-fat dairy for higher-fat dairy and using herbs and spices to add flavor rather than loads of butter, cream and salt.

This book can change your life because it provides simple, healthy and quick solutions to one of the biggest dilemmas in our increasingly crowded lives: what to have for dinner. There are over 200 recipes in this book that take less than 45 minutes to prepare start to finish. (*See page 495 for a list of quick entrees.*) When you use the hundreds of recipes, tips, tools and techniques that are sprinkled throughout this book you will not only start to prefer cooking the EATINGWELL way, you too will make healthy eating a way of life.

How to Eat Well for Life

1. Load Up on Fruits & Vegetables. Since our offices in Charlotte, Vermont, are surrounded by farmland, our recipes are inspired by what we find growing each season, in much the same way my mother's dinners were decided by what sprouted in her garden. Our recipes start with each season's freshest fruits and vegetables (that's why you'll always see a whole fruit or vegetable on our magazine covers).

At present, only one in four Americans gets the 5 to 13 daily servings of fruits and vegetables the USDA recommends. Simply upping your consumption of fruits and vegetables—foods packed with vitamins, minerals and antioxidants—helps to lower your risk of heart disease and diabetes. Not to mention all the other benefits: for example, beta carotene in carrots and sweet potatoes helps keep your eyes, bones and immune system healthy, and lycopene in tomatoes, watermelon and pink grapefruit may help protect against prostate and breast cancers. With foods like this, who wants supplements?

Most of our recipes (from pizzas to desserts) include plenty of fruits and vegetables. Even meat and poultry dishes, such as Grilled Duck with Strawberry-Fig Sauce (*page 343*), shine with a fruit-filled sauce. When in doubt, our recipe developers and testers always add more vegetables. Sautéed onions, shredded zucchini or baby spinach are easy to incorporate into many dishes. And don't worry if you can't always find fresh vegetables or fruits. Frozen ones are great too because they're usually picked at their prime, when they have the most nutrients, and then those nutrients are sealed in when they're frozen.

2. Make the Most of Meats. Protein is essential for our bodies. It's a component of every cell in our body, it helps us build and repair tissues and gives us energy. The foods highest in protein, such as beef, chicken and seafood, often are at the heart of a meal. And that's where they should be—at the heart of it, not the whole meal. Americans have become used to making a big slab of meat the center of the meal, whereas in many other cultures (think of an Italian meat sauce or a Chinese stir-fry) meat is part of but not the entire plate. We recommend that you fill just a quarter of your plate with a protein, such as chicken, fish, tofu, lean beef or pork, a quarter with a whole grain like brown rice or a starch like a potato, and half with vegetables.

In EatingWell recipes we use the USDA recommended 3 ounces of cooked meat per serving. Plus we use lean cuts of beef and pork and show you how to make rich-tasting chicken dishes without the skin (which adds as much as 4 grams of fat). Try the Baked Chicken with Onions & Leeks (*page 331*) for proof.

3. Serve More Seafood. The American Heart Association recommends eating two servings of fish and seafood a week. Why? Seafood is a good lean source of protein. And many fish, especially fatty fish like salmon, tuna and sardines, have something that's hard to get from other foods: omega-3 fatty acids and specifically DHA and EPA, healthy fats that have been linked to improving everything from heart health to brain functioning to depression. We love seafood in everything from soups and salads to main dishes. Who knew that you may become happier, smarter and healthier just by serving up Grilled Salmon & Zucchini with Red Pepper Sauce (*page 295*)?

4. Go for Good Fats. Not all fat is bad—and some, like the unsaturated fat in olive oil and canola, may actually help reduce "bad" LDL cholesterol, which in turn may help to lower your risk of heart disease. But regardless of what kind of fat we use in a recipe, we still use all fats in moderation because they are high in calories. Over the years, we've perfected plenty of ways to make cooking with less fat easy and tasty too. For instance, make sure you have a set of nonstick or cast-iron skillets so you can cook with teaspoons of oil rather than tablespoons. Skip tossing cooked vegetables in butter. Instead try roasting them with a little olive oil (*see page 165 for a guide to roasting vegetables*) or serve them with a squeeze of lemon and a sprinkling of fresh herbs. Try replacing some of the butter in baked goods with better-for-you canola oil.

The myth that you need butter and cream to make food taste better is just that: a myth. As for dairy—milk, sour cream and yogurt are good sources of calcium, which helps keep your bones strong and healthy. But we like to cut down saturated fat without sacrificing flavor by replacing them with low-fat or nonfat versions.

5. Make It Flavorful. Probably the biggest criticism of "healthy" cooking has been that it is bland or flavorless. It doesn't have to be—and our recipes certainly aren't. Use plenty of spices, herbs and citrus to make your food taste great. And use salt, too—it is essential to bring out the flavors in food—but it's wise to watch your sodium intake, as sodium can contribute to high blood pressure, which can lead to heart disease. The USDA recommends consuming less than 2,300 mg of sodium (about 1 teaspoon salt) daily. The majority of Americans' sodium intake comes from processed foods, so if you're cooking with mostly whole, natural foods, you're already on your way to keeping your sodium intake in check.

For other, less "virtuous" seasonings, such as bacon or cheese, we choose varieties with big flavor like extra-sharp Cheddar cheese or a super-smoky bacon. That way you can add a moderate amount to your food for the biggest impact. That's what my mom did with her kale salad and I knew that was good, even as a kid.

6. Be a Savvy Shopper. One of the best ways to make healthy cooking a breeze is to be a smart shopper. That starts with planning meals and making a detailed shopping list grouped by the layout of your supermarket before you head to the store. It makes your trip much less stressful (not to mention faster) if you don't have to backtrack when you're already at the register because you realize that you forgot the carrots. Concentrate your shopping in the outer sections of most supermarkets—produce, seafood, meat and dairy departments—where the healthiest and least-processed ingredients tend to be. In the freezer section, head for frozen vegetables and fruits. In the inner aisles, go for healthy staples like whole grains, canned or dried beans, canned tomatoes, spices and plenty of tasty condiments.

And when you're picking up those foods that have nutrition labels, make sure you always read them. Check the nutrition information and also look at what ingredients are in the product. A general rule: the simpler the ingredient list is to read, the better. The label's a great spot to look out for trans fats—don't just rely on the marketing that says "0 grams trans fats," but check to make sure there are no partially hydrogenated oils in the ingredient list. (*For more on how to read a label, turn to page 474.*)

We also believe in keeping a well-stocked pantry. When your pantry is full of staples, you'll find you won't need to run to the store in the middle of cooking dinner to get a bottle of soy sauce. Plus it makes it easier to improvise a dinner on the fly when you don't already have something planned. Ingredients like pasta, canned beans and canned fish can be the basis of spur-of-the-moment meals. (*You'll find three easy soups that can be made from pantry staples on page 62 and our recommendations for what to keep stocked in a healthy pantry on page 480.*)

7. Eat What You Love. Eating well is not about deprivation—it's about that good feeling you get when you eat something that is flavorful, wholesome and satisfying. No food should be off limits. Studies show that depriving yourself of the foods you love, especially in the name of dieting, may cause you to overeat later. The art of EATINGWELL is about embracing a delicious and healthy way of eating that you can sustain for your whole life.

That's why we believe you should satisfy your cravings. We love sweets, but when we develop our recipes for desserts and baked goods we limit added sugars. (Added sugars of any kind—whether it's corn syrup, white sugar, maple syrup or agave—all add calories and don't offer any nutritional value.) So go ahead and enjoy a slice of that Dark Cherry Bundt Cake (*page 411*). Savor it slowly so you really enjoy it without feeling guilty. But the bottom line is that maintaining a healthy weight comes down to balancing the amount of calories you eat with the amount you expend during the day. So if you're going to have that piece of cake, think about cutting back somewhere else or exercising a little longer.

8. Make Cooking Fun. If you never learned to cook or you think cooking is drudgery, this book will change your mind. Cooking should be relaxing, creative and delicious. Here at EATINGWELL we keep things interesting by constantly looking for new inspiration from top chefs, foreign countries, our readers, even taco trucks.

If you're not experienced in the kitchen, perhaps you cook the same few things over and over. You can start broadening your skills by slowly adding new, easy recipes to your repertoire—pick one new recipe to try each week. The more things you cook, the more confident you'll feel about experimenting and the more fun you'll have in the kitchen. Think of this book as your guide to healthy, delicious and enjoyable cooking, every step of the way. Try starting with the delicious menus on the following pages.

Lebanese Potato Salad

Menus

MEATLESS MONDAY
Inside-Out Lasagna (*page 237*)
Spring Green Salad with Rouille Dressing (*page 85*)
Chocolate-Covered Brownie Bites (*page 385*)

20 MINUTES TO DINNER
Greek Salad with Sardines (*page 96*)
Warm whole-wheat pita bread
Roasted Pineapple (*page 385*)

FIRE UP THE GRILL
Tomato-Herb Marinated Flank Steak (*page 363*)
Pesto-Topped Grilled Zucchini (*page 164*)
Lebanese Potato Salad (*page 148*)

SLOW-COOKER HEAVEN
Greek Chicken & Vegetable Ragout (*page 336*)
Brown basmati rice with Mint & Feta seasoning (*page 185*)
Green Salad with Asparagus & Peas (*page90*)

PACK A PICNIC
Picnic Oven-Fried Chicken (*page 331*)
Cheddar Cornmeal Biscuits with Chives (*page 189*)
Crunchy Bok Choy Slaw (*page 112*)
Stone-Fruit Bars (*page 446*)

PIZZA NIGHT
Pesto & Spinach Pizza (*page 227*)
Sautéed Mushroom Salad (*page 93*)
Gingersnap-Banana Frozen Yogurt (*page 385*)

KIDS RULE
Steak & Potato Kebabs with Creamy Cilantro Sauce (*page 364*)
Roasted Acorn Squash with Cider Drizzle (*page 163*)
Vanilla-Orange Freezer Pops (*page 388*)

LAZY SUMMER SUNDAY BRUNCH
Tomato-Jalapeño Bloody Mary (*page 46*)
Mushroom & Wild Rice Frittata (*page 458*)
Roasted potatoes with Mustard-Rosemary seasoning
    (*page 150*)
Skillet-Seared Tomatoes with Melted Gruyère (*page 159*)
Banana-Blueberry-Almond Quick Bread (*page 467*)

Banana-Blueberry-Almond Quick Bread

Picnic Oven-Fried Chicken

Roasted Acorn Squash with Cider Drizzle

Real Cornbread

Spicy Green Salad with Soy & Roasted Garlic Dressing

Spicy Lamb Meatballs in Tomato Sauce

Roasted Garlic & Meyer Lemon-Rubbed Turkey

Salty Chihuahua

Roasted Garlic Guacamole

Smoked Trout Crackers with Lemon-Dill Mayonnaise

Scallop & Shrimp Dumplings

Appetizers & Drinks

Spiced Spanish Almonds

H↑F H♥H

MAKES: 3 cups

ACTIVE TIME: 10 minutes | TOTAL: 1½ hours

TO MAKE AHEAD: Store in an airtight container for up to 1 week.

Salty, sweet and laced with smoke—the perfect kind of almond for a party. If any remain the next day, savor them over a salad topped with sliced ripe pears and shaved Manchego cheese. **Shopping Tip:** *Spanish Marcona almonds have recently become more popular and more available. They're flatter than ordinary almonds, with a richer flavor. Always skinned, most Marcona almonds have already been sautéed in oil and lightly salted when you get them. For this recipe, select unsalted and oil-free nuts if you can, though either will work well. Find them at specialty stores or online at* tienda.com.

¼	cup light brown sugar
2	teaspoons ground cumin
1	teaspoon hot paprika
1	teaspoon dried thyme
1	teaspoon kosher salt
¼	teaspoon cayenne pepper
1	large egg white
1	tablespoon water
1	pound (about 3 cups) Marcona *or* raw whole almonds (*see Shopping Tip*)

1. Preheat oven to 275°F. Coat a large rimmed baking sheet with cooking spray.

2. Whisk brown sugar, cumin, paprika, thyme, salt and cayenne in a large bowl. Whisk egg white and water in a medium bowl until foamy. Add almonds and stir to coat; pour through a sieve to drain off excess egg white. Transfer the almonds to the bowl of spices; stir well to coat. Spread evenly on the prepared baking sheet.

3. Bake the almonds for 30 minutes. Stir, reduce the oven temperature to 200° and bake until the almonds are dry and golden, about 30 minutes more. Let cool before serving, about 20 minutes.

PER 1/4-CUP SERVING: 245 calories; 19 g fat (1 g sat, 12 g mono); 0 mg cholesterol; 12 g carbohydrate; 4 g added sugars; 8 g protein; 5 g fiber; 99 mg sodium; 5 mg potassium.

EatingWell Tip

Keep almonds on hand and store them in the freezer to keep them fresh. Spice them up for an appetizer, toss them in a salad or eat a handful for a snack. **Almonds have been shown to reduce cholesterol levels.**

Tomato Toast with Sardines & Mint

MAKES: 12 toasts

ACTIVE TIME: 15 minutes | TOTAL: 30 minutes

TO MAKE AHEAD: Cover and refrigerate the sardine mixture (Step 2) for up to 2 days.

This recipe was developed for EATINGWELL *by Washington, D.C.-based chef Barton Seaver, who is a passionate advocate for the health of the oceans. Seaver wanted to create a recipe featuring the humble sardine because its wild population is healthy and stable. We think he has truly elevated the canned sardine with this fresh-tasting and simple appetizer.*

- 1 **4-ounce can boneless, skinless sardines packed in olive oil, preferably smoked**
- 2 **tablespoons finely chopped fresh mint**
- 2 **teaspoons extra-virgin olive oil**
- ⅛ **teaspoon salt**
- 3 **slices multigrain bread** *or* **12 slices baguette, preferably whole-grain**
- ½ **medium ripe tomato**
- 1 **tablespoon very thinly sliced yellow onion**

1. Preheat oven to 350°F.

2. Flake sardines with a fork into a mixing bowl. (The pieces should not be mashed, but should be no bigger than a dime.) Add mint, oil and salt; toss gently to combine.

3. If using whole slices of bread, cut off the crusts and cut each into four triangles. Place the triangles or baguette slices on a baking sheet and bake until crispy and golden brown, 12 to 14 minutes. As soon as you remove them from the oven, rub each slice with the cut side of the tomato. As you progress, the tomato will break down until only the skin remains.

4. Top each toast with about 1½ teaspoons of the sardine mixture. Top the sardine mixture with a couple of onion slices and serve immediately.

PER TOAST: 41 calories; 2 g fat (0 g sat, 1 g mono); 5 mg cholesterol; 3 g carbohydrate; 0 g added sugars; 3 g protein; 1 g fiber; 113 mg sodium; 63 mg potassium.

EatingWell Tip

Take a lesson from Spain and try rubbing toasty bread with a tomato half rather than oil or butter. You'll **save calories and fat** but still get plenty of flavor.

◄ Smoked Trout Crackers with Lemon-Dill Mayonnaise

MAKES: 20 crackers
ACTIVE TIME: 15 minutes | TOTAL: 15 minutes

A simple lemon-dill mayonnaise adds a touch of sophistication to smoked trout on crackers.

- ⅓   **cup low-fat mayonnaise**
- 1   **teaspoon freshly grated lemon zest**
- 1   **tablespoon lemon juice**
- 1   **tablespoon minced fresh dill**
- ½   **teaspoon freshly ground pepper**
- 20   **thin whole-grain crackers**
- 4   **ounces thinly sliced smoked trout**

Combine mayonnaise, lemon zest, lemon juice, dill and pepper in a small bowl. Top crackers with a spoonful of the lemon-dill mayonnaise; divide trout among the crackers.

PER CRACKER: 22 calories; 1 g fat (0 g sat, 0 g mono); 4 mg cholesterol; 2 g carbohydrate; 0 g added sugars; 2 g protein; 0 g fiber; 40 mg sodium; 42 mg potassium.

EatingWell Tip

Read the label when you're shopping for crackers and pick ones with **fiber-rich whole grains**, as few ingredients as possible and no hydrogenated oils, a source of trans fats. We like a number of the crackers imported from Scandinavia, especially Finn Crisps.

Caramelized Onion & Shrimp Bruschetta

MAKES: 24 bruschetta
ACTIVE TIME: 50 minutes | TOTAL: 1 hour 20 minutes
TO MAKE AHEAD: Prepare through Step 3, cover and refrigerate for up to 3 days. Bring the spread to room temperature before assembling.

Caramelized onions and golden raisins add sweet balance to shrimp in this easy bruschetta. It can be assembled in just a few minutes if you make the onion spread ahead of time. For a vegetarian option, top with crumbled feta.

- ½   **cup golden raisins**
- 2   **tablespoons canola oil**
- 4   **cups chopped yellow onions**
- 2   **tablespoons capers, rinsed and chopped**
- 2   **tablespoons minced fresh dill**
- ½   **teaspoon freshly ground pepper**
- ¼   **teaspoon salt**
- 24   **thin slices baguette, toasted**
- 24   **peeled and deveined cooked shrimp (26-30 per pound)**

1. Place raisins in a small bowl and cover with boiling water; set aside for 30 minutes.

2. Meanwhile, heat oil in a large skillet over medium heat. Add onions and cook, stirring often, until softened and beginning to color, 5 to 10 minutes. Cover, reduce heat to medium-low, and continue cooking, stirring occasionally, until the onions are golden brown, 15 to 25 minutes more.

3. Drain and chop the raisins; add to the onions along with capers, dill, pepper and salt. Cook, uncovered, stirring, for 5 minutes. Transfer to a bowl and let cool for at least 30 minutes.

4. Top each slice of baguette with 1 tablespoon of the onion spread and 1 shrimp.

PER BRUSCHETTA: 61 calories; 2 g fat (0 g sat, 1 g mono); 26 mg cholesterol; 8 g carbohydrate; 0 g added sugars; 4 g protein; 1 g fiber; 100 mg sodium; 95 mg potassium.

Festive Olives

H✕W   H♥H

MAKES: 4 pints (8 cups)
ACTIVE TIME: 20 minutes | TOTAL: 45 minutes
TO MAKE AHEAD: Cover and refrigerate for up to 1 month.

Chiles, cranberries, kumquats and mint add color and flavor to your favorite black and green olives.

¼ cup extra-virgin olive oil
2 cloves garlic, crushed and peeled
7 dried hot red chiles, divided
1 pound imported black olives packed in brine, undrained
1 pound imported green olives packed in brine, undrained
1 cup fresh cranberries
1 cup kumquats, stem ends removed, sliced into ¼-inch-thick rounds
½ cup fresh mint leaves, slivered

1. Heat oil in a small skillet over low heat. Add garlic cloves and 3 chiles; cook until the garlic is golden, about 1 minute. Remove the pan from the heat, cover and let stand for 10 minutes. Discard the garlic and chiles, reserving the oil.

2. Gently stir olives with brine, cranberries, kumquats, mint and the infused oil in a large bowl. Divide the mixture among four 1-pint sterilized jars (*see How To*), making sure the olives are covered with liquid. Place 1 of the remaining chiles in each jar. Close lids and refrigerate for at least 1 week. Before serving, allow the mixture to come to room temperature.

PER 1/4-CUP SERVING: 63 calories; 6 g fat (0 g sat, 3 g mono); 0 mg cholesterol; 3 g carbohydrate; 0 g added sugars; 0 g protein; 1 g fiber; 347 mg sodium; 19 mg potassium.

How To

Sterilize Jars | Steam jars upside down, with their lids alongside, in a closed steamer for 10 minutes. Or place jars and lids in a large pot, add water to cover by 1 inch and boil for 10 minutes.

Tapenade with Crostini

MAKES: about 36 crostini
ACTIVE TIME: 20 minutes | TOTAL: 20 minutes
TO MAKE AHEAD: Cover and refrigerate the tapenade (Step 1) for up to 1 week. The crostini (Steps 2-3) may be baked several hours in advance, allowed to cool to room temperature, then wrapped and stored at room temperature.

Along the French Riviera, this black-olive spread invariably contains an anchovy or two, but you may make it without.

1 cup black olives, pitted
2 tablespoons drained capers, rinsed
1½ tablespoons rum *or* brandy
1½ teaspoons extra-virgin olive oil
1½ teaspoons fresh thyme *or* ½ teaspoon dried
1 anchovy fillet (optional)
1 small clove garlic, crushed
½-1 teaspoon lemon juice, divided
½ cup fresh breadcrumbs (*see How To, page 43*)
   Freshly ground pepper to taste
1 small baguette *or* loaf of Italian bread

1. Combine olives, capers, rum (or brandy), oil, thyme, anchovy (if using), garlic and ½ teaspoon lemon juice in a food processor. Pulse until the mixture is finely chopped. Add breadcrumbs and pulse just until mixed. Season with pepper and additional lemon juice, if desired.

2. Preheat oven to 400°F.

3. Slice bread diagonally into rounds about ½ inch thick. Arrange in a single layer on a large baking sheet. Bake until just beginning to brown, about 8 minutes. Spread the tapenade on the crostini just before serving.

PER CROSTINI: 31 calories; 1 g fat (0 g sat, 0 g mono); 0 mg cholesterol; 5 g carbohydrate; 0 g added sugars; 1 g protein; 1 g fiber; 71 mg sodium; 1 mg potassium.

Deviled Eggs

MAKES: 24 deviled eggs
ACTIVE TIME: 10 minutes | TOTAL: 10 minutes

Try experimenting with this basic recipe by adding your favorite mix-ins—like pickle relish, finely chopped red bell pepper or salsa—to the yolk mixture.

- 12 hard-boiled eggs (*see Tip, page 484*), peeled
- ½ cup low-fat mayonnaise
- 2 tablespoons chopped fresh chives
- 2 teaspoons Dijon mustard
- ¼ teaspoon salt
- ¼ teaspoon freshly ground pepper
   Paprika for garnish

1. Slice eggs in half lengthwise. Scoop out the yolks, discarding half and putting the rest in a small bowl.

2. Thoroughly mash the yolks with a fork. Stir in mayonnaise, chives and mustard. Season with salt and pepper.

3. Spoon the yolk mixture into the hollows in the egg whites; sprinkle with paprika, if desired. Arrange on a platter.

PER DEVILED EGG: 29 calories; 1 g fat (0 g sat, 1 g mono); 53 mg cholesterol; 1 g carbohydrate; 0 g added sugars; 3 g protein; 0 g fiber; 84 mg sodium; 30 mg potassium.

EatingWell Tip

Try omitting some of the egg yolks in recipes to **save on fat and calories**. One yolk has 5 grams of fat and 54 calories compared with only 16 calories and no fat for an egg white.

New Potatoes with Caviar

MAKES: 24 pieces
ACTIVE TIME: 30 minutes | TOTAL: 45 minutes

New potatoes topped with a bit of sour cream and caviar are a sophisticated addition to your cocktail party spread. **Shopping Tip:** *Caviar (salted sturgeon eggs) from U.S. farmed sturgeon is considered the best choice for the environment. Most imported caviar comes from overfished wild sturgeon that are at risk of extinction.*

- 12 very small new potatoes
- ½ cup reduced-fat sour cream
- ¼ cup nonfat plain yogurt
- ¼ cup finely chopped fresh chives
- 2 ounces black caviar (¼ cup; *see Shopping Tip*)
   Freshly ground pepper (optional)

1. Place potatoes in a medium saucepan, add water to cover and bring to a boil. Reduce heat to low and cook until tender, 10 to 15 minutes. Drain the potatoes and cool under running water. Refrigerate until chilled.

2. Combine sour cream and yogurt. When potatoes are thoroughly chilled, cut them in half. Cut a small slice off each rounded end so that the potatoes sit without rolling. Place a teaspoonful of the sour cream mixture on each potato. Top with chives and ½ teaspoon of caviar. Garnish with freshly ground pepper, if desired.

PER PIECE: 76 calories; 1 g fat (0 g sat, 0 g mono); 16 mg cholesterol; 14 g carbohydrate; 0 g added sugars; 2 g protein; 1 g fiber; 48 mg sodium; 395 mg potassium.
NUTRITION BONUS: Vitamin C (15% daily value).

◀ Tuna-Stuffed Peppers

MAKES: about 24 stuffed peppers
ACTIVE TIME: 35 minutes | TOTAL: 35 minutes
TO MAKE AHEAD: Cover and refrigerate stuffed peppers and balsamic syrup separately for up to 4 hours. Drizzle the peppers with the syrup just before serving.

These tuna-stuffed peppers are easy to make and pretty to serve to guests. **Shopping Tip:** *Look for red and/or green, jarred, mild (or sweet) cherry peppers near pickles and olives or in the "olive bar" at well-stocked supermarkets and specialty-food stores.*

- 24 whole jarred mild *or* sweet cherry peppers (from two 16-ounce jars; *see Shopping Tip*)
- 1 5- to 6-ounce can water-packed chunk light tuna (*see Tip, page 490*), drained well
- 1 tablespoon lemon juice
- 1 tablespoon extra-virgin olive oil
- 1 tablespoon capers, rinsed and finely chopped
- 2 anchovy fillets, finely chopped (optional)
  Freshly ground pepper to taste
- ¼ cup balsamic vinegar

1. Select 24 whole peppers. (Refrigerate any remaining peppers in a jar, with brine to cover, for another use.) Cut off and discard the pepper stems. Scoop out the seeds with a small spoon (a measuring teaspoon works well). Rinse the peppers to remove any residual seeds, and set in a colander to drain.

2. Combine tuna, lemon juice, oil, capers and anchovies (if using) in a medium bowl.

3. Fill each pepper with about 1 teaspoon of the tuna mixture and place them on a serving plate. (Depending on the size of the peppers, you may not fill all 24.) Grind some pepper over the stuffed peppers.

4. Bring vinegar to a boil in a very small saucepan; simmer until syrupy and reduced to about 2 teaspoons, 3 to 3½ minutes. Drizzle the syrup over the peppers.

PER PEPPER: 16 calories; 1 g fat (0 g sat, 0 g mono); 1 mg cholesterol; 1 g carbohydrate; 0 g added sugars; 1 g protein; 0 g fiber; 129 mg sodium; 11 mg potassium.

Classic Hummus

H✕W   H⬆F   H♥H

MAKES: 1½ cups
ACTIVE TIME: 10 minutes | TOTAL: 10 minutes
TO MAKE AHEAD: Cover and refrigerate for up to 5 days.

It's easy to make hummus at home with just a few pantry items. Serve drizzled with your best-quality extra-virgin olive oil and chopped parsley. Mop it up with warm whole-wheat pita bread or cut-up vegetables. **Shopping Tip:** *Tahini is a thick paste of ground sesame seeds. Look for it at large supermarkets in the Middle Eastern section or near other nut butters.*

- 1 clove garlic, smashed and peeled
- 1 15-ounce can chickpeas, rinsed
- 3 tablespoons fresh lemon juice
- 3 tablespoons extra-virgin olive oil
- 1 tablespoon tahini (*see Shopping Tip*)
- ½ teaspoon salt

With the motor running, drop garlic through the feed tube of a food processor fitted with a steel blade attachment; process until finely minced. Scrape down the sides of the workbowl and add chickpeas, lemon juice, oil, tahini and salt. Process until completely smooth, stopping to scrape down the sides as necessary, 1 to 2 minutes.

PER 1/4-CUP SERVING: 144 calories; 9 g fat (1 g sat, 6 g mono); 0 mg cholesterol; 13 g carbohydrate; 0 g added sugars; 3 g protein; 3 g fiber; 298 mg sodium; 114 mg potassium.

Black-Eyed Pea Spread

H✖W   H♥H

MAKES: about 1¼ cups
ACTIVE TIME: 15 minutes | TOTAL: 15 minutes
TO MAKE AHEAD: Cover and refrigerate for up to 2 days.

Serve this delectable, garlicky black-eyed pea spread with pita chips or toasted slices of baguette.

1	15-ounce can black-eyed peas, rinsed
¼	cup tightly packed fresh parsley leaves
2	tablespoons lemon juice
2	tablespoons extra-virgin olive oil
1½	teaspoons chopped garlic (1 large clove)
½	teaspoon dried tarragon
¼	teaspoon freshly ground pepper
¼	teaspoon salt, or to taste

Reserve a few black-eyed peas for garnish and place the remaining peas in a food processor, along with parsley, lemon juice, oil, garlic, tarragon and pepper. Process until smooth. Taste and adjust seasonings, adding salt if desired. Transfer to a serving bowl and garnish with the reserved peas.

PER 1/4-CUP SERVING: 104 calories; 6 g fat (1 g sat, 4 g mono); 0 mg cholesterol; 10 g carbohydrate; 0 g added sugars; 3 g protein; 2 g fiber; 242 mg sodium; 140 mg potassium.
NUTRITION BONUS: Vitamin C (15% daily value).

▶ French Onion Dip

H✖W

MAKES: about 2½ cups
ACTIVE TIME: 50 minutes | TOTAL: 1 hour 40 minutes
TO MAKE AHEAD: Cover and refrigerate the onion mixture (Step 1) for up to 3 days or freeze for up to 2 months. Cover and refrigerate the dip for up to 3 days.

In our homemade version of French onion dip, we simmer chopped onions in broth and use reduced-fat sour cream and yogurt for the familiar rich and creamy flavor. The result: 12 grams less fat per serving than the original.

1	tablespoon extra-virgin olive oil
4	cups chopped onions
¾	teaspoon salt
1	14-ounce can reduced-sodium beef broth *or* 1¾ cups mushroom broth (*see Tip, page 482*)
2	teaspoons onion powder
2	tablespoons distilled white vinegar
1	cup reduced-fat sour cream
⅓	cup nonfat plain yogurt

1. Heat oil in a large skillet over medium-high heat. Add onions and salt; cook, stirring occasionally, until beginning to brown, 6 to 10 minutes. Add broth, scrape up any browned bits, and simmer until the liquid is almost evaporated, 10 to 20 minutes. Reduce heat to medium-low and cook until the onions are deep golden brown, 5 to 8 minutes more. Stir in onion powder, then stir in vinegar and cook until evaporated, 1 to 2 minutes. Remove from the heat and let cool for 20 minutes.

2. Combine sour cream and yogurt in a medium bowl. Stir in the onions. Chill for at least 30 minutes.

PER 1/4-CUP SERVING: 80 calories; 4 g fat (2 g sat, 2 g mono); 11 mg cholesterol; 8 g carbohydrate; 0 g added sugars; 2 g protein; 1 g fiber; 282 mg sodium; 176 mg potassium.

EatingWell Tip

Replace full-fat sour cream with reduced-fat sour cream and nonfat plain yogurt. You'll **save calories and fat** and still have a rich-tasting dip.

Roasted Garlic Guacamole with Help-Yourself Garnishes (*Guacamole de Ajo Asado con Sabores a Escoger*)

H ⬆ F

MAKES: 4 cups guacamole

ACTIVE TIME: 30 minutes | TOTAL: 30 minutes

TO MAKE AHEAD: Cover and refrigerate the guacamole (Step 1) for up to 1 day.

This recipe was developed by chef Rick Bayless, who thinks a key part of any great fiesta is the food. "I like to welcome guests with this guacamole bar," he says. "I start off with a basic guacamole made with roasted garlic and set out bowls of toppings so everyone can customize each bite."

GUACAMOLE

- 6 large cloves garlic, unpeeled
- 6 ripe medium avocados
- ½ cup coarsely chopped fresh cilantro, loosely packed
- 2 tablespoons fresh lime juice, plus more if desired
- 1 teaspoon salt

GARNISHES

- ¾ cup Mexican *queso fresco* (*see Tip, page 488*), *queso añejo*, salted pressed farmer's cheese, firm goat cheese, mild feta *or* Romano, finely crumbled or grated
- ¾ cup toasted pumpkin seeds (*see How To*)
- ¾ cup sliced pickled jalapeños
- ½ cup crumbled crisp-fried bacon *or* ¾ cup coarsely crumbled *chicharrón* (Mexican crisp-fried pork rind)
- 1 16-ounce bag large, sturdy tortilla chips

1. **To prepare guacamole:** Place unpeeled garlic in a small dry skillet over medium heat; cook, turning occasionally, until soft and blackened in spots, 10 to 15 minutes. Cool, then slip off the skins; finely chop. Scoop avocado flesh into a large bowl. Add the garlic, cilantro and lime juice to taste. Coarsely mash everything together. Season with salt. Transfer to a serving bowl and place plastic wrap directly on the surface of the guacamole. Refrigerate until ready to serve.

2. **To set up the guacamole bar:** Scoop garnishes into small serving bowls and put the chips in a large basket or bowl. Encourage guests to spoon a little guacamole on a chip and top with garnishes that appeal.

PER 1/4-CUP SERVING: 310 calories; 21 g fat (4 g sat, 10 g mono); 7 mg cholesterol; 28 g carbohydrate; 0 g added sugars; 7 g protein; 7 g fiber; 510 mg sodium; 505 mg potassium.
NUTRITION BONUS: Folate (16% daily value).

How To

Toast Pumpkin Seeds | Place in a small dry skillet and cook over medium-low heat, stirring constantly, until fragrant and lightly browned, 2 to 4 minutes.

Southwestern Layered Bean Dip

H✖W   H⬆F

MAKES: 6 cups

ACTIVE TIME: 20 minutes | TOTAL: 20 minutes

TO MAKE AHEAD: Prepare through Step 1, cover and refrigerate for up to 1 day. To serve, continue with Steps 2-3.

Plenty of black beans, salsa and chopped fresh vegetables mean a healthy amount of dietary fiber in this Tex-Mex layered dip. We use reduced-fat sour cream along with full-fat (and full-flavored) cheese to make the dip lighter without compromising great taste. Be sure to have lots of tortilla chips on hand when you serve it.

1	16-ounce can nonfat refried beans, preferably "spicy"
1	15-ounce can black beans, rinsed
4	scallions, sliced
½	cup prepared salsa
½	teaspoon ground cumin
½	teaspoon chili powder
¼	cup pickled jalapeño slices, chopped
1	cup shredded Monterey Jack *or* Cheddar cheese
½	cup reduced-fat sour cream
1½	cups chopped romaine lettuce
1	medium tomato, chopped
1	medium avocado, chopped
¼	cup canned sliced black olives (optional)

1. Combine refried beans, black beans, scallions, salsa, cumin, chili powder and jalapeños in a medium bowl. Transfer to a shallow 2-quart microwavable dish; sprinkle with cheese.

2. Microwave on High until the cheese is melted and the beans are hot, 3 to 5 minutes.

3. Spread sour cream evenly over the hot bean mixture, then scatter with lettuce, tomato, avocado and olives (if using).

PER 1/2-CUP SERVING: 145 calories; 7 g fat (3 g sat, 3 g mono); 12 mg cholesterol; 15 g carbohydrate; 0 g added sugars; 7 g protein; 5 g fiber; 310 mg sodium; 256 mg potassium.
NUTRITION BONUS: Vitamin A (17% daily value).

EatingWell Tip

Don't shy away from avocados because they're high in calories. They provide lutein, an antioxidant that **helps keep eyes healthy**. Plus, most of the fats in the buttery fruit are monounsaturated, which are associated with cardiovascular health.

Chile con Queso

H)(W

MAKES: 4 cups

ACTIVE TIME: 20 minutes | TOTAL: 20 minutes

TO MAKE AHEAD: Cover and refrigerate for up to 3 days. Slowly reheat on the stove over medium heat or on Medium in the microwave.

Our healthier version of chile con queso will have ooey-gooey-cheese lovers celebrating. Now you can enjoy this Tex-Mex dip without all the fat and calories. We replaced some of the cheese with a low-fat white sauce and used sharp Cheddar plus a splash of beer to boost the flavor. Our version cuts the calories in half and reduces total fat and saturated fat by nearly 60 percent. Serve with Chile-Lime Tortilla Chips (opposite). **Shopping Tip:** *We like the flavor of Rotel brand diced tomatoes with green chiles the best in this dip. Choose original or mild, depending on your spice preference.*

- 2 teaspoons extra-virgin olive oil
- 1 medium onion, chopped
- 2 cloves garlic, minced
- ½ cup pale ale *or* other light-colored beer
- 1½ cups low-fat milk, divided
- 3 tablespoons cornstarch
- 1¾ cups shredded sharp Cheddar, preferably orange
- 1 10-ounce can diced tomatoes with green chiles (*see Shopping Tip*), drained, *or* 1¼ cups drained petite-diced tomatoes
- 2 tablespoons lime juice
- 1 teaspoon salt
- 1 teaspoon chili powder
  Cayenne pepper to taste (optional)
- ¼ cup sliced scallions
- 2 tablespoons chopped fresh cilantro

1. Heat oil in a large saucepan over medium heat. Add onion and garlic and cook, stirring, until soft and beginning to brown, 4 to 5 minutes. Add beer and cook until reduced slightly, about 1 minute. Add 1 cup milk and bring to a simmer.

2. Meanwhile, whisk the remaining ½ cup milk and cornstarch in a small bowl. Add to the pan and cook, stirring vigorously, until bubbling and thickened, 1 to 2 minutes. Reduce heat to low, add cheese and cook, stirring, until melted. Stir in drained tomatoes, lime juice, salt, chili powder and cayenne (if using). Serve warm, garnished with scallions and cilantro.

PER 1/4-CUP SERVING: 84 calories; 5 g fat (3 g sat, 2 g mono); 14 mg cholesterol; 5 g carbohydrate; 0 g added sugars; 4 g protein; 0 g fiber; 315 mg sodium; 36 mg potassium.

EatingWell Tip

Try cooking with beer. It **adds depth of flavor without packing in a ton of calories and saturated fat.** Mix it into sauces (see Lamb Chops with Beer & Mustard Sauce, *page 359*), stews, chili or even a cheese dip, as in this recipe.

Fresh Tomato Salsa

H✗W H♥H

MAKES: 5 cups
ACTIVE TIME: 30 minutes | TOTAL: 30 minutes
TO MAKE AHEAD: Cover and refrigerate for up to 3 days.

Fresh and easy, this recipe yields about 5 cups of salsa, so it's good for a party. If you like spicy salsa, use the full amount of jalapeños and add more cayenne pepper.

- 4 cups diced tomatoes (5-6 medium)
- ¾ cup finely diced red onion (about 1 small)
- ¼ cup red-wine vinegar
- 1-2 jalapeños, seeded and minced
- ½ cup chopped fresh cilantro
- ½ teaspoon salt
  Pinch of cayenne pepper, or more to taste

Combine tomatoes, onion, vinegar, jalapeño to taste, cilantro, salt and cayenne in a medium bowl. Refrigerate until ready to serve.

PER 1/2-CUP SERVING: 19 calories; 0 g fat (0 g sat, 0 g mono); 0 mg cholesterol; 4 g carbohydrate; 0 g added sugars; 1 g protein; 1 g fiber; 121 mg sodium; 196 mg potassium.
NUTRITION BONUS: Vitamin C (18% daily value).

Chile-Lime Tortilla Chips

MAKES: 6 servings, 8 chips each
ACTIVE TIME: 30 minutes | TOTAL: 30 minutes
TO MAKE AHEAD: Store in an airtight container for 1 to 2 days.

These tortilla chips are baked, not fried, and a squeeze of lime and a sprinkle of chili powder add flavor without tons of calories. Plus with 5 grams less fat per serving than a packaged version, they deliver all the crunch without the guilt.

- 12 6-inch corn tortillas
  Canola oil cooking spray
- 2 tablespoons lime juice
- ½ teaspoon chili powder
- ¼ teaspoon salt

1. Position oven racks in the middle and lower third of oven; preheat to 375°F.

2. Coat both sides of each tortilla with cooking spray and cut into quarters. Place tortilla wedges in a single layer on 2 large baking sheets. Combine lime juice and chili powder in a small bowl. Brush the mixture on each tortilla wedge and sprinkle with salt.

3. Bake the tortillas, switching the baking sheets halfway through, until golden and crisp, 15 to 20 minutes (depending on the thickness of the tortillas).

PER SERVING: 142 calories; 2 g fat (0 g sat, 0 g mono); 0 mg cholesterol; 29 g carbohydrate; 0 g added sugars; 2 g protein; 2 g fiber; 169 mg sodium; 10 mg potassium.

BBQ Chicken Tenders

MAKES: about 24 tenders
ACTIVE TIME: 40 minutes | TOTAL: 1½ hours (including 30 minutes marinating time)

These crispy chicken "wings," made with boneless, skinless chicken breast tenders, stay crispy with only a light coating of oil—no deep-frying needed. Serve as an appetizer or try them for dinner with crunchy vegetables and dip on the side.

1	cup prepared barbecue sauce
2	tablespoons Dijon mustard
2	tablespoons honey
1½	pounds chicken tenders (*see Tip, page 482*)
½	cup all-purpose flour
½	teaspoon salt
½	teaspoon freshly ground pepper
2	large eggs
1¾	cups coarse dry breadcrumbs, preferably whole-wheat (*see How To*)
	Olive oil *or* canola oil cooking spray

1. Combine barbecue sauce, mustard and honey in a large bowl. Set aside ½ cup of the sauce in a small bowl. Cut any large chicken tenders in half lengthwise, then add all the tenders to the large bowl with the remaining sauce; stir to coat. Marinate in the refrigerator for 30 minutes to 1 hour.

2. Preheat oven to 450°F. Coat a large rimmed baking sheet with cooking spray.

3. Combine flour, salt and pepper in a shallow dish. Lightly beat eggs in another shallow dish. Place breadcrumbs in a third shallow dish. Coat each tender in flour, shaking off any excess. Dip in egg and let any excess drip off. Then roll in the breadcrumbs, shaking off any excess. Place the tenders on the prepared baking sheet. Generously coat both sides of each tender with cooking spray.

4. Bake for 10 minutes. Turn each tender over and continue baking until the outside is crisp and the tenders are cooked through, about 10 minutes more. Serve with the reserved sauce for dipping.

PER TENDER: 67 calories; 0 g fat (0 g sat, 0 g mono); 28 mg cholesterol; 8 g carbohydrate; 2 g added sugars; 8 g protein; 1 g fiber; 141 mg sodium; 7 mg potassium.

How To

Make Coarse Dry Breadcrumbs | Trim crusts from firm sandwich bread, preferably whole-wheat. Tear the bread into pieces and process in a food processor until coarse crumbs form. Spread on a baking sheet and bake at 250°F until dry, 10 to 15 minutes. One slice of bread makes about ⅓ cup dry breadcrumbs.

EatingWell Tip

Try oven-frying instead of deep-frying to **reduce calories and fat**. Just spray breaded foods with canola or olive oil and bake them in the oven.

Vegetable Satay

MAKES: 12 skewers
ACTIVE TIME: 30 minutes | TOTAL: 2½ hours (including 2 hours marinating time) | TO MAKE AHEAD: Prepare through Step 2, cover and refrigerate for up to 1 day.
EQUIPMENT: 12 skewers

Although usually made with strips of chicken or beef, this Indonesian-style satay is made with fresh broccoli and cauliflower florets. **Shopping Tip:** *We use bottled ginger juice (pressed gingerroot) to add the taste of fresh ginger without the work of mincing or grating. Use it to flavor drinks, stir-fries, marinades or anywhere you'd use fresh ginger. Find it at specialty stores or online at* gingerpeople.com.

> 24 **broccoli florets**
> 24 **cauliflower florets**
> 1 **tablespoon reduced-sodium soy sauce**
> 1 **tablespoon rice vinegar**
> 1 **tablespoon toasted sesame oil**
> 1 **tablespoon minced fresh ginger *or* ginger juice (*see Shopping Tip*)**
> 1 **tablespoon smooth natural peanut butter**
> 1 **clove garlic, minced**
> 1 **teaspoon hot Madras curry powder**
> ¼ **teaspoon salt**

1. Bring a large saucepan of water to a boil over high heat. Add broccoli and cauliflower; cook until tender-crisp, about 3 minutes. Drain; rinse under cool water.

2. Whisk soy sauce, vinegar, oil, ginger (or ginger juice), peanut butter, garlic, curry and salt in a large bowl until smooth. Add the florets; gently toss to coat. Let marinate at room temperature for at least 2 hours or cover and refrigerate for up to 1 day.

3. To serve, thread 2 broccoli and 2 cauliflower florets onto each skewer. (Reserve marinade.) Arrange the skewers on a platter in a single layer and drizzle with the marinade.

PER SKEWER: 33 calories; 2 g fat (0 g sat, 1 g mono); 0 mg cholesterol; 3 g carbohydrate; 0 g added sugars; 2 g protein; 1 g fiber; 100 mg sodium; 156 mg potassium.
NUTRITION BONUS: Vitamin C (50% daily value).

Rustic Pesto Tart

H✳W   H♥H

MAKES: 12 appetizer servings
ACTIVE TIME: 15 minutes | TOTAL: 45 minutes
TO MAKE AHEAD: Prepare up to 2 hours ahead; serve at room temperature.

Talk about easy! Almost everything in this pesto-cranberry tart is premade. Although the tart can be enjoyed shortly after it comes out of the oven, it's just as good served at room temperature. **Shopping Tip:** *Look for fresh or frozen balls of whole-wheat pizza dough at your supermarket. Check the ingredient list to make sure the dough doesn't contain any hydrogenated oils.*

> 1 **pound whole-wheat pizza dough, store-bought (*see Shopping Tip*) or Thin-Crust Whole-Wheat Pizza Dough (see *page 226*)**
> ¼ **cup prepared pesto**
> 6 **tablespoons dried cranberries**
> ½ **cup shredded fontina *or* Swiss cheese**

1. Preheat oven to 400°F. Coat a large baking sheet with cooking spray.

2. Sprinkle work surface and dough with flour. Press dough out and roll, stretch or toss it into a 14-inch circle. Place on the prepared baking sheet. Spread pesto on the dough to within ⅛ inch of the edge. Sprinkle cranberries and cheese evenly over the pesto. Fold 1 to 1½ inches of the border over the filling all the way around, leaving the center exposed.

3. Bake the tart until browned and bubbling, 20 to 22 minutes. Cool on the pan for 5 minutes before cutting into 12 pieces.

PER SERVING: 134 calories; 4 g fat (2 g sat, 2 g mono); 7 mg cholesterol; 18 g carbohydrate; 3 g added sugars; 5 g protein; 1 g fiber; 175 mg sodium; 18 mg potassium.

Spinach-Feta Rolls

MAKES: 36 rolls
ACTIVE TIME: 25 minutes | TOTAL: 1 hour
TO MAKE AHEAD: Cover and refrigerate for up to 2 days. Reheat in a 350°F oven until heated through, 10 to 12 minutes.

Inspired by the Greek appetizer spanakopita, *these spinach-and-feta-filled rolls are easy to make for a crowd.* **Timing Tip:** *Thaw frozen phyllo in the refrigerator for at least 8 hours or according to package directions, before preparing the recipe.*

SPINACH-FETA FILLING

- 1¼ **pounds fresh spinach, stemmed**
- 1 **tablespoon extra-virgin olive oil**
- 3 **bunches scallions, trimmed and chopped (1½ cups)**
- ¼ **cup crumbled feta cheese**
- 2 **tablespoons freshly grated Parmesan cheese**
- 2 **tablespoons chopped fresh dill**
- 1 **tablespoon lemon juice**
- ¼ **teaspoon salt**
  Freshly ground pepper to taste
- 2 **large egg whites, lightly beaten**

PHYLLO PASTRY

- 1 **large egg white**
- 2 **tablespoons extra-virgin olive oil**
- ¼ **teaspoon salt**
- 8 **sheets phyllo dough (14x18 inches), thawed (see Timing Tip)**
- 1 **teaspoon poppy seeds or sesame seeds or a combination (optional)**

1. **To prepare filling:** Place spinach with water still clinging to the leaves in a large pot. Cover and cook over medium heat until the spinach is wilted, about 5 minutes. Drain and refresh with cold water. Squeeze the spinach dry and chop.

2. Heat 1 tablespoon oil in a medium nonstick skillet over medium heat. Add scallions and cook, stirring, until softened, 2 to 3 minutes. Transfer to a medium bowl and stir in the spinach, feta, Parmesan, dill and lemon juice. Season with salt and pepper. Stir in 2 egg whites.

3. Position rack in upper third of oven; preheat to 350°F. Lightly coat a baking sheet with cooking spray or line with parchment paper.

4. **To make phyllo rolls:** Whisk egg white, 2 tablespoons oil and salt in a small bowl.

5. Lay one sheet of phyllo on a work surface with a short side toward you. Brush the lower half of the sheet with the egg-white mixture and fold the top half over. Brush the top with the egg-white mixture. Repeat this step with a second sheet of phyllo and set it on top of the first. Spoon one-fourth of the spinach filling along one long edge of the phyllo stack. Tuck in the short sides and roll up, jelly-roll fashion. Place on the prepared baking sheet. Repeat with the remaining phyllo, egg-white mixture and filling, making 4 rolls in all.

6. Brush the tops of the rolls lightly with the egg-white mixture and sprinkle with seeds, if desired. Bake until golden, 25 to 30 minutes. Cool for 5 minutes. With a serrated knife, cut each roll diagonally into 9 pieces and serve hot.

PER ROLL: 38 calories; 2 g fat (0 g sat, 1 g mono); 1 mg cholesterol; 5 g carbohydrate; 0 g added sugars; 2 g protein; 1 g fiber; 92 mg sodium; 121 mg potassium.
NUTRITION BONUS: Vitamin A (32% daily value).

Shrimp Summer Rolls

H✖W   H♥H

MAKES: 6 spring rolls
ACTIVE TIME: 35 minutes | TOTAL: 35 minutes
TO MAKE AHEAD: Cover and refrigerate the filling for up to 8 hours. Prepare rolls up to 2 hours in advance; wrap in a damp kitchen towel, place in a plastic bag and store in the refrigerator or a cooler.

These pretty little rolls are super-fresh-tasting and easy to make. Serve with your choice of dipping sauces (right). **Shopping Tip:** *Rice-paper wrappers are translucent round sheets made from rice flour. They need to briefly soak in warm water to make them soft and pliable before using. Find them in the Asian section of large supermarkets or at Asian food stores.*

12	ounces raw shrimp (21-25 per pound; *see Tip, page 489*), peeled and deveined
1½	cups mung bean sprouts *or* sunflower sprouts
4	scallions, chopped
2	tablespoons chopped fresh mint
1	tablespoon fish sauce (*see Tip, page 484*)
1	tablespoon lime juice
6	8½-inch rice-paper wrappers (*see Shopping Tip*)

1. Cook shrimp in boiling water just until curled and opaque in the center, 1 to 2 minutes. Drain and refresh under cold running water. Transfer to a clean cutting board to cool, then chop.

2. Combine the shrimp with sprouts, scallions, mint, fish sauce and lime juice in a large bowl. Working with one wrapper at a time, soak in a large bowl of very warm water until softened, about 30 seconds. Place the soaked wrapper on a clean, damp dish towel. Put a generous ⅓ cup of the shrimp filling in the center, fold the wrapper over the filling and roll into a tight cylinder, folding in the sides as you go. Repeat with the remaining wrappers and filling. Cut each roll in half before serving.

PER SPRING ROLL: 116 calories; 1 g fat (0 g sat, 0 g mono); 86 mg cholesterol; 13 g carbohydrate; 0 g added sugars; 13 g protein; 1 g fiber; 371 mg sodium; 183 mg potassium.

SPICY PEANUT SAUCE

MAKES: ⅓ cup
ACTIVE TIME: 5 minutes | TOTAL: 5 minutes

2	tablespoons smooth natural peanut butter
2	tablespoons "lite" coconut milk
1	tablespoon lime juice
2	teaspoons reduced-sodium soy sauce
1	teaspoon brown sugar
½	teaspoon crushed red pepper, or to taste

Whisk peanut butter, coconut milk, lime juice, soy sauce, brown sugar and crushed red pepper in a small bowl until smooth.

PER TABLESPOON: 50 calories; 4 g fat (1 g sat, 0 g mono); 0 mg cholesterol; 3 g carbohydrate; 1 g added sugars; 2 g protein; 0 g fiber; 78 mg sodium; 13 mg potassium.

VIETNAMESE DIPPING SAUCE

MAKES: ½ cup
ACTIVE TIME: 5 minutes | TOTAL: 5 minutes

3	tablespoons lime juice
3	tablespoons water
2	tablespoons fish sauce (*see Tip, page 484*)
1	tablespoon sugar
1	clove garlic, minced
1	serrano pepper, minced, *or* ½ teaspoon crushed red pepper
1	scallion, minced (optional)

Stir together lime juice, water, fish sauce, sugar, garlic, serrano (or crushed red pepper) and scallion (if using) in a small bowl until the sugar is dissolved.

PER TABLESPOON: 13 calories; 0 g fat (0 g sat, 0 g mono); 0 mg cholesterol; 3 g carbohydrate; 2 g added sugars; 1 g protein; 0 g fiber; 298 mg sodium; 11 mg potassium.

Scallop & Shrimp Dumplings

MAKES: 36 dumplings

ACTIVE TIME: 1 hour | TOTAL: 1 hour | TO MAKE AHEAD: Prepare filling (Step 1); cover and refrigerate for up to 2 days or freeze for up to 1 week.

Crisp, pan-fried dumplings don't have to be loaded with fat. Cooking them in a mix of water and oil makes them crisp on the bottom, tender and juicy inside. (Photograph: page 16.) **Shopping Tip:** *The best dumpling wrappers for this recipe are round "gyoza" wrappers. Look for them at Asian markets. Or substitute square wonton wrappers and use a 3- to 3½-inch round cookie cutter to cut each wrapper into a circle (they need not be perfectly round).*

8	ounces scallops, minced
4	ounces raw shrimp, peeled and deveined (*see Tip, page 489*), minced
½	cup minced scallions
1	tablespoon minced fresh ginger
3	cloves garlic, minced
2	tablespoons reduced-sodium soy sauce
2	teaspoons toasted sesame oil
¼	teaspoon freshly ground pepper
36	round (*gyoza*) dumpling wrappers (*see Shopping Tip*)
2	tablespoons canola oil, divided
¾	cup water, divided
	Ginger-Garlic Dipping Sauce (*right*), optional

1. Combine scallops, shrimp, scallions, ginger, garlic, soy sauce, sesame oil and pepper in a large bowl.

2. Organize your work area with a bowl of cold water, your stack of dumpling wrappers and a floured baking sheet to hold filled dumplings.

3. Working with one dumpling wrapper at a time, dip your finger into the water and moisten the edges. Spoon about 1½ teaspoons of filling into the center. Fold the wrapper over to form a half circle. Pinch the edges together to seal. Repeat with the remaining wrappers and filling. Cover the wrappers and finished dumplings with moist paper towels to prevent drying.

4. Preheat oven to 200°F.

5. Mix 1 tablespoon canola oil with ¼ cup water in a large nonstick skillet and place over medium heat; bring to a simmer. Carefully arrange one-third of the dumplings in the skillet so they are not touching; cover and cook until the dumplings puff up and are light brown on the bottom, 4 to 5 minutes. Carefully flip the dumplings with tongs and cook for 1 minute more. Transfer the dumplings to a baking sheet and keep warm in the oven.

6. Repeat with the remaining 1 tablespoon canola oil, another ¼ cup water and half the remaining dumplings. Cook the final batch of dumplings in the remaining ¼ cup water, adjusting the heat as necessary to prevent scorching. (There will be enough oil left in the pan for the final batch.) Serve hot with Ginger-Garlic Dipping Sauce, if desired.

PER DUMPLING: 42 calories; 1 g fat (0 g sat, 1 g mono); 7 mg cholesterol; 5 g carbohydrate; 0 g added sugars; 2 g protein; 0 g fiber; 83 mg sodium; 40 mg potassium.

GINGER-GARLIC DIPPING SAUCE

MAKES: ¾ cup

ACTIVE TIME: 10 minutes | TOTAL: 40 minutes

TO MAKE AHEAD: Cover and refrigerate for up to 3 days.

In addition to being a delicious dipping sauce for dumplings, this can be used as a marinade for chicken, pork or tofu.

½	cup reduced-sodium soy sauce
2	tablespoons lemon juice
2	tablespoons rice vinegar
2	cloves garlic, minced
2	tablespoons chopped fresh cilantro
1	tablespoon minced ginger
2	teaspoons toasted sesame oil

Combine soy sauce, lemon juice, vinegar, garlic, cilantro, ginger and sesame oil in a small bowl. Cover and refrigerate for at least 30 minutes to allow flavors to blend.

PER TEASPOON: 5 calories; 0g fat (0 g sat, 0 g mono); 0 mg cholesterol; 0 g carbohydrate; 0 g added sugars; 0 g protein; 0 g fiber; 87 mg sodium; 12 mg potassium.

Spicy Lamb Meatballs in Tomato Sauce

MAKES: 48 meatballs

ACTIVE TIME: 45 minutes | TOTAL: 1¼ hours

TO MAKE AHEAD: Cover and refrigerate for up to 1 day. Just before serving, reheat over medium-low.

These succulent meatballs can be served on little plates with plenty of bread for sopping up the rich tomato sauce or simply with toothpicks (and a napkin!). They are best served warm. (Photograph: page 14.)

12	ounces ground lamb
12	ounces 93%-lean ground turkey
1	cup fresh whole-wheat breadcrumbs (*see How To*)
1	large egg white
1	cup minced onion, divided
6	cloves garlic, minced, divided
4	tablespoons chopped fresh mint, divided
1	teaspoon ground coriander
½	teaspoon ground cumin
½	teaspoon kosher salt, divided
1	tablespoon extra-virgin olive oil
½	cup red wine
¼	teaspoon cayenne pepper
1	28-ounce can crushed tomatoes

1. Preheat oven to 350°F. Coat a baking sheet with cooking spray.

2. Combine lamb, turkey, breadcrumbs, egg white, ½ cup onion, half the garlic, 2 tablespoons mint, coriander, cumin and ¼ teaspoon salt in a large bowl. Gently mix to combine. Shape into 48 little meatballs, about 1 tablespoon each. Place on the prepared baking sheet.

3. Bake the meatballs for 10 minutes. Set aside.

4. Meanwhile, heat oil in a large saucepan over medium heat. Add the remaining ½ cup onion and cook, stirring, until golden, 3 to 5 minutes. Stir in the remaining garlic, wine, cayenne and the remaining ¼ teaspoon salt. Simmer over medium-low heat until the wine has reduced significantly, 3 to 5 minutes. Add tomatoes and return to a simmer. Reduce heat to low and simmer, partially covered, for 20 minutes.

5. Add the meatballs to the sauce and cook until heated through, about 5 minutes. Garnish with the remaining 2 tablespoons mint.

PER MEATBALL: 48 calories; 2 g fat (1 g sat, 1 g mono); 9 mg cholesterol; 3 g carbohydrate; 0 g added sugars; 3 g protein; 1 g fiber; 46 mg sodium; 77 mg potassium.

How To

Make Fresh Breadcrumbs | Trim crusts from firm whole-wheat sandwich bread. Tear the bread into pieces and process in a food processor into coarse crumbs. One slice of bread makes about ⅓ cup crumbs.

Country-Style Chicken Liver Mousse

H H

MAKES: 3 cups
ACTIVE TIME: 1 hour | TOTAL: 2½ hours (including 1 hour chilling time) | TO MAKE AHEAD: Cover and refrigerate for up to 1 week.

What makes this chicken liver mousse so special is its coarse texture and use of very little fat. Most recipes for mousse made from cooked chicken livers contain copious amounts of butter or other fats for a moist and creamy texture. This version gets moisture, flavor and texture from onions, shallots and apple. For best results, do not overcook the chicken livers, which should be pink on the inside. Serve with mustard and crackers or toasted bread. **Shopping Tip:** *Look for fresh chicken livers that have not been previously frozen. Previously frozen livers exude more liquid when cooking so they don't brown properly, which results in a watery, less pleasant texture for the mousse.*

- 2 tablespoons extra-virgin olive oil
- 1 pound fresh chicken livers (*see Shopping Tip*), patted dry
- 1 teaspoon salt, divided
- 1 teaspoon freshly ground pepper, divided
- ⅛ teaspoon freshly grated nutmeg, divided
- 1 pound onions (3-4 medium), cut into 1-inch chunks
- ½ cup coarsely chopped shallots
- 2 cloves garlic, peeled
- 1 tart apple, peeled and cut into 1-inch cubes
- ⅓ cup brandy
- 10 fresh sage leaves
- 1 teaspoon chopped fresh thyme

1. Heat oil in a large heavy nonstick skillet over medium heat. Add chicken livers and sprinkle with ¼ teaspoon each salt and pepper and a pinch of nutmeg. Cook until beginning to brown on the bottom, 3 to 5 minutes. Turn over using tongs and sprinkle with another ¼ teaspoon each salt and pepper and pinch of nutmeg. Cook until the livers are firm to the touch and pink on the inside when cut into, about 3 minutes more. Transfer to a bowl with the tongs (leave any remaining oil in the pan), cover and refrigerate for at least 30 minutes or up to 1 hour.

2. Meanwhile, add onions, shallots and garlic to the pan. Sprinkle with ¼ teaspoon each salt and pepper. Cover and cook over medium heat, stirring occasionally, until browning and beginning to soften, 8 to 10 minutes. Stir in apple, brandy, sage and thyme and scrape up any browned bits. Cover and continue cooking, stirring frequently, until the onions are very soft and the apple is beginning to break down, 6 to 8 minutes more. Transfer the mixture to a shallow bowl and refrigerate for 30 minutes.

3. Spoon the cooled livers and any juices into a food processor; pulse several times until the livers are coarsely chopped (individual pieces should be about ¼ inch). Using a rubber spatula, scrape the mixture into a medium bowl. Add the onion mixture to the food processor and pulse to coarsely chop until it resembles cooked oatmeal. Transfer to the bowl and stir the liver and onions to form a lumpy, homogenous paste. Season with ¼ teaspoon each salt and pepper, or more to taste. Spoon the liver mousse into a deep bowl just large enough to hold it. Press plastic wrap directly onto the surface and refrigerate for at least 1 hour.

PER 1/4-CUP SERVING: 104 calories; 4 g fat (1 g sat, 2 g mono); 130 mg cholesterol; 6 g carbohydrate; 0 g added sugars; 7 g protein; 1 g fiber; 223 mg sodium; 171 mg potassium.
NUTRITION BONUS: Vitamin A (87% daily value), Folate (56% dv), Iron (21% dv), Vitamin C (18% dv).

Tomato-Jalapeño Bloody Mary

MAKES: 4 servings
ACTIVE TIME: 15 minutes | TOTAL: 2¼ hours (including 2 hours chilling time)

Make this zesty garden-fresh drink when summer tomatoes and peppers are at their peak. Garnish with dilly beans (to make your own, see page 133). **Shopping Tip:** *Capers are dried and pickled small flower buds from a shrub native to the Mediterranean. Caperberries are the more mature fruit produced by the shrub. They are about the size of an olive, starchier than the smaller caper and usually sold with the stem still attached. They are typically used as a drink garnish, but can also be served as an appetizer—like olives. Look for them at well-stocked supermarkets near olives and pickles or find them online at* tienda.com. NONALCOHOLIC VARIATION: *Omit the vodka.*

    3   large ripe tomatoes, cut into wedges
    ¼   cup lemon juice
    2   jalapeños, stemmed and seeded
  2-3   teaspoons prepared horseradish
    1   teaspoon Worcestershire sauce
    1   teaspoon sugar
    ½   teaspoon celery salt
    ½   teaspoon freshly ground pepper
    6   ounces (¾ cup) vodka
    4   caperberries (*see Shopping Tip*) *or* large green
          olives for garnish
    4   pickled dilly beans for garnish

1. Puree tomatoes in a blender with lemon juice, jalapeños, horseradish to taste, Worcestershire, sugar, celery salt and pepper, scraping down the sides as necessary. Stir in vodka. Refrigerate until chilled, about 2 hours.

2. Divide the mixture among 4 ice-filled glasses. Spear caperberries (or olives) and dilly beans on toothpicks to garnish the drinks, if desired.

PER SERVING: 136 calories; 0 g fat (0 g sat, 0 g mono); 0 mg cholesterol; 9 g carbohydrate; 1 g added sugars; 1 g protein; 2 g fiber; 154 mg sodium; 375 mg potassium.
NUTRITION BONUS: Vitamin C (45% daily value), Vitamin A (25% dv).

▶ Bourbon-Cherry Seltzers

MAKES: 4 servings
ACTIVE TIME: 25 minutes | TOTAL: 25 minutes plus 1 week marinating time for bourbon cherries
TO MAKE AHEAD: Store the bourbon cherries (Step 1) in the refrigerator for up to 1 month.

Homemade cherry-infused bourbon (or rum) is the base for this adult seltzer. The bourbon syrup from the cherries is sweet, but if you like a sweeter cocktail, use ginger ale in place of the seltzer.

    1   cup bourbon, such as Maker's Mark, *or* dark rum
    ¾   cup packed dark brown sugar
    2   cups whole fresh cherries, stems left on
   16   ounces (2 cups) seltzer water

1. Microwave bourbon (or rum) and brown sugar in a microwavable dish until hot, about 1 minute. (*Alternatively, heat in a small saucepan over medium heat, stirring occasionally, until hot.*) Stir until the sugar is dissolved. Pack cherries into a small jar and pour the hot liquid over them; gently press on the cherries to make sure they are submerged. Cover and refrigerate for at least 1 week or up to 1 month.

2. **To prepare seltzers:** Fill four 12-ounce rocks glasses with ice, add 1½ ounces (3 tablespoons) cherry-infused bourbon (or rum) to each glass and top with about 4 ounces (½ cup) seltzer each. Garnish with 2 or 3 whole bourbon cherries. (*Refrigerate the remaining bourbon cherries for up to 1 month.*)

PER SERVING: 219 calories; 0 g fat (0 g sat, 0 g mono); 0 mg cholesterol; 32 g carbohydrate; 30 g added sugars; 0 g protein; 0 g fiber; 10 mg sodium; 57 mg potassium.

Cucumber-Lemonade Chiller

◄ Cucumber-Lemonade Chiller

MAKES: 4 servings

ACTIVE TIME: 15 minutes | **TOTAL:** 15 minutes

Pick up rosemary, cucumbers and lemons to concoct this grown-up lemonade that will keep you cool on a hot day. **Shopping Tip:** *Agave syrup or nectar is the naturally sweet juice extracted from the agave plant. It has a lower glycemic index than table sugar, but is even sweeter. Use it in moderation when substituting for table sugar. Look for it near other sweeteners at natural-foods stores.* NONALCOHOLIC VARIATION: *Omit the gin.*

- 3 large cucumbers
- 1 tablespoon chopped fresh rosemary, plus 4 sprigs for garnish
- 1 cup water
- 6 ounces (¾ cup) gin
- ½ cup lemon juice
- 3 tablespoons agave syrup (*see Shopping Tip*)

1. Cut 12 thin slices of cucumber for garnish.

2. Peel and chop the rest of the cucumber; transfer to a food processor, add chopped rosemary and puree. Pour the puree through a fine-mesh strainer set over a medium bowl or large measuring cup. Press on the solids to extract all the juice. Add water, gin, lemon juice and agave syrup to the cucumber juice; stir until the agave is dissolved. Divide among 4 ice-filled glasses. Garnish with cucumber slices and rosemary sprigs.

PER SERVING: 169 calories; 0 g fat (0 g sat, 0 g mono); 0 mg cholesterol; 18 g carbohydrate; 12 g added sugars; 1 g protein; 1 g fiber; 6 mg sodium; 241 mg potassium. NUTRITION BONUS: Vitamin C (32% daily value).

Watermelon Gin Fizz

Salty Chihuahua

MAKES: 4 servings
ACTIVE TIME: 10 minutes | TOTAL: 10 minutes

This is a Mexican-inspired take on the Salty Dog (usually made with grapefruit juice, vodka and salt). (Photograph: page 16.)

Coarse salt (optional)
4   ounces tequila, divided
2   ounces orange-flavored liqueur, such as Cointreau, divided
3   cups grapefruit juice, divided
4   grapefruit slices for garnish

Wet the rims of 4 glasses and coat with coarse salt (if desired); fill the glasses with ice. Pour 1 ounce tequila and ½ ounce liqueur into each. Top each with ¾ cup grapefruit juice and stir. Garnish with a slice of grapefruit.

PER COCKTAIL: 188 calories; 0 g fat (0 g sat, 0 g mono); 0 mg cholesterol; 23 g carbohydrate; 6 g added sugars; 1 g protein; 0 g fiber; 3 mg sodium; 303 mg potassium. NUTRITION BONUS: Vitamin C (117% daily value), Vitamin A (16% dv).

Island Limeade

MAKES: 4 servings
ACTIVE TIME: 10 minutes | TOTAL: 1 hour (including chilling time)

Take a trip to the islands in this simple tropical cocktail. NONALCOHOLIC VARIATION: *Omit the rum.*

⅓-½   cup sugar
3   cups boiling water
1¼   cups freshly squeezed lime juice
6   ounces dark rum

Stir sugar to taste into water. Chill. Add lime juice. Divide rum and the limeade among 4 ice-filled glasses.

PER COCKTAIL: 183 calories; 0 g fat (0 g sat, 0 g mono); 0 mg cholesterol; 23 g carbohydrate; 17 g added sugars; 0 g protein; 0 g fiber; 7 mg sodium; 93 mg potassium. NUTRITION BONUS: Vitamin C (38% daily value).

◄ Watermelon Gin Fizz

MAKES: 4 servings
ACTIVE TIME: 10 minutes | TOTAL: 45 minutes (including freezing time)

This pretty pink cocktail would be perfect for a bridal shower luncheon. Any leftover pureed juice is refreshing on its own. NONALCOHOLIC VARIATION: *Omit the gin.*

5   cups diced seeded watermelon, divided
6   ounces gin, divided
8   tablespoons lime juice, divided
1⅓   cups ginger ale, divided
Lime wedges for garnish

1. Freeze 1 cup watermelon for garnish.

2. Puree the remaining 4 cups watermelon in a blender or food processor. Strain; divide the juice among 4 ice-filled glasses. Top each with 1½ ounces gin, 2 tablespoons lime juice and ⅓ cup ginger ale. Garnish with the frozen watermelon and lime wedges.

PER COCKTAIL: 179 calories; 0 g fat (0 g sat, 0 g mono); 0 mg cholesterol; 21 g carbohydrate; 7 g added sugars; 1 g protein; 1 g fiber; 8 mg sodium; 208 mg potassium. NUTRITION BONUS: Vitamin C (37% daily value), Vitamin A (18% dv).

Sausage & Vegetable Soup

Roasted Parsnip Soup

Root Vegetable Stew with Herbed Dumplings

Tilapia Corn Chowder

Soups

Simple Vegetable Soups

A simple pureed vegetable soup makes a great starter or accompaniment to a hearty salad for dinner. Plus leftovers are nice for lunch the next day. Here's a basic method and variations for carrot, potato, broccoli and pea soup.

Pureed Vegetable Soup

H✖W   H⬆F   H♥H

MAKES: 8 servings, about 1 cup each
ACTIVE TIME: 35-45 minutes | TOTAL: 35-50 minutes
TO MAKE AHEAD: Cover and refrigerate for up to 4 days or freeze for up to 3 months.

- 1 **tablespoon butter**
- 1 **tablespoon extra-virgin olive oil**
- 1 **medium onion, chopped**
- 1 **stalk celery, chopped**
- 2 **cloves garlic, chopped**
- 1 **teaspoon chopped fresh thyme *or* parsley**
  Vegetable of choice (*see Variations, right*)
  Water (*see Variations*)
- 4 **cups reduced-sodium chicken broth,**
  "no-chicken" broth (*see Tip, page 482*)
  ***or* vegetable broth**
- ½ **cup half-and-half (optional)**
- ½ **teaspoon salt**
  Freshly ground pepper to taste

1 Heat butter and oil in a Dutch oven over medium heat until the butter melts. Add onion and celery; cook, stirring occasionally, until softened, 4 to 6 minutes. Add garlic and thyme (or parsley); cook, stirring, until fragrant, about 10 seconds.

2. Stir in vegetable of choice. Add water and broth; bring to a lively simmer over high heat. Reduce heat to maintain a lively simmer and cook until very tender. (*See Variations, right, for timing.*)

3. Puree the soup in batches in a blender until smooth. (Use caution when pureeing hot liquids.) Stir in half-and-half (if using), salt and pepper.

CARROT SOUP:
- 5 **cups chopped carrots**
- 2 **cups water**
Simmer for about 25 minutes.
PER SERVING: 77 calories; 3 g fat (1 g sat, 2 g mono); 4 mg cholesterol; 10 g carbohydrate; 0 g added sugars; 3 g protein; 3 g fiber; 484 mg sodium; 397 mg potassium.
NUTRITION BONUS: Vitamin A (269% daily value).

PEA SOUP:
- 6 **cups peas (fresh *or* frozen)**
- ½ **cup water**
Simmer for 1 minute.
PER SERVING: 132 calories; 4 g fat (1 g sat, 2 g mono); 4 mg cholesterol; 18 g carbohydrate; 0 g added sugars; 8 g protein; 6 g fiber; 433 mg sodium; 405 mg potassium.
NUTRITION BONUS: Vitamin C (75% daily value), Folate (20% dv), Vitamin A (18% dv).

POTATO SOUP:
- 5 **cups chopped peeled potatoes**
- 2 **cups water**
Simmer for about 15 minutes.
PER SERVING: 128 calories; 3 g fat (1 g sat, 2 g mono); 4 mg cholesterol; 22 g carbohydrate; 0 g added sugars; 4 g protein; 2 g fiber; 434 mg sodium; 460 mg potassium.
NUTRITION BONUS: Vitamin C (15% daily value).

BROCCOLI SOUP:
- 8 **cups chopped broccoli**
  (stems and florets)
- 2 **cups water**
Simmer for about 8 minutes.
PER SERVING: 69 calories; 4 g fat (1 g sat, 2 g mono); 4 mg cholesterol; 7 g carbohydrate; 0 g added sugars; 4 g protein; 3 g fiber; 458 mg sodium; 349 mg potassium.
NUTRITION BONUS: Vitamin C (80% daily value), Vitamin A (23% dv), Folate (21% dv).

Cold Cucumber Soup

H✻W   H♥H

MAKES: 4 servings, about 1 cup each
ACTIVE TIME: 10 minutes | TOTAL: 10 minutes

Tangy buttermilk and fresh mint make this chilled soup a refreshing starter in the summer.

- 1 small clove garlic, crushed and peeled
- ½ teaspoon salt
- 4 cups peeled, seeded and chopped cucumbers (about 3 cucumbers), divided
- 1½ cups buttermilk (*see Tip, page 482*)
- ¼ cup fresh mint leaves, plus sprigs for garnish
- 1 tablespoon red wine vinegar
- 2 ice cubes
  Freshly ground pepper to taste

1. Place garlic clove on a cutting board and sprinkle with salt. Mash with the side of a chef's knife into a smooth paste. Transfer to a blender.

2. Reserving ½ cup of cucumbers for garnish, add the remaining cucumbers to the blender along with buttermilk, mint leaves, vinegar and ice cubes; blend until smooth. Taste and adjust seasonings with salt and pepper. Ladle into bowls and garnish with the reserved cucumbers and mint sprigs.

PER SERVING: 57 calories; 1 g fat (1 g sat, 0 g mono); 4 mg cholesterol; 8 g carbohydrate; 0 g added sugars; 4 g protein; 1 g fiber; 392 mg sodium; 349 mg potassium.

Watermelon Gazpacho

H✻W   H♥H

MAKES: 6 servings, generous 1 cup each
ACTIVE TIME: 20 minutes | TOTAL: 20 minutes
TO MAKE AHEAD: Cover and refrigerate for up to 1 day.

The delicate flavors of cucumber and watermelon go hand in hand to create a sweet-and-savory chilled soup, perfect as a first course on a hot night.

- 8 cups finely diced seedless watermelon (about 6 pounds with the rind)
- 1 medium cucumber, peeled, seeded and finely diced
- ½ red bell pepper, finely diced
- ¼ cup chopped fresh basil
- ¼ cup chopped flat-leaf parsley
- 3 tablespoons red-wine vinegar
- 2 tablespoons minced shallot
- 2 tablespoons extra-virgin olive oil
- ¾ teaspoon salt

Mix watermelon, cucumber, bell pepper, basil, parsley, vinegar, shallot, oil and salt in a large bowl. Puree 3 cups of the mixture in a blender or food processor to the desired consistency; transfer to another large bowl. Puree another 3 cups and add to the bowl. Stir in the remaining diced watermelon mixture. Serve at room temperature or chilled.

PER SERVING: 114 calories; 5 g fat (1 g sat, 4 g mono); 0 mg cholesterol; 17 g carbohydrate; 0 g added sugars; 2 g protein; 1 g fiber; 296 mg sodium; 324 mg potassium.
NUTRITION BONUS: Vitamin C (57% daily value), Vitamin A (37% dv).

EatingWell Tip

Start your meal with soup. Research has shown that starting a meal with a vegetable-based soup resulted in people consuming 20 percent fewer calories over the course of their meal.

Roast Peppers | In the oven or on the grill.

1. **Oven-Roasting:** Place on a baking sheet and bake at 450°F, turning occasionally, until soft, wrinkled and blackened in spots, 20 to 30 minutes.
2. **Grill-Roasting:** Preheat grill to high or prepare a hot charcoal fire. Grill peppers, turning frequently, until the skin is blistered on all sides and blackened in spots, about 10 minutes.
3. Transfer the roasted peppers to a large bowl and cover with plastic wrap. Let steam for 10 minutes to loosen the skins. Uncover and let cool.
4. Peel off the skin with your hands or a paring knife. Remove the stems and seeds.

Golden Gazpacho

H✖W   H⬆F   H❤H

MAKES: 6 servings, 1 generous cup each
ACTIVE TIME: 35 minutes | TOTAL: 3 hours (including 2 hours chilling time) | TO MAKE AHEAD: Cover and refrigerate for up to 1 day.

Inspired by Spanish pureed gazpachos, this recipe uses orange peppers and yellow or orange tomatoes to turn the soup a lovely golden hue.

1	large orange *or* yellow bell pepper, roasted and peeled (*see How To*)
3½	pounds yellow *or* orange tomatoes, peeled (*see Tip, page 490*) and cored, divided
1	cup coarsely chopped sweet onion
2	tablespoons extra-virgin olive oil
1	teaspoon salt
	Freshly ground pepper to taste
2-3	red *or* green jalapeño peppers, seeded and minced, for garnish

Place roasted pepper, half the tomatoes, onion and oil in a blender and puree until smooth. Transfer to a large metal bowl. Puree the remaining tomatoes until smooth and add to the bowl; stir to combine. Refrigerate the gazpacho until chilled, at least 2 hours. Season with salt and pepper. Serve garnished with jalapeños, if desired.

PER SERVING: 104 calories; 5 g fat (1 g sat, 4 g mono); 0 mg cholesterol; 13 g carbohydrate; 0 g added sugars; 3 g protein; 3 g fiber; 452 mg sodium; 804 mg potassium.
NUTRITION BONUS: Vitamin C (142% daily value), Folate (25% dv), Potassium (23% dv).

Roasted Parsnip Soup

H✳W   H⬆F   H♥H

MAKES: 6 servings, generous 1 cup each
ACTIVE TIME: 40 minutes | TOTAL: 1 hour

The earthy flavor of parsnips goes especially well with fragrant pears, but carrots or even rutabaga work nicely in this soup as well. Serve it as a first course or as a light main dish with a crusty whole-grain bread.

2	pounds parsnips, peeled and woody core removed (*see How To*)
2	pears, peeled and cut into eighths
1	small yellow *or* white onion, peeled and cut into eighths
1	tablespoon canola oil
1	teaspoon salt, divided
¼	teaspoon freshly ground pepper
1	cup balsamic vinegar
2¼	cups reduced-sodium chicken broth *or* vegetable broth
2¼	cups low-fat milk

1. Position rack in lower third of oven; preheat to 450°F.

2. Toss parsnips, pears, onion, oil, ½ teaspoon salt and pepper in a roasting pan. Roast, stirring every 10 minutes, until very soft and starting to brown, about 40 minutes.

3. Meanwhile, boil vinegar in a small saucepan until syrupy and reduced to about ¼ cup, 10 to 14 minutes. (Watch the syrup carefully during the last few minutes of reducing to prevent burning.) Remove from the heat.

4. Puree half of the parsnip mixture with broth in a blender until very smooth; transfer to a large saucepan. Puree the other half with milk until very smooth. Add to the saucepan and stir in the remaining ½ teaspoon salt. Heat the soup over medium heat, stirring often, about 5 minutes. Gently reheat the balsamic syrup if it has become thicker than syrup while standing. Ladle the soup into bowls and drizzle with the balsamic syrup.

PER SERVING: 246 calories; 4 g fat (1 g sat, 2 g mono); 6 mg cholesterol; 49 g carbohydrate; 0 g added sugars; 7 g protein; 9 g fiber; 671 mg sodium; 764 mg potassium.
NUTRITION BONUS: Vitamin C (50% daily value), Folate (28% dv), Potassium (22% dv), Calcium (19% dv).

How To

Prep Parsnips | Remove the peel with a vegetable peeler, then quarter the parsnip lengthwise and cut out the fibrous, woody core with a paring knife.

Leek & Potato Soup

H✁W   H❤H

MAKES: 6 servings, about 1 cup each
ACTIVE TIME: 25 minutes | TOTAL: 45 minutes

Our lightened version of potato-leek soup uses just a touch of reduced-fat sour cream to make it rich and creamy.

1½	teaspoons canola oil
3	leeks, trimmed, thinly sliced and rinsed (3 cups)
2	cloves garlic, minced
1½	teaspoons chopped fresh thyme *or* ½ teaspoon dried
6	cups reduced-sodium chicken broth
1¼	pounds all-purpose potatoes (about 3 medium), peeled and cut into small chunks
½	cup reduced-fat sour cream
¼	teaspoon salt
¼	teaspoon freshly ground pepper

1. Heat oil in a large heavy saucepan over low heat. Add leeks and cook, stirring, until softened, about 10 minutes. Add garlic and thyme; cook for 2 minutes more. Pour in broth, increase heat to medium and bring to a boil. Reduce heat to low and simmer for 10 minutes.

2. Pour the soup through a strainer set over a large bowl. Puree the leeks in a food processor or blender until smooth, adding some of the broth if necessary. Return the puree and broth to the saucepan. Add potatoes and simmer, covered, until the potatoes are soft, 10 to 15 minutes. Remove from the heat and mash the potatoes thoroughly with a potato masher.

3. Stir in sour cream, salt and pepper. Return to low heat and heat until hot, but not boiling. Serve hot or chilled.

PER SERVING: 152 calories; 4 g fat (2 g sat, 1 g mono); 8 mg cholesterol; 25 g carbohydrate; 0 g added sugars; 7 g protein; 2 g fiber; 620 mg sodium; 712 mg potassium.
NUTRITION BONUS: Vitamin C (40% daily value), Potassium (20% dv), Vitamin A (17% dv).

▶ Roasted Pumpkin-Apple Soup

H✁W   H⬆F   H❤H

MAKES: 12 servings, about 1 cup each
ACTIVE TIME: 30 minutes | TOTAL: 1 hour 10 minutes
TO MAKE AHEAD: Cover and refrigerate for up to 3 days.

Try this velvety soup as a delightful first course for a special meal or for dinner with grilled Cheddar sandwiches.

4	pounds pie pumpkin *or* butternut squash, peeled, seeded and cut into 2-inch chunks
4	large sweet-tart apples, such as Empire, Cameo *or* Braeburn, unpeeled, cored and cut into eighths
¼	cup extra-virgin olive oil
1¼	teaspoons salt, divided
¼	teaspoon freshly ground pepper
1	tablespoon chopped fresh sage
6	cups reduced-sodium chicken broth *or* vegetable broth, divided
⅓	cup chopped hazelnuts, toasted (*see Tip, page 486*)
2	tablespoons hazelnut oil

1. Preheat oven to 450°F.

2. Toss pumpkin (or squash), apples, olive oil, 1 teaspoon salt and pepper in a large bowl. Spread evenly on a large rimmed baking sheet. Roast, stirring once, for 30 minutes. Stir in sage; continue roasting until very tender and starting to brown, 15 to 20 minutes more.

3. Transfer about one-third of the pumpkin (or squash) and apples to a blender along with 2 cups broth. Puree until smooth. Transfer to a Dutch oven and repeat for two more batches. Season with the remaining ¼ teaspoon salt and heat through over medium-low heat, stirring constantly to prevent splattering, for about 6 minutes. Serve each portion topped with hazelnuts and a drizzle of hazelnut oil.

PER SERVING: 180 calories; 9 g fat (1 g sat, 7 g mono); 0 mg cholesterol; 25 g carbohydrate; 0 g added sugars; 3 g protein; 6 g fiber; 525 mg sodium; 570 mg potassium.
NUTRITION BONUS: Vitamin A (288% daily value), Vitamin C (40% dv), Potassium (16% dv).

Cheddar Cauliflower Soup

H✖W

MAKES: 8 servings, 1 cup each
ACTIVE TIME: 35 minutes | TOTAL: 35 minutes

Start your meal off with a bowl of this satisfying, easy cheesy cauliflower soup.

2	tablespoons extra-virgin olive oil
2	large leeks, white and light green parts only, thinly sliced and rinsed
4	cups chopped cauliflower florets (from 1 medium head)
2½	cups low-fat milk, divided
2	cups water
1	bay leaf
1	teaspoon salt
½	teaspoon white *or* black pepper
3	tablespoons all-purpose flour
1½	cups shredded extra-sharp Cheddar cheese
1	tablespoon lemon juice

1. Heat oil in a large saucepan over medium heat. Add leeks and cook, stirring, until very soft, about 5 minutes. Add cauliflower, 2 cups milk, water, bay leaf, salt and pepper. Bring to a boil over medium-high heat, stirring often. Reduce heat to a simmer, cover and cook, stirring occasionally, until the cauliflower is soft, about 8 minutes.

2. Meanwhile, whisk the remaining ½ cup milk and flour in a small bowl. When the cauliflower is soft, remove the bay leaf and stir in the milk mixture. Cook over medium-high heat, stirring, until the soup has thickened slightly, about 2 minutes more. Remove from the heat. Stir in cheese and lemon juice.

PER SERVING: 187 calories; 11 g fat (5 g sat, 3 g mono); 27 mg cholesterol; 13 g carbohydrate; 0 g added sugars; 10 g protein; 2 g fiber; 489 mg sodium; 206 mg potassium.
NUTRITION BONUS: Vitamin C (50% daily value), Calcium (27% dv), Vitamin A (15% dv).

EatingWell Tip

Use stronger cheeses like extra-sharp Cheddar—they give a bigger flavor impact so you can use less and cut saturated fat and calories.

Making Soup from the Pantry

If you have a well-stocked pantry, the answer to "What's for dinner?" can be as simple as "Soup!" Just add a salad (*see page 82 for ideas*) and some crusty bread and dinner can be on the table in no time. Here are our favorite ingredients to keep handy for satisfying soups, plus three easy recipes for soups from the pantry.

Soup Ingredients to Keep on Hand

IN YOUR PANTRY:

Cans or boxes of reduced-sodium chicken, beef, mushroom, "no-chicken" and/or vegetable broth

Dried herbs and spices, assorted

Canned tomatoes (whole, diced, crushed); tomato paste

Salsa

Small whole-wheat pasta, such as orzo and elbows

Brown rice (regular or instant)

Barley (pearl or quick-cooking)

Canned or dried beans

Canned artichoke hearts

Garlic

Potatoes

Onions

IN YOUR REFRIGERATOR AND FREEZER:

Carrots

Celery

Frozen corn, peas, spinach, lima beans, chopped okra, edamame, broccoli

Sausage (chicken, turkey or pork)

Frozen homemade broth (*see page 78*)

3 Easy Soups from the Pantry

◀ **BLACK BEAN SOUP**

H✖W   H⬆F   H❤H

MAKES: 4 servings, about 1¼ cups each

ACTIVE TIME: 15 minutes | TOTAL: 25 minutes

TO MAKE AHEAD: Cover and refrigerate for up to 3 days. Garnish with sour cream and cilantro, if desired, just before serving.

- 1   tablespoon canola oil
- 1   small onion, chopped
- 1   tablespoon chili powder
- 1   teaspoon ground cumin
- 2   15-ounce cans black beans, rinsed
- 3   cups water
- ½   cup prepared salsa
- ¼   teaspoon salt
- 1   tablespoon lime juice
- 4   tablespoons reduced-fat sour cream (optional)
- 2   tablespoons chopped fresh cilantro (optional)

1. Heat oil in a large saucepan over medium heat. Add onion and cook, stirring, until beginning to soften, 2 to 3 minutes. Add chili powder and cumin and cook, stirring, 1 minute more. Add beans, water, salsa and salt. Bring to a boil; reduce heat and simmer for 10 minutes. Remove from the heat and stir in lime juice.

2. Transfer half the soup to a blender and puree (use caution when pureeing hot liquids). Stir the puree back into the saucepan. Serve garnished with sour cream and cilantro, if desired.

PER SERVING: 207 calories; 4 g fat (0 g sat, 2 g mono); 0 mg cholesterol; 34 g carbohydrate; 0 g added sugars; 10 g protein; 10 g fiber; 424 mg sodium; 586 mg potassium. NUTRITION BONUS: Folate (24% daily value), Iron (19% dv), Potassium & Vitamin C (17% dv).

QUICK TOMATO SOUP

H�metaW   H↑F   H♥H

MAKES: 6 servings, about 1½ cups each
ACTIVE TIME: 15 minutes | TOTAL: 30 minutes
TO MAKE AHEAD: Cover and refrigerate for up to 3 days.

- 1   tablespoon extra-virgin olive oil
- 3   cloves garlic, minced
- 1   teaspoon dried herbs, such as thyme, oregano, rosemary *or* basil
- ¼   teaspoon crushed red pepper (optional)
- 2   28-ounce cans crushed tomatoes
- 1   cup water
- 2   teaspoons sugar
- 2   cups nonfat *or* low-fat milk

Heat oil in a large saucepan over medium heat. Add garlic, herbs and crushed red pepper (if using); cook, stirring, until fragrant, about 30 seconds. Add tomatoes, water and sugar. Bring to a boil; reduce heat and simmer for 10 minutes. Stir in milk and heat through, about 1 minute.

PER SERVING: 142 calories; 3 g fat (0 g sat, 2 g mono); 2 mg cholesterol; 25 g carbohydrate; 1 g added sugars; 7 g protein; 5 g fiber; 385 mg sodium; 911 mg potassium.
NUTRITION BONUS: Vitamin C (42% daily value), Vitamin A (37% dv), Potassium (26% dv), Calcium & Iron (20% dv), Magnesium (16% dv).

PASTA & CHICKPEA SOUP

H�metaW   H↑F   H♥H

MAKES: 6 servings, 1½ cups each
ACTIVE TIME: 30 minutes | TOTAL: 30 minutes

- 2   teaspoons extra-virgin olive oil
- 2   cloves garlic, finely chopped
- 1   14-ounce can plum tomatoes, drained
- 1   large sprig fresh rosemary *or* 1½ teaspoons crushed dried
- 2   15-ounce cans reduced-sodium beef broth
- 2   cups water
- 2   19-ounce cans chickpeas, rinsed, divided
- 6   ounces whole-wheat elbow macaroni *or* cavatappi
- ½   teaspoon freshly ground pepper
- ⅓   cup grated Pecorino Romano *or* Parmesan cheese

1. Heat oil in a Dutch oven over low heat. Add garlic and cook, stirring, until golden, about 1 minute. Add tomatoes and rosemary; simmer for 5 minutes, crushing tomatoes with a fork or potato masher. Pour in broth and water; bring to a simmer over medium heat.

2. Meanwhile, mash 1 cup chickpeas in a small bowl with a fork or potato masher. Stir the mashed chickpeas, pasta and pepper into the tomato-broth mixture. Simmer, uncovered, until the pasta is tender, 8 to 10 minutes or according to package directions. Stir in the remaining whole chickpeas and heat through. If using fresh rosemary, remove the sprig. Serve the soup with a sprinkling of grated cheese.

PER SERVING: 307 calories; 5 g fat (2 g sat, 2 g mono); 8 mg cholesterol; 54 g carbohydrate; 0 g added sugars; 14 g protein; 10 g fiber; 657 mg sodium; 386 mg potassium. NUTRITION BONUS: Folate (26% daily value), Magnesium (20% dv), Iron (16% dv).

Cream of Mushroom & Barley Soup

H✕W   H↑F

MAKES: 4 servings, about 1¾ cups each
ACTIVE TIME: 50 minutes | TOTAL: 1¼ hours
TO MAKE AHEAD: Prepare soup through Step 4. Cover and refrigerate the soup and cooked barley separately for up to 3 days. To serve, combine (Step 5) and reheat.

This take on cream of mushroom soup is rich with earthy porcini mushrooms and has the added goodness of whole-grain barley. **Shopping Tips:** *Look for* **mushroom broth** *in aseptic containers at well-stocked supermarkets or natural-foods stores.* **Sherry** *is fortified wine originally from southern Spain. Don't use the "cooking sherry" sold in many supermarkets—it can be surprisingly high in sodium. Instead, purchase dry sherry that's sold with other fortified wines at your wine or liquor store.*

½	cup pearl barley
4½	cups reduced-sodium chicken broth *or* mushroom broth (*see Shopping Tips*), divided
1	ounce dried porcini mushrooms
2	cups boiling water
2	teaspoons butter
1	tablespoon extra-virgin olive oil
1	cup minced shallots (about 4 medium)
8	cups sliced white mushrooms (about 20 ounces)
2	stalks celery, finely chopped
1	tablespoon minced fresh sage *or* 1 teaspoon dried
¼	teaspoon salt
½	teaspoon freshly ground pepper
2	tablespoons all-purpose flour
1	cup dry sherry (*see Shopping Tips*)
½	cup reduced-fat sour cream
¼	cup minced fresh chives

1. Bring barley and 1½ cups broth to a boil in a small saucepan over high heat. Cover, reduce heat to low and simmer until tender, 30 to 35 minutes.

2. Meanwhile, combine porcinis and boiling water in a medium bowl and soak until softened, about 20 minutes. Line a sieve with paper towels, set it over a bowl and pour in mushrooms and soaking liquid. Reserve the soaking liquid. Transfer the mushrooms to a cutting board and finely chop.

3. Heat butter and oil in a Dutch oven over medium-high heat. Add shallots and cook, stirring often, until softened, about 2 minutes. Add white mushrooms and cook, stirring often, until they start to brown, 8 to 10 minutes. Add the porcinis, celery, sage, salt and pepper and cook, stirring often, until beginning to soften, about 3 minutes. Sprinkle flour over the vegetables and cook, stirring, until the flour is incorporated, about 1 minute. Add sherry and cook, stirring, until most of the sherry has evaporated, about 1 minute.

4. Add the soaking liquid and the remaining 3 cups broth; increase heat to high and bring to a boil. Reduce heat and simmer, stirring occasionally, until the soup has thickened, 18 to 22 minutes.

5. Add the cooked barley and continue cooking, stirring occasionally, until heated through, about 5 minutes more. Stir in sour cream. Garnish with chives.

PER SERVING: 333 calories; 10 g fat (4 g sat, 4 g mono); 17 mg cholesterol; 38 g carbohydrate; 0 g added sugars; 13 g protein; 6 g fiber; 822 mg sodium; 1,209 mg potassium.
NUTRITION BONUS: Potassium (35% daily value), Iron (21% dv), Vitamin A (18% dv).

EatingWell Tip

In creamy soups, try replacing heavy cream with reduced-fat sour cream. You **save 190 calories and 17 grams of saturated fat** per ½ cup and still get a velvety texture.

Tilapia Corn Chowder

H ✄ W   H ❤ H

MAKES: 6 servings, about 1¼ cups each
ACTIVE TIME: 45 minutes | TOTAL: 45 minutes

Use fresh corn in this light fish chowder when it's in season. (Photograph: page 50.)

2	ounces bacon (about 2 slices)
1	teaspoon canola oil
1	stalk celery, diced
1	leek, white part only, halved lengthwise, rinsed and thinly sliced
½	teaspoon salt
½	teaspoon freshly ground pepper
4	cups reduced-sodium chicken broth
8	ounces Yukon Gold potatoes, diced
2	cups fresh corn kernels (about 4 ears; *see Tip, page 483*) *or* frozen
1½	pounds tilapia fillets, cut into bite-size pieces
1	teaspoon finely chopped fresh thyme
1	cup half-and-half
2	teaspoons lemon juice
2	tablespoons chopped fresh chives (optional)

1. Chop bacon and cook in a Dutch oven over medium heat until crispy, 3 to 4 minutes. Drain on paper towels.

2. Add oil to the pan. Add celery, leek, salt and pepper and cook until the vegetables just begin to soften, about 2 minutes. Add broth, potatoes and corn. Bring to a gentle simmer. Cook until the potatoes are just tender and the corn is cooked through, about 8 minutes. Stir in tilapia and thyme; return to a gentle simmer. Cook until the tilapia is cooked through, about 4 minutes more. Remove from the heat.

3. Stir in half-and-half, lemon juice and the reserved bacon. Garnish with chives, if using.

PER SERVING: 279 calories; 9 g fat (4 g sat, 3 g mono); 75 mg cholesterol; 21 g carbohydrate; 0 g added sugars; 30 g protein; 2 g fiber; 729 mg sodium; 728 mg potassium.
NUTRITION BONUS: Vitamin C (25% daily value), Potassium (21% dv), Folate (17% dv), Magnesium (15% dv).

Southeast Asian–Inspired Salmon Soup

H ✄ W   H ❤ H

MAKES: 6 servings, about 2 cups each
ACTIVE TIME: 35 minutes | TOTAL: 35 minutes

A touch of chile-garlic sauce and hot sesame oil add heat to this delicately flavored salmon soup.

2	ounces bean thread noodles (*see Tip, page 481*)
2	tablespoons canola oil
3	tablespoons thinly sliced garlic
7	cups reduced-sodium chicken broth
1	15-ounce can petite diced tomatoes
1	tablespoon fish sauce (*see Tip, page 484*)
1	tablespoon chile-garlic sauce (*see Tip, page 482*)
2	teaspoons hot sesame oil, *or* to taste
1¼	pounds wild salmon fillet, skinned (*see Tip, page 489*) and cut into ½-inch cubes
1	cup thinly sliced scallions
½	cup loosely packed cilantro leaves
	Lime wedges for garnish

1. Place noodles in a large bowl, cover with hot tap water and soak until softened, 20 to 25 minutes. Drain.

2. Meanwhile, heat canola oil over medium heat in a Dutch oven. Add garlic and cook, stirring often, until golden brown, about 3 minutes. Transfer to a paper towel with a slotted spoon.

3. Carefully pour broth into the pan (it may spatter a little); bring to a boil. Stir in tomatoes and their juice, fish sauce, chile-garlic sauce and hot sesame oil. Stir in salmon, reduce heat and gently simmer until nearly cooked through, about 2 minutes. Stir in the noodles and scallions; simmer 1 minute more.

4. Top with cilantro and the crispy garlic. Serve with lime wedges, if desired.

PER SERVING: 284 calories; 13 g fat (2 g sat, 6 g mono); 60 mg cholesterol; 16 g carbohydrate; 0 g added sugars; 26 g protein; 1 g fiber; 1,140 mg sodium; 649 mg potassium.
NUTRITION BONUS: Vitamin C (28% daily value), Potassium (19% dv), Vitamin A (17% dv), omega-3s.

Minestrone with Endive & Pepperoni

H✂W   H⬆F   H❤H

MAKES: 6 servings, about 1½ cups each
ACTIVE TIME: 30 minutes | TOTAL: 30 minutes

Considering that this minestrone incorporates mostly frozen vegetables, it is remarkably savory and aromatic. Look for frozen soup or stew vegetables with potatoes, carrots, celery and onion in the mix to give the soup the best flavor. Although pepperoni isn't traditionally part of minestrone, you'll find it's a great shortcut to add spicy, complex flavor.

1	tablespoon extra-virgin olive oil
½	cup chopped fresh *or* frozen (thawed) bell peppers, any color
5	cups reduced-sodium beef broth
1½	teaspoons dried oregano
1	teaspoon dried thyme
⅔	cup whole-wheat elbow noodles *or* other small pasta
1	pound frozen mixed soup (*or* stew) vegetables (including potatoes, carrots, celery, onion), thawed, chopped
1	cup frozen baby lima beans, thawed
1	15-ounce can diced tomatoes with garlic and onion
½	cup diced pepperoni
3	cups lightly packed coarsely chopped curly endive *or* chard, tough stems removed
	Freshly ground pepper to taste
	Freshly grated Parmesan cheese for garnish

1. Heat oil in a large saucepan or Dutch oven over medium-high heat. Add bell peppers and cook, stirring, for 3 minutes. Add broth, oregano and thyme; bring to a rolling boil over high heat. Add pasta and cook for 3 minutes less than the package directions.

2. Add mixed soup (or stew) vegetables and lima beans. Bring to a boil over medium-high heat; boil until the vegetables are almost tender, about 3 minutes. Stir in tomatoes, pepperoni and endive (or chard); return to a boil. Adjust the heat and simmer until the endive (or chard) is just tender, about 5 minutes. Season with pepper and garnish with Parmesan, if desired.

PER SERVING: 213 calories; 7 g fat (2 g sat, 3 g mono); 14 mg cholesterol; 28 g carbohydrate; 0 g added sugars; 9 g protein; 5 g fiber; 721 mg sodium; 352 mg potassium.
NUTRITION BONUS: Vitamin C (48% daily value), Vitamin A (28% dv).

EatingWell Tip

Meat doesn't have to be the centerpiece of the meal. Try using just a little bit of meats like pepperoni as flavor enhancers to add complexity to a dish without being the star ingredient.

Chicken & Spinach Soup with Fresh Pesto

H✖W   H⬆F   H♥H

MAKES: 5 servings, about 1½ cups each
ACTIVE TIME: 30 minutes | TOTAL: 30 minutes

This fragrant, Italian-flavored soup takes advantage of quick-cooking ingredients—boneless, skinless chicken breast, bagged baby spinach and canned beans. It features a simple homemade basil pesto swirled in at the end to add a fresh herb flavor. If you are very pressed for time, you can substitute 3 to 4 tablespoons of a store-bought basil pesto.

2	teaspoons plus 1 tablespoon extra-virgin olive oil, divided
½	cup chopped carrot *or* diced red bell pepper
1	large boneless, skinless chicken breast (about 8 ounces), cut into quarters
1	large clove garlic, minced
5	cups reduced-sodium chicken broth
1½	teaspoons dried marjoram
6	ounces baby spinach, coarsely chopped
1	15-ounce can cannellini beans *or* great northern beans, rinsed
¼	cup grated Parmesan cheese
⅓	cup lightly packed fresh basil leaves
	Freshly ground pepper to taste
¾	cup whole-grain croutons (*see How To*) for garnish

1. Heat 2 teaspoons oil in a large saucepan or Dutch oven over medium-high heat. Add carrot (or bell pepper) and chicken; cook, turning the chicken and stirring frequently, until the chicken begins to brown, 3 to 4 minutes. Add garlic and cook, stirring, for 1 minute more. Stir in broth and marjoram; bring to a boil over high heat. Reduce the heat and simmer, stirring occasionally, until the chicken is cooked through, about 5 minutes.

2. With a slotted spoon, transfer the chicken pieces to a clean cutting board to cool. Add spinach and beans to the pot and bring to a gentle boil. Cook for 5 minutes to blend the flavors.

3. Combine the remaining 1 tablespoon oil, Parmesan and basil in a food processor (a mini processor works well). Process until a coarse paste forms, adding a little water and scraping down the sides as necessary.

4. Cut the chicken into bite-size pieces. Stir the chicken and pesto into the pot. Season with pepper. Heat until hot. Garnish with croutons, if desired.

PER SERVING: 204 calories; 8 g fat (2 g sat, 4 g mono); 29 mg cholesterol; 16 g carbohydrate; 0 g added sugars; 18 g protein; 6 g fiber; 691 mg sodium; 529 mg potassium.
NUTRITION BONUS: Vitamin A (111% daily value), Folate & Vitamin C (20% dv), Potassium (15% dv).

How To

Make Your Own Croutons | Remove the crusts from 3 slices whole-wheat country bread (5-6 ounces); tear the bread into ½- to 1-inch pieces or dice into cubes. Toss on a large baking sheet with 1 tablespoon extra-virgin olive oil and freshly ground pepper to taste. Bake at 400°F until golden brown and crisp, 10 to 12 minutes. (*Store airtight at room temperature for up to 3 days.*)
MAKES: **about 2 cups** | PER 1/2-CUP SERVING: 119 calories; 5 g fat (1 g sat, 3 g mono); 0 mg cholesterol; 15 g carbohydrate; 2 g added sugars; 5 g protein; 2 g fiber; 167 mg sodium; 89 mg potassium.

Sausage & Vegetable Soup

H✂W   H⬆F   H❤H

MAKES: 12 servings, about 2 cups each
ACTIVE TIME: 30 minutes | TOTAL: 1 hour
TO MAKE AHEAD: Cover and refrigerate for up to 1 day.

Chock-full of vegetables, thick with kidney beans and gently seasoned with garlic and anise, this soup typifies the Portuguese way of cooking. (Photograph: page 50.)

    8   ounces hot Italian turkey sausage,
            casings removed
    8   ounces sweet Italian turkey sausage,
            casings removed
    5   cups water
    3   large white potatoes (about 2½ pounds),
            cut into ½-inch cubes
    3   stalks celery, sliced
    1   small zucchini, sliced
    1   medium onion, chopped
    1   28-ounce can whole tomatoes, chopped,
            juice reserved
    1   15-ounce can kidney beans, rinsed
   ¾   cup sliced olives
    2   cloves garlic, minced
    1   teaspoon aniseed
   ½   teaspoon freshly ground pepper

1. Cook hot and sweet sausages in a Dutch oven over medium heat, breaking them up into small pieces with a wooden spoon, until browned and cooked through, about 6 minutes. Drain fat.

2. Stir in water, potatoes, celery, zucchini, onion, tomatoes with their juice, beans, olives, garlic, aniseed and pepper. Bring to a boil. Reduce heat to low, cover and simmer until vegetables are tender, about 30 minutes.

PER SERVING: 205 calories; 6 g fat (1 g sat, 0 g mono); 23 mg cholesterol; 27 g carbohydrate; 0 g added sugars; 11 g protein; 4 g fiber; 422 mg sodium; 552 mg potassium. NUTRITION BONUS: Vitamin C (35% daily value), Potassium (16% dv).

Soup Beans

H✂W   H⬆F   H❤H

MAKES: 8 servings, ¾ cup each
ACTIVE TIME: 20 minutes | TOTAL: 2 hours 10 minutes
TO MAKE AHEAD: Cover and refrigerate for up to 3 days or freeze for up to 3 months.

These days "soup beans" speak instant comfort to anyone who had familial connections from Appalachia, where every garden produced shelling beans that could be eaten fresh or grown to maturity for dry beans. Serve this thick, stewlike soup with cornbread, pickle relish and diced sweet onion.

    1   pound pinto, yellow-eyed or other dried beans,
            sorted and rinsed (2½ cups)
   12   cups water
    8   ounces finely diced ham (about 1½ cups)
    1   medium onion, peeled
    1   clove garlic, peeled
   ½   teaspoon salt
    1   teaspoon freshly ground pepper
   ¼   teaspoon crushed red pepper

1. Place beans, water, ham, onion, garlic, salt, pepper and crushed red pepper in a large Dutch oven; bring to a boil. Reduce heat and simmer, stirring occasionally, until the beans are very tender and beginning to burst, 1½ to 2 hours. If necessary, add ½ to 1 cup water more while simmering to keep the beans just submerged in cooking liquid.

2. Remove from the heat; discard the onion and garlic. Transfer 2 cups of the beans to a medium bowl and coarsely mash with a fork or potato masher. Return the mashed beans to the pot; stir to combine.

PER SERVING: 236 calories; 2 g fat (1 g sat, 1 g mono); 16 mg cholesterol; 35 g carbohydrate; 0 g added sugars; 19 g protein; 12 g fiber; 534 mg sodium; 679 mg potassium. NUTRITION BONUS: Folate (58% daily value), Potassium (19% dv), Iron (17% dv).

Louisiana Gumbo

H✂W H♥H

MAKES: 4 servings, about 1¾ cups each
ACTIVE TIME: 20 minutes | TOTAL: 50 minutes

This flavorful stew packed with shrimp, chicken, sausage, okra and tomatoes is a staple in Louisiana. Serve with Real Cornbread (page 190). **Shopping Tip:** *Andouille sausage is a smoky, mildly spicy pork sausage commonly used in Cajun cooking. Look for it near other smoked sausages at large supermarkets or specialty food stores.*

¼	cup all-purpose flour
1	tablespoon canola oil
1	onion, chopped
1	large green bell pepper, diced
1	stalk celery, minced
4	cloves garlic, minced
4	cups reduced-sodium chicken broth
1	14-ounce can whole tomatoes, drained and chopped
10	okra pods, trimmed and cut into ½-inch-long pieces (1 cup)
½	teaspoon freshly ground pepper
¼	teaspoon dried thyme
¼	teaspoon dried oregano
⅛	teaspoon cayenne pepper
1	bay leaf
½	cup long-grain white rice
6	ounces medium raw shrimp, peeled and deveined (*see Tip, page 489*)
4	ounces boneless, skinless chicken breast *or* thigh meat, trimmed and cut into ½-inch pieces
2	ounces andouille sausage (*see Shopping Tip*) *or* kielbasa, thinly sliced
	Hot sauce to taste

1. Heat a heavy cast-iron skillet over medium heat. Add flour and cook, stirring constantly with a wooden spoon, until the flour turns a deep golden color, 7 to 10 minutes. Transfer the flour to a plate and let cool. (There will be a strong aroma similar to burnt toast. Be careful not to let the flour burn; reduce the heat if flour seems to be browning too quickly.) (*Alternatively, toast the flour in a pie plate in a 400°F oven for 20 minutes.*)

2. Heat oil in a heavy stockpot or Dutch oven over medium heat. Add onion, bell pepper, celery and garlic; cook, stirring occasionally, until the onions are lightly browned, about 7 minutes. Stir in the toasted flour. Gradually stir in broth and bring to a simmer, stirring. Add tomatoes, okra, pepper, thyme, oregano, cayenne and bay leaf. Cover and cook for 15 minutes. Stir in rice and cook, covered, for 15 minutes longer.

3. Add shrimp, chicken and sausage; simmer until the shrimp is opaque inside, the chicken is no longer pink and the rice is tender, about 5 minutes longer. Discard the bay leaf. Ladle into bowls and serve with hot sauce.

PER SERVING: 309 calories; 6 g fat (1 g sat, 3 g mono); 92 mg cholesterol; 37 g carbohydrate; 0 g added sugars; 25 g protein; 4 g fiber; 830 mg sodium; 767 mg potassium.
NUTRITION BONUS: Vitamin C (83% daily value), Folate (29% dv), Iron & Potassium (22% dv), Magnesium (16% dv).

EatingWell Tip

Most store-bought broth is high in sodium. Look for reduced-sodium varieties (aim for a brand with 554 mg, or lower, per cup). Or make your own broth with no added sodium (*see page 78*).

Quick Pepperpot Soup

H✹W

MAKES: 6 servings, about 1½ cups each
ACTIVE TIME: 40 minutes | TOTAL: 40 minutes

Jamaican pepperpot soup is usually a long-simmered preparation made with tough cuts of meat and vegetables. This version uses quick-cooking sirloin instead to get it on the table fast. If you're not a fan of beef, try the soup with shrimp instead. **Shopping Tips:** *One of the hottest chile peppers,* **Scotch bonnets** *come in vivid shades of red, orange and green and have a distinctive citrus note. If you can't find Scotch bonnet peppers, habaneros can be substituted. More commonly referred to as amaranth in the U.S.,* **callaloo** *is the ubiquitous cooking green in Jamaica. Some farmers consider it to be simply a weed, but if you're lucky to find it in bunches at your farmers' market or a Caribbean market, snap it up! It has a texture somewhere between that of collard greens and spinach, both of which are fine substitutes.*

- 1 **tablespoon canola oil**
- 1 **pound sirloin steak, trimmed, cut into ½-inch pieces**
- 1½ **teaspoons salt, divided**
- 1 **small white onion, diced**
- 1 **clove garlic, minced**
- 1 **teaspoon minced Scotch bonnet chile pepper** (*see Shopping Tips*), *or* **to taste**
- 1 **teaspoon chopped fresh thyme** *or* **¼ teaspoon dried**
- 4 **cups water**
- 1 **teaspoon cornstarch**
- 1 **pound sweet potato (about 1 large), cut into ½-inch pieces**
- 1 **cup chopped (½-inch) okra, fresh** *or* **frozen** (*not* **thawed**)
- 3 **cups chopped callaloo (***see Shopping Tips***), collard greens** *or* **spinach**
- 3 **scallions, sliced**
- 1 **14-ounce can "lite" coconut milk, well shaken**

1. Heat oil in a Dutch oven over medium heat. Add steak and ½ teaspoon salt; cook, stirring occasionally, until no longer pink on the outside, 3 to 4 minutes. Transfer to a plate.

2. Add onion, garlic, chile pepper and thyme to the pot and cook, stirring, for 1 minute. Whisk water and cornstarch in a bowl or large measuring cup; add to the pot along with sweet potato and okra. Bring to a boil over high heat; boil for 1 minute. Reduce heat to a simmer and cook until the vegetables are almost tender, 3 to 5 minutes. Stir in callaloo (or collards or spinach) and the remaining 1 teaspoon salt; cook until tender, 2 to 3 minutes more. Add scallions and the steak plus any accumulated juices. Cook until the steak is hot and just cooked through, 1 to 2 minutes more. Remove from the heat and stir in coconut milk.

PER SERVING: 240 calories; 10 g fat (5 g sat, 3 g mono); 28 mg cholesterol; 20 g carbohydrate; 1 g added sugars; 18 g protein; 4 g fiber; 680 mg sodium; 628 mg potassium.
NUTRITION BONUS: Vitamin A (80% daily value), Vitamin C (35% dv), Zinc (20% dv), Potassium (18% dv).

Root Vegetable Stew
with Herbed Dumplings

H♣F

MAKES: 6 servings, about 1½ cups stew &
3 dumplings each
ACTIVE TIME: 50 minutes | TOTAL: 1 hour

This root vegetable stew is flecked with sausage and topped with whole-wheat herbed dumplings. Turn up the heat by using hot Italian sausage or make it crowd-pleasing with sweet sausage. If you find beets or turnips with their greens still attached, the greens of one bunch should yield just enough for this dish. Otherwise use whatever dark leafy greens look fresh at the market.

STEW

4	teaspoons extra-virgin olive oil, divided
8	ounces Italian sausage links, hot *or* sweet
2	pounds assorted root vegetables, such as carrots, turnips, parsnips, beets *or* celeriac, peeled (*see How To*) and diced
1	large onion, diced
4	cloves garlic, minced
1	tablespoon chopped fresh sage *or* rosemary
2	cups reduced-sodium chicken broth
2	cups water
3	cups chopped dark leafy greens, such as beet, turnip, kale *or* chard

DUMPLINGS

1¼	cups whole-wheat pastry flour (*see Tip, page 485*)
½	cup cake flour
1	tablespoon chopped fresh sage *or* rosemary
1	tablespoon baking powder
¼	teaspoon salt
1	large egg, lightly beaten
½	cup low-fat milk

1. **To prepare stew:** Heat 2 teaspoons oil in a medium skillet over medium heat. Add sausages and cook until browned on all sides, 5 to 6 minutes. Transfer to a cutting board. Let cool slightly; cut into 1-inch pieces.

2. If using parsnips, quarter lengthwise and remove the woody core before dicing. Heat the remaining 2 teaspoons oil in a Dutch oven over medium heat. Cook onion, stirring occasionally, until barely tender, about 4 minutes. Add root vegetables and cook for 5 minutes. Add garlic and sage (or rosemary) and cook until fragrant, about 30 seconds. Add broth and water and bring to a simmer, stirring often.

3. **To prepare dumplings:** Meanwhile, whisk whole-wheat flour, cake flour, sage (or rosemary), baking powder and salt in a medium bowl. Add egg and milk and stir until a stiff batter forms.

4. When the stew reaches a simmer, stir in greens and the sausage and return to a simmer. Drop the dough, about 1 tablespoon at a time, over the stew, making about 18 dumplings. Adjust the heat to maintain a gentle simmer, cover and cook undisturbed until the dumplings are puffed, the vegetables are tender and the sausage is cooked through, about 10 minutes.

PER SERVING: 407 calories; 17 g fat (5 g sat, 8 g mono); 65 mg cholesterol; 50 g carbohydrate; 0 g added sugars; 14 g protein; 8 g fiber; 885 mg sodium; 858 mg potassium.
NUTRITION BONUS: Vitamin A (151% daily value), Vitamin C (43% dv), Folate (32% dv), Calcium (28% dv), Potassium (25% dv), Iron (16% dv).

How To

Peel Root Vegetables | Beets, carrots and parsnips are easily peeled with a vegetable peeler, but for tougher-skinned roots like celeriac, rutabaga and turnips, removing the peel with a knife can be easier. Cut off one end of the root to create a flat surface to keep it steady on the cutting board. Follow the contour of the vegetable with your knife. If you use a vegetable peeler on the tougher roots, peel around each vegetable at least three times to ensure all the fibrous skin has been removed.

Bouillabaisse with Spicy Rouille

H✱W H♥H

MAKES: 6 servings, about 1⅓ cups each
ACTIVE TIME: 1¼ hours | TOTAL: 1½ hours
TO MAKE AHEAD: Prepare through Step 1. Cover and refrigerate for up to 1 day. Reheat and proceed with Step 2.

This famous Provençal stew was traditionally made with fishermen's catch of the day. Our version uses ocean-friendly calamari, tilapia and scallops. **Shopping Tips:** *Be sure to buy* **"dry" sea scallops**. *"Wet" scallops, which have been treated with sodium tripolyphosphate (STP), are not only mushy and less flavorful, but will not brown properly. Some scallops will have a small white muscle on the side; remove it before cooking.* **Calamari**, *also known as squid, is sold frozen or fresh in the seafood department of the grocery store. Look for cleaned calamari, with its cartilage and ink removed; otherwise ask at the fish counter to have it cleaned.*

- **1 tablespoon extra-virgin olive oil**
- **2 leeks, white parts only, halved lengthwise, thinly sliced and washed**
- **1 stalk celery, diced**
- **4 cloves garlic, minced**
- **½ teaspoon fennel seeds, crushed**
- **4 plum tomatoes, diced**
- **2 large red potatoes, diced (½-inch pieces)**
- **1 cup dry white wine**
- **2 8-ounce bottles clam juice (*see Tip, page 483*)**
- **1 cup water**
- **2 4-inch strips orange peel (*see Tip, page 483*)**
- **2 bay leaves**
- **Pinch of saffron (*see Tip, page 488*)**
- **8 ounces tilapia fillets, cut into thirds**
- **8 ounces large dry sea scallops (*see Shopping Tips*), halved**
- **8 ounces cleaned, sliced calamari (squid) tubes and tentacles (*see Shopping Tips*)**
- **Spicy Rouille (*right*)**

1. Heat oil in a Dutch oven over medium-high heat. Add leeks, celery, garlic and fennel seeds and cook, stirring often, until the leeks are softened, 3 to 4 minutes. Add tomatoes and potatoes; cook, stirring often, until the tomatoes begin to break down, about 4 minutes. Add wine, increase heat to high, bring to a boil, and cook, stirring often, until reduced, 2 to 3 minutes. Add clam juice, water, orange peel, bay leaves and saffron and bring to a boil. Reduce heat and simmer, stirring occasionally, until the potatoes are just tender, about 15 minutes.

2. Carefully submerge tilapia and scallops in the soup, return to a simmer and cook for 2 minutes. Add calamari, submerge in the soup, and simmer until cooked through, about 3 minutes. Discard orange peel and bay leaves. Serve the soup with a spoonful of Spicy Rouille on top.

PER SERVING: 243 calories; 5 g fat (1 g sat, 2 g mono); 122 mg cholesterol; 22 g carbohydrate; 0 g added sugars; 23 g protein; 2 g fiber; 405 mg sodium; 936 mg potassium.
NUTRITION BONUS: Vitamin C (42% daily value), Potassium & Vitamin A (27% dv), Magnesium (21% dv).

SPICY ROUILLE

MAKES: ⅓ cup, for 6 servings
ACTIVE TIME: 5 minutes | TOTAL: 5 minutes
TO MAKE AHEAD: Cover and refrigerate for up to 4 days.

This bright red garlicky sauce (pronounced "roo-EE") has a nice kick of cayenne. Traditionally an accompaniment for bouillabaisse, it's also great served as a condiment for Easy Sautéed Fish Fillets (page 284).

- **¼ cup chopped jarred roasted red peppers**
- **3 tablespoons low-fat mayonnaise**
- **2 teaspoons lemon juice**
- **1 teaspoon minced garlic**
- **¼ teaspoon salt**
- **¼ teaspoon freshly ground pepper**
- **¼ teaspoon cayenne pepper**
- **Pinch of saffron (*see Tip, page 488*)**

Combine red peppers, mayonnaise, lemon juice, garlic, salt, pepper, cayenne and saffron in a food processor; pulse, scraping down the sides as necessary, until smooth.

PER SERVING: 12 calories; 1 g fat (0 g sat, 0 g mono); 0 mg cholesterol; 2 g carbohydrate; 0 g added sugars; 0 g protein; 0 g fiber; 196 mg sodium; 7 mg potassium.

Making Your Own Broth

Store-bought broth is great for convenience, but making your own is actually quite easy and the great full flavor is worth the effort. Plus there's no added sodium when you make it at home. You can substitute homemade broths in any recipe calling for broth or stock—just taste and adjust the salt accordingly.

Roasted Vegetable Broth

MAKES: 16 cups

ACTIVE TIME: 30 minutes | TOTAL: 3 hours

TO MAKE AHEAD: Cover and refrigerate for up to 1 week or freeze for up to 3 months. | EQUIPMENT: 2 roasting pans

Roasting the vegetables yields rich and flavorful results; use this broth in any recipe that calls for vegetable broth.

- 6 **large carrots, cut into 1-inch pieces**
- 5 **large onions, cut into 1-inch pieces**
- 1 **bulb fennel, cored and cut into 1-inch pieces**
- 2 **tablespoons canola oil**
- 2 **tablespoons tomato paste**
- 1 **cup dry white wine, divided**
- 20 **cups water**
- 4 **stalks celery, cut into 1-inch pieces**
- ½ **bunch parsley (about 10 sprigs)**
- ½ **bunch thyme (about 8 sprigs)**
- 12 **black peppercorns**
- 6 **cloves garlic, crushed and peeled**
- 4 **bay leaves**

1. Preheat oven to 425°F.

2. Combine carrots, onions and fennel in a large roasting pan. Toss with oil. Transfer half the vegetables to a second roasting pan. Roast the vegetables for 45 minutes, stirring every 15 minutes and switching the position of the pans each time you stir.

3. In one pan, push the vegetables to one side and spread tomato paste in the other side. Continue roasting (both pans) until the tomato paste begins to blacken (PHOTO 1), about 15 minutes more.

4. Transfer the roasted vegetables to a large stockpot. Pour ½ cup wine into each roasting pan and place each pan over two burners on the stovetop. Bring to a boil over medium-high heat. Cook, scraping up any browned bits, for 1 to 2 minutes (PHOTO 2). Add the contents of the roasting pans to the stockpot, along with water, celery, parsley, thyme, peppercorns, garlic and bay leaves. Cover and bring to a simmer. Uncover and simmer for 1 hour without stirring, adjusting heat as necessary to maintain the simmer.

5. Strain the broth through a colander (PHOTO 3), pressing on the solids to remove all liquid. Discard solids. If not using immediately, cool the broth before storing (*see How To, opposite*).

ANALYSIS NOTE: After straining and skimming, broth has negligible calories and nutrients.

How To: Make Roasted Vegetable Broth

Rich Homemade Chicken Broth

MAKES: 8 cups

ACTIVE TIME: 15 minutes | TOTAL: 4¼ hours

TO MAKE AHEAD: Cover and refrigerate for up to 1 week or freeze for up to 3 months.

This chicken broth is extra rich and tasty because we use whole leg quarters with the meat on. If you want a thriftier, but still tasty, broth (or some might call it "stock"), try the recipe made from a leftover roast chicken carcass on page 338.

4	pounds chicken leg quarters, cut in half
1	small carrot, peeled and cut into 2-inch pieces
1	small stalk celery, cut into 2-inch pieces
1	small onion, root end trimmed, peeled and cut into eighths
6	sprigs fresh parsley
2	sprigs fresh thyme
1	bay leaf
1	clove garlic, crushed and peeled
20	black peppercorns
20	cups water

1. Place chicken, carrot, celery, onion, parsley, thyme, bay leaf, garlic and peppercorns in a stockpot or large (10-quart) Dutch oven (PHOTO 1). Add water. Bring to a boil over high heat, then reduce heat to maintain a simmer. Skim any foam and fat that rises to the surface (PHOTO 2). Simmer for 4 hours.

2. Place a colander over a large bowl and strain the broth, pressing on the solids to release as much liquid as possible (PHOTO 3). Discard solids. If not using immediately, cool the broth before storing (*see How To*).

3. Once the broth is cool, use a spoon to remove any congealed fat from the surface (PHOTO 4).

ANALYSIS NOTE: After straining and skimming, broth has negligible calories and nutrients

How To

Cool Broth Quickly | Set the bowl of broth into a larger bowl of ice water. Let stand in the ice water until the broth is at room temperature.

How To: Make Chicken Broth

Smoked Trout Salad with Herb & Horseradish Dressing

Watercress & Watermelon Salad with Goat Cheese

Coconut-Lime Chicken & Snow Peas

Sautéed Mushroom Salad

Salads

Building a Better Side Salad

Add a salad to your meal to pack more vegetable servings into your day. And when you make a salad with a variety of colors, you get an array of healthful nutrients. These mix-and-match salad ideas will re-invigorate your salad routine. **Pick from each category to build a delicious salad that serves 4.**

1 Start with 4 cups of greens:

ARUGULA is an aromatic green that lends a peppery mustard flavor to salads.

BELGIAN ENDIVE has compact, slender, elongated heads with cream-colored leaves that have yellow or pink tips.

BUTTERHEAD LETTUCES (Boston and Bibb) are soft, buttery-textured lettuces with mild flavor.

ESCAROLE is a type of chicory with tender, broad, pale green leaves that can be eaten raw or lightly cooked.

LEAF LETTUCES are lettuces that grow leaves from a single stalk rather than forming a tight head.

RADICCHIO heads have thick purple-red leaves streaked with white veins. Try it along with other salad greens to balance its bitter flavor.

ROMAINE grows in tall, cylindrical heads and is the lettuce of choice for Caesar salad.

SPINACH is a tender, mild-flavored green. Baby spinach is harvested earlier than large-leaved mature spinach. Remove the tough stems from mature spinach.

Make Your Own Croutons Remove the crusts from 3 slices **whole-wheat country bread** (5-6 ounces); tear the bread into ½- to 1-inch pieces or dice into cubes. Toss on a large baking sheet with 1 tablespoon extra-virgin **olive oil** and freshly ground **pepper** to taste. Bake at 400°F until golden brown and crisp, 10 to 12 minutes. (*Store airtight at room temperature for up to 3 days.*) | MAKES: about 2 cups.
PER 1/2-CUP SERVING: 119 calories; 5 g fat (1 g sat, 3 g mono); 0 mg cholesterol; 15 g carbohydrate; 2 g added sugars; 5 g protein; 2 g fiber; 167 mg sodium; 89 mg potassium.

2 Add a total of 1 cup of vegetables:

Artichoke hearts (canned), chopped
Beets, raw, shredded, *or* cooked *or* canned pickled, diced
Bell pepper, diced
Broccoli *or* cauliflower, chopped
Cabbage (red), shredded
Carrots, shredded
Corn kernels, fresh *or* frozen (thawed)
Cucumbers, sliced
Onion (red), slivered
Peas, frozen (thawed)
Radishes, sliced
Scallions, sliced
Snow peas, thinly sliced
Tomatoes, diced, *or* grape *or* cherry tomatoes, halved

3 Sprinkle up to ½ cup of add-ons on top:

Avocado, diced
Bacon, cooked, crumbled
Beans (canned), rinsed
Cheese, such as blue, feta, Cheddar, Parmesan, Asiago
      or Swiss, shredded *or* crumbled
Croutons, whole-wheat (*see recipe, left*)
Eggs, hard-boiled (*see How To, page 85*), chopped
Dried fruit, such as raisins, currants *or* cranberries,
      or chopped dried apricots, pineapple *or* mangoes
Nuts, toasted (*see Tip, page 486*), chopped
Olives, chopped *or* sliced
Orange *or* grapefruit segments

4 Toss with ¼ cup dressing (*opposite*):

Ranch Dressing
Orange-Sesame Dressing
Blue Cheese Vinaigrette
Raspberry Vinaigrette
Poppy Seed Dressing
Creamy Garlic Dressing
Tomato-Herb Dressing
Garlic-Dijon Vinaigrette
Herb & Horseradish Dressing

9 Easy Salad Dressings

Refrigerate these dressings for 3 to 5 days.

RANCH DRESSING Whisk ⅔ cup nonfat **buttermilk**, 6 tablespoons low-fat **mayonnaise**, ¼ cup chopped fresh **dill** (or 4 teaspoons dried), 2 tablespoons minced **red onion**, 4 teaspoons **white-wine vinegar**, ½ teaspoon each **garlic powder** and **salt** and freshly ground **pepper** to taste in a bowl until blended. MAKES: about 1¼ cups. | PER TABLESPOON: 8 calories; 0 g fat (0 g sat, 0 g mono).

ORANGE-SESAME DRESSING Whisk ¼ cup each **orange juice** and **cider vinegar** (or rice vinegar), 2 tablespoons each **canola oil**, **sugar** and reduced-sodium **soy sauce** and 2 teaspoons **toasted sesame oil** in a bowl until the sugar has dissolved. MAKES: about ¾ cup. | PER TABLESPOON: 37 calories; 3 g fat (0 g sat, 2 g mono).

BLUE CHEESE VINAIGRETTE Blend ⅓ cup crumbled **blue cheese**, ¼ cup reduced-sodium **chicken broth** (or water), 3 tablespoons each extra-virgin **olive oil**, **canola oil** and **tarragon vinegar** (or white-wine vinegar), 1 tablespoon minced **shallot**, 1 teaspoon Dijon **mustard**, ¼ teaspoon **salt** and ½ teaspoon freshly ground **pepper** in a blender until combined. (*Alternatively, mash blue cheese and broth or water in a bowl with a fork. Add oils, vinegar, shallot, mustard, salt and pepper and whisk until combined.*) MAKES: about 1 cup. PER TABLESPOON: 58 calories; 6 g fat (1 g sat, 4 g mono).

RASPBERRY VINAIGRETTE Whisk ⅔ cup **grapeseed oil** (or canola oil), ¼ cup **raspberry vinegar**, ¼ teaspoon **salt** and freshly ground **pepper** to taste in a bowl until blended. MAKES: about 1 cup. | PER TABLESPOON: 81 calories; 9 g fat (1 g sat, 1 g mono).

POPPY SEED DRESSING Whisk ½ cup each **buttermilk** and reduced-fat **sour cream**, 2 tablespoons **honey**, 1 tablespoon **lemon juice** and 1½ teaspoons toasted **poppy seeds** in a bowl until smooth. MAKES: about 1 cup. | PER TABLESPOON: 23 calories; 1 g fat (1 g sat, 0 g mono).

CREAMY GARLIC DRESSING Blend ½ cup **buttermilk**, ¼ cup low-fat **mayonnaise**, 2 tablespoons grated **Parmesan cheese**, 1½ tablespoons **lemon juice**, 2 teaspoons reduced-sodium **soy sauce**, 1 minced **garlic** clove, ⅛ teaspoon **salt** and freshly ground **pepper** to taste in a blender until smooth. MAKES: about 1 cup. PER TABLESPOON: 10 calories; 0 g fat (0 g sat, 0 g mono).

TOMATO-HERB DRESSING Whisk ⅔ cup **tomato juice**, 2 tablespoons each extra-virgin **olive oil** and whole-grain **mustard**, 1½ tablespoons **red-wine vinegar**, 1 tablespoon each chopped fresh **tarragon** and **chives**, 2 minced **garlic** cloves, ¼ teaspoon **salt** and freshly ground **pepper** to taste in a bowl until blended. MAKES: about 1 cup. | PER TABLESPOON: 21 calories; 2 g fat (0 g sat, 1 g mono).

GARLIC-DIJON VINAIGRETTE Whisk ½ cup extra-virgin **olive oil** and ¼ cup each **lemon juice** and **red-wine vinegar** in a medium bowl. Add 2 tablespoons Dijon **mustard** and 2 minced small **garlic** cloves; whisk until smooth. Season with ¼ teaspoon **salt** and freshly ground **pepper** to taste. MAKES: about 1 cup. PER TABLESPOON: 65 calories; 7 g fat (1 g sat, 5 g mono).

HERB & HORSERADISH DRESSING Whisk 1 cup **crème fraîche** (or reduced-fat sour cream), ⅔ cup finely chopped mixed fresh **herbs** (such as chives, dill, flat-leaf parsley), ¼ cup prepared **horseradish**, ¼ teaspoon **salt** and freshly ground **pepper** to taste in a bowl until combined. MAKES: about 1 cup. | PER TABLESPOON: 51 calories; 5 g fat (3 g sat, 0 g mono).

◄ Watercress & Endive Salad

H✖W   H⬆F   H♥H

MAKES: 4 servings, about 1 cup each
ACTIVE TIME: 15 minutes | TOTAL: 15 minutes

Watercress and Belgian endive are topped with fresh corn kernels, grated egg and a simple lemon vinaigrette for a stunning first-course salad.

- ¾ teaspoon freshly grated lemon zest
- 2 tablespoons lemon juice
- 1 tablespoon extra-virgin olive oil
- ¼ teaspoon salt
- 4 cups watercress, tough stems removed
- 2 hard-boiled eggs (*see How To*), grated through the large holes of a box grater
- ½ cup fresh corn kernels (*see Tip, page 483*)
- 2 heads Belgian endive, trimmed and leaves separated
  Freshly ground pepper to taste

Whisk lemon zest, lemon juice, oil and salt in a large bowl. Add watercress, egg and corn; toss to combine. To serve, arrange about 6 endive leaves on each salad plate and top with about 1 cup of the salad. Season with pepper.

PER SERVING: 135 calories; 7 g fat (2 g sat, 4 g mono); 106 mg cholesterol; 13 g carbohydrate; 0 g added sugars; 8 g protein; 9 g fiber; 250 mg sodium; 1,009 mg potassium.
NUTRITION BONUS: Vitamin A (136% daily value), Folate (97% dv), Vitamin C (60% dv), Potassium (29% dv), Calcium (19% dv), Zinc (16% dv).

How To

Hard-Boil Eggs | Place eggs in a single layer in a saucepan; cover with water. Bring to a simmer over medium-high heat. Reduce heat to low and cook at the barest simmer for 10 minutes. Remove from heat, pour out hot water and cover the eggs with ice-cold water. Let stand until cool enough to handle before peeling.

Spring Green Salad with Rouille Dressing

H✖W   H♥H

MAKES: 6 servings, 1⅓ cups each
ACTIVE TIME: 20 minutes | TOTAL: 20 minutes

Fresh greens are set off by a dressing that takes its cue from the nutty, creamy mélange that's stirred into bouillabaisse. **Shopping Tip:** *White balsamic vinegar is unaged balsamic made from Italian white wine grapes and grape musts (unfermented crushed grapes). Its mild flavor and clear color make it ideal for salad dressing.*

ROUILLE DRESSING
- ⅓ cup chopped hazelnuts
- ½ cup jarred pimiento peppers, rinsed
- ½ teaspoon chopped garlic
- 2 tablespoons water
- 1½ tablespoons white balsamic vinegar (*see Shopping Tip*) *or* white-wine vinegar
- ½ teaspoon salt
- ½ teaspoon freshly ground pepper

SALAD
- 1 large cucumber, peeled, halved, seeded and cut into thin half-moons
- 2 stalks celery, thinly sliced
- 4 cups bite-size pieces romaine lettuce
- 1 cup baby spinach leaves
- 24 fresh basil leaves, chopped

1. **To prepare dressing:** Toast hazelnuts in a small dry skillet over medium-low heat, stirring often, until lightly browned, 2 to 4 minutes. Transfer to a food processor; let cool for 5 minutes. Add pimientos, garlic, water, vinegar, salt and pepper. Process until smooth.

2. **To prepare salad:** Combine cucumber, celery, romaine, spinach and basil in a salad bowl. Add the dressing, toss gently, and serve.

PER SERVING: 73 calories; 4 g fat (0 g sat, 3 g mono); 0 mg cholesterol; 6 g carbohydrate; 0 g added sugars; 2 g protein; 2 g fiber; 354 mg sodium; 256 mg potassium.
NUTRITION BONUS: Vitamin A (73% daily value), Vitamin C (22% dv), Folate (18% dv).

Watercress & Watermelon Salad with Goat Cheese

H✖W

MAKES: 5 servings, 2 cups each
ACTIVE TIME: 20 minutes | TOTAL: 20 minutes

The contrasting flavors and textures of crisp, sweet watermelon and creamy, tangy goat cheese are magical partners. (Photograph: page 80.) Top with sliced grilled chicken (see page 479) to make it a meal.

- 3 tablespoons extra-virgin olive oil
- 3 tablespoons orange juice
- 1 tablespoon red-wine vinegar
- ¼ teaspoon salt
  Freshly ground pepper to taste
- 8 cups watercress, tough stems removed,
  or mixed salad greens (5 ounces)
- 4 cups diced seedless watermelon
  (about 3 pounds with the rind)
- ¼ cup very thinly sliced red onion
- 2 ounces goat cheese, crumbled
- ½ cup chopped hazelnuts, toasted (*see Tip, page 486*)

Whisk oil, orange juice, vinegar, salt and pepper in a large bowl until well combined. Add watercress, watermelon and red onion; toss to coat. Divide among 5 plates. Top with goat cheese and hazelnuts to serve.

PER SERVING: 227 calories; 18 g fat (3 g sat, 12 g mono); 5 mg cholesterol; 13 g carbohydrate; 0 g added sugars; 6 g protein; 2 g fiber; 182 mg sodium; 425 mg potassium.
NUTRITION BONUS: Vitamin C (65% daily value), Vitamin A (51% dv).

► Caprese Salad

H✖W

MAKES: 4 servings, about 1¼ cups each
ACTIVE TIME: 15 minutes | TOTAL: 15 minutes

Summer-ripe tomatoes and fresh mozzarella need only a sprinkling of fresh herbs, salt and pepper to shine in this simple summer salad.

- 2 medium red tomatoes, cut into wedges
- 2 medium yellow tomatoes, cut into wedges
- ¾ cup diced fresh mozzarella cheese
- ¼ cup chopped fresh parsley
- 2 tablespoons chopped fresh basil
- ¼ teaspoon salt
  Freshly ground pepper to taste

Gently toss tomatoes, mozzarella, parsley, basil and salt together in a large bowl. Season with pepper.

PER SERVING: 93 calories; 5 g fat (3 g sat, 1 g mono); 17 mg cholesterol; 6 g carbohydrate; 0 g added sugars; 6 g protein; 2 g fiber; 308 mg sodium; 461 mg potassium.
NUTRITION BONUS: Vitamin C (38% daily value), Vitamin A (21% dv).

Warm Dandelion Greens with Roasted Garlic Dressing

H✖W H⬆F

MAKES: 4 servings, about 1½ cups each
ACTIVE TIME: 20 minutes | TOTAL: 1¼ hours (including garlic-roasting time)

Though the blooming of the season's first dandelions may trigger an impulse to get out the lawnmower, a delicious option is to pick them for salads. Eating spring greens, especially dandelion and spinach, is part of the natural rhythm of the seasons and in the olden days signaled the move from the heavy meat-based diet of winter into summer's lighter fare. The sweet flavor of Roasted Garlic Dressing served warm over the greens tenderizes them for a melt-in-your-mouth salad.

ROASTED GARLIC DRESSING

- 1   large head garlic, roasted (*see How To*)
- 3   tablespoons extra-virgin olive oil
- 2   tablespoons balsamic vinegar *or* red-wine vinegar
- 1   tablespoon lime juice
- ⅛   teaspoon salt
     Freshly ground pepper to taste

SALAD

- 1   medium shallot, finely chopped
- 6   cups bite-size pieces dandelion greens *or* spinach (about 1 bunch), tough stems removed
- ¼   cup pine nuts, toasted (*see Tip, page 486*)
- 2   ounces goat cheese, crumbled
     Freshly ground pepper to taste

1. **To prepare dressing:** Squeeze roasted garlic pulp into a blender or food processor (discard the skins). Add oil, vinegar, lime juice, salt and pepper and blend or process until smooth.

2. **To prepare salad:** Transfer the dressing to a small saucepan and place over medium heat until warm, 1 to 2 minutes. Add shallot and simmer until the shallot is softened, 3 to 5 minutes.

3. Place dandelion greens (or spinach) in a large salad bowl. Pour the warm dressing over the greens and toss until they are wilted and coated. Add pine nuts and goat cheese and toss again, slightly melting the cheese with the warm greens. Season with pepper.

PER SERVING: 263 calories; 22 g fat (4 g sat, 12 g mono); 7 mg cholesterol; 14 g carbohydrate; 0 g added sugars; 7 g protein; 3 g fiber; 192 mg sodium; 441 mg potassium.
NUTRITION BONUS: Vitamin A (172% daily value), Vitamin C (33% dv), Iron (20% dv), Calcium (19% dv).

How To

Roast Garlic | Rub off the excess papery skin from 1 large head of garlic without separating the cloves. Slice the tip off the head, exposing the ends of the cloves. Place the garlic on a piece of foil, drizzle with 1 tablespoon extra-virgin olive oil and wrap into a package. Bake at 400°F in a small baking dish until the garlic is very soft, 40 minutes to 1 hour. Unwrap and let cool slightly before using.

Green Salad with Asparagus & Peas

H✠W H⬆F H♥H

MAKES: 8 servings, about 2 cups each
ACTIVE TIME: 35 minutes | TOTAL: 35 minutes
TO MAKE AHEAD: Cover and refrigerate the dressing
for up to 5 days.

This salad combines two stars of the spring garden, asparagus and peas. Since the asparagus goes into the mix raw, you'll want to look for the freshest, most tender spears you can find and slice them into very thin rounds. (Photograph: page 5.)

2	teaspoons freshly grated lemon zest
¼	cup lemon juice
¼	cup canola oil *or* extra-virgin olive oil
1	teaspoon sugar
½	teaspoon salt
¼	teaspoon freshly ground pepper
2	heads Boston *or* Bibb lettuce, torn into bite-size pieces
2	cups very thinly sliced fresh asparagus (about 1 bunch)
2	cups shelled fresh peas (about 3 pounds unshelled)
1	pint grape *or* cherry tomatoes, halved
2	tablespoons minced fresh chives *or* scallion greens

Combine lemon zest and juice, oil, sugar, salt and pepper in a large salad bowl. Add lettuce, asparagus, peas, tomatoes and chives (or scallion greens); toss to coat.

PER SERVING: 113 calories; 7 g fat (1 g sat, 4 g mono); 0 mg cholesterol; 10 g carbohydrate; 1 g added sugars; 3 g protein; 3 g fiber; 152 mg sodium; 340 mg potassium.
NUTRITION BONUS: Vitamin A & Vitamin C (45% daily value), Folate (19% dv).

▶ Raspberry, Avocado & Mango Salad

H✠W H⬆F H♥H

MAKES: 5 servings, about 2 cups each
ACTIVE TIME: 25 minutes | TOTAL: 25 minutes

Pureed berries give the tangy wine vinegar dressing a creamy texture that gently clings to the lettuce and fruit. This is a salad to enjoy when fresh berries are in the market.

1½	cups fresh raspberries, divided
¼	cup extra-virgin olive oil
¼	cup red-wine vinegar
1	small clove garlic, coarsely chopped
¼	teaspoon kosher salt
⅛	teaspoon freshly ground pepper
8	cups mixed salad greens
1	ripe mango, diced (*see Tip, page 486*)
1	small ripe avocado, diced
½	cup thinly sliced red onion
¼	cup toasted chopped hazelnuts *or* sliced almonds (*see Tip, page 486*; optional)

1. Puree ½ cup raspberries, oil, vinegar, garlic, salt and pepper in a blender until combined.

2. Combine greens, mango, avocado and onion in a large bowl. Pour the dressing on top and gently toss to coat. Divide the salad among 5 salad plates. Top each with the remaining raspberries and sprinkle with nuts, if using.

PER SERVING: 215 calories; 16 g fat (2 g sat, 12 g mono); 0 mg cholesterol; 18 g carbohydrate; 0 g added sugars; 3 g protein; 7 g fiber; 82 mg sodium; 564 mg potassium.
NUTRITION BONUS: Vitamin C (65% daily value), Vitamin A (55% dv), Folate (36% dv), Potassium (16% dv).

EatingWell Tip

Add ingredients like fruit that have big bright flavors to your salad to **keep every bite flavorful without having to pile on more dressing**.

◀ Melon Panzanella

H✂W   H↑F   H♥H

MAKES: 6 servings, about 1 cup each
ACTIVE TIME: 30 minutes | TOTAL: 50 minutes

Traditional panzanella, Italian bread salad, was the inspiration for this dish. This variation uses sweet, ripe melon instead of tomatoes, plus peppery arugula and a touch of sizzled prosciutto to complement the taste of the melon. Try firm-textured orange- or green-fleshed melons, such as honeydew, casaba, cantaloupe or Galia. We even like it with watermelon.

    4   ounces whole-grain bread, torn into bite-size
          pieces (about 2½ cups)
    3   tablespoons extra-virgin olive oil
    1   ounce thinly sliced prosciutto, cut into thin
          strips (about ⅓ cup)
    2   cloves garlic, minced
    2   tablespoons red-wine vinegar
    ¼   teaspoon salt
    ¼   teaspoon freshly ground pepper
    4   cups torn arugula leaves
    2   cups cubed firm ripe melon
    2   tablespoons chopped fresh basil

1. Preheat oven to 250°F.

2. Spread bread pieces on a baking sheet. Bake until lightly toasted, about 20 minutes.

3. Meanwhile, heat oil in a large nonstick skillet over medium heat. Add prosciutto and cook, stirring occasionally, until crisp, 3 to 4 minutes. Add garlic and cook, stirring, 30 seconds more. Remove from the heat and stir in vinegar, salt and pepper.

4. Place arugula, melon, basil and the bread in a large bowl. Add the prosciutto mixture and toss to combine. Let stand for about 20 minutes before serving so the bread can absorb some of the dressing.

PER SERVING: 130 calories; 8 g fat (1 g sat, 5 g mono); 4 mg cholesterol; 13 g carbohydrate; 1 g added sugars; 3 g protein; 3 g fiber; 277 mg sodium; 150 mg potassium.
NUTRITION BONUS: Vitamin C (16% daily value).

Sautéed Mushroom Salad

H✂W   H♥H

MAKES: 6 servings, about 1⅓ cups each
ACTIVE TIME: 25 minutes | TOTAL: 25 minutes

Here we make a warm sherry-mushroom dressing to toss over bitter greens. The dressing wilts the greens until they are just tender. (Photograph: page 80.)

    2   tablespoons extra-virgin olive oil, divided
    1   small onion, halved and sliced
    1   pound white *or* cremini mushrooms, quartered
    2   cloves garlic, minced
  1½   teaspoons chopped fresh thyme
          or ½ teaspoon dried
    3   tablespoons dry sherry (*see Tip, page 489*)
    2   tablespoons lemon juice
    ¼   teaspoon salt
    ¼   teaspoon freshly ground pepper
    8   cups bitter salad greens, such as frisee, arugula
          or baby dandelion greens
    2   tablespoons grated Parmesan cheese

1. Heat 1 tablespoon oil in a large nonstick skillet over medium heat. Add onion and cook until softened, about 3 minutes. Add mushrooms and cook, stirring, until they release their juices, 10 to 12 minutes.

2. Add garlic and thyme and stir until fragrant, about 30 seconds. Add sherry and cook until mostly evaporated, about 3 minutes. Stir in the remaining 1 tablespoon oil, lemon juice, salt and pepper and continue cooking for 1 minute more. Pour over greens in a large bowl and toss to coat. Sprinkle with Parmesan.

PER SERVING: 85 calories; 6 g fat (1 g sat, 4 g mono); 1 mg cholesterol; 6 g carbohydrate; 0 g added sugars; 4 g protein; 1 g fiber; 135 mg sodium; 377 mg potassium.
NUTRITION BONUS: Vitamin C (15% daily value).

Smoked Trout Salad with Herb & Horseradish Dressing

H ✘ W

MAKES: 4 servings, about 3 cups each
ACTIVE TIME: 10 minutes | TOTAL: 10 minutes
TO MAKE AHEAD: Cover and refrigerate the dressing for 3 to 5 days.

Smoked trout tops heart-shaped watercress and mixed greens tossed with creamy horseradish dressing, creating a wonderful appetizer salad. (Photograph: page 80.)
Shopping Tip: *Mâche (pronounced "mosh"), also known as lamb's lettuce or corn salad, is a tangy green that resembles watercress. Popular in Europe, it is enjoyed in the first salads of spring. Look for it at specialty stores, large supermarkets and farmers' markets.*

1   head butterhead lettuce, torn into bite-size pieces
4   cups bite-size pieces watercress *or* arugula
       (about 1 bunch), tough stems removed
1   cup mâche (*see Shopping Tip*) *or* mixed salad
       greens
½   cup Herb & Horseradish Dressing (*page 83*)
4   ounces smoked trout fillet, skin removed
4   scallions, sliced
1   tablespoon capers, rinsed (optional)

Gently toss lettuce, watercress (or arugula) and mâche (or mixed greens) in a large bowl. Toss with Herb & Horseradish Dressing to coat. (*Cover and refrigerate the remaining dressing for up to 5 days.*) Divide the greens among 4 plates. Flake 1 ounce trout over each salad and sprinkle with scallions and capers (if using).

PER SERVING: 173 calories; 13 g fat (7 g sat, 0 g mono); 30 mg cholesterol; 4 g carbohydrate; 0 g added sugars; 10 g protein; 2 g fiber; 429 mg sodium; 325 mg potassium.
NUTRITION BONUS: Vitamin A (63% daily value), Vitamin C (42% dv), Folate (17% dv).

▶ Greek Salad with Sardines

H ✘ W   H ⬆ F   H ❤ H

MAKES: 4 servings, about 2 cups each
ACTIVE TIME: 20 minutes | TOTAL: 20 minutes

The fresh, tangy elements of a Greek salad—tomato, cucumber, feta, olives and lemony vinaigrette—pair well with rich-tasting sardines. Look for sardines with skin and bones (which are edible): they have more than four times the amount of calcium as skinless, boneless ones. If you have fresh sardines available in your supermarket, try them in place of canned. Lightly dredge them in salt-and-pepper-seasoned flour and cook in a little olive oil.

3   tablespoons lemon juice
2   tablespoons extra-virgin olive oil
1   clove garlic, minced
2   teaspoons dried oregano
½   teaspoon freshly ground pepper
3   medium tomatoes, cut into large chunks
1   large English cucumber, cut into large chunks
1   15-ounce can chickpeas, rinsed
⅓   cup crumbled feta cheese
¼   cup thinly sliced red onion
2   tablespoons sliced Kalamata olives
2   4-ounce cans sardines with bones,
       packed in olive oil *or* water, drained

Whisk lemon juice, oil, garlic, oregano and pepper in a large bowl until well combined. Add tomatoes, cucumber, chickpeas, feta, onion and olives; gently toss to combine. Divide the salad among 4 plates and top with sardines.

PER SERVING: 320 calories; 19 g fat (4 g sat, 10 g mono); 67 mg cholesterol; 25 g carbohydrate; 0 g added sugars; 18 g protein; 7 g fiber; 686 mg sodium; 587 mg potassium.
NUTRITION BONUS: Vitamin C (35% daily value), Calcium (26% dv), Vitamin A (20% dv), Potassium (17% dv).

EatingWell Tip
Top your salad with a 3-ounce serving of sardines and you'll **get a whopping 1,950 mg of heart-healthy omega-3s**—the most from any fish available.

Grilled Halibut Salad Niçoise

H✕W   H▲F   H♥H

MAKES: 6 servings
ACTIVE TIME: 1 hour 10 minutes | TOTAL: 1½ hours
TO MAKE AHEAD: Prepare potatoes and green beans (Step 2), cover and refrigerate separately for up to 3 days.

Salad niçoise, a classic French salad, is typically made with tuna. Here we use sweet grilled halibut (in season in mid-summer) or striped bass. To make it quicker, substitute 2 or 3 cans of drained chunk light tuna. Or skip the fish altogether for a vegetarian main-course salad. We call for serving it on a platter, but it's just as beautiful individually plated. **Shopping Tip:** *Wild-caught halibut from the Pacific is sustainably fished and has a larger, more stable population, according to Monterey Bay Aquarium Seafood Watch (seafoodwatch.org).*

DRESSING

1	medium clove garlic
¼	teaspoon salt
5	tablespoons extra-virgin olive oil
6	tablespoons fresh orange juice, plus more to taste
¼	cup white-wine vinegar *or* red-wine vinegar
1	tablespoon Dijon mustard

SALAD

1½	pounds red potatoes (5-6 medium), scrubbed and halved
1¼	pounds green beans, trimmed
	Juice of 1 large lemon
2	tablespoons extra-virgin olive oil
½	teaspoon salt, divided
1	pound Pacific halibut *or* striped bass (*see Shopping Tip*)
¼	teaspoon coarsely ground pepper, plus more to taste
1	large head Boston lettuce
1½	cups grape tomatoes
3	hard-boiled eggs (*see How To, page 85*), peeled and cut into wedges
¼	cup sliced pitted black Niçoise *or* Kalamata olives
¼	cup finely chopped fresh parsley

1. **To prepare dressing:** Peel the garlic and smash with the side of a chef's knife. Using a fork, mash the garlic with ¼ teaspoon salt in a small bowl to form a coarse paste. Whisk in 5 tablespoons oil. Add 6 tablespoons orange juice, vinegar and mustard; whisk until well blended. Taste and whisk in up to 4 tablespoons more juice to mellow the flavor; season with more salt, if desired. Set aside at room temperature.

2. **To prepare salad:** Bring 1 inch of water to a boil in a large saucepan fitted with a steamer basket. Add potatoes; cook until tender, 10 to 15 minutes. Remove to a cutting board to cool. Add green beans to the steamer basket; cook until bright green and just tender, 4 to 6 minutes. Rinse in a colander with cold water until cool. Drain well.

3. When the potatoes are cool enough to handle, slice and place in a shallow bowl. Drizzle with ⅓ cup dressing; set aside. Place the green beans in a medium bowl and toss with 2 tablespoons dressing; set aside.

4. Combine lemon juice, 2 tablespoons oil and ¼ teaspoon salt in a sturdy sealable plastic bag; shake until the salt dissolves. Add fish and marinate for up to 20 minutes while you ready the grill.

5. Preheat grill to medium-high for 10 minutes, then reduce heat to medium. (For a charcoal grill, wait until the flames subside and only coals and some ash remain—flames will cause the oil on the fish to burn.)

6. Drain the fish and pat dry with paper towels. Season with the remaining ¼ teaspoon salt and ¼ teaspoon pepper. Oil the grill rack (*see Tip, page 485*). Grill the fish, turning once, until browned and just cooked through, 4 to 5 minutes per side for halibut; 3 to 4 minutes per side for bass.

7. Arrange lettuce leaves on a large serving platter. Arrange the fish (whole or flaked into large chunks), potatoes, green beans and tomatoes on top. Drizzle with the remaining dressing. Garnish with eggs, olives, parsley and pepper to taste.

PER SERVING: 448 calories; 23 g fat (4 g sat, 16 g mono); 130 mg cholesterol; 36 g carbohydrate; 0 g added sugars; 24 g protein; 6 g fiber; 565 mg sodium; 1,343 mg potassium.
NUTRITION BONUS: Vitamin C (75% daily value), Vitamin A (47% dv), Potassium (38% dv), Magnesium (30% dv), Folate (29% dv), Iron (17% dv).

Scallop Salad with Mirin-Soy Vinaigrette

H✕W   H♥H

MAKES: 4 servings
ACTIVE TIME: 25 minutes | TOTAL: 25 minutes

⏱ *An elegant main-course salad gets an Asian twist with a mirin-soy dressing. Serve with sesame breadsticks.*

- 2 tablespoons extra-virgin olive oil *or* peanut oil, divided
- 1 tablespoon mirin (*see Tip, page 486*)
- 1 tablespoon reduced-sodium soy sauce
- 1 tablespoon sherry vinegar *or* cider vinegar
- 1 tablespoon very finely chopped shallots
- ⅛ teaspoon salt
   Freshly ground pepper to taste
- 1 red bell pepper, cut into rings
- 1 pound dry sea scallops (*see Tip, page 489*), patted dry
- 4 cups mixed salad greens

1. Combine 1 tablespoon oil, mirin, soy sauce, vinegar and shallots in a small saucepan; bring to a boil and remove from the heat. Season with salt and pepper and set the vinaigrette aside.

2. Heat 1½ teaspoons oil in a large nonstick skillet over medium-high heat. Add bell pepper; cook, stirring, until wilted and lightly browned, 2 to 3 minutes. Remove with tongs and set aside.

3. Add the remaining 1½ teaspoons oil to the pan; add scallops. Season with salt and pepper. Cook until browned on both sides and opaque in the middle, 2 to 3 minutes per side.

4. Toss greens with 2 tablespoons of the reserved vinaigrette. Toss the scallops and bell pepper with the remaining vinaigrette. Serve on top of the greens.

PER SERVING: 195 calories; 8 g fat (1 g sat, 5 g mono); 37 mg cholesterol; 8 g carbohydrate; 0 g added sugars; 21 g protein; 2 g fiber; 368 mg sodium; 622 mg potassium.
NUTRITION BONUS: Vitamin C (85% daily value), Vitamin A (50% dv), Folate (24% dv), Magnesium (20% dv), Potassium (18% dv).

Coconut-Lime Chicken & Snow Peas

H✕W   H♥H

MAKES: 2 servings, about 3 cups each
ACTIVE TIME: 35 minutes | TOTAL: 35 minutes
TO MAKE AHEAD: The dressing (Step 2) will keep for up to 2 days.

⏱ *Double the flavor, halve the work—simply by using the same tangy combination of coconut milk, lime juice and brown sugar for both poaching the chicken and dressing the salad. Crisp romaine lettuce, cabbage and snow peas add freshness and an irresistible crunch. (Photograph: page 80.)*

- 1 cup "lite" coconut milk (*see Tip, page 483*)
- ¼ cup lime juice
- 2 tablespoons brown sugar
- ½ teaspoon salt
- 8 ounces chicken tenders
- 4 cups shredded romaine lettuce
- 1 cup shredded red cabbage
- 1 cup sliced snow peas
- 3 tablespoons minced fresh cilantro
- 2 tablespoons minced red onion

1. Preheat oven to 400°F.

2. Whisk coconut milk, lime juice, sugar and salt in an 8-inch glass baking dish. Set aside ¼ cup of the dressing in a large bowl. Place chicken in the baking dish; bake until cooked through, about 20 minutes.

3. Meanwhile, add lettuce, cabbage, snow peas, cilantro and onion to the large bowl with the dressing; toss to coat. Divide between 2 plates.

4. Transfer the chicken to a clean cutting board and thinly slice. Arrange the chicken slices on top of the salads. Drizzle 1 tablespoon of the coconut cooking liquid over each of the salads.

PER SERVING: 178 calories; 3 g fat (1 g sat, 0 g mono); 67 mg cholesterol; 13 g carbohydrate; 3 g added sugars; 29 g protein; 4 g fiber; 189 mg sodium; 407 mg potassium.
NUTRITION BONUS: Vitamin A (174% daily value), Vitamin C (102% dv), Folate (37% dv).

Spring Chicken & Blue Cheese Salad

H✻W

MAKES: 4 servings, about 2 cups greens & 3 ounces chicken each
ACTIVE TIME: 15 minutes | TOTAL: 55 minutes

This main-dish chicken salad has bright flavors of tarragon in a creamy blue cheese dressing with just a touch of sweetness from honey. **Shopping Tip:** *Thick and creamy Greek-style yogurt is made by removing the whey from cultured milk. Because the whey has been removed, you can cook with Greek yogurt without the normal separation that occurs when cooking with regular yogurt. Either can be used in this recipe, but we recommend using Greek yogurt if it's available at your supermarket.*

CHICKEN

- **1 cup nonfat Greek yogurt (see *Shopping Tip*)**
- **1 clove garlic, minced**
- **2 tablespoons extra-virgin olive oil**
- **2 tablespoons finely chopped fresh tarragon *or* 1 tablespoon dried**
- **1 pound boneless, skinless chicken breast, trimmed**
- **¼ teaspoon salt**
- **¼ teaspoon freshly ground pepper**

CREAMY BLUE CHEESE-TARRAGON DRESSING

- **2 ounces blue cheese**
- **3 tablespoons extra-virgin olive oil**
- **2 tablespoons red-wine vinegar**
- **1 tablespoon finely chopped fresh tarragon *or* 1 teaspoon dried**
- **1 tablespoon honey**
- **1-2 tablespoons nonfat Greek yogurt (see *Shopping Tip*; optional)**
- **⅛ teaspoon salt**
- **Freshly ground pepper to taste**

SALAD

- **1 head butterhead lettuce, torn into bite-size pieces**
- **½ head radicchio, cored and very thinly sliced**
- **1 cup baby arugula *or* mixed baby greens**
- **½ cup walnuts, toasted (see *Tip, page 486*) and chopped**

1. Preheat oven to 350°F.

2. **To prepare chicken:** Combine yogurt, garlic, oil and tarragon in a large bowl. Season chicken with salt and pepper and add to the bowl; turn to coat. Place the chicken in a baking dish and cover completely with the yogurt mixture.

3. Bake until the chicken is cooked through and an instant-read thermometer inserted into the thickest part registers 165°F, 35 to 45 minutes. Transfer to a clean cutting board. Thinly slice the chicken when cool enough to handle.

4. **To prepare dressing:** Mash blue cheese, oil, vinegar, tarragon and honey together in a medium bowl with a fork until well combined. For a creamier dressing, add yogurt 1 tablespoon at a time, if desired. Season with salt and pepper.

5. **To assemble salad:** Gently toss lettuce, radicchio and arugula (or mixed greens) in a large bowl. Divide the greens among 4 plates, top with equal portions of the chicken, spoon 2 tablespoons of the dressing over each salad and sprinkle with walnuts.

PER SERVING: 420 calories; 29 g fat (6 g sat, 14 g mono); 73 mg cholesterol; 9 g carbohydrate; 4 g added sugars; 31 g protein; 2 g fiber; 487 mg sodium; 444 mg potassium.
NUTRITION BONUS: Vitamin A (37% daily value), Folate (17% dv), Calcium (15% dv).

Mâche & Chicken Salad with Honey-Tahini Dressing

H✄W   H↑F   H♥H

MAKES: 4 servings, about 2 cups each
ACTIVE TIME: 40 minutes | TOTAL: 55 minutes
TO MAKE AHEAD: Cover and refrigerate the dressing (Step 1) for up to 3 days.

In this salad, mâche (also known as lamb's lettuce) is tossed with spring ingredients—new red-skinned potatoes and fresh peas—and a lemony tahini dressing and chicken. If you can't find mâche at the supermarket, baby spinach is a good substitute. **Shopping Tip:** *Tahini is a thick paste of ground sesame seeds. Look for it at large supermarkets in the Middle Eastern section or near other nut butters.*

HONEY-TAHINI DRESSING

- ½ cup lemon juice
- ⅓ cup extra-virgin olive oil
- ⅓ cup tahini (*see Shopping Tip*)
- 2 tablespoons honey
- 2 cloves garlic, minced
- 1 teaspoon salt
   Freshly ground pepper to taste

SALAD

- 1 pound new *or* baby red potatoes
- 1 pound chicken tenders
- ¼ teaspoon plus pinch of salt, divided
- ¼ teaspoon freshly ground pepper
- 1 tablespoon extra-virgin olive oil
- ½ small clove garlic
- 4 cups mâche (*see Tip, page 485*) *or* baby spinach
- 1 cup shelled English peas (about 1½ pounds unshelled) *or* thawed frozen peas
- 1 tablespoon finely chopped shallot

1. **To prepare dressing:** Combine lemon juice, ⅓ cup oil, tahini, honey and minced garlic in a blender, a jar with a tight-fitting lid or a medium bowl. Blend, shake or whisk until smooth. Season with 1 teaspoon salt and pepper.

2. **To prepare salad:** Place a steamer basket in a large saucepan, add 1 inch of water and bring to a boil. Put potatoes in the basket and steam until barely tender when pierced with a skewer, 15 to 20 minutes, depending on size. When cool enough to handle, slice or quarter.

3. Meanwhile, toss chicken with ¼ teaspoon salt and pepper. Heat 1 tablespoon oil in a large nonstick skillet over medium heat. Add the chicken and cook until golden brown and cooked through, about 4 minutes per side. Transfer to a clean cutting board to cool. Shred into bite-size pieces.

4. Season a wooden salad bowl by rubbing with ½ clove garlic and a pinch of salt. Chop the garlic and add to the bowl along with the potatoes and mâche (or spinach). Pour ½ cup dressing over the potatoes and greens; gently toss to coat. (*Cover and refrigerate the remaining ¾ cup dressing for up to 3 days.*) Add peas, shallot and the shredded chicken; gently toss and serve.

PER SERVING: 382 calories; 16 g fat (2 g sat, 10 g mono); 67 mg cholesterol; 31 g carbohydrate; 3 g added sugars; 32 g protein; 5 g fiber; 532 mg sodium; 803 mg potassium.
NUTRITION BONUS: Vitamin A (71% daily value), Vitamin C (52% dv), Folate (27% dv), Potassium (23% dv), Iron (18% dv), Magnesium (17% dv).

EatingWell Tip

Use olive oil whenever you can for its health benefits. **Olive oil is rich in monounsaturated fat,** which promotes "good" HDL cholesterol, and it contains antioxidants that may help keep your heart healthy.

Southwest Grilled Chicken Caesar

H✂W H⬆F

MAKES: 4 servings, about 3 cups each
ACTIVE TIME: 30 minutes | TOTAL: 30 minutes

Avocado stands in for raw egg and some of the oil in this rich, creamy dressing.

- **1 pound boneless, skinless chicken breasts, tenders removed (see *Tip, page 482*)**
- **1¼ teaspoons ground cumin, divided**
- **1¼ teaspoons chili powder, divided**
- **1¼ teaspoons kosher salt, divided**
- **1 avocado, diced, divided**
- **½ cup shredded Asiago *or* Parmesan cheese, divided**
- **3 anchovy fillets, chopped**
- **3 tablespoons water**
- **2 tablespoons lemon juice**
- **1 tablespoon extra-virgin olive oil**
- **1 clove garlic, chopped**
- **¼ teaspoon freshly ground pepper, or to taste**
- **10 cups chopped romaine lettuce**
- **1 cup croutons, preferably whole-wheat (*page 82*)**

1. Preheat grill to high.

2. Pound chicken breasts between 2 pieces of plastic wrap with a meat mallet to an even ¾-inch thickness. Combine 1 teaspoon each cumin and chili powder and ½ teaspoon salt; sprinkle on the chicken.

3. Oil the grill rack (*see Tip, page 485*). Grill the chicken until no longer pink, 3 to 4 minutes per side.

4. Puree half the avocado, ¼ cup cheese, anchovies, water, lemon juice, oil, garlic, pepper and the remaining cumin, chili powder and salt in a food processor until smooth. Gently toss with romaine, croutons, the remaining avocado and cheese in a large bowl. Serve topped with the grilled chicken.

PER SERVING: 357 calories; 20 g fat (5 g sat, 10 g mono); 66 mg cholesterol; 18 g carbohydrate; 1 g added sugars; 26 g protein; 7 g fiber; 745 mg sodium; 733 mg potassium. NUTRITION BONUS: Vitamin A (215% daily value), Vitamin C (63% dv), Folate (55% dv), Potassium (21% dv), Calcium (18% dv).

▶ Blueberry, Steak & Walnut Salad

H✂W H♥H

MAKES: 4 servings, about 2 cups each
ACTIVE TIME: 30 minutes | TOTAL: 30 minutes

Blueberries are terrific in both sweet and savory dishes. Add steak, walnuts and feta cheese to this simple salad for a light and satisfying supper.

- **1 pound sirloin steak *or* strip steak (1-1¼ inches thick), trimmed**
- **½ teaspoon salt, divided**
- **½ teaspoon freshly ground pepper**
- **1 cup fresh blueberries, divided**
- **½ cup chopped walnuts, toasted (see *Tip, page 486*)**
- **3 tablespoons fruity vinegar, such as raspberry**
- **1 tablespoon minced shallot**
- **1 teaspoon sugar**
- **3 tablespoons walnut oil *or* canola oil**
- **8 cups baby spinach**
- **¼ cup crumbled feta cheese**

1. Preheat grill to medium.

2. Sprinkle steak with ¼ teaspoon salt and pepper. Oil the grill rack (*see Tip, page 485*). Grill the steak about 5 minutes per side for medium-rare, 6 minutes per side for medium. Let rest on a clean cutting board for 5 minutes. Thinly slice crosswise.

3. Pulse ¼ cup blueberries, ¼ cup walnuts, vinegar, shallot, sugar and the remaining ¼ teaspoon salt in a food processor to form a chunky paste. With the motor running, add oil until incorporated. Toss spinach in a large bowl with the dressing. To serve, top the spinach with the steak, feta and the remaining blueberries and walnuts.

PER SERVING: 392 calories; 26 g fat (5 g sat, 7 g mono); 50 mg cholesterol; 11 g carbohydrate; 1 g added sugars; 29 g protein; 3 g fiber; 494 mg sodium; 748 mg potassium. NUTRITION BONUS: Vitamin A (114% daily value), Zinc (36% dv), Vitamin C (35% dv), Folate (34% dv), Magnesium (26% dv), Iron & Potassium (21% dv).

Asparagus & Radish Salad

Broccoli Rabe with Garlic & Anchovies

Lebanese Potato Salad

*Roasted Brussels Sprouts with
Hazelnut Brown Butter*

Vegetables

Artichoke | PEAK SEASON: Spring, Fall | LOOK FOR: Tight heads with no bruising. | STORE: Refrigerate in a plastic bag for up to 1 week.

Artichoke & Potato Gratin

H✹W H⬆F H♥H

MAKES: 6 servings

ACTIVE TIME: 45 minutes | TOTAL: 2 hours

Fresh artichokes and potatoes combine in this tasty gratin.

- ⅔ **cup freshly grated Parmesan cheese**
- 2 **cloves garlic, very finely chopped**
- 1 **whole lemon, plus 2 tablespoons lemon juice**
- 4 **large artichokes**
- 1½ **pounds Yukon Gold potatoes, peeled**
- ½ **teaspoon salt**
- ¼ **teaspoon freshly ground pepper**
- ½ **cup reduced-sodium chicken broth *or* vegetable broth**
- ⅓ **cup fresh breadcrumbs, preferably whole-wheat (see *Tip*, page 481)**

1. Preheat oven to 375°F. Coat a 1½-quart gratin dish or other shallow baking dish with cooking spray. Combine Parmesan and garlic in a small bowl; set aside.

2. To prepare artichokes, fill a large bowl with cold water. Juice the lemon and add to the water; add the lemon halves to the water as well. Peel away all the outer leaves of the artichokes, snapping the leaves off at the base until the fuzzy choke is visible. Trim off the leaves with a paring knife, removing any fibrous green portions. Trim the bottom ¼ inch off the stem and pare away the tough outer skin. Remove the choke with a melon baller or knife. Slice the stem and base into thin slices and drop into the lemon water. Repeat with the remaining artichokes.

3. Cut potatoes into ¼-inch-thick slices (a food processor does the job nicely) and spread half of them in the prepared dish. Drain the artichokes, discarding the lemon halves, and place them on top of the potatoes. Sprinkle 2 tablespoons lemon juice, followed by salt, pepper and half of the Parmesan mixture over the artichokes. Layer the remaining potatoes on top. Pour broth over the vegetables and cover the dish tightly with foil. Bake until the potatoes are very tender, 1 to 1¼ hours.

4. Combine breadcrumbs with the remaining Parmesan mixture and sprinkle over the potatoes. Bake, uncovered, until the top is golden, 10 to 15 minutes more.

PER SERVING: 186 calories; 3 g fat (2 g sat, 1 g mono); 8 mg cholesterol; 33 g carbohydrate; 0 g added sugars; 10 g protein; 9 g fiber; 518 mg sodium; 912 mg potassium.
NUTRITION BONUS: Vitamin C (65% daily value), Folate & Potassium (26% dv), Magnesium (24% dv), Calcium (17% dv), Iron (15% dv).

EatingWell Tip

Take advantage of fresh artichokes in spring and fall when they're in season. They're loaded with **fiber (about 9 grams per large artichoke)**.

Artichokes with Balsamic Vinaigrette

H✖W   H⬆F   H♥H

MAKES: 4 servings
ACTIVE TIME: 20 minutes | TOTAL: 50 minutes

Dipping artichoke leaves one by one into balsamic vinaigrette until you reach the meaty heart is a leisurely way to begin a meal.

- 1   lemon
- 3   quarts plus 1 tablespoon water, divided
- ½   cup dry white wine
- 2   sprigs fresh parsley
- 2   sprigs fresh thyme *or* ½ teaspoon dried thyme leaves
- 1   bay leaf
- 2   teaspoons salt
- 4   medium artichokes
- 1   tablespoon balsamic vinegar
- 1   tablespoon extra-virgin olive oil
- 1   teaspoon Dijon mustard
- 1   clove garlic, finely chopped
     Freshly ground pepper to taste

1. Cut lemon in half. Slice 1 half and reserve the other half for rubbing over artichokes. Place 3 quarts water, wine, parsley, thyme, bay leaf, salt and the lemon slices in a large pot. Bring to a simmer, cover and cook over medium-low heat for 10 minutes.

2. Meanwhile, trim artichokes (*see How To*).

3. Add the artichokes to the pot and simmer, covered, until tender, about 30 minutes. Drain, discarding lemon slices and herbs, and let cool slightly.

4. Whisk vinegar, oil, mustard, garlic and remaining 1 tablespoon water in a small bowl. Season with salt and pepper. Serve the artichokes with the vinaigrette for dipping.

PER SERVING: 95 calories; 4 g fat (1 g sat, 3 g mono); 0 mg cholesterol; 14 g carbohydrate; 0 g added sugars; 4 g protein; 7 g fiber; 525 mg sodium; 481 mg potassium.
NUTRITION BONUS: Vitamin C (25% daily value), Folate (22% dv), Magnesium (19% dv).

How To

Trim an Artichoke

1. Using a sharp knife, remove ½ inch of leaves from the cone-shaped artichoke top. Trim ½ to 1 inch off the stem end.

2. Remove the small, tough outer layer(s) of leaves from the stem end and snip all remaining spiky tips from the rest of the outer leaves using a pair of kitchen shears. Rub the whole artichoke, especially the cut portions, with the cut side of a lemon half.

Asparagus | PEAK SEASON: Spring | LOOK FOR: Sturdy spears with tight, clean heads; the cut ends should not look dried out, wrinkled or woody. Fresh asparagus should snap when bent. | STORE: Trim the ends of spears and stand them upright in about an inch of water, cover with plastic and store in the refrigerator for up to 3 days. Or wrap ends with a damp paper towel and store in a plastic bag for up to 3 days. | PREP: Trim or snap off stem ends; peel more woody, mature stalk ends with a vegetable peeler, if desired.

Prosciutto-Wrapped Asparagus

H✕W H♥H

MAKES: 4 servings
ACTIVE TIME: 20 minutes | TOTAL: 20 minutes

These prosciutto-wrapped bundles of grilled asparagus are a delicious addition to a spring brunch or elegant dinner.

- 16 spears asparagus (about 1 bunch), trimmed
- 1 teaspoon extra-virgin olive oil
  Pinch of salt
  Freshly ground pepper to taste
- 2 very thin slices prosciutto, cut in half lengthwise

1. Preheat grill to medium.

2. Toss asparagus with oil, salt and pepper in a medium bowl. Wrap 1 length of prosciutto around the middle of 4 asparagus spears. Repeat, making 4 bundles. Oil the grill rack (*see Tip, page 485*). Grill the bundles, turning once or twice, until the asparagus is tender and charred in spots, about 10 minutes.

PER SERVING: 39 calories; 2 g fat (0 g sat, 1 g mono); 6 mg cholesterol; 3 g carbohydrate; 0 g added sugars; 3 g protein; 1 g fiber; 235 mg sodium; 135 mg potassium.
NUTRITION BONUS: Folate (22% daily value).

Asparagus & Radish Salad

H✕W H⬆F H♥H

MAKES: 4 servings, scant 1 cup each
ACTIVE TIME: 15 minutes | TOTAL: 15 minutes

This colorful asparagus and radish salad is dressed with a sesame-soy vinaigrette. Pair it with grilled shrimp and rice noodles. (Photograph: page 106.)

- 1 bunch asparagus (about 1 pound), trimmed
- 2 tablespoons white vinegar
- 1 tablespoon reduced-sodium soy sauce
- 2 teaspoons canola oil
- 1 teaspoon toasted sesame oil
- ½ teaspoon grated fresh ginger
- 2-3 dashes Asian red chile sauce, such as sriracha (optional)
- 1 bunch radishes, trimmed and cut into wedges
- 2 tablespoons finely chopped scallion

1. Fill a medium bowl with ice water and place by the stove. Bring 1 inch of water to a boil in a large saucepan fitted with a steamer basket.

2. Thinly slice asparagus stalks on the diagonal, leaving the tips whole. Place in the steamer basket and steam until tender-crisp, about 1 minute. Transfer the asparagus to the ice water. Drain.

3. Combine vinegar, soy sauce, canola oil, sesame oil, ginger and chile sauce (if using) in a large bowl. Add the asparagus, radishes and scallion; toss to combine. Serve warm or room temperature.

PER SERVING: 67 calories; 4 g fat (0 g sat, 2 g mono); 0 mg cholesterol; 7 g carbohydrate; 0 g added sugars; 3 g protein; 3 g fiber; 129 mg sodium; 379 mg potassium.
NUTRITION BONUS: Folate (46% daily value), Vitamin C (27% dv), Vitamin A (25% dv).

Beets | PEAK SEASON: Spring, Fall | LOOK FOR: Firm beets. The most common are dark red, but other types, such as golden and 'Chioggia'—an heirloom variety with concentric rings of red and white flesh—are also available and have a similar sweet, earthy flavor. They are sold with or without their greens attached. | STORE: Refrigerate for up to 1 month. If the greens are attached, trim and store them separately in a plastic bag. PREP: Cut off greens (reserve for another use, if desired).

Beets & Greens Salad with Cannellini Beans

H✖W H⬆F

MAKES: 4 servings, ¾ cup each
ACTIVE TIME: 30 minutes | TOTAL: 2 hours (including 1½ hours to roast beets) | TO MAKE AHEAD: Prepare through Step 1, cover and refrigerate for up to 2 days.

Sometimes beets have beautiful, unblemished, tender greens attached. When that happens, blanch the greens and toss with beans and vinaigrette, using some of the beets to garnish the salad, as in this recipe. Use the leftover cooked beets for other dishes. If you buy beet greens on their own, you can make the salad just with them. Either way is delicious. Soaking the onion in ice water for 10 minutes or more renders it less pungent and more crisp.

2	bunches beets with greens *or* 8 cups lightly packed beet greens *or* chard and 4 beets
2	cloves garlic, crushed and peeled
½	teaspoon salt
3	tablespoons red-wine vinegar
⅓	cup extra-virgin olive oil
1	teaspoon dried oregano *or* 2 teaspoons fresh oregano leaves, minced
	Freshly ground pepper to taste
1	15-ounce *or* 19-ounce can cannellini beans, rinsed
¼	cup thinly slivered red onion

1. If using beets, preheat oven to 400°F. Cut greens from beets, leaving about 1 inch of stem attached; reserve about 8 cups greens, lightly packed. Wash and dry the beets. Wrap the beets in foil and roast until tender, 1¼ to 1½ hours, depending on the size. (*Alternatively, place beets in a microwave-safe dish, add ¼ cup water, cover and microwave on high for 20 to 25 minutes.*) When the beets are cool enough to handle, peel 4 of them and cut into ½-inch wedges. You should have about 2 cups. Place in a medium bowl. (Reserve any remaining beets for another use.)

2. Using a mortar and pestle or the side of a chef's knife, mash garlic and salt into a paste. Transfer to a large bowl. Add vinegar and whisk to blend. Add oil, oregano and pepper, whisking until blended. Measure out 1 tablespoon and add to the beet wedges; toss to coat. Add beans to the remaining dressing and toss to coat. Let marinate at room temperature until ready to use.

3. Place onion in a small bowl, cover with cold water and add a handful of ice cubes; let stand for 10 minutes, or until ready to use.

4. Meanwhile, bring 2 cups lightly salted water to a boil in a large wide pan. Wash beet greens (or chard) in several changes of water; trim the stems. Add the greens to boiling water, cover and cook until tender, about 5 minutes. Drain well, pressing on the greens with the back of a spoon to remove excess moisture. Cut into 1-inch pieces.

5. Drain the onion. Add to the beans along with greens; toss to coat. Spoon the salad onto a serving platter or individual plates and garnish with the beets, if using. Serve immediately.

PER SERVING: 298 calories; 19 g fat (3 g sat, 13 g mono); 0 mg cholesterol; 27 g carbohydrate; 0 g added sugars; 8 g protein; 9 g fiber; 825 mg sodium; 1,049 mg potassium.
NUTRITION BONUS: Vitamin A (92% daily value), Vitamin C (33% dv), Potassium (30% dv), Folate (28% dv), Iron (19% dv), Magnesium (22% dv).

Roasted Beets with Mustard

H✂W   H⬆F   H♥H

MAKES: 4 servings
ACTIVE TIME: 20 minutes | TOTAL: 50 minutes

Try a variety of beets in this dish. The simple Dijon vinaigrette really makes the earthy beet flavor sing.

- 2 **pounds small beets, greens removed**
- 2 **teaspoons extra-virgin olive oil**
- ¼ **cup sliced scallions**
- 2 **tablespoons Dijon mustard**
- 1 **tablespoon lemon juice**
- ¼ **teaspoon salt**
  Freshly ground pepper to taste

1. Preheat oven to 425°F.

2. Cut off stems and root ends from beets. Scrub the beets well and cut in half lengthwise. Toss with oil on a rimmed baking sheet. Arrange cut-side down and roast until tender when pierced with a fork, about 30 minutes. Let cool for 5 minutes, then peel off and discard the skins.

3. Cut the beets into matchsticks. Place in a serving bowl and toss with scallions, mustard and lemon juice. Season with salt and pepper.

PER SERVING: 122 calories; 3 g fat (0 g sat, 2 g mono);
0 mg cholesterol; 23 g carbohydrate; 0 g added sugars;
4 g protein; 7 g fiber; 421 mg sodium; 760 mg potassium.
NUTRITION BONUS: Folate (63% daily value), Vitamin C (23% dv),
Potassium (22% dv).

Bok Choy | PEAK SEASON: Spring, Fall, Winter | LOOK FOR: Green leaves with silky white stalks. The leaves should not appear wilted or blemished. Look for it in smaller "baby" or larger mature sizes. | STORE: Refrigerate in a plastic bag for up to 3 days. | PREP: Wash well.

Crunchy Bok Choy Slaw

H✂W   H♥H

MAKES: 8 servings, ¾ cup each
ACTIVE TIME: 20 minutes | TOTAL: 20 minutes

A versatile side dish to go with grilled meats or poultry—crispy, crunchy and thoroughly delicious.

- ¼ **cup rice vinegar**
- 1 **tablespoon toasted sesame oil**
- 2 **teaspoons sugar**
- 2 **teaspoons Dijon mustard**
- ¼ **teaspoon salt**
- 6 **cups very thinly sliced bok choy**
  (about 1-pound head, trimmed)
- 2 **medium carrots, shredded**
- 2 **scallions, thinly sliced**

Whisk vinegar, oil, sugar, mustard and salt in a large bowl until the sugar dissolves. Add bok choy, carrots and scallions; toss to coat with the dressing.

PER SERVING: 34 calories; 2 g fat (0 g sat, 1 g mono);
0 mg cholesterol; 4 g carbohydrate; 1 g added sugars;
1 g protein; 1 g fiber; 137 mg sodium; 202 mg potassium.
NUTRITION BONUS: Vitamin A (102% daily value), Vitamin C (45% dv).

Broccoli | PEAK SEASON: Spring, Fall, Winter | LOOK FOR: Sturdy, dark-green spears with tight buds and a high floret-to-stem ratio; there should be no yellowing. | STORE: Refrigerate in a plastic bag for 3 to 5 days.

Broccoli & Tomatoes with Rice Wine-Oyster Sauce

H✂W   H♥H

MAKES: 4 servings, ¾ cup each
ACTIVE TIME: 15 minutes | TOTAL: 15 minutes
TO MAKE AHEAD: Prep the broccoli up to 4 hours ahead.

When stir-frying firm vegetables like broccoli, cover the wok for 30 seconds after adding the sauce. Cooking the vegetables covered, even for a short time, helps get them tender but still crisp. If Chinese broccoli is available in your market, use this same method but cut the stalks and leaves into 2-inch pieces. **Shopping Tips: Shao Hsing** *(or Shaoxing) is a seasoned rice wine. It is available at most Asian specialty markets and in the Asian section of some larger supermarkets. If unavailable, dry sherry is the best substitute.* **Oyster sauce** *is a richly flavored Chinese condiment made from oysters and brine. Vegetarian oyster sauces substitute mushrooms for the oysters. Both can be found at large supermarkets or Asian specialty markets.*

RICE WINE-OYSTER SAUCE

   1   tablespoon Shao Hsing rice wine (*see Shopping Tips*) **or** dry sherry
   2   teaspoons oyster-flavored sauce *or* vegetarian oyster sauce (*see Shopping Tips*)
   ¼   teaspoon sugar
   ⅛   teaspoon salt

BROCCOLI & TOMATOES

   1   tablespoon canola oil
   1   tablespoon finely chopped fresh ginger
   8   ounces broccoli, florets cut into bite-size pieces and stems cut into ¼-inch slices (3 cups)
   1   cup cherry tomatoes, halved
   1   teaspoon sesame oil

1. **To prepare sauce:** Whisk rice wine (or sherry), oyster sauce, sugar and salt in a small bowl.

2. **To stir-fry:** Heat a 14-inch wok or large skillet over high heat until a bead of water vaporizes within 1 to 2 seconds of contact. Swirl canola oil into the pan, add ginger and stir-fry for 10 seconds. Add broccoli and stir-fry until bright green, 1 to 2 minutes. Add tomatoes and stir-fry for 15 seconds. Stir the sauce and swirl it into the pan; cover and cook for 30 seconds. Stir-fry until the vegetables are just tender but the broccoli is still bright green, 1 to 2 minutes. Stir in sesame oil. Serve immediately.

PER SERVING: 74 calories; 5 g fat (0 g sat, 3 g mono); 0 mg cholesterol; 6 g carbohydrate; 1 g added sugars; 2 g protein; 2 g fiber; 218 mg sodium; 280 mg potassium.
NUTRITION BONUS: Vitamin C (97% daily value), Vitamin A (40% dv).

EatingWell Tip

Include broccoli and any of the other vegetables from the cruciferous family, such as cabbage, turnips and cauliflower, in your diet. **They contain sulforaphane, a compound that may reduce your risk of cancer.**

◀ Broccoli Salad with Creamy Feta Dressing

H✖W   H↑F   H♥H

MAKES: 4 servings, 1 cup each
ACTIVE TIME: 20 minutes | TOTAL: 20 minutes
TO MAKE AHEAD: Cover and refrigerate for up to 1 day.

Finely chopped raw broccoli is tender and mild. Here it's tossed with a creamy dressing, chickpeas and sweet bell pepper.

⅓   cup crumbled feta cheese
¼   cup nonfat plain yogurt
1   tablespoon lemon juice
1   clove garlic, minced
¼   teaspoon freshly ground pepper
8   ounces broccoli crowns, trimmed and finely chopped (about 3 cups)
1   7-ounce can chickpeas, rinsed
½   cup chopped red bell pepper

1. Whisk feta, yogurt, lemon juice, garlic and pepper in a medium bowl until combined.

2. Add broccoli, chickpeas and bell pepper; toss to coat. Serve at room temperature or chilled.

PER SERVING: 113 calories; 3 g fat (2 g sat, 1 g mono); 11 mg cholesterol; 15 g carbohydrate; 0 g added sugars; 7 g protein; 4 g fiber; 245 mg sodium; 349 mg potassium.
NUTRITION BONUS: Vitamin C (133% daily value), Vitamin A (47% dv), Folate (21% dv).

Broccoli Rabe | PEAK SEASON: Spring, Fall, Winter | LOOK FOR: Thin stalks and crisp leaves. | STORE: Loosely wrap in a damp paper towel and refrigerate in a plastic bag for 3 to 5 days. PREP: Wash thoroughly; trim tough ends from stalks.

Broccoli Rabe with Garlic & Anchovies

H✖W   H↑F   H♥H

MAKES: 8 servings, generous ½ cup each
ACTIVE TIME: 25 minutes | TOTAL: 25 minutes

Pungent broccoli rabe (or broccoli rape, broccoli raab or rapini) is tossed with a rich mixture of garlic, olive oil and anchovies in this easy side dish. (Photograph: page 106.)

2   pounds broccoli rabe, stem ends trimmed, chopped
3   tablespoons extra-virgin olive oil
6   cloves garlic, chopped
6   anchovy fillets, chopped
¼   teaspoon crushed red pepper (optional)
¼   teaspoon salt
    Freshly ground pepper to taste

1. Bring a large pot or Dutch oven of water to a boil. Add broccoli rabe and cook until tender when pierced with a fork, 3 to 5 minutes. Drain well.

2. Heat oil in a large skillet over medium heat. Add garlic, anchovies and crushed red pepper (if using); cook, stirring, until the garlic is very light brown, 1 to 2 minutes. Add the broccoli rabe, toss to coat, and cook, stirring occasionally, for 2 minutes more. Season with salt and pepper.

PER SERVING: 82 calories; 6 g fat (1 g sat, 4 g mono); 3 mg cholesterol; 4 g carbohydrate; 0 g added sugars; 5 g protein; 3 g fiber; 221 mg sodium; 248 mg potassium.
NUTRITION BONUS: Vitamin A (59% daily value), Vitamin C (40% dv), Folate (24% dv), Iron (15% dv).

Brussels Sprouts | PEAK SEASON: Fall, Winter | LOOK FOR: Tight, firm, small deep-green heads without brown or yellow leaves or insect holes. | STORE: Refrigerate sprouts in a plastic bag for up to 1 week. | PREP: Peel off outer leaves; trim stem.

Roasted Brussels Sprouts with Hazelnut Brown Butter

H✷W   H⬆F   H❤H

MAKES: 4 servings, ¾ cup each
ACTIVE TIME: 10 minutes | TOTAL: 25 minutes

Browning butter brings out a mellow nuttiness that complements the strong flavor of the sprouts. Browned butter can be an excellent flavor addition to any sauté. (Photograph: page 106.)

- 1 tablespoon butter
- 1 pound Brussels sprouts, trimmed and quartered
- ¼ cup chopped hazelnuts
- ¼ teaspoon salt
  Freshly ground pepper to taste
- 3 tablespoons water

1. Position rack in bottom third of oven; preheat to 450°F.

2. Place butter on a large rimmed baking sheet and roast until the butter is melted, browned and fragrant, 4 to 5 minutes. Remove the baking sheet from the oven; toss Brussels sprouts and hazelnuts with the browned butter and sprinkle with salt and pepper. Return to the oven and roast for 7 minutes. Sprinkle with water; toss and continue roasting until the sprouts are tender and lightly browned, 7 to 9 minutes more.

PER SERVING: 111 calories; 8 g fat (2 g sat, 3 g mono); 8 mg cholesterol; 9 g carbohydrate; 0 g added sugars; 4 g protein; 4 g fiber; 170 mg sodium; 409 mg potassium.
NUTRITION BONUS: Vitamin C (118% daily value), Vitamin A (20% dv), Folate (19% dv).

Shredded Brussels Sprouts with Bacon & Onions

H✷W   H❤H

MAKES: 6 servings, ½ cup each
ACTIVE TIME: 30 minutes TOTAL: 30 minutes

A small amount of bacon goes a long way to flavor these very thinly sliced Brussels sprouts—the results may even win over sprout skeptics.

- 2 slices bacon
- 1 small yellow onion, thinly sliced
- ¼ teaspoon salt
- ¾ cup water
- 1 teaspoon Dijon mustard
- 1 pound Brussels sprouts, trimmed, halved and very thinly sliced
- 1 tablespoon cider vinegar

1. Cook bacon in a large skillet over medium heat, turning once, until crisp, 5 to 7 minutes. Drain on a paper towel. Crumble.

2. Add onion and salt to the drippings in the pan. Cook over medium heat, stirring often, until tender and browned, about 3 minutes. Add water and mustard and scrape up any browned bits. Add Brussels sprouts and cook, stirring often, until tender, 4 to 6 minutes. Stir in vinegar and top with the crumbled bacon.

PER SERVING: 46 calories; 1 g fat (0 g sat, 0 g mono); 2 mg cholesterol; 7 g carbohydrate; 0 g added sugars; 3 g protein; 2 g fiber; 175 mg sodium; 292 mg potassium.
NUTRITION BONUS: Vitamin C (87% daily value).

Cabbage | PEAK SEASON: Fall, Winter | LOOK FOR: Vividly colored, tightly closed heads that feel heavy and look crisp. STORE: Refrigerate for up to 2 weeks. | PREP: Remove any damaged outer leaves and cut head into quarters through the stem end. Remove stem core.

Cabbage Slaw

H✖W   H♥H

MAKES: 4 servings, about ½ cup each
ACTIVE TIME: 15 minutes | TOTAL: 15 minutes
TO MAKE AHEAD: Cover and refrigerate for up to 1 day.

This colorful, vinegar-dressed coleslaw can be made in just 15 minutes. Use preshredded cabbage to make it even quicker.

  2 cups finely shredded green cabbage
  ½ cup thinly sliced red bell pepper
  ⅓ cup thinly sliced red onion
  2 tablespoons seasoned rice vinegar
  2 tablespoons extra-virgin olive oil
  ¼ teaspoon salt
  ⅛ teaspoon freshly ground pepper

Toss cabbage, bell pepper, onion, vinegar and oil in a large bowl. Season with salt and pepper; toss again to combine.

PER SERVING: 82 calories; 7 g fat (1 g sat, 5 g mono); 0 mg cholesterol; 4 g carbohydrate; 0 g added sugars; 1 g protein; 1 g fiber; 153 mg sodium; 114 mg potassium.
NUTRITION BONUS: Vitamin C (62% daily value).

Warm Red Cabbage Salad

H✖W   H♥H

MAKES: 6 servings, generous ¾ cup each
ACTIVE TIME: 20 minutes | TOTAL: 20 minutes

In this quick German-inspired side dish, red cabbage is cooked until just tender and combined with sweet apples, caraway and a tangy vinaigrette. Serve with roasted pork loin or turkey kielbasa.

  1 tablespoon extra-virgin olive oil
  4 cups thinly sliced red cabbage (¼ large head)
  ¾ teaspoon caraway seeds
  ½ teaspoon salt
  1 crisp, sweet apple, such as Braeburn *or* Gala, cut into matchsticks
  1 shallot, minced
  1 tablespoon red-wine vinegar
  ½ teaspoon Dijon mustard
  ½ teaspoon freshly ground pepper
  2 tablespoons chopped walnuts, toasted
     (*see Tip, page 486*)

Heat oil in a large saucepan over medium heat. Add cabbage, caraway seeds and salt. Cook, covered, stirring occasionally, until tender, 8 to 10 minutes. Remove from the heat. Add apple, shallot, vinegar, mustard and pepper and stir until combined. Serve sprinkled with toasted walnuts.

PER SERVING: 76 calories; 4 g fat (1 g sat, 2 g mono); 0 mg cholesterol; 10 g carbohydrate; 0 g added sugars; 2 g protein; 2 g fiber; 216 mg sodium; 193 mg potassium.
NUTRITION BONUS: Vitamin C (60% daily value).

Carrots | PEAK SEASON: Year-round. | LOOK FOR: Brightly colored, firm carrots without any gray or shriveled spots on the skin. The greens should preferably still be attached. STORE: Trim greens and refrigerate carrots in a plastic bag for up to 3 weeks. | PREP: Peel.

Marinated Carrots

H✂W   H⬆F   H❤H

MAKES: 4 servings
ACTIVE TIME: 20 minutes | TOTAL: 30 minutes

Keep carrots on hand so you can make this easy side dish anytime.

6   carrots (12 ounces), cut into ¼-inch-by-2-inch matchsticks
4   cloves garlic, peeled and crushed
1   tablespoon balsamic vinegar
2   teaspoons extra-virgin olive oil
2   teaspoons chopped fresh thyme *or*
    ½ teaspoon dried
    Pinch of sugar
¼   teaspoon salt
    Freshly ground pepper to taste

1. Place carrots and garlic in a small saucepan and cover with cold water. Bring to a boil over medium-high heat and boil for 30 seconds. (*Alternatively, place carrots, garlic and ¼ cup water in a 1-quart casserole; cover with lid or vented plastic wrap and microwave on High until crisp-tender, 5 to 7 minutes, stirring midway.*)

2. Immediately drain the carrots and garlic; transfer to a medium bowl. Add vinegar, oil, thyme and sugar and toss well. Let cool for 10 minutes, stirring occasionally. Discard the garlic and season with salt and pepper.

PER SERVING: 66 calories; 3 g fat (0 g sat, 2 g mono); 0 mg cholesterol; 11 g carbohydrate; 0 g added sugars; 1 g protein; 3 g fiber; 210 mg sodium; 311 mg potassium. NUTRITION BONUS: Vitamin A (306% daily value).

▶ Carrot & Celery Root Salad with Honey-Lemon Dressing

H✂W   H⬆F   H❤H

MAKES: 4 servings, about ¾ cup each
ACTIVE TIME: 15 minutes | TOTAL: 15 minutes

Here we combine carrots and celery root (also known as celeriac) in a quick shredded slaw. Try it as a change from an ordinary mixed green salad.

2   tablespoons walnut oil *or* canola oil
2   tablespoons lemon juice
1   tablespoon honey
1   small shallot, minced
½   teaspoon salt
¼   teaspoon freshly ground pepper
2   cups shredded carrots (about 4 medium)
1   cup peeled and shredded celery root (*see How To*)
¼   cup golden raisins
¼   cup chopped walnuts, toasted (*see Tip, page 486*)

Whisk oil, lemon juice, honey, shallot, salt and pepper in a large bowl. Add carrots, celery root, raisins and walnuts; toss to combine.

PER SERVING: 190 calories; 12 g fat (1 g sat, 2 g mono); 0 mg cholesterol; 22 g carbohydrate; 4 g added sugars; 2 g protein; 3 g fiber; 357 mg sodium; 385 mg potassium. NUTRITION BONUS: Vitamin A (204% daily value), Vitamin C (16% dv).

How To

Peel Celery Root | Cut off one end to create a flat surface to keep it steady. Cut off the skin with your knife, following the contour of the root. Or use a vegetable peeler and peel around the root at least three times to ensure all the fibrous skin has been removed.

Cauliflower | PEAK SEASON: Spring, Fall, Winter | LOOK FOR: Tight heads without black, brown or yellow spots; the green leaves at the stem should still be attached firmly to the head, not limp or withered. | STORE: Refrigerate in a plastic bag for up to 5 days.

Skillet Cauliflower Gratin

H✖W

MAKES: 4 servings, about 1 cup each
ACTIVE TIME: 30 minutes | TOTAL: 30 minutes

Nonfat milk and a bit of sharp Cheddar combine to make a rich sauce without all the butter usually found in gratins.

4	cups 1-inch cauliflower florets (about ½ large head; *see How To*)
1½	cups nonfat milk, divided
¼	teaspoon salt
½	cup dry breadcrumbs, preferably whole-wheat (*see Tip, page 481*)
¾	cup shredded sharp Cheddar cheese, divided
½	teaspoon extra-virgin olive oil
2	tablespoons all-purpose flour
1	tablespoon chopped fresh chives
1	teaspoon Dijon mustard
¼	teaspoon white pepper

1. Position rack in upper third of oven; preheat broiler.

2. Bring cauliflower, 1¼ cups milk and salt to a boil in a large ovenproof skillet over medium-high heat. Reduce heat, cover and simmer until the cauliflower is tender, about 5 minutes.

3. Meanwhile, combine breadcrumbs, ¼ cup cheese and oil in a small bowl. Whisk flour and the remaining ¼ cup milk in another small bowl until smooth; stir the mixture into the pan and cook, stirring, until thickened, about 1 minute. Stir in the remaining ½ cup cheese, chives, mustard and pepper. Sprinkle with the breadcrumb mixture. Broil until the top is crispy and beginning to brown, 1 to 2 minutes.

PER SERVING: 184 calories; 8 g fat (5 g sat, 2 g mono); 24 mg cholesterol; 17 g carbohydrate; 0 g added sugars; 11 g protein; 2 g fiber; 357 mg sodium; 303 mg potassium.
NUTRITION BONUS: Vitamin C (37% daily value), Calcium (28% dv).

How To

Prep Cauliflower | To prepare florets from a whole head of cauliflower, remove outer leaves. Slice off the thick stem. With the head upside down and holding a knife at a 45° angle, slice into the smaller stems with a circular motion—removing a "plug" from the center of the head. Break or cut florets into the desired size.

Chard | PEAK SEASON: Spring, Fall, Winter | LOOK FOR: Crisp, brightly colored greens; avoid those that are wilted or blemished. | STORE: Store unwashed; wrap stem ends in damp paper towels and refrigerate in a plastic bag for up to 10 days. | PREP: Wash well and coarsely chop. The stems are edible; keep them separate when prepping and cook for 3 to 5 minutes longer than the leaves. One pound of greens cooks down to 1-2 cups.

Chipotle Cheddar Chard

H✖W

MAKES: 6 servings, about ⅔ cup each
ACTIVE TIME: 25 minutes | TOTAL: 25 minutes
TO MAKE AHEAD: Cover and refrigerate for up to 2 days.

If you like, make a double batch of this spicy, cheesy dish and enjoy it as a quesadilla filling.

1	pound chard
2	teaspoons canola oil
1	small onion, halved and thinly sliced
1	medium tomato, chopped
¼	cup reduced-sodium chicken broth *or* water
¼-½	teaspoon ground chipotle pepper
¼	teaspoon salt
⅔	cup shredded sharp Cheddar cheese

1. Wash chard and let water cling to the leaves (it helps steam the chard and keeps the dish from drying out); separate stems and leaves and chop.

2. Heat oil in a large skillet over medium heat. Add the stems and onion; cook, stirring often, until softened, 3 to 5 minutes. Add tomato, broth (or water), chipotle to taste and salt; bring to a simmer. Add the leaves; cook, covered, stirring once, until just tender, about 2 minutes. Scatter cheese on top and cook, uncovered, until it is melted, 1 to 2 minutes more. Serve.

PER SERVING: 89 calories; 6 g fat (3 g sat, 2 g mono); 13 mg cholesterol; 5 g carbohydrate; 0 g added sugars; 5 g protein; 2 g fiber; 335 mg sodium; 503 mg potassium.
NUTRITION BONUS: Vitamin A (99% daily value), Vitamin C (28% dv).

▶ Garlic Creamed Chard

H✖W

MAKES: 4 servings, about ⅔ cup each
ACTIVE TIME: 35 minutes | TOTAL: 35 minutes

Our lightened, garlic-infused cream sauce is perfect with tender chard. Try this creamy dish alongside broiled New York strip steak.

1	pound chard
1	tablespoon extra-virgin olive oil
2	tablespoons minced garlic
4	teaspoons unsalted butter
4	teaspoons all-purpose flour
⅔	cup low-fat milk
¼	teaspoon salt
⅛	teaspoon ground nutmeg
⅛	teaspoon freshly ground pepper

1. Wash chard and let water cling to the leaves (it helps steam the chard and keeps the dish from drying out); separate stems and leaves and chop.

2. Heat oil in a Dutch oven over medium heat. Add the stems and cook, stirring often, until softened, 3 to 5 minutes. Stir in the leaves and cook, stirring constantly, until wilted, about 2 minutes. Cover and cook, stirring once, until tender, about 2 minutes more. Transfer to a colander placed in the sink and press with a wooden spoon to remove excess liquid. Return the chard to the pot, cover and keep warm.

3. Cook garlic and butter in a small saucepan over medium heat until the garlic is fragrant but not browned, about 2 minutes. Whisk in flour and cook until bubbling, about 30 seconds. Add milk, salt, nutmeg and pepper; cook, whisking constantly, until thickened, 1 to 2 minutes. Stir the chard into the sauce and serve immediately.

PER SERVING: 136 calories; 8 g fat (3 g sat, 4 g mono); 12 mg cholesterol; 10 g carbohydrate; 0 g added sugars; 4 g protein; 2 g fiber; 367 sodium; 688 mg potassium.
NUTRITION BONUS: Vitamin A (143% daily value), Vitamin C (33% dv), Magnesium (26% dv), Potassium (20% dv), Iron (15% dv).

Corn | PEAK SEASON: Summer | LOOK FOR: Pale to dark green husks with moist silks. The cob should fill the husk, and the cut at the stem should look fresh. | STORE: Refrigerate, with the husks left on, in a plastic bag, for up to 2 days. PREP: Husk corn.

◀ Mexican Grilled Corn

H✖W   H♥H

MAKES: 4 servings
ACTIVE TIME: 25 minutes | TOTAL: 25 minutes

Street vendors across Mexico sell this style of roasted or grilled corn—topped with mayonnaise, chili powder and Cotija cheese. Serve the unadorned corn on a platter with small bowls of the sauce, cheese and lime on the side so everyone can make their own. **Shopping Tip:** *Cotija cheese, also called* queso añejo *or* queso añejado, *is an aged Mexican cheese similar in texture and flavor to Parmesan. Find it near other specialty cheeses or at Mexican grocery stores.*

2   tablespoons low-fat mayonnaise
2   tablespoons nonfat plain yogurt
½   teaspoon chili powder
4   ears corn, husked
4   tablespoons finely shredded Cotija (*see Shopping Tip*) *or* Parmesan cheese
1   lime, quartered

1. Preheat grill to medium-high.

2. Combine mayonnaise, yogurt and chili powder in a small bowl.

3. Grill corn, turning occasionally, until marked and tender, 8 to 12 minutes total. Spread each ear with 1 tablespoon of the sauce and sprinkle with 1 tablespoon Cotija (or Parmesan). Serve with lime wedges.

PER SERVING: 100 calories; 2 g fat (1 g sat, 0 g mono); 2 mg cholesterol; 20 g carbohydrate; 1 g added sugars; 4 g protein; 2 g fiber; 118 mg sodium; 282 mg potassium.
NUTRITION BONUS: Vitamin C (16% daily value).

Cool Fresh Corn Relish

H✖W   H♥H

MAKES: 12 servings, about ⅓ cup each
ACTIVE TIME: 25 minutes | TOTAL: 25 minutes
TO MAKE AHEAD: Cover and refrigerate for up to 3 days.

Serve this fresh summertime treat as a side dish or as a condiment with your favorite grilled meat or fish.

5   large ears corn, unhusked
1½   cups finely diced sweet onion
¾   cup finely chopped flat-leaf parsley (1-2 bunches)
3   tablespoons lime juice
2   tablespoons extra-virgin olive oil
¼   teaspoon salt

1. Microwave corn, in the husks, on High until steaming and just tender, 7 to 9 minutes. When cool enough to handle, remove the husks and silk. (*Alternatively, remove husks and silk and cook corn in a large pot of boiling water until just tender, about 5 minutes.*) Slice the kernels from the corn using a sharp knife (*see How To*).

2. Combine the corn kernels, onion, parsley, lime juice, oil and salt in a bowl. Serve room temperature or cold.

PER SERVING: 84 calories; 3 g fat (1 g sat, 2 g mono); 0 mg cholesterol; 14 g carbohydrate; 0 g added sugars; 2 g protein; 2 g fiber; 62 mg sodium; 220 mg potassium.
NUTRITION BONUS: Vitamin C (19% daily value).

How To

Cut Corn from a Cob | Stand an ear of corn on one end and slice the kernels off with a sharp knife.

Old Corn

H✖W H♥H

MAKES: 4 servings, generous ½ cup each
ACTIVE TIME: 25 minutes | TOTAL: 25 minutes
TO MAKE AHEAD: Cover and refrigerate for up to 3 days.

There is no form of corn that a Southerner can't use. This recipe is designed for corn that was picked a few days ago or has otherwise lost some of its sweetness. In the country it's called fried corn, but the corn's really boiled in milk or cream to soften and sweeten it.

- 2 slices bacon
- 2 teaspoons canola oil
- 3 cups fresh corn kernels (about 4 ears; *see How To, page 125*) or frozen
- ¼ teaspoon freshly ground pepper
- ⅔ cup nonfat milk, plus more if needed

1. Cook bacon in a large heavy skillet over medium heat until crispy, 2 to 4 minutes per side. Drain the bacon on a paper towel; discard fat. Heat oil in the same pan over high heat. Add corn and pepper and cook, stirring often, until the corn begins to brown, 4 to 5 minutes.

2. Add milk and bring to a simmer, stirring to scrape up any browned bits. Reduce heat to medium-low and simmer until most of the milk has evaporated, about 5 minutes. Add more milk to prevent sticking, a tablespoon at a time, if the liquid boils away before the corn is tender. Remove from the heat. Crumble the bacon into the corn; stir to combine. Serve immediately.

PER SERVING: 146 calories; 5 g fat (1 g sat, 3 g mono); 4 mg cholesterol; 22 g carbohydrate; 0 g added sugars; 6 g protein; 2 g fiber; 107 mg sodium; 377 mg potassium.

Cucumber | PEAK SEASON: Summer | LOOK FOR: Firm cucumbers without any soft or wrinkled spots. | STORE: Refrigerate for up to 3 days. | PREP: Peel if skin is waxy, otherwise peel and seed if desired or according to recipe.

Tropical Cucumber Salad

H✖W H⬆F H♥H

MAKES: 4 servings, about 1 cup each
ACTIVE TIME: 15 minutes | TOTAL: 15 minutes
TO MAKE AHEAD: Cover and refrigerate for up to 1 hour.

Combine cucumber, avocado and mango with a salty-sweet dressing for a taste of the tropics. **Shopping Tip:** *Fish sauce is a pungent Southeast Asian condiment made from salted, fermented fish. Find it in the Asian-food section of large supermarkets and at Asian specialty markets. We use Thai Kitchen fish sauce, lower in sodium than other brands, in our recipe testing and nutritional analyses.*

- 3-5 teaspoons fish sauce (*see Shopping Tip*)
- 1 teaspoon freshly grated lime zest, plus more for garnish
- 2 tablespoons lime juice
- 1 tablespoon canola oil
- 2 teaspoons light brown sugar
- 1 teaspoon rice vinegar
- ¼ teaspoon crushed red pepper
- 1 medium English cucumber, cut into ¾-inch dice
- 1 avocado, cut into ¾-inch dice
- 1 mango, cut into ¾-inch dice (*see Tip, page 486*)
- ¼ cup chopped fresh cilantro

Whisk fish sauce to taste, lime zest, lime juice, oil, brown sugar, vinegar and crushed red pepper in a large bowl until combined. Add cucumber, avocado, mango and cilantro; gently toss to coat. Serve garnished with lime zest, if desired.

PER SERVING: 168 calories; 11 g fat (1 g sat, 7 g mono); 0 mg cholesterol; 18 g carbohydrate; 1 g added sugars; 2 g protein; 5 g fiber; 305 mg sodium; 450 mg potassium.
NUTRITION BONUS: Vitamin C (42% daily value), Folate (15% dv).

Eggplant | PEAK SEASON: Summer, Fall | LOOK FOR: Smooth, glossy skins without wrinkles or spongy spots. | STORE: Refrigerate for up to 1 week. | PREP: The skin is edible. Peel, if desired, or according to recipe.

Indian Eggplant-Shallot Stew

H�W   H⬆F   H♥H

MAKES: 6 servings, generous ½ cup each
ACTIVE TIME: 30 minutes | TOTAL: 30 minutes
TO MAKE AHEAD: Cover and refrigerate for up to 2 days. Reheat on the stovetop or in the microwave.

This simple combination of coarsely mashed eggplant and shallots makes a quick side dish to go with roast chicken or seared salmon. Or serve with whole-wheat couscous or brown basmati rice as a vegetarian main dish. **Shopping Tip:** *Highly acidic, tart and complex-tasting tamarind fruit is used extensively in southern Indian cooking. The pulp is extracted and stored in paste form as tamarind concentrate. It is widely available at Indian grocery stores and other ethnic supermarkets. It will keep in a covered container in the refrigerator for up to 1 year. Lime juice is an acceptable substitute.*

  1 tablespoon canola oil
  1 tablespoon coriander seeds
  1 dried red chile, such as Thai, cayenne
       or chile de arbol

  1 teaspoon tamarind concentrate (*see Shopping Tip*)
       or juice of 1 large lime
  1 cup water
  1 teaspoon black *or* yellow mustard seeds
1½ pounds eggplant, peeled and cut into ½-inch
       cubes (6 cups)
  1 cup thinly sliced shallots (about 3 large)
½ teaspoon salt
  2 tablespoons finely chopped fresh cilantro

1. Heat oil in a large saucepan over medium-high heat; add coriander seeds and chile; toast until the coriander turns reddish brown and the chile is slightly blackened, about 30 seconds. With a slotted spoon, transfer spices to a plate to cool. Grind in spice grinder or mortar and pestle until the mixture is the texture of coarsely ground black pepper.

2. Dissolve tamarind concentrate (or lime juice) in water. Reheat the oil over medium-high heat; add mustard seeds. When the seeds begin to pop, cover the pan. As soon as the popping stops, add eggplant and shallots; cook, stirring constantly, for 1 minute. Add the tamarind (or lime juice) mixture, salt and the ground spices; bring to a boil. Reduce heat to medium-low, cover and simmer until the eggplant is fork-tender, 3 to 5 minutes. Coarsely mash the stew with a potato masher. Sprinkle with cilantro and serve.

PER SERVING: 74 calories; 3 g fat (0 g sat, 2 g mono);
0 mg cholesterol; 12 g carbohydrate; 0 g added sugars;
2 g protein; 4 g fiber; 201 mg sodium; 367 mg potassium.

Ratatouille à la Casablancaise

H✂W   H⬆F   H♥H

MAKES: 8 servings, about ½ cup each
ACTIVE TIME: 40 minutes | TOTAL: 40 minutes
TO MAKE AHEAD: Cover and refrigerate for up to 3 days.

Ratatouille—a cooked eggplant and tomato dish combined with other seasonal vegetables and olive oil—has many regional variations. This one is made with cinnamon, a signature spice in Moroccan cooking. Try it as an appetizer with toasted bread or as a sandwich filling.

1	large eggplant (1¼-1½ pounds), peeled and cut into ¼-inch cubes
1½	teaspoons salt, divided
3	tablespoons plus 1 teaspoon extra-virgin olive oil, divided
1	medium yellow summer squash, peeled and cut into ¼-inch cubes
1	red bell pepper, diced
3	medium tomatoes, peeled (*see Tip, page 490*), seeded and diced, *or* 1 cup drained canned diced tomatoes
2	cloves garlic, minced
1¼	teaspoons ground cinnamon
1	teaspoon sugar
¼	teaspoon freshly ground pepper

1. Place eggplant on a baking sheet and sprinkle with 1 teaspoon salt; let stand for 30 minutes. Rinse and pat dry.

2. Heat 3 tablespoons oil in a nonstick skillet over medium-high heat. Add the eggplant, squash and bell pepper. Cook, stirring, until the vegetables are soft, 8 to 10 minutes. Transfer to a large bowl.

3. Add the remaining 1 teaspoon oil to the pan. Add tomatoes, garlic, cinnamon, sugar, the remaining ½ teaspoon salt and pepper. Cook, stirring, until the tomatoes begin to break down, 3 to 5 minutes. Add to the bowl with the eggplant mixture and stir to combine. Cool to room temperature before serving, for the best flavor.

PER SERVING: 88 calories; 6 g fat (1 g sat, 5 g mono); 0 mg cholesterol; 8 g carbohydrate; 0 g added sugars; 2 g protein; 3 g fiber; 224 mg sodium; 342 mg potassium.
NUTRITION BONUS: Vitamin C (52% daily value), Vitamin A (18% dv).

EatingWell Tip

Did you know that cooking tomatoes makes them even healthier? **The lycopene that helps protect against cancer is more available to your body in cooked versus raw tomatoes.**

Fennel | PEAK SEASON: Spring, Fall, Winter | LOOK FOR: Small, white, unbruised bulbs with bright green stalks and feathery fronds. | STORE: Refrigerate in a plastic bag for 3 to 5 days.

How To

Prep Fennel | Cut off the stalks and fronds where they meet the bulb, remove any damaged outer layers and cut ¼ inch off the bottom. Quarter the bulb lengthwise and cut out the core. The edible fronds are a delicious garnish for any dish containing the bulb.

Fennel & Lemon Green Bean Salad

H✖W   H↑F   H♥H

MAKES: 6 servings
ACTIVE TIME: 20 minutes | TOTAL: 50 minutes (including 30 minutes chilling time)

The Italians often enjoy fennel the way North Americans eat celery: raw in salads. This salad is aromatic and crisp with a fresh lemon dressing.

- 4 ounces green beans, trimmed and cut into 1½-inch pieces
- 4 bulbs fennel, trimmed and cored (*see How To*), thinly sliced and fronds reserved
- 4 ounces mushrooms, trimmed and quartered
- 1 2-by-½-inch strip lemon zest, julienned
- 2 tablespoons balsamic vinegar
- 2 tablespoons water
- 1 tablespoon lemon juice
- 1 tablespoon extra-virgin olive oil
- ¼ teaspoon salt
   Freshly ground pepper to taste

1. Bring 1 inch of water to a boil in a medium sauce-pan fitted with a steamer basket. Steam beans until tender-crisp, 3 to 5 minutes. Rinse under cold water. Place them in a salad bowl.

2. Add sliced fennel bulb to the salad bowl along with mushrooms and lemon zest. Whisk vinegar, water, lemon juice and oil in a small bowl until well blended. Pour the dressing over the salad and add 2 tablespoons minced fennel fronds. Toss lightly. Season with salt and pepper. Cover and chill for 30 minutes to 1 hour.

PER SERVING: 84 calories; 3 g fat (0 g sat, 2 g mono); 0 mg cholesterol; 14 g carbohydrate; 0 g added sugars; 3 g protein; 6 g fiber; 182 mg sodium; 754 mg potassium.
NUTRITION BONUS: Vitamin C (38% daily value), Potassium (22% dv).

Braised Fennel with Tomatoes & Potatoes

H✖W   H⬆F   H♥H

MAKES: 4 servings, 1 cup each
ACTIVE TIME: 25 minutes | TOTAL: 1 hour

Braised fennel, tomatoes and potatoes make a rich and hearty side dish. Serve with grilled or pan-seared veal chops, chicken breasts and any broiled or baked fish.

- 1   tablespoon extra-virgin olive oil
- 1   large bulb fennel, trimmed and cored (*see How To, page 129*), thinly sliced and fronds reserved
- 1   teaspoon fennel seeds
- ¼   teaspoon salt
  Freshly ground pepper to taste
- 2   large tomatoes, diced
- 1   pound Yukon Gold potatoes, peeled and cut into ¾-inch cubes
- ½-¾ cup reduced-sodium chicken broth *or* water, divided
- 2   tablespoons Pernod *or* other anise-flavored liqueur (optional)
- 2   tablespoons finely chopped flat-leaf parsley *or* fennel fronds for garnish

Heat oil in a 12-inch cast-iron skillet over high heat. Add fennel and cook, stirring often, until it starts to brown, 4 to 5 minutes. Season with fennel seeds, salt and pepper. Add tomatoes, bring to a simmer and cook until the tomato juices are slightly reduced, about 4 minutes. Add potatoes and ½ cup broth (or water); cover the pan tightly and simmer over medium-low heat. Check after 10 minutes to make sure the pan juices don't run dry. If necessary, add more broth (or water), 2 tablespoons at a time, to prevent scorching. Simmer until the potatoes are tender, about 10 minutes more. Uncover, add Pernod (or other liqueur), if using, and simmer for 3 to 4 minutes more. Serve garnished with parsley (or fennel fronds), if desired.

PER SERVING: 148 calories; 4 g fat (1 g sat, 3 g mono); 0 mg cholesterol; 26 g carbohydrate; 0 g added sugars; 4 g protein; 6 g fiber; 259 mg sodium; 954 mg potassium.
NUTRITION BONUS: Vitamin C (68% daily value), Potassium (28% dv), Vitamin A (17% dv).

Green Beans | PEAK SEASON: Summer | LOOK FOR: Small, thin, firm beans. | STORE: Refrigerate in a plastic bag for 3 to 5 days. PREP: Trim stem ends.

▶ Braised Green Beans & Summer Vegetables

H✖W   H⬆F   H♥H

MAKES: 6 servings, about 1 cup each
ACTIVE TIME: 30 minutes | TOTAL: 30 minutes

When green beans, summer squash and cherry tomatoes are plentiful in backyard gardens and farmers' markets, try this quick braise. We like the salty, nutty flavor of Parmesan, but you can use any flavorful cheese.

- 1   tablespoon extra-virgin olive oil
- 1   small onion, halved and sliced
- 1   tablespoon finely chopped fresh oregano *or* 1 teaspoon dried
- ½   cup dry white wine *or* reduced-sodium chicken broth
- 1   pound green beans, trimmed
- 1   medium summer squash *or* zucchini, halved and cut into 1-inch pieces
- 1   cup halved cherry tomatoes *or* grape tomatoes
- ¼   teaspoon salt
- ¼   teaspoon freshly ground pepper
- ¼   cup finely shredded Parmesan cheese

Heat oil in a large skillet over medium heat. Add onion and oregano; cook, stirring, until softened and beginning to brown, about 2 minutes. Add wine (or broth); bring to a boil. Add green beans, reduce heat, cover and simmer for 10 minutes, stirring once or twice. Add squash (or zucchini) and tomatoes; cover and cook until the vegetables are tender, 8 to 10 minutes more. Season with salt and pepper. Sprinkle with Parmesan.

PER SERVING: 92 calories; 4 g fat (1 g sat, 2 g mono); 2 mg cholesterol; 10 g carbohydrate; 0 g added sugars; 3 g protein; 3 g fiber; 158 mg sodium; 291 mg potassium.
NUTRITION BONUS: Vitamin C (28% daily value), Vitamin A (17% dv).

◄ Quick Chile Dilly Beans

H✖W H♥H

MAKES: about 5 cups (drained) beans
ACTIVE TIME: 40 minutes | TOTAL: 1 day
TO MAKE AHEAD: Refrigerate for up to 1 month.
EQUIPMENT: 2-quart canning jar or similar-size tempered-glass or heatproof-plastic container

Traditionalists might say dilly beans are best after a month or so of marinating, but you can get that long-marinated taste in just one day with this quick technique.

- 1 **pound green beans, trimmed**
- 3 **cups water**
- 2 **cups distilled white vinegar**
- 2 **tablespoons salt**
- 1 **tablespoon pickling spice**
- 1 **teaspoon whole black peppercorns**
- ½ **teaspoon dried dill seed *or* 4 fresh dill seed heads**
- 2 **shallots, peeled and sliced, leaving root end intact**
- 1-2 **small fresh red chile peppers, quartered lengthwise**
- 2 **cloves garlic, peeled and sliced lengthwise**

1. Place a large bowl of ice water by the stove. Bring a large pot of water to a boil. Cook green beans until tender-crisp, 3 to 4 minutes. Use a slotted spoon to transfer the beans to the ice water to cool. Drain.

2. Meanwhile, combine 3 cups water, vinegar, salt, pickling spice and peppercorns in a medium saucepan. Bring to a boil and stir until the salt dissolves. Boil for 5 minutes. Remove from the heat and let stand for 10 minutes to cool slightly.

3. Place dill seed (or dill seed heads), shallots, chiles to taste and garlic in a 2-quart canning jar (or similar-size tempered-glass or heatproof-plastic container with a lid). Add the beans. Carefully pour the hot brine through a sieve into the jar. Make sure all the beans are submerged. Cool to room temperature. Cover and refrigerate for 1 day to marinate.

PER 1/2-CUP SERVING: 16 calories; 0 g fat (0 g sat, 0 g mono); 0 mg cholesterol; 4 g carbohydrate; 0 g added sugars; 1 g protein; 1 g fiber; 156 mg sodium; 65 mg potassium.

Green & Yellow Beans with Wild Mushrooms

H✖W H⬆F H♥H

MAKES: 10 servings, about ¾ cup each
ACTIVE TIME: 35 minutes | TOTAL: 35 minutes
TO MAKE AHEAD: Prepare through Step 1, cover and refrigerate for up to 1 day.

Simply prepared green and yellow beans with wild mushrooms are easy holiday fare. **Shopping Tip:** *If you can't find wild mushrooms, use button or cremini mushrooms.*

- 1 **pound green beans, trimmed**
- 1 **pound yellow wax beans, trimmed**
- 3 **tablespoons extra-virgin olive oil**
- 2 **cloves garlic, minced**
- 8 **ounces wild mushrooms, such as chanterelle, oyster *or* porcini (*see Shopping Tip*), trimmed and sliced**
- ½ **teaspoon kosher salt, divided**
  Freshly ground pepper to taste

1. Bring a large pot of water to a boil. Add green beans and wax beans and cook until tender-crisp, about 4 minutes. (Cook for another minute or two if you like your green beans more tender.) Drain well.

2. Meanwhile, heat oil in a large heavy skillet over medium heat. Add garlic and cook, stirring, until fragrant, about 1 minute. Stir in mushrooms and cook, stirring, until they release their juices and most of the liquid has evaporated, about 5 minutes. Season with ¼ teaspoon salt and pepper.

3. Reserve 1 tablespoon of the mushrooms for garnish. Add the cooked beans to the mushrooms in the pan and cook, stirring to combine, until heated through, 1 to 3 minutes. Season with the remaining ¼ teaspoon salt and pepper. Serve topped with the reserved mushrooms.

PER SERVING: 77 calories; 5 g fat (1 g sat, 3 g mono); 0 mg cholesterol; 9 g carbohydrate; 0 g added sugars; 2 g protein; 3 g fiber; 62 mg sodium; 296 mg potassium.
NUTRITION BONUS: Vitamin C (15% daily value).

Green Bean Casserole

H✻W   H⬆F   H❤H

MAKES: 6 servings

ACTIVE TIME: 45 minutes | TOTAL: 1 hour

TO MAKE AHEAD: Prepare through Step 4; store the onion topping, toasted breadcrumbs and sauce in separate containers in the refrigerator for up to 2 days.

This tasty makeover of the Thanksgiving classic has out standing flavor. We like the convenience of frozen green beans in this recipe, but you can easily substitute ½ pound fresh green beans for frozen. Simply trim and cut into 1-inch lengths. Then blanch the beans for 1 to 2 minutes in boiling water, refresh under cold water, drain well and spread in the baking dish.

ONION TOPPING

- ½   **teaspoon canola oil**
- 1   **large onion, thinly sliced**
- ½   **cup fresh breadcrumbs, preferably whole-wheat (*see Tip, page 481*)**

SAUCE & GREEN BEANS

- 2   **cups nonfat milk**
- 6   **black peppercorns**
- 1   **bay leaf**
  Pinch of grated nutmeg
- ½   **teaspoon canola oil**
- 1   **small onion, finely chopped**
- 8   **ounces mushrooms, trimmed and sliced**
- 1   **clove garlic, finely chopped**
- ¼   **cup all-purpose flour**
- ¼   **cup reduced-fat sour cream**
- 1   **teaspoon salt**
- ½   **teaspoon freshly ground pepper**
- 1   **9-ounce package frozen green beans (2 cups)**

1. **To prepare onion topping:** Heat oil in a large non-stick skillet over low heat. Add sliced onion and cook, stirring occasionally, until very tender and golden, about 30 minutes. Set aside.

2. Meanwhile, preheat oven to 350°F. Spread breadcrumbs on a baking sheet and toast, stirring once, until lightly browned, 5 to 10 minutes. Set aside.

3. **To prepare sauce:** Combine milk, peppercorns, bay leaf and nutmeg in a medium saucepan and heat over low until steaming. Remove from heat, let stand for 5 minutes and strain into a measuring cup. (Discard peppercorns and bay leaf.)

4. Meanwhile, heat oil in a large saucepan over medium heat. Add chopped onion and cook, stirring often, until golden, 3 to 4 minutes. Add mushrooms and garlic and cook, stirring, until tender, 3 to 4 minutes. Sprinkle flour over the vegetables and cook, stirring, for 1 minute. Slowly pour in the milk, whisking constantly. Bring to a boil, stirring. Reduce heat to low and cook, stirring, until thickened, about 1 minute. Remove from heat. Whisk in sour cream, salt and pepper.

5. **To assemble and bake casserole:** Preheat oven to 425°F. Spread green beans evenly over the bottom of a shallow 2-quart baking dish and pour the sauce over the top. Toss together the reserved onions and breadcrumbs in a small bowl and spread over the beans. Bake until bubbling, 15 to 25 minutes.

PER SERVING: 126 calories; 3 g fat (1 g sat, 1 g mono); 6 mg cholesterol; 21 g carbohydrate; 0 g added sugars; 7 g protein; 3 g fiber; 438 mg sodium; 390 mg potassium.

EatingWell Tip

Skip canned vegetables and opt for frozen when you're looking for convenience. **Canned veggies usually have added sodium while frozen vegetables don't.**

Sizzled Green Beans with Crispy Prosciutto & Pine Nuts

H✂W   H↑F   H♥H

MAKES: 8 servings, ¾ cup each
ACTIVE TIME: 30 minutes I TOTAL: 45 minutes
TO MAKE AHEAD: Prepare through Step 1 and refrigerate
for up to 2 days.

Sizzling green beans in a little oil helps to bring out their natural sweetness. Prosciutto, pine nuts and lemon zest dress up the flavor without adding a lot of fat.

-     2 pounds green beans, trimmed
- 2½ teaspoons extra-virgin olive oil, divided
-     2 ounces thinly sliced prosciutto, cut into ribbons
-     4 cloves garlic, minced
-     2 teaspoons minced fresh sage
-   ¼ teaspoon salt, divided
        Freshly ground pepper to taste
-   ¼ cup toasted pine nuts (see *Tip, page 486*)
- 1½ teaspoons freshly grated lemon zest
-     1 teaspoon lemon juice

1. Bring a large pot of water to a boil. Add beans, return to a boil, and simmer until crisp-tender, 3 to 4 minutes. Drain.

2. Heat ½ teaspoon oil in a large nonstick skillet over medium heat. Add prosciutto; cook, stirring, until crispy, 4 to 5 minutes. Drain on a paper towel.

3. Wipe out the pan; heat the remaining 2 teaspoons oil over medium heat. Add the beans, garlic, sage, ⅛ teaspoon salt and several grinds of pepper. Cook, stirring occasionally, until the beans are browned in places, 3 to 4 minutes. Stir in pine nuts, lemon zest and the prosciutto. Season with lemon juice, the remaining ⅛ teaspoon salt and pepper.

PER SERVING: 98 calories; 5 g fat (1 g sat, 2 g mono); 6 mg cholesterol; 10 g carbohydrate; 0 g added sugars; 5 g protein; 4 g fiber; 264 mg sodium; 196 mg potassium.
NUTRITION BONUS: Vitamin C (20% daily value), Vitamin A (16% dv).

Kale I PEAK SEASON: Spring, Fall, Winter I LOOK FOR: Crisp, brightly colored greens; avoid those that are wilted or blemished. I STORE: Store unwashed; wrap stem ends in damp paper towels and refrigerate in a plastic bag for up to 10 days. I PREP: Wash well and discard the tough stems.

Kale & Potato Hash

H✂W   H↑F   H♥H

MAKES: 4 servings, ½ cup each
ACTIVE TIME: 35 minutes I TOTAL: 35 minutes

Fresh, partially cooked, shredded potatoes for hash browns can be found in the refrigerated produce section and sometimes in the dairy section of most super-markets. Alternatively, boil potatoes until they can just be pierced with a fork but are not completely tender. Let cool slightly, then shred.

-   8 cups torn kale leaves (about ½ large bunch)
-   2 tablespoons horseradish
-   1 medium shallot, minced
-   ½ teaspoon freshly ground pepper
-   ¼ teaspoon salt
-   2 cups cooked shredded potatoes
-   3 tablespoons extra-virgin olive oil

1. Place kale in a large microwavable bowl, cover and microwave until wilted, about 3 minutes. Drain, cool slightly, and finely chop. Mix horseradish, shallot, pepper and salt in the bowl. Add potatoes and the chopped kale; stir to combine.

2. Heat oil in a large nonstick skillet over medium heat. Add the kale-potato mixture in an even layer; cook, stirring every 3 to 4 minutes and spreading out again, until the potatoes begin to turn golden brown and crisp, 12 to 15 minutes total.

PER SERVING: 208 calories; 11 g fat (2 g sat, 8 g mono); 0 mg cholesterol; 24 g carbohydrate; 0 g added sugars; 5 g protein; 5 g fiber; 219 mg sodium; 359 mg potassium.
NUTRITION BONUS: Vitamin A (385% daily value), Vitamin C (100% dv).

Mushrooms | PEAK SEASON: Year-round (depending on region and mushroom variety). | LOOK FOR: Firm mushrooms with a fresh, smooth appearance. They should appear dry, but not dried out. | STORE: Refrigerate in their original container up to 1 week. Once opened, store in a paper bag. Do not store fresh mushrooms in airtight containers, which will cause condensation and speed up spoilage. PREP: Wipe off any dirt with a damp paper towel.

◀ Garlic-Rosemary Mushrooms

H✖W   H⬆F   H♥H

MAKES: 4 servings, about ¾ cup each
ACTIVE TIME: 20 minutes | TOTAL: 20 minutes

These simple sautéed mushrooms work as a quick, weeknight side dish. To turn them into a main course, toss with cooked pasta and a generous handful of Parmesan cheese or fold into an omelet with Gruyère or fontina (see omelet guide, page 455).

1	ounce bacon (about 1½ slices), chopped
1½	pounds mixed mushrooms, such as cremini, shiitake (stemmed) and portobello, cut into ¼-inch slices
2	medium cloves garlic, finely chopped
1½	teaspoons chopped fresh rosemary *or* ½ teaspoon dried
¼	teaspoon salt
	Freshly ground pepper to taste
¼	cup dry white wine

Cook bacon in a large skillet over medium heat until just beginning to brown, about 4 minutes. Add mushrooms, garlic, rosemary, salt and pepper and cook, stirring occasionally, until almost dry, 8 to 10 minutes. Pour in wine and cook until most of the liquid has evaporated, 30 seconds to 1 minute.

PER SERVING: 75 calories; 2 g fat (0 g sat, 0 g mono); 3 mg cholesterol; 10 g carbohydrate; 0 g added sugars; 5 g protein; 3 g fiber; 213 mg sodium; 660 mg potassium.
NUTRITION BONUS: Potassium (19% daily value).

Sesame Roasted Mushrooms & Scallions

H✖W   H⬆F   H♥H

MAKES: 6 servings, about ⅔ cup each
ACTIVE TIME: 20 minutes | TOTAL: 45 minutes

Roasting brings out the natural sweetness of mushrooms. Here they are paired with full-flavored sesame oil, ginger, garlic and scallions. Using a variety of mixed mushrooms makes this dish special. Serve with Lemon-Pepper Catfish (page 288).

2	tablespoons toasted sesame oil
2	tablespoons reduced-sodium soy sauce
1	tablespoon grated fresh ginger
1	tablespoon minced garlic
4	teaspoons rice vinegar
½	teaspoon freshly ground pepper
1½	pounds mixed mushrooms, such as shiitake (stemmed), oyster and white, thickly sliced
2	bunches scallions, cut into 2-inch pieces
1	tablespoon toasted sesame seeds (*see How To*)

1. Preheat oven to 450°F.

2. Combine oil, soy sauce, ginger, garlic, vinegar and pepper in a large bowl. Add mushrooms and scallions and toss to coat. Transfer to a roasting pan.

3. Roast, stirring once or twice, until browned and cooked through, about 25 minutes. Sprinkle with sesame seeds.

PER SERVING: 106 calories; 6 g fat (1 g sat, 2 g mono); 0 mg cholesterol; 12 g carbohydrate; 0 g added sugars; 5 g protein; 4 g fiber; 152 mg sodium; 554 mg potassium.
NUTRITION BONUS: Potassium (16% daily value).

How To

Toast Sesame Seeds | Heat a small dry skillet over low heat. Add seeds and cook, stirring constantly, until golden and fragrant, about 2 minutes. Transfer to a small bowl and let cool.

Okra | PEAK SEASON: Summer | LOOK FOR: Pods vary in shape and size (from 2 to 7 inches long); all should be relatively firm, bright and free of spots or mold. | STORE: Store in a paper bag in the upper (usually warmer) part of the refrigerator. Keep it dry. | PREP: Wash and dry okra before trimming. To use whole, trim off the tip of the stem, taking care not to open the pod and expose the seeds. For sliced okra, cut off and discard the whole top end, then slice the pod.

Spicy Pickled Okra

MAKES: about 12 cups
ACTIVE TIME: 30 minutes | TOTAL: 30 minutes (plus 1 week)
TO MAKE AHEAD: Cover and refrigerate for up to 1 month.
EQUIPMENT: 6 pint-size (2-cup) canning jars or tempered-glass or heatproof-plastic containers with lids

These are the perfect tangy and crunchy treat to turn anyone on to the beauty of this underappreciated vegetable.

- 2 **pounds okra (about 12 cups)**
- 6 **whole habanero peppers**
- 3 **cups distilled white vinegar *or* cider vinegar**
- 3 **cups water**
- 2 **tablespoons plus 2 teaspoons sea salt**
- 2 **tablespoons sugar**

1. Cook okra in a pot of boiling water for 2 minutes. Transfer it to a bowl of ice water to cool. Drain.

2. Divide the okra among 6 pint-size (2-cup) canning jars (or tempered-glass or heatproof-plastic containers with lids). Add 1 habanero to each jar.

3. Combine vinegar, 3 cups water, salt and sugar in a large saucepan. Bring to a boil and stir until the salt and sugar dissolve. Boil for 2 minutes. Carefully fill jars (or containers) with the brine to within ½ inch of the rim, covering the okra completely. Place the lids on the jars (or containers) and refrigerate for at least 1 week before serving.

PER 1/4-CUP SERVING: 8 calories; 0 g fat (0 g sat, 0 g mono); 0 mg cholesterol; 2 g carbohydrate; 0 g added sugars; 1 g protein; 1 g fiber; 54 mg sodium; 76 mg potassium.

Stewed Okra & Tomatoes

H✖W   H⬆F   H❤H

MAKES: 6 servings, ¾ cup each
ACTIVE TIME: 25 minutes | TOTAL: 1 hour 10 minutes
TO MAKE AHEAD: Cover and refrigerate for up to 3 days.

Stewing okra with onion and tomatoes is absolutely traditional all through the South. Small amounts of meat are often added for seasoning. Add corn to this, too, if you like, and serve it over rice, hot cornbread or grits.

- 4 **ounces breakfast sausage, preferably spicy, casings removed if necessary**
- 1 **medium onion, chopped**
- 1 **pound okra, sliced**
- 3 **cups chopped tomatoes (3-4 medium)**
- ⅔ **cup reduced-sodium tomato juice *or* water**
- ¼ **teaspoon salt**
- ½ **teaspoon crushed red pepper *or* ½ jalapeño, minced**

1. Cook sausage in a large saucepan or Dutch oven over medium heat, breaking it up as it cooks, until it is no longer pink, 2 to 3 minutes. Add onion and cook, stirring frequently, until soft and translucent, about 5 minutes.

2. Increase heat to high; add okra, tomatoes, tomato juice (or water), salt and crushed red pepper (or jalapeño) and cook, stirring often, until bubbling. Reduce heat to a gentle simmer and cook, stirring occasionally, until the mixture is thick and the vegetables are very tender, 35 to 45 minutes.

PER SERVING: 88 calories; 4 g fat (1 g sat, 2 g mono); 7 mg cholesterol; 11 g carbohydrate; 0 g added sugars; 4 g protein; 4 g fiber; 201 mg sodium; 561 mg potassium.
NUTRITION BONUS: Vitamin C (58% daily value), Vitamin A (22% dv), Folate (19% dv), Potassium (16% dv).

Onions | PEAK SEASON: Spring, Summer, Fall | LOOK FOR: Firm, heavy onions without cuts, bruises or sprouting. Scallions should have a firm white base and bright, fresh-looking greens. | STORE: Keep in a cool, dry, dark, well-ventilated place away from potatoes, which give off moisture and gas that can cause onions to spoil quickly. Refrigerate scallions and chives for up to 5 days.

Baked Stuffed Onions

H✂W   H♥H

MAKES: 6 servings
ACTIVE TIME: 40 minutes | TOTAL: 1 hour 10 minutes
TO MAKE AHEAD: Prepare through Step 3; cover and refrigerate for up to 8 hours.

These baked onions are stuffed with a savory combination of mushrooms, breadcrumbs and capers.

3	Spanish onions
3	ounces day-old Italian bread (about six ½-inch-thick slices), crust removed
½	cup nonfat milk
1	large egg, lightly beaten
3	ounces mushrooms (6 large), chopped
2	tablespoons capers, rinsed and chopped
1	tablespoon chopped fresh parsley
1	clove garlic, minced
½	teaspoon salt
¼	teaspoon freshly ground pepper
¼	cup fine dry unseasoned breadcrumbs
1½	teaspoons extra-virgin olive oil

1. Preheat oven to 375°F.

2. Keeping the whole onions intact, peel away the outer layer. Carefully trim root ends with a paring knife, so they are flat. Cook the onions in a large pot of boiling water until tender, about 10 minutes. Drain and let cool.

3. Meanwhile, combine bread with milk in a small bowl; let soak for 10 minutes. Squeeze bread almost dry and, with your fingers, break it into a large bowl. Stir in egg, mushrooms, capers, parsley, garlic, salt and pepper. Set aside.

4. Cut onions in half horizontally. Scoop out some of the center of each onion and chop coarsely. (Reserve the onion halves). Add the chopped onion to the bread mixture and mix well. Fill the onion halves with the bread mixture and sprinkle with dry breadcrumbs.

5. Arrange the onions in a shallow 2-quart baking dish and drizzle with oil. Bake, uncovered, until the tops are golden and the onions are heated through, about 25 minutes.

PER SERVING: 113 calories, 3 g fat (1 g sat, 1 g mono); 36 mg cholesterol; 17 g carbohydrate; 0 g added sugars; 5 g protein; 2 g fiber; 363 mg sodium; 201 mg potassium.
NUTRITION BONUS: Folate (18% daily value).

Onion Rings

H✳W H♥H

MAKES: 6 servings, 6-7 onion rings each
ACTIVE TIME: 40 minutes | TOTAL: 1 hour

We couldn't get enough of these crunchy onion rings in the EatingWell Test Kitchen. Try any seasoning blend that you have on hand to add flavor to the breading or substitute 1 teaspoon salt instead. Seasoned whole-wheat breadcrumbs are available in some supermarkets and natural-foods stores. If you can find them, try them in place of the plain breadcrumbs and seasoning blend.

2	**medium yellow onions**
¾	**cup all-purpose flour**
2	**teaspoons baking powder**
3	**large eggs**
1½	**cups fine dry breadcrumbs, preferably whole-wheat (see How To)**
1	**tablespoon seasoning blend, such as Cajun, jerk *or* Old Bay**
	Olive oil or canola oil cooking spray

1. Position racks in upper and lower thirds of oven; preheat to 450°F. Coat 2 large rimmed baking sheets with cooking spray.

2. Cut off both ends of each onion and peel. Slice into ½-inch-thick slices; separate into rings. (Discard the smallest rings or reserve for another use.) Place the rings in a medium bowl; cover with cold water.

3. Combine flour and baking powder in a shallow dish. Lightly beat eggs in another shallow dish. Combine breadcrumbs and seasoning in a third shallow dish. Working with one ring at time, remove from the water, letting any excess drip off. Coat in flour, shaking off any excess. Dip in egg and let any excess drip off. Then coat in the breadcrumb mixture, shaking off any excess. Place on the prepared baking sheets. Generously coat the onion rings with cooking spray.

4. Bake for 10 minutes. Turn each onion ring over and return to the oven, switching the positions of the baking sheets. Continue baking until brown and very crispy, 8 to 10 minutes more.

PER SERVING: 175 calories; 3 g fat (1 g sat, 1 g mono); 79 mg cholesterol; 29 g carbohydrate; 0 g added sugars; 7 g protein; 2 g fiber; 557 mg sodium; 136 mg potassium.

How To

Make Fine Dry Breadcrumbs | Trim crusts from firm whole-wheat sandwich bread. Tear the bread into pieces and process in a food processor until very fine. Spread on a baking sheet and bake at 250°F until dry, about 10 to 15 minutes. One slice of bread makes about ⅓ cup dry breadcrumbs. Look for fine dry whole-wheat breadcrumbs in the natural-foods section of large supermarkets or natural-foods stores.

Creamed Onions

H✂W   H♥H

MAKES: 12 servings, about ½ cup each
ACTIVE TIME: 1 hour | TOTAL: 1 hour 50 minutes
TO MAKE AHEAD: Cover and refrigerate for up to 2 days.
Reheat in the microwave on High, covered, stirring
frequently, or on the stovetop over medium-low heat.

*A holiday staple in many households, creamed onions are
usually bathed in a rich white sauce made with heavy
cream. In this version, we roast the onions for an added layer
of flavor and lighten up the sauce with low-fat milk. The
result is a luxuriously silky sauce with a sweet roasted onion
flavor for far fewer calories and less fat. We like the smaller
size of pearl onions, but boiling onions also work well.*

3	pounds pearl onions, fresh *or* frozen, *or* boiling onions
3	tablespoons extra-virgin olive oil, divided
1	teaspoon salt, divided
½	cup reduced-sodium beef broth
1	tablespoon butter
¼	cup all-purpose flour
3	cups low-fat milk
1	bay leaf
1	teaspoon chopped fresh thyme
¼	teaspoon white *or* black pepper
2	teaspoons lemon juice

1. Preheat oven to 400°F.

2. If using fresh onions, bring a large pot of water to a boil. Add onions and cook 1 minute to loosen the skins. Drain. When cool enough to handle, trim both ends, leaving enough of the root end to keep the onions whole while roasting. Peel off the skins. Toss the prepared fresh onions (or frozen onions) with 1 tablespoon oil and ¼ teaspoon salt in a large bowl. Spread in an even layer in a roasting pan large enough to accommodate all the onions in a single layer. (If you're using fresh onions, a 9-by-13-inch pan is large enough; if using frozen, you may need a larger pan.) Roast the onions, stirring occasionally, until soft and brown in spots, 45 minutes to 1 hour.

3. Remove the roasting pan from the oven and add broth, stirring and scraping up any brown bits. Return the pan to the oven and roast for 10 minutes more.

4. About 30 minutes after the onions start roasting, start the cream sauce. Melt butter with the remaining 2 tablespoons oil in a large saucepan over medium heat. Add flour and cook, whisking, until the mixture bubbles and is free of lumps, about 30 seconds. Whisk in milk, then add bay leaf, thyme, pepper and the remaining ¾ teaspoon salt; bring to a gentle boil, whisking often. Reduce heat to the barest simmer and cook, whisking often, until the sauce has thickened to the consistency of thick gravy, about 5 minutes. Remove from the heat. Discard the bay leaf.

5. Stir the roasted onions and any broth from the pan into the cream sauce. Stir in lemon juice. Transfer to a serving dish and serve warm.

PER SERVING: 119 calories; 5 g fat (2 g sat, 3 g mono);
6 mg cholesterol; 15 g carbohydrate; 0 g added sugars;
4 g protein; 2 g fiber; 249 mg sodium; 159 mg potassium.

Lebanese Potato Salad

H❌W   H❤H

MAKES: 8 servings, about ⅔ cup each
ACTIVE TIME: 20 minutes | TOTAL: 1¼ hours (including cooling time) | TO MAKE AHEAD: Prepare through Step 2; cover and refrigerate for up to 2 days. Add additional lemon juice and/or salt to taste.

Dressed with a tangy lemon vinaigrette and fresh mint, this invigorating—and dairy-free—potato salad makes the perfect summer potluck contribution. (Photograph: page 106.)

- 2 **pounds russet potatoes, scrubbed (about 3 medium)**
- ¼ **cup lemon juice**
- 3 **tablespoons extra-virgin olive oil**
- ½ **teaspoon salt**
   Freshly ground pepper to taste
- 4 **scallions, thinly sliced**
- ¼ **cup chopped fresh mint**

1. Place potatoes in a large saucepan or Dutch oven and cover with lightly salted water. Bring to a boil and cook until tender, 25 to 30 minutes. Drain and rinse with cold water. Transfer to a cutting board. Let cool for 20 minutes. Cut the cooled potatoes into ½-inch pieces.

2. Whisk lemon juice, oil, salt and pepper in a large bowl. Add the potatoes and toss to coat.

3. Just before serving, add scallions and mint to the salad and toss gently.

PER SERVING: 143 calories; 5 g fat (1 g sat, 4 g mono); 0 mg cholesterol; 22 g carbohydrate; 0 g added sugars; 3 g protein; 2 g fiber; 153 mg sodium; 517 mg potassium.
NUTRITION BONUS: Vitamin C (20% daily value), Potassium (15% dv).

▶ Country Potato Salad

H❌W   H❤H

MAKES: 8 servings, about 1 cup each
ACTIVE TIME: 40 minutes | TOTAL: 1 hour
TO MAKE AHEAD: Cover and refrigerate for up to 1 day. Taste and adjust seasoning if desired.

This updated picnic potato salad gets subtle flavor from smoked ham.

- 2 **pounds small potatoes, scrubbed**
- 1 **cup chopped celery**
- 2 **ounces smoked ham, sliced into strips**
- ¼ **cup chopped fresh parsley**
- 2 **tablespoons chopped fresh chives *or* scallions**
- 2 **tablespoons chopped fresh mint *or* dill**
- ¾ **cup buttermilk (*see Tip, page 482*)**
- 1 **tablespoon lemon juice**
- 1 **tablespoon peanut oil *or* canola oil**
- ½ **teaspoon salt**
   Freshly ground pepper to taste
- 2 **large hard-boiled eggs (*see Tip, page 484*), peeled and coarsely chopped**

1. Place potatoes in a large saucepan, cover with water and bring to a simmer over medium-high heat. Reduce heat to medium and cook, partially covered, until just tender, 12 to 20 minutes, depending on their size. Drain and let cool for about 15 minutes.

2. When the potatoes are cool enough to handle, taste a bit of skin—if it's bitter or tough, peel them. Otherwise, leave the skins on. Cut the potatoes into bite-size pieces and put them in a large salad bowl.

3. Add celery, ham, parsley, chives (or scallions) and mint (or dill) to the potatoes. Toss to combine. Add buttermilk, lemon juice, oil, salt and pepper; stir to combine. Gently stir in chopped egg. Serve at room temperature or chilled.

PER SERVING: 137 calories; 4 g fat (1 g sat, 1 g mono); 57 mg cholesterol; 20 g carbohydrate; 0 g added sugars; 6 g protein; 2 g fiber; 269 mg sodium; 615 mg potassium.
NUTRITION BONUS: Vitamin C (23% daily value), Potassium (18% dv).

Cooking Potatoes

Potatoes are versatile and delicious. They're also nutritious—potatoes are rich in vitamin C and potassium and offer some fiber, especially when eaten with the skin on. Here are easy ways to enjoy potatoes roasted, baked or mashed.

Roasted Potatoes

Preheat oven to 450°F. Cut 2 pounds scrubbed **potatoes** (peeled if desired) into ¾-inch chunks. Toss in a large roasting pan with 1 tablespoon extra-virgin **olive oil**, ½ teaspoon **salt** and ¼ teaspoon **pepper**. Roast potatoes in upper third of oven, stirring occasionally, until golden brown and tender, 30 to 35 minutes. MAKES: 6 servings. PER SERVING: 134 calories.

Toss with potatoes *before* roasting:
CUMIN: 1 teaspoon ground **cumin**, ½ teaspoon ground **coriander** and a pinch of **cayenne pepper**.
LEMON-OREGANO: 1 teaspoon each freshly grated **lemon zest** and dried **oregano**.
MUSTARD-ROSEMARY: 1 tablespoon each Dijon **mustard** and chopped fresh **rosemary**.

Or toss with potatoes *after* roasting:
HERBS: 2 tablespoons chopped fresh **herbs**, such as parsley or dill.
SALT & VINEGAR: A sprinkling of **malt vinegar** (or white vinegar) and **coarse salt**.

Baked Potatoes

Scrub 1 medium **russet potato** per person; pierce in several places with a fork. Microwave the potatoes on Medium, turning once or twice, until cooked through, about 20 minutes. Or use the "potato setting" on your microwave and cook according to the manufacturer's directions. (*Alternatively, bake potatoes directly on the center rack in a 400°F oven until cooked through, 45 to 60 minutes.*) | PER POTATO: 219 calories.

Top each baked potato with:
CURRY SAUCE: 1 tablespoon nonfat plain **yogurt** mixed with 2 teaspoons chopped **scallions**, ¼-½ teaspoon **curry powder** and ¼ teaspoon **salt**.
FETA & OLIVE: 1 tablespoon crumbled **feta cheese**, 2 teaspoons chopped fresh **herbs** and 1 teaspoon chopped black **olives**.
SALSA: 1 tablespoon each prepared salsa and **Monterey Jack cheese** and 1 teaspoon reduced-fat **sour cream**.
SCALLION-RANCH: 1 tablespoon low-fat **ranch dressing** and 2 teaspoons chopped **scallions**.
TOMATO-PESTO: 1 tablespoon prepared **pesto** and 1 chopped small plum **tomato**.

Mashed Potatoes

Scrub and peel (if desired) 2 pounds all-purpose **potatoes**. Cut into chunks and place in a large heavy saucepan. Add lightly salted water to cover. Bring to a boil. Reduce heat to medium, cover, and cook until the potatoes are very tender, 10 to 15 minutes. When the potatoes are done, drain in a colander and return to the pan. Place the pan over low heat and shake for about 1 minute to dry the potatoes. Mash the potatoes with ⅔ cup **buttermilk** (or low-fat milk or low-fat plain yogurt) and **salt** & **pepper** to taste, plus one of the following combinations, if desired. MAKES: 6 servings. | PER SERVING: 119 calories.

Stir into mashed potatoes:
CHEDDAR-CHIVE: 1 cup shredded extra-sharp **Cheddar cheese** and 3 tablespoons sliced fresh **chives** (or scallion greens).
GARLIC MASHED: Cook 6 peeled **garlic** cloves with the potatoes. *After mashing:* Add 2 teaspoons melted **butter**.
GOAT CHEESE: 2 teaspoons melted **butter** and 3 ounces crumbled **goat cheese**.
HERBED: 2 teaspoons extra-virgin **olive oil**, 3 tablespoons minced fresh **chives** and/or **thyme**.
PARSLEY-BUTTERMILK: 2 minced **scallions**, ¼ cup minced **parsley** and 2 tablespoons **butter**.

Rutabaga | PEAK SEASON: Fall, Winter | LOOK FOR: Firm, unblemished bulbs. They're often thinly coated with wax to prolong storage. They have an earthy, buttery flavor. STORE: Keep in a cool, dark place for up to 2 weeks or refrigerate for up to 1 month. | PREP: To peel a rutabaga, cut off one end to create a flat surface to keep it steady. Cut off the skin with your knife, following the contour of the bulb. Or use a vegetable peeler and peel around the bulb at least three times to ensure all the fibrous skin has been removed.

Glazed Rutabagas & Potatoes

H❌W   H⬆F   H❤H

MAKES: 8 servings
ACTIVE TIME: 20 minutes | TOTAL: 1½ hours

Roasted earthy rutabagas and potatoes are simply glazed in this easy side dish.

2½ pounds boiling potatoes, peeled and cut into 1-inch cubes (6 cups)
2   pounds rutabaga, peeled and cut into 1-inch cubes (6 cups)
2   tablespoons canola oil
3   tablespoons sugar
1   teaspoon salt
½   teaspoon freshly ground pepper

1. Position rack in lower third of oven. Preheat to 425°F.

2. Toss together potatoes, rutabaga and oil in a large bowl. Spread out on a large baking sheet. Cover with foil and roast until just tender, about 45 minutes.

3. Sprinkle the vegetables with sugar, salt and pepper; toss gently to coat. Return to the oven and roast, uncovered, until golden brown and glazed, about 25 minutes more.

PER SERVING: 205 calories; 4 g fat (0 g sat, 2 g mono); 0 mg cholesterol; 41 g carbohydrate; 5 g added sugars; 4 g protein; 5 g fiber; 320 mg sodium; 821 mg potassium.
NUTRITION BONUS: Vitamin C (63% daily value), Potassium (23% dv).

Spinach | PEAK SEASON: Spring, Fall, Winter | LOOK FOR: Supple, deeply colored leaves without mushy spots. | STORE: If spinach is damp, dry on kitchen towels, wrap in dry towels and refrigerate in a plastic bag for 3 to 5 days. | PREP: Trim stems. Wash leaves in several changes of water.

Creamed Spinach Gratin

H❌W   H⬆F   H❤H

MAKES: 4 servings
ACTIVE TIME: 10 minutes | TOTAL: 20 minutes

This homey spinach casserole is perfect served with grilled steaks and baked potatoes topped with a little sauce of horseradish stirred into reduced-fat sour cream.

3   teaspoons extra-virgin olive oil, divided
1   pound frozen spinach, thawed and squeezed dry
2   cloves garlic, minced
⅓   cup low-fat milk
⅓   cup low-fat mayonnaise
¼   teaspoon salt
    Freshly ground pepper to taste
¼   cup seasoned breadcrumbs
2   tablespoons freshly grated Parmesan cheese

1. Preheat oven to 450°F. Coat a baking dish or gratin dish with cooking spray.

2. Heat 2 teaspoons oil in a medium skillet over medium-high heat. Add spinach and garlic; cook, stirring, until fragrant. Remove from heat; stir in milk and mayonnaise. Season with salt and pepper.

3. Place the spinach mixture in the prepared baking dish. Combine breadcrumbs, Parmesan and the remaining 1 teaspoon oil; sprinkle over the spinach. Bake for 10 to 15 minutes.

PER SERVING: 135 calories; 7 g fat (1 g sat, 3 g mono); 3 mg cholesterol; 14 g carbohydrate; 0 g added sugars; 7 g protein; 4 g fiber; 582 mg sodium; 450 mg potassium.
NUTRITION BONUS: Vitamin A (267% daily value), Folate (45% dv), Magnesium (23% dv), Calcium (22% dv).

Spicy Stewed Potatoes & Spinach with Buttermilk (*Aloo chaas*)

H✖W   H⬆F   H♥H

MAKES: 4 servings, 1 cup each
ACTIVE TIME: 30 minutes | TOTAL: 45 minutes

This stewlike Indian potato-and-spinach curry can be served as a side dish or as part of a vegetarian buffet. The touch of cream prevents the buttermilk from curdling when it's heated and helps balance the heat from the pungent chiles. Serve with basmati rice and roast chicken or grilled fish.

1	pound russet *or* Yukon Gold potatoes, peeled and cut into 2-inch chunks
2	dried red chiles, such as Thai, cayenne *or* chile de arbol, stemmed
1	cup boiling water
½	cup firmly packed fresh cilantro
4	large cloves garlic, peeled
¾	teaspoon salt
1	tablespoon canola oil
¼	teaspoon ground turmeric
½	cup buttermilk (*see Tip, page 482*)
1	tablespoon whipping cream
8	ounces baby spinach

1. Place potatoes in a medium bowl; cover with cold water to prevent browning. Place chiles in a small heatproof bowl and pour the boiling water over them. Set aside until they are reconstituted, about 15 minutes. Reserving the chile-soaking water, coarsely chop the chiles (do not seed).

2. Pile cilantro, garlic, salt and the chopped chiles in a mortar. Pound the ingredients to a pulpy mass with the pestle, using a spatula to contain the mixture in the center for a concentrated pounding. (*Alternatively, pulse the ingredients in a food processor until minced.*)

3. Heat oil in a large skillet over medium-high heat. Add the spice paste and cook, stirring, until the garlic is honey-brown and the chiles are pungent, 1 to 2 minutes. (Make sure to use adequate ventilation.) Drain the potatoes and add to the pan along with turmeric; cook, stirring to coat the potatoes with the yellow spice, about 30 seconds. Pour in the reserved chile-soaking water and scrape the pan to loosen any browned bits; bring to a boil. Reduce heat to a gentle simmer, cover and cook, stirring occasionally, until the potatoes are fork-tender, 15 to 20 minutes.

4. Whisk buttermilk and cream in a small bowl.

5. When the potatoes are tender, pile the spinach leaves over them, cover and cook until the spinach is wilted, 3 to 4 minutes. Remove from the heat and stir in the buttermilk mixture.

PER SERVING: 172 calories; 5 g fat (1 g sat, 3 g mono); 5 mg cholesterol; 28 g carbohydrate; 0 g added sugars; 5 g protein; 4 g fiber; 520 mg sodium; 776 mg potassium.
NUTRITION BONUS: Vitamin A (114% daily value), Vitamin C (97% dv), Folate (32% dv), Potassium (22% dv), Magnesium (19% dv).

Meringue-Topped Sweet Potato Casserole

H✂W   H↑F   H♥H

MAKES: 10 servings, about ½ cup each
ACTIVE TIME: 30 minutes | **TOTAL:** 1¼ hours

Here's a lightened-up take on the classic Thanksgiving sweet potato casserole topped with marshmallows. We skip the butter in the filling and make it creamy with low-fat evaporated milk and add a tangy sweetness with chunks of pineapple. We top it with an airy, slightly sweet meringue. You can pipe the meringue to make it look fancy or simply spread it neatly with a rubber spatula.

SWEET POTATO CASSEROLE

- 2½ **pounds sweet potatoes (about 3 medium), peeled and cut into 2-inch chunks**
- 2 **large eggs**
- 2 **tablespoons brown sugar**
- ¼ **teaspoon ground cinnamon**
- 1 **tablespoon canola oil**
- 1 **cup low-fat evaporated milk**
- 1 **teaspoon vanilla extract**
- ½ **teaspoon salt**
- 1 **8-ounce can crushed pineapple, undrained**
- ½ **cup chopped pecans, toasted (see Tip, page 486)**

MERINGUE TOPPING

- 2 **large egg whites, at room temperature, *or* equivalent dried egg whites (see Tip, page 484), reconstituted according to package directions**
- ¼ **cup granulated sugar**

1. Place sweet potatoes in a large saucepan and cover with water. Bring to a boil. Reduce heat to a simmer and cook until tender, 10 to 15 minutes. Drain well and transfer to a food processor. Process until smooth.

2. Preheat oven to 350°F. Coat an 8-inch-square (or similar 2-quart) broiler-safe baking dish (*see Tip, page 481*) with cooking spray.

3. Whisk whole eggs, brown sugar, cinnamon, oil, evaporated milk, vanilla and salt in a large bowl until smooth. Add the sweet potato; whisk until smooth. Stir in pineapple and juice. Spread the mixture in the prepared baking dish. Sprinkle pecans over the top.

4. Bake the casserole until heated through and the edges are bubbling, 35 to 45 minutes. Set aside while you make the topping.

5. **To prepare meringue topping:** Position rack in top third of oven; preheat broiler. Beat egg whites in a medium bowl with an electric mixer at high speed until soft peaks form (*see Tip, page 484*). Beat in ¼ cup sugar in a slow, steady stream. Continue beating until stiff peaks form. Spoon the meringue into a gallon-size sealable bag (*see How To,* PHOTO 1). Seal the bag, pressing out as much air as possible. Cut a ½-inch hole in one corner (PHOTO 2). Pipe the meringue onto the casserole, making marshmallow-size dots. (*Alternatively, use a pastry bag fitted with a ½-inch tip or spread the meringue over the casserole as if you were frosting a cake.*) Broil until lightly browned, watching carefully to prevent burning, 30 to 90 seconds.

PER SERVING: 200 calories; 7 g fat (1 g sat, 3 g mono); 46 mg cholesterol; 30 g carbohydrate; 10 g added sugars; 5 g protein; 3 g fiber; 194 mg sodium; 362 mg potassium.
NUTRITION BONUS: Vitamin A (281% daily value), Vitamin C (23% dv).

How To: Improvise a Pastry Bag

Curried Sweet Potatoes

H✱W   H↑F   H♥H

MAKES: 10 servings
ACTIVE TIME: 35 minutes | TOTAL: 45 minutes
TO MAKE AHEAD: Cover and refrigerate for up to 2 days. Reheat on the stovetop or in the microwave.

Dried apricots, raisins and curry powder make unusual but delectable partners for sweet potatoes in this traditional Southern recipe. Try it with roasted pork tenderloin, turkey or chicken.

4½	pounds sweet potatoes (8 or 9 medium), peeled and cut into 1-inch pieces
1	teaspoon salt, plus more to taste
1	cup dried apricots (3 ounces), cut into ¼-inch slivers
½	cup raisins
1	cup boiling water
1	tablespoon canola oil
1	onion, finely chopped
2	teaspoons curry powder
	Freshly ground pepper to taste

1. Place sweet potatoes in a large pot and add enough cold water to cover by 1 inch. Add 1 teaspoon salt and bring to a boil over high heat. Reduce heat to medium and cook until tender but not mushy, 8 to 12 minutes. Drain well.

2. Combine apricots, raisins and boiling water in a small bowl; let sit until plumped, about 10 minutes.

3. Heat oil in a large wide pot over medium-high heat. Add onion; cook, stirring often, until softened, about 2 minutes. Add curry powder; cook, stirring, until fragrant, about 2 minutes. Add the cooked sweet potatoes, apricots, raisins and the fruit-soaking liquid. Season with salt and pepper. Stir gently over medium-low heat until warmed through.

PER SERVING: 183 calories; 2 g fat (0 g sat, 1 g mono); 0 mg cholesterol; 41 g carbohydrate; 0 g added sugars; 3 g protein; 6 g fiber; 280 mg sodium; 818 mg potassium.
NUTRITION BONUS: Vitamin A (487% daily value), Vitamin C (43% dv), Potassium (23% dv).

Tomatillos | PEAK SEASON: Summer | LOOK FOR: Tart, plum-size green fruit that look like small, husk-covered green tomatoes. Husks should be brightly colored, not brown. | STORE: Refrigerate in their husks in a plastic bag for up to 2 weeks. | PREP: Remove outer husks and rinse well before using.

Tomatillo Salsa

MAKES: about 1½ cups
ACTIVE TIME: 20 minutes | TOTAL: 20 minutes
TO MAKE AHEAD: Cover and refrigerate for up to 4 days.

Grilling the tomatillos in this salsa adds a lovely smoky flavor and aroma.

12	ounces fresh tomatillos (about 8), husked, rinsed and dried
2	small serrano chiles *or* jalapeño peppers, seeded and coarsely chopped
2	cloves garlic, peeled
3	tablespoons chopped fresh cilantro
1	tablespoon lime juice
	Pinch of sugar
¼	teaspoon salt

1. Preheat grill or broiler.

2. Grill or broil tomatillos, turning occasionally, until softened and blackened in spots, 6 to 8 minutes. Halve the tomatillos.

3. Combine the tomatillos, serranos (or jalapeños) and garlic in a food processor or blender; process until smooth. Transfer to a small bowl. Stir in cilantro and lime juice. Season with sugar and salt.

PER TABLESPOON: 5 calories; 0 g fat (0 g sat, 0 g mono); 0 mg cholesterol; 1 g carbohydrate; 0 g added sugars; 0 g protein; 0 g fiber; 25 mg sodium; 42 mg potassium.

Tomatoes | PEAK SEASON: Summer, Fall | LOOK FOR: Plump, shiny tomatoes that give slightly when pressed. Smell the stem end for that distinctive aroma. | STORE: Tomatoes continue to ripen after they are picked. Refrigeration destroys their flavor; store at room temperature, away from sunlight.

Green Tomato Chutney

H✖W   H♥H

MAKES: 3 cups
ACTIVE TIME: 10 minutes | TOTAL: 40 minutes

Here's a great way to use up green tomatoes from the garden. Serve this sweet-and-sour chutney as an accompaniment for grilled chicken or pork.

1¼	pounds green tomatoes, diced
1	cup diced onion
½	cup currants
⅓	cup sweet vermouth
2	tablespoons brown sugar
1	tablespoon cider vinegar
2	teaspoons mustard seeds
½	teaspoon salt

Combine tomatoes, onion, currants, vermouth, brown sugar, vinegar, mustard seeds and salt in a large saucepan. Bring to a boil. Cover, reduce heat and simmer until tender, 30 to 40 minutes.

PER 1/3-CUP SERVING: 68 calories; 0 g fat (0 g sat, 0 g mono); 0 mg cholesterol; 14 g carbohydrate; 4 g added sugars; 1 g protein; 2 g fiber; 140 mg sodium; 241 mg potassium.
NUTRITION BONUS: Vitamin C (27% daily value).

▶ Tomato & Fennel Salad

H✖W   H⬆F   H♥H

MAKES: 4 servings, about 1 cup each
ACTIVE TIME: 10 minutes | TOTAL: 10 minutes

We like to use heirloom tomatoes in this simple salad. They're at their peak during the summer months and worth seeking out at your local grocery store or farmers' market. Which varieties you choose is up to you—any will work well here.

1	tablespoon extra-virgin olive oil
1	tablespoon champagne vinegar *or* white-wine vinegar
½	teaspoon salt
	Freshly ground pepper to taste
1	pound tomatoes, cut into wedges
2	cups thinly sliced cored fennel bulb (*see Tip, page 484*)
¼	cup chopped fresh parsley
⅓	cup toasted pine nuts (*see Tip, page 486*)

Whisk oil, vinegar, salt and pepper in a large bowl until combined. Add tomatoes, fennel, parsley and pine nuts; toss to coat.

PER SERVING: 141 calories; 12 g fat (1 g sat, 5 g mono); 0 mg cholesterol; 9 g carbohydrate; 0 g added sugars; 3 g protein; 3 g fiber; 321 mg sodium; 513 mg potassium.
NUTRITION BONUS: Vitamin C (38% daily value), Vitamin A (25% dv), Potassium (15% dv).

◀ Skillet-Seared Tomatoes with Melted Gruyère

MAKES: 4 servings
ACTIVE TIME: 20 minutes | TOTAL: 30 minutes

Serve these as a savory side dish with chicken or steak, to complement a meatless meal or as a sandwich on toasted whole-grain bread. A pinch of sugar helps balance the tomatoes' acidity.

- 2   tablespoons extra-virgin olive oil
- 4   large ripe but firm plum tomatoes, halved lengthwise (about 1¼ pounds)
- 2   tablespoons finely chopped flat-leaf parsley
- 1   medium clove garlic, minced
- ½   teaspoon sugar (optional)
- ½   teaspoon kosher salt
      Freshly ground pepper to taste
- ¾   cup shredded Gruyère, Comte, fontina *or* mozzarella cheese

1. Heat a 12-inch heavy stainless-steel or cast-iron skillet over medium heat until hot enough to sizzle a drop of water. Add oil. Arrange tomatoes cut-side down in the pan and cook, uncovered, until just tender and the undersides are darkened, 10 to 15 minutes.

2. Meanwhile, mix parsley and garlic in a small bowl.

3. Using a wide spatula, carefully turn each tomato cut-side up. Reduce the heat to medium-low. Sprinkle each tomato with sugar (if using), salt and pepper, followed by equal portions of the parsley mixture and shredded cheese. Cover and cook until the cheese is melted, about 2 minutes. Serve warm.

PER SERVING: 178 calories; 14 g fat (5 g sat, 8 g mono); 22 mg cholesterol; 7 g carbohydrate; 0 g added sugars; 7 g protein; 2 g fiber; 222 mg sodium; 345 mg potassium.
NUTRITION BONUS: Vitamin C (67% daily value), Vitamin A (25% dv), Calcium (22% dv).

Tomato Gratin

H✖W   H♥H

MAKES: 6 servings
ACTIVE TIME: 20 minutes | TOTAL: 30 minutes

A gratin is any dish topped with cheese or bread-crumbs mixed with butter, then heated until browned—but it needn't be heavy. This one has plenty of garden-fresh tomatoes and herbs, a touch of full-flavored cheese and a crispy crumb topping.

- 4   slices whole-grain bread, torn into quarters
- 1   tablespoon minced garlic
- 1   tablespoon extra-virgin olive oil
- ⅓   cup finely shredded Pecorino Romano *or* Parmesan cheese
- 4   medium tomatoes, sliced
- ¼   cup chopped fresh basil
- ½   teaspoon freshly ground pepper
- ¼   teaspoon salt

1. Preheat oven to 450°F. Coat a shallow 2-quart baking dish with nonstick spray.

2. Place bread in a food processor and pulse until coarse crumbs form. Add garlic, oil and cheese; pulse to combine. Spread the seasoned breadcrumbs on a baking sheet and bake until beginning to brown, about 5 minutes.

3. Meanwhile, layer tomato slices in the prepared baking dish, sprinkling each layer with basil, pepper and salt. Bake the tomatoes for 10 minutes; sprinkle with the toasted breadcrumbs, and bake for 10 minutes more. Serve immediately.

PER SERVING: 104 calories; 4 g fat (1 g sat, 3 g mono); 4 mg cholesterol; 12 g carbohydrate; 1 g added sugars; 5 g protein; 2 g fiber; 257 mg sodium; 259 mg potassium.
NUTRITION BONUS: Vitamin C (18% daily value), Vitamin A (16% dv).

Turnips | PEAK SEASON: Fall, Winter | LOOK FOR: Smaller turnips with firm skins that are not bruised, soft or shriveled. Usually just the turnip bulb is available without the greens attached. If you find turnips with greens, make sure they're not wilted. STORE: If greens are attached, trim the greens and refrigerate the turnips for up to 1 week. | PREP: Cut off greens and trim the ends. To peel a turnip, use a vegetable peeler and peel around the root, making sure the fibrous layer below the skin has been removed.

Mashed Potatoes & Turnips with Greens

H✖W   H⬆F   H♥H

MAKES: 10 servings, 1 cup each
ACTIVE TIME: 30 minutes | TOTAL: 55 minutes
TO MAKE AHEAD: Prepare through Step 1; keep warm for up to 1 hour.

In summer, if you can find small sweet turnips with their greens, then by all means use those greens. Otherwise, large turnips and broccoli rabe—both widely available in super-markets—are excellent in this recipe.

3	**medium russet potatoes, peeled and cut into 1-inch pieces**
3-4	**medium turnips, peeled and cut into 1-inch pieces**
1	**sprig fresh thyme *or* ¼ teaspoon dried**
4	**teaspoons extra-virgin olive oil, divided**
½	**cup freshly grated Parmesan cheese *or* aged goat cheese, optional**
½	**teaspoon salt, or to taste** **Freshly ground pepper to taste**
2	**large onions, cut in half and sliced about ¼ inch thick**
1	**bunch broccoli rabe, stems trimmed, cut into 1-inch pieces**

1. Place potatoes, turnips and thyme in a large pot. Cover with lightly salted water and bring to a boil. Cook, uncovered, over medium-high heat, until the vegetables are tender, 20 to 25 minutes. Drain, reserving the cooking liquid. Place the potatoes and turnips in a large bowl; discard thyme sprig, if using. Mash with a potato masher, adding a little cooking water, if needed, to achieve the desired consistency. Stir in 2 teaspoons oil and cheese, if using. Season with salt and pepper. To keep warm, set the bowl over simmering water and cover with parchment paper or foil.

2. Meanwhile, heat the remaining 2 teaspoons oil in a large cast-iron or nonstick skillet over medium-high heat. Add onions and cook, stirring often, until golden and very tender, 10 to 15 minutes. Remove from heat.

3. Bring a large pot of lightly salted water to a boil. Add broccoli rabe and cook until tender, 5 to 8 minutes. Drain and add to the onions; toss to mix.

4. To serve, mound the mashed vegetables in a bowl or onto individual plates and top with the onions and broccoli rabe.

PER SERVING: 144 calories; 3 g fat (1 g sat, 2 g mono); 4 mg cholesterol; 24 g carbohydrate; 0 g added sugars; 6 g protein; 3 g fiber; 227 mg sodium; 514 mg potassium.
NUTRITION BONUS: Vitamin C (98% daily value), Vitamin A (59% dv), Potassium (15% dv).

EatingWell Tip

Eat your potatoes with a side of greens...dark leafy greens, to be specific. Many of them, such as turnip greens and broccoli rabe, are an excellent source of vitamin K, which may help **build and maintain strong bones**.

Winter Squash | PEAK SEASON: Fall, Winter | LOOK FOR: Hard squash that does not look shiny and has a remnant of the dried-out stem still attached. Look for vivid colors during harvest season. Later in the year, after the squash has been stored, the skin color may fade as the flesh becomes sweeter. STORE: Store in a cool spot with good air circulation for up to 1 month. | PREP: No need to remove the skin if you're planning to cook it with the skin on. Remove the skin with a vegetable peeler or paring knife, if desired, or according to recipe. Once opened, clean out the seeds and stringy fibers with a spoon.

Roasted Squash & Root Vegetables with Chermoula

H✕W   H⬆F   H♥H

MAKES: 6 servings, about 1¼ cups each
ACTIVE TIME: 30 minutes | TOTAL: 1¼ hours

Here, a medley of vegetables are roasted with chermoula (also spelled charmoula), a quintessential Moroccan spice blend. (Any combination of vegetables will work in this dish; start with about 12 cups of peeled pieces.) **Shopping Tip:** *Look for already peeled, seeded and quartered butternut squash in the produce department.*

- ¼ cup extra-virgin olive oil
- 3 cloves garlic, minced
- 2 teaspoons paprika, preferably sweet Hungarian
- 2 teaspoons ground cumin
- 1 teaspoon salt
- 8 ounces peeled and seeded butternut squash, cut into 1-inch chunks (*see Shopping Tip*)
- 1 medium rutabaga, peeled and cut into 1-inch chunks
- 1 medium sweet potato, peeled and cut into 1-inch chunks
- 1 medium baking potato, peeled and cut into 1-inch chunks
- 1 medium turnip, peeled and cut into 1-inch chunks
- 2 medium carrots, cut into ½-inch slices

1. Preheat oven to 425°F.

2. Place oil, garlic, paprika, cumin and salt in a food processor or blender and pulse or blend until smooth. Place squash, rutabaga, sweet potato, potato, turnip and carrots in a roasting pan large enough to accommodate the pieces in a single layer. Toss with the spiced oil mixture until well combined.

3. Roast the vegetables, stirring once or twice, until tender, 45 to 50 minutes.

PER SERVING: 235 calories; 10 g fat (1 g sat, 7 g mono); 0 mg cholesterol; 35 g carbohydrate; 0 g added sugars; 4 g protein; 7 g fiber; 461 mg sodium; 844 mg potassium.
NUTRITION BONUS: Vitamin A (296% daily value), Vitamin C (78% dv), Potassium (24% dv).

◀ Roasted Acorn Squash with Cider Drizzle

H✕W   H⬆F   H❤H

MAKES: 4 servings
ACTIVE TIME: 15 minutes | TOTAL: 45 minutes

Roasting squash in the oven caramelizes its natural sugars. Here we serve acorn squash with a cider reduction that's spiced with cinnamon and cloves.

1	medium acorn squash (about 1¾ pounds)
1	teaspoon extra-virgin olive oil
¼	teaspoon salt
¼	teaspoon freshly ground pepper
2	cups apple cider
1	tablespoon packed brown sugar
1	3-inch cinnamon stick
3-5	whole cloves
2	teaspoons butter

1. Preheat oven to 400°F. Coat a baking sheet with cooking spray.

2. Cut squash in half lengthwise and scoop out seeds. Cut each half in half again lengthwise. Brush the cut sides of the squash with oil and season with salt and pepper. Place the squash, cut-side down, on the prepared baking sheet. Roast for 20 minutes, turn the squash over so the opposite cut side is down, and continue roasting until tender, 15 to 20 minutes more.

3. Meanwhile, combine cider, brown sugar, cinnamon stick and cloves to taste in a small saucepan; bring to a boil over medium-high heat. Cook, stirring occasionally, until reduced to a thin, syrupy glaze, 20 to 25 minutes. (Watch carefully toward the end to prevent burning.) Remove from the heat; discard the cinnamon stick and cloves. Stir in butter until melted. Serve the roasted squash with the cider drizzle.

PER SERVING: 195 calories; 3 g fat (2 g sat, 1 g mono); 5 mg cholesterol; 43 g carbohydrate; 3 g added sugars; 2 g protein; 7 g fiber; 153 mg sodium; 743 mg potassium.
NUTRITION BONUS: Vitamin C (30% daily value), Potassium (21% dv), Magnesium (18% dv), Vitamin A (16% dv).

Delicata Squash with Orange & Pistachios

H✕W   H❤H

MAKES: 4 servings
ACTIVE TIME: 35 minutes | TOTAL: 35 minutes

If you haven't tried delicata squash, it's worth seeking out. The skin is tender enough to eat when cooked, so there's no peeling involved. All you have to do is slice it and then cook it. Here we sauté it with olive oil and a little orange juice and zest, then add a sprinkling of pistachios to make it special.

1	tablespoon extra-virgin olive oil
2	shallots, halved and sliced
1	large delicata squash, halved lengthwise, seeded and thinly sliced (about 4 cups)
1	teaspoon freshly grated orange zest
¾	cup orange juice
½	teaspoon salt
¼	teaspoon freshly ground pepper
2	tablespoons chopped salted pistachios

Heat oil in a large nonstick skillet over medium heat. Add shallots and cook, stirring, until softened and beginning to brown, about 2 minutes. Add squash, orange zest and juice, salt and pepper. Reduce heat to medium-low, cover and cook, stirring once, until the squash is almost tender, 6 to 8 minutes. Uncover and cook, stirring occasionally, until the liquid is absorbed and the squash is tender and beginning to brown, 12 to 15 minutes more. Garnish with pistachios.

PER SERVING: 122 calories; 5 g fat (1 g sat, 4 g mono); 0 mg cholesterol; 17 g carbohydrate; 0 g added sugars; 3 g protein; 2 g fiber; 308 mg sodium; 169 mg potassium.
NUTRITION BONUS: Vitamin A (98% daily value), Vitamin C (62% dv).

Zucchini & Summer Squash | PEAK SEASON: Summer

LOOK FOR: No breaks, gashes or soft spots; smaller squash (under 8 inches) are sweeter and have fewer seeds; do not peel, but scrub gently under running water. | STORE: Refrigerate in a plastic bag for 4 to 5 days. | PREP: Cut off both ends.

Pesto-Topped Grilled Zucchini

H✂W   H♥H

MAKES: 4 servings
ACTIVE TIME: 30 minutes | TOTAL: 30 minutes

Rustic pesto takes simple grilled squash from ordinary to exceptional with tangy lemon and fresh garlic. Serve as a side dish or chop the grilled squash, combine with the pesto and toss with pasta for a light entree.

- ½   cup chopped fresh basil
- ¼   cup toasted pine nuts (*see Tip, page 486*)
- 1   tablespoon extra-virgin olive oil
- 1   tablespoon grated Parmesan cheese
- 1   clove garlic, minced
- 2   teaspoons lemon juice
- ¼   teaspoon salt
- 2   medium zucchini *or* summer squash (about 1 pound), sliced diagonally ¼ inch thick
     Canola *or* olive oil cooking spray

1. Preheat grill to medium-high.

2. Combine basil, pine nuts, oil, Parmesan, garlic, lemon juice and salt in a small bowl.

3. Coat both sides of squash slices with cooking spray. Grill the squash until browned and tender, 2 to 3 minutes per side. Serve topped with the pesto.

PER SERVING: 115 calories; 10 g fat (1 g sat, 4 g mono); 1 mg cholesterol; 6 g carbohydrate; 0 g added sugars; 3 g protein; 2 g fiber; 167 mg sodium; 371 mg potassium. NUTRITION BONUS: Vitamin C (35% daily value).

Parmesan-Squash Cakes

H✂W

MAKES: 4 servings
ACTIVE TIME: 25 minutes | TOTAL: 35 minutes

In this recipe we shred summer squash and use it like shredded potatoes to make tasty little pancakes flavored with Parmesan cheese and shallots.

- 1   large egg
- ⅔   cup finely chopped shallots
- 1   tablespoon chopped flat-leaf parsley
- ¼   teaspoon salt
- ¼   teaspoon freshly ground pepper
- 2   cups shredded seeded summer squash (2-3 medium, about 1 pound; *see How To*)
- ½   cup freshly grated Parmesan cheese
- 1   tablespoon extra-virgin olive oil

1. Preheat oven to 400°F.

2. Beat egg in a large bowl. Stir in shallots, parsley, salt and pepper. Wrap shredded squash in a clean kitchen towel and twist to squeeze out any liquid. Add the squash and cheese to the bowl; stir to combine.

3. Heat oil in a large ovenproof nonstick skillet over medium heat. Pack a ⅓-cup measuring cup with the squash mixture and unmold it into the pan; gently pat it down to form a 3-inch cake. Repeat, making 4 squash cakes. Cook until browned and crispy on the bottom, 3 to 4 minutes. Gently turn the cakes over and transfer the pan to the oven. Bake for 10 minutes. Serve immediately.

PER SERVING: 130 calories; 8 g fat (3 g sat, 4 g mono); 62 mg cholesterol; 9 g carbohydrate; 0 g added sugars; 7 g protein; 1 g fiber; 322 mg sodium; 407 mg potassium. NUTRITION BONUS: Vitamin C (37% daily value), Calcium & Vitamin A (15% dv).

How To

Seed & Shred Summer Squash | Cut squash in half lengthwise and scrape out seeds with a spoon. To shred, use the large-holed side of a box grater.

Roasting Vegetables

Roasting vegetables is a quick way to give them tons of rich flavor with barely any work. TO ROAST VEGETABLES: Preheat oven to 450°F. Prepare the vegetable of your choice. Toss with 4 teaspoons **olive oil** or **canola oil**, ½ teaspoon **salt** and ¼ teaspoon **pepper**—or with any of the seasoning combinations on page 169. Spread on a baking sheet and roast. See the chart below for prep instructions and cooking times.

VEGETABLE	AMOUNT FOR 4 SERVINGS	ROASTING TIME	ANALYSIS PER SERVING
Beets & Turnips	1½ pounds without greens, ends trimmed, peeled, cut into 1-inch pieces or wedges	20-25 minutes	BEETS: 115 calories; 16 g carbohydrate; 5 g fiber I TURNIPS: 90 calories; 11 g carbohydrate; 3 g fiber
Broccoli & Cauliflower	1 pound, cut into 1-inch florets	15-20 minutes	BROCCOLI: 74 calories; 6 g carbohydrate; 3 g fiber I CAULIFLOWER: 71 calories; 6 g carbohydrate; 2 g fiber
Brussels Sprouts	1 pound, outer leaves removed, stems trimmed; larger ones quartered, smaller ones halved	15-20 minutes	91 calories; 10 g carbohydrate; 4 g fiber
Cabbage	1½ pounds (1 small head), cored, cut into 1-inch squares	15-20 minutes	75 calories; 7 g carbohydrate; 3 g fiber
Carrots & Parsnips	1½ pounds, peeled or scrubbed, woody core removed from parsnips; cut into ¼-inch slices	20-25 minutes	CARROTS: 104 calories; 15 g carbohydrate; 4 g fiber I PARSNIPS: 137 calories; 23 g carbohydrate; 5 g fiber
Fennel	2 large bulbs, stalks and fronds trimmed from the bulb, the bulb cored and cut into 1-inch wedges	25-30 minutes	79 calories; 9 g carbohydrate; 4 g fiber
Green Beans	1 pound, stem ends trimmed	15-20 minutes	77 calories; 8 g carbohydrate; 3 g fiber
Sweet Potatoes	1½ pounds, scrubbed (peeled if desired), cut into 1-inch pieces or wedges	20-25 minutes	195 calories; 35 g carbohydrate; 6 g fiber
Winter Squash, Butternut	2 pounds, peeled, seeded, cut into 1-inch pieces	25-35 minutes	119 calories; 20 g carbohydrate; 6 g fiber

Steaming Vegetables

Steamed vegetables can't be beat for simplicity or health. Serve them plain with a drizzle of olive oil and a little salt and pepper or season them with one of our flavor combinations (*see page 169*). TO STEAM VEGETABLES: Bring an inch of water to a steady boil in a large saucepan over high heat. Prepare the vegetable of your choice and place in a steamer basket in the saucepan. Cover and steam until just tender. See the chart below for prep instructions and timing.

VEGETABLE	AMOUNT FOR 4 SERVINGS	STEAMING TIME	ANALYSIS PER SERVING
Asparagus	1½ pounds (1-2 bunches), trimmed	4 minutes	37 calories; 7 g carbohydrate; 3 g fiber
Beets	1½ pounds without greens, ends trimmed, peeled, cut into 1-inch pieces or wedges	10-15 minutes	75 calories; 17 g carbohydrate; 3 g fiber
Broccoli & Cauliflower	1 pound broccoli, 1½-2 pounds cauliflower (about 1 head), cut into 1-inch florets	5-6 minutes	BROCCOLI: 32 calories; 6 g carbohydrate; 3 g fiber	CAULIFLOWER: 39 calories; 7 g carbohydrate; 4 g fiber
Brussels Sprouts	1 pound, stems trimmed	6-8 minutes	41 calories; 8 g carbohydrate; 3 g fiber
Carrots	1½ pounds, cut into ⅛-inch-thick rounds	4 minutes	60 calories; 14 g carbohydrate; 5 g fiber
Green Beans	1 pound, stem ends trimmed	5 minutes	40 calories; 9 g carbohydrate; 4 g fiber
Peas, Snap or Snow	1 pound, trimmed	3-5 minutes	53 calories; 9 g carbohydrate; 3 g fiber
Potatoes (baby), Red or Yukon Gold	1½ pounds, scrubbed	10-15 minutes	140 calories; 30 g carbohydrate; 2 g fiber

Grilling Vegetables

Grilling imparts a delicious smokiness to vegetables. And if the grill's already going, why not put some vegetables on too? TO GRILL VEGETABLES: Preheat grill to medium-high. Prepare the vegetables of your choice. Brush the vegetables with 1 tablespoon **olive oil** or **canola oil** and sprinkle with ¼ teaspoon each **salt** and **pepper**—or with one of the flavor combinations on page 169. Grill the vegetables, turning occasionally, until lightly charred and tender. See the chart below for prep instructions and timing.

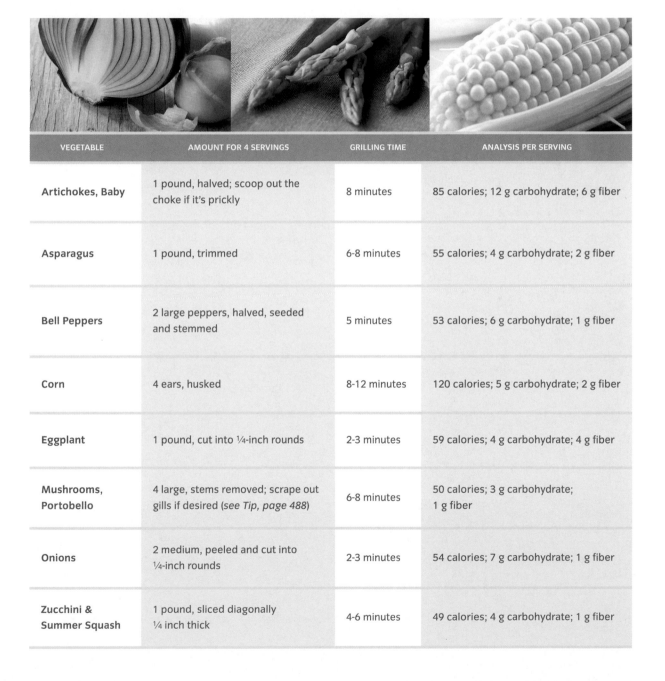

VEGETABLE	AMOUNT FOR 4 SERVINGS	GRILLING TIME	ANALYSIS PER SERVING
Artichokes, Baby	1 pound, halved; scoop out the choke if it's prickly	8 minutes	85 calories; 12 g carbohydrate; 6 g fiber
Asparagus	1 pound, trimmed	6-8 minutes	55 calories; 4 g carbohydrate; 2 g fiber
Bell Peppers	2 large peppers, halved, seeded and stemmed	5 minutes	53 calories; 6 g carbohydrate; 1 g fiber
Corn	4 ears, husked	8-12 minutes	120 calories; 5 g carbohydrate; 2 g fiber
Eggplant	1 pound, cut into ¼-inch rounds	2-3 minutes	59 calories; 4 g carbohydrate; 4 g fiber
Mushrooms, Portobello	4 large, stems removed; scrape out gills if desired (see Tip, page 488)	6-8 minutes	50 calories; 3 g carbohydrate; 1 g fiber
Onions	2 medium, peeled and cut into ¼-inch rounds	2-3 minutes	54 calories; 7 g carbohydrate; 1 g fiber
Zucchini & Summer Squash	1 pound, sliced diagonally ¼ inch thick	4-6 minutes	49 calories; 4 g carbohydrate; 1 g fiber

Sautéing Vegetables

Sautéing is an easy way to cook vegetables in a flash. TO SAUTÉ VEGETABLES: Prepare the vegetable of your choice. Heat 1 tablespoon **olive oil** or **canola oil** or **butter** in a large skillet over medium heat. Add the vegetables to the pan and cook, stirring frequently, until tender. See the chart below for prep instructions and timing. Season with one of our flavor combinations (*opposite*), if desired.

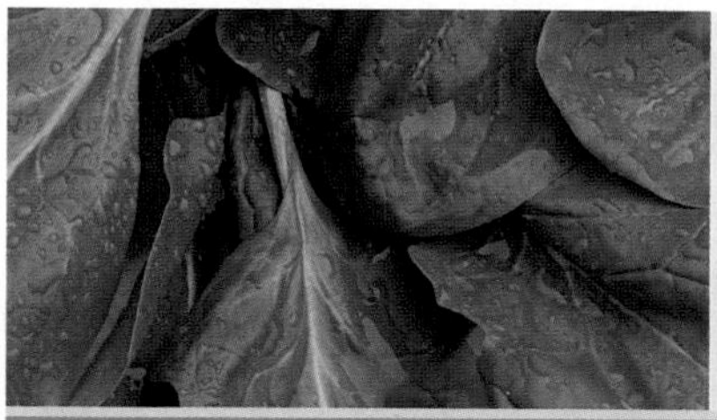

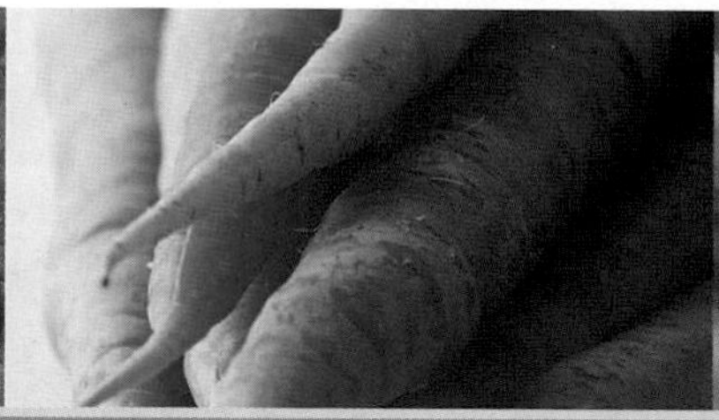

VEGETABLE	AMOUNT FOR 4 SERVINGS	SAUTÉING TIME	ANALYSIS PER SERVING
Asparagus	1 pound, trimmed and cut into 1-inch pieces	5-7 minutes	55 calories; 4 g carbohydrate; 2 g fiber
Carrots	1 pound, cut into ⅛-inch rounds	4-6 minutes	78 calories; 11 g carbohydrate; 3 g fiber
Chard & Collard Greens	1¼ pounds, trimmed and leaves chopped	4-6 minutes	CHARD: 57 calories; 5 g carbohydrate; 3 g fiber | COLLARD GREENS: 74 calories; 8 g carbohydrate; 5 g fiber
Corn	4 ears, remove kernels from cobs (*see How To, page 125*)	3-5 minutes	119 calories; 19 g carbohydrate; 2 g fiber
Green Beans	1 pound, stem ends trimmed	8-10 minutes	70 calories; 9 g carbohydrate; 4 g fiber
Peas, Snap or Snow	1 pound, trimmed	2-3 minutes	79 calories; 9 g carbohydrate; 3 g fiber
Spinach	1¼ pounds, trimmed, tough stems removed	2-4 minutes	57 calories; 4 g carbohydrate; 3 g fiber
Winter Squash, Delicata	1 large, halved lengthwise, seeded, thinly sliced	10 minutes	72 calories; 9 g carbohydrate; 1 g fiber
Zucchini & Summer Squash	1 pound, ¼-inch slices	6-8 minutes	51 calories; 4 g carbohydrate; 1 g fiber

Seasoning Vegetables

For grilled or roasted vegetables

Toss prepared vegetables (*see chart, page 167 or page 165*) with any of these easy flavor combinations.

CHILE-GARLIC & SOY: *Before grilling or roasting:* Toss the vegetables with 4 teaspoons extra-virgin **olive oil** (or canola oil), 1 tablespoon each **chile-garlic sauce** and reduced-sodium **soy sauce** and ⅛ teaspoon ground **white pepper**.

CHILI-LIME: *Before grilling or roasting:* Toss the vegetables with 4 teaspoons **canola oil**, ¾ teaspoon each **chili powder** and ground **cumin** and ½ teaspoon **salt**. *After grilling or roasting:* Toss with 2 tablespoons chopped fresh **cilantro** and **lime juice** to taste.

GARLIC-THYME: *Before grilling or roasting:* Toss the vegetables with 2 tablespoons extra-virgin **olive oil**, 1 tablespoon chopped fresh **thyme** (or 1 teaspoon dried), ½ teaspoon **garlic powder** and ¼ teaspoon each **salt** and freshly ground **pepper**. *After grilling or roasting:* Toss with 2 tablespoons chopped **fennel fronds**, if desired.

MAPLE BUTTER: *Before grilling or roasting:* Toss the vegetables with 2 tablespoons pure **maple syrup**, 1 tablespoon melted **butter**, 1½ teaspoons **lemon juice**, ½ teaspoon **salt** and freshly ground **pepper** to taste.

SPICY ORANGE: *Before grilling or roasting:* Toss the vegetables with 4 teaspoons extra-virgin **olive oil**, the zest of 1 **orange**, ½ teaspoon **salt** and ¼-½ teaspoon **crushed red pepper**.

For steamed vegetables

Toss or top steamed vegetables (*see chart, page 166*) with any of these easy flavor combinations.

BACON-HORSERADISH: Finely chop 4 strips crisp-cooked **bacon**; combine with ¼ cup reduced-fat **sour cream**, 2 teaspoons prepared **horseradish**, ¼ teaspoon **salt** and ⅛ teaspoon freshly ground **pepper**.

FRESH TOMATO & SHALLOT: Combine 2 chopped **tomatoes**, 1 minced **shallot**, 1 tablespoon each extra-virgin **olive oil** and **balsamic vinegar**, and ¼ teaspoon each **salt** and freshly ground **pepper**.

LEMON-DILL: Whisk 4 teaspoons chopped fresh **dill**, 1 tablespoon each minced **shallot**, extra-virgin **olive oil** and **lemon juice**, 1 teaspoon whole-grain **mustard**, and ¼ teaspoon each **salt** and freshly ground **pepper**.

For sautéed vegetables

Toss sautéed vegetables (*see chart, opposite*) with any of these easy flavor combinations.

CAPER & PARSLEY: Combine ⅓ cup chopped **shallot**, ¼ cup flat-leaf **parsley** leaves, 3 tablespoons rinsed **capers**, 2 tablespoons **white-wine vinegar**, and ¼ teaspoon each **salt** and freshly ground **pepper**.

MUSTARD-SCALLION: Combine ¼ cup sliced **scallions**, 2 tablespoons Dijon **mustard**, 1 tablespoon **lemon juice**, ¼ teaspoon each **salt** and freshly ground **pepper**.

SESAME-ORANGE: Combine 3 tablespoons **orange juice**, 1 teaspoon **sesame oil**, and ¼ teaspoon each **salt** and freshly ground **pepper**. Sprinkle with 2 teaspoons toasted **sesame seeds**.

Basque Vegetable Rice

Farro with Pistachios & Herbs

Crunchy-Munchy Corn & Millet Bread

Fresh Herb & Lemon Bulgur Pilaf

Grains & Breads

Fresh Herb & Lemon Bulgur Pilaf

H↑F H♥H

MAKES: 6 servings, about 1 cup each
ACTIVE TIME: 30 minutes | TOTAL: 50 minutes
TO MAKE AHEAD: Cover and refrigerate for up to 2 days.
Add more lemon juice and/or salt to taste before serving.

This pilaf, made with nutty bulgur, gets plenty of bright flavor from fresh dill, mint, parsley, ginger and lemon. (Photograph: page 170.) **Shopping Tip:** *Bulgur is made by parboiling, drying and coarsely grinding or cracking wheat berries. Don't confuse bulgur with cracked wheat, which is simply that—cracked wheat. Since the parboiling step is skipped, cracked wheat must be cooked for up to an hour whereas bulgur simply needs a quick soak in hot water for most uses. Look for it in the natural-foods section of large supermarkets, near other grains, or online at* kalustyans.com.

- 2 tablespoons extra-virgin olive oil
- 2 cups chopped onion
- 1 clove garlic, finely chopped
- 1½ cups bulgur, preferably medium *or* coarse
  (*see Shopping Tip*)
- ½ teaspoon ground turmeric
- ½ teaspoon ground cumin
- 2 cups vegetable broth *or* reduced-sodium
  chicken broth
- 1½ cups chopped carrot
- 2 teaspoons grated *or* finely chopped fresh ginger
- 1 teaspoon coarse salt
- ¼ cup lightly packed finely chopped fresh dill
- ¼ cup lightly packed finely chopped fresh mint
- ¼ cup lightly packed finely chopped flat-leaf parsley
- 3 tablespoons lemon juice, or more to taste
- ½ cup chopped walnuts, toasted (*see How To*)

1. Heat oil in a large high-sided skillet or broad shallow saucepan with a tight-fitting lid over medium heat until hot enough to sizzle a piece of onion. Add onion, reduce heat to medium-low and cook, stirring often, until golden brown, 12 to 18 minutes. Stir in garlic and cook, stirring, for 1 minute. Add bulgur, turmeric and cumin and cook, stirring, until the bulgur is coated with oil, about 1 minute.

2. Add broth, carrot, ginger and salt and bring to a boil, stirring. Cover and cook over medium-low heat until all the broth is absorbed and there are "eyes" or indentations in the surface of the bulgur, about 15 minutes. (Do not stir the pilaf.) Remove from the heat and let stand, covered, for 5 minutes.

3. Stir dill, mint, parsley and lemon juice into the pilaf. Serve topped with walnuts.

PER SERVING: 277 calories; 12 g fat (1 g sat, 5 g mono); 0 mg cholesterol; 39 g carbohydrate; 0 g added sugars; 7 g protein; 10 g fiber; 507 mg sodium; 420 mg potassium.
NUTRITION BONUS: Vitamin A (122% daily value), Vitamin C (23% dv), Magnesium (22% dv).

How To

Toast Small or Chopped Nuts | Cook in a small dry skillet over medium-low heat, stirring constantly, until fragrant and lightly browned, 2 to 6 minutes.

EatingWell Tip

Stock bulgur in your pantry. It's convenient because it's quick-cooking plus it's a whole grain. Studies have shown whole grains may **protect against cancer, diabetes, heart disease and obesity**.

Wild Rice Salad with Smoked Turkey

H✕W   H↑F   H♥H

MAKES: 8 servings, about 1 cup each
ACTIVE TIME: 30 minutes | TOTAL: 50 minutes

Wild and white rice, smoked turkey, apples and watercress combine for a colorful salad that's great for a potluck.

- 3 **cups water, divided**
- ¾ **cup wild rice, rinsed**
- ½ **teaspoon salt, divided**
- ½ **cup long-grain white rice**
- 8 **ounces smoked turkey breast, diced (2 cups)**
- 2 **red apples, such as McIntosh, diced**
- 5 **scallions, sliced**
- 1 **stalk celery, diced**
- ½ **cup apple juice concentrate, thawed**
- ¼ **cup cider vinegar**
- 1 **teaspoon dried tarragon *or* thyme**
  Freshly ground pepper to taste
- 1 **bunch watercress, trimmed**
- 2 **tablespoons chopped toasted pecans (*see How To, opposite*)**

1. Combine 2 cups water, wild rice and ¼ teaspoon salt in a saucepan; bring to a boil. Cover and simmer over low heat until the rice is tender, 40 to 50 minutes. Bring the remaining 1 cup water and ¼ teaspoon salt to a boil in another saucepan. Add white rice, cover and simmer over low heat until the rice is tender and most of the water has been absorbed, about 20 minutes. Transfer the wild and white rice to a sieve and refresh under cold water to cool.

2. Combine the wild and white rice, turkey, apples, scallions and celery in a large bowl. Whisk apple juice concentrate, vinegar and tarragon (or thyme), and pepper in a small bowl. Pour over the salad and toss well. Serve on watercress, sprinkled with pecans.

PER SERVING: 202 calories; 2 g fat (0 g sat, 1 g mono); 12 mg cholesterol; 37 g carbohydrate; 0 g added sugars; 9 g protein; 3 g fiber; 422 mg sodium; 348 mg potassium.
NUTRITION BONUS: Vitamin C (38% daily value), Folate (15% dv).

Farro with Pistachios & Herbs

H✕W   H↑F   H♥H

MAKES: 10 servings, about ⅔ cup each
ACTIVE TIME: 35 minutes | TOTAL: 35 minutes
TO MAKE AHEAD: Prepare up to 2 hours ahead. Hold at room temperature and reheat over low until warm.

Here we stir fresh parsley and crunchy pistachios into farro for an easy side dish. (Photograph: page 170.)
Shopping Tip: *Farro is a whole grain commonly used in Italian cooking. Find it at natural-foods stores and amazon.com. Five cups cooked barley (see guide, page 184) can substituted for the cooked farro.*

- 2 **cups farro (*see Shopping Tip*)**
- 4 **cups water**
- 1 **teaspoon kosher salt, divided**
- 2 **tablespoons plus ½ teaspoon extra-virgin olive oil, divided**
- 1 **large yellow onion, chopped**
- 2 **cloves garlic, minced**
- 4 **ounces salted shelled pistachios (about 1 cup), toasted (*see How To, opposite*) and chopped**
- ½ **teaspoon freshly ground pepper, divided**
- ½ **cup chopped fresh parsley**

1. Combine farro, water and ¾ teaspoon salt in a large heavy saucepan and bring to a boil. Stir and reduce the heat to a simmer; cook, uncovered, until the farro is tender, 15 to 20 minutes.

2. Meanwhile, heat 2 tablespoons oil in a medium skillet over medium heat. Add onion and garlic and cook, stirring, until translucent, 4 to 6 minutes. Remove from the heat.

3. Combine pistachios, the remaining ½ teaspoon oil and ¼ teaspoon pepper in a large bowl.

4. Drain the farro and add to the bowl along with the onion mixture and parsley. Season with the remaining ¼ teaspoon salt and pepper. Toss to combine.

PER SERVING: 220 calories; 9 g fat (1 g sat, 5 g mono); 0 mg cholesterol; 30 g carbohydrate; 0 g added sugars; 8 g protein; 5 g fiber; 163 mg sodium; 161 mg potassium.

Jeweled Golden Rice

H⬆F H❤H

MAKES: 8 servings, ¾ cup each
ACTIVE TIME: 30 minutes | TOTAL: 2 hours 10 minutes
(including 1 hour chilling time)
TO MAKE AHEAD: Cover and refrigerate for up to 2 days.

Inspired by a classic Persian recipe, this eye-catching fruit-and nut-studded rice dish goes well with roast poultry or pork. Here, the colorful "jewels" are fresh and dried cherries, chopped celery, green onion and mixed nuts. The dish is prepared ahead, making it convenient for entertaining. **Shopping Tip:** *Saffron adds flavor and golden color to a variety of Middle Eastern, African and European foods. Find it in the specialty-herb section of large supermarkets and gourmet-food shops or at* tienda.com. *It will keep in an airtight container for several years.*

1	**cup brown basmati rice**
1	**14-ounce can reduced-sodium chicken broth**
⅓	**cup water**
1	**tablespoon mild *or* hot curry powder**
½	**teaspoon ground turmeric**
1	**generous pinch finely crumbled saffron threads (see *Shopping Tip*)**
3	**tablespoons canola oil**
⅓	**cup lemon juice**
3	**tablespoons honey**
1	**tablespoon freshly grated orange zest**
1	**tablespoon minced fresh ginger**
¼	**teaspoon salt**
2	**cups chopped celery**

¾	**cup coarsely chopped dried cherries**
½	**cup chopped scallions *or* chives, divided**
1	**cup fresh dark sweet cherries, pitted and chopped**
¾	**cup unsalted mixed nuts, preferably pistachios, almonds and cashews, chopped, divided**

1. Combine rice, broth, water, curry powder, turmeric and saffron in a medium saucepan. Bring to a boil, stir once, cover with a tight-fitting lid, reduce heat to a simmer and cook until the liquid is absorbed, about 35 minutes. Remove from heat and let stand, covered, 5 minutes more. Fluff with a fork.

2. Combine oil, lemon juice, honey, orange zest, ginger and salt in a large, nonreactive bowl (*see Tip, page 486*). Stir in the cooked rice, celery, dried cherries and ¼ cup scallions (or chives). Cover and refrigerate for at least 1 hour and up to 2 days.

3. To serve, fold fresh cherries and ½ cup mixed nuts into the rice mixture. Serve at room temperature, garnished with the remaining ¼ cup scallions (or chives) and mixed nuts.

PER SERVING: 287 calories; 12 g fat (1 g sat, 7 g mono);
0 mg cholesterol; 41 g carbohydrate; 6 g added sugars;
6 g protein; 5 g fiber; 213 mg sodium; 269 mg potassium.
NUTRITION BONUS: Vitamin C (16% daily value).

EatingWell Tip

Opt for brown rice over white rice whenever possible to **add fiber to your diet**. One cup of brown rice has 3 more grams of fiber than white.

◄ Wild Rice with Dried Apricots & Pistachios

H✖W   H⬆F   H❤H

MAKES: 6 servings, ⅔ cup each
ACTIVE TIME: 35 minutes | TOTAL: 1 hour 10 minutes

Colorful apricots, scallions and pistachios make this vibrant dish worthy of any holiday table. It's also just as good served cold or room temperature at a potluck.

7	cups water
1	cup wild rice, rinsed
2	teaspoons extra-virgin olive oil
1	small red onion, chopped
1	medium red bell pepper, seeded and diced
2	cloves garlic, minced
1½	teaspoons ground cumin
½	cup dried apricots, diced
½	cup orange juice
¼	teaspoon salt, or to taste
	Freshly ground pepper to taste
⅔	cup thinly sliced scallion greens
⅓	cup shelled pistachios, coarsely chopped

1. Bring water to a boil in a large saucepan. Add wild rice, cover, reduce heat to medium-low and cook at a lively simmer until the grains are tender and starting to split, 45 to 55 minutes. Drain in a fine sieve.

2. Shortly before the wild rice is ready, heat oil in a large nonstick skillet over medium-high heat. Add onion and cook, stirring often, until softened, 2 to 3 minutes. Add bell pepper, garlic and cumin; cook, stirring, for 1 minute. Add apricots, orange juice, salt and pepper; simmer until the apricots have plumped and the liquid has reduced slightly, 1 to 2 minutes. Stir in the wild rice. Remove from the heat and stir in scallion greens. Serve topped with chopped pistachios.

PER SERVING: 218 calories; 5 g fat (1 g sat, 3 g mono);
0 mg cholesterol; 37 g carbohydrate; 0 g added sugars;
7 g protein; 5 g fiber; 112 mg sodium; 472 mg potassium.
NUTRITION BONUS: Vitamin C (65% daily value), Vitamin A (27% dv).

Whole-Wheat Couscous with Parmesan & Peas

H✖W   H⬆F   H❤H

MAKES: 6 servings, ⅔ cup each
ACTIVE TIME: 15 minutes | TOTAL: 20 minutes

Couscous, which is actually a type of tiny pasta, makes an almost-instant side dish. Happily, the whole-wheat variety is just as fast to prepare as regular couscous. Lemon zest is a delicious accent to nutty Parmesan in this Italian-inspired couscous.

1	14-ounce can reduced-sodium chicken broth *or* vegetable broth
¼	cup water
2	teaspoons extra-virgin olive oil
1	cup whole-wheat couscous
1½	cups frozen peas
2	tablespoons chopped fresh dill
1	teaspoon freshly grated lemon zest
¼	teaspoon salt
	Freshly ground pepper to taste
½	cup freshly grated Parmesan cheese

1. Combine broth, water and oil in a large saucepan; bring to a boil. Stir in couscous and remove from heat. Cover and let plump for 5 minutes.

2. Meanwhile, cook peas on the stovetop or in the microwave according to package directions.

3. Add the peas, dill, lemon zest, salt and pepper to the couscous; mix gently and fluff with a fork. Serve hot, sprinkled with cheese.

PER SERVING: 213 calories; 4 g fat (1 g sat, 2 g mono);
6 mg cholesterol; 35 g carbohydrate; 0 g added sugars;
11 g protein; 7 g fiber; 376 mg sodium; 104 mg potassium.
NUTRITION BONUS: Vitamin A (16% daily value).

EatingWell Tip

When it comes to **getting heart-healthy whole grains into your diet**, it doesn't get any easier than whole-wheat couscous. Boil water, add the couscous, cover for 5 minutes and it's done!

Sausage Stuffing

H✖W   H⬆F   H❤H

MAKES: 8 cups, enough to stuff one 12-pound turkey
or to serve 8 as a side dish
ACTIVE TIME: 40 minutes | TOTAL: 40 minutes (not including
baking the stuffing separately)

*This classic stuffing pairs turkey sausage with the tangy
sweetness of apples. Using turkey instead of pork
sausages halves the fat content in this recipe.*

8	cups cubed whole-wheat bread (12 slices)
8	ounces bulk turkey sausage
1½	teaspoons canola oil
3	stalks celery, chopped
2	onions, chopped
1	clove garlic, finely chopped
3	Golden Delicious *or* McIntosh apples, peeled, cored and chopped
2	tablespoons chopped fresh sage *or* 2 teaspoons rubbed dried sage
1	teaspoon chopped fresh thyme *or* ½ teaspoon dried
½	teaspoon dried basil
1½-2	cups reduced-sodium chicken broth
¼	teaspoon salt
	Freshly ground pepper to taste

1. Preheat oven to 350°F. Spread bread on a baking sheet and bake until lightly toasted, 15 to 20 minutes.

2. Cook sausage in a large nonstick skillet over medium heat, stirring with a wooden spoon to break it up, until no longer pink, 5 to 10 minutes. Drain in a colander to remove excess fat.

3. Add oil to the pan and heat over medium-low heat. Add celery, onions and garlic; cook, stirring, until softened, about 5 minutes. Add apples and cook, stirring, until tender, 8 to 10 minutes more. Transfer to a large bowl and add the sausage, toasted bread, sage, thyme and basil. Toss well.

4. Drizzle 1½ cups broth over the bread mixture and toss until evenly moistened. Season with salt and pepper. If baking separately (rather than stuffing a bird), add the remaining ½ cup broth. Cover and bake in a lightly oiled casserole dish at 325°F until heated through, 35 to 45 minutes. If you want a crisp top, uncover for the last 15 minutes.

PER SERVING: 202 calories; 5 g fat (1 g sat, 2 g mono);
21 mg cholesterol; 29 g carbohydrate; 2 g added sugars;
12 g protein; 4 g fiber; 556 mg sodium; 358 mg potassium.

Basque Vegetable Rice

H✖W   H⬆F   H♥H

MAKES: 8 servings, about 1 cup each
ACTIVE TIME: 40 minutes | TOTAL: 1½ hours

This dish can work with all sorts of combinations. Try adding other vegetables, such as mushrooms and peas, or if you like something heartier, some slightly spicy Italian sausage is a good choice. (Photograph: page 170.) **Shopping Tip:** *Valencia rice (sometimes called paella rice) is Spanish-grown, short-grain rice classically used when making paella. It differs from other short-grain rice because of its ability to absorb moisture without breaking down. When fully cooked, the individual grains of rice remain whole. 'Bomba' is the best variety. Find it at specialty markets or online at tienda.com. Arborio rice can be used as a substitute, but yields a creamier dish.*

- 2   tablespoons extra-virgin olive oil
- 1   small dried red chile pepper, such as chile de arbol, broken
- 1   medium onion, quartered and thinly sliced
- 2   cloves garlic, minced
- 2   large ripe tomatoes, seeded and diced
- 1   medium zucchini, diced
- 1   red bell pepper, diced
- 1   green bell pepper, thinly sliced
- 1   teaspoon paprika, preferably Spanish
- 1   teaspoon dried thyme
- ½   teaspoon salt
- ⅛   teaspoon freshly ground pepper
- 1¼   cups short-grain white rice, preferably Valencia (*see Shopping Tip*)
- 3   cups vegetable broth *or* reduced-sodium chicken broth
- 2   tablespoons finely minced fresh flat-leaf parsley for garnish
- 6   lemon wedges for garnish

1. Heat oil in a 12-inch cast-iron skillet over medium heat. Add chile pepper, onion and garlic and cook, stirring often, until the onion is soft but not browned, about 6 minutes.

2. Add tomatoes, zucchini, bell peppers, paprika, thyme, salt and pepper; cover and simmer, stirring occasionally, for 15 minutes.

3. Add rice; stir to coat well with the tomato mixture. Add broth; bring to a boil. Reduce heat to low, cover and simmer until the rice is tender, 25 to 30 minutes. Serve hot directly from the pan, garnished with parsley and lemon wedges, if desired.

PER SERVING: 158 calories; 4 g fat (1 g sat, 3 g mono); 0 mg cholesterol; 27 g carbohydrate; 0 g added sugars; 3 g protein; 3 g fiber; 325 mg sodium; 320 mg potassium.
NUTRITION BONUS: Vitamin C (70% daily value), Vitamin A (37% dv), Folate (22% dv).

Wild Mushroom & Barley Risotto

H✣W   H⬆F   H♥H

MAKES: 10 servings, ¾ cup each
ACTIVE TIME: 1 hour | TOTAL: 1 hour

In this pungent mushroom risotto, we substitute fiber-rich barley for the more traditional arborio rice. Any combination of mushrooms will work; if you use shiitakes, remove the stems from the caps before using.

6	cups vegetable, mushroom *or* reduced-sodium chicken broth
1½	cups water
2	tablespoons extra-virgin olive oil
1	small onion, minced
2	cloves garlic, minced
3	cups mixed wild mushrooms, coarsely chopped
1½	cups pearl barley, rinsed
½	cup red wine
6	cups baby arugula
⅓	cup freshly grated Parmesan cheese
1	tablespoon butter
2	teaspoons balsamic vinegar
	Freshly ground pepper to taste

1. Bring broth and water to a simmer in a large saucepan. Adjust heat to maintain a steady simmer.

2. Heat oil in a large Dutch oven over medium-high heat. Add onion and garlic and cook, stirring, until the onion is translucent, about 2 minutes. Add mushrooms and cook, stirring, until they begin to release their juices, 2 to 3 minutes. Add barley and cook, stirring, for 1 minute. Add wine and simmer, stirring, until most of the liquid has evaporated, about 1 minute more. Reduce heat to medium.

3. Add ½ cup hot broth to the barley and cook, stirring, until most of the liquid has been absorbed. Continue adding ½ cup hot broth at a time and stirring until the liquid has been absorbed after each addition, adjusting the heat to maintain a gentle simmer, until the barley is tender and creamy but still somewhat firm, 35 to 45 minutes. (You might not use all the broth.)

4. Stir in arugula and cook, stirring, until it is wilted, about 1 minute. Remove from the heat. Stir in cheese, butter and vinegar. Season with pepper.

PER SERVING: 200 calories; 5 g fat (2 g sat, 2 g mono); 5 mg cholesterol; 31 g carbohydrate; 0 g added sugars; 6 g protein; 6 g fiber; 326 mg sodium; 253 mg potassium.
NUTRITION BONUS: Vitamin A (19% daily value).

EatingWell Tip

Try making risotto with barley instead of the traditional arborio rice. The texture will be a bit less creamy, but it has a great nutty taste and you'll get **more dietary fiber, which can help you feel full longer**.

Red-Wine Risotto

H✂W   H♥H

MAKES: 8 servings, about ¾ cup each
ACTIVE TIME: 50 minutes | TOTAL: 50 minutes

Rich, red-wine-infused risotto is served as a first course or side dish all over Northern Italy. The type of wine used varies according to region. In Piedmont, a local Barbera or Barbaresco is the wine of choice. Any dry red wine that's good enough to drink can be used in its place.

4½	cups reduced-sodium beef broth
2	tablespoons extra-virgin olive oil
1	medium onion, finely chopped
2	cloves garlic, minced
1½	cups arborio, carnaroli *or* other Italian "risotto" rice
¼	teaspoon salt
1¾	cups dry red wine, such as Barbera, Barbaresco *or* Pinot Noir
2	teaspoons tomato paste
1	cup finely shredded Parmigiano-Reggiano cheese, divided
	Freshly ground pepper to taste

1. Place broth in a medium saucepan; bring to a simmer over medium-high heat. Reduce the heat so the broth remains steaming, but is not simmering.

2. Heat oil in a Dutch oven over medium-low heat. Add onion and cook, stirring occasionally, for 5 minutes. Add garlic and cook, stirring, until the onion is very soft and translucent, about 2 minutes. Add rice and salt and stir to coat.

3. Stir ½ cup of the hot broth and a generous splash of wine into the rice; reduce heat to a gentle simmer and cook, stirring constantly, until the liquid has been absorbed. Add more broth, ½ cup at a time along with some wine, stirring after each addition until most of the liquid has been absorbed. After about 10 minutes, stir in tomato paste. Continue to cook, adding broth and wine and stirring after each addition until most of the liquid is absorbed; the risotto is done when you've used all the broth and wine and the rice is creamy and just tender, 20 to 30 minutes more.

4. Remove the risotto from the heat; stir in ¾ cup cheese and pepper. Serve sprinkled with the remaining ¼ cup cheese.

PER SERVING: 193 calories; 6 g fat (2 g sat, 4 g mono); 10 mg cholesterol; 18 g carbohydrate; 0 g added sugars; 6 g protein; 1 g fiber; 493 mg sodium; 175 mg potassium.

Cooking Grains

Start with **1 cup uncooked grain**; serving size is ½ cup cooked. See the chart below for cooking instructions.

GRAIN (1 CUP)	LIQUID (WATER/BROTH)	DIRECTIONS	YIELD	ANALYSIS PER 1/2-CUP SERVING
Barley, Pearl*	2½ cups	Bring barley and liquid to a boil. Reduce heat to low and simmer, covered, 35-50 minutes.	3-3½ cups	97 calories; 22 g carbohydrate; 3 g fiber
Bulgur (*see Tip, page 482*)	1½ cups	Bring bulgur and liquid to a boil. Reduce heat to low; simmer, covered, until tender and most of the liquid has been absorbed, 10-15 minutes.	2½-3 cups	76 calories; 17 g carbohydrate; 4 g fiber
Couscous, Whole-Wheat	1¾ cups	Bring liquid to a boil; stir in couscous. Remove from heat and let stand, covered, for 5 minutes. Fluff with a fork.	3-3½ cups	70 calories; 15 g carbohydrate; 2 g fiber
Grits, Quick-Cooking	4 cups	Bring liquid and ½ teaspoon salt to a boil; slowly stir in grits. Reduce heat to medium-low; cook, stirring occasionally, until thickened, about 5 minutes.	3 cups	96 calories; 21 g carbohydrate; 1 g fiber
Polenta (Cornmeal)	4⅓ cups	Bring cold water and 1 teaspoon salt to a boil. Slowly whisk in cornmeal until smooth. Reduce heat to low, cover and cook, stirring occasionally, until very thick and creamy, 10 to 15 minutes.	4-4⅓ cups	55 calories; 12 g carbohydrate; 1 g fiber
Quinoa (*see Tip, page 488*)	2 cups	Rinse in several changes of cold water. Bring quinoa and liquid to a boil. Reduce heat to low and simmer, covered, until tender and most of the liquid has been absorbed, 15-20 minutes. Fluff with a fork.	3 cups	111 calories; 20 g carbohydrate; 3 g fiber
Rice, Brown*	2½ cups	Bring rice and liquid to a boil. Reduce heat to low and simmer, covered, until tender and most of the liquid has been absorbed, 40-50 minutes. Let stand for 5 minutes, then fluff with a fork.	3 cups	109 calories; 23 g carbohydrate; 2 g fiber
Rice, Wild*	At least 4 cups	Cook rice in a large saucepan of lightly salted boiling water until tender, 45-55 minutes. Drain.	2-2½ cups	83 calories; 18 g carbohydrate; 1 g fiber

*ONLY HAVE 10 MINUTES? Make quick-cooking barley, instant brown rice or quick-cooking wild rice (follow package directions).

Jazzing Up Whole Grains

Add any of these flavor combinations to 2 to 4 cups cooked grains (*see chart, opposite*).

APRICOT NUT: ⅓ cup chopped dried **apricots**, ¼ cup chopped toasted **nuts** (walnuts, pecans or pistachios), 3 tablespoons **orange juice**, 1 teaspoon extra-virgin **olive oil**, and **salt** & freshly ground **pepper** to taste.

LIME-CILANTRO: ⅔ cup coarsely chopped fresh **cilantro**, ⅓ cup chopped **scallions**, 2 tablespoons **lime juice**, and **salt** & freshly ground **pepper** to taste.

MEDITERRANEAN: 1 chopped medium **tomato**, ¼ cup chopped Kalamata **olives**, ½ teaspoon **herbes de Provence**, and **salt** & freshly ground **pepper** to taste.

MINT & FETA: ¾ cup sliced **scallions**, ¼ cup each finely crumbled **feta** cheese and sliced fresh **mint**, and **salt** & freshly ground **pepper** to taste.

PARMESAN & BALSAMIC: ¼ cup freshly grated **Parmesan** cheese, 1 teaspoon **butter**, 2 teaspoons balsamic **vinegar**, and **salt** & freshly ground **pepper** to taste.

PARMESAN-DILL: ⅓ cup freshly grated **Parmesan** cheese, 2 tablespoons chopped fresh **dill**, 1 teaspoon freshly grated **lemon zest**, and **salt** & freshly ground **pepper** to taste.

PEAS & LEMON: 1 cup frozen **peas**; cover and let stand for 5 minutes. Stir in 3 tablespoons chopped fresh **parsley**, 1½ teaspoons extra-virgin **olive oil**, 1 teaspoon freshly grated **lemon zest**, and **salt** & freshly ground **pepper** to taste.

SPICY & SWEET SESAME-SOY: 3 tablespoons **rice-wine vinegar**, 1 tablespoon reduced-sodium **soy sauce**, 2 teaspoons each **sesame oil** and finely chopped fresh **ginger**, 1 teaspoon each **chile-garlic sauce** and **honey**, and ¼ cup chopped toasted **cashews**.

SPINACH: 3 cups sliced baby **spinach** (or arugula); cover and let stand for 5 minutes. Season with **salt** & freshly ground **pepper** to taste.

TOMATO-TARRAGON: ¾ cup chopped **tomatoes**, 3 tablespoons minced fresh **tarragon** (or parsley or thyme), and **salt** & freshly ground **pepper** to taste.

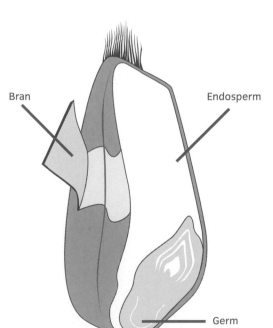

Bran

Endosperm

Germ

What exactly is a whole grain?

Grains are made up of three parts: the bran, germ and endosperm. The bran is the high-fiber outer coating. The germ is the protein- and nutrient-dense portion. The endosperm is a source of carbohydrate along with some protein. A grain is "whole" if these three parts have been left intact. If it's processed (e.g., cracked, rolled or cooked), it's still considered a whole grain if it retains its original balance of nutrients. When grains are refined the bran and germ are removed (taking many nutrients with them), leaving just the endosperm. Examples of a refined grain are white flour or white rice (though refined grains are often enriched to replace some of the nutrients stripped during processing).

Honey Oat Quick Bread

H✖W   H↑F   H♥H

MAKES: 12 slices

ACTIVE TIME: 15 minutes | TOTAL: 1¾ hours (including cooling time) | TO MAKE AHEAD: Wrap airtight and keep at room temperature for up to 1 day.

This bread has a moist, tender crumb. It calls for ingredients usually in the pantry, and is tasty yet healthful. Plus it only takes about 15 minutes to stir together the batter. Home-made bread doesn't get much easier than that.

2	tablespoons plus 1 cup old-fashioned rolled oats *or* quick-cooking (*not* instant) oats, divided
1⅓	cups whole-wheat flour *or* white whole-wheat flour (*see Tip, page 484*)
1	cup all-purpose flour
2¼	teaspoons baking powder
¼	teaspoon baking soda
1¼	teaspoons salt
8	ounces (scant 1 cup) nonfat *or* low-fat plain yogurt
1	large egg
¼	cup canola oil
¼	cup clover honey *or* other mild honey
¾	cup nonfat *or* low-fat milk

1. Position rack in middle of oven; preheat to 375°F. Coat a 9-by-5-inch (or similar size) loaf pan with cooking spray. Sprinkle 1 tablespoon oats in the pan and tip to coat the sides and bottom with oats.

2. Thoroughly stir together whole-wheat flour, all-purpose flour, baking powder, baking soda and salt in a large bowl. Using a fork, beat the remaining 1 cup oats, yogurt, egg, oil and honey in a medium bowl until well blended. Stir in milk. Gently stir the yogurt mixture into the flour mixture just until thoroughly incorporated but not overmixed (excess mixing can cause toughening). Immediately scrape the batter into the pan, spreading to the edges. Sprinkle the remaining 1 tablespoon oats on top.

3. Bake the loaf until well browned on top and a toothpick inserted in the center comes out clean, 40 to 50 minutes. (It's normal for the top to crack.) Let stand in the pan on a wire rack for 15 minutes. Run a table knife around and under the loaf to loosen it and turn it out onto the rack. Let cool until barely warm, about 45 minutes.

PER SLICE: 199 calories; 6 g fat (1 g sat, 3 g mono); 18 mg cholesterol; 31 g carbohydrate; 5 g added sugars; 6 g protein; 3 g fiber; 399 mg sodium; 146 mg potassium.

EatingWell Tip

To **get the added fiber and nutrients from whole grains**, try replacing about half of the all-purpose flour in baked goods with whole-wheat or white whole-wheat flour (as we did in this recipe).

Cheddar Cornmeal Biscuits with Chives

H✖W

MAKES: 12 biscuits

ACTIVE TIME: 20 minutes | TOTAL: 35 minutes

These chive-flecked cornmeal biscuits taste best made with extra-sharp Cheddar, but any Cheddar will work. **Shopping Tip:** *Find stone-ground cornmeal at the supermarket, natural-foods stores and at* kingarthurflour.com *or* bobsredmill.com.

1½	**cups all-purpose flour**
½	**cup cornmeal, preferably stone-ground (see Shopping Tip)**
1	**tablespoon baking powder**
½	**teaspoon baking soda**
½	**teaspoon salt**
¼	**teaspoon freshly ground pepper**
½	**cup shredded extra-sharp Cheddar cheese**
2	**tablespoons cold butter, cut into ½-inch cubes**
¾	**cup reduced-fat sour cream**
¼	**cup finely chopped fresh chives**
1	**tablespoon honey (optional)**
3 5	**tablespoons low-fat milk**

1. Preheat oven to 400°F.

2. Combine flour, cornmeal, baking powder, baking soda, salt and pepper in a food processor. Pulse a few times to mix. Add cheese and butter and pulse again until the mixture looks pebbly with small oat-size lumps. Transfer the mixture to a large bowl.

3. Add sour cream, chives and honey (if using) and stir with a rubber spatula until almost combined. Add 3 tablespoons milk, stirring, just until the dough comes together; add more milk as needed until the dough holds together in a shaggy mass. Don't overmix.

4. On a lightly floured surface, lightly pat the dough into a rectangle about 9 by 5 inches and just over ½ inch thick. Using a large chef's knife, divide the dough evenly into 12 biscuits. Place on an ungreased baking sheet.

5. Bake the biscuits until lightly browned on top, 14 to 16 minutes. Serve warm or at room temperature.

PER SERVING: 132 calories; 5 g fat (3 g sat, 1 g mono); 15 mg cholesterol; 17 g carbohydrate; 0 g added sugars; 3 g protein; 1 g fiber; 320 mg sodium; 60 mg potassium.

Real Cornbread

H✷W   H♥H

MAKES: 8 servings
ACTIVE TIME: 10 minutes | TOTAL: 30 minutes
TO MAKE AHEAD: The cornbread can be made up to
3 hours in advance. Reheat, wrapped in foil, in
a warm oven.

*This traditional cornbread is made without flour,
isn't sweet and has a crumbly texture. You can change
the adaptable recipe to suit your cornbread preference.
For a variation, substitute ½ teaspoon baking soda for
the baking powder and use buttermilk instead of milk. If
you're looking for a more muffinlike texture, substitute
flour for half the cornmeal. (Photograph: page 14.)*

3	tablespoons canola oil
2	cups yellow *or* white cornmeal
1	teaspoon baking powder
½	teaspoon salt
1	large egg, beaten
1½	cups nonfat milk *or* buttermilk (*see Tip, page 482*)

1. Preheat oven to 450°F. Place oil in a 9-inch cast-iron skillet or similar-size glass baking dish and transfer to the preheating oven.

2. Mix cornmeal, baking powder and salt in a medium bowl. Add egg and milk (or buttermilk); stir until just combined. Remove the pan from the oven and swirl the oil to coat the bottom and a little way up the sides. Very carefully pour the excess hot oil into the cornmeal mixture; stir until just combined. Pour the batter into the hot pan.

3. Bake until the bread is firm in the middle and lightly golden, about 20 minutes. Let cool for 5 minutes before slicing. Serve warm.

PER SERVING: 186 calories; 7 g fat (1 g sat, 4 g mono); 29 mg cholesterol; 26 g carbohydrate; 0 g added sugars; 5 g protein; 2 g fiber; 254 mg sodium; 165 mg potassium.

Parmesan Skillet Flatbreads

H⬆F   H♥H

MAKES: 6 flatbreads
ACTIVE TIME: 40 minutes | TOTAL: 1½-2 hours
TO MAKE AHEAD: Store in a plastic bag for up to 2 days.

*Cooking these rustic rounds on the stovetop is fun to do
and gives them a toasty exterior and moist center.*

1	cup lukewarm water
1	tablespoon extra-virgin olive oil
1	package active dry yeast (2¼ teaspoons)
1	teaspoon sugar
1½-2	cups all-purpose flour
1	cup whole-wheat flour
¾	cup finely shredded Parmigiano-Reggiano cheese
1¼	teaspoons salt

1. Whisk water, oil, yeast and sugar in a large bowl; let stand until foamy, about 5 minutes. Stir in 1½ cups all-purpose flour, whole-wheat flour, cheese and salt. Add just enough of the remaining ½ cup flour to make a smooth but slightly sticky dough. Turn out onto a lightly floured work surface and knead until smooth but still soft, about 5 minutes, adding more flour as needed.

2. Oil a clean bowl, add the dough and turn to coat with oil. Cover with plastic wrap and set in a warm place until doubled in size, 1 to 1½ hours.

3. Punch down the dough and divide into 6 equal balls. Dust with flour. Place a large skillet over medium-high heat until very hot. Roll or stretch each ball into a circle about 7 inches in diameter. Cook one at a time, turning once, until browned on both sides and cooked through, 30 seconds to 1 minute per side. Adjust the heat as necessary to prevent burning. Stack the cooked flatbreads on top of each other on a plate and cover with a clean towel. Let cool completely before storing.

PER FLATBREAD: 258 calories; 7 g fat (2 g sat, 3 g mono); 7 mg cholesterol; 40 g carbohydrate; 0 g added sugars; 10 g protein; 4 g fiber; 658 mg sodium; 136 mg potassium.
NUTRITION BONUS: Folate (32% daily value).

Crunchy-Munchy Corn & Millet Bread

H✣W H♥H

MAKES: 1 large loaf, 14 slices
ACTIVE TIME: 30 minutes | TOTAL: 24 hours
TO MAKE AHEAD: Wrap airtight and keep at room temperature for up to 3 days or freeze for up to 2 months.

This no-knead bread is crunchy on the outside and moist and soft on the inside; if you can't find millet (look for it near other grains), substitute sesame seeds. A 9- to 10-inch-diameter pot produces a nicely domed loaf, while a wider pot allows the dough to spread out and form a flatter loaf. (Photograph: page 170.)

⅔ cup plus 2 tablespoons whole-grain *or* stone-ground yellow cornmeal, divided
⅓ cup yellow corn grits *or* very coarse-grained uncooked polenta
1 cup boiling water
2 cups unbleached bread flour (*see Tip, page 484*), plus more as needed
⅔ cup whole-wheat flour, preferably white whole-wheat (*see Tip, page 484*)
5 tablespoons millet *or* sesame seeds, divided
2 tablespoons sugar
1½ teaspoons table salt
¾ teaspoon instant, quick-rising *or* bread-machine yeast (*not* active dry yeast)
⅓ cup nonfat *or* low-fat plain yogurt
2 tablespoons corn oil, canola oil *or* other flavorless vegetable oil
¾ cup ice water, plus more as needed

1. **Mix dough:** Place ⅔ cup cornmeal and corn grits (or polenta) in a medium bowl. Gradually stir in boiling water until well blended and lump-free. Let stand until barely warm. Thoroughly stir 2 cups bread flour, whole-wheat flour, 3 tablespoons millet (or sesame seeds), sugar, salt and yeast in a 4-quart (or larger) bowl. Thoroughly stir yogurt and oil into the cornmeal mixture. Stir ¾ cup ice water into the cornmeal mixture until smoothly incorporated. Stir the cornmeal mixture into the flour mixture, scraping down the sides and mixing just until the ingredients are thoroughly blended; it may seem too dry initially, but it usually comes together with sufficient stirring. The dough should be moist and somewhat sticky, but fairly stiff. If the mixture is still too dry, stir in just enough additional ice water to facilitate mixing, but don't overmoisten. If the dough is too wet, stir in just enough flour to stiffen slightly. Lightly coat the top with oil. Cover the bowl with plastic wrap.

2. **First rise:** Let the dough rise at room temperature (about 70°F) for 12 to 18 hours; if convenient, stir once partway through the rise. For convenience (and improved flavor), you may refrigerate the dough for 3 to 12 hours before starting the first rise.

3. **Second rise:** Generously coat a 3½- to 5-quart Dutch oven (or similar ovenproof pot) with oil. Coat the bottom and sides with 1 tablespoon each cornmeal and millet (or sesame seeds). Vigorously stir the dough to deflate it. If it's soft and very sticky, stir in just enough bread flour to yield a firm but moist dough (it should be fairly hard to stir). Transfer the dough to the pot. Lightly coat the dough with oil, then smooth the top. Sprinkle with the remaining 1 tablespoon each cornmeal and millet (or sesame seeds) and pat down. Put the lid on the pot or tightly cover with foil.

4. Let rise at warm room temperature until the dough is double the deflated size, 1½ to 2½ hours. (For an accelerated rise, *see How To, page 192.*)

5. **15 minutes before baking:** Position a rack in lower third of oven; preheat to 450°F. Generously sprinkle or spritz the loaf with water.

6. **Bake, cool, slice:** Bake the loaf on the lower rack, covered, until lightly browned and crusty, 60 to 70 minutes. Uncover and continue baking until nicely browned and a skewer inserted in the center comes out with just a few crumbs on the tip (or until an instant-read thermometer registers 204-206°), 10 to 15 minutes longer. Cool in the pot on a wire rack for 10 to 15 minutes. Turn the loaf out on the rack and let cool to at least warm before serving. The loaf is good warm but slices best when cool.

PER SLICE: 175 calories; 3 g fat (0 g sat, 1 g mono);
0 mg cholesterol; 33 g carbohydrate; 2 g added sugars;
5 g protein; 2 g fiber; 258 mg sodium; 79 mg potassium.
NUTRITION BONUS: Folate (18% daily value).

Parmesan-Herb Focaccia

H✂W H♥H

MAKES: 12 servings
ACTIVE TIME: 25 minutes | **TOTAL:** 24 hours
TO MAKE AHEAD: Wrap airtight and keep at room temperature for up to 3 days or freeze for up to 2 months.

Puffy, chewy and fragrant, this easy, no-knead focaccia goes well with soups and stews. Use only fresh herbs and avoid the temptation to stir them into the dough (sprinkle them over it); many herbs, including the ones called for here, inhibit yeast growth when combined in dough.

- 2 **cups unbleached all-purpose flour** *or* **unbleached bread flour (*see Tip, page 484*), plus more as needed**
- 1 **cup whole-wheat flour** *or* **white whole-wheat flour**
- 4 **tablespoons good-quality grated Parmesan cheese, divided**
- 1 **teaspoon table salt**
- 1½ **teaspoons instant, quick-rising** *or* **bread-machine yeast (*not* active dry yeast)**
- 1½ **cups ice water, plus more as needed**
- 2 **tablespoons chopped fresh oregano, chives** *or* **rosemary, divided**
- 2 **teaspoons extra-virgin olive oil**
- 2 **teaspoons fennel seeds (optional)**
- ½ **teaspoon sea salt** *or* **other coarse salt**

1. **Mix dough:** Thoroughly stir 2 cups all-purpose (or bread) flour, whole-wheat flour, 3 tablespoons Parmesan, the table salt and yeast in a 4-quart (or larger) bowl. Vigorously stir in 1½ cups ice water, scraping down the sides and mixing just until the dough is thoroughly blended. The dough should be barely moist and fairly stiff. If the mixture is too dry, stir in just enough additional ice water to facilitate mixing, but don't overmoisten. If the dough is too wet, stir in just enough flour to stiffen slightly. Lightly coat the top with oil. Cover the bowl with plastic wrap.

2. **First rise:** Let the dough rise at room temperature (about 70°F) for 12 to 18 hours; if convenient, stir once partway through the rise. For convenience (and improved flavor), you may refrigerate the dough for 3 to 12 hours before starting the first rise.

3. **Second rise:** Coat a 9-by-13-inch (or similar) baking pan with oil, then line it with a sheet of parchment paper. Lightly coat the paper with oil. Stir the dough just until deflated. If it is soft, stir in just enough all-purpose (or bread) flour to yield a firm but moist dough (it should be fairly hard to stir). Sprinkle 1 tablespoon chopped herbs over the dough (don't stir them in), then invert the dough into the pan so the herbs are underneath. Drizzle the dough with 2 teaspoons olive oil. With well-oiled hands, lightly pat and press the dough out until it fills the pan and is evenly thick; if it springs back and is resistant, let it rest for 10 minutes, then proceed. Sprinkle with the remaining 1 tablespoon Parmesan and herbs, and fennel seeds (if using), and pat down. Tent the pan with foil.

4. Let rise in a warm spot (*see How To*) until the dough is double the deflated size, 45 minutes to 2½ hours (depending on the temperature of where it's rising).

5. **20 minutes before baking:** Position a rack in lowest part of oven; preheat to 500°F. Lightly spritz or sprinkle the dough with water. With oiled fingertips, make deep indentations, or dimples, all over the top. Sprinkle evenly with sea salt (or other coarse salt).

6. **Bake, cool, slice:** Reduce oven temperature to 475°. Bake on the lowest rack, turning the pan from front to back halfway through for even browning, until golden brown and an instant-read thermometer inserted into the center registers 204-206°, 25 to 30 minutes. Cool in the pan on a wire rack for 10 to 15 minutes before slicing. Best served warm.

PER SERVING: 124 calories; 2 g fat (0 g sat, 1 g mono); 1 mg cholesterol; 23 g carbohydrate; 0 g added sugars; 4 g protein; 2 g fiber; 295 mg sodium; 74 mg potassium.
NUTRITION BONUS: Folate (16% daily value).

How To

Create a Warm Environment for Rising Bread | Cooler temperatures will slow the rising time. If your room is cool or you want to try to speed up the rising process, create a warm environment by microwaving ½ cup water in a 1-cup glass measure just to boiling. Set the water in one corner of the microwave, place the covered dough on the other side of the turned-off microwave and close the door.

Black Olive & Herb Yeast Loaves

H✖W   H↑F   H♥H

MAKES: 2 large loaves, about 12 slices each
ACTIVE TIME: 30 minutes | TOTAL: 3¼-4½ hours (depending on rising times) | TO MAKE AHEAD: Store cooled loaves, tightly wrapped, for 3 days at room temperature or freeze for up to 2 weeks. If frozen, thaw completely and, if desired, warm (wrapped in foil) at 350°F before serving.

These rustic olive- and herb-flecked loaves are light-textured, flavorful, aromatic and crisp on top. To simplify preparations, kneading is skipped and the gluten is developed by beating the dough with an electric mixer.

1½	tablespoons (about 2 packets) active dry yeast *or* 1 tablespoon quick-rising yeast
⅔	cup lukewarm (100-105°F) water, plus 2½ cups hot (110-115°F) water
3½	cups all-purpose flour
2½	tablespoons flavorful olive oil, plus more for brushing
3	tablespoons sugar
3	tablespoons finely chopped fresh chives *or* 2 teaspoons dried
1¼	teaspoons (generous) each dried oregano and dried thyme leaves *or* 3½ tablespoons finely minced fresh rosemary leaves
2¼	teaspoons salt
3¼	cups whole-wheat flour *or* white whole-wheat flour (*see Tip, page 484*), plus a little more for dusting
⅔	cup well-drained, pitted and finely chopped Niçoise, Kalamata *or* other very flavorful brined black olives

1. In a 1-cup measure, sprinkle yeast over ⅔ cup lukewarm water. Let stand, stirring occasionally, until the yeast dissolves.

2. Place all-purpose flour, oil, sugar, chives, oregano and thyme (or rosemary) and salt in a large mixing bowl. Beat in the 2½ cups hot water with an electric mixer on low speed (using a paddle attachment if possible) until well blended and smooth. Slowly beat in the yeast mixture until evenly incorporated. Gradually raise the speed to medium (or almost to the point the mixture begins to splatter), and beat for 4 minutes if using a heavy-duty stand mixer or 5 minutes if using a hand mixer.

3. Using a large wooden spoon, vigorously stir whole-wheat flour and olives into the dough until evenly incorporated; it's all right if the dough is slightly sticky and wet. Turn out the dough into a very large lightly oiled bowl. Lightly brush the top of the dough with olive oil until evenly covered. Tightly cover the bowl with plastic wrap and set in a warm spot (*see How To, page 192*) until the dough doubles in bulk, 45 minutes to 1 hour (depending on the temperature of where it's rising).

4. Generously coat 2 round 1½- to 2-quart (6- to 8-cup capacity) ovenproof casseroles or soufflé dishes with cooking spray. Coat your hand with cooking spray; press down the dough in the bowl, then divide it between the prepared baking dishes. Drizzle a little olive oil over the top of each; with your fingertips, smooth out the dough and evenly brush it with the oil. Sprinkle each loaf with about 1 tablespoon whole-wheat flour until evenly coated. Loosely cover the dishes with plastic wrap. Set in a warm spot (*see How To, page 192*) until the dough rises to the plastic wrap, 45 minutes to 1½ hours).

5. Remove the plastic wrap; let the dough rise until it's about ¼ to ½ inch above the rims, 15 to 30 minutes. Meanwhile, preheat the oven to 400°F.

6. Transfer the loaves to the middle of the oven; avoid jarring, as they may deflate. Bake until the tops are nicely browned, about 30 minutes. Remove the loaves from the dishes (run a table knife around the edge to loosen if necessary), place top-side up on a baking sheet, and continue baking until they are well browned on top and sound hollow when tapped on the bottom, 10 to 15 minutes more. Let the loaves cool for at least 15 minutes before serving. Cut into thick wedges.

PER SLICE: 154 calories; 3 g fat (0 g sat, 1 g mono); 0 mg cholesterol; 28 g carbohydrate; 2 g added sugars; 4 g protein; 3 g fiber; 282 mg sodium; 95 mg potassium.
NUTRITION BONUS: Folate (20% daily value).

Soft Whole-Wheat Dinner Rolls

H✕W H♥H

MAKES: 2 dozen rolls
ACTIVE TIME: 40 minutes | **TOTAL:** 4 hours
TO MAKE AHEAD: Prepare through Step 4 and refrigerate overnight. Remove from the refrigerator and let rise until almost doubled in size, about 3½ hours. Continue to Step 6.

Here's a not-too-big dinner roll you can feel good about serving for the holidays or any special occasion.

1½	**cups warm (about 120°F) low-fat milk**
¼	**cup sugar**
¼	**cup unsalted butter, melted**
¼	**cup canola oil**
3	**large eggs, divided**
1	**package quick-rising yeast (about 2¼ teaspoons), such as Fleischmann's RapidRise**
3	**cups whole-wheat flour**
2	**cups cake flour, divided, plus more for dusting**
1¼	**teaspoons salt**
2	**tablespoons wheat germ**

1. Whisk milk, sugar, butter, oil and 2 eggs in a large bowl. Whisk yeast, whole-wheat flour, 1½ cups cake flour and salt in a medium bowl. Gradually stir the dry ingredients into the wet ingredients using a wooden spoon. The dough will be very sticky.

2. Sprinkle ½ cup cake flour on a work surface. Turn out the dough onto it and knead until all the flour is incorporated, 1 to 2 minutes. Coat a large bowl with cooking spray. Transfer the dough to the bowl, coat the top with cooking spray and cover with plastic wrap. Let rise at room temperature (about 70°F) until doubled in volume, 1¼ to 2 hours.

3. Coat a 9-by-13-inch metal baking pan with cooking spray. Turn the dough out onto a lightly floured surface; pat into a rough 7-by-10-inch rectangle. Cut lengthwise into 4 equal strips (PHOTO 1) using a bench knife or butter knife. Then cut each strip crosswise into 6 equal portions (PHOTO 2). (Each portion will weigh 1¼ to 1½ ounces.)

4. Working with one portion of dough at a time, gather and pinch the edges together, shaping the dough into a rough ball. The spot where the edges come together is the bottom of the ball (PHOTO 3). Place each ball, bottom down, on a clean work surface. With a slightly cupped hand, move the ball around in a circular motion, keeping the bottom in place while tucking the loose edges into it and stretching the surface of the dough tight (PHOTO 4). (If the outer skin breaks, set the roll aside and let it rest while rounding the remaining rolls. Reroll once the dough relaxes.) Arrange the rolls in the prepared pan. Cover with plastic wrap. (If following make-ahead instructions, refrigerate the rolls now.)

5. Let the rolls rise at room temperature until almost doubled in size, about 1¼ hours (PHOTO 5).

6. Preheat oven to 400°F. Whisk the remaining egg in a small bowl, and brush the tops of the rolls with it (you'll have some left over); sprinkle with wheat germ. Bake the rolls until light brown on top, about 20 minutes.

PER ROLL: 154 calories; 5 g fat (2 g sat, 2 g mono); 25 mg cholesterol; 23 g carbohydrate; 2 g added sugars; 4 g protein; 2 g fiber; 136 mg sodium; 114 mg potassium.

How To: Make Dinner Rolls

Salmon Salad Sandwich

Crab Salad Melts

Turkish Lamb Pita Burgers

Vietnamese Steak Sandwich

Sandwiches & Burgers

Mozzarella en Carrozza

H✖W

MAKES: 2 servings
ACTIVE TIME: 25 minutes | TOTAL: 25 minutes

Loosely translated as "mozzarella in a carriage," Mozzarella en Carrozza is a fried mozzarella sandwich with a pungent anchovy-butter sauce. For this healthier rendition, we brown one side on the stovetop and finish the sandwich in a hot oven. The result: a crisp "carriage" and creamy, savory mozzarella filling. Enjoy with a glass of dry Italian white wine.

- ½ **cup shredded part-skim mozzarella**
- 1 **tablespoon low-fat mayonnaise**
- 2 **teaspoons Dijon mustard**
- 2 **anchovy fillets, rinsed and finely chopped**
- 1 **teaspoon drained capers**
   Freshly ground pepper to taste
- 4 **½-inch-thick slices Italian bread**
- 1 **large egg**
- ¼ **cup nonfat milk**
- ¼ **cup all-purpose flour**
   Pinch of cayenne pepper
- 1 **teaspoon extra-virgin olive oil**

1. Preheat oven to 450°F.

2. Combine mozzarella, mayonnaise, mustard, anchovies, capers and pepper in a small bowl. Spread the mixture over 2 slices of bread. Top with the remaining bread to form sandwiches.

3. Whisk egg and milk in a small shallow dish. Combine flour and cayenne in another small shallow dish. Dip each sandwich into the egg mixture and turn to coat, letting the excess drip off. Dredge lightly in flour and dip again in the egg mixture.

4. Brush a heavy ovenproof skillet, preferably cast-iron, with oil. Heat over medium-high heat. Add the sandwiches and cook until the underside is golden, about 1 minute. Turn the sandwiches over and transfer the pan to the oven. Bake until golden and heated through, 8 to 10 minutes. Serve immediately.

PER SERVING: 335 calories; 13 g fat (5 g sat, 5 g mono); 125 mg cholesterol; 36 g carbohydrate; 0 g added sugars; 18 g protein; 2 g fiber; 750 mg sodium; 194 mg potassium.
NUTRITION BONUS: Folate (46% daily value), Calcium (30% dv), Iron (15% dv).

BBQ Tofu Sandwich

H✕W   H⬆F   H♥H

MAKES: 4 servings
ACTIVE TIME: 25 minutes | TOTAL: 25 minutes

Though vegetarian BBQ may be an oxymoron, once you take a bite of this delicious tofu sandwich topped with coleslaw and dill pickles you won't worry about the contradiction. Serve with baked beans and corn on the cob. **Shopping Tip:** *Look for preshredded cabbage-and-carrot "coleslaw mix" near other prepared vegetables in the produce section.*

¼	**cup thinly sliced onion**
1	**14-ounce package extra-firm or firm water-packed tofu, drained**
⅛	**teaspoon salt**
1	**tablespoon canola oil**
½	**cup prepared barbecue sauce**
1½	**cups coleslaw mix (*see Shopping Tip*) *or* finely shredded cabbage**
2	**tablespoons low-fat mayonnaise**
2	**teaspoons red-wine vinegar**
¼	**teaspoon garlic powder**
	Freshly ground pepper to taste
4	**whole-wheat hamburger buns, toasted**
4	**dill pickle sandwich slices**

1. Place onion in a small bowl, cover with cold water and set aside. Stand tofu on its long narrow side. Cut lengthwise into 4 rectangular slabs, each about ½ inch thick, and pat dry. Sprinkle with salt.

2. Heat oil in a large nonstick skillet over medium heat. Add the tofu slabs (depending on the size of your pan, the tofu may slope up the sides a little). Cook until browned on both sides, about 4 minutes per side. Reduce heat to low. Add barbecue sauce and carefully turn the tofu to coat with the sauce. Cover and cook for 3 minutes more.

3. Meanwhile, combine coleslaw (or cabbage), mayonnaise, vinegar, garlic powder and pepper in a medium bowl. Drain the onion.

4. To assemble sandwiches, place about ⅓ cup of the coleslaw (or cabbage) mixture on each bun and top with a tofu slab, a pickle slice and a few onion slices. Spread any sauce remaining in the pan on the top buns.

PER SERVING: 259 calories; 10 g fat (1 g sat, 4 g mono); 0 mg cholesterol; 32 g carbohydrate; 7 g added sugars; 12 g protein; 5 g fiber; 724 mg sodium; 335 mg potassium.
NUTRITION BONUS: Calcium (26% daily value), Magnesium (20% dv), Vitamin C (17% dv), Iron (16% dv).

EatingWell Tip

Choose whole-wheat bread or buns for sandwiches. They **add fiber to your meal**, which may help you stay satisfied longer.

Fried Green Tomato Sandwiches with Rémoulade Sauce

H✕W   H↑F   H♥H

MAKES: 4 servings
ACTIVE TIME: 35 minutes | TOTAL: 35 minutes

Technically, these tomatoes aren't fried but they are breaded and lightly browned in a skillet, then finished in the oven. A tangy sauce with sweet gherkins and capers is the perfect complement.

GREEN TOMATOES

- ¾ **cup buttermilk (see *Tip*, page 482)**
- 1 **large egg white**
- 1½ **cups yellow cornmeal**
- ½ **teaspoon salt**
- ½ **teaspoon cayenne pepper**
- 2 **large green tomatoes, cored and cut into ¼-inch-thick slices**
- 2 **teaspoons extra-virgin olive oil, divided**
- 2 **teaspoons butter, divided**

RÉMOULADE SAUCE

- 2 **tablespoons low-fat mayonnaise**
- 2 **tablespoons reduced-fat sour cream *or* nonfat plain yogurt**
- 1 **tablespoon prepared horseradish**
- 1 **tablespoon Dijon mustard**
- 2 **teaspoons lemon juice**
- ½ **teaspoon cayenne pepper**
- 2 **scallions, chopped**
- 2 **sweet gherkins, chopped, *or* 1 tablespoon sweet pickle relish**
- 1 **tablespoon capers, rinsed and chopped**

- 4 **leaves iceberg lettuce**
- 4 **hamburger buns, preferably whole-wheat**

1. Preheat oven to 450°F.

2. **To prepare tomatoes:** Whisk buttermilk and egg white in a medium bowl. Mix cornmeal, salt and cayenne in a shallow dish. Dip half the tomato slices into the buttermilk mixture, then gently turn each slice in the cornmeal mixture to coat.

3. Heat 1 teaspoon oil and 1 teaspoon butter in a large nonstick skillet over medium heat until foamy. Add the tomato slices and cook until the undersides are golden brown, 4 to 5 minutes. Transfer the slices to a baking sheet, browned-side up. Repeat with the remaining tomato slices, dipping them in the buttermilk and cornmeal, cooking them in the remaining oil and butter and transferring them to the baking sheet.

4. Transfer the baking sheet to the oven and bake the tomatoes until well browned on both sides, 8 to 12 minutes.

4. **To prepare rémoulade sauce:** Combine mayonnaise, sour cream (or yogurt), horseradish, mustard, lemon juice, cayenne, scallions, gherkins (or relish) and capers in a small bowl.

5. **To assemble sandwiches:** Layer lettuce, tomato slices and rémoulade sauce on buns.

PER SERVING: 333 calories; 9 g fat (3 g sat, 3 g mono); 9 mg cholesterol; 57 g carbohydrate; 3 g added sugars; 10 g protein; 7 g fiber; 666 mg sodium; 509 mg potassium.
NUTRITION BONUS: Vitamin C (43% daily value), Magnesium (24% dv), Vitamin A (21% dv), Iron (16% dv).

Salmon Salad Sandwich

H✳W H♥H

MAKES: 4 servings
ACTIVE TIME: 15 minutes | **TOTAL:** 15 minutes

Salmon salad served on tangy pumpernickel bread is an easy dinner. Make a double batch and you'll have lunch for the next day. (Photograph: page 198.)

2 6- to 7-ounce cans boneless, skinless wild Alaskan salmon, drained
¼ cup minced red onion
2 tablespoons lemon juice
1 tablespoon extra-virgin olive oil
¼ teaspoon freshly ground pepper
4 tablespoons reduced-fat cream cheese (Neufchâtel)
8 slices pumpernickel bread, toasted
8 slices tomato
2 large leaves romaine lettuce, cut in half

Combine salmon, onion, lemon juice, oil and pepper in a medium bowl. Spread 1 tablespoon cream cheese on each of 4 slices of bread. Spread ½ cup salmon salad over the cream cheese. Top with 2 tomato slices, a piece of lettuce and another slice of bread.

PER SERVING: 286 calories; 9 g fat (3 g sat, 4 g mono); 34 mg cholesterol; 29 g carbohydrate; 0 g added sugars; 22 g protein; 4 g fiber; 645 mg sodium; 263 mg potassium.
NUTRITION BONUS: Folate (22% daily value), Iron & Vitamin C (17% dv), omega-3s.

EatingWell Tip

Try canned wild salmon in your sandwiches and salads. It is an inexpensive and convenient source of **heart-healthy omega-3s**.

Crab Salad Melts

H✳W H⬆F ♥H

MAKES: 4 servings
ACTIVE TIME: 25 minutes | **TOTAL:** 25 minutes

Here's a great light spring dinner. You can use any type of crabmeat, including more affordable options available in pouches or cans near other canned fish or in tubs in the seafood department. Serve with a tossed salad. (Photograph: page 198.)

3 asparagus spears *or* 12 snow peas, trimmed and thinly sliced (about ⅓ cup)
8 ounces crabmeat, any shells *or* cartilage removed
⅓ cup finely chopped celery
¼ cup finely chopped red bell pepper
1 scallion, finely chopped
4 teaspoons lemon juice
1 tablespoon low-fat mayonnaise
¼ teaspoon Old Bay seasoning
2-5 dashes hot sauce
Freshly ground pepper to taste
4 whole-wheat English muffins, split and toasted
½ cup shredded Swiss cheese

1. Place rack in the upper third of the oven; preheat broiler.

2. Place asparagus (or snow peas) in a medium microwavable bowl with 1 teaspoon water. Cover and microwave until tender, about 30 seconds. Add crab, celery, bell pepper, scallion, lemon juice, mayonnaise, Old Bay seasoning, hot sauce to taste and pepper; stir to combine.

3. Place English muffin halves, cut-side up, on a large baking sheet. Spread a generous ¼ cup of the crab salad on each muffin half and sprinkle each with 1 tablespoon cheese. Broil until the cheese is melted, 3 to 6 minutes.

PER SERVING: 252 calories; 6 g fat (3 g sat, 1 g mono); 52 mg cholesterol; 30 g carbohydrate; 4 g added sugars; 22 g protein; 5 g fiber; 629 mg sodium; 239 mg potassium.
NUTRITION BONUS: Calcium (33% daily value), Vitamin C (27% dv), Folate (15% dv).

Shrimp Po' Boy

H✱W H↑F H♥H

MAKES: 4 servings
ACTIVE TIME: 30 minutes | TOTAL: 30 minutes

This twist on the Louisiana favorite piles grilled shrimp and creamy-dressed cabbage onto a crusty bun. Bread that's soft on the inside and crusty on the outside is perfect for a Po' Boy sandwich. We grill both sides of a whole-wheat bun for that added crunch. You may need a few extra napkins to enjoy it, but this sandwich is well worth it. **Shopping Tip:** *Look for already peeled and deveined small shrimp for this recipe. Shrimp are usually sold by the number needed to make one pound, not by the size name. For example, "51-60 count" means there will be 51 to 60 shrimp in a pound. If you can't find them already peeled and deveined,* *see Tip, page 489.*

- **2 cups finely shredded red cabbage**
- **2 tablespoons dill pickle relish**
- **2 tablespoons low-fat mayonnaise**
- **2 tablespoons nonfat plain yogurt**
- **1 pound peeled and deveined raw shrimp (51-60 per pound; *see Shopping Tip*)**
- **4 teaspoons canola oil, divided**
- **1 teaspoon chili powder**
- **½ teaspoon paprika**
- **¼ teaspoon freshly ground pepper**
- **4 whole-wheat hot dog buns *or* small sub rolls, split**
- **4 tomato slices, halved**
- **¼ cup thinly sliced red onion**

1. Preheat grill to medium-high.

2. Combine cabbage, relish, mayonnaise and yogurt in a medium bowl.

3. Toss shrimp with 2 teaspoons oil, chili powder, paprika and pepper in a medium bowl. Place the remaining 2 teaspoons oil in a small bowl. Dip a pastry brush in water, then in the oil and lightly brush the inside of each bun (or roll).

4. Place a grill basket (*see How To*) on the grill. Add the shrimp and spread in a single layer. Grill, stirring occasionally, until the shrimp are pink and just cooked through, about 3 minutes. Open the buns and grill, turning once, until toasted on both sides, about 1 minute total.

5. To assemble the sandwiches, divide tomato and onion among the buns. Spread about ⅓ cup cabbage mixture down the middle of each and top with about ½ cup grilled shrimp.

PER SERVING: 308 calories; 9 g fat (1 g sat, 4 g mono); 173 mg cholesterol; 29 g carbohydrate; 3 g added sugars; 28 g protein; 5 g fiber; 597 mg sodium; 509 mg potassium.
NUTRITION BONUS: Vitamin C (43% daily value), Iron (24% dv), Magnesium (23% dv), Vitamin A (22% dv), Zinc (16% dv).

How To

Grill Small Shrimp | Use a grill basket when grilling small shrimp so they don't fall into the fire. If you don't have one, fold a 24-inch-long piece of heavy-duty foil in half and crimp up the edges to create a lip; this "basket" will prevent the shrimp from sliding off.

EatingWell Tip

Hold the mayo! Make a creamy spread with **less fat and calories** by combining half low-fat mayonnaise and half nonfat yogurt.

Spicy Black Bean Sandwiches with Chipotle Mayonnaise

H✳W   H↑F   H♥H

MAKES: 4 servings
ACTIVE TIME: 20 minutes | TOTAL: 20 minutes

Canned chipotle peppers add a rich, smoky flavor to these black bean sandwiches.

1   15-ounce can black beans, rinsed
¾   cup chopped red onion
3   tablespoons chopped fresh cilantro
1   clove garlic, finely chopped
1   tablespoon chili powder
1   teaspoon ground cumin
2   tablespoons lime juice
¼   teaspoon salt
1   tablespoon low-fat mayonnaise
3   tablespoons reduced-fat sour cream *or* nonfat plain yogurt
2   teaspoons chopped chipotle peppers in adobo sauce (*see Tip, page 487*)
4   6-inch pita breads, preferably whole-wheat
½   small head iceberg lettuce, shredded
1   ripe avocado, sliced
1   ripe tomato, sliced

1. Combine black beans, onion, cilantro, garlic, chili powder, cumin and lime juice in a large bowl; season with salt. Slightly mash the beans while stirring, until all ingredients are incorporated and the mixture just holds together. Stir together mayonnaise, sour cream (or yogurt) and chipotle in a small bowl.

2. Slice off the top third of each pita; open them up and spread the bean mixture inside. Top with the chipotle mayonnaise, shredded lettuce, sliced avocado and tomato. Serve within 30 minutes.

PER SERVING: 450 calories; 12 g fat (2 g sat, 5 g mono); 4 mg cholesterol; 73 g carbohydrate; 2 g added sugars; 17 g protein; 18 g fiber; 653 mg sodium; 840 mg potassium. NUTRITION BONUS: Vitamin C (30% daily value), Folate (28% dv), Potassium & Vitamin A (24% dv), Magnesium (20% dv).

► Roasted Vegetable Sandwiches

H✳W   H↑F   H♥H

MAKES: 4 servings
ACTIVE TIME: 20 minutes | TOTAL: 50 minutes
TO MAKE AHEAD: Individually wrap and refrigerate for 4 to 6 hours.

These hearty sandwiches may be assembled ahead of time and are perfect for a summer picnic.

1   small eggplant, thinly sliced into rounds
1   zucchini, thinly sliced
1   yellow summer squash, thinly sliced
1   red bell pepper, thinly sliced
4   teaspoons extra-virgin olive oil
2   cloves garlic, finely chopped
¼   teaspoon salt
¼   teaspoon freshly ground pepper
¼   cup reduced-fat sour cream *or* nonfat plain yogurt
2   tablespoons low-fat mayonnaise
1   tablespoon chopped fresh basil
1   teaspoon lemon juice
1   16-inch-long baguette, split lengthwise and cut into 4 pieces
1   bunch watercress, large stems removed (about 2 cups)

1. Preheat oven to 450°F. Toss eggplant, zucchini, yellow squash and bell pepper with oil and garlic in a large roasting pan. Season with salt and pepper. Roast the vegetables, stirring occasionally, until tender and starting to brown, 30 to 35 minutes. Let cool.

2. Meanwhile, whisk sour cream (or yogurt), mayonnaise, basil and lemon juice in a small bowl. Reserve in the refrigerator.

3. Spread the mayonnaise mixture on both of the bread halves and arrange watercress on the bottom layer. Top with the vegetable mixture and the bread tops.

PER SERVING: 270 calories; 8 g fat (2 g sat, 4 g mono); 6 mg cholesterol; 43 g carbohydrate; 0 g added sugars; 9 g protein; 7 g fiber; 562 mg sodium; 670 mg potassium. NUTRITION BONUS: Vitamin C (105% daily value), Vitamin A (35% dv), Potassium (19% dv), Folate (17% dv), Iron (15% dv).

Guinness-Marinated Bison Steak Sandwiches

H ✂ W   H ♥ H

MAKES: 4 servings
ACTIVE TIME: 40 minutes | TOTAL: 40 minutes
(plus 12-18 hours marinating time)

This open-face, "fork and knife" sandwich is piled with slices of Guinness-marinated bison steak, mushrooms and red onion. Rib-eyes are great-tasting bison steaks, but they must be cut thick, at least 1½ inches, so you can sear and brown the outside without overcooking the inside. Because bison is so lean, it's important to cook the steaks no more than medium-rare to keep them juicy and tender. You can also make this with regular beef rib-eye steaks.

1	cup Guinness beer *or* other stout
½	cup finely chopped sweet onion
⅓	cup reduced-sodium soy sauce
2	tablespoons molasses (*not* blackstrap)
1	tablespoon chopped fresh rosemary *or* 1 teaspoon dried
1	tablespoon minced garlic
¼	teaspoon Worcestershire sauce
1	pound boneless bison rib-eye steaks, 1½-2 inches thick
24	cremini mushrooms, stems removed
1	large red onion, cut into ¼-inch-thick slices
2	tablespoons extra-virgin olive oil
½	teaspoon kosher salt
	Freshly ground pepper to taste
4	slices rye bread, ½-¾ inch thick

1. Combine beer, sweet onion, soy sauce, molasses, rosemary, garlic and Worcestershire sauce in a large sealable plastic bag. Add steaks. Seal the bag, shake and turn it, and refrigerate, flipping over and shaking the bag from time to time, for 12 to 18 hours.

2. Preheat a grill to medium. Remove the steaks from the marinade and pat dry. Reserve 1 cup marinade (discard the rest). Brush mushroom caps and onion slices with oil, sprinkle with salt and pepper and place in a grilling basket. (No grill basket? *See Tip, page 485.*) Place the basket on the grill; place the steaks directly on the grill rack. Grill the steaks and vegetables until browned on the first side, 5 to 7 minutes. Turn everything over and grill until an instant-read thermometer inserted into the center of the steak registers 125°F for medium-rare and the vegetables are soft and lightly browned, about 5 minutes more. Remove from the grill and let rest for 5 to 10 minutes. Lightly grill or toast the bread.

3. Meanwhile, place the reserved 1 cup marinade in a small saucepan and bring to a simmer over medium-high heat. Boil until reduced by about half, 7 to 10 minutes.

4. Divide the mushrooms and onions among the pieces of toast and drizzle each with about 1 tablespoon of the reduced sauce. Slice the steak; divide among the sandwiches and drizzle with more sauce. Pour any accumulated juice from the steak over the sandwiches and serve with a fork and knife.

PER SERVING: 337 calories; 10 g fat (2 g sat, 7 g mono); 70 mg cholesterol; 29 g carbohydrate; 3 g added sugars; 31 g protein; 3 g fiber; 591 mg sodium; 1,038 mg potassium.
NUTRITION BONUS: Zinc (33% daily value), Potassium (30% dv), Iron (26% dv), Folate (20% dv), Magnesium (15% dv).

EatingWell Tip

Keep calories low by serving sandwiches open-face. In this steak sandwich, you'll **save about 80 calories** by having just one piece of bread.

Spanish Pork Burgers

H✕W   H⬆F

MAKES: 4 servings

ACTIVE TIME: 55 minutes | TOTAL: 55 minutes

TO MAKE AHEAD: Cover and refrigerate the lemon-saffron mayonnaise (Step 5) for up to 5 days.

This Spanish-themed burger is boldly flavored with sautéed onions (which keep it moist), paprika, garlic and green olives. The creamy mayonnaise spread is tangy with lemon and a hint of earthy saffron. Look for 90%-lean or leaner pork for this burger. If you can't find it, you can grind your own from a lean cut, such as tenderloin or loin. (See guide, page 215, to learn how.) **Shopping Tips:** *Spain is known for its superb paprika called* **Pimentón de la Vera**, *which has a smoky flavor, and for intensely flavored peppers called* **Piquillos**. *Look for these specialty ingredients at well-stocked supermarkets, gourmet-food shops or online at spanishtable.com or tienda.com.*

    1   tablespoon extra-virgin olive oil
    3   cups thinly sliced Spanish onion
    ¾   teaspoon freshly ground pepper, divided
    ¼   teaspoon salt, divided
    1   pound lean ground pork
    1   tablespoon finely chopped Spanish green olives,
        such as Manzanilla
    2   teaspoons minced garlic
    2   teaspoons *Pimentón de la Vera* (*see Shopping Tips*)
        or Hungarian paprika
    ¼   cup shredded Manchego *or* Monterey Jack cheese
    ¼   cup low-fat mayonnaise
    2   teaspoons freshly grated lemon zest
    1   tablespoon lemon juice
        Pinch of saffron (*see Tip, page 488*)

    4   whole-wheat hamburger buns, toasted
    2   whole jarred Piquillo peppers (*see Shopping Tips*)
        or jarred pimientos, halved lengthwise

1. Heat oil in a large skillet over medium heat. Add onion, ¼ teaspoon pepper and ⅛ teaspoon salt. Cover and cook, stirring occasionally, until soft and translucent, about 10 minutes. Set aside half the onion for topping; finely chop the other half.

2. Preheat grill to medium.

3. Place the chopped onion in a large bowl; add pork, olives, garlic, paprika, the remaining ½ teaspoon pepper and ⅛ teaspoon salt. Gently combine, without overmixing, until evenly incorporated. Form into 4 equal patties, about ½ inch thick.

4. Oil the grill rack (*see Tip, page 485*). Grill the burgers, turning once, until an instant-read thermometer inserted in the center registers 165°F, 10 to 12 minutes total. Top with cheese and cook until it is melted, about 1 minute more.

5. Combine mayonnaise, lemon zest, lemon juice and saffron in a small bowl. Assemble the burgers on toasted buns with the lemon-saffron mayonnaise, some of the reserved onions and half a pepper.

PER SERVING: 383 calories; 13 g fat (4 g sat, 5 g mono); 72 mg cholesterol; 38 g carbohydrate; 3 g added sugars; 31 g protein; 6 g fiber; 643 mg sodium; 685 mg potassium.
NUTRITION BONUS: Vitamin C & Zinc (22% daily value), Potassium (20% dv), Magnesium (19% dv), Iron (15% dv).

Lamb Burgers Topped with Mâche Salad

H❌W   H⬆F   H♥H

MAKES: 4 servings

ACTIVE TIME: 30 minutes | TOTAL: 30 minutes

TO MAKE AHEAD: Refrigerate the dressing (Step 1) for up to 1 day. Cover and refrigerate the lamb mixture (Step 2) for up to 4 hours.

These juicy lamb burgers are mounded with a generous portion of greens and sandwiched on a crusty bun.
Shopping Tip: *Look for Meyer lemons in late winter and early spring in well-stocked supermarkets and specialty grocers. Regular lemon works well as a substitute in this recipe.*

- 4 teaspoons extra-virgin olive oil
- ¾ teaspoon lemon zest, preferably Meyer lemon (*see Shopping Tip*), divided
- 2 tablespoons lemon juice, preferably Meyer lemon
- 1 teaspoon honey, preferably orange-blossom honey
- ½ teaspoon Dijon mustard
- ½ teaspoon poppy seeds
- ¾ teaspoon salt, divided
- Freshly ground pepper to taste
- ¼ cup unseasoned dry breadcrumbs, preferably whole-wheat (*see Tip, page 481*)
- 2 tablespoons chopped fresh chives
- 1 clove garlic, minced
- 1 pound lean ground lamb, preferably from the leg (*see guide, page 215*)

- 4 sandwich buns, preferably whole-wheat
- 4 cups mâche (*see Tip, page 485*) *or* coarsely chopped butterhead lettuce
- ½ cup fresh mint leaves

1. Whisk oil, ¼ teaspoon lemon zest, lemon juice, honey, mustard, poppy seeds, ½ teaspoon salt and pepper to taste in a large bowl. Set aside.

2. Combine breadcrumbs, chives, garlic and the remaining ½ teaspoon lemon zest, ¼ teaspoon salt and ½ teaspoon pepper in a medium bowl. Add lamb and gently knead until combined. Form into 4 patties.

3. Coat a large nonstick skillet with cooking spray and heat over medium heat. Add the patties; cook until there is just a hint of pink in the center, 3 to 5 minutes per side. Transfer to a plate; tent with foil to keep warm.

4. Meanwhile, warm or toast buns, if desired. Add mâche (or lettuce) and mint to the bowl with the dressing; toss to coat. Place the lamb burgers on the buns and top with salad greens (a generous ¾ cup each).

PER SERVING: 343 calories; 12 g fat (3 g sat, 6 g mono); 73 mg cholesterol; 30 g carbohydrate; 4 g added sugars; 29 g protein; 5 g fiber; 732 mg sodium; 650 mg potassium.
NUTRITION BONUS: Vitamin A (47% daily value), Zinc (36% dv), Iron (30% dv), Folate (24% dv), Magnesium (21% dv), Potassium (18% dv).

GUIDE:

Making a Better Burger

Burgers get a bum rap for being unhealthy, and healthier burgers have the reputation of being bland and dry. Here are 6 tips to make a healthy burger taste great.

1. **ADD A LEANER, NEUTRAL-TASTING MEAT LIKE GROUND TURKEY** to a fattier cut like lamb to reduce saturated fat and cholesterol.
2. **INCORPORATE INGREDIENTS THAT ADD MOISTURE** to lean meat so that your burgers don't dry out. Try adding shredded cheese, cooked grains and flavorful sauces, which add flavor too.
3. **STUD WHITE-MEAT BURGERS WITH COLOR,** such as bright green sliced scallions or diced red bell peppers.
4. **GET CREATIVE** and use flavor combinations from your favorite ethnic foods to season burgers. Green olives, *Pimentón de la Vera*, saffron and Manchego cheese give the Spanish Pork Burger (*page 217*) flair.
5. **MIX SALT, PEPPER AND/OR SPICES INTO THE MEAT** instead of just sprinkling them on your burgers before cooking, so every bite is full of flavor.
6. **DON'T OVERWORK THE MEAT** or your burger may be tough. Mix the ingredients until they're just combined.

Turkish Lamb Pita Burgers

H↑F

MAKES: 6 servings

ACTIVE TIME: 1 hour | TOTAL: 1 hour | TO MAKE AHEAD: Store the toasted spices (Step 2) in an airtight container for up to 1 week. Cover and refrigerate the yogurt sauce (Step 3) for up to 3 days.

Heavy on exotic spices, this decadent sandwich is a great way to familiarize yourself with the joys of Turkish cooking. Lean turkey blended with lamb lightens the mix. Stuff the patties into warm pita bread or roll the mixture into meatballs and serve with the yogurt sauce as an hors d'oeuvre.

- ⅓ cup bulgur (*see Tip, page 482*)
- 1 cup boiling water
- 2 teaspoons whole coriander seeds
- 2 teaspoons whole cumin seeds
- ¾ cup nonfat plain yogurt, preferably Greek (*see Tip, page 490*)
- ¼ cup finely chopped scallion greens
- ¼ cup chopped flat-leaf parsley, divided
- 2 tablespoons chopped fresh mint
- 1 tablespoon chopped fresh oregano
- 1 teaspoon freshly grated lemon zest
- 1 tablespoon lemon juice
- 1 teaspoon sugar
- 1½ teaspoons freshly ground pepper, divided
- 2 cups diced tomato
- ½ cup finely chopped red onion
- 2 tablespoons extra-virgin olive oil
- 12 ounces ground lamb (*see guide, page 215*)
- 4 ounces 93%-lean ground turkey
- 1 cup finely chopped yellow onion
- 1 large egg
- 2 tablespoons chopped garlic
- ½ teaspoon cayenne pepper
- ½ teaspoon salt
- ¼ teaspoon ground allspice
  Pinch of ground cinnamon
- 6 whole-wheat pita breads, warmed

1. Combine bulgur and water in a small bowl; let stand until the water is absorbed and the bulgur is tender, 20 to 30 minutes. Drain any excess liquid.

2. Meanwhile, heat coriander and cumin seeds in a small skillet over medium heat until they begin to pop and are fragrant and lightly toasted, about 2 minutes. Scrape into a small bowl to cool, then crush in a mortar and pestle or spice grinder.

3. Combine 2 teaspoons of the spice mixture with yogurt, scallion greens, 2 tablespoons parsley, mint, oregano, lemon zest, lemon juice, sugar and ½ teaspoon pepper in a small bowl. Cover and refrigerate.

4. Mix tomato, red onion and oil in another small bowl.

5. Preheat broiler (*or see Grilling Variation*). Coat a broiler pan with cooking spray.

6. Place the reserved bulgur, the remaining spice mixture, the remaining 2 tablespoons parsley and the remaining 1 teaspoon pepper in a large bowl. Add lamb, turkey, yellow onion, egg, garlic, cayenne, salt, allspice and cinnamon. Gently combine, without overmixing, until evenly incorporated. Form into 12 equal balls, then form each into an oval patty about ½ inch thick.

7. Place the patties on the prepared broiler pan. Broil, turning once, until browned and an instant-read thermometer inserted in the center registers 165°F, 8 to 10 minutes total.

8. Slice open the warmed pita breads. Fill with 2 burgers, about ⅓ cup tomato mixture and 2 generous tablespoons yogurt sauce each.

PER SERVING: 567 calories; 23 g fat (7 g sat, 10 g mono); 88 mg cholesterol; 64 g carbohydrate; 3 g added sugars; 28 g protein; 12 g fiber; 648 mg sodium; 698 mg potassium.
NUTRITION BONUS: Vitamin C (32% daily value), Magnesium (26% dv), Potassium (20% dv), Vitamin A & Zinc (19% dv), Iron (17% dv).

GRILLING VARIATION

To grill the lamb patties, preheat a grill to medium-high. Oil the grill rack (*see Tip, page 485*). Grill the patties, turning once, until an instant-read thermometer inserted in the center registers 165°F, 8 to 10 minutes total.

"Fajita" Burgers

H✖W   H⬆F

MAKES: 4 servings
ACTIVE TIME: 50 minutes | TOTAL: 50 minutes
TO MAKE AHEAD: Cover and refrigerate the chipotle mayonnaise (*Step 3*) for up to 5 days.

This spicy burger is served on an oblong roll, slathered with a spicy chipotle mayonnaise and topped with roasted Anaheim peppers and a delicious slaw.

1	pound 90%-lean ground beef
¾	cup chopped fresh cilantro, divided
½	cup finely chopped red onion
¼	cup chopped scallions
2	teaspoons minced garlic
1	tablespoon chili powder, preferably New Mexican
1	teaspoon ground cumin
½	teaspoon dried oregano, preferably Mexican
½	teaspoon freshly ground pepper
¼	teaspoon salt
⅓	cup low-fat mayonnaise
1	tablespoon lime juice
1	tablespoon chopped chipotle chile in adobo (*see Tip, page 487*)
2	roasted Anaheim *or* poblano peppers (*see Tip, page 487*)
½	cup shredded Monterey Jack cheese
4	French rolls, preferably whole-wheat, split and toasted
1	cup shredded green cabbage
4	slices tomato
4	thin slices red onion

1. Preheat grill to medium-high.

2. Place beef, ¼ cup cilantro, onion, scallions, garlic, chili powder, cumin, oregano, pepper and salt in a large bowl. Gently combine, without overmixing, until evenly incorporated. Form into 4 equal patties, about ½ inch thick and oval-shaped to match the rolls.

3. Combine the remaining ½ cup cilantro, mayonnaise, lime juice and chipotle in a small bowl.

4. Peel the roasted peppers, halve lengthwise and remove the seeds.

5. Oil the grill rack (*see Tip, page 485*). Grill the burgers until an instant-read thermometer inserted in the center registers 165°F, about 6 minutes per side. Top with cheese; cook until it is melted, about 1 minute more.

6. Assemble the burgers on toasted rolls with the chipotle mayonnaise, half a roasted pepper, cabbage, tomato and onion.

PER SERVING: 402 calories; 17 g fat (7 g sat, 6 g mono); 82 mg cholesterol; 34 g carbohydrate; 3 g added sugars; 30 g protein; 7 g fiber; 695 mg sodium; 626 mg potassium.
NUTRITION BONUS: Zinc (46% daily value), Vitamin C (33% dv), Iron (27% dv), Vitamin A (26% dv), Calcium (22% dv), Magnesium (19% dv), Potassium (18% dv).

EatingWell Tip

To make sure you are buying "whole-wheat" rolls or buns, check the ingredients list. **Whole-wheat flour should be one of the first ingredients** listed on the label. It contains valuable fiber which may protect your heart and lower your risk of diabetes. Rolls just labeled "wheat" may contain only refined flour, which has had a lot of its fiber stripped.

Best Veggie Burgers

H⁂W H↑F H♥H

MAKES: 6 burgers

ACTIVE TIME: 40 minutes | TOTAL: 40 minutes

TO MAKE AHEAD: Cool the baked patties, individually wrap and freeze for up to 3 months. Defrost overnight in the refrigerator. Reheat in an oiled nonstick skillet over medium heat until golden brown.

These tofu burgers are packed with fresh broccoli, carrots, onion and red bell pepper, which gives them a garden-fresh flavor and great texture. Try doubling the recipe and freezing the extra patties to have on hand for a quick dinner.

- Canola *or* olive oil cooking spray
- 1 14-ounce package firm *or* extra-firm water-packed tofu, drained
- 1 cup coarse dry breadcrumbs, preferably whole-wheat (see *Tip, page 481*)
- 1 cup finely chopped broccoli florets
- 1 medium carrot, finely chopped
- ⅓ cup finely chopped red onion
- ⅓ cup finely chopped red bell pepper
- 2 tablespoons Dijon mustard
- 2 teaspoons minced garlic, divided
- ½ teaspoon salt
- ½ teaspoon freshly ground pepper
- 2 large eggs, beaten
- ⅓ cup low-fat mayonnaise
- ¾ teaspoon paprika, preferably smoked (see *Tip, page 486*)
- 6 hamburger buns, preferably whole-wheat
- 6 lettuce leaves (optional)
- 6 tomato slices (optional)

1. Preheat oven to 425°F. Coat a large baking sheet with cooking spray.

2. Finely crumble tofu and squeeze out extra water with your hands. Place in a large bowl and stir in breadcrumbs, broccoli, carrot, onion, bell pepper, mustard, 1 teaspoon garlic, salt and pepper. Add eggs and thoroughly combine the mixture with your hands until it holds together enough to form patties.

3. Form the mixture into six 3½-inch patties (using about ¾ cup of the mixture each) and place on the prepared baking sheet. (If the mixture crumbles a little as you transfer it to the pan, gently pat and squeeze the patty back together on the pan.) Coat the top of each patty with cooking spray.

4. Bake the burgers until firm to the touch and starting to brown, about 20 minutes.

5. Combine mayonnaise, paprika and the remaining 1 teaspoon garlic in a small bowl. Serve the burgers on buns with the seasoned mayonnaise, lettuce and tomato (if using).

PER SERVING: 285 calories; 8 g fat (2 g sat, 2 g mono); 71 mg cholesterol; 41 g carbohydrate; 3 g added sugars; 14 g protein; 6 g fiber; 753 mg sodium; 386 mg potassium.

NUTRITION BONUS: Vitamin A (51% daily value), Vitamin C (38% dv), Calcium (24% dv), Folate, Iron & Magnesium (20% dv).

Tortellini Primavera

Grilled Garden Pizza

Creamy Scallop & Pea Fettuccine

Inside-Out Lasagna

Pizza & Pasta

Grilled Garden Pizza

H⬆F

MAKES: 4 servings
ACTIVE TIME: 40 minutes | TOTAL: 40 minutes

Bell pepper, zucchini and a fresh tomato sauce give this vegetarian pizza a taste of summer.

- 4 whole baby *or* 1 medium zucchini, halved lengthwise
- 1 pint cherry tomatoes
- 2 tablespoons tomato paste
- 8 fresh basil leaves
- 2 teaspoons minced fresh oregano
- ¼ teaspoon salt
- ½ teaspoon freshly ground pepper
  Yellow cornmeal for dusting
- 1 pound whole-wheat pizza dough, store-bought (*see EatingWell Tip*) *or* Thin-Crust Whole-Wheat Pizza Dough (*page 226*)
- 4 ounces fresh mozzarella cheese, thinly sliced
- 1 medium yellow bell pepper, diced
- 3 tablespoons grated Parmesan cheese

1. Preheat grill to medium-high (*or see Oven Variation*).

2. Grill zucchini until marked and softened, about 4 minutes. Thinly slice. Reduce heat to low.

3. Process tomatoes, tomato paste, basil, oregano, salt and pepper in a food processor until smooth, scraping down the sides as needed.

4. Sprinkle cornmeal onto a pizza peel or the bottom of a large baking sheet. Roll out the dough (*see How To, page 226*) and transfer it to the prepared peel or baking sheet, making sure the underside of the dough is completely coated with cornmeal.

5. Slide the crust onto the grill rack; close the lid. Cook until lightly browned, 3 to 4 minutes.

6. Using a large spatula, flip the crust. Spread the tomato mixture on the crust, leaving a 1-inch border. Quickly top with mozzarella, bell pepper and the zucchini. Sprinkle with Parmesan.

7. Close the lid again and grill until the cheese has melted and the bottom of the crust has browned, about 8 minutes.

PER SERVING: 383 calories; 9 g fat (5 g sat, 2 g mono); 26 mg cholesterol; 59 g carbohydrate; 1 g added sugars; 19 g protein; 7 g fiber; 682 mg sodium; 576 mg potassium.
NUTRITION BONUS: Vitamin C (125% daily value), Folate (48% dv), Calcium (23% dv), Iron (21% dv), Magnesium & Vitamin A (20% dv).

OVEN VARIATION

Place a pizza stone on the lowest rack; preheat oven to 450°F for at least 20 minutes. Roll out dough and place on a cornmeal-dusted pizza peel or inverted baking sheet, using enough cornmeal so that the dough slides easily. Slide the dough onto the preheated stone and cook until the bottom begins to crisp, about 3 minutes. Remove the crust from the oven using a large spatula and place it uncooked-side down on the peel or baking sheet, making sure the underside of the crust is completely coated with cornmeal. Quickly add the toppings and slide the pizza back onto the stone. Continue baking until the toppings are hot and the bottom of the crust has browned, 12 to 15 minutes.

EatingWell Tip
Avoid trans fats by looking for fresh or frozen whole-wheat pizza dough without any hydrogenated oils at your supermarket.

Grilled Eggplant Parmesan Pizza

H✕W   H↑F   H♥H

MAKES: 4 servings
ACTIVE TIME: 20 minutes | TOTAL: 35 minutes

Eggplant Parm is spun into a pizza with grilled egg-plant, marinara, fresh basil and Parmigiano-Reggiano cheese. Use a vegetable peeler to shave curls off a block of hard cheese like Parmigiano-Reggiano.

1	small eggplant (about 12 ounces)
	Yellow cornmeal for dusting
1	pound whole-wheat pizza dough, store-bought (*see EatingWell Tip, page 228*) *or* Thin-Crust Whole-Wheat Pizza Dough (*page 226*)
¾	cup prepared marinara sauce
2	tablespoons chopped fresh basil
1	medium clove garlic, minced
¾	cup thinly shaved Parmigiano-Reggiano cheese

1. Preheat grill to medium-high (*or see Oven Variation, page 228*).

2. Cut eggplant into ½-inch thick rounds. Grill, turning once, until marked and softened, 4 to 6 minutes. Let cool slightly, then thinly slice into strips. Reduce heat to low.

3. Sprinkle cornmeal onto a pizza peel or the bottom of a large baking sheet. Roll out the dough (*see How To, page 226*) and transfer it to the prepared peel or baking sheet, making sure the underside of the dough is completely coated with cornmeal.

4. Slide the crust onto the grill rack; close the lid. Cook until lightly browned, 3 to 4 minutes.

5. Using a large spatula, flip the crust. Spread marinara sauce on the crust, leaving a 1-inch border. Quickly top with the eggplant, basil and garlic. Lay the Parmigiano-Reggiano shavings on top.

6. Close the lid again and grill until the cheese has melted and the bottom of the crust has browned, about 8 minutes.

PER SERVING: 369 calories; 7 g fat (3 g sat, 2 g mono); 12 mg cholesterol; 62 g carbohydrate; 1 g added sugars; 17 g protein; 10 g fiber; 741 mg sodium; 541 mg potassium.
NUTRITION BONUS: Folate (47% daily value), Calcium (23% dv), Iron & Magnesium (20% dv), Potassium & Zinc (15% dv).

EatingWell Tip

Many store-bought marinara sauces have a lot of sodium, but the amounts vary widely among brands. **Check nutrition labels for sodium** and aim for brands that have around 400 mg or less per ½-cup serving.

Macaroni & Cheese

H↑F

MAKES: 4 servings
ACTIVE TIME: 20 minutes | **TOTAL:** 55 minutes

This simple mac-and-cheese uses low-fat cottage cheese with just a cup of sharp Cheddar to add flavor.

8	ounces (2 cups) whole-wheat elbow macaroni
1½	cups low-fat cottage cheese
1	cup nonfat milk, divided
1	tablespoon all-purpose flour
1	cup shredded sharp Cheddar cheese (4 ounces)
¼	teaspoon freshly grated nutmeg
¼	teaspoon salt
⅛	teaspoon cayenne pepper
	Freshly ground pepper to taste
2	tablespoons freshly grated Parmesan cheese
2	tablespoons fine dry breadcrumbs

1. Preheat oven to 375°F. Coat a shallow 2-quart baking dish with cooking spray.

2. Bring a large pot of water to a boil. Add macaroni; cook until just tender, 8 to 10 minutes or according to package directions. Drain in a colander and rinse with cold water; set aside. Puree cottage cheese in a food processor or blender until smooth; set aside.

3. Heat ¾ cup milk in a large heavy saucepan over medium heat until steaming. Whisk flour and the remaining ¼ cup milk in a small bowl until smooth. Stir into the hot milk and cook, whisking, until the sauce is smooth and thick, about 2 minutes. Remove from the heat and stir in the pureed cottage cheese, Cheddar, nutmeg, salt, cayenne and pepper. Stir in the cooked macaroni. Spoon into the prepared baking dish. Sprinkle with Parmesan and breadcrumbs. Bake until bubbling and brown, about 35 minutes.

PER SERVING: 425 calories; 12 g fat (7 g sat, 3 g mono); 36 mg cholesterol; 52 g carbohydrate; 0 g added sugars; 30 g protein; 7 g fiber; 758 mg sodium; 332 mg potassium.
NUTRITION BONUS: Calcium (39% daily value), Magnesium (26% dv), Zinc (20% dv), Folate (16%), Iron (15%).

▶ Brothy Chinese Noodles

H✖W   H↑F   H♥H

MAKES: 6 servings, about 1⅓ cups each
ACTIVE TIME: 30 minutes | **TOTAL:** 30 minutes

This dish was inspired by Chinese Dan Dan noodles— ground pork and noodles in a spicy sauce. We use ground turkey and omit the traditional Sichuan peppercorns for convenience. **Shopping Tips: Dried Chinese noodles**, *often used in Chinese soups and lo mein, cook up quickly and can be found along with* **hot sesame oil** *in the Asian-food section of most supermarkets.*

2	tablespoons hot sesame oil (*see Shopping Tips*), divided
1	pound 93%-lean ground turkey
1	bunch scallions, sliced, divided
2	cloves garlic, minced
1	tablespoon minced fresh ginger
4	cups reduced-sodium chicken broth
¾	cup water
3	cups thinly sliced bok choy
8	ounces dried Chinese noodles (*see Shopping Tips*)
3	tablespoons reduced-sodium soy sauce
1	tablespoon rice vinegar
1	small cucumber, sliced into matchsticks

1. Heat 1 tablespoon oil in a large saucepan over medium heat. Add ground turkey, all but 2 tablespoons of the scallions, garlic and ginger and cook, stirring and breaking up the turkey, until no longer pink, about 5 minutes. Transfer to a plate.

2. Add broth, water, bok choy, noodles, soy sauce, vinegar and the remaining 1 tablespoon oil to the pan. Bring to a boil over medium-high heat. Cook, stirring occasionally, until the noodles are tender, 3 to 5 minutes. Return the turkey mixture to the pan and stir to combine. Serve topped with the reserved 2 tablespoons scallions and cucumber.

PER SERVING: 292 calories; 10 g fat (2 g sat, 2 g mono); 43 mg cholesterol; 32 g carbohydrate; 0 g added sugars; 22 g protein; 6 g fiber; 633 mg sodium; 509 mg potassium.
NUTRITION BONUS: Vitamin A (32% daily value), Vitamin C (22% dv), Iron (20% dv).

Pasta Salad Niçoise

H✗W   H↑F   H♥H

MAKES: 6 servings, 1⅓ cups each
ACTIVE TIME: 30 minutes | TOTAL: 30 minutes
TO MAKE AHEAD: If not serving immediately, toss the cooled pasta with 1 teaspoon oil. Refrigerate the pasta and the tuna mixture separately for up to 1 day.

Toss canned tuna, roasted red peppers and lots of fresh herbs with pasta for a quick weeknight supper. **Shopping Tip:** *Harissa, a fiery North African chile paste, is available at specialty-food stores or at* amazon.com. *Harissa in a tube will be much hotter than that in a jar. You can use Chinese or Thai chile-garlic sauce instead.*

2	**cloves garlic, crushed and peeled**
½	**teaspoon salt**
2	**5- to 6-ounce cans water-packed chunk light tuna (see *Tip, page 490*), drained and flaked**
½	**cup diced jarred roasted red peppers**
¼	**cup chopped fresh basil**
¼	**cup chopped fresh chives *or* scallions**
¼	**cup chopped pitted black olives**
2	**tablespoons capers, rinsed**
2	**tablespoons extra-virgin olive oil**
2	**tablespoons balsamic vinegar**
2	**tablespoons lemon juice**
½	**teaspoon freshly ground pepper**
½	**teaspoon harissa (see *Shopping Tip*)**
12	**ounces small whole-wheat pasta shells**

1. Put a large pot of water on to boil.

2. Mash garlic and salt into a paste with a chef's knife or a spoon. Transfer to a large bowl and add tuna, peppers, basil, chives (or scallions), olives, capers, oil, vinegar, lemon juice, pepper and harissa, if using. Toss gently to combine. Let stand for 15 minutes to allow the flavors to blend.

3. Meanwhile, cook pasta until just tender, 8 to 10 minutes or according to package directions. Drain in a colander and rinse under cold water until cool. Drain well. Add the pasta to the tuna mixture and toss gently to combine.

PER SERVING: 301 calories; 6 g fat (1 g sat, 4 g mono); 8 mg cholesterol; 46 g carbohydrate; 0 g added sugars; 16 g protein; 5 g fiber; 489 mg sodium; 162 mg potassium.
NUTRITION BONUS: Magnesium (15% daily value).

EatingWell Tip

Keep your sodium intake in check by enjoying savory gems like olives and capers in moderation. These tasty treats are high in sodium.

Penne with Artichoke Hearts
(*Penne al carciofi*)

H⬆F H♥H

MAKES: 6 servings

ACTIVE TIME: 35 minutes | TOTAL: 35 minutes

Artichokes, ricotta cheese, lemon juice and zest form the sauce for this quick pasta dish.

1	9-ounce package frozen artichoke hearts
10	ounces whole-wheat penne *or* rigatoni
2	teaspoons extra-virgin olive oil
1	small onion, thinly sliced
1	clove garlic, finely chopped
1½	teaspoons chopped fresh oregano *or* ½ teaspoon dried
¼	teaspoon salt
¼	teaspoon freshly ground pepper
¼	cup water
¼	cup dry white wine
2	tablespoons lemon juice
½	cup part-skim ricotta cheese
1	tablespoon freshly grated lemon zest

1. Bring a large pot of water to a boil. Add artichokes and cook for 1 minute. Remove with a slotted spoon to a cutting board. When cool enough to handle, slice about two-thirds of the artichokes into small wedges and set aside; finely chop the remaining artichokes into a paste and set aside.

2. Add pasta to the boiling water and cook until just tender, 8 to 10 minutes or according to package directions.

3. Meanwhile, heat oil in a large nonstick skillet over medium heat. Add onion and garlic; cook, stirring, for 1 minute. Add oregano, salt and a generous grinding of pepper. Stir in ¼ cup water and cook until the water has evaporated and the onions are soft, about 2 minutes. Reduce heat to low, stir in wine, lemon juice and the reserved artichoke wedges and chopped artichokes. Simmer, stirring, until heated through, about 1 minute. (If the mixture becomes dry, add 1 or 2 tablespoons of water.) Add ricotta and stir until creamy.

4. When the pasta is ready, drain and add to the pan with the sauce; toss well. Remove from heat and stir in lemon zest. Taste and adjust seasonings with salt and pepper. Serve immediately.

PER SERVING: 364 calories; 7 g fat (2 g sat, 3 g mono); 10 mg cholesterol; 63 g carbohydrate; 0 g added sugars; 16 g protein; 13 g fiber; 234 mg sodium; 435 mg potassium.
NUTRITION BONUS: Folate (36% daily value), Magnesium (33% dv), Vitamin C (20% dv), Iron (17% dv), Calcium (16% dv).

◄ Tortellini Primavera

H↑F

MAKES: 5 servings, about 1¼ cups each
ACTIVE TIME: 25 minutes | TOTAL: 25 minutes

This creamy tortellini and vegetable pasta is a real crowd pleaser. To make it even quicker, use frozen chopped vegetables instead of fresh. Serve with a green salad and whole-grain baguette.

1   14-ounce can vegetable broth *or* reduced-sodium chicken broth
2   tablespoons all-purpose flour
1   tablespoon extra-virgin olive oil
3   cloves garlic, sliced
1   cup shredded fontina cheese *or* ¾ cup shredded Parmesan cheese
1   tablespoon chopped fresh tarragon, dill *or* chives *or* 1 teaspoon dried tarragon
⅛   teaspoon salt
4   cups chopped vegetables, such as broccoli, carrots and snap peas, *or* 16-ounce bag frozen mixed vegetables
1   16-ounce package frozen cheese tortellini

1. Put a large pot of water on to boil.

2. Whisk broth and flour in a small bowl. Heat oil in a large skillet over medium heat. Add garlic and cook, stirring, until just beginning to brown, 1 to 2 minutes. Add the broth mixture to the pan, bring to a boil and cook, stirring occasionally, until the sauce is thick enough to coat the back of a spoon, about 3 minutes. Remove from the heat and stir in cheese, tarragon (or dill or chives) and salt.

3. Add vegetables and tortellini to the boiling water; return the water to a simmer and cook until the vegetables and tortellini are tender, 3 to 5 minutes. Drain; add to the pan with the sauce and stir to coat.

PER SERVING: 424 calories; 15 g fat (8 g sat, 4 g mono); 68 mg cholesterol; 55 g carbohydrate; 0 g added sugars; 14 g protein; 5 g fiber; 566 mg sodium; 321 mg potassium.
NUTRITION BONUS: Vitamin A (126% daily value), Calcium (29% dv), Vitamin C (17% dv), Folate (16% dv).

Inside-Out Lasagna

H✕W   H↑F   H♥H

MAKES: 4 servings, about 1½ cups each
ACTIVE TIME: 25 minutes | TOTAL: 25 minutes

Here we take basic lasagna ingredients—ricotta cheese, pasta and tomatoes—and skip the layering and long baking time to make a super-quick and satisfying meal for the whole family. Serve with steamed broccoli and a whole-grain baguette. (Photograph: page 224.)

8   ounces whole-wheat rotini *or* fusilli
1   tablespoon extra-virgin olive oil
1   small onion, chopped
3   cloves garlic, sliced
8   ounces sliced white mushrooms (about 3½ cups)
½   teaspoon salt
¼   teaspoon freshly ground pepper
1   14-ounce can diced tomatoes with Italian herbs
8   cups baby spinach
½   teaspoon crushed red pepper (optional)
¾   cup part-skim ricotta cheese

1. Bring a large pot of water to a boil. Add pasta; cook until just tender, 8 to 10 minutes or according to package directions. Drain and transfer to a large bowl.

2. Heat oil in a large nonstick skillet over medium heat. Add onion and garlic; cook, stirring, until soft and beginning to brown, about 3 minutes. Add mushrooms, salt and pepper; cook, stirring, until the mushrooms release their liquid, 4 to 6 minutes.

3. Add tomatoes, spinach and crushed red pepper (if using). Increase heat to medium-high; cook, stirring once halfway through, until the spinach is wilted, about 4 minutes.

4. Toss the sauce with the pasta and divide among 4 bowls. Dollop each serving with ricotta.

PER SERVING: 364 calories; 9 g fat (3 g sat, 4 g mono); 14 mg cholesterol; 55 g carbohydrate; 0 g added sugars; 16 g protein; 7 g fiber; 588 mg sodium; 788 mg potassium.
NUTRITION BONUS: Vitamin A (90% daily value), Vitamin C (50% dv), Folate (25% dv), Potassium (22% dv), Calcium (21% dv).

Gnocchi with Tomatoes, Pancetta & Wilted Watercress

H ♥ H

MAKES: 4 servings, about 1 cup each
ACTIVE TIME: 30 minutes | TOTAL: 30 minutes

Pancetta—cured Italian-style bacon—balances the sweet tomatoes and peppery watercress in this pasta. **Shopping Tip:** *We like the texture of "shelf-stable" prepared gnocchi found in the Italian section of most supermarkets, but frozen and fresh gnocchi also work here.*

2	ounces pancetta, chopped
3	cloves garlic, minced
2	large tomatoes, chopped
½	teaspoon sugar
¼	teaspoon crushed red pepper
2	teaspoons red-wine vinegar
¼	teaspoon salt
1	pound gnocchi (*see Shopping Tip*)
4	ounces watercress, tough stems removed, coarsely chopped (6 cups packed)
⅓	cup freshly grated Parmesan cheese

1. Put a large pot of water on to boil.

2. Cook pancetta in a large nonstick skillet over medium heat, stirring occasionally, until it begins to brown, 4 to 5 minutes. Add garlic and cook, stirring, for 30 seconds. Add tomatoes, sugar and crushed red pepper and cook, stirring, until the tomatoes are almost completely broken down, about 5 minutes. Stir in vinegar and salt. Remove from the heat.

3. Cook gnocchi in the boiling water until they float, 3 to 5 minutes or according to package directions. Place watercress in a colander and drain the gnocchi over the watercress, wilting it slightly. Add the gnocchi and watercress to the sauce in the pan; toss to combine. Serve immediately, with Parmesan.

PER SERVING: 378 calories; 7 g fat (3 g sat, 1 g mono); 16 mg cholesterol; 63 g carbohydrate; 0 g added sugars; 14 g protein; 3 g fiber; 686 mg sodium; 330 mg potassium.
NUTRITION BONUS: Vitamin C (52% daily value), Vitamin A (35% dv), Iron (17% dv), Calcium (16% dv).

EatingWell Tip

Get cruciferous vegetables like the watercress in this pasta into your diet. They contain isothiocyanates, antioxidants that **amp up your body's detoxifying enzymes**. Other crucifers include broccoli, Brussels sprouts, cauliflower and cabbage.

Vermicelli with Tomatoes, Olives & Capers (*Vermicelli alla puttanesca*)

H↑F H♥H

MAKES: 6 servings
ACTIVE TIME: 30 minutes I TOTAL: 30 minutes

Chopped fresh tomatoes are the base of this raw pasta sauce, flavored with briny olives and parsley.

1	pound whole-wheat vermicelli *or* spaghettini
4	large tomatoes, coarsely chopped, *or* one 28-ounce can plum tomatoes, drained and coarsely chopped (3½ cups)
¼	cup chopped flat-leaf parsley
16	large black olives (packed in brine), pitted and chopped
4	anchovy fillets, rinsed and finely chopped
3	large cloves garlic, finely chopped
3	tablespoons capers, rinsed and minced
2	tablespoons extra-virgin olive oil
½	teaspoon freshly ground pepper
¼	cup freshly grated Pecorino Romano *or* Parmesan cheese

1. Bring a large pot of water to a boil. Add pasta; cook until just tender, 8 to 10 minutes or according to package directions.

2. Meanwhile, combine tomatoes, parsley, olives, anchovies, garlic, capers, oil and pepper in a serving bowl.

3. Drain the pasta and add it to the bowl with the sauce. Toss to combine. Taste and adjust seasonings. Sprinkle with cheese and serve immediately.

PER SERVING: 383 calories; 10 g fat (2 g sat, 4 g mono); 5 mg cholesterol; 64 g carbohydrate; 0 g added sugars; 14 g protein; 11 g fiber; 394 mg sodium; 493 mg potassium. NUTRITION BONUS: Magnesium & Vitamin C (32% daily value), Vitamin A (25% dv), Iron (20% dv), Folate (17% dv), Zinc (15% dv).

Eggplant Pomodoro Pasta

H✂W H↑F H♥H

MAKES: 6 servings
ACTIVE TIME: 35 minutes I TOTAL: 35 minutes

Diced eggplant turns tender and tasty sautéed with garlic and olive oil. Toss with fresh plum tomatoes, green olives and capers and you have a simple light summer sauce. We like it over angel hair pasta, but any type of pasta will work.

2	tablespoons extra-virgin olive oil
1	medium eggplant (about 1 pound), cut into ½-inch cubes
2	cloves garlic, minced
4	plum tomatoes, diced
⅓	cup chopped pitted green olives
2	tablespoons red-wine vinegar
4	teaspoons capers, rinsed
¾	teaspoon salt
½	teaspoon freshly ground pepper
¼	teaspoon crushed red pepper (optional)
12	ounces whole-wheat angel hair pasta
¼	cup chopped fresh parsley *or* basil

1. Put a large pot of water on to boil.

2. Heat oil in a large nonstick skillet over medium heat. Add eggplant; cook, stirring occasionally, until just softened, about 5 minutes. Add garlic; cook, stirring, until fragrant, 30 seconds to 1 minute. Add tomatoes, olives, vinegar, capers, salt, pepper and crushed red pepper (if using); cook, stirring, until the tomatoes begin to break down, 5 to 7 minutes more.

3. Meanwhile, cook pasta in boiling water until just tender, about 6 minutes or according to package directions. Drain and divide the pasta among 6 shallow bowls. Spoon the sauce over the pasta and sprinkle parsley (or basil) on top.

PER SERVING: 282 calories; 7 g fat (1 g sat, 5 g mono); 0 mg cholesterol; 50 g carbohydrate; 0 g added sugars; 10 g protein; 10 g fiber; 467 mg sodium; 419 mg potassium. NUTRITION BONUS: Magnesium (25% daily value), Vitamin C (18% dv), Folate & Iron (15% dv).

Fusilli with Roasted Tomatoes, Asparagus & Shrimp

H✖W   H⬆F   H♥H

MAKES: 6 servings
ACTIVE TIME: 20 minutes | TOTAL: 45 minutes

Roasted tomatoes, asparagus, garlic and shrimp make a tasty topping for whole-wheat fusilli.

12	plum tomatoes, quartered lengthwise
4	teaspoons extra-virgin olive oil, divided
	Freshly ground pepper to taste
1	small head garlic
1	pound thin asparagus, trimmed and cut into 2-inch lengths (*or* larger stalks, peeled and halved lengthwise before cutting)
1	pound raw shrimp (21-25 per pound; *see Tip, page 489*), peeled and deveined
12	ounces whole-wheat fusilli *or* rotini
2	teaspoons lemon juice
1	tablespoon chopped fresh oregano *or* 1 teaspoon dried
1	tablespoon chopped fresh thyme *or* 1 teaspoon dried
¼	teaspoon salt

1. Position oven rack in lower third of oven; preheat to 450°F.

2. Toss tomatoes with 2 teaspoons oil and a generous grinding of pepper in a large roasting pan. Rub off the excess papery skin from garlic without separating the cloves. Slice the tip off the head, exposing the ends of the cloves. Wrap in foil and add to the roasting pan.

3. Roast without stirring until the tomatoes are wrinkled and beginning to brown, about 20 minutes. Scatter the asparagus and shrimp over the tomatoes and roast until the shrimp are pink and firm and the asparagus is tender, about 10 minutes more. Remove the garlic from the pan, unwrap and let cool for 5 minutes. Cover the roasting pan to keep warm.

4. Meanwhile, bring a large pot of water to a boil. Add pasta; cook until just tender, 8 to 10 minutes or according to package directions.

5. While the pasta is cooking, separate the garlic cloves and squeeze out the soft pulp. Mash to a paste with the flat side of a knife.

6. Drain the pasta and return to the pot. Add the remaining 2 teaspoons oil, mashed garlic, lemon juice, oregano, thyme, salt and pepper, tossing to evenly coat the pasta. Transfer the pasta to the roasting pan and toss gently to combine, making sure to scrape up any bits from the bottom of the pan. Serve immediately.

PER SERVING: 345 calories; 6 g fat (1 g sat, 3 g mono); 115 mg cholesterol; 52 g carbohydrate; 0 g added sugars; 26 g protein; 9 g fiber; 226 mg sodium; 668 mg potassium.
NUTRITION BONUS: Vitamin C (40% daily value), Magnesium (33% dv), Vitamin A (32% dv), Folate (27% dv), Iron (26% dv), Potassium (19% dv), Zinc (18% dv).

Creamy Scallop & Pea Fettuccine

H ⬆ F

MAKES: 5 servings, about 1½ cups each
ACTIVE TIME: 40 minutes | TOTAL: 40 minutes

This rich pasta dish is full of sweet seared scallops and plump peas. Low-fat milk and flour thicken the sauce, giving it a creamy texture without the extra calories and fat found in traditional cream sauces. Serve with a small Caesar salad on the side. **Shopping Tip:** *Some bottled clam juices are very high in sodium, so salt the recipe accordingly. We like the Bar Harbor brand (120 mg sodium per 2-ounce serving). Look for it in the canned-fish section or the seafood department of your supermarket.*

8	ounces whole-wheat fettuccine
1	pound large dry sea scallops (*see Tip, page 489*)
¼	teaspoon salt, divided
1	tablespoon extra-virgin olive oil
1	8-ounce bottle clam juice (*see Shopping Tip*)
1	cup low-fat milk
3	tablespoons all-purpose flour
¼	teaspoon ground white pepper
3	cups frozen peas, thawed
¾	cup finely shredded Romano cheese, divided
⅓	cup chopped fresh chives
½	teaspoon freshly grated lemon zest
1	teaspoon lemon juice

1. Bring a large pot of water to a boil. Add fettuccine; cook until just tender, 8 to 10 minutes or according to package directions. Drain.

2. Meanwhile, pat scallops dry and sprinkle with ⅛ teaspoon salt. Heat oil in a large nonstick skillet over medium-high heat. Add the scallops and cook until golden brown, 2 to 3 minutes per side. Transfer to a plate.

3. Add clam juice to the pan. Whisk milk, flour, white pepper and the remaining ⅛ teaspoon salt in a medium bowl until smooth. Whisk the milk mixture into the clam juice. Bring the mixture to a simmer, stirring constantly. Continue stirring until thickened, 1 to 2 minutes. Return the scallops and any accumulated juices to the pan along with peas and return to a simmer. Stir in the fettuccine, ½ cup Romano cheese, chives, lemon zest and juice until combined. Serve with the remaining cheese sprinkled on top.

PER SERVING: 430 calories; 10 g fat (4 g sat, 2 g mono); 47 mg cholesterol; 55 g carbohydrate; 0 g added sugars; 34 g protein; 10 g fiber; 728 mg sodium; 670 mg potassium.
NUTRITION BONUS: Vitamin A (42% daily value), Magnesium (37% dv), Vitamin C (33% dv), Calcium (29% dv), Folate (23% dv), Iron (20% dv), Potassium & Zinc (19% dv).

EatingWell Tip

Use whole-wheat pasta in place of white pasta to **add an additional 4 grams of fiber** per 2-ounce serving.

Seafood Linguine

H↑F H♥H

MAKES: 4 servings
ACTIVE TIME: 35 minutes | TOTAL: 35 minutes

This restaurant-worthy mixed seafood pasta is a snap to make and an easy way to impress guests. We like the sweet taste and extra-saucy consistency of canned diced San Marzano tomatoes in sauces like this one. Marjoram pairs well with the seafood, but basil or even parsley work too. Serve with an arugula salad with Creamy Garlic Dressing (page 83).

8	ounces whole-wheat linguine *or* spaghetti
2	tablespoons extra-virgin olive oil
4	cloves garlic, chopped
1	tablespoon chopped shallot
1	28-ounce can diced tomatoes, drained
½	cup dry white wine
½	teaspoon salt
¼	teaspoon freshly ground pepper
12	littleneck *or* small cherrystone clams (about 1 pound), scrubbed
8	ounces dry sea scallops
8	ounces tilapia *or* other flaky white fish, cut into 1-inch strips
1	tablespoon chopped fresh marjoram *or* 1 teaspoon dried, plus more for garnish
¼	cup grated Parmesan cheese (optional)

1. Bring a large pot of water to a boil. Add pasta; cook until just tender, 8 to 10 minutes, or according to package directions. Drain and rinse.

2. Meanwhile, heat oil in a large skillet over medium heat. Add garlic and shallot and cook, stirring, until beginning to soften, about 1 minute.

3. Increase the heat to medium-high. Add tomatoes, wine, salt and pepper. Bring to a simmer and cook for 1 minute. Add clams, cover and cook for 2 minutes. Stir in scallops, fish and marjoram. Cover and cook until the scallops and fish are cooked through and the clams have opened, 3 to 5 minutes more. (Discard any clams that don't open.)

4. Spoon the sauce and clams over the pasta and sprinkle with additional marjoram and Parmesan (if using).

PER SERVING: 465 calories; 10 g fat (2 g sat, 6 g mono); 62 mg cholesterol; 55 g carbohydrate; 0 g added sugars; 36 g protein; 8 g fiber; 805 mg sodium; 658 mg potassium.
NUTRITION BONUS: Vitamin C (58% daily value), Iron (55% dv), Magnesium (34% dv), Vitamin A (23%), Potassium (19% dv), Zinc (18% dv), Folate (16% dv).

EatingWell Tip

Use high-quality Parmesan cheese to garnish your pasta dishes. We like imported Parmigiano-Reggiano because it has a strong flavor so you can **use less and still get a big flavor impact**.

Iberian-Style Sausage & Chicken Ragù

H✂W   H♥H

MAKES: about 8 cups, for 16 servings
ACTIVE TIME: 1 hour | TOTAL: 2 hours 10 minutes
TO MAKE AHEAD: Refrigerate in an airtight container for up to 5 days or freeze for up to 3 months.

This Spanish-inspired sausage and chicken ragù is best served over a heartier pasta, such as whole-wheat penne, or gnocchi. Garnish with grated sheep's-milk cheese, such as Manchego. **Shopping Tips:** *Look for* **linguiça** *or Spanish-style* **chorizo** *near other refrigerated cured sausages. Spain is known for its superb smoky paprika called* **Pimentón de la Vera**. *Regular smoked paprika can be used as a substitute.* **Saffron** *adds flavor and golden color to a variety of Middle Eastern, African and European foods. Look for* Pimentón de la Vera *and saffron in the spice section of well-stocked supermarkets, gourmet-food shops or at* tienda.com.

- 1 **tablespoon extra-virgin olive oil**
- 8 **ounces linguiça (Portuguese-style sausage)** *or* **Spanish-style chorizo (see** *Shopping Tips***), diced**
- 3 **cups chopped onion**
- 2 **tablespoons finely chopped garlic**
- 2 **tablespoons** *Pimentón de la Vera* **(see** *Shopping Tips***)**
- 2 **pounds boneless, skinless chicken thighs, trimmed and cut into 1-inch chunks**
- ½ **teaspoon kosher salt**
  Freshly ground pepper to taste
- 3 **cups white wine**

- 4 **cups diced seeded tomatoes** *or* **canned diced tomatoes**
- 2 **cups reduced-sodium chicken broth**
- ¼ **cup chopped flat-leaf parsley**
- 1 **generous pinch saffron threads (see** *Shopping Tips***)**

1. Heat oil in a large pot or Dutch oven over medium heat and add sausage. Cook, stirring occasionally, until the edges begin to color, 5 to 10 minutes. Add onion and garlic. Cover and cook for 10 minutes, stirring occasionally, until the onion is quite soft.

2. Sprinkle *Pimentón de la Vera* over the onion mixture; stir to coat. Cook for 1 minute. Add chicken, salt and pepper; stir to coat. Cook, stirring, for 5 minutes. Add wine and increase heat to high; cook until the wine is reduced by about a third, about 8 minutes.

3. Stir in tomatoes, broth, parsley and saffron; reduce heat to maintain a simmer and cook, uncovered, until the chicken is tender and the sauce is beginning to thicken, 1 to 1¼ hours. Season with more pepper, if desired.

PER 1/2-CUP SERVING: 185 calories; 7 g fat (2 g sat, 2 g mono); 38 mg cholesterol; 7 g carbohydrate; 0 g added sugars; 16 g protein; 1 g fiber; 230 mg sodium; 312 mg potassium.
NUTRITION BONUS: Vitamin A (18% daily value), Vitamin C (17% dv).

EatingWell Tip
Trim the fat from boneless, skinless chicken thighs before cooking to **cut down on saturated fat**.

Homemade Potato Gnocchi

H)(W H♥H

MAKES: about 12 dozen (6 cups) gnocchi, for 6 servings
ACTIVE TIME: 1 hour | TOTAL: 2¼ hours
TO MAKE AHEAD: Toss cooked gnocchi with olive oil and refrigerate in a single layer for up to 2 days. (Or freeze cooked gnocchi in a single layer on a lined baking sheet, transfer to an airtight container and freeze for up to 3 months. Defrost in the refrigerator.) Reheat gnocchi in boiling water until they float.

Traditional homemade gnocchi (little Italian dumplings) are made with just potato, flour, egg and salt. Be sure not to work the dough too much or the gnocchi will be tough. Toss them with your favorite sauce and dinner is served!

2 pounds medium Yukon Gold *or* russet potatoes
¾ teaspoon salt
1 large egg yolk, beaten
1-1¼ cups all-purpose flour, divided

1. Preheat oven to 400°F.

2. Pierce potatoes in several spots with a fork. Bake directly on the center rack until tender when pierced with a knife, 45 minutes to 1¼ hours, depending on the size and type of your potatoes. Remove to a wire rack and let stand until cool enough to handle, 15 to 20 minutes.

3. Scoop the insides out of the potato skins and push through a potato ricer fitted with a fine disc onto a clean counter (PHOTO 1, *opposite*). (If you don't have a ricer, mash the potatoes until smooth.) Gather the potato into a mound on the counter, sprinkle with salt and let cool, about 15 minutes.

4. Put a large pot of water on to boil.

5. Pour egg yolk over the cooled potato (*or for Spinach or Sun-Dried Tomato Gnocchi, see right*). Sprinkle 1 cup flour on top (PHOTO 2). Use a bench knife or metal spatula to gently fold the flour and egg into the potatoes (PHOTO 3) until combined (it will not look like dough at this point). Gently squeeze, knead and pat the dough until it holds together and resembles biscuit or cookie dough (PHOTO 4). The dough will be a little sticky; if it's very sticky, add more flour, about 1 tablespoon at a time, as necessary. Be careful not to overwork the dough: overworked dough will yield tougher gnocchi.

6. Pat the dough into a 1½-inch-thick disk and then divide it into 4 equal pieces (PHOTO 5). Working on a lightly floured surface with lightly floured hands, roll each portion into a 24- to 26-inch-long "snake," ½ to ¾ inch wide. Start at the center of the dough and roll out using your fingertips and very light pressure (PHOTO 6); gently pull the dough out as you roll. Cut the snake into ¾-inch pieces (PHOTO 7). Use your fingertip to make an indentation (or "dimple") in the center of each gnocchi (PHOTO 8). Place the gnocchi on a lightly floured baking sheet as they are made. Repeat with remaining dough.

7. Adjust the heat so the water is at a gentle boil. Add about one-quarter of the gnocchi at a time. When the gnocchi float to the top (PHOTO 9), transfer to a parchment or wax paper-lined baking sheet with a slotted spoon. Continue boiling the gnocchi in batches until they are all cooked, returning the water to a gentle boil between batches. Serve immediately or, to give them a golden-brown crust, cook about one-fourth of them at a time in 1 teaspoon extra-virgin olive oil in a large nonstick skillet over medium-high heat, stirring gently, about 2 minutes.

PER SERVING: 197 calories; 1 g fat (0 g sat, 0 g mono); 35 mg cholesterol; 43 g carbohydrate; 0 g added sugars; 6 g protein; 3 g fiber; 292 mg sodium; 659 mg potassium.
NUTRITION BONUS: Vitamin C (45% daily value), Potassium (19% dv), Folate (16% dv).

SPINACH AND SUN-DRIED TOMATO VARIATIONS (PHOTO 9)

For Spinach Gnocchi | Boil 5 ounces frozen thawed (or chopped fresh) spinach until tender, 2 to 3 minutes. Drain and squeeze out liquid; transfer to a food processor. Add the egg yolk and pulse until pureed.

For Sun-Dried Tomato Gnocchi | Soak ⅓ cup sun-dried tomatoes (*not* oil-packed) in boiling water until soft, 10 to 20 minutes. Drain; transfer to a food processor. Add the egg yolk and pulse until pureed.

In **Step 5**, pour the spinach puree or the sun-dried tomato puree over the cooled potatoes.

Neapolitan Meatballs

H✕W   H↑F

MAKES: 8 servings, 2-3 meatballs each
ACTIVE TIME: 1 hour | TOTAL: 2 hours
TO MAKE AHEAD: Cover and refrigerate for up to 3 days or freeze for up to 3 months.

A touch of cinnamon distinguishes these delicious tomato-sauced meatballs. Adding whole-grain bulgur allows you to use less meat, resulting in meatballs with less than half the total fat and saturated fat of the original. Plus a vibrant-tasting combination of fresh and canned tomatoes in the sauce helps reduce the sodium by two-thirds. Serve with pasta, polenta or even on a whole-grain roll with a bit of melted part-skim mozzarella for a meatball sub.

½	**cup bulgur (*see Tip, page 482*)**
2	**tablespoons extra-virgin olive oil, divided**
8	**cloves garlic, very thinly sliced**
¾	**teaspoon dried oregano**
¼	**teaspoon crushed red pepper**
2	**28-ounce cans diced tomatoes**
4	**cups diced plum tomatoes (about 1½ pounds)**
2	**cups cubed whole-wheat country bread**
1	**large egg**
1	**large egg white**
1	**pound 93%-lean ground beef**
½	**cup finely shredded Parmesan cheese**
½	**teaspoon ground cinnamon**
½	**teaspoon freshly ground pepper, plus more to taste**
⅛	**teaspoon salt**
½	**teaspoon sugar (optional)**

1. Place bulgur in a medium bowl and cover generously with hot water. Let soak for 30 minutes. Drain in a fine sieve, pressing to remove excess liquid.

2. Meanwhile, heat 1 tablespoon oil in a large Dutch oven over medium-low heat. Add garlic, oregano and crushed red pepper; cook, stirring, until softened but not browned, about 1 minute. Stir in canned tomatoes and plum tomatoes; increase heat to medium-high and bring to a simmer. Reduce heat to low. Partially cover and let simmer while you prepare meatballs.

3. Place bread in a medium bowl and cover with cold water. Let soak for a few minutes. Drain and squeeze out moisture.

4. Whisk egg and egg white in a large bowl. Add the bulgur, the bread, beef, Parmesan, cinnamon, pepper and salt. Gently combine with a potato masher and/or your hands. Form into 20 oval meatballs about 2 inches long.

5. Heat the remaining 1 tablespoon oil in a large nonstick skillet over medium-high heat. Add half the meatballs and cook, turning occasionally, until browned all over, 3 to 4 minutes. Transfer to a paper towel-lined plate; blot with paper towels. Brown the remaining meatballs.

6. Mash the simmering tomato sauce with a potato masher to break down any large chunks of tomato. Add the meatballs to the sauce. Simmer over low heat, partially covered, for 50 minutes.

7. Taste the sauce and add sugar, if it seems tart, and additional pepper to taste. Serve the meatballs with the sauce.

PER SERVING: 289 calories; 11 g fat (4 g sat, 5 g mono); 73 mg cholesterol; 23 g carbohydrate; 0 g added sugars; 23 g protein; 5 g fiber; 665 mg sodium; 462 mg potassium.
NUTRITION BONUS: Vitamin C (72% daily value), Vitamin A (38% dv), Zinc (27% dv), Iron (19% dv).

EatingWell Tip

Reduce the amount of ground beef in recipes by replacing some of it with bulgur. You'll still get a meaty taste and texture, but with **more fiber and less saturated fat**.

Fresh Tomato Sauce

H❌W H❤H

MAKES: 2 quarts (8 cups)
ACTIVE TIME: 1 hour | TOTAL: 1½ hours
TO MAKE AHEAD: Cover and refrigerate for up to 5 days or freeze for up to 6 months.

Take advantage of the summer harvest to stock your freezer with this sauce and you'll be one step closer to a garden-fresh meal.

4½	pounds plum tomatoes
¼	cup extra-virgin olive oil
¾	cup chopped garlic (about 2 heads)
4	cups diced onions (3-4 medium)
1½	teaspoons salt
¼	cup tomato paste
1	teaspoon dried oregano
½	cup red wine
2	tablespoons red-wine vinegar
½	cup chopped fresh basil
	Freshly ground pepper to taste

1. Peel, seed and chop tomatoes (*see How To*).

2. Heat oil in a Dutch oven over medium heat. Add garlic; cook, stirring constantly, until fragrant and just beginning to color, 2 to 3 minutes. Add onions and salt, stir to coat, cover and cook, stirring often and adjusting heat as necessary to prevent burning, until soft and turning golden, 10 to 15 minutes.

3. Stir in tomato paste and oregano and cook, stirring often, until the tomato paste is beginning to brown on the bottom of the pan, 2 to 4 minutes. Pour in wine and vinegar; bring to a simmer, scraping up any browned bits with a spoon. Cook until reduced slightly, about 2 minutes. Add the tomatoes and any juice from the bowl; return to a simmer, stirring often. Reduce heat to maintain a gentle simmer and cook, stirring occasionally, until the tomatoes are mostly broken down, about 25 minutes.

4. Remove from the heat; stir in basil and pepper. Transfer the sauce, in batches, to a blender or food processor. (Use caution when pureeing hot liquids.) Process to desired consistency. For a smooth sauce, puree it all; for a chunky sauce, puree just half and mix it back into the rest of the sauce.

PER 1/2-CUP SERVING: 88 calories; 4 g fat (1 g sat, 3 g mono); 0 mg cholesterol; 12 g carbohydrate; 0 g added sugars; 2 g protein; 2 g fiber; 223 mg sodium; 416 mg potassium.
NUTRITION BONUS: Vitamin C (35% daily value), Vitamin A (22% dv).

How To

Peel and Seed Fresh Tomatoes

1. Bring a large pot of water to a boil. Place a large bowl of ice water next to the stove. Using a sharp paring knife, core the tomatoes and score a small X into the flesh on the bottom.
2. Place the tomatoes in the boiling water, in batches, until the skins are slightly loosened, 30 seconds to 2 minutes.
3. Using a slotted spoon, transfer the tomatoes to the ice water and let sit for 1 minute before removing.
4. Place a sieve over a bowl; working over it, peel the tomatoes using a paring knife, and let the skins fall into the sieve.
5. Halve the tomatoes crosswise and scoop out the seeds with a hooked finger, letting the sieve catch the seeds. Press on the seeds and skins to extract any extra juice. Coarsely chop the peeled tomatoes.

Turkey Lasagna

H✂W   H↑F

MAKES: 9 servings

ACTIVE TIME: 45 minutes | TOTAL: 2 hours

TO MAKE AHEAD: Prepare through Step 6; refrigerate for up to 1 day. In Step 7, bake the lasagna, covered, for 1 hour before removing foil and topping with cheese.

Stealth veggies and lean ground turkey make over classic meat lasagna. The picky eaters in your family will never guess that this lasagna is loaded with healthy vegetables. When the more than 3 cups of vegetables take a trip through the food processor and cook down they disappear into the meat.

8	ounces lasagna noodles, preferably whole-wheat
3	cloves garlic, smashed and peeled
8	ounces cremini mushrooms, large ones cut in half
1	large carrot, cut into 2-inch pieces
1	stalk celery, cut into 2-inch pieces
1	large onion, peeled and cut into 2-inch pieces
2	teaspoons extra-virgin olive oil
1	pound lean (90-93%) ground turkey *or* beef
1½	teaspoons Italian seasoning
1	teaspoon fennel seeds
½	teaspoon freshly ground pepper
¼	teaspoon salt
2	cups part-skim ricotta cheese
1	large egg
1	24-ounce jar prepared marinara sauce
2	cups (8 ounces) Italian blend shredded cheese *or* shredded part-skim mozzarella, divided

1. Bring a large pot of water to a boil. Add noodles; cook until not quite tender, about 2 minutes less than the package directions. Drain; return the noodles to the pot and cover with cool water. Set aside.

2. With the food processor motor running, drop garlic through the feed tube and process until minced. Add mushrooms, carrot and celery and process until finely chopped. Turn the machine off, add onion and pulse until coarsely chopped.

3. Heat oil in a large skillet over medium-high heat. Add turkey (or beef) and cook, breaking up with a wooden spoon, until no longer pink, 4 to 6 minutes. Reduce heat to medium and add the vegetable mixture, Italian seasoning, fennel seeds, pepper and salt. Cook, stirring often, until the mushrooms' liquid has evaporated, the mixture has cooked down, the vegetables are soft and the skillet is dry, 12 to 15 minutes.

4. Combine ricotta and egg in a medium bowl.

5. Preheat oven to 350°F. Coat a 9-by-13-inch baking pan with cooking spray.

6. **To assemble lasagna:** Drain the noodles and spread out on a clean kitchen towel. Spread half the marinara in the prepared baking dish. Layer 3 noodles over the sauce. Spread half the ricotta mixture over the noodles. Top with half the meat mixture, one-third of the remaining marinara and one-third of the shredded cheese. Continue with another layer of noodles, the remaining ricotta, the remaining meat mixture, half the remaining marinara and half the remaining shredded cheese. Top with a third layer of noodles and the remaining marinara. Cover the lasagna with foil.

7. Bake until bubbling, about 45 minutes. Remove the foil; sprinkle the remaining shredded cheese on top. Bake until the cheese is just melted but not browned, 10 to 15 minutes more. Let stand for 10 to 20 minutes before serving.

PER SERVING: 400 calories; 16 g fat (7 g sat, 4 g mono); 84 mg cholesterol; 37 g carbohydrate; 0 g added sugars; 29 g protein; 6 g fiber; 726 mg sodium; 685 mg potassium.
NUTRITION BONUS: Vitamin A (46% daily value), Calcium (40% dv), Potassium (20% dv), Magnesium (19% dv), Zinc (18% dv), Iron (17% dv).

EatingWell Tip
Sneak some finely chopped vegetables into your ground-meat mixture for lasagna, meatloaf or chili to make servings generous but **keep calories and fat in check**.

Caramelized Onion Lasagna

H✖W   H⬆F

MAKES: 9 servings
ACTIVE TIME: 1 hour 10 minutes | **TOTAL:** 1 hour 40 minutes
TO MAKE AHEAD: Cover and refrigerate the caramelized onion filling (Step 2) for up to 1 day.

This lasagna with portobello mushrooms, sweet onions, spinach and Gorgonzola cheese has a rich, complex flavor. It's also great with goat cheese instead of Gorgonzola, if you prefer.

  8 **ounces lasagna noodles, preferably whole-wheat**

CARAMELIZED ONION FILLING
  3 **tablespoons extra-virgin olive oil**
  3 **large sweet onions, thinly sliced (about 10 cups)**
  4 **medium portobello mushroom caps, gills removed (see Tip, page 488), diced**
½ **cup red wine**
  1 **teaspoon salt**
    Freshly ground pepper to taste

SPINACH & CHEESE FILLING
  4 **cups baby spinach**
  2 **cups part-skim ricotta cheese**
½ **cup chopped fresh basil**
½ **teaspoon salt**

WHITE SAUCE & TOPPING
  2 **tablespoons extra-virgin olive oil**
  3 **tablespoons all-purpose flour**
  2 **cups low-fat milk**
½ **teaspoon salt**
  2 **ounces crumbled Gorgonzola cheese**
⅓ **cup chopped walnuts**
¼ **cup chopped fresh basil**

1. Bring a large pot of water to a boil. Add noodles; cook until not quite tender, about 2 minutes less than the package directions. Drain; return the noodles to the pot and cover with cool water. Set aside.

2. **To prepare onion filling:** Meanwhile, heat 3 table-spoons oil in a large skillet over medium heat. Add onions and cook, stirring frequently, until golden brown and very soft, about 25 minutes. (If they begin to stick, add water ¼ cup at a time to release them and prevent burning.) Add mushrooms and cook, stirring, until just beginning to soften, about 3 minutes. Add wine and 1 teaspoon salt and continue cooking until most of the liquid is absorbed, 2 to 3 minutes. Remove from heat; stir in pepper.

3. **To prepare spinach filling:** Place spinach, ricotta, basil and ½ teaspoon salt in a food processor and process until smooth.

4. **To prepare white sauce:** Heat 2 tablespoons oil in a medium saucepan over medium-high heat. Add flour and stir until bubbling, about 30 seconds. Gradually whisk in milk and ½ teaspoon salt and bring to a boil, whisking constantly. Cook, whisking, until the sauce has the consistency of thick gravy, about 1 minute. Add Gorgonzola and gently whisk until it is melted. Remove from the heat. (The sauce will continue to thicken as it sits.)

5. Preheat oven to 375°F. Coat a 9-by-13-inch baking pan with cooking spray.

6. **To assemble lasagna:** Drain the noodles and spread out on a clean kitchen towel. Spread ½ cup white sauce in the prepared pan. Place a layer of noodles over the sauce. Spread half of the spinach filling over the noodles and top with one-third of the onion fill-ing. Evenly spread ½ cup white sauce over the onions. Repeat with another layer of noodles, the remaining spinach filling, half the remaining onion filling and half the remaining white sauce. To finish, top with a third layer of noodles, spread the remaining onion fill-ing over the noodles and then spread or dollop the re-maining white sauce on top. Sprinkle with walnuts and basil.

7. Bake until hot and bubbling, about 30 minutes. Let stand for 5 minutes before serving.

PER SERVING: 387 calories; 18 g fat (6 g sat, 8 g mono); 25 mg cholesterol; 41 g carbohydrate; 0 g added sugars; 17 g protein; 6 g fiber; 720 mg sodium; 614 mg potassium.
NUTRITION BONUS: Vitamin A (33% daily value), Calcium (32% dv), Folate & Magnesium (22% dv), Potassium (18% dv), Zinc (15% dv).

Tandoori Tofu

Rice & Corn Cakes with Spicy Black Beans

Risotto with Edamame, Arugula & Porcini

Bean & Butternut Tacos with Green Salsa

Vegetarian

Tofu & Broccoli Stir-Fry

H✄W   H♥H

MAKES: 4 servings, 1¼ cups each
ACTIVE TIME: 30 minutes | TOTAL: 30 minutes

We like broccoli best in this tofu stir-fry, but any mixture of vegetables you have on hand will work. One way to get great tofu texture without deep-frying is to toss the tofu in cornstarch before stir-frying. Let it cook for several minutes without stirring to help it develop a little crust. Serve with Chinese egg noodles or rice noodles and a glass of Riesling.
Shopping Tip: *Sherry is a type of fortified wine originally from southern Spain. Don't use "cooking sherry" sold in many supermarkets—it can be surprisingly high in sodium. Instead, get dry sherry that's sold with other fortified wines at your wine or liquor store.*

½ **cup vegetable broth *or* reduced-sodium chicken broth**

¼ **cup dry sherry (*see Shopping Tip*) *or* rice wine**

3 **tablespoons reduced-sodium soy sauce**

3 **tablespoons cornstarch, divided**

2 **tablespoons plus 1 teaspoon sugar**

¼ **teaspoon crushed red pepper, *or* more to taste**

1 **14-ounce package extra-firm water-packed tofu, drained**

¼ **teaspoon salt**

2 **tablespoons canola oil, divided**

1 **tablespoon minced garlic**

1 **tablespoon minced fresh ginger**

6 **cups broccoli florets**

3 **tablespoons water**

1. Combine broth, sherry (or rice wine), soy sauce, 1 tablespoon cornstarch, sugar and crushed red pepper in a small bowl. Set aside.

2. Cut tofu into ¾-inch cubes and pat dry, then sprinkle with salt. Place the remaining 2 tablespoons cornstarch in a large bowl. Add the tofu; toss gently to coat. Heat 1 tablespoon oil in a large nonstick skillet or wok over medium-high heat. Add the tofu; cook, undisturbed, until browned, about 3 minutes. Gently turn and cook, stirring occasionally, until browned all over, 2 to 3 minutes more. Transfer to a plate.

3. Reduce heat to medium. Add the remaining 1 tablespoon oil, garlic and ginger; cook until fragrant, about 30 seconds. Add broccoli and water; cover and cook, stirring once or twice, until tender-crisp, 2 to 4 minutes. Stir the reserved broth mixture and add to the pan. Cook until the sauce has thickened, 1 to 2 minutes. Return the tofu to the pan; toss to combine with the broccoli and sauce.

PER SERVING: 258 calories; 13 g fat (1 g sat, 9 g mono); 0 mg cholesterol; 23 g carbohydrate; 7 g added sugars; 14 g protein; 4 g fiber; 544 mg sodium; 539 mg potassium.
NUTRITION BONUS: Vitamin C (168% daily value), Vitamin A (65% dv), Calcium (26% dv), Folate (23% dv), Magnesium (21% dv), Iron (17% dv), Potassium (15% dv).

EatingWell Tip

Use reduced-sodium soy sauce instead of regular soy sauce. You'll save about 370 mg of sodium per tablespoon.

Tandoori Tofu

H✖W H♥H

MAKES: 6 servings
ACTIVE TIME: 30 minutes | TOTAL: 30 minutes

A tandoori-inspired spice rub and smokiness from the grill flavor these tofu "steaks." While you're there, grill some vegetables, too, to serve alongside. Skewer cherry tomatoes and chunks of eggplant to grill along with the tofu.

- 2   teaspoons paprika
- 1   teaspoon salt, divided
- ½   teaspoon ground cumin
- ½   teaspoon ground coriander
- ¼   teaspoon ground turmeric
- 3   tablespoons extra-virgin olive oil
- 1   tablespoon minced garlic
- 1   tablespoon lime juice
- 2   14-ounce packages extra-firm *or* firm water-packed tofu, drained
- ⅔   cup nonfat plain yogurt
- 6   tablespoons sliced scallions *or* chopped fresh cilantro for garnish

1. Preheat grill to medium-high.

2. Combine paprika, ½ teaspoon salt, cumin, coriander and turmeric in a small bowl. Heat oil in a small skillet over medium heat. Add garlic, lime juice and the spice mixture; cook, stirring, until sizzling and fragrant, about 1 minute. Remove from the heat.

3. Slice each tofu block crosswise into 6 slices; pat dry. Use about 3 tablespoons of the spiced oil to brush both sides of the tofu slices; sprinkle with the remaining ½ teaspoon salt. (Reserve the remaining spiced oil.)

4. Oil the grill rack (*see Tip, page 485*). Grill the tofu until it has grill marks and is heated through, 2 to 3 minutes per side.

5. Combine yogurt with the reserved spiced oil in a small bowl. Serve the grilled tofu with the yogurt sauce, garnished with scallions (or cilantro), if desired.

PER SERVING: 173 calories; 13 g fat (2 g sat, 7 g mono); 1 mg cholesterol; 6 g carbohydrate; 0 g added sugars; 12 g protein; 2 g fiber; 419 mg sodium; 224 mg potassium.
NUTRITION BONUS: Calcium (31% daily value).

GUIDE:

6 Tasty Ways to Try Tofu

Tofu is an economical, low-fat and cholesterol-free protein source. And consuming 25 grams of soy protein a day, such as that in tofu, may help reduce the risk of heart disease. Here are some easy ways to incorporate tofu into your diet.

1. **START YOUR DAY WITH A TOFU-FRUIT SMOOTHIE:** Whirl ¼ cup **silken tofu**, ½ cup **frozen berries** (or peaches), ¾ cup **orange juice** and **sugar** (or honey) to taste in a blender.

2. **SCRAMBLE TOFU INSTEAD OF EGGS.** Sauté crumbled **tofu** (regular or silken) in a little **olive oil** and season with chopped fresh **herbs**, **salt** and **pepper**.

3. **SUBSTITUTE CUBES OF FIRM REGULAR TOFU FOR CHICKEN OR SEAFOOD** in stews, soups and stir-fries.

4. **GIVE CAESAR SALAD DRESSING CREAMY TEXTURE WITHOUT RAW EGG:** Blend ¼ cup **silken tofu**, 3 tablespoons grated **Parmesan cheese**, 2 tablespoons each low-fat **mayonnaise** and **lemon** juice, ½ teaspoon **anchovy paste**, ¼ teaspoon **Worcestershire sauce** and 1 minced **garlic** clove until smooth in a food processor or blender. (*Cover and refrigerate for up to 2 days.*)

5. **MAKE SANDWICHES WITH FLAVORED BAKED TOFU** (available in well-stocked supermarkets and natural-foods stores) instead of cold cuts and cheese.

6. **MAKE AN EGG-FREE TOFU MAYONNAISE** by pureeing 1 cup **silken tofu**, 2 tablespoons extra-virgin **olive oil**, 1 tablespoon **lemon juice**, 1 teaspoon Dijon **mustard**, ¼ teaspoon **sugar**, and **salt** and **pepper** to taste in a food processor.

Indian Mango Dal

H✕W   H↑F   H♥H

MAKES: 6 servings, about 1 cup each
ACTIVE TIME: 30 minutes | TOTAL: 40 minutes

Many types of dal (or dhal) are made across India. The basic dish contains lentils or other legumes flavored with aromatics and spices. Here, yellow lentils (toor dal) and mango are cooked in a more traditionally Southern India style—more souplike. Both ripe and underripe mango will work: less-ripe mango imparts a tart flavor and holds its shape, while riper mango breaks down more during cooking and gives the dish a sweeter taste. Serve over basmati rice or with roasted chicken.

1	cup yellow lentils
4	cups water
1	teaspoon salt, divided
½	teaspoon ground turmeric
1	tablespoon canola oil
½	teaspoon cumin seeds
1	medium onion, chopped
4	cloves garlic, minced
1	tablespoon minced fresh ginger
½	teaspoon ground coriander
¼	teaspoon cayenne pepper
2	mangoes, peeled and diced (*see How To*)
½	cup chopped fresh cilantro

1. Place lentils in a colander and rinse until the water runs clear. Combine lentils, 4 cups water, ½ teaspoon salt and turmeric in a large saucepan. Bring to a boil. Reduce heat to a simmer, partially cover and cook, stirring occasionally, for 15 minutes.

2. Meanwhile, heat oil in a large nonstick skillet over medium heat. Add cumin seeds and cook until fragrant and starting to brown, about 30 seconds. Add onion; cook, stirring, until soft and beginning to brown, 4 to 6 minutes. Add garlic, ginger, coriander, cayenne and the remaining ½ teaspoon salt and cook, stirring, for 1 minute more.

3. Stir the garlic mixture and mangoes into the lentils. Return to a simmer; cook, stirring occasionally, until the lentils are falling apart, 10 to 15 minutes more. Stir in cilantro.

PER SERVING: 186 calories; 3 g fat (0 g sat, 2 g mono); 0 mg cholesterol; 33 g carbohydrate; 0 g added sugars; 9 g protein; 9 g fiber; 398 mg sodium; 511 mg potassium.
NUTRITION BONUS: Folate (45% daily value), Vitamin C (40% dv), Iron (20% dv), Vitamin A (15% dv).

How To: Peel and Slice a Mango

   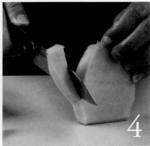

1. Slice both ends off the mango, revealing the long, slender seed inside.
2. Set the fruit upright on a work surface and cut off the skin with a sharp knife.
3. With the seed perpendicular to you, slice the fruit from both sides of the seed, yielding two large pieces.
4. Turn the seed parallel to you and slice the two smaller pieces of fruit from each side. Cut into desired size.

Sweet Potato, Corn & Black Bean Hash

H↑F H♥H

MAKES: 2 servings, about 2 cups each
ACTIVE TIME: 35 minutes | TOTAL: 35 minutes

This quick and easy hash is a fabulous one-pot meal. Serve with warm cornbread or tortillas.

- 2 teaspoons canola oil
- 2 medium onions, chopped
- 1 medium sweet potato, peeled and cut into ½-inch dice
- 2 large cloves garlic, minced
- 1 jalapeño pepper, seeded and minced
- 4 teaspoons ground cumin
- ½ teaspoon salt
- ¾ cup water
- ¾ cup frozen corn kernels
- 1 15-ounce can black beans, rinsed
- 2 tablespoons chopped fresh cilantro
  Freshly ground pepper to taste
- 1 lime, cut into wedges

Heat oil in a large skillet, preferably cast-iron, over medium-high heat. Add onions and cook, stirring occasionally, until browned in spots, 3 to 5 minutes. Add sweet potato and cook, stirring, until it starts to brown in spots, 5 to 7 minutes. Add garlic, jalapeño, cumin and salt; cook, stirring, until fragrant, about 30 seconds. Add water and cook, scraping up any browned bits, until liquid is absorbed, 3 to 5 minutes. Stir in corn and black beans and cook until heated through, 1 to 2 minutes. Stir in cilantro and season with salt and pepper. Serve with lime wedges.

PER SERVING: 377 calories; 7 g fat (1 g sat, 3 g mono); 0 mg cholesterol; 71 g carbohydrate; 0 g added sugars; 14 g protein; 17 g fiber; 756 mg sodium; 1,009 mg potassium. NUTRITION BONUS: Vitamin A (243% daily value), Vitamin C (63% dv), Folate (36% dv), Iron (31% dv).

EatingWell Tip
Most canned beans are high in sodium. Always rinse them before you use them—you'll **cut the sodium by about 35 percent**. Or make your own (see page 269).

▶ Hilary's Heavenly Eggs

H✖W H↑F

MAKES: 4 servings
ACTIVE TIME: 35 minutes | TOTAL: 35 minutes

This unusual combination of eggs braised in tomato sauce served on crusty bread is out of this world. Also try it over angel hair pasta. Serve with steamed broccolini.

- 2 tablespoons extra-virgin olive oil
- 1 medium onion, thinly sliced
- 2 cloves garlic, sliced
- 2 cups prepared marinara sauce
- 4 large eggs
- 6 large fresh basil leaves, torn into small pieces
- 1 tablespoon grated Parmesan cheese
- ¼ teaspoon freshly ground pepper
- 4 slices whole-wheat country bread, toasted

1. Heat oil in large skillet over medium heat. Add onion and garlic. Cook, stirring occasionally, until soft and beginning to brown, 4 to 6 minutes.

2. Reduce heat to medium-low. Add marinara and adjust heat to maintain a simmer. Crack an egg into a small bowl, taking care not to break the yolk. Make a well in the sauce roughly large enough to hold the egg and slip it in so that the yolk and most of the white is contained (some white may spread out). Repeat with the remaining eggs, evenly spacing them around the pan. Sprinkle the sauce with basil; cover and cook until the eggs are the desired doneness, 6 to 8 minutes for medium-set. Remove from the heat and sprinkle with Parmesan and pepper.

3. To serve, top each slice of toasted bread with an egg and sauce. Serve immediately.

PER SERVING: 345 calories; 17 g fat (4 g sat, 8 g mono); 215 mg cholesterol; 38 g carbohydrate; 1 g added sugars; 13 g protein; 6 g fiber; 768 mg sodium; 530 mg potassium. NUTRITION BONUS: Vitamin A (25% daily value), Iron (20% dv), Potassium (15% dv).

Risotto with Edamame, Arugula & Porcini

H✴W   H⬆F   H♥H

MAKES: 4 servings, 1½ cups each
ACTIVE TIME: 30 minutes | TOTAL: 40 minutes

Not up for 20 minutes of leaning over the stove? You can still enjoy this main-course risotto, studded with tasty green soybeans, because the microwave eliminates much of the constant stirring required for preparing a stovetop risotto.

- 1   **ounce dried porcini mushrooms** *or other* **dried mushrooms**
- 2   **cups water**
- 1   **10-ounce package frozen shelled edamame (about 2 cups)**
- 1½   **cups arborio rice**
- ¼   **cup chopped shallot**
- 1½   **tablespoons extra-virgin olive oil**
- 1   **teaspoon freshly grated lemon zest**
- 1   **tablespoon lemon juice**
- ½   **teaspoon salt**
- ½   **teaspoon freshly ground pepper**
- 2   **cups arugula, torn into bite-size pieces**
- ½   **cup freshly grated Parmesan cheese (1 ounce), plus shaved Parmesan for garnish**

1. Bring mushrooms and water to a boil in a small saucepan over high heat. Cover the pan and remove from the heat; let stand until the mushrooms are softened, about 10 minutes. Line a fine-mesh sieve with a wet paper towel and place over a large measuring cup or medium bowl. Pour the mushrooms and liquid into the sieve. Reserve the liquid. Transfer the mushrooms to a cutting board and let cool slightly, then coarsely chop. Add enough water to the strained liquid to equal 4½ cups; set aside the mushrooms and liquid for Step 4.

2. Cover edamame with water in a small saucepan and bring to a boil over high heat. Reduce heat to medium and simmer for 2 minutes; set aside in the cooking water.

3. Meanwhile, place rice and shallot in a shallow 3-quart baking dish that will fit and rotate properly in your microwave. Stir in oil until the rice is evenly coated. Spread the rice evenly in the dish and microwave, uncovered, on High until it looks opaque and is just beginning to color in one or two spots, 3 minutes.

4. Add lemon zest and juice, salt, pepper, the reserved chopped mushrooms and the mushroom water; stir well. Microwave on High for 9 minutes. Stir well, then microwave until the rice is tender but still firm in the center and most of the liquid has been absorbed, 9 minutes more. Depending on the power of your microwave, this last cooking time will vary. After 9 minutes, cook in 3-minute intervals, stopping to stir and test rice for doneness. Drain the edamame and add to the risotto along with arugula and Parmesan; stir until the arugula is wilted. Garnish with shaved Parmesan, if desired. Serve immediately.

PER SERVING: 325 calories; 12 g fat (3 g sat, 5 g mono); 9 mg cholesterol; 40 g carbohydrate; 0 g added sugars; 16 g protein; 5 g fiber; 458 mg sodium; 434 mg potassium.
NUTRITION BONUS: Folate (57% daily value), Iron (20% dv), Calcium (18% dv).

EatingWell Tip

Edamame (green soybeans) have a creamy texture. Stir them into main dishes, such as risotto, or toss them in salads to **add protein and fiber**. Look for shelled edamame in the freezer section of the supermarket.

Bean & Butternut Tacos with Green Salsa

H✂W H⬆F H❤H

MAKES: 4 servings, 2 tacos each
ACTIVE TIME: 1¼ hours | TOTAL: 1¼ hours
TO MAKE AHEAD: Prepare salsa (Steps 1-3), cover and refrigerate for up to 2 days.

Beans and roasted squash make an outstanding vegetarian taco filling. (Photograph: page 256.) **Shopping Tips: Tomatillos** *are tart, plum-size fruits that look like small, husk-covered green tomatoes. Find them in the produce section near the tomatoes. Remove husks and rinse well before using. For the best flavor, use fresh, good-quality* **Mexican oregano** *and* **chili powder**. *Find both at Latin markets or in the bulk spice section at well-stocked natural-foods stores.*

SALSA

- 8 ounces tomatillos (*see Shopping Tips*)
- 2 cloves garlic, unpeeled
- 1 jalapeño pepper
- ¼ cup sliced white onion
- ½ ripe avocado, diced
- 3 tablespoons chopped fresh cilantro
- ¼ teaspoon salt
  Freshly ground pepper to taste

TACOS

- 4 cups diced (½-inch) peeled butternut squash
- 3-4 small dried red chiles
- 2 cloves garlic, unpeeled, smashed and left whole
- 1 tablespoon extra-virgin olive oil
- ¾ teaspoon dried oregano, preferably Mexican (*see Shopping Tips*), divided
- ½ teaspoon salt, divided
- ¼ teaspoon cumin seeds, plus ½ teaspoon ground toasted cumin seeds (*see Tip, page 489*), divided
- 2 cups cooked pinto beans, drained (*see guide, opposite*)
- ½ teaspoon chili powder (*see Shopping Tips*)
  Freshly ground pepper to taste
- 8 6-inch corn tortillas
- ½ cup fresh cilantro leaves
- ½ cup finely shredded red *or* green cabbage
- 8 teaspoons crumbled *queso fresco* (*see Tip, page 488*) *or* feta cheese

1. **To prepare salsa:** Bring a pot of water to a boil. Remove husks from tomatillos and rinse well. Cook the tomatillos in the boiling water until soft, 5 to 8 minutes. Drain and set aside.

2. Toast garlic cloves, jalapeño and onion in a dry medium skillet over medium heat, turning occasionally, until browned, fragrant and soft, 5 to 7 minutes.

3. When cool enough to handle, peel the garlic. Remove the jalapeño stem and remove seeds if desired. Combine the tomatillos, garlic, jalapeño, onion and avocado in a blender or food processor. Process until smooth. Stir in cilantro, salt and pepper. Set aside for topping the tacos.

4. **To prepare tacos:** Preheat oven to 400°F.

5. Put squash in a medium bowl and, using kitchen shears, finely snip chiles to taste into small pieces (seeds and all) into the bowl. Add garlic, oil, ½ teaspoon oregano, ¼ teaspoon salt and whole cumin seeds; toss to coat. Arrange on a baking sheet in a single layer. Bake until soft and beginning to brown, 20 to 25 minutes. Peel and finely chop the garlic when cool enough to handle; stir into the squash.

6. Meanwhile, combine beans in a small saucepan with the remaining ¼ teaspoon oregano and ¼ teaspoon salt, ground cumin, chili powder and pepper. Heat over medium-low heat for about 10 minutes.

7. Warm tortillas one at a time in a dry large cast-iron (or similar heavy) skillet over medium heat until soft and pliable. Wrap in a clean towel to keep warm as you go. Spoon ¼ cup of the warm beans into each tortilla; divide the roasted squash evenly among the tacos and top each with cilantro, cabbage, ½ cup of the salsa and cheese. (*Refrigerate the remaining ½ cup salsa for up to 2 days.*)

PER SERVING: 406 calories; 9 g fat (2 g sat, 4 g mono); 3 mg cholesterol; 71 g carbohydrate; 0 g added sugars; 13 g protein; 14 g fiber; 518 mg sodium; 1,006 mg potassium. NUTRITION BONUS: Vitamin A (254% daily value), Vitamin C (60% dv), Folate (49% dv), Potassium (28% dv), Magnesium (25% dv), Iron (20% dv), Calcium (16% dv).

Multi-Bean Chili

H✖W H⬆F H♥H

MAKES: 6 servings, scant 2 cups each
ACTIVE TIME: 20 minutes | TOTAL: 35 minutes
TO MAKE AHEAD: Cover and refrigerate for up to 3 days
or freeze for up to 2 months.

Even confirmed carnivores will love this meatless chili because it's rib-sticking thick. Serve with a dollop of reduced-fat sour cream, minced scallions and a little shredded Cheddar.

1	tablespoon canola oil
1	large onion, diced
4	cloves garlic, minced
3	tablespoons chili powder
1	tablespoon ground cumin
¼-½	teaspoon ground chipotle chile (*see Tip, page 487*) *or* cayenne pepper, or to taste
1	28-ounce can crushed tomatoes
3	medium tomatoes, chopped
1	15-ounce can dark red kidney beans, rinsed
1	15-ounce can small white beans, such as navy beans, rinsed
1	15-ounce can black beans, rinsed
3	cups water
½	teaspoon freshly ground pepper

Heat oil in a Dutch oven over medium heat. Add onion and cook, stirring, until beginning to soften, 2 to 3 minutes. Reduce heat to medium-low and cook, stirring often, until very soft and just beginning to brown, 3 to 4 minutes. Add garlic, chili powder, cumin and chipotle (or cayenne) to taste and cook, stirring constantly, until fragrant, 30 seconds to 1 minute. Stir in canned and fresh tomatoes, kidney, white and black beans, water and pepper. Increase heat to high and bring to a boil, stirring often. Reduce heat to a simmer and cook, stirring occasionally, until the chili has reduced slightly, 10 to 15 minutes.

PER SERVING: 263 calories; 4 g fat (0 g sat, 2 g mono); 0 mg cholesterol; 49 g carbohydrate; 0 g added sugars; 14 g protein; 15 g fiber; 761 mg sodium; 868 mg potassium. NUTRITION BONUS: Vitamin C (60% daily value), Vitamin A (45% dv), Iron (29% dv), Potassium (25% dv), Folate (21% dv).

GUIDE:

Cooking Beans

We always keep canned beans on hand because they're convenient and healthy. But if you have time, cooking your own dried beans is a great option: you'll save money, reduce sodium and get better flavor. Try substituting homemade cooked beans for canned beans in any recipe. Freeze any extra cooked beans to use in soups, salads and dips.

Equivalents

- A pound of dried beans (about 2 cups) will yield 5 to 6 cups cooked beans.
- One 19-ounce can yields about 2 cups cooked beans; a 15-ounce can, about 1½ cups.

Soaking

To soak or not to soak? Soaking beans before cooking helps them to cook more evenly and cuts down on the total cooking time. So if you've planned ahead, soak them. If you don't have time, skip the soaking, but plan to cook them longer.

OVERNIGHT SOAK: Rinse and pick over the beans, then place in a large bowl with enough cold water to cover by 2 inches. Let the beans soak for at least 8 hours or overnight. Drain.

QUICK SOAK: Rinse and pick over the beans, then place them in a large pot with enough cold water to cover them by 2 inches. Bring to a boil. Boil for 2 minutes. Remove from the heat and let stand, covered, for 1 hour; drain.

Cooking

CONVENTIONAL METHOD: Place the drained, soaked beans in a large pot and add enough cold water to cover them by 2 inches (about 2 quarts of water for 1 pound of beans). Bring to a boil, skimming off any debris that rises to the surface. Reduce the heat to low and simmer gently, stirring occasionally, until the beans are tender, 20 minutes to 3 hours (cooking time will vary with the type and age of bean). Add salt to taste.

SLOW-COOKER METHOD: Place the drained, soaked beans in a slow cooker and pour in 5 cups boiling water. Cover and cook on High until tender, 2 to 3½ hours. Add salt to taste, and cook 15 minutes more.

Rice & Corn Cakes
with Spicy Black Beans

H✖W   H⬆F   H❤H

MAKES: 4 servings
ACTIVE TIME: 35 minutes | **TOTAL:** 50 minutes

These crispy fried patties get a swift kick from the easy-to-make bean-and-salsa accompaniment. Instant brown rice only takes about 10 minutes, a great shortcut on a busy night. Garnish with lime wedges and scallions.

- 1 **cup instant brown rice**
- 6 **scallions, trimmed and sliced**
- 2 **teaspoons minced garlic**
- 1½ **teaspoons chopped fresh thyme *or* ½ teaspoon dried, crushed**
- 1 **cup frozen corn**
- 1 **cup fresh whole-wheat breadcrumbs (*see Tip, page 481*)**
- ½ **teaspoon salt**
- ¼ **teaspoon freshly ground pepper**
- 2 **large eggs**
- 4 **teaspoons extra-virgin olive oil, divided**
- 1 **15-ounce can black beans, rinsed**
- 1 **cup tomato salsa**

1. Cook rice according to package directions, adding scallions, garlic and thyme to the water. Remove from heat and stir in corn, breadcrumbs, salt and pepper. Let stand for about 5 minutes to cool slightly.

2. Whisk eggs in a large bowl until frothy. Add the rice mixture and mash with a potato masher until the mixture holds together (it will be fairly soft), about 1 minute. Shape the mixture into 8 patties.

3. Heat 2 teaspoons oil in a medium nonstick skillet over medium-high heat. Carefully transfer 4 patties to the pan with a spatula and cook until browned and crispy, about 3 minutes per side. Transfer to a plate; cover to keep warm. Wipe out the pan with a paper towel, add the remaining 2 teaspoons oil and repeat with the remaining 4 patties.

4. Meanwhile, combine beans and salsa in a small saucepan and cook over medium-high heat, stirring occasionally, until hot, about 5 minutes. To serve, divide the beans among 4 plates and top with 2 patties each.

PER SERVING: 368 calories; 9 g fat (2 g sat, 5 g mono); 106 mg cholesterol; 61 g carbohydrate; 0 g added sugars; 15 g protein; 9 g fiber; 655 mg sodium; 566 mg potassium.
NUTRITION BONUS: Vitamin C (25% daily value), Folate (22% dv), Iron (17% dv), Potassium (16% dv).

EatingWell Tip

Always keep frozen vegetables on hand for those last-minute dinners when you don't have any fresh vegetables in the crisper. **They're picked and frozen at their peak of ripeness when they are most nutrient-packed.**

Brown Rice & Tofu Maki

H✂W   H♥H

MAKES: 8 servings, 6 pieces each
ACTIVE TIME: 1 hour 5 minutes | TOTAL: 2 hours
EQUIPMENT: Bamboo sushi rolling mat (maki rolling mat)

Maki is the Japanese name for "sushi rolls." Short-grain rice is full of amylopectin, a sticky starch, which gives it its characteristic chewiness. Serve with wasabi, soy sauce and pickled ginger. **Shopping Tips: Mirin** *is a low-alcohol rice wine essential to Japanese cooking. Toasted* **nori** *sheets are thin, dried seaweed wrappers used for maki rolls. Be sure to choose nori that is labeled "toasted" when making maki— untoasted nori is too chewy. Look for both ingredients in the Asian section of the supermarket or at Asian markets.*

4¼	cups water
2¼	cups short-grain brown rice
3	tablespoons mirin (*see Shopping Tips*)
3	tablespoons reduced-sodium soy sauce
3½	teaspoons sugar, divided
⅓	cup rice vinegar
½	teaspoon salt
8	sheets toasted nori seaweed (*see Shopping Tips*)
32	matchstick strips flavored baked tofu, such as Thai *or* teriyaki (about 3 ounces)
32	matchstick strips red bell pepper (about 1 small pepper)
32	matchstick strips peeled and seeded cucumber (about ½ small)
5	tablespoons unsalted roasted peanuts, chopped

1. Bring water to a boil in a large saucepan over medium heat. Stir in rice, reduce heat to low, cover, and simmer at the lowest bubble until the rice is tender, about 50 minutes (*see How To*). Remove from the heat and let stand, covered, for 10 minutes.

2. Meanwhile, stir mirin, soy sauce and 1½ teaspoons sugar in a small skillet. Bring to a simmer and cook until slightly thickened, about 3 minutes.

3. Spread the warm rice evenly on a large rimmed baking sheet. Whisk vinegar, the remaining 2 teaspoons sugar and salt in a small bowl; drizzle over the rice. Toss with 2 spatulas until cool enough to handle and slightly sticky.

4. Place a nori sheet on a sushi-rolling mat—shiny side down with a shorter end close to you. Wet your hands and pat about ¾ cup of the seasoned rice into a thin layer on the sheet (PHOTO 1), leaving a 1-inch border at the top (the short side on the far end of the mat). Drizzle 1 teaspoon of the mirin sauce about 1 inch from the bottom of the rice; place 4 strips each baked tofu, bell pepper and cucumber over the sauce (PHOTO 2); then sprinkle with about 2 teaspoons chopped peanuts. Using the bamboo mat to help you, roll the maki closed, getting the mat out from inside the maki as it rolls up (PHOTO 3). Gently press the closed mat over the roll to seal the roll (PHOTO 4). Trim any ragged edges and slice into 6 pieces with a wet sharp knife.

5. Repeat Step 4 with the remaining nori, rice, tofu, vegetables and peanuts. Serve with any remaining sauce.

PER SERVING: 287 calories; 5 g fat (1 g sat, 2 g mono); 0 mg cholesterol; 48 g carbohydrate; 2 g added sugars; 9 g protein; 3 g fiber; 393 mg sodium; 230 mg potassium.
NUTRITION BONUS: Vitamin A (61% daily value), Vitamin C (28% dv), Magnesium (23% dv).

How To

Cook Rice | Perfectly cooked rice can be tricky. To cook whole-grain rice, we recommend a pan with a tight-fitting lid, cooking on your coolest (or simmer) burner and making sure the rice is simmering at the "lowest bubble."

Red Onion & Goat Cheese Pancake

H✖W H♥H

MAKES: 4 main-dish servings *or* 8 side-dish servings
ACTIVE TIME: 30 minutes | TOTAL: 40 minutes

The technique for this pancake is similar to that for a Dutch baby or German pancake, but the savory onion and goat cheese combination is a surprise for those who think of pancakes as breakfast food only. Serve with a mixed green salad for a light supper or as a side dish with grilled or roasted meat.

1	tablespoon extra-virgin olive oil
2	large red onions, sliced (*see How To*)
2	tablespoons water
2	tablespoons chopped fresh thyme
½	cup all-purpose flour
½	cup low-fat milk
2	large eggs
2	large egg whites
1	tablespoon canola oil
1	tablespoon sugar
¼	teaspoon salt
¼	teaspoon freshly ground pepper
¼	cup crumbled goat cheese
1	cup balsamic vinegar
2	teaspoons honey

1. Heat olive oil in a large cast-iron or ovenproof nonstick skillet over medium-high heat. Reduce heat to medium, add onions and cook, stirring occasionally, until they are tender and light golden brown, 15 to 20 minutes. Stir in water and thyme, scraping up any browned bits.

2. Meanwhile, position rack in middle of oven; preheat to 450°F.

3. Blend flour, milk, eggs, egg whites, canola oil, sugar, salt and pepper in a blender until smooth. Pour the batter over the onions. Sprinkle with cheese.

4. Bake the pancake until it is puffed and golden, about 15 minutes.

5. Meanwhile, combine vinegar and honey in a small saucepan. Bring to a boil over medium-high heat and cook until syrupy and reduced to ⅓ cup, 12 to 15 minutes. (Watch carefully during the last few minutes to prevent burning.) Cut the pancake into wedges and serve immediately with the balsamic syrup.

PER MAIN-DISH SERVING: 308 calories; 12 g fat (3 g sat, 6 g mono); 111 mg cholesterol; 38 g carbohydrate; 6 g added sugars; 10 g protein; 2 g fiber; 267 mg sodium; 314 mg potassium.

How To

Cut Onions Without Crying | Onions contain a volatile compound called a lachrymator that reacts with the fluid in your eyes and makes them water. To chop them without crying, try wearing goggles or burning a candle nearby.

Savory Carrot & Tarragon Tart

H ✖ W

MAKES: 8 servings

ACTIVE TIME: 45 minutes | TOTAL: 1¾ hours

TO MAKE AHEAD: Prepare the crust (Step 2), wrap tightly and refrigerate for up to 3 days. Loosely cover and refrigerate the baked tart for up to 1 day. | EQUIPMENT: 9- to 10-inch tart pan (with or without removable bottom)

The bright orange carrots in this savory tart are a feast for the eyes and the palate. Tarragon lends bold flavor; other herbs, such as thyme or rosemary, would be delicious too.

CRUST

1	cup all-purpose flour
½	cup whole-wheat flour
1½	teaspoons fresh tarragon leaves *or* ½ teaspoon dried
½	teaspoon salt
4	tablespoons cold unsalted butter, cut into small pieces
¼	cup extra-virgin olive oil *or* canola oil
¼	cup low-fat plain yogurt

FILLING

2	tablespoons extra-virgin olive oil *or* canola oil
1	cup thinly sliced red onion
1½	cups grated carrots
2	tablespoons dry sherry (*see Tip, page 489*) *or* rice vinegar, divided
1	tablespoon Dijon mustard
½	cup shredded reduced-fat Cheddar cheese
½	cup low-fat plain yogurt
½	cup low-fat milk
2	large eggs
2	teaspoons finely chopped fresh tarragon *or* ¾ teaspoon dried
¼	teaspoon salt
⅛	teaspoon freshly ground pepper

1. Preheat oven to 350°F.

2. **To prepare crust:** Coat a 9- to 10-inch tart pan with cooking spray. Place all-purpose flour, whole-wheat flour, tarragon and ½ teaspoon salt in a food processor; pulse to combine. Add butter one piece at a time, pulsing once or twice after each addition, until incorporated. Add ¼ cup oil and ¼ cup yogurt and pulse just until the dough starts to come together. Transfer the dough to the prepared pan (it will be crumbly), spread evenly and press firmly into the bottom and all the way up the sides to form a crust.

3. Bake the crust until set but not browned, about 15 minutes. Let cool on a wire rack.

4. **To prepare filling:** Heat 2 tablespoons oil in a large skillet over medium heat. Add onion and cook, stirring occasionally, until tender, about 5 minutes. Stir in carrots and 1 tablespoon sherry (or rice vinegar) and cook, stirring, for 2 minutes. Remove from the heat.

5. Spread mustard over the crust. Sprinkle with Cheddar, then evenly spread the carrot mixture in the tart shell.

6. Whisk ½ cup yogurt, milk, eggs, tarragon, the remaining 1 tablespoon sherry (or rice vinegar), ¼ teaspoon salt and pepper in a medium bowl. Place the tart pan on a baking sheet and pour in the filling.

7. Bake the tart until the filling is firm and the edges are golden brown, 40 to 45 minutes. Let cool for 15 minutes before slicing. Serve warm or chilled.

PER SERVING: 297 calories; 19 g fat (7 g sat, 9 g mono); 72 mg cholesterol; 24 g carbohydrate; 0 g added sugars; 8 g protein; 2 g fiber; 342 mg sodium; 248 mg potassium.
NUTRITION BONUS: Vitamin A (75% daily value), Folate (17% dv).

Sweet Potato, Red Onion & Fontina Tart

H⬆F

MAKES: 12 servings
ACTIVE TIME: 40 minutes | TOTAL: 1¾ hours
TO MAKE AHEAD: Prepare the crust (Step 2), wrap tightly and refrigerate for up to 3 days or freeze for up to 6 months. Cool, cover and refrigerate the baked tart for up to 1 day. Reheat at 350°F for about 20 minutes.

Try this roasted-vegetable free-form tart as a vegetarian main dish or as an appetizer or side dish for a special dinner. The pastry dough is very forgiving and quite easy to roll out on parchment paper or a nonstick baking mat. The walnut-studded crust is crisper served warm, but you can enjoy the tart at room temperature or even cold.

CRUST

- ¾ cup walnuts
- 1¼ cups whole-wheat pastry flour (*see Tip, page 485*)
- 1¼ cups all-purpose flour, plus more for dusting
- 2 tablespoons chopped fresh thyme *and/or* rosemary
- ¾ teaspoon salt
- ¾ teaspoon freshly ground pepper
- ½ cup extra-virgin olive oil
- 7 tablespoons ice-cold water

FILLING

- 1½ pounds sweet potatoes, peeled and sliced into ¼-inch-thick slices
- 1 tablespoon plus 2 teaspoons extra-virgin olive oil, divided
- ½ teaspoon salt
- ¼ teaspoon freshly ground pepper
- 1½ cups thinly sliced red onion
- 1 cup shredded fontina *or* Cheddar cheese
- 1 large egg white mixed with 1 teaspoon water
- 1 teaspoon chopped fresh thyme *and/or* rosemary

1. Preheat oven to 425°F.

2. **To prepare crust:** Pulse walnuts in a food processor until finely ground. Combine in a large bowl with whole-wheat flour, all-purpose flour, 2 tablespoons thyme and/or rosemary, ¾ teaspoon each salt and pepper. Make a well in the center and add ½ cup oil and water. Gradually stir the wet ingredients into the dry ingredients to form a soft dough (it will seem wetter than other types of pastry dough). Knead in the bowl just until the dough comes together. Pat it into a disk, wrap in plastic and refrigerate for at least 15 minutes or up to 3 days.

3. **To prepare filling:** Combine sweet potatoes, 1 tablespoon oil, ½ teaspoon salt and ¼ teaspoon pepper in a large bowl. Spread on three-fourths of a large rimmed baking sheet. Toss onion in the bowl with 1 teaspoon oil. Spread evenly on the remaining one-fourth of the baking sheet. Roast for 10 minutes. Remove from the oven. Reduce temperature to 375°.

4. Line a work surface with parchment paper or a non-stick baking mat, lightly dust with flour and dust the top of the dough with flour. Roll the dough into a rustic 15-inch circle, adding more flour, if necessary, to prevent sticking. Transfer the crust to a baking sheet with the parchment or baking mat in place.

5. Leaving a 2-inch border, sprinkle cheese evenly over the crust. Make an overlapping ring of the larger sweet potato slices over the cheese, leaving the 2-inch border. Spread the onion slices in another ring closer to the center. Using the rest of the sweet potato slices, make an overlapping circle in the center of the crust (the pattern will look like a bull's-eye). Pick up the edges of the crust using a spatula and fold over the filling, making pleats in the dough as necessary (it's OK if the dough cracks a little as you fold it); the filling will not be completely covered. Brush the crust with the egg-white wash. Drizzle the vegetables with the remaining 1 teaspoon oil and sprinkle with 1 teaspoon thyme and/or rosemary.

6. Bake the tart until lightly browned on the edges, about 50 minutes. Cool for 10 minutes before slicing.

PER SERVING: 309 calories; 18 g fat (4 g sat, 10 g mono); 10 mg cholesterol; 30 g carbohydrate; 0 g added sugars; 7 g protein; 3 g fiber; 332 mg sodium; 180 mg potassium.
NUTRITION BONUS: Vitamin A (140% daily value).

Black Bean & Salmon Tostadas

Seared Scallops with Sautéed Cucumbers

Arctic Char on a Bed of Kale

Sugar Snap Pea & Shrimp Curry

Fish & Seafood

Sugar Snap Pea & Shrimp Curry

H✂W H♥H

MAKES: 4 servings
ACTIVE TIME: 25 minutes | TOTAL: 25 minutes

This dish is best done at the last minute so the snap peas keep their crisp texture. The pink of the shrimp and the green peas make it as pretty as it is tasty. (Photograph: page 278.)

2	tablespoons canola oil
2	tablespoons Madras curry powder
1½	pounds raw shrimp (16-20 per pound; *see Tip, page 489*), peeled and deveined
1	pound sugar snap peas, trimmed
1	cup "lite" coconut milk
¼	cup lemon juice
½	teaspoon salt

Heat oil in a wok or large skillet over medium heat. Add curry powder and cook, stirring, until fragrant, 1 to 2 minutes. Add shrimp and peas and cook, stirring, until the shrimp are almost cooked through, about 4 minutes. Stir in coconut milk, lemon juice and salt. Bring to a boil and cook until the shrimp have cooked through, about 2 minutes more.

PER SERVING: 349 calories; 15 g fat (4 g sat, 5 g mono); 259 mg cholesterol; 15 g carbohydrate; 1 g added sugars; 39 g protein; 4 g fiber; 563 mg sodium; 593 mg potassium.
NUTRITION BONUS: Vitamin C (125% daily value), Iron (40% dv), Vitamin A (30% dv), Magnesium (24% dv), Potassium (17% dv), Calcium & Zinc (15% dv).

EatingWell Tip

Keep a bag of shrimp in your freezer and you'll have a **quick, healthy dinner option at your fingertips**. Shrimp take only a couple minutes to thaw and then cook, and a 3-ounce serving has about 85 calories.

Black Bean & Salmon Tostadas

H✂W H↑F H♥H

MAKES: 4 servings, 2 tostadas each
ACTIVE TIME: 25 minutes | TOTAL: 25 minutes

Tostadas made with your own crispy shells are a great way to perk up canned salmon. Serve with lime wedges. (Photograph: page 278.)

8	6-inch corn tortillas
	Canola oil cooking spray
1	6- to 7-ounce can boneless, skinless wild Alaskan salmon (*see Tip, page 488*), drained
1	ripe avocado, diced
2	tablespoons minced pickled jalapeños, plus 2 tablespoons pickling juice from the jar, divided
2	cups coleslaw mix (*see Tip, page 483*) or shredded cabbage
2	tablespoons chopped cilantro
1	15-ounce can black beans, rinsed
3	tablespoons reduced-fat sour cream
2	tablespoons prepared salsa
2	scallions, chopped

1. Position racks in upper and lower thirds of the oven; preheat to 375°F.

2. Coat tortillas on both sides with cooking spray. Place on 2 baking sheets. Bake, turning once, until light brown, 12 to 14 minutes.

3. Combine salmon, avocado and jalapeños in a bowl. Combine the pickling juice with coleslaw mix (or cabbage) and cilantro in another bowl. Process black beans, sour cream, salsa and scallions in a food processor until smooth. Transfer to a microwavable bowl. Cover and microwave on High until hot, about 2 minutes. To assemble tostadas, spread each tortilla with some bean mixture and some salmon mixture and top with the cabbage salad.

PER SERVING: 319 calories; 11 g fat (2 g sat, 6 g mono); 16 mg cholesterol; 43 g carbohydrate; 0 g added sugars; 16 g protein; 12 g fiber; 352 mg sodium; 670 mg potassium.
NUTRITION BONUS: Vitamin C (60% daily value), Folate (27% dv), Potassium (19% dv), Iron (18% dv), omega-3s.

Choosing Seafood

You know you're supposed to be eating fish and seafood for your health, but on the flip side you're bombarded with bad news about wild fish populations, mercury in fish and problems with fish farms. There's a lot to consider when it comes to deciding which seafood to eat. At EATINGWELL we only develop recipes using fish and seafood that is OK to eat according to the experts.

A Healthy Choice:

Studies have shown that eating fish at least twice a week is associated with a 30 percent lower risk of developing heart disease. And eating seafood that's high in DHA and EPA, two types of omega-3 fatty acids, has an even more positive effect on heart disease. Plus, omega-3s have been linked with a reduced risk of depression, improved brain development and reduced inflammation. The only catch with omega-3s: some of the best sources are larger fish, such as tuna, which tend to have higher levels of mercury contamination. So it's a balancing act—sardines, mussels, rainbow trout and wild Alaskan salmon are all good options because they have low levels of mercury *and* are also good sources of omega-3s.

Rules of Thumb:

THE SMALLER THE BETTER: Fish that are lower on the food chain are less contaminated with toxins and reproduce quickly so their populations tend to be more stable. Good examples include anchovies, sardines, herring and mackerel.

FISH FARMS: When it comes to aquaculture, typically the best option is fish raised in closed-system freshwater farms. U.S. farmed catfish, rainbow trout and tilapia are all best choices for the environment, readily available and inexpensive.

FARMED BIVALVES: Farmed clams, mussels and oysters are best choices for the environment. They can actually improve water quality in areas where they are farmed because they filter and clean water as they feed.

U.S. FISHERIES: The U.S. has been a lot more aggressive about regulating fisheries and aquaculture than many other countries. So it's often a better choice environmentally to go with U.S. fish and seafood as opposed to imported.

Helpful Tools:

CARRY A POCKET GUIDE. Blue Ocean Institute (*blueocean.org*), Seafood Watch (*seafoodwatch.org*) and Environmental Defense Fund (*edf.org*) have handy wallet-size guides for seafood and sushi that you can download or order.

PHONE IT IN! Text 30644 with the word "fish" followed by a space and the seafood you are considering. In about 10 seconds you will get up-to-date facts and sustainability ratings from the Blue Ocean Institute. Or try the iPhone app from Seafood Watch, which provides all their recommendations on sustainable seafood choices.

LOOK FOR THE MSC BLUE ECO LABEL. The independent, nonprofit Marine Stewardship Council (MSC) certifies wild fishcries that are well-managed and sustainable. (At present it does not look at farmed fish.)

For info on the specific fish or seafood recommended in the recipes in this book, check the glossary, pages 481-490. (The recipes and information in this book are based on the guidelines from Monterey Bay Aquarium as of spring 2010.)

Artichoke & Olive Tuna Salad

H✕W H♥H

MAKES: 5 servings, about ¾ cup each
ACTIVE TIME: 15 minutes | TOTAL: 15 minutes
TO MAKE AHEAD: Cover and refrigerate for up to 2 days.

Serve this salad with sliced tomato on a bed of lettuce or on French bread.

2   5- to 6-ounce cans water-packed chunk
    light tuna (*see Tip, page 490*), drained
    and flaked
1   cup chopped canned artichoke hearts
½   cup chopped olives
⅓   cup low-fat mayonnaise
2   teaspoons lemon juice
1½ teaspoons chopped fresh oregano
    or ½ teaspoon dried

Combine tuna, artichokes, olives, mayonnaise, lemon juice and oregano in a medium bowl.

PER SERVING: 113 calories; 5 g fat (1 g sat, 2 g mono);
14 mg cholesterol; 8 g carbohydrate; 1 g added sugars;
10 g protein; 2 g fiber; 467 mg sodium; 87 mg potassium.

EatingWell Tip

Get more fatty fish like tuna and salmon into your diet. They contain omega-3 fatty acids that have been linked to **improving heart health and brain function**.

▶ Pistachio-Crusted Tuna Steaks

H✕W H♥H

MAKES: 4 servings
ACTIVE TIME: 30 minutes | TOTAL: 30 minutes

A pistachio crust teams up with a savory mustard-dill sauce for an exceptional tuna dish.

1   tablespoon thinly sliced shallot
1   bay leaf
½   cup dry white wine
3   tablespoons reduced-fat sour cream
2   teaspoons lemon juice
2   teaspoons chopped fresh dill, divided
1   teaspoon whole-grain mustard
½   teaspoon salt, divided
¼   cup coarse dry breadcrumbs, preferably
    whole-wheat (*see Tip, page 481*)
¼   cup shelled pistachios
4   4-ounce tuna steaks, 1-1¼ inches thick
    (*see Tip, page 490*)
1   teaspoon extra-virgin olive oil

1. Place shallot, bay leaf and wine in a small saucepan and bring to a boil. Reduce until the wine is almost evaporated, about 5 minutes. Transfer to a small bowl; discard bay leaf. Add sour cream, lemon juice, 1 teaspoon dill, mustard and ¼ teaspoon salt; stir to combine.

2. Put breadcrumbs, pistachios, the remaining dill and ¼ teaspoon salt in a blender or food processor. Process until finely ground. Transfer to a shallow bowl. Dredge both sides of the tuna in the pistachio mixture.

3. Heat oil in a large nonstick skillet over medium heat. Add the tuna and cook until browned, adjusting the heat as necessary to prevent burning, 4 to 5 minutes per side for medium-rare. Serve with the lemon-dill sauce.

PER SERVING: 239 calories; 7 g fat (2 g sat, 3 g mono);
55 mg cholesterol; 8 g carbohydrate; 0 g added sugars;
29 g protein; 1 g fiber; 371 mg sodium; 631 mg potassium.
NUTRITION BONUS: Magnesium & Potassium (18% daily value).

Sautéing Fish

Do your body good—eat more fish! Fish is an excellent source of lean protein. Plus thin fillets cook up in minutes to get dinner on the table fast. Just top them with one of these easy no-cook sauces for a restaurant-worthy entree.

Easy Sautéed Fish Fillets

H✂W   H❤H

MAKES: 4 servings
ACTIVE TIME: 15 minutes | TOTAL: 15 minutes

Here's an easy method for quickly cooking fish fillets. Any thin white fish fillet will work in this recipe. Sustainable choices include Pacific sole or U.S. farm-raised catfish or tilapia.

- ⅓ **cup all-purpose flour**
- ½ **teaspoon salt**
- ¼ **teaspoon freshly ground pepper**
- 1 **pound catfish, tilapia, Pacific sole *or* other white fish fillets, cut into 4 portions**
- 1 **tablespoon extra-virgin olive oil**

1. Combine flour, salt and pepper in a shallow dish; thoroughly dredge fillets (discard any leftover flour).

2. Heat oil in a large nonstick skillet over medium-high heat. Add the fish, working in batches if necessary, and cook until lightly browned and just opaque in the center, 3 to 4 minutes per side. Serve immediately.

PER SERVING: 173 calories; 5 g fat (1 g sat, 3 g mono); 54 mg cholesterol; 8 g carbohydrate; 0 g added sugars; 22 g protein; 0 g fiber; 383 mg sodium; 422 mg potassium.

EatingWell Tip

Use a nonstick skillet when you're sautéing fish. You can **use less oil and delicate fish won't stick to the pan** or break apart.

No-Cook Sauces

TARTAR SAUCE

MAKES: about ½ cup
ACTIVE TIME: 10 minutes | TOTAL: 10 minutes
TO MAKE AHEAD: Cover and refrigerate for up to 5 days.

Combine ½ cup low-fat **mayonnaise**, 1 chopped **cornichon** (or sour gherkin pickle), 1 minced **anchovy fillet**, 1 tablespoon minced **shallot** and 1 teaspoon each chopped **capers**, dried **tarragon** and chopped fresh **parsley** in a small bowl. Stir in 2 teaspoons **lemon juice** and freshly ground **pepper** to taste.

PER TABLESPOON: 51 calories; 4 g fat (0 g sat, 1 g mono); 8 mg cholesterol; 4 g carbohydrate; 1 g added sugars; 1 g protein; 0 g fiber; 364 mg sodium; 15 mg potassium.

CUCUMBER RAITA

MAKES: 1½ cups
ACTIVE TIME: 10 minutes | TOTAL: 10 minutes
TO MAKE AHEAD: Cover and refrigerate for up to 2 days.

Peel, seed and dice 1 small **cucumber**. Combine with 1 cup low-fat plain **yogurt**, 2 tablespoons chopped fresh **mint**, 1 minced small **garlic** clove, 1 tablespoon **lime juice**, ½ teaspoon ground **cumin** and ¼ teaspoon each **salt** and freshly ground **pepper** in a small bowl. Serve immediately or cover and refrigerate for 30 minutes to allow flavors to blend.

PER 1/4-CUP SERVING: 32 calories; 1 g fat (0 g sat, 0 g mono); 2 mg cholesterol; 4 g carbohydrate; 0 g added sugars; 2 g protein; 0 g fiber; 129 mg sodium; 146 mg potassium.

GREEN GODDESS SAUCE

MAKES: 1¼ cups
ACTIVE TIME: 10 minutes | **TOTAL:** 10 minutes
TO MAKE AHEAD: Cover and refrigerate for up to 3 days.

Combine ¾ cup low-fat **mayonnaise**, ¼ cup reduced-fat **sour cream**, 4 chopped **anchovy fillets**, 3 tablespoons chopped fresh **chives**, 2 tablespoons chopped fresh **parsley**, 1 tablespoon rinsed **capers**, 2 teaspoons freshly grated **lemon zest**, 1 teaspoon **lemon juice**, ⅛ teaspoon **salt** and freshly ground **pepper** to taste in a food processor. Pulse to combine.

PER TABLESPOON: 29 calories; 2 g fat (1 g sat, 1 g mono); 4 mg cholesterol; 2 g carbohydrate; 0 g added sugars; 0 g protein; 0 g fiber; 110 mg sodium; 15 mg potassium.

CILANTRO PESTO

MAKES: about ⅔ cup
ACTIVE TIME: 20 minutes | **TOTAL:** 20 minutes
TO MAKE AHEAD: Cover and refrigerate for up to 2 days.

Drop 2 crushed **garlic** cloves into a food processor or blender with the motor running. Add 2 tablespoons toasted slivered **almonds** and process until ground. Add 2 cups lightly packed **cilantro** leaves and ¼ teaspoon each **salt** and freshly ground **pepper**; process until finely chopped. With the motor running, gradually add 2 tablespoons each **canola oil** and nonfat plain **yogurt** and 1 tablespoon **lime juice**; process until the mixture forms a paste. Taste and adjust seasonings.

PER TABLESPOON: 39 calories; 4 g fat (0 g sat, 2 g mono); 0 mg cholesterol; 1 g carbohydrate; 0 g added sugars; 1 g protein; 0 g fiber; 63 mg sodium; 42 mg potassium.

BLACK BEAN-GARLIC SAUCE

MAKES: about ¼ cup
ACTIVE TIME: 5 minutes | **TOTAL:** 5 minutes

Combine 1 tablespoon each **black bean-garlic sauce** (*see Tip, page 481*), finely chopped **scallion**, **rice vinegar** and **water**, 1 teaspoon **canola oil** and ⅛ teaspoon **crushed red pepper** in a small bowl.

PER TABLESPOON: 18 calories; 1 g fat (0 g sat, 1 g mono); 0 mg cholesterol; 1 g carbohydrate; 0 g added sugars; 0 g protein; 0 g fiber; 318 mg sodium; 5 mg potassium.

▲ PINEAPPLE & JALAPEÑO SALSA

MAKES: about 4 cups
ACTIVE TIME: 20 minutes | **TOTAL:** 1 hour 20 minutes (including chilling time) | **TO MAKE AHEAD:** Cover and refrigerate for up to 3 days.

Cut the top and skin off 1 small ripe **pineapple**, remove the eyes and core. Finely dice the pineapple and place in a nonreactive bowl (*see Tip, page 486*). Add ¼ cup minced **scallions**, 3 tablespoons each chopped fresh **cilantro** and **lime juice**, 2 tablespoons minced **jalapeño** and 1 tablespoon **canola oil**. Toss to mix. Season with ¼ teaspoon **salt** and freshly ground **pepper** to taste. Chill at least 1 hour before serving to allow flavors to meld.

PER 1/4-CUP SERVING: 30 calories; 1 g fat (0 g sat, 1 g mono); 0 mg cholesterol; 6 g carbohydrate; 0 g added sugars; 0 g protein; 1 g fiber; 37 mg sodium; 54 mg potassium.
NUTRITION BONUS: Vitamin C (35% daily value).

Catfish & Potato Hash

H✖W H♥H

MAKES: 4 servings

ACTIVE TIME: 30 minutes | TOTAL: 30 minutes

Hash isn't just for corned beef. It's also great made with catfish—or other flaky white fish. Any ham adds flavor to the hash, but we think a higher-quality smoked ham will give you the biggest flavor-bang for your buck. Serve with a poached egg on top (see How To) and a green salad.

2   **small russet potatoes**
3   **teaspoons canola oil, divided**
1   **pound catfish fillets, patted dry and coarsely chopped**
1   **medium red bell pepper, diced**
1   **bunch scallions, sliced**
½   **cup diced ham**
1   **tablespoon whole-grain mustard**
¼   **teaspoon salt**
¼   **teaspoon freshly ground pepper**
1   **lemon, quartered**

1. Pierce potatoes several times and microwave on High until tender, 10 to 12 minutes. Cut the potatoes in half and set aside; coarsely chop when cool enough to handle.

2. Meanwhile, heat 1 teaspoon oil in a large nonstick skillet over medium heat. Add catfish and cook, stirring often, until just cooked through and opaque, 4 to 6 minutes. Transfer to a plate with a slotted spoon and discard any liquid in the pan. Add the remaining 2 teaspoons oil, bell pepper, scallions and ham and cook, stirring, until the vegetables are soft, about 4 minutes.

3. Return the catfish to the pan along with the chopped potatoes, mustard, salt and pepper. Continue to cook, stirring gently, until combined and heated through, about 2 minutes more. Serve with lemon wedges.

PER SERVING: 291 calories; 14 g fat (3 g sat, 7 g mono); 63 mg cholesterol; 17 g carbohydrate; 0 g added sugars; 24 g protein; 2 g fiber; 521 mg sodium; 732 mg potassium.
NUTRITION BONUS: Vitamin C (80% daily value), Vitamin A (25% dv), Potassium (21% dv).

How To

Poach Eggs

1. Fill a large, straight-sided skillet or Dutch oven with 2 inches of water; bring to a boil. Add ¼ cup distilled white vinegar. Reduce to a gentle simmer: the water should be steaming and small bubbles should come up from the bottom of the pan.

2. Working with one at a time, break an egg into a small bowl, submerge the lip of the bowl into the simmering water and gently add the egg. (Don't poach more than 4 eggs at a time in a large skillet or pot.)

3. Cook for 4 minutes for soft set, 5 minutes for medium set and 8 minutes for hard set. Using a slotted spoon, transfer the eggs to a clean dish towel to drain for a minute before serving.

Lemon-Pepper Catfish

H✄W H♥H

MAKES: 4 servings
ACTIVE TIME: 15 minutes | **TOTAL:** 45 minutes

Though catfish is tender enough to be quickly sautéed, its firm flesh also stands up well to the grill. This recipe works best with thicker fillets.

2	tablespoons lemon juice
2	tablespoons extra-virgin olive oil
1-2	teaspoons finely crushed black peppercorns
½	teaspoon salt
4	catfish fillets (about 1 pound total)
1	lemon, cut into 4 wedges

1. Whisk lemon juice, oil, pepper and salt in a shallow nonreactive dish (*see Tip, page 486*). Add catfish and turn to coat with marinade. Cover and refrigerate for 30 minutes.

2. Preheat grill or broiler to high.

3. Oil the grill rack (*see Tip, page 485*). Grill or broil the fish (about 4 inches from the heat if broiling), turning once, until it is opaque, 3 to 5 minutes per side. Serve with lemon wedges.

PER SERVING: 222 calories; 16 g fat (3 g sat, 9 g mono); 53 mg cholesterol; 2 g carbohydrate; 0 g added sugars; 18 g protein; 0 g fiber; 351 mg sodium; 370 mg potassium.
NUTRITION BONUS: Vitamin C (16% daily value).

▶ Catfish Etouffée

H✄W H♥H

MAKES: 4 servings
ACTIVE TIME: 15 minutes | **TOTAL:** 40 minutes

Although the classic Cajun stew, étouffée, is usually made with crayfish, it's also delicious with easier-to-find catfish. We added a bit of reduced-fat sour cream and stewed tomatoes to make the sauce rich and flavorful without a lot of extra calories.

1	tablespoon butter
1	tablespoon all-purpose flour
1	large onion, sliced
1	cup sliced celery
1	green bell pepper, diced
1	14-ounce can stewed tomatoes
	Pinch of cayenne pepper (optional)
1	pound catfish fillets, cut into 4 portions
¼	teaspoon salt
¼	cup reduced-fat sour cream

1. Melt butter in a large saucepan over medium heat. Add flour and cook, stirring until the flour is brown and fragrant, about 1 minute.

2. Add onion, celery, bell pepper, tomatoes and cayenne (if using); bring to a simmer. Cover and cook on medium-low, stirring occasionally, until the vegetables are very soft, about 15 minutes.

3. Sprinkle catfish with salt and place in the saucepan on top of the vegetables. Reduce heat to maintain a low simmer, cover and cook until the catfish is just cooked through and opaque, 8 to 10 minutes more. Remove from the heat.

4. Remove the catfish from the pan with a slotted spoon. Stir sour cream into the vegetables. Serve the catfish over the stewed vegetables.

PER SERVING: 257 calories; 14 g fat (5 g sat, 5 g mono); 67 mg cholesterol; 14 g carbohydrate; 0 g added sugars; 20 g protein; 3 g fiber; 454 mg sodium; 739 mg potassium.
NUTRITION BONUS: Vitamin C (60% daily value), Potassium (21% dv).

Arctic Char on a Bed of Kale

H✕W   H♥H

MAKES: 4 servings
ACTIVE TIME: 30 minutes | TOTAL: 30 minutes

Arctic char, related to salmon and trout, has a mild flavor and cooks up quickly. We like the taste and texture of Lacinato (a.k.a. Dinosaur) kale in this dish, but any variety of kale will work.

1	tablespoon extra-virgin olive oil
1	large shallot, thinly sliced
1	cup reduced-sodium chicken broth
¼	cup water
1-1½	pounds kale, tough stems removed, coarsely chopped (14-16 cups)
1	pound arctic char *or* wild-caught salmon fillet (*see Tip, page 488*), skinned and cut into 4 portions
¼	teaspoon salt
¼	teaspoon freshly ground pepper
¼	cup reduced-fat sour cream
2	teaspoons prepared horseradish
1	tablespoon chopped fresh dill *or* 1 teaspoon dried
4	lemon wedges for garnish

1. Heat oil in a large skillet over medium heat. Cook shallot, stirring, until beginning to soften, about 2 minutes. Add broth, water and half the kale; cook, stirring, until slightly wilted, about 1 minute. Add the remaining kale and cook until tender, about 8 minutes.

2. Sprinkle fish with salt and pepper and place on the kale. Cover and cook until the fish is just cooked through, 5 to 7 minutes.

3. Meanwhile, combine sour cream, horseradish and dill in a bowl. Serve the fish and kale with the sauce and lemon wedges.

PER SERVING: 335 calories; 16 g fat (3 g sat, 8 g mono); 90 mg cholesterol; 14 g carbohydrate; 0 g added sugars; 35 g protein; 2 g fiber; 424 mg sodium; 1,136 mg potassium.
NUTRITION BONUS: Vitamin A (353% daily value), Vitamin C (230% dv), Potassium (32% dv), Calcium & Iron (24% dv), Magnesium (19% dv), omega-3s.

EatingWell Tip

Steam your fish on a bed of kale as we do here. Steaming is a **quick low-calorie method to give fish a delicate texture**. Plus you get a serving of kale, which is packed with beta carotene that may help protect your eyes from the sun's damaging rays.

Salmon Pinwheels

H♥H

MAKES: 4 servings
ACTIVE TIME: 15 minutes | TOTAL: 30 minutes

Don't be intimidated by this fancy-looking breaded-salmon pinwheel—it's quite easy to do. This technique works best when you use "center-cut" salmon fillet. If you don't have a center-cut fillet or want to simplify the preparation, leave the fillet whole, spread the mayonnaise over it, top with the breadcrumb mixture and bake. To cut down on prep time, ask your fishmonger to skin the salmon for you. Serve with roasted potatoes and sautéed spinach.

½ cup coarse dry breadcrumbs, preferably whole-wheat (*see Tip, page 481*)
1 tablespoon extra-virgin olive oil
1 tablespoon whole-grain mustard
1 tablespoon chopped shallot
1 tablespoon lemon juice
1 teaspoon chopped rinsed capers
1 teaspoon chopped fresh thyme *or* ½ teaspoon dried
1¼ pounds center-cut wild-caught salmon fillet (*see Tip, page 488*), skinned and cut lengthwise into 4 strips
4 teaspoons low-fat mayonnaise

1. Preheat oven to 400°F. Coat a 9-by-13-inch baking dish with cooking spray.

2. Mix breadcrumbs, oil, mustard, shallot, lemon juice, capers and thyme in a small bowl until combined.

3. Working with one at a time, spread each salmon strip with 1 teaspoon mayonnaise. Spread about 3 tablespoons of the breadcrumb mixture over the mayonnaise. Starting at one end, roll the salmon up tightly, tucking in any loose filling as you go. Insert a toothpick though the end to keep the pinwheel from unrolling. Place in the prepared dish. Repeat with the remaining salmon strips.

4. Bake the pinwheels until just cooked through, 15 to 20 minutes. Remove the toothpicks before serving.

PER SERVING: 385 calories; 24 g fat (5 g sat, 8 g mono); 79 mg cholesterol; 9 g carbohydrate; 0 g added sugars; 31 g protein; 1 g fiber; 211 mg sodium; 530 mg potassium.
NUTRITION BONUS: Potassium (15% daily value), omega-3s.

EatingWell Tip

Choose wild salmon over farmed. **It's not only a better choice for the environment, it can also save you calories.** Farmed salmon are fattened to increase their weight and they don't have much room to swim, so their flesh is usually fattier.

Grilled Salmon & Zucchini with Red Pepper Sauce

H✂W   H♥H

MAKES: 4 servings
ACTIVE TIME: 35 minutes | TOTAL: 35 minutes

Jazz up simply grilled salmon and summer vegetables with a zesty sauce based on the classic Spanish romesco. Made with roasted red peppers, tomatoes and almonds, this sauce is a great match for any seafood, poultry or vegetables. Using smoked paprika brings out the flavors from the grill.

⅓	cup sliced almonds, toasted (*see Tip, page 486*)
¼	cup chopped jarred roasted red peppers
¼	cup halved grape tomatoes *or* cherry tomatoes
1	small clove garlic
1	tablespoon extra-virgin olive oil
1	tablespoon sherry vinegar *or* red-wine vinegar
1	teaspoon paprika, preferably smoked
¾	teaspoon salt, divided
½	teaspoon freshly ground pepper, divided
1¼	pounds wild-caught salmon fillet (*see Tip, page 488*), skinned (*see How To*) and cut crosswise into 4 portions
2	medium zucchini *or* summer squash (*or* 1 of each), halved lengthwise
	Canola *or* olive oil cooking spray
1	tablespoon chopped fresh parsley for garnish

1. Preheat grill to medium.

2. Process almonds, peppers, tomatoes, garlic, oil, vinegar, paprika, ¼ teaspoon salt and ¼ teaspoon pepper in a food processor or blender until smooth; set aside.

3. Coat salmon and zucchini (and/or summer squash) on both sides with cooking spray, then sprinkle with the remaining ½ teaspoon salt and ¼ teaspoon pepper. Grill, turning once, until the salmon is just cooked through and the squash is soft and browned, about 3 minutes per side.

4. Transfer the squash to a clean cutting board. When cool enough to handle, slice into ½-inch pieces. Toss in a bowl with half of the reserved sauce. Divide the squash among 4 plates along with a piece of salmon topped with some of the remaining sauce. Garnish with parsley, if desired.

PER SERVING: 281 calories; 13 g fat (2 g sat, 7 g mono); 66 mg cholesterol; 8 g carbohydrate; 0 g added sugars; 32 g protein; 2 g fiber; 599 mg sodium; 874 mg potassium.
NUTRITION BONUS: Vitamin C (37% daily value), Magnesium (20% dv), Vitamin A (19% dv), omega-3s.

How To

Skin a Salmon Fillet | Place salmon on a clean cutting board, skin side down. Starting at the tail end, slip the blade of a long, sharp knife between the fish flesh and the skin, holding the skin down firmly with your other hand. Gently push the blade along at a 30° angle, separating the fillet from the skin without cutting through either.

Salmon & Escarole Packets with Lemon-Tarragon Butter

H✕W H♥H

MAKES: 4 servings

ACTIVE TIME: 40 minutes | TOTAL: 1 hour

EQUIPMENT: Parchment paper or foil

This company-worthy salmon is steamed on a bed of escarole and basted in a rich lemon-butter sauce. Rainbow trout or arctic char are good substitutes for the salmon.

2	tablespoons butter
2	lemons
2	tablespoons minced fresh tarragon *or* 1 teaspoon dried
2	cloves garlic, minced
6	cups chopped escarole, romaine lettuce *or* spinach
1	bunch scallions, thinly sliced
¾	teaspoon salt, divided
½	teaspoon freshly ground pepper, divided
1-1¼	pounds wild-caught salmon fillet (*see Tip, page 488*), skinned and cut into 4 portions

1. Preheat oven to 400°F (*or see Grill Variation, page 298*).

2. You'll need four 20- to 24-inch-long pieces of parchment paper or foil. Fold in half crosswise (PHOTO 1). Draw half a heart shape on one side of the fold as if you were making a Valentine (PHOTO 2). Use scissors to cut it out (PHOTO 3). Open up the heart (PHOTO 4).

3. Combine butter with the juice of 1 lemon in a small pan and melt over low heat. Stir in tarragon and garlic; reserve 2 tablespoons. Combine the rest of the sauce in a large bowl with escarole (or lettuce or spinach), scallions, ¼ teaspoon each salt and pepper; toss to coat.

4. Place one-fourth of the greens mixture on one side of each open heart fairly close to the crease and leaving at least a 1-inch border around the edges for folding. Place 1 piece of fish on top of each portion of greens (PHOTO 5). Season with the remaining ½ teaspoon salt and ¼ teaspoon pepper. Brush the reserved sauce on the fish. Slice the remaining lemon and top the fish with the lemon slices.

5. Close the packet (PHOTO 6). Starting at the top, seal by folding the edges together in a series of small, tight folds (PHOTO 7). Twist the tip and tuck it under to help keep the packet closed (PHOTO 8). Place the packets on a large rimmed baking sheet (they may overlap slightly). Bake until the fish is just cooked through and the greens are wilted, about 15 minutes. (Open one carefully to check for doneness—be cautious of the steam.) Let the packets rest unopened for 5 minutes before serving.

PER SERVING: 215 calories; 10 g fat (5 g sat, 2 g mono); 68 mg cholesterol; 7 g carbohydrate; 0 g added sugars; 24 g protein; 3 g fiber; 512 mg sodium; 766 mg potassium.
NUTRITION BONUS: Vitamin A (45% daily value), Vitamin C (40% dv), Folate (34% dv), Potassium (22% dv), omega-3s.

How To: Make a Parchment-Paper Packet

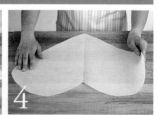

Fish Packets with Potatoes, Lemon & Capers

H✂W   H♥H

MAKES: 4 servings
ACTIVE TIME: 35 minutes | TOTAL: 50 minutes

In this packet, the golden, crusty potato cake takes on the tangy flavors of lemon and capers. The delicate fish fillets are quite thin so be careful not to overcook. For step-by-step photos of how to assemble the packets, see page 296.

- ¼ **cup chopped shallots**
- 2 **tablespoons finely chopped fresh parsley**
- 2 **tablespoons capers, rinsed and chopped**
- ¼ **cup lemon juice**
- 2 **tablespoons dry white wine**
- 2 **tablespoons extra-virgin olive oil**
- 2 **teaspoons Dijon mustard**
- 1 **pound yellow-fleshed potatoes, such as Yukon Gold, peeled and sliced ⅛ inch thick**
- ¼ **teaspoon salt, divided**
- 1 **pound Pacific sole (*see Tip, page 489*) or flounder fillets, cut into 4 portions**

1. Preheat oven to 400°F (*or see Grill Variation*).

2. You'll need four 20- to 24-inch-long pieces of parchment paper or foil. Fold in half crosswise (PHOTO 1, *page 296*). Draw half a heart shape on one side of the fold as if you were making a Valentine (PHOTO 2). Use scissors to cut it out (PHOTO 3). Open up the heart (PHOTO 4).

3. Combine shallots, parsley and capers in a small bowl. Whisk lemon juice, wine, oil and mustard in another small bowl or glass measuring cup.

4. Arrange one-fourth of the potatoes on one side of each open heart, slightly overlapping, to form a 5- to 6-inch circle fairly close to the crease and leaving at least a 1-inch border around the edges for folding. Sprinkle with a dash of salt; set a piece of fish on the potatoes. Top with one-fourth of the shallot mixture and 1 tablespoon of the lemon juice mixture.

5. Close the packet (PHOTO 6). Starting at the top, seal by folding the edges together in a series of small, tight folds (PHOTO 7). Twist the tip and tuck it under to help keep the packet closed (PHOTO 8). Place the packets on a large rimmed baking sheet (they may overlap slightly). Bake until the potatoes are tender and the fish is opaque in the center, about 20 minutes, depending on the thickness. (Open one carefully to check for doneness—be cautious of the steam.) Let the packets rest unopened for 5 minutes before serving. Top with the remaining lemon juice mixture.

PER SERVING: 254 calories; 8 g fat (1 g sat, 6 g mono); 53 mg cholesterol; 22 g carbohydrate; 0 g added sugars; 21 g protein; 3 g fiber; 342 mg sodium; 805 mg potassium. NUTRITION BONUS: Vitamin C (55% daily value), Potassium (23% dv), Magnesium (19% dv).

GRILL VARIATION

Cooking in packets is great for the grill, but it's not safe to put parchment paper over an open flame, so use foil. To prepare packets for grilling, start with eight 20- to 24-inch-long pieces of foil. Layer two sheets for each of four packets (the double layers will help protect the contents from burning). Arrange the ingredients on one half of each double layer. Fold the foil over the ingredients and tightly seal the packets by crimping and folding the edges together. Grill over medium heat for 8 to 10 minutes, rotating the packets to another spot on the grill about halfway through to ensure even cooking.

Roasted Cod, Tomatoes, Orange & Onions

H✕W   H♥H

MAKES: 4 servings
ACTIVE TIME: 30 minutes | TOTAL: 1½ hours

For amazing flavor and texture with barely any effort, this recipe for roasting fish can't be beat. Try it with mahi-mahi or wild salmon also.

- 1 **pound ripe but firm small round *or* plum tomatoes, cut into ½-inch-thick wedges**
- 2 **medium yellow onions, cut into ¼-inch-thick wedges**
- 1 **tablespoon finely slivered orange zest (*see Tip, page 483*)**
- 1 **tablespoon extra-virgin olive oil**
- 1 **tablespoon chopped fresh thyme**
- ½ **teaspoon kosher salt, divided**
   Freshly ground pepper to taste
- 1 **pound boneless, skinless Pacific cod (*see Tip, page 483*) *or* other thick-cut, firm-fleshed fish, cut into 4 portions**

1. Preheat oven to 400°F.

2. Combine tomatoes, onions, orange zest, oil and chopped thyme in a 3-quart glass or ceramic baking dish. Sprinkle with ¼ teaspoon salt and pepper; stir to combine. Roast, stirring occasionally, until the onions are golden and brown on the edges, about 45 minutes. Remove from the oven. Increase oven temperature to 450°F.

3. Push the vegetables aside, add fish and season with the remaining ¼ teaspoon salt and pepper; spoon the vegetables over the fish. Return to the oven and bake until the fish is opaque in the center, about 10 to 12 minutes.

PER SERVING: 162 calories; 5 g fat (1 g sat, 3 g mono); 43 mg cholesterol; 11 g carbohydrate; 0 g added sugars; 20 g protein; 2 g fiber; 214 mg sodium; 531 mg potassium.
NUTRITION BONUS: Vitamin C (67% daily value), Vitamin A (16% dv), Potassium (15% dv).

Shrimp & Cheddar Grits

H✕W   H♥H

MAKES: 4 servings
ACTIVE TIME: 25 minutes | TOTAL: 25 minutes

The South's version of creamy polenta, grits are easy to make on a weeknight—especially when topped with quickly broiled shrimp and scallions. Use the sharpest Cheddar you can find for these cheesy grits.
Shopping Tip: *Look for quick grits near oatmeal and other hot cereals or near cornmeal in the baking aisle.*

- 1 **14-ounce can reduced-sodium chicken broth**
- 1½ **cups water**
- ¾ **cup quick grits (*not* instant; *see Shopping Tip*)**
- ½ **teaspoon freshly ground pepper, divided**
- ¾ **cup shredded extra-sharp *or* sharp Cheddar cheese**
- 1 **pound raw shrimp (16-20 per pound; *see Tip, page 489*), peeled and deveined**
- 1 **bunch scallions, trimmed, cut into 1-inch pieces**
- 1 **tablespoon extra-virgin olive oil**
- ¼ **teaspoon garlic powder**
- ⅛ **teaspoon salt**

1. Position rack in upper third of oven; preheat broiler.

2. Bring broth and water to a boil in a large saucepan over medium-high heat. Whisk in grits and ¼ teaspoon pepper. Reduce heat to medium-low, cover and cook, stirring occasionally, until thickened, 5 to 7 minutes. Remove from heat and stir in cheese. Cover to keep warm.

3. Meanwhile, toss shrimp, scallions, oil, garlic powder, the remaining ¼ teaspoon pepper and salt in a medium bowl. Transfer to a rimmed baking sheet. Broil, stirring once, until the shrimp are pink and just cooked through, 5 to 6 minutes. Serve the grits topped with the broiled shrimp and scallions.

PER SERVING: 377 calories; 13 g fat (5 g sat, 5 g mono); 195 mg cholesterol; 30 g carbohydrate; 0 g added sugars; 32 g protein; 2 g fiber; 612 mg sodium; 426 mg potassium.
NUTRITION BONUS: Iron (25% daily value), Folate (24% dv), Calcium (23% dv), Magnesium & Zinc (16% dv).

Puerto Rican Fish Stew (*Bacalao*)

H⋈W H♥H

MAKES: 4 servings, about 1 cup each
ACTIVE TIME: 25 minutes | **TOTAL:** 45 minutes

Bacalao, salted dried codfish, is the defining ingredient in traditional Puerto Rican fish stew, but salt cod requires overnight soaking and several rinses in cool water before it can be used, so we opt for fresh fish in this quick version. Serve with crusty rolls to soak up the juices. **Shopping Tip:** *Opt for firmer hook-and-line-caught haddock or U.S.-farmed tilapia. Pacific cod also works, but will be more flaky.*

- 2 tablespoons extra-virgin olive oil
- 1 medium onion, chopped
- 4 cloves garlic, minced
- 1 pound firm white fish, such as haddock, tilapia *or* Pacific cod (*see Shopping Tip*), cut into 1½-inch pieces
- 1 14-ounce can diced tomatoes
- 1 Anaheim *or* poblano pepper, chopped
- ¼ cup packed chopped fresh cilantro
- 2 tablespoons sliced pimiento-stuffed green olives
- 1 tablespoon capers, rinsed
- 1 teaspoon dried oregano
- ½ teaspoon salt
- ½ cup water, as needed
- 1 ripe avocado, chopped (optional)

Heat oil in a large high-sided skillet or Dutch oven over medium heat. Add onion and cook, stirring occasionally, until softened, about 2 minutes. Add garlic and cook, stirring, for 1 minute. Add fish, tomatoes and their juice, chile pepper, cilantro, olives, capers, oregano and salt; stir to combine. Add up to ½ cup water if the mixture seems dry. Cover and simmer for 20 minutes. Remove from the heat. Serve warm or at room temperature, garnished with avocado (if using).

PER SERVING: 207 calories; 9 g fat (1 g sat, 6 g mono); 65 mg cholesterol; 9 g carbohydrate; 0 g added sugars; 23 g protein; 2 g fiber; 607 mg sodium; 639 mg potassium.
NUTRITION BONUS: Vitamin C (70% daily value), Iron & Vitamin A (15% dv).

Curried Fish

H⋈W H♥H

MAKES: 6 servings, about 1 cup each
ACTIVE TIME: 35 minutes | **TOTAL:** 35 minutes

Though curried goat, chicken and shrimp are more popular in Jamaica than fish, this version with mild mahi-mahi is a delicious and light alternative. Serve over rice. **Kitchen Tip:** *One of the hottest chile peppers, Scotch bonnets come in red, orange and green. Though they look similar to habaneros, Scotch bonnets have a citrus note that makes them undeniably different. You can control the heat of a dish a little by discarding the membranes that hold the seeds, which are the spiciest part of chile peppers, along with the seeds themselves. Be sure to wash your hands thoroughly after handling hot peppers or wear rubber gloves. Habaneros can be substituted.*

- 3 tablespoons canola oil
- 2 tablespoons curry powder
- 1 medium onion, finely chopped
- 1 green bell pepper, diced
- 2 cloves garlic, minced
- 1 teaspoon minced Scotch bonnet chile pepper (*see Kitchen Tip*), or to taste
- 1 teaspoon chopped fresh thyme *or* ¼ teaspoon dried
- 1 14-ounce can "lite" coconut milk
- 2 pounds mahi-mahi fillets (*see Tip, page 486*), skinned, cut into 1-inch pieces
- 3 scallions, thinly sliced
- 1 teaspoon salt

Heat oil in a large skillet over medium heat. Add curry powder and cook for 1 minute. Add onion, bell pepper, garlic, chile pepper and thyme. Cook, stirring, until fragrant, about 2 minutes. Add coconut milk and bring to a simmer. Stir in fish and scallions; cover and cook until the fish is just cooked through, 5 to 7 minutes. Stir in salt and serve immediately.

PER SERVING: 265 calories; 13 g fat (4 g sat, 5 g mono); 110 mg cholesterol; 7 g carbohydrate; 1 g added sugars; 30 g protein; 2 g fiber; 541 mg sodium; 752 mg potassium.
NUTRITION BONUS: Vitamin C (35% daily value), Potassium (21% dv), Iron (15% dv).

Grilled Fish Tacos

H✂W   H↑F   H♥H

MAKES: 6 servings, 2 tacos each

ACTIVE TIME: 30 minutes | TOTAL: 50 minutes

TO MAKE AHEAD: Prepare Adobo Rub (Step 1) and refrigerate for up to 3 days. Prepare coleslaw (Step 3) up to 4 hours ahead.

Often in fish tacos, the fish is cut into strips, battered and deep-fried. Not only does that make them high in fat and calories, but it's also more of a chore. Coat the fish with a flavor-packed chile rub and grill it to add a nice smoky flavor. Make sure the fillets are no more than ½ to ¾ inch thick so they cook quickly. Sometimes flipping fish on the grill can be tricky since it can stick. The solution is to invest in a grill basket that easily holds 4 to 6 fish fillets and secures them for easy flipping. If you don't have a basket, make sure the grill is hot and well oiled before adding the fish. Serve with fresh cilantro, avocado, salsa and jalapeños so everyone can top their tacos just the way they like. **Shopping Tip:** *Mildly spicy dried chiles, such as ancho or New Mexico, add moderate heat and rich flavor to Mexican sauces like mole. Chili powder made from these chiles has more flavor than American-style blends. Look for whole dried chiles in the produce section of large supermarkets and New Mexico or ancho chili powder in the specialty-spice section of large supermarkets or online at* penzeys.com.

ADOBO RUB

- 4 teaspoons chili powder, preferably made with New Mexico *or* ancho chiles (*see Shopping Tip*)
- 2 tablespoons lime juice
- 2 tablespoons extra-virgin olive oil
- 1 teaspoon ground cumin
- 1 teaspoon onion powder
- 1 teaspoon garlic powder
- 1 teaspoon salt
- ½ teaspoon freshly ground pepper

FISH

- 2 pounds mahi-mahi *or* Pacific halibut (*see Tip, page 485*), ½-¾ inch thick, skinned and cut into 4 portions

COLESLAW

- ¼ cup reduced-fat sour cream
- ¼ cup low-fat mayonnaise
- 2 tablespoons chopped fresh cilantro

- 1 teaspoon lime zest
- 2 tablespoons lime juice
- 1 teaspoon sugar
- ⅛ teaspoon salt
  Freshly ground pepper to taste
- 3 cups finely shredded red *or* green cabbage

- 12 corn tortillas, warmed (*see How To*)

1. **To prepare Adobo Rub:** Combine chili powder, lime juice, oil, cumin, onion powder, garlic power, salt and pepper in a small bowl.

2. **To prepare fish:** Rub the Adobo Rub all over fish. Let stand 20 to 30 minutes for the fish to absorb the flavor.

3. **To prepare coleslaw:** Combine sour cream, mayonnaise, cilantro, lime zest, lime juice, sugar, salt and pepper in a medium bowl; mix until smooth and creamy. Add cabbage and toss to combine. Refrigerate until ready to use.

4. Preheat grill to medium-high.

5. Oil the grill rack (*see Tip, page 485*) or use a grilling basket. Grill the fish until it is cooked through and easily flakes with a fork, 3 to 5 minutes per side. Transfer to a platter and separate into large chunks.

6. Serve the tacos family-style by passing the fish, tortillas and coleslaw separately.

PER SERVING: 319 calories; 9 g fat (2 g sat, 5 g mono); 110 mg cholesterol; 29 g carbohydrate; 1 g added sugars; 31 g protein; 5 g fiber; 702 mg sodium; 827 mg potassium.
NUTRITION BONUS: Vitamin C (30% daily value), Potassium (24% dv), Magnesium (22% dv), Vitamin A (17% dv), Iron (16% dv).

How To

Warm Corn Tortillas | Microwave: Wrap stacks of up to 12 tortillas in barely damp paper towels; microwave on High for 30 to 45 seconds. Wrap tortillas in a clean towel to keep warm. **Oven:** Wrap stacks of 6 tortillas in foil; place in a 375°F oven for 10 to 15 minutes. Wrap tortillas in a clean towel to keep warm.

Cooking Mussels

Mussels are gourmet fast food—they cook up into a bistro meal in just 45 minutes and you dirty just one pot in the process. Start with one of the 6 flavor variations, with inspiration from France to Thailand, then follow our master method to cook up your mussels. Don't forget lots of crusty whole-grain baguette to soak up the juices!

Mussel Tips

SHOP & STORE: Look for closed mussels—or those open only a fraction of an inch. When you get them home, store them in a large bowl with a few damp paper towels on top for up to 1 day.

TO CLEAN: Discard mussels with broken shells or whose shell remains open after you tap it. Hold mussels under running water and use a stiff brush to remove any barnacles; pull off any black fibrous "beards" (*see photo*). (Some mussels may not have a beard.) Mussels should be "debearded" no more than 30 minutes before cooking.

Master Mussels Recipe

MAKES: 4 servings
ACTIVE TIME: 45 minutes | **TOTAL:** 45 minutes

> Meat (*see Variations, opposite*)
> Oil (*see Variations*)
> Vegetables & Aromatics (*see Variations*)
> Liquid & Seasoning (*see Variations*)
> 4 pounds mussels, cleaned (*see Tips, left*)
> Garnish (*see Variations*), optional

1. Cook MEAT (if any) in a large Dutch oven over medium heat, stirring, until starting to brown, 5 to 7 minutes. Transfer to a paper towel-lined plate; pour off the fat from the pan and wipe out any remaining fat.

2. Add OIL to the pan and heat over medium heat. Add VEGETABLES & AROMATICS and cook, stirring often, until the vegetables are just starting to brown, 30 seconds to 4 minutes (depending on the amount and type of vegetables used).

3. Add LIQUID & SEASONING; bring to a boil over high heat. Stir in mussels. Cover and cook just until the mussels have opened, 4 to 6 minutes. Remove from the heat (discard any unopened mussels). Stir in GARNISH (if any) and/or the cooked MEAT. Serve with the sauce from the pan.

Variations: Mussels 6 Ways

MUSSELS WITH CIDER & BACON
MEAT: 4 slices bacon, chopped
OIL: 2 tablespoons extra-virgin olive oil
VEGETABLES & AROMATICS: 4 minced garlic cloves, 1 finely diced medium onion
LIQUID & SEASONING: 1½ cups apple cider, 2 teaspoons cider vinegar, 1 tablespoon chopped fresh sage, ¼ teaspoon each salt & freshly ground pepper
PER SERVING: 281 calories; 13 g fat (2 g sat, 7 g mono); 42 mg cholesterol; 23 g carbohydrate; 0 g added sugars; 18 g protein; 1 g fiber; 528 mg sodium; 310 mg potassium.
NUTRITION BONUS: Iron (25% daily value), Vitamin C (23% dv), Folate (15% dv).

MUSSELS WITH TOMATOES & WHITE WINE
OIL: 1 tablespoon extra-virgin olive oil
VEGETABLES & AROMATICS: 4 minced garlic cloves, 1 finely diced medium onion, 1 chopped fennel bulb
LIQUID & SEASONING: 2 cups chopped plum tomatoes, 1 cup dry white wine, 1 cup fish or seafood stock (or bottled clam juice, *see Tip, page 483*, or reduced-sodium chicken broth), ¼ teaspoon each salt & freshly ground pepper
GARNISH: 2 tablespoons chopped fennel fronds (or chopped fresh basil)
PER SERVING: 258 calories; 7 g fat (1 g sat, 4 g mono); 36 mg cholesterol; 20 g carbohydrate; 0 g added sugars; 19 g protein; 4 g fiber; 509 mg sodium; 815 mg potassium.
NUTRITION BONUS: Vitamin C (52% daily value), Iron (29% dv), Potassium (23% dv), Folate (22% dv), Vitamin A (18% dv), Magnesium (15% dv).

MUSSELS WITH THAI SEASONINGS
OIL: 1 tablespoon canola oil (or extra-virgin olive oil)
VEGETABLES & AROMATICS: 2 minced garlic cloves
LIQUID & SEASONING: 14-ounce can "lite" coconut milk, 2 tablespoons lime juice, 2 teaspoons Thai green curry paste (or to taste), 1 tablespoon brown sugar, 1 tablespoon Thai fish sauce (or ¼ teaspoon salt)
GARNISH: ½ cup chopped fresh basil and/or cilantro
PER SERVING: 238 calories; 13 g fat (6 g sat, 3 g mono); 35 mg cholesterol; 12 g carbohydrate; 4 g added sugars; 17 g protein; 0 g fiber; 601 mg sodium; 187 mg potassium.
NUTRITION BONUS: Iron (24% daily value), Vitamin C (18% dv).

MUSSELS WITH SAFFRON CREAM SAUCE
OIL: 1 tablespoon extra-virgin olive oil
VEGETABLES & AROMATICS: 2 minced garlic cloves, 1 finely diced small onion, 1 chopped celery stalk
LIQUID & SEASONING: 2 cups diced plum tomatoes, 1 cup fish or seafood stock (or bottled clam juice, *see Tip, page 483*), ½ teaspoon saffron threads, ¼ teaspoon each salt & freshly ground pepper. After discarding any unopened mussels, stir in ½ cup heavy cream.
GARNISH: ½ cup chopped flat-leaf parsley
PER SERVING: 278 calories; 18 g fat (8 g sat, 7 g mono); 77 mg cholesterol; 11 g carbohydrate; 0 g added sugars; 18 g protein; 1 g fiber; 493 mg sodium; 513 mg potassium.
NUTRITION BONUS: Vitamin C (33% daily value), Iron & Vitamin A (26% dv), Folate (17% dv).

HOT-&-SOUR MUSSELS
OIL: 1 tablespoon canola oil (or extra-virgin olive oil)
VEGETABLES & AROMATICS: 2 minced garlic cloves, 1 sliced bunch scallions, 1 tablespoon minced fresh ginger
LIQUID & SEASONING: 1 cup fish or seafood stock (or bottled clam juice, *see Tip, page 483*, or reduced-sodium chicken broth), 2 tablespoons reduced-sodium soy sauce, 1 tablespoon Chinkiang vinegar (*see Tip, page 483*; or distilled white vinegar), ¾ teaspoon ground white pepper
GARNISH: ¼ cup sliced scallion greens
PER SERVING: 171 calories; 7 g fat (1 g sat, 3 g mono); 36 mg cholesterol; 9 g carbohydrate; 0 g added sugars; 18 g protein; 1 g fiber; 992 mg sodium; 342 mg potassium.
NUTRITION BONUS: Iron (27% daily value), Folate (16% dv).

MEXICAN-INSPIRED MUSSELS
MEAT: ⅓ cup diced Spanish chorizo (*see Tip, page 483*)
OIL: 1 tablespoon extra-virgin olive oil
VEGETABLES & AROMATICS: 1 diced large onion, 2 teaspoons ground cumin
LIQUID & SEASONING: 1 cup beer (preferably dark Mexican beer, such as Negra Modelo), 2 diced plum tomatoes, ¼ cup drained canned chopped green chiles, ½ teaspoon freshly ground pepper
GARNISH: ½ cup chopped fresh cilantro
PER SERVING: 242 calories; 11 g fat (3 g sat, 5 g mono); 45 mg cholesterol; 13 g carbohydrate; 0 g added sugars; 19 g protein; 1 g fiber; 392 mg sodium; 343 mg potassium.
NUTRITION BONUS: Vitamin C (33% daily value), Iron (28% dv).

Seared Scallops with Sautéed Cucumbers

H✂W   H♥H

MAKES: 4 servings

ACTIVE TIME: 25 minutes | TOTAL: 1 hour

Sweet sea scallops pair beautifully with lightly sautéed cucumbers. Try adding a handful of julienned snow peas to the cucumbers, for extra crunch. Serve simply with crusty bread or a few boiled new potatoes.

2	large English cucumbers
½	teaspoon kosher salt, divided
	Freshly ground pepper to taste
3	teaspoons butter, divided
3	teaspoons extra-virgin olive oil, divided
¼	cup reduced-fat sour cream
1¼	pounds large dry sea scallops (*see Tip, page 489*)
1	tablespoon minced fresh dill *or* flat-leaf parsley for garnish

1. Cut cucumbers in half lengthwise, scrape out seeds with a spoon and cut crosswise into ¼-inch-thick slices. Transfer to a colander set over a bowl. Toss with ¼ teaspoon salt and set aside for 30 minutes to drain.

2. Heat 1 teaspoon butter and 2 teaspoons oil in a 12-inch cast-iron skillet over high heat. Add the drained cucumbers and cook, stirring, until wilted and beginning to brown, 2 to 4 minutes. Stir in sour cream and cook, stirring, for 1 minute. Transfer to a small bowl.

3. Wipe out the pan. Heat the remaining 2 teaspoons butter and 1 teaspoon oil over high heat. Add scallops, season with the remaining ¼ teaspoon salt and pepper and cook until lightly browned and cooked through, 2 to 3 minutes per side. Gently stir the cucumber mixture into the scallops. Serve garnished with dill (or parsley), if desired.

PER SERVING: 230 calories; 9 g fat (4 g sat, 3 g mono); 60 mg cholesterol; 11 g carbohydrate; 0 g added sugars; 25 g protein; 1 g fiber; 378 mg sodium; 754 mg potassium.
NUTRITION BONUS: Magnesium (26% daily value), Potassium (22% dv), Vitamin C (16% dv).

EatingWell Tip

Instead of using all butter, use a little bit of butter mixed with olive oil. It's an easy way to **cut back on saturated fat** while still enjoying a rich buttery flavor.

Grilled Sea Scallops with Cilantro & Black Bean Sauce

H✱W   H♥H

MAKES: 6 servings, about 4 scallops & 1½ tablespoons sauce each
ACTIVE TIME: 45 minutes | **TOTAL:** 45 minutes
EQUIPMENT: Six 10-inch skewers | **TO MAKE AHEAD:** The sauce (Steps 1-2) will keep for up to 5 days in the refrigerator.

Here, Chinese fermented black beans are stir-fried with garlic and ginger, flavor-enhanced with Chinese or Japanese rice wine, and blended into a delicate puree that makes a delicious dip to complement all sorts of grilled seafood, including plump sea scallops. Sweet mirin counterbalances the saltiness of the beans. **Shopping Tip:** *Fermented black beans, oxidized soybeans that are salt-dried, have a savory, salty and slightly bitter flavor. They are frequently used in Chinese stir-fries, marinades and sauces. Before using, they should be soaked in water for 10 to 30 minutes to get rid of excess salt. When purchasing fermented black beans, look for shiny, firm beans (avoid dull and dry beans with salt spots). Once open, store airtight in the refrigerator for up to 1 year. If you can't find fermented black beans, substitute black bean-garlic sauce, available at well stocked supermarkets.*

  2 tablespoons fermented black beans (*see Shopping Tip*) *or* 1 tablespoon black bean-garlic sauce
  2 tablespoons canola oil, divided
  2 large cloves garlic, peeled and finely grated *or* minced
  2 tablespoons finely grated fresh ginger
  ⅓ cup Shao Hsing rice wine (*see Tip, page 489*) *or* Japanese sake
  ¼ cup mirin (*see Tip, page 486*)
  2 teaspoons toasted sesame oil
  ½ bunch fresh cilantro, stems trimmed, plus sprigs for garnish
  3 tablespoons lemon juice
  1½ pounds (24-30) large dry sea scallops (*see Tip, page 489*)
  ¼ teaspoon freshly ground pepper, *or* to taste

1. If using fermented black beans, place them in a small bowl, cover with water and let stand for 10 minutes. Drain and rinse.

2. Heat 1 tablespoon oil in a large skillet or wok over high heat. Add garlic and ginger and cook, stirring, until light golden and fragrant, 30 to 45 seconds. Add the black beans (or black bean-garlic sauce) and cook, stirring, for 1 minute. Carefully pour in rice wine (or sake), mirin and sesame oil; lower the heat to medium-low and simmer, lightly crushing the black beans, until the liquid is reduced by about half, about 3 minutes. Remove from heat.

3. Preheat grill to high.

4. Put cilantro, lemon juice and the remaining 1 tablespoon oil in a blender; process until smooth. Transfer the marinade to a large bowl, add scallops and gently toss to coat with the marinade. Divide the scallops among 6 skewers, spacing about ½ inch apart. Season with pepper. (Discard marinade.) Oil the grill rack (*see Tip, page 485*). Grill the scallops until golden and crisp on the edges and cooked through, 2 to 4 minutes per side. Serve with the black bean sauce and garnish with cilantro sprigs.

PER SERVING: 197 calories; 6 g fat (1 g sat, 2 g mono); 37 mg cholesterol; 8 g carbohydrate; 0 g added sugars; 20 g protein; 0 g fiber; 183 mg sodium; 385 mg potassium.
NUTRITION BONUS: Magnesium (17% daily value).

Shrimp & Summer Squash with Saffron Rice

H✖W   H↑F   H♥H

MAKES: 4 servings, 1½ cups sauté & 1 cup rice each
ACTIVE TIME: 40 minutes | TOTAL: 1 hour

Golden saffron and a bounty of herbs and summer vegetables make this a beautiful and fresh-tasting dish. Don't overseason; let the flavors sing. **Shopping Tip:** *Saffron adds flavor and golden color to a variety of Middle Eastern, African and European foods. Find it in the specialty-herb section of large supermarkets and gourmet-food shops and at* tienda.com. *It will keep in an airtight container for several years.*

  2½ **cups water**
  1   **teaspoon salt, divided**
¼-½ **teaspoon saffron threads (see Shopping Tip)**
  1   **cup long-grain brown rice**
  2   **tablespoons extra-virgin olive oil**
  3   **medium yellow summer squash, quartered lengthwise and cut into ¼-inch-thick slices**
  1   **pound raw shrimp (21-25 per pound; see Tip, page 489), peeled and deveined (see How To)**
  ⅓ **cup tightly packed fresh mint leaves, finely chopped**
  2   **tablespoons lemon juice**
      Freshly ground pepper to taste

1. Bring water, ½ teaspoon salt and saffron to taste to a boil in a medium saucepan. Add rice, return to a boil, cover and reduce the heat to maintain a gentle simmer. Cook until the water is absorbed and the rice is tender, 40 to 45 minutes. Fluff with a fork.

2. About 10 minutes before the rice is done, heat oil in a large skillet over medium heat. Add squash and cook, stirring occasionally, until just tender (do not brown), 5 to 7 minutes. Stir in shrimp and cook, stirring constantly, for 2 minutes. Stir in mint and cook for 30 seconds. Stir in lemon juice; remove from heat. Season with the remaining ½ teaspoon salt and pepper. Serve over the rice.

PER SERVING: 384 calories; 11 g fat (2 g sat, 6 g mono); 172 mg cholesterol; 43 g carbohydrate; 0 g added sugars; 29 g protein; 5 g fiber; 767 mg sodium; 710 mg potassium.
NUTRITION BONUS: Vitamin C (53% daily value), Magnesium (35% dv), Iron (27% dv), Potassium (20% dv), Zinc (18% dv), Vitamin A (16% dv), Folate (15% dv).

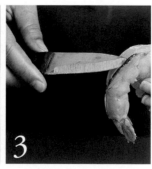

How To

Peel and Devein Shrimp
1. To peel, grasp the legs and hold onto the tail while you twist off the shell. 2. To devein, use a paring knife to make a slit along the length of the shrimp. 3. Remove the dark digestive tract (or "vein") with the knife tip.

Summer Paella

H✕W   H♥H

MAKES: 6 servings
ACTIVE TIME: 1 hour 20 minutes | TOTAL: 1 hour 20 minutes
TO MAKE AHEAD: Prepare peppers and onion (Steps 1-3), cover and refrigerate for up to 2 days.
EQUIPMENT: Three 12-inch skewers; 13-inch paella pan or large high-sided skillet

Paella started as an outdoor dish. Grilling seafood, zesty sausage and vegetables before combining them with saffron-scented rice replicates that traditional character. The first time, for simplicity, do the grilling and slicing before cooking the rice. If you have a side-by-side grill and burner, later you can perform both tasks simultaneously, which makes you look like a cooking wizard. Perfectly done paella rice will be dry and the slightest bit toothsome.

1	green bell pepper
1	red *or* orange bell pepper
1	small red onion, sliced in ½-inch-thick rounds
	Olive oil cooking spray
12	ounces raw shrimp (21-25 per pound; *see Tip, page 489*), peeled and deveined, tails left on
3	tablespoons extra-virgin olive oil
2	teaspoons minced garlic
4	cups reduced-sodium chicken broth
1	scant teaspoon crumbled saffron threads
¼	teaspoon kosher salt
2	cups short-grain white rice, such as bomba, Valencia *or* arborio
12	hard-shell clams, such as littlenecks *or* cherrystones, *or* mussels
10	ounces raw spicy turkey *or* chicken sausage links
½	cup frozen baby peas, thawed
¼	cup halved pitted briny black olives
¼	cup halved pitted briny green olives
¼	cup minced fresh parsley

1. Preheat grill to medium-high.

2. Grill bell peppers, turning occasionally, until softened and charred in spots, about 8 minutes. Coat onion slices lightly with olive oil spray and grill, turning once, until slightly softened and beginning to caramelize, about 2 minutes per side.

3. Transfer the peppers to a plastic bag and let steam until cool enough to handle. Peel off the skins; discard the stems and seeds. Chop the peppers and onion.

4. Thread shrimp onto three 12-inch skewers. Lightly coat with olive oil spray.

5. Heat oil in a 13-inch paella pan or large high-sided skillet over medium heat. Add the bell peppers, onion and garlic and cook, stirring, until fragrant, 1 to 2 minutes. Stir in broth, saffron and salt; bring to a boil. Add rice, stir just to combine and spread to form a thin, even layer in the pan. Reduce heat to a gentle simmer and cook the rice, uncovered, for 10 minutes.

6. After 10 minutes, gently fold the outside portions of rice into the center of the pan to ensure even cooking. Continue simmering, without stirring, until the rice looks dry and is just tender (it will still be a little toothsome), about 10 minutes more. Watch carefully and be prepared to shift the pan partially off the burner as necessary to keep the rice cooking at the same rate and prevent burning.

7. Meanwhile, place the skewered shrimp, clams (or mussels) and sausage on the grill. Grill the shrimp until firm and pink, 1 to 2 minutes per side. Remove from the skewers and place in a large bowl. Grill the clams (or mussels) until their shells pop open, 2 to 4 minutes total. (Discard any clams or mussels that don't open.) Add to the bowl with the shrimp, keeping them level to avoid losing their juices. Grill the sausage, turning occasionally, until cooked through, 10 to 14 minutes. When cool enough to handle, thinly slice and add to the bowl with the seafood.

8. When the rice is done, remove from the heat, cover with a lid or heavy kitchen towel and let stand for 5 minutes. Gently stir in peas and black and green olives. Scatter the sausage and seafood plus any accumulated juices over the rice and sprinkle with parsley.

PER SERVING: 379 calories; 15 g fat (3 g sat, 7 g mono); 124 mg cholesterol; 32 g carbohydrate; 0 g added sugars; 29 g protein; 2 g fiber; 958 mg sodium; 465 mg potassium.
NUTRITION BONUS: Vitamin C (88% daily value), Iron (41% dv), Vitamin A (27% dv).

Barbecue Pulled Chicken

Pomegranate-Glazed Turkey with Roasted Fennel

Brazilian Chicken & Peanut Stew

Simple Herb-Roasted Chicken

Poultry

GUIDE:

Sautéing Chicken

One of the easiest dinners around is a seared chicken breast with a quick pan sauce. Here's the master method for sautéing chicken and three simple sauce combinations to get you started. Once you've got the method down, you can experiment with items from your pantry to make a sauce (think: olives, capers, tomatoes and white wine, or leeks, apple cider and sage).

Master Chicken Sauté

H✱W H♥H

MAKES: 4 servings
ACTIVE TIME: 30 minutes | TOTAL: 30 minutes

- **4 boneless, skinless chicken breasts (1¼-1½ pounds total), trimmed and tenders removed (*see Tip, page 482*)**
- **¼ cup all-purpose flour**
- **½ teaspoon salt, divided**
- **¼ teaspoon freshly ground pepper**
- **3 teaspoons extra-virgin olive oil *or* canola oil, divided**

1. Prepare AROMATICS (*right*). Pound chicken breasts between 2 pieces of plastic wrap with a rolling pin, meat mallet or heavy skillet until flattened to an even thickness, about ½ inch. Combine flour, ¼ teaspoon salt and pepper in a shallow dish. Dredge the chicken, shaking off excess. Heat 1½ teaspoons oil in a large nonstick skillet over medium-high heat. Add the chicken and cook until well browned and no longer pink in the center, 3 to 5 minutes per side. Transfer to a plate, cover and keep warm.

2. Whisk LIQUIDS in a measuring cup. Add the remaining 1½ teaspoons oil to the pan, then add the AROMATICS and cook, stirring, for 1 minute. Add the LIQUIDS. Simmer until slightly thickened, 3 to 5 minutes.

3. Return chicken and accumulated juices to the pan; simmer until heated through, 1 to 2 minutes. Transfer the chicken to a serving platter. Stir SEASONINGS into the sauce; add the remaining ¼ teaspoon salt and pepper to taste (*omit for Scallion & Ginger Spiced Chicken*). Spoon the sauce over the chicken; GARNISH.

SCALLION & GINGER SPICED CHICKEN

AROMATICS: **¼ cup minced scallion whites**
3 cloves garlic, minced
1 tablespoon minced fresh ginger
LIQUIDS: **¾ cup reduced-sodium chicken broth**
⅓ cup rice-wine vinegar
2 tablespoons hoisin sauce (*see Tip, page 485*)
2 teaspoons sugar
SEASONINGS: **1 tablespoon reduced-sodium soy sauce**
GARNISH: **½ cup sliced scallion greens**

PER SERVING: 223 calories; 7 g fat (1 g sat, 4 g mono); 73 mg cholesterol; 14 g carbohydrate; 4 g added sugars; 26 g protein; 1 g fiber; 885 mg sodium; 545 mg potassium.

ROSEMARY-ORANGE CHICKEN

AROMATICS: **¼ cup finely chopped shallots**
1 clove garlic, minced
LIQUIDS: **¾ cup fresh orange juice**
½ cup reduced-sodium chicken broth
SEASONINGS: **1 teaspoon butter**
1 teaspoon chopped fresh rosemary
½ teaspoon white-wine vinegar

PER SERVING: 208 calories; 8 g fat (2 g sat, 4 g mono); 75 mg cholesterol; 9 g carbohydrate; 0 g added sugars; 25 g protein; 0 g fiber; 494 mg sodium; 580 mg potassium. NUTRITION BONUS: Vitamin C (43% daily value), Potassium (17% dv).

◀ LEMON & DILL CHICKEN

AROMATICS: **¼ cup finely chopped onion**
3 cloves garlic, minced
LIQUIDS: **1 cup reduced-sodium chicken broth**
2 teaspoons all-purpose flour
1 tablespoon chopped fresh dill
1 tablespoon lemon juice
GARNISH: **1 tablespoon chopped fresh dill**

PER SERVING: 186 calories; 7 g fat (1 g sat, 4 g mono); 73 mg cholesterol; 5 g carbohydrate; 0 g added sugars; 26 g protein; 0 g fiber; 562 mg sodium; 506 mg potassium.

Chicken Breasts with Mushroom Cream Sauce

H✖W

MAKES: 4 servings

ACTIVE TIME: 30 minutes | TOTAL: 30 minutes

This delicious creamy sauce contains a bountiful amount of mushrooms and is served over chicken breasts. It would also be great with seared pork chops.

- 4 5-ounce boneless, skinless chicken breasts, trimmed and tenders removed (*see Tip, page 482*)
- 1 teaspoon freshly ground pepper
- ½ teaspoon salt
- 2 tablespoons canola oil
- 2 medium shallots, minced
- 2 cups thinly sliced shiitake mushroom caps
- ¼ cup dry vermouth *or* dry white wine
- ½ cup reduced-sodium chicken broth
- ¼ cup heavy cream
- ¼ cup minced fresh chives *or* scallion greens

1. Season chicken with pepper and salt on both sides.

2. Heat oil in a large skillet over medium heat. Add the chicken and cook, turning once or twice and adjusting the heat to prevent burning, until brown and an instant-read thermometer inserted into the thickest part registers 165°F, 12 to 16 minutes. Transfer to a plate and tent with foil to keep warm.

3. Add shallot to the pan and cook, stirring, until fragrant, about 30 seconds. Add mushrooms; cook, stirring occasionally, until tender, about 2 minutes. Pour in vermouth (or wine); simmer until almost evaporated, scraping up any browned bits, about 1 minute. Pour in broth and cook until reduced by half, 1 to 2 minutes. Stir in cream and chives (or scallions); return to a simmer. Return the chicken to the pan, turn to coat with sauce and cook until heated through, about 1 minute.

PER SERVING: 274 calories; 15 g fat (5 g sat, 7 g mono); 83 mg cholesterol; 5 g carbohydrate; 0 g added sugars; 25 g protein; 1 g fiber; 281 mg sodium; 381 mg potassium.

EatingWell Tip
Develop flavors using wine and broth as the base of a creamy sauce and add just a small amount of cream at the end to **save on calories and saturated fat**.

Turkish Chicken Thighs

H✴W   H♥H

MAKES: 4 servings
ACTIVE TIME: 10 minutes | TOTAL: 1 hour 40 minutes
(including 1 hour of marinating)

The acidity of yogurt helps tenderize chicken and keep it moist when you use it in a marinade. If you can't find hot paprika, substitute 2 teaspoons sweet paprika and ¼ teaspoon cayenne.

    8   bone-in chicken thighs (about 3½ pounds total),
        skin removed, trimmed
    1   tablespoon lemon juice
    1   cup low-fat plain yogurt
    2   cloves garlic, minced
    1   tablespoon minced fresh ginger
    2   teaspoons hot paprika
 1½   teaspoons dried mint
    ½   teaspoon salt

1. Place chicken in a large bowl. Add lemon juice and toss to coat. Whisk yogurt, garlic, ginger, paprika, mint and salt in a separate bowl. Pour the yogurt mixture over the chicken and stir to coat. Cover with plastic wrap and refrigerate for at least 1 hour or up to 24 hours.

2. Position rack in upper third of oven; preheat broiler. Remove the chicken from the marinade (discard marinade). Place the chicken on a broiler rack and broil until browned on top, about 15 minutes. Reduce oven temperature to 400°F and bake until the chicken is just cooked through and an instant-read thermometer inserted into the thickest part registers 165°F, about 15 minutes more. Serve immediately.

PER SERVING: 207 calories; 10 g fat (3 g sat, 4 g mono); 83 mg cholesterol; 4 g carbohydrate; 0 g added sugars; 24 g protein; 0 g fiber; 284 mg sodium; 320 mg potassium.
NUTRITION BONUS: Zinc (31% daily value), Potassium (18% dv), Magnesium (16% dv).

▶ Quick Chicken Cordon Bleu

H✴W

MAKES: 4 servings
ACTIVE TIME: 35 minutes | TOTAL: 35 minutes

This easy take on chicken Cordon Bleu keeps the flavors the same, but skips the fussy layering and breading steps. Serve with delicata squash and broccoli.

    4   boneless, skinless chicken breasts
        (1¼-1½ pounds), trimmed and tenders
        removed (see Tip, page 482)
    ½   teaspoon freshly ground pepper, divided
    ¼   teaspoon salt
    ⅓   cup shredded Gruyère *or* Swiss cheese
    2   tablespoons reduced-fat cream cheese
    ¼   cup coarse dry whole-wheat breadcrumbs
        (see Tip, page 481)
    1   tablespoon chopped fresh parsley *or* thyme
    4   teaspoons extra-virgin olive oil, divided
    ¼   cup chopped ham (about 1 ounce)

1. Preheat oven to 400°F.

2. Sprinkle chicken with ¼ teaspoon pepper and salt. Combine cheese and cream cheese in a bowl. Combine the remaining ¼ teaspoon pepper with breadcrumbs, parsley (or thyme) and 2 teaspoons oil in another bowl.

3. Heat the remaining 2 teaspoons oil in a large, oven-proof nonstick skillet over medium heat. Cook the chicken until browned on both sides, about 2 minutes per side. Move the chicken to the center so all pieces are touching. Spread with the cheese mixture, sprinkle with ham, then top with the breadcrumb mixture.

4. Bake until the chicken is no longer pink in the center and an instant-read thermometer registers 165°F, 5 to 7 minutes.

PER SERVING: 245 calories; 12 g fat (4 g sat, 6 g mono); 82 mg cholesterol; 4 g carbohydrate; 0 g added sugars; 28 g protein; 1 g fiber; 314 mg sodium; 215 mg potassium.

Thai Chicken & Mango Stir-Fry

H✻W   H♥H

MAKES: 6 servings, about 1 cup each
ACTIVE TIME: 45 minutes | TOTAL: 45 minutes

Both ripe and underripe mango work well in this chicken and vegetable stir-fry. If the mangoes you have are less ripe, use 2 teaspoons brown sugar. If they're ripe and sweet, use just 1 teaspoon or omit the brown sugar altogether. **Shopping Tip:** *Fish sauce is a pungent Southeast Asian condiment made from salted, fermented fish. Find it in the Asian-food section of large supermarkets and at Asian specialty markets. We use Thai Kitchen fish sauce, lower in sodium than other brands (1,190 mg per tablespoon), in our recipe testing and nutritional analyses.*

  2 **tablespoons plus 1 teaspoon fish sauce**
      (see Shopping Tip)
  2 **tablespoons lime juice**
1½ **teaspoons cornstarch**
1-2 **teaspoons brown sugar**
  4 **teaspoons canola oil, divided**
  1 **pound chicken tenders, cut into 1-inch pieces**
  2 **cloves garlic, minced**
  1 **teaspoon minced fresh ginger**
1-2 **fresh small red *or* green chile peppers, stemmed and sliced, *or* ½-¾ teaspoon crushed red pepper**
  4 **cups bite-size broccoli florets**
¼ **cup water**

  2 **mangoes, peeled and sliced (*see Tip, page 486*)**
  1 **bunch scallions, cut into 1-inch pieces**
¼ **cup chopped fresh cilantro**
¼ **cup chopped fresh basil, preferably Thai**
¼ **cup chopped fresh mint**
  1 **lime, cut into 6 wedges (optional)**

1. Combine fish sauce, lime juice, cornstarch and brown sugar to taste in a small bowl.

2. Heat 2 teaspoons oil in a wok or large skillet over high heat. Add chicken; cook, stirring, until just cooked through, 5 to 7 minutes. Transfer to a plate.

3. Add the remaining 2 teaspoons oil, garlic, ginger and chiles (or crushed red pepper) to the pan. Cook, stirring, until fragrant, about 15 seconds. Add broccoli and water; cook, stirring, until beginning to soften, about 2 minutes. Add mangoes and scallions; cook, stirring, for 1 minute. Add the reserved sauce and chicken; cook, stirring, until the sauce is thickened and the chicken is heated through, about 1 minute. Stir in cilantro, basil and mint. Serve with lime wedges, if desired.

PER SERVING: 192 calories; 5 g fat (1 g sat, 3 g mono); 42 mg cholesterol; 19 g carbohydrate; 1 g added sugars; 18 g protein; 4 g fiber; 518 mg sodium; 491 mg potassium.
NUTRITION BONUS: Vitamin C (133% daily value), Vitamin A (49% dv), Folate & Potassium (16% dv).

Pomegranate-Glazed Turkey with Roasted Fennel

H✂W   H⬆F   H♥H

MAKES: 4 servings

ACTIVE TIME: 30 minutes | TOTAL: 30 minutes

Pair turkey cutlets with roasted fennel and a rich pomegranate pan sauce for a simple yet elegant dish. Garnish with jewel-like fresh pomegranate seeds if available—they are in season from September through January. Turkey scallopini (thinner and smaller than cutlets) will also work in this recipe, but will need to be cooked in batches. Serve with bulgur or quinoa.

4	medium fennel bulbs, cored and thickly sliced
5	teaspoons canola oil, divided
½	teaspoon chopped fresh thyme, plus 1 sprig
1	teaspoon kosher salt, divided
¾	teaspoon freshly ground pepper, divided
4	turkey cutlets, ¼ inch thick (1 pound)
1	cup pomegranate juice
¼	cup reduced-sodium chicken broth *or* water
1	teaspoon cornstarch

1. Preheat oven to 450°F.

2. Toss fennel, 3 teaspoons oil, chopped thyme and ¼ teaspoon each salt and pepper in a medium bowl. Spread on a rimmed baking sheet. Roast, stirring twice, until tender and golden, about 25 minutes.

3. Meanwhile, sprinkle both sides of turkey with the remaining ¾ teaspoon salt and ½ teaspoon pepper. Heat the remaining 2 teaspoons oil in a large skillet over medium-high heat. Add the turkey and cook until browned, 1 to 3 minutes per side. Transfer to a plate.

4. Add pomegranate juice and thyme sprig to the pan; bring to a boil. Boil, stirring often, until reduced to ¼ cup, 6 to 10 minutes. Discard the thyme. Whisk broth (or water) and cornstarch; add to the pan and cook, stirring constantly, until thickened, about 15 seconds. Reduce heat to medium, return the turkey and any accumulated juices to the pan, turning to coat with sauce, and cook for 1 minute. To serve, top roasted fennel with turkey and sauce.

PER SERVING: 336 calories; 13 g fat (2 g sat, 6 g mono); 66 mg cholesterol; 27 g carbohydrate; 0 g added sugars; 29 g protein; 7 g fiber; 496 mg sodium; 1,353 mg potassium. NUTRITION BONUS: Vitamin C (47% daily value), Potassium (39% dv), Iron (17% dv).

EatingWell Tip

One of the keys to **getting more vegetables into your diet** is making them taste great. Try roasting them (as we do with fennel in this recipe) to bring out their rich, nutty flavor. (*See page 165 for how to roast 12 vegetables.*)

Choosing Poultry

North Americans eat more poultry than any other meat—nearly 100 pounds per capita annually. And with good reason: chicken and turkey—both white and dark meat—are good sources of protein, and low in fat and calories, particularly *sans* skin. But simple succulence, economy and versatility are the fundamental reasons why poultry is so well loved.

Healthy Choices: Chicken

Boneless, skinless chicken breasts are very low in fat, only 1 to 2 grams of fat per serving. When preparing, trim any excess fat from the outer edge of the breast. Dark meat (thigh and drumstick) has a slightly higher fat content so it's more forgiving of overcooking. There's also a little more iron and almost twice the zinc—not bad for a small increment in calories (3 ounces cooked thigh has 164 calories and 9 grams fat versus 122 calories and 3 grams fat for breast). To trim them well, use kitchen shears to snip the fat away from the meat.

A SERVING OF CHICKEN: For recipes where you want to serve one boneless chicken breast per person, look for relatively small ones. One 4- to 5-ounce breast yields a healthy 3-ounce cooked portion when you remove the tender, the small strip of meat attached to the underside of the breast. Don't throw those tenders away—freeze them in an airtight container until you've gathered enough to make a meal. (Chicken tenders can also be purchased separately.) Four 1-ounce tenders will yield a 3-ounce cooked portion. If you want to serve one thigh per person, buy them at the butcher counter; prepackaged thighs vary dramatically in size. Ask for one 6-ounce boneless, skinless thigh per person. After trimming, you'll have a 4-ounce portion.

Healthy Choices: Turkey

Ground turkey is typically available ground 93%-lean, made from light and dark meat or 99%-lean, made from turkey breast only. We usually prefer 93%-lean because it's juicier and more flavorful. If you use 99%-lean ground turkey, you'll save 30 calories, 5½ grams total fat, 2 grams saturated fat and 20 milligrams cholesterol per serving. Turkey cutlets are thin, quick-cooking cuts of turkey breast and they vary widely in size and weight. Purchase 4 ounces raw cutlet per serving.

What's in a label?

FREE RANGE is a USDA-regulated term that means birds are granted access to the outdoors. Birds do not necessarily live on a grassy range—they may live in a building, but have access to an outdoor area.

CERTIFIED ORGANIC, another USDA-regulated label, means that all feed given to birds must be certified organic, (no chemical fertilizers, pesticides, animal by-products or other additives.) And birds must be given access to the outdoors.

NO HORMONES OR HORMONE-FREE on a label doesn't set one bird apart from another because the USDA prohibits the use of hormones in poultry.

RAISED WITHOUT ANTIBIOTICS indicates that birds were raised without antibiotics to maintain health or treat disease.

NATURAL means that no additives or preservatives were introduced after the poultry was processed (although certain sodium-based broths can be added; read the fine print if this is a concern). "Natural" has nothing to do with standards of care, type of feed or administration of medications.

PERCENT RETAINED WATER is a label required by the USDA that shows the maximum amount of water that may be retained during processing. Birds absorb water when they are dipped in a cold bath after they are slaughtered, in order to quickly lower their temperature, to control pathogens like *Salmonella*. Some producers "air-chill" birds, a process that does not result in any retained water.

CERTIFIED HUMANE RAISED & HANDLED is overseen by a nonprofit endorsed by the American Society for the Prevention of Cruelty to Animals and the Humane Society of the United States, and ensures the bird received basic standards of care.

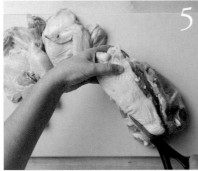

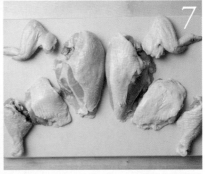

How To

Cut Up a Whole Chicken | Here are 7 steps for cutting a whole chicken into 2 breast halves, 2 thighs, 2 drumsticks and 2 wings.

1. Lay the bird on its back. Wiggle a wing to determine where the joint attaches to the breast. To separate the wing from the breast, use a sharp knife to cut through the ball joint where it meets the breast. Repeat with the other wing.

2. Pull a leg away from the body to see where it attaches. To remove the whole leg, first cut through the skin between the thigh and the breast.

3. Continue to pull on the leg and wiggle it a bit to determine where the thigh meets the socket in the back. Cut through that joint. Repeat with the other leg.

4. Place each leg skin-side down. Flex to see where the ball joint between the drumstick and thigh is located. Look for the thin line of fat that was perpendicular to the body. Cut through the line of fat to separate the thigh and drumstick, wiggling the joint as needed to determine where it is. Repeat with the other leg.

5. To remove the backbone, turn the bird over; start at the head end and cut through the rib cage on one side of the backbone with kitchen shears or a sharp knife. Repeat on the other side of the backbone to remove it completely. (Reserve the backbone to add to the pot when you're cooking chicken stock, if desired; see page 338.)

6. To cut the breast into 2 halves, place it skin-side down, exposing the breastbone. To protect your hand, fold up a kitchen towel and place it on top of a heavy, sharp knife. Use a lot of pressure to cut through the reddish breast bone and whitish cartilage right down the center of the breast. Now you have 2 breast halves. Cut each breast half in half again, crosswise, if desired. (The wishbone is located at the thick part of the breast. If desired, tease the meat away from the 2 pieces of wishbone using your hands and/or a sharp knife to scrape the meat from the bone.)

7. Now you have 8 pieces of chicken.

REFRIGERATE OR FREEZE POULTRY as soon as possible after purchase. Freeze poultry for up to 9 months. If freezing poultry for longer than two weeks, wrap in heavy-duty foil, freezer paper or freezer bags to prevent freezer burn. Frozen poultry should be defrosted in the refrigerator, never at room temperature, to prevent bacterial growth.

◀ Baked Chicken with Onions & Leeks

H✂W   H♥H

MAKES: 6 servings
ACTIVE TIME: 35 minutes | TOTAL: 1 hour 20 minutes

This mustard-glazed chicken is roasted on a bed of sliced onions, leeks and garlic that you can serve alongside it. To save money, try cutting up a whole chicken for this recipe (see page 329) instead of buying chicken parts.

2	cups thinly sliced onions
1	cup thinly sliced leek, white and light green part only, rinsed
4	cloves garlic, thinly sliced
3	tablespoons extra-virgin olive oil, divided
2	teaspoons fresh thyme leaves
¼	teaspoon salt
2½-3	pounds bone-in chicken pieces (thighs, drumsticks *and/or* breasts), skin removed, trimmed
¼	cup Dijon mustard
2	teaspoons minced shallot
1½	teaspoons chopped fresh rosemary
1	teaspoon reduced-sodium soy sauce
¾	teaspoon freshly ground pepper

1. Preheat oven to 400°F.

2. Toss onions, leek, garlic, 2 tablespoons oil, thyme and salt in a large bowl to coat. Spread the mixture in a nonreactive 9-by-13-inch baking dish (*see Tip, page 486*). Cut any chicken breasts in half crosswise so they'll cook more quickly. Place the chicken pieces on the vegetables. Bake for 10 minutes.

3. Meanwhile, whisk mustard, shallot, rosemary, soy sauce and pepper in a small bowl; gradually whisk in the remaining 1 tablespoon oil. After 10 minutes, brush the chicken with the mustard glaze. Continue baking until an instant-read thermometer inserted into the thickest part of a leg or breast (without touching bone) registers 165°F, 30 to 45 minutes more. Serve the chicken with the vegetables.

PER SERVING: 260 calories; 13 g fat (3 g sat, 8 g mono); 78 mg cholesterol; 8 g carbohydrate; 0 g added sugars; 26 g protein; 1 g fiber; 332 mg sodium; 338 mg potassium.

Picnic Oven-Fried Chicken

H✂W   H♥H

MAKES: 4 servings
ACTIVE TIME: 20 minutes | TOTAL: 1 hour 35 minutes (including 30 minutes marinating time)
TO MAKE AHEAD: Marinate the chicken for up to 8 hours.

It's true: crunchy, flavorful fried chicken can be healthy! (Photograph: page 13.)

½	cup nonfat buttermilk (*see Tip, page 482*)
1	tablespoon Dijon mustard
2	cloves garlic, minced
1	teaspoon hot sauce
2½-3	pounds whole chicken legs, skin removed, trimmed and cut into thighs and drumsticks
½	cup whole-wheat flour
2	tablespoons sesame seeds
1½	teaspoons paprika
1	teaspoon dried thyme
1	teaspoon baking powder
⅛	teaspoon salt
	Freshly ground pepper to taste
	Olive oil cooking spray

1. Whisk buttermilk, mustard, garlic and hot sauce in a shallow glass dish until well blended. Add chicken and turn to coat. Cover and marinate in the refrigerator for at least 30 minutes or for up to 8 hours.

2. Preheat oven to 425°F. Line a baking sheet with foil. Set a wire rack on it and coat with cooking spray.

3. Combine flour, sesame seeds, paprika, thyme, baking powder, salt and pepper in a sealable bag. Tapping off excess marinade, place one or two pieces of chicken at a time in the bag and shake to coat. Tap off excess flour; place the chicken on the prepared rack. Spray the chicken pieces with cooking spray.

4. Bake the chicken until golden brown and no longer pink in the center, 40 to 50 minutes.

PER SERVING: 226 calories; 7 g fat (2 g sat, 2 g mono); 130 mg cholesterol; 5 g carbohydrate; 0 g added sugars; 34 g protein; 1 g fiber; 258 mg sodium; 406 mg potassium.

Brazilian Chicken & Peanut Stew

H✖W   H♥H

MAKES: 8 servings

ACTIVE TIME: 50 minutes | TOTAL: 1 hour 10 minutes

TO MAKE AHEAD: Cover and refrigerate for up to 3 days
or freeze for up to 1 month.

*Ground peanuts, shrimp and coconut in this stew reflects
the distinct African influence in Brazilian food. This stew
has an amazing robust flavor, so pair it with something
subtle like brown rice or whole-wheat noodles.* **Shopping
Tips: Dried shrimp** *are tiny dried crustaceans often used in
Asian and Latin American cooking. They have a distinctive,
pungent, fishy flavor. Look for them at Asian markets or at
amazon.com.* **Fish sauce** *is a pungent Southeast Asian
sauce made from salted, fermented fish. It can be found
in the Asian section of large supermarkets and at Asian
specialty markets.*

4	teaspoons extra-virgin olive oil, divided
2	pounds boneless, skinless chicken breasts, trimmed and cut into bite-size pieces
¼	teaspoon salt
	Pinch of freshly ground pepper
1	large onion, chopped
1	red bell pepper, chopped
6	plum tomatoes, chopped
¼	cup chopped fresh parsley
4	cloves garlic, minced
¼	cup dried shrimp *or* 3 tablespoons fish sauce (*see Shopping Tips*), optional
¼	cup roasted peanuts
1	14-ounce can reduced-sodium chicken broth
¾	cup "lite" coconut milk

1. Heat 2 teaspoons oil in a Dutch oven over medium-high heat. Add chicken, salt and pepper and sauté, stirring often, until cooked through, about 5 minutes. Transfer to a medium bowl and set aside.

2. Heat the remaining 2 teaspoons oil in the pot over medium heat. Add onion and bell pepper and cook, stirring occasionally, until softened, 3 to 5 minutes. Add tomatoes, parsley and garlic, reduce to a simmer and cook, stirring occasionally, until thick and bubbly, 10 to 15 minutes.

3. Meanwhile, place dried shrimp (if using) in a food processor and process until finely ground. Transfer to a small bowl. Add peanuts to the processor and process until finely ground. Combine the ground shrimp (or fish sauce), if using, with the ground peanuts.

4. Add broth, coconut milk and the peanut mixture to the pot. Increase heat to medium, bring to a simmer and cook, stirring occasionally, until slightly thickened, 10 to 15 minutes. Add the reserved chicken and cook until heated through, about 2 minutes.

PER SERVING: 216 calories; 9 g fat (3 g sat, 4 g mono);
63 mg cholesterol; 7 g carbohydrate; 0 g added sugars;
26 g protein; 2 g fiber; 243 mg sodium; 459 mg potassium.
NUTRITION BONUS: Vitamin C (62% daily value), Vitamin A (24% dv).

Barbecue Pulled Chicken

H✖W   H♥H

MAKES: 8 servings

ACTIVE TIME: 25 minutes | SLOW-COOKER TIME: 5 hours

TO MAKE AHEAD: Cover and refrigerate for up to 3 days or freeze for up to 1 month. | PREP AHEAD: Combine sauce ingredients (in Step 1) in a bowl. Trim chicken thighs. Chop onion and mince garlic. Refrigerate in separate covered containers for up to 1 day. | EQUIPMENT: 6-quart slow cooker

This fanciful reinterpretation of pulled pork uses chicken and lots of tomato sauce. Serve on buns topped with sliced red onions, with coleslaw on the side.

1	**8-ounce can reduced-sodium tomato sauce**
1	**4-ounce can chopped green chiles, drained**
3	**tablespoons cider vinegar**
2	**tablespoons honey**
1	**tablespoon sweet *or* smoked paprika**
1	**tablespoon tomato paste**
1	**tablespoon Worcestershire sauce**
2	**teaspoons dry mustard**
1	**teaspoon ground chipotle chile (*see Tip, page 487*)**
½	**teaspoon salt**
2½	**pounds boneless, skinless chicken thighs, trimmed**
1	**small onion, finely chopped**
1	**clove garlic, minced**

1. Stir tomato sauce, chiles, vinegar, honey, paprika, tomato paste, Worcestershire sauce, mustard, ground chipotle and salt in a 6-quart slow cooker until smooth. Add chicken, onion and garlic; stir to combine.

2. Put the lid on and cook on Low until the chicken can be pulled apart, about 5 hours.

3. Transfer the chicken to a clean cutting board and shred with a fork. Return the chicken to the sauce, stir well and serve.

PER SERVING: 210 calories; 9 g fat (2 g sat, 3 g mono); 74 mg cholesterol; 10 g carbohydrate; 4 g added sugars; 21 g protein; 1 g fiber; 312 mg sodium; 389 mg potassium.
NUTRITION BONUS: Vitamin C (18% daily value), Vitamin A & Zinc (15% dv).

> **EatingWell Tip**
>
> Tender chicken thighs are a good stand-in for fattier cuts of meat like pork shoulder. Using thighs in this recipe instead of pork **saves you 32 calories and 3 grams of fat** per 3-ounce serving.

Greek Chicken & Vegetable Ragout

H ♥ H

MAKES: 6 servings, about 1⅓ cups each
ACTIVE TIME: 40 minutes | SLOW-COOKER TIME: 2½-3 hours on High *or* 4-4½ hours on Low | TO MAKE AHEAD: Cover and refrigerate for up to 2 days. Freezing is not recommended.
PREP AHEAD: Peel and cut potatoes; cover with water. Trim chicken thighs. Combine broth, wine and minced garlic. Refrigerate in separate covered containers for up to 1 day.
EQUIPMENT: 4-quart or larger slow cooker

Chicken thighs stay moist and succulent during slow cooking, infusing the accompanying vegetables with superb flavor. This easy braise has a luxurious finish of avgolémono, *a versatile Greek sauce made with egg, lemon and fresh dill. Serve with whole-wheat orzo or crusty bread to soak up the sauce.*

1   **pound carrots, cut into 1¼-inch pieces,** *or* **3 cups baby carrots**
1   **pound (3-4 medium) yellow-fleshed potatoes, such as Yukon Gold, peeled and cut lengthwise into 1¼-inch-wide wedges**
2   **pounds boneless, skinless chicken thighs, trimmed**
1   **14-ounce can reduced-sodium chicken broth**
⅓   **cup dry white wine**
4   **cloves garlic, minced**
¾   **teaspoon salt**
1   **15-ounce can artichoke hearts, rinsed and quartered if large**
1   **large egg**
2   **large egg yolks**
⅓   **cup lemon juice**
⅓   **cup chopped fresh dill**
    Freshly ground pepper to taste

1. Spread carrots and potatoes over the bottom and up the sides of a 4-quart or larger slow cooker. Arrange chicken on top of the vegetables. Bring broth, wine, garlic and salt to a simmer in a medium saucepan over medium-high heat. Pour over the chicken and vegetables. Cover and cook until the chicken is cooked through and vegetables are tender, 2½ to 3 hours on High or 4 to 4½ hours on Low.

2. Add artichokes to the slow cooker, cover and cook on High for 5 minutes. Meanwhile, whisk egg, egg yolks and lemon juice in a medium bowl.

3. Transfer the chicken and vegetables to a serving bowl using a slotted spoon. Cover and keep warm. Ladle about ½ cup of the cooking liquid into the egg mixture. Whisk until smooth. Whisk the egg mixture into the remaining cooking liquid in the slow cooker. Cover and cook on High, whisking 2 or 3 times, until slightly thickened and sauce reaches 160°F on an instant-read thermometer, 15 to 20 minutes. Stir in dill and pepper. Pour the sauce over the chicken and vegetables and serve.

PER SERVING: 357 calories; 13 g fat (4 g sat, 5 g mono); 192 mg cholesterol; 29 g carbohydrate; 0 g added sugars; 30 g protein; 5 g fiber; 761 mg sodium; 804 mg potassium.
NUTRITION BONUS: Vitamin A (206% daily value), Vitamin C (38% dv), Potassium (23% dv).

EatingWell Tip

Fresh herbs **flavor dishes healthfully**. Add tender herbs, such as dill, cilantro and parsley, just before serving to give maximum flavor impact.

Roasting Chicken & Loving the Leftovers

If you're looking for a way to make your food dollars and cooking efforts go further, roast a whole chicken or two. If you're cooking for two, one roast chicken yields at least two meals' worth of meat: eat the freshly roasted chicken one night and use the leftover meat as the base of your meal the next night. (*See recipes on pages 339-341 for what to do with leftover chicken.*) If you're cooking for four or more: roasting two chickens at once is hardly any more work. You can make a quick broth out of the roasted bones to get even more for your money (*see recipe below*).

Two Simple Herb-Roasted Chickens

MAKES: 12-16 servings (depending on size of chickens)
ACTIVE TIME: 20 minutes | TOTAL: 2 hours
EQUIPMENT: Kitchen string

Season your chicken with whatever herbs you like—we've included some basic suggestions in the recipe to get you started. Though we like to roast two birds at once, you can also easily halve all the ingredients and just roast one. (Photograph: page 314.)

- ¼ **cup chopped fresh herbs, such as parsley, sage, rosemary *and/or* thyme**
- 2 **cloves garlic, minced**
- 2 **tablespoons extra-virgin olive oil**
- 2 **teaspoons kosher salt**
- 1 **teaspoon freshly ground pepper**
- 2 **4- to 5-pound whole chickens, giblets reserved for making Chicken Stock**

1. Preheat oven to 375°F. Lightly coat a large roasting pan with cooking spray.

2. Mix herbs, garlic, oil, salt and pepper in a small bowl to form a paste. Rub the herb mixture all over the chickens, under the skin and over the breast and thigh meat. Tie the legs together with kitchen string. Place the chickens in the prepared pan, breast-side up, preferably not touching each other.

3. Roast the chickens for 45 minutes. Rotate the pan 180 degrees and continue roasting until a thermometer inserted into the thickest part of the thigh, without touching the bone, registers 165°F, 45 minutes to 1 hour more. (Be sure to check the temperature of each chicken. One might be done before the other.) Transfer to a clean cutting board; let rest for 10 minutes before removing the string and carving (*see How To, page 345*).

PER 3-OUNCE SERVING: 165 calories; 7 g fat (2 g sat, 3 g mono); 69 mg cholesterol; 1 g carbohydrate; 0 g added sugars; 23 g protein; 0 g fiber; 206 mg sodium; 201 mg potassium.

CHICKEN STOCK

MAKES: about 12 cups
ACTIVE TIME: 15 minutes | TOTAL: 2¼ hours | TO MAKE AHEAD: Refrigerate for up to 2 days or freeze for up to 6 months.

Use the leftovers of a roasted chicken dinner (after removing the meat) to make savory broth.

- 2 **roast chicken carcasses, meat removed, plus reserved giblets**
- 1 **onion, quartered**
- 1 **carrot, quartered**
- 1 **stalk celery, quartered**
- 6 **cloves garlic, unpeeled**
- 16 **cups water**
   Several sprigs each fresh parsley and thyme
- 1 **teaspoon whole black peppercorns**
- 1 **teaspoon salt**

Place carcasses and giblets in a large pot. Add onion, carrot, celery, garlic and water. Bring to a boil, skimming foam. Reduce heat to low and add herbs, peppercorns and salt; simmer gently, uncovered, for 2 hours. Strain through a fine sieve into a large bowl. (Discard solids.) If not using immediately, cool the stock before storing (*see How To, page 79*). Once the stock is cool, use a spoon to remove any congealed fat from the surface.

ANALYSIS NOTE: After straining and skimming, stock has negligible calories and nutrients.

4 Quick Meals with Leftover Chicken

▼ 1. MOROCCAN CHICKEN SALAD

H✖W   H♥H

MAKES: 4 servings, about 1⅓ cups each

ACTIVE TIME: 20 minutes | TOTAL: 20 minutes

⅓ cup orange juice

¼ cup reduced-sodium chicken broth

2 tablespoons lemon juice

2 tablespoons chopped fresh mint

2 tablespoons chopped fresh cilantro

2 teaspoons extra-virgin olive oil

½ teaspoon ground cinnamon

⅛ teaspoon cayenne pepper

2 cups shredded cooked chicken

2 cups cooked rice (*see guide, page 184*)

2 cups shredded carrots

¼ cup sliced scallions

¼ cup chopped Kalamata olives

½ teaspoon salt

Freshly ground pepper to taste

Whisk orange juice, broth, lemon juice, mint, cilantro, oil, cinnamon and cayenne in a large bowl. Add chicken, rice, carrots, scallions and olives. Toss to coat. Season with salt and pepper.

PER SERVING: 326 calories; 12 g fat (3 g sat, 6 g mono); 67 mg cholesterol; 32 g carbohydrate; 0 g added sugars; 22 g protein; 3 g fiber; 515 mg sodium; 484 mg potassium.

NUTRITION BONUS: Vitamin A (192% daily value), Vitamin C (35% dv), Folate (28% dv), Iron & Zinc (16% dv).

Korean Chicken Soup

Shredded Chicken & Pinto Bean Burritos

◀ 2. KOREAN CHICKEN SOUP

H✖W H♥H

MAKES: 6 servings, generous 1 cup each
ACTIVE TIME: 20 minutes | TOTAL: 35 minutes

- 8   cups reduced-sodium chicken broth
- 2   tablespoons finely chopped garlic
- 2   tablespoons finely grated fresh ginger
- ½   cup uncooked white rice
- 1   tablespoon reduced-sodium soy sauce
- 1   teaspoon toasted sesame oil
- 1-2 teaspoons hot chile paste *or* hot chile sauce
- 1   cup shredded cooked chicken (*see page 338 or How To, below*)
- 2   scallions, finely chopped
- 1   tablespoon sesame seeds, toasted (*see Tip, page 489*)

Combine broth, garlic and ginger in a Dutch oven; bring to a boil over high heat. Add rice, reduce the heat to medium-low and simmer until the rice is tender, 12 to 15 minutes. Stir in soy sauce and sesame oil; add chile paste (or sauce) to taste. Add chicken and heat through. Garnish with scallions and sesame seeds.

PER SERVING: 149 calories; 2 g fat (0 g sat, 1 g mono); 20 mg cholesterol; 18 g carbohydrate; 0 g added sugars; 13 g protein; 1 g fiber; 857 mg sodium; 392 mg potassium.
NUTRITION BONUS: Folate (16% daily value).

How To

Poach Chicken Breasts | If you don't have leftover chicken but you want to make a recipe that calls for cooked chicken, the easiest way to cook it is to poach it. Place boneless, skinless chicken breasts in a medium skillet or saucepan. Add lightly salted water (or chicken broth) to cover and bring to a boil. Cover, reduce heat to low and simmer gently until the chicken is cooked through and no longer pink in the middle, 10 to 15 minutes. (1 pound raw chicken = about 2½ cups chopped or shredded cooked chicken)

3. CURRIED CHICKEN & PASTA SALAD

H↑F H♥H

MAKES: 6 servings, about 1¼ cups each
ACTIVE TIME: 25 minutes | TOTAL: 25 minutes

- 12 ounces large whole-wheat pasta shells *or* penne
- 2 tablespoons slivered almonds
- 1 tablespoon curry powder, preferably Madras
- ½ cup low-fat mayonnaise
- ½ cup low-fat plain yogurt *or* reduced-fat sour cream
- ⅓ cup mango chutney (*see Tip, page 486*)
- 1 teaspoon turmeric
- ¼ teaspoon ground cinnamon
  Pinch of cayenne pepper, or to taste
- 2 cups cooked chicken (*see page 338 or How To, opposite*), cut into 1-inch pieces
- ½ cup raisins
- 4 scallions, chopped
- ½ cup diced celery
- ⅛ teaspoon salt
  Freshly ground pepper to taste

1. Cook pasta in a large pot of lightly salted water until just tender, about 10 minutes. Drain and rinse. Set aside.

2. Toast almonds in a small dry skillet over low heat, stirring constantly, until golden, about 2 minutes. Transfer to a plate to cool. Return the pan to the stovetop and add curry powder. Toast, stirring constantly, over low heat until fragrant, about 30 seconds. Transfer to a small bowl; stir in mayonnaise, yogurt, chutney, turmeric, cinnamon and cayenne.

3. Combine chicken, raisins, scallions, celery and the reserved pasta in a large bowl. Add the dressing and toss to coat. Taste and adjust seasonings with salt, pepper and cayenne. Sprinkle the toasted almonds on top.

PER SERVING: 452 calories; 9 g fat (1 g sat, 2 g mono); 46 mg cholesterol; 70 g carbohydrate; 9 g added sugars; 24 g protein; 7 g fiber; 473 mg sodium; 573 mg potassium.
NUTRITION BONUS: Iron & Potassium (16% daily value).

◀ 4. SHREDDED CHICKEN & PINTO BEAN BURRITOS

H↑F

MAKES: 6 servings
ACTIVE TIME: 20 minutes | TOTAL: 40 minutes

- 1 tablespoon canola oil
- 1 medium onion, halved and sliced
- 2 cloves garlic, minced
- 1 tablespoon ground cumin
- 1 teaspoon chili powder
- 1 15-ounce can diced tomatoes with green chiles, undrained
- 2 tablespoons lime juice
- 4 cups shredded cooked chicken (*see page 338 or How To, opposite*)
- 1 15-ounce can pinto beans, rinsed
- 6 10-inch whole-wheat flour tortillas
- ¾ cup grated Monterey *or* pepper Jack cheese
- 2 cups shredded green cabbage

Heat oil in a large saucepan over medium heat. Add onion and cook, stirring, until softened, about 2 minutes. Stir in garlic, cumin and chili powder and cook for 30 seconds. Add tomatoes and lime juice; bring to a boil. Reduce heat to a simmer and cook until the onions are very soft, 16 to 20 minutes. Stir in chicken and beans and continue cooking until the mixture is heated through, 3 to 5 minutes more. Divide the mixture among tortillas. Top each with cheese and cabbage, roll into burritos and serve.

PER SERVING: 512 calories; 14 g fat (5 g sat, 4 g mono); 92 mg cholesterol; 52 g carbohydrate; 0 g added sugars; 42 g protein; 7 g fiber; 970 mg sodium; 464 mg potassium.
NUTRITION BONUS: Calcium (31% daily value), Iron (25% dv), Vitamin C (22% dv).

Grilled Duck with Strawberry-Fig Sauce

H ✖ W

MAKES: 4 servings
ACTIVE TIME: 50 minutes | TOTAL: 50 minutes
TO MAKE AHEAD: Cover and refrigerate the sauce (Steps 1-2) for up to 2 days.

Here we pair a luscious strawberry-fig sauce with grilled duck for an elegant main dish. Serve with rice pilaf and grilled vegetables. **Shopping Tip:** *Boneless duck breasts range widely in weight, from about ½ to 1 pound, depending on the breed of duck. For this recipe, we recommend using smaller (about ½-pound) breasts—we prefer their milder flavor. Look for them near other poultry in the fresh or frozen specialty-meat section of large supermarkets or online at* mapleleaffarms.com *or* dartagnan.com.

1	tablespoon extra-virgin olive oil
1	medium shallot, sliced
⅓	cup port (*see Tip, page 488*)
2	tablespoons chopped dried figs
2½	cups halved fresh strawberries (about 12 ounces), divided
1	cup plus 2 tablespoons reduced-sodium chicken broth, divided
1	tablespoon plus 1 teaspoon balsamic vinegar, divided
½	teaspoon salt, divided
½	teaspoon freshly ground pepper, divided
1	teaspoon cornstarch
1½-2	pounds boneless duck breasts (*see Shopping Tip*), trimmed, skin removed
1	tablespoon chopped fresh basil

1. Heat oil in a large saucepan over medium heat. Add shallot and cook, stirring, until beginning to soften, about 1 minute. Add port and figs and cook, stirring, 1 minute. Add 1½ cups strawberries, 1 cup broth, 1 tablespoon vinegar, ¼ teaspoon salt and ¼ teaspoon pepper; bring to a boil. Reduce heat to a simmer and cook, stirring occasionally, until the strawberries are very soft and broken down and the sauce has reduced slightly, about 15 minutes.

2. Strain the sauce through a fine-mesh strainer into a 2-cup glass measuring cup or bowl (discard the solids). You should have about 1 cup liquid. (If you have more than that, return the sauce to the pan and continue reducing until you have about 1 cup.) Combine the remaining 2 tablespoons broth and cornstarch in a small bowl. Return the strained sauce to the pan along with the cornstarch mixture; cook over medium heat, stirring, until the sauce is thick enough to coat the back of a spoon and has reduced by half, 5 to 7 minutes. Combine 1 tablespoon of the sauce with the remaining 1 teaspoon vinegar in a small bowl to use as a basting sauce. Cover the remaining sauce to keep warm.

3. Meanwhile, preheat grill to medium.

4. Season duck breasts with the remaining ¼ teaspoon salt and pepper. Oil the grill rack (*see Tip, page 485*). Grill the duck, basting twice, until an instant-read thermometer inserted into the thickest part registers 150°F for medium, 4 to 8 minutes per side, depending on the thickness. Transfer to a clean cutting board and let rest for 5 minutes.

5. While the duck is resting, chop the remaining 1 cup strawberries. Slice the duck and serve with the sauce, garnished with the chopped strawberries and basil.

PER SERVING: 298 calories; 16 g fat (5 g sat, 7 g mono); 95 mg cholesterol; 7 g carbohydrate; 0 g added sugars; 26 g protein; 1 g fiber; 519 mg sodium; 400 mg potassium.
NUTRITION BONUS: Vitamin C (42% daily value), Zinc (19% dv), Iron (18% dv).

EatingWell Tip

Despite its rich reputation, duck is actually a **lean and healthy source of protein**—when you serve it without the skin. Duck breast has 139 calories and 5 grams of fat per 3-ounce serving with the skin removed.

Roasted Garlic & Meyer Lemon-Rubbed Turkey

H✁W   H♥H

MAKES: 12 servings, 3 ounces each, plus leftovers
ACTIVE TIME: 45 minutes | TOTAL: 5 hours
TO MAKE AHEAD: Prepare through Step 4; cover and refrigerate for up to 1 day. | EQUIPMENT: Kitchen string

Mellow white miso paste (found in natural-foods stores and well-stocked supermarkets) is the secret ingredient in this amazing Meyer lemon and garlic rub. The miso gives the turkey a mildly salted taste without the hassle of brining. (Photograph: page 15.) **Shopping Tip:** *Look for* **Meyer lemons** *in late winter and early spring in well-stocked supermarkets and specialty grocers. If you can't find them, use 2 teaspoons lemon zest and 1 teaspoon orange zest plus 2 tablespoons lemon juice and 2 teaspoons orange juice in Step 3. Place lemon and orange skins into the cavity in Step 6.*

2	heads garlic
3	Meyer lemons (*see Shopping Tip*)
¼	cup sweet white miso (*see Tip, page 486*)
2	tablespoons canola oil
1	tablespoon chopped fresh thyme, plus 3 sprigs
½	teaspoon freshly ground pepper
1	10- to 12-pound turkey
1	medium yellow onion, peeled and quartered, divided
2	cups water, plus more as needed
	Citrus Gravy (*opposite*)

1. Position rack in lower third of oven; preheat to 400°F.

2. Rub off excess papery skin from garlic heads without separating the cloves. Slice the tips off, exposing the ends of the cloves. Place the heads on a square of foil (or in a ceramic garlic roaster). Sprinkle with 4 teaspoons water and wrap into a package. Roast until very soft, 40 to 45 minutes. Unwrap and let cool.

3. Zest lemons. Place the zest in a medium bowl; juice the lemons into the bowl through a strainer to catch the seeds. Reserve the squeezed lemon skins.

4. Add miso, oil, chopped thyme and pepper to the lemon mixture. Squeeze the garlic cloves out of their skins into the bowl. Whisk until the mixture forms a paste.

5. Reduce oven temperature to 350°. Remove giblets and neck from turkey cavities; reserve for making Turkey Giblet Stock, if desired. Pat the turkey dry with paper towels.

6. Loosen the skin over the breast and thigh meat. Rub the paste under the skin onto the breast meat and leg meat and a little inside the cavity. Tuck the wing tips under the turkey. Place the reserved squeezed lemon skins, thyme sprigs and 2 onion quarters in the cavity. (You may not use all the citrus skins.) Tie the legs together with kitchen string. Place the turkey breast-side up on a roasting rack set in a large roasting pan.

7. Roast the turkey for 1 hour. Add 2 cups water and the remaining onion to the pan, tent with foil and continue roasting for 1 hour more. Baste the turkey with pan drippings and continue roasting, basting every 15 minutes or so, until an instant-read thermometer inserted into the thickest part of a thigh without touching bone registers 165°F, 1½ to 2 hours more. Add more water 1 cup at a time if the pan is dry.

8. Transfer the turkey to a clean cutting board (reserve the pan juices). Let the turkey rest while you make Citrus Gravy. Remove the string and carve (*see How To, opposite*).

PER 3 OUNCES MEAT & 2 TABLESPOONS GRAVY: 185 calories; 6 g fat (1 g sat, 2 g mono); 63 mg cholesterol; 4 g carbohydrate; 0 g added sugars; 26 g protein; 1 g fiber; 219 mg sodium; 299 mg potassium. NUTRITION BONUS: Zinc (17% daily value).

How To

Make Turkey Giblet Stock | Combine **neck and giblets** (except liver) from a 10- to 12-pound turkey, 6 cups **water**, 1 peeled and quartered medium **onion**, 1 medium chopped **carrot** and 1 chopped **celery** stalk in a large saucepan; bring to a boil. Add 1 **bay leaf**, 1 sprig fresh **thyme** and 1 teaspoon whole black **peppercorns**. Reduce heat and simmer, skimming and discarding any foam, for 1 hour. Strain stock through a fine-mesh sieve into a medium bowl and let cool. Discard solids. If necessary, add enough water (or reduced-sodium chicken broth) to measure 4 cups stock.

CITRUS GRAVY

MAKES: about 2½ cups

ACTIVE TIME: 25 minutes | TOTAL: 25 minutes

This rich gravy has the added brightness of lemon. Make it while the turkey rests.

4 cups Turkey Giblet Stock (*see How To, opposite*) *or* reduced-sodium chicken broth, divided
¼ cup all-purpose flour
1 cup dry white wine
2 tablespoons Meyer lemon juice *or* 4 teaspoons lemon juice plus 2 teaspoons orange juice
¼ teaspoon salt
Freshly ground pepper to taste

1. When you remove the turkey from the roasting pan (*Step 8, opposite*), leave the roasted onions behind. Skim off any visible fat from the pan juices.

2. Whisk ½ cup of the stock (or chicken broth) and flour in a small bowl until smooth; set aside.

3. Set the roasting pan over two burners on medium heat. Add wine; bring to a boil and cook, scraping up the browned bits, until the liquid is reduced by about half, 2 to 4 minutes. Add the remaining 3½ cups stock (or broth). Increase heat to medium-high; return to a boil, stirring often. Boil until the liquid is reduced by about half, 6 to 8 minutes.

4. Whisk the reserved flour-stock mixture and add it to the pan, whisking constantly, until the gravy is thickened, 1 to 3 minutes. Stir in lemon juice (or lemon and orange juices). Remove from the heat and pour the gravy through a fine sieve into a large measuring cup. (Discard the solids.) Season with salt and pepper.

PER 2-TABLESPOON SERVING: 16 calories; 0 g fat (0 g sat, 0 g mono); 0 mg cholesterol; 2 g carbohydrate; 0 g added sugars; 0 g protein; 0 g fiber; 31 mg sodium; 13 mg potassium.

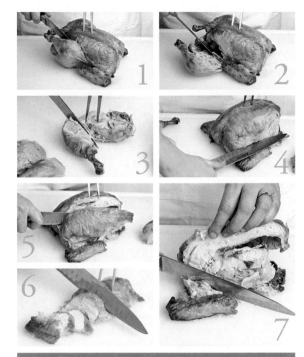

How To

Carve a Turkey or Chicken | After the bird is roasted, let it rest for up to 30 minutes before carving. Then, follow these easy step-by-step instructions.

1. Place the roasted bird on a cutting board. Hold it steady with a carving fork and cut through the skin between the leg and body using a large sharp carving knife.

2. Cut through the hip joint, removing the entire leg from the body. Repeat with the other leg.

3. Place a leg skin-side down and cut through the joint between the drumstick and thigh. Repeat with the other leg. (For turkey, slice the meat away from the bone of the thigh and slice the thigh meat thinly. Hold the drumstick and slice the meat off parallel to the bone.)

4. To remove the breast meat, make a horizontal cut near the base.

5. Then, hold near the breastbone with the carving fork. Use a boning knife to make a cut along one side of the breast down to the horizontal cut you made at the base of the body. Repeat with the second breast half on the other side of the breastbone.

6. Cut the breast meat into slices, if desired.

7. Bend a wing away from the body and use a knife to remove the wing piece. Repeat with the other wing. Cut off the wingtips, if desired.

Game Hens with Brussels Sprouts & Chestnuts

H✖W   H⬆F   H♥H

MAKES: 8 servings, ½ game hen & about ¾ cup vegetables each
ACTIVE TIME: 40 minutes | TOTAL: 1 hour 25 minutes
EQUIPMENT: Kitchen string

Game hens are easy to prepare and will help make your celebration more festive. Their buttery flavor complements roasted Brussels sprouts and chestnuts. **Shopping Tip:** *Cooked peeled chestnuts are available in jars in the baking aisle or with seasonal foods at many supermarkets.*

- 1 **tablespoon chopped fresh thyme**
- 2 **teaspoons salt**
- 1 **teaspoon freshly ground pepper**
- 4 **Cornish game hens, 1-1½ pounds each**
- 2 **teaspoons butter**
- 2 **teaspoons extra-virgin olive oil**
- 1 **large red onion, peeled and cut through the root end into 8 wedges**
- 2 **pounds Brussels sprouts, trimmed and cut in half if large (about 6 cups)**
- 16 **ounces jarred roasted chestnuts (2½ cups; see Shopping Tip)**
- 2 **tablespoons white-wine vinegar**

1. Preheat oven to 375°F. Combine thyme, salt and pepper in a small bowl.

2. Remove giblets (if included) from game hens and trim any excess skin. Loosen the skin over the breast and thigh meat and rub half the thyme mixture under the skin. Tie legs together with kitchen string.

3. Heat butter and oil in a large roasting pan set over 2 burners on medium heat. Add the game hens; brown on all sides, turning occasionally, 10 to 12 minutes.

4. Add onion to the pan, transfer to the oven and roast for 10 minutes. Add Brussels sprouts and roast for 20 minutes. Stir chestnuts and the remaining thyme mixture into the pan. Continue roasting until an instant-read thermometer inserted into a thigh registers 165°F, 10 to 15 minutes more.

5. Transfer the game hens to a large clean cutting board and let rest for 10 minutes. Place the roasting pan over 2 burners on medium heat. Toss the vegetables with vinegar and bring to a simmer, gently stirring and scraping up any browned bits. Remove the string from the game hens, turn breast-side down and slice in half lengthwise using a large heavy knife, cutting straight through to the breast side. Serve the game hens with the vegetables.

PER SERVING: 324 calories; 7 g fat (2 g sat, 3 g mono); 93 mg cholesterol; 41 g carbohydrate; 0 g added sugars; 25 g protein; 7 g fiber; 663 mg sodium; 978 mg potassium.
NUTRITION BONUS: Vitamin C (173% daily value), Potassium (28% dv), Folate (27% dv), Vitamin A (18% dv), Iron (16% dv).

EatingWell Tip
Remove the skin from poultry before you eat it. You'll save about 6 grams of fat and 2 grams of saturated fat for each 3-ounce serving.

Butterflied Grilled Chicken with a Chile-Lime Rub

H✳W   H❤H

MAKES: 6 servings

ACTIVE TIME: 30 minutes | TOTAL: 1 hour 25 minutes
(plus 12-24 hours marinating time)

A quick and efficient way to cook a whole bird on the grill is to butterfly it. In this recipe, we sear the chicken over direct heat then finish cooking over indirect heat. That way we avoid the all-too-common grilling problem of chicken burned on the outside and raw in the center. For best flavor, let the chicken marinate in the rub overnight in the refrigerator. Serve with lime wedges and fresh salsa.

3	tablespoons chile powder, preferably New Mexico, *or* Hungarian paprika
2	tablespoons extra-virgin olive oil
2	teaspoons freshly grated lime zest
3	tablespoons lime juice
1	tablespoon minced garlic
1	teaspoon ground coriander
1	teaspoon ground cumin
1	teaspoon dried oregano, preferably Mexican
1½	teaspoons kosher salt
1	teaspoon freshly ground pepper
	Pinch of ground cinnamon
1	3½- to 4-pound chicken

1. Combine chile powder (or paprika) and oil in a small bowl with lime zest and juice, garlic, coriander, cumin, oregano, salt, pepper and cinnamon to form a wet paste.

2. Using kitchen shears, cut the chicken down one side of the backbone, through the ribs (PHOTO 1). Make an identical cut on the opposite side to remove the backbone completely (PHOTO 2); discard (or reserve it for stock). Place the chicken cut-side down and flatten with the heel of your hand (PHOTO 3). Generously smear the spice rub under and over the skin and on the interior of the bird. Place in a nonreactive baking dish (*see Tip, page 486*). Cover with plastic wrap and refrigerate overnight or up to 24 hours.

3. Preheat half the grill to medium-high (or build a medium-high heat fire on one side of a charcoal grill); leave the other half unheated. Have a squirt bottle of water ready by the grill.

4. Leave all the spice rub on the chicken. Place the chicken skin-side down over the heat and grill until the skin begins to color and grill marks form, about 5 minutes. (Extinguish any flare-ups with the squirt bottle.) Flip over and grill 5 minutes more. Move the chicken to the unheated side. Close the lid and cook, making sure the chicken is flat against the grate, until an instant-read thermometer inserted into the thickest part of a thigh without touching bone registers 165°F, 30 to 40 minutes. Transfer to a platter and let rest for 5 to 10 minutes before carving (*see How To, page 345*).

PER SERVING (WITHOUT SKIN): 213 calories; 9 g fat (2 g sat, 5 g mono); 88 mg cholesterol; 4 g carbohydrate; 0 g added sugars; 28 g protein; 2 g fiber; 422 mg sodium; 420 mg potassium. NUTRITION BONUS: Vitamin A (25% daily value).

How To: Butterfly a Whole Chicken

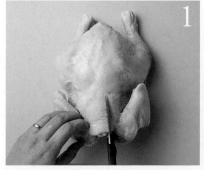

Pork Chops with Peach Barbecue Sauce

Steak & Potato Kebabs with Creamy Cilantro Sauce

Ragout of Pork & Prunes

Steak Diane

Meat

Making Spice Rubs & Marinades

One of our favorite ways to make a healthy dinner in a hurry: season steaks or pork chops with a spice rub or marinade and throw them on the grill. You can buy rubs and marinades at the supermarket, but they're simple to make at home and they're a great way to use up spices and condiments in your pantry. And rubs and marinades aren't just good for meats—use them with chicken, seafood, tofu and even vegetables. (*See chart, page 479, for grilling times.*)

Coat your chosen protein generously with one of these spice rubs just before grilling. Store any leftover rub in an airtight container.

TUSCAN SPICE RUB
MAKES: about 1 cup
USE ON: Boneless, skinless chicken thighs, salmon steaks or lamb chops.

Grind 1 tablespoon **fennel seeds** in a spice grinder (such as a clean coffee grinder) or a mortar and pestle until coarsely ground. Combine with 6 tablespoons dried **basil**, 3 tablespoons each **garlic powder** and **kosher salt**, 2 tablespoons each dried **rosemary** and dried **oregano** in a bowl.
PER TEASPOON: 5 calories; 211 mg sodium.

SPANISH RUB
MAKES: about 1 cup
USE ON: Pork chops, tenderloin, salmon steaks or shrimp.

Combine 6 tablespoons **smoked paprika** (*see Tip, page 486*), 3 tablespoons each **regular paprika**, dried **cilantro** and **kosher salt**, 1 tablespoon ground dried **lemon peel** and 1½ teaspoons freshly ground **pepper** in a bowl.
PER TEASPOON: 4 calories; 211 mg sodium.

COFFEE RUB
MAKES: about 1 cup
USE ON: Chicken thighs, duck, beef or lamb.

Mix ½ cup finely ground **coffee**, ¼ cup coarsely ground **pepper** and 3 tablespoons **kosher salt** together in a bowl.
PER TEASPOON: 5 calories; 383 mg sodium.

Marinate 1 to 2 pounds of your chosen protein in one of these marinades; discard marinade before grilling. (*See chart, page 479, for marinating times.*)

FIVE-SPICE MARINADE
MAKES: about ¼ cup
USE ON: Beef, duck, lamb or chicken.

Whisk ¼ cup reduced-sodium **soy sauce** and 3 tablespoons **sugar** in a small bowl until the sugar is dissolved. Stir in 1 teaspoon **five-spice powder** and 1 grated large **garlic** clove.
PER TEASPOON: 17 calories; 130 mg sodium.

OREGANO-GARLIC MARINADE
MAKES: about 1 cup
USE ON: Tuna, shrimp, chicken or vegetables.

Combine ½ cup fresh **lemon juice**, ⅓ cup dry **white wine**, 2 tablespoons extra-virgin **olive oil**, 2 minced **garlic** cloves, 1 tablespoon dried **oregano**, 1 teaspoon **salt** and ½ teaspoon freshly ground **pepper** in a small bowl. Use ½ cup to marinate; reserve remaining marinade for basting.
PER TEASPOON: 8 calories; 49 mg sodium.

PINEAPPLE-CHIPOTLE MARINADE
MAKES: about 1 cup
USE ON: Chicken, pork or shrimp.

Combine ½ cup **cider vinegar**, ⅓ cup **frozen pineapple juice concentrate**, 2 tablespoons each **molasses** and **chipotle peppers in adobo sauce**, 1 tablespoon **canola oil** and 2 teaspoons **salt** in a small bowl. Use ½ cup to marinate; reserve remaining marinade for basting.
PER TEASPOON: 9 calories; 100 mg sodium.

Steak Diane

H✂W   H♥H

MAKES: 4 servings
ACTIVE TIME: 35 minutes | TOTAL: 35 minutes

A brandied mixed mushroom sauce tops seared strip steak in our healthy version of the classic dish Steak Diane. (Photograph: page 350.) *Serve with garlic mashed potatoes* (see page 150) *and steamed green beans* (see page 166).

1	pound boneless strip steak, such as top loin *or* New York, ¾-1 inch thick, trimmed and cut into 4 portions
¼	teaspoon freshly ground pepper, plus more to taste
⅛	teaspoon salt
1	tablespoon extra-virgin olive oil
3	cups sliced mixed mushrooms, such as shiitake, oyster and cremini
½	cup brandy
1	15-ounce can reduced-sodium beef broth
1	teaspoon butter, softened
1	teaspoon all-purpose flour
2	teaspoons Dijon mustard
1	tablespoon chopped fresh chives

1. Season steaks on both sides with ¼ teaspoon pepper and salt. Heat oil in a large skillet over medium-high heat. Reduce heat to medium, add the steaks and cook 3 to 5 minutes per side for medium. Transfer to a plate and tent with foil to keep warm.

2. Add mushrooms to the pan and cook, stirring, until golden brown and beginning to release their juices, about 3 minutes. Add brandy and cook, stirring, until almost evaporated, about 1 minute. Add broth, bring to a boil and cook until reduced by half, 8 to 10 minutes.

3. Meanwhile, combine butter and flour in a small bowl to form a paste. When the pan sauce is reduced by half, whisk in mustard, then gradually whisk in the butter-flour paste a few bits at a time and cook until the sauce thickens, about 1 minute. Reduce heat to medium-low. Return the steak to the pan along with any accumulated juice. Turn to coat with the sauce and cook until heated through, about 1 minute. Top the steak with the sauce and sprinkle with chives.

PER SERVING: 273 calories; 10 g fat (3 g sat, 5 g mono); 55 mg cholesterol; 5 g carbohydrate; 0 g added sugars; 24 g protein; 1 g fiber; 392 mg sodium; 488 mg potassium.
NUTRITION BONUS: Zinc (30% daily value).

> **EatingWell Tip**
> Add mushrooms to beef dishes—the flavors complement each other beautifully. Plus the mushrooms **bulk up the serving size without a lot of extra calories.**

Filet Mignon with Madeira-Prune Sauce

H✖W

MAKES: 4 servings
ACTIVE TIME: 40 minutes | TOTAL: 40 minutes

Prunes and Madeira meld in this sweet and savory sauce that's a snap to make. If you're in the mood to splurge, filet mignon is incomparably tender in this recipe. But our tasters loved it with sirloin as well. **Shopping Tip:** *Madeira, a fortified wine from the Portuguese island of Madeira, has a sweet, mellow flavor somewhat like sherry. Find it at liquor stores or in the wine section of the supermarket.*

- 5 large shallots, peeled and halved
- 3 teaspoons extra-virgin olive oil, divided
- 1 tablespoon coarsely chopped fresh thyme
- ½ teaspoon kosher salt
- ½ teaspoon freshly ground pepper
- 4 4-ounce filet mignon *or* sirloin steaks, 1¼ inches thick, trimmed
- ¾ cup Madeira (*see Shopping Tip*)
- 1 14-ounce can reduced-sodium beef broth
- 1 teaspoon butter, softened
- 1 teaspoon all-purpose flour
- 1 teaspoon tomato paste
- ¼ cup pitted prunes, coarsely chopped

1. Preheat oven to 425°F.

2. Toss shallots with 1 teaspoon oil in a small baking pan. Roast until beginning to brown, about 25 minutes.

3. Meanwhile, combine thyme, salt and pepper in a small bowl; rub the mixture all over steaks. Heat the remaining 2 teaspoons oil in a large nonstick skillet over medium-high heat. Add the steaks and cook, adjusting the heat as necessary to prevent burning, 4 to 6 minutes per side for medium-rare. Transfer to a plate; tent with foil to keep warm.

4. Add Madeira to the pan and cook for 1 minute. Add broth and bring to a boil; continue cooking until the liquid is reduced by about half, 10 to 12 minutes.

5. Combine butter and flour in a small bowl. Stir tomato paste into the pan until dissolved, then add the butter-flour paste in small bits, breaking up any lumps with a wooden spoon, until it's dissolved. Add prunes and continue cooking until the sauce has thickened, about 3 minutes more. Add the roasted shallots and steaks to the pan along with any accumulated juices. Turn to coat and cook until heated through, 1 to 2 minutes. Serve the steaks with the pan sauce.

PER SERVING: 335 calories; 15 g fat (5 g sat, 7 g mono); 60 mg cholesterol; 20 g carbohydrate; 0 g added sugars; 19 g protein; 1 g fiber; 402 mg sodium; 495 mg potassium.
NUTRITION BONUS: Zinc (33% daily value).

EatingWell Tip

Beef can be part of a healthy diet—just **keep portion sizes reasonable**. A healthy serving is 3 ounces cooked, about the size of a deck of cards.

Pork Medallions with Fig & Port Wine Sauce

H ♥ H

MAKES: 4 servings

ACTIVE TIME: 45 minutes | TOTAL: 45 minutes

⏱ *This is a great dish to wow guests with. The sauce is magical with the pork, but the real beauty is how simple it is. Serve with mashed potatoes* (see page 150) *and a medley of green beans and wax beans.*

16	small dried Mission figs, stemmed
1	cup tawny port (*see Tip, page 488*)
2	teaspoons plus 1 tablespoon extra-virgin olive oil, divided
1	cup thinly sliced onion
1	cup reduced-sodium chicken broth
1	teaspoon chopped fresh thyme
1	bay leaf
1	teaspoon balsamic vinegar, *or* more to taste
½	teaspoon kosher salt, divided
	Freshly ground pepper to taste
1	pork tenderloin (1-1¼ pounds), trimmed and sliced into 1-inch-thick medallions
¼	cup all-purpose flour

1. Place figs in a small microwavable bowl and cover with port. Cover the bowl and microwave on High for 3 minutes.

2. Heat 2 teaspoons oil in a small saucepan over medium heat. Add onion and cook, stirring, until soft and translucent, 4 to 6 minutes. Add broth, thyme, bay leaf and the fig-port mixture. Bring to a boil and cook until reduced by half, 10 to 12 minutes. Season with vinegar, ¼ teaspoon salt and pepper. Set aside.

3. Sprinkle both sides of pork medallions with the remaining ¼ teaspoon salt and pepper and dredge lightly with flour, shaking off the excess.

4. Heat the remaining 1 tablespoon oil in a large nonstick skillet over medium-high heat. Add the medallions and cook until browned, 2 to 3 minutes per side. Add the reserved fig-port sauce; bring to a simmer and cook until the pork is cooked, but still a little pink in the center, about 2 minutes. The sauce should be syrupy. If not, remove the medallions with a slotted spoon to a platter and tent with foil to keep warm. Boil the sauce until it's reduced and syrupy. Discard the bay leaf. Serve the sauce over the medallions.

PER SERVING: 395 calories; 9 g fat (2 g sat, 5 g mono); 74 mg cholesterol; 38 g carbohydrate; 0 g added sugars; 27 g protein; 4 g fiber; 349 mg sodium; 828 mg potassium.
NUTRITION BONUS: Potassium (24% daily value), Zinc (17% dv).

EatingWell Tip

Pair pork with fruit. The sweet and tart flavors of fruit balance the richness of pork, plus you'll get the added benefit of more fruit in your diet. Here, figs offer **an added boost of fiber and potassium**.

Cider-Brined Pork Chops

H❓W H♥H

MAKES: 4 servings

ACTIVE TIME: 50 minutes | TOTAL: 4¼ hours (including 3 hours brining) | TO MAKE AHEAD: Brine chops (*Steps 1-2*) for up to 8 hours.

Once brined, these chops can be pan-fried, broiled or grilled. The main caution here is not to overcook them. Brining (soaking in a salt solution) helps keep the chops firm and juicy, but even brining will not prevent dry hard chops if overcooked. Bone-in rib chops at least 1 inch thick are the best choice for this recipe, and each one is typically large enough to feed two people. Using the thicker chops makes it easier to avoid overcooking the meat. Divide them before serving.

CIDER BRINE

- 2 cups apple cider
- 1 cup water
- ¼ cup kosher salt
- ¼ cup honey
- ⅛ teaspoon ground cinnamon
- 2 cups ice

PORK CHOPS & SAUTÉED APPLES

- 2 bone-in pork rib chops (about 1¾ pounds, 1-1¼ inch thick), trimmed
- 1 teaspoon chopped fresh sage
- 1 teaspoon freshly ground pepper
- ¼ teaspoon ground ginger, divided
- 2 teaspoons extra-virgin olive oil
- 1 teaspoon butter
- ½ cup thinly sliced onion
- ½ cup white wine
- 1 tart apple, peeled and thinly sliced
- ½ cup apple cider

1. **To prepare cider brine:** Pour 2 cups cider and water into a bowl and stir in salt until dissolved, then stir in honey and cinnamon until the honey is dissolved. Stir in ice and check to see that the mixture registers 45°F or lower on an instant-read thermometer.

2. **To prepare chops & apples:** Place chops in a large sealable plastic bag. Carefully add the brine to the bag, seal, then place the bag in a bowl in case of any leaks. Refrigerate for at least 3 hours or up to 8 hours.

3. Combine sage, pepper and ⅛ teaspoon ginger in a small bowl. Remove the chops from the brine. (Discard bag and brine.) Sprinkle both sides of the chops with the sage mixture.

4. Heat a large heavy skillet over medium heat. Add oil and the chops. Cook until lightly browned, 2 to 3 minutes per side. Transfer the chops to a plate.

5. Melt butter in the pan; add onion, stir to coat, cover and cook, stirring often, until starting to brown, 2 to 3 minutes. Add wine and stir, scraping up any browned bits; cook for 1 minute. Stir in apple, ½ cup cider and ⅛ teaspoon ginger; bring to a boil. Nestle the chops into the sauce, reduce heat to a simmer, cover and cook for 3 minutes. Turn the chops, cover and cook until an instant-read thermometer inserted into the center registers 145°F, 3 to 5 minutes. Transfer the chops to a warm platter and tent with foil.

6. Bring the sauce in the pan to a boil and cook until it is syrupy, 3 to 4 minutes. Spoon the sauce over the chops and serve.

PER SERVING: 259 calories; 11 g fat (3 g sat, 5 g mono); 60 mg cholesterol; 12 g carbohydrate; 0 g added sugars; 23 g protein; 1 g fiber; 344 mg sodium; 402 mg potassium.

◄ Grilled Lamb Chops with Eggplant Salad

H✖W   H↑F   H♥H

MAKES: 4 servings
ACTIVE TIME: 35 minutes | **TOTAL:** 35 minutes

Here we grill eggplant slices and red onion to toss in a salad with fresh mint and parsley to accompany grilled lamb chops. Serve with whole-grain rice pilaf and green beans.

- 1 medium eggplant (about 1 pound), peeled and sliced into ¼-inch rounds
- 1 medium red onion, sliced into ¼-inch rounds
  Canola *or* olive oil cooking spray
  Juice of 1 lemon
- ¼ cup chopped fresh parsley
- 2 tablespoons chopped fresh mint
- 1 tablespoon extra-virgin olive oil
- 1 teaspoon salt, divided
  Pinch of cayenne pepper
- 8 lamb loin chops, 1-1½ inches thick, trimmed (1½-1¾ pounds total)
- ¼ teaspoon freshly ground pepper

1. Preheat grill to medium-high.

2. Spray both sides of eggplant and onion rounds with cooking spray. Grill the vegetables, turning once, until browned on both sides, 2 to 3 minutes per side. Transfer to a cutting board. When cool enough to handle, chop the eggplant and onion and combine in a medium bowl with lemon juice, parsley, mint, oil, ½ teaspoon salt and cayenne.

3. Meanwhile, sprinkle lamb chops with pepper and the remaining ½ teaspoon salt. Grill the chops until browned on both sides and cooked to desired doneness, about 4 minutes per side for medium. Serve with the eggplant salad.

PER SERVING: 231 calories; 11 g fat (3 g sat, 6 g mono); 68 mg cholesterol; 11 g carbohydrate; 0 g added sugars; 23 g protein; 5 g fiber; 648 mg sodium; 627 mg potassium.
NUTRITION BONUS: Vitamin C (28% daily value), Zinc (22% dv), Potassium (18% dv).

Lamb Chops with Beer & Mustard Sauce

MAKES: 4 servings
ACTIVE TIME: 30 minutes | **TOTAL:** 30 minutes

H✖W   H♥H

Dark beers are too, well, dark for this sauce. Try a lager instead.

- 8 lamb rib chops (about 1½ pounds), trimmed
- 2 cloves garlic, peeled and cut in half
- 1 teaspoon canola oil
- ¼ teaspoon salt
  Freshly ground pepper to taste
- 1 cup reduced-sodium beef broth
- 1 12-ounce bottle beer, divided
- 1 tablespoon molasses
- 1½ tablespoons whole-grain mustard
- 1 teaspoon cornstarch

1. Preheat oven to 400°F.

2. Rub lamb chops with one of the garlic halves, brush lightly with oil and season with salt and pepper.

3. Heat a large nonstick skillet over medium-high heat. Add the chops and brown well, 2 to 3 minutes per side. Transfer to an ovenproof dish. Roast until desired doneness, about 10 minutes for medium-rare.

4. Meanwhile, pour beef broth and 1 cup beer into the pan; stir in molasses and the remaining garlic. Bring to a boil over medium-high heat and cook until the liquid has reduced by half, 8 to 10 minutes. Remove the garlic; stir in mustard.

5. Combine cornstarch and 2 tablespoons beer (the rest of the beer is for the cook) in a small bowl. Add to the sauce in the pan and whisk until slightly thickened. Serve immediately.

PER SERVING: 232 calories; 9 g fat (3 g sat, 4 g mono); 69 mg cholesterol; 9 g carbohydrate; 3 g added sugars; 23 g protein; 0 g fiber; 435 mg sodium; 391 mg potassium.
NUTRITION BONUS: Zinc (20% daily value).

Pork Chops with Peach Barbecue Sauce

H❳❲W   H♥H

MAKES: 4 servings

ACTIVE TIME: 40 minutes | TOTAL: 1¼ hours (including 30 minutes brining time) | TO MAKE AHEAD: Brine the pork chops (Step 1) for up to 4 hours. Refrigerate the peach barbecue sauce (Step 3) for up to 5 days.

The tangy peach barbecue sauce that glazes these pork chops is incredible on grilled chicken or salmon as well. Bone-in pork chops (as opposed to boneless) are less likely to dry out. Just make sure to trim away as much fat as possible for healthier results.

- ¼ cup plus ½ teaspoon kosher salt, divided
- ¼ cup firmly packed brown sugar
- 2 cups boiling water
- 3 cups ice cubes
- 4 bone-in, center-cut pork chops, ½-¾ inch thick (1¾-2 pounds), trimmed
- 2 ripe but firm peaches, pitted and quartered, *or* 3 cups frozen sliced peaches
- 1 medium tomato, quartered and seeded
- 2 tablespoons cider vinegar
- 1 tablespoon canola oil
- ½ cup chopped onion, preferably Vidalia
- 2 teaspoons finely chopped fresh ginger
- 2 tablespoons honey
- ¼ teaspoon freshly ground pepper, plus more to taste

1. Place ¼ cup salt and brown sugar in a medium heat-proof bowl. Pour in boiling water and stir to dissolve. Add ice cubes and stir to cool. Add pork chops, cover and refrigerate for at least 30 minutes or up to 4 hours.

2. Puree peaches, tomato and vinegar in a food processor until smooth.

3. About 30 minutes before you're ready to cook the pork chops, heat oil in a medium saucepan over medium-high heat. Add onion and cook, stirring occasionally, until golden brown, 5 to 7 minutes. Add ginger and cook, stirring frequently, until fragrant, 1 to 2 minutes. Add the peach puree, the remaining ½ teaspoon salt, honey and pepper to taste. Bring to a boil over high heat, then reduce the heat to a simmer. Cook until reduced by about half, 20 to 25 minutes. Reserve ¼ cup of the sauce for basting the chops; keep the remaining sauce warm in the saucepan until ready to serve.

4. Preheat grill to medium.

5. Remove the pork chops from the brine (discard brine), rinse well, and thoroughly dry with paper towels. Season the chops with ¼ teaspoon pepper and brush both sides with some of the reserved sauce.

6. Grill the pork chops, turning once, until an instant-read thermometer inserted into the center registers 145°F, 2 to 4 minutes per side. Transfer to a plate, tent with foil and let rest for 5 minutes. Serve with the warm peach barbecue sauce on the side.

PER SERVING: 280 calories; 11 g fat (2 g sat, 5 g mono); 83 mg cholesterol; 18 g carbohydrate; 10 g added sugars; 27 g protein; 1 g fiber; 506 mg sodium; 564 mg potassium.
NUTRITION BONUS: Potassium & Zinc (16% daily value), Vitamin C (15% dv).

Tomato-Herb Marinated Flank Steak

H✕W   H♥H

MAKES: 6 servings

ACTIVE TIME: 35 minutes | TOTAL: 4 hours 35 minutes
(including 4 hours marinating time)

TO MAKE AHEAD: Marinate steak for up to 24 hours.

*In this recipe, we make a dual-purpose sauce from garden-
fresh tomatoes, shallot, marjoram and rosemary. We use
half the sauce to marinate the steak and the other half
as a basting sauce.*

1	medium tomato, chopped
1	shallot, peeled and quartered
¼	cup red-wine vinegar
2	tablespoons chopped fresh marjoram
1	tablespoon chopped fresh rosemary
1	teaspoon salt
½	teaspoon freshly ground pepper
1½	pounds flank steak, trimmed

1. Puree tomato, shallot, vinegar, marjoram, rosemary, salt and pepper in a blender until smooth. Set aside ½ cup in the refrigerator. Scrape the remaining puree into a large, sealable plastic bag. Add steak and turn to coat. Refrigerate for 4 hours or up to 24 hours.

2. Preheat grill to medium-high. Remove the steak from the marinade (discard the marinade). Oil the grill rack (*see Tip, page 485*). Grill the steak 4 to 5 minutes per side for medium-rare or 6 to 7 minutes per side for medium, turning once and brushing the cooked side with some of the reserved sauce. When the steak is cooked, turn it over again and brush with more sauce. Transfer to a clean cutting board; let rest for 5 minutes. Thinly slice the steak crosswise and serve with any remaining sauce spooned on top.

PER SERVING: 164 calories; 6 g fat (2 g sat, 2 g mono);
37 mg cholesterol; 1 g carbohydrate; 0 g added sugars;
25 g protein; 0 g fiber; 289 mg sodium; 425 mg potassium.
NUTRITION BONUS: Zinc (29% daily value).

GUIDE:

Choosing Beef

If you've cut back on beef because you think it's unhealthy, there is good reason to take a second look. We love to cook beef because it's delicious, versatile and when you eat a reasonable 3-ounce serving of a lean cut it's also healthy. Beef is an excellent source of protein and a good source of iron, and few foods provide as much zinc, a mineral vital to growth and a healthy immune system. Beef also contains conjugated linoleic acid (CLA), a healthy type of fat that, according to preliminary research, may help with weight loss and could play a role in reducing risk for heart disease and maintaining strong bones. Here are some guidelines to help you shop for beef.

HEALTHY CHOICES: Tender cuts in the "loin" category, such as tenderloin, top loin and sirloin, and flavorful cuts like flank and strip steak are lean and best for quick-cooking, dry-heat techniques like sautéing, grilling and broiling. Tough cuts like chuck and round become tender in long, moist-heat cooking, such as stewing or braising. Always trim visible fat from whichever cut of beef you choose.

WHAT DO THE GRADES MEAN? Beef is given quality grades determined by the amount of marbling and the age of the animal, both of which affect the tenderness, juiciness and flavor of the meat. The USDA assigns three possible grades: Prime, Choice and Select. Prime meat has the most marbling, or fat, within the meat, making it juicy and flavorful, but also increasing its fat content (including saturated fat); Select has the least marbling; Choice is in the middle.

WHAT TO LOOK FOR: Fresh beef should be bright red. Vacuum-packaged beef will be maroon because of the lack of oxygen. It should be firm to the touch with little to no excess moisture in the package and the packaging should be in good condition. Be sure to check the "sell-by" date.

Steak & Potato Kebabs
with Creamy Cilantro Sauce

H✹W   H♥H

MAKES: 4 servings
ACTIVE TIME: 40 minutes | TOTAL: 40 minutes
EQUIPMENT: Eight 10- to 12-inch skewers

Steak kebabs get a Southwestern spin with poblano peppers and a creamy sauce spiked with cilantro, chili powder, cumin and vinegar. The potatoes are partially cooked in the microwave before putting them on the grill so they're done at the same time as faster-cooking steak, peppers and onions. Serve with a green salad and Spanish rice.

½ **cup packed fresh cilantro leaves, minced**
2 **tablespoons red-wine vinegar *or* cider vinegar**
2 **tablespoons reduced-fat sour cream**
1 **small clove garlic, minced**
1 **teaspoon chili powder**
½ **teaspoon ground cumin**
½ **teaspoon salt, divided**
8 **new *or* baby red potatoes**
1¼ **pounds strip steak, trimmed and cut into
      1½-inch pieces**
2 **poblano peppers *or* 1 large green bell pepper,
      cut into 1-inch pieces**
1 **teaspoon extra-virgin olive oil**
1 **large sweet onion, cut into 1-inch chunks**

1. Combine cilantro, vinegar, sour cream, garlic, chili powder, cumin and ¼ teaspoon salt in a small bowl. Set aside.

2. Preheat grill to high.

3. Place potatoes in a microwavable container. Cover and microwave on High until just tender when pierced with a fork, 3 to 3½ minutes.

4. Toss the potatoes, steak and pepper pieces with oil and the remaining ¼ teaspoon salt in a large bowl. Thread the potatoes, steak, peppers and onion chunks onto 8 skewers. Grill, turning once or twice, until the steak reaches desired doneness, about 6 minutes for medium. Serve the kebabs with the reserved sauce.

PER SERVING: 272 calories; 9 g fat (3 g sat, 4 g mono); 65 mg cholesterol; 17 g carbohydrate; 0 g added sugars; 30 g protein; 2 g fiber; 368 mg sodium; 786 mg potassium.
NUTRITION BONUS: Vitamin C & Zinc (37% daily value), Potassium (22% dv), Iron (15% dv).

EatingWell Tip
Leave the skins on your potatoes. The skin and the layer just below contain **potassium, which may help regulate blood pressure**, and a little extra fiber.

Shish Kebab with Tahini Sauce

H✳W

MAKES: 8 servings
ACTIVE TIME: 35 minutes | TOTAL: 2½ hours
TO MAKE AHEAD: Marinate steak (Step 1) and refrigerate
for up to 1 day. | EQUIPMENT: Nine 12-inch skewers

*Roasted and grilled meats are ubiquitous throughout the
Middle East. This marinade, infused with allspice and
cinnamon, would be excellent on lamb or chicken as well.
Tuck the grilled chunks of meat and onion into warm
whole-wheat pitas.*

   6   cloves garlic, crushed
   ½   cup lemon juice
   ¼   cup plus 1 tablespoon canola oil, divided
   1   teaspoon kosher salt
   ½   teaspoon ground allspice
   ¼   teaspoon ground cinnamon
   ¼   teaspoon freshly ground pepper
   2   pounds sirloin steak, trimmed and cut into
         1-inch pieces
   2   large onions, cut into 8 wedges each
         Tahini Sauce (*right*)

1. Combine garlic, lemon juice, ¼ cup oil, salt, allspice,
   cinnamon and pepper in a medium bowl. Place beef in
   a large sealable plastic bag and pour in the marinade.
   Refrigerate for at least 2 hours or up to 1 day.

2. Preheat grill to high.

3. Remove the beef from the bag. (Discard the marinade.)
   Brush onions with the remaining 1 tablespoon oil.
   Divide the beef among 6 skewers and the onions
   among the remaining 3 skewers. Grill the onions until
   charred and tender, 10 to 12 minutes per side. Grill
   the beef, turning once or twice, until slightly charred
   but still pink in the middle, about 6 minutes. Serve
   with Tahini Sauce.

PER SERVING: 286 calories; 17 g fat (3 g sat, 8 g mono);
42 mg cholesterol; 9 g carbohydrate; 0 g added sugars;
26 g protein; 2 g fiber; 229 mg sodium; 443 mg potassium.
NUTRITION BONUS: Zinc (33% daily value), Vitamin C (23% dv).

TAHINI SAUCE

MAKES: about 1 cup
ACTIVE TIME: 15 minutes | TOTAL: 15 minutes
TO MAKE AHEAD: Cover and refrigerate for up to 5 days.

*This garlicky tahini sauce is traditionally served with chicken
kebabs, but we love it with beef as well.* **Shopping Tip:**
*Tahini is a thick paste made from ground sesame seeds.
Look for it at large supermarkets in the Middle Eastern
section or near other nut butters.*

   2   cloves garlic, minced
   ¾   teaspoon kosher salt
   ½   cup tahini (*see Shopping Tip*)
   7   tablespoons lemon juice
   3   tablespoons water

Mash garlic and salt in a medium bowl using the back of
a spoon until a paste forms. Whisk in tahini, lemon juice
and water.

PER 2-TABLESPOON SERVING: 93 calories; 8 g fat (1 g sat, 3 g mono);
0 mg cholesterol; 5 g carbohydrate; 0 g added sugars;
3 g protein; 1 g fiber; 111 mg sodium; 88 mg potassium.

EatingWell Tip

For grilling, try sirloin. **It's one of the leanest cuts
around** with only 151 calories and 2 grams saturated fat
per 3-ounce serving.

Lion's Head Meatballs

H✂W   H♥H

MAKES: 10 meatballs, for 5 main-dish
or 10 appetizer servings
ACTIVE TIME: 45 minutes | TOTAL: 45 minutes
TO MAKE AHEAD: Cover and refrigerate the meatball
mixture (Step 2) for up to 2 days.

This is a famous dish along the Yangtze River in China, with many regional variations. Serve with rice and sautéed bok choy for dinner. Or serve as an appetizer at a party.

1	cup "lite" coconut milk
2½	tablespoons reduced-sodium soy sauce
1	tablespoon curry powder
1	pound lean ground pork *or* beef
½	cup chopped scallions
¼	cup minced leek, white and pale green part only, rinsed
2	tablespoons cornstarch
1	tablespoon all-purpose flour
1	tablespoon toasted sesame oil
1	tablespoon finely chopped fresh ginger
2	teaspoons seeded and minced fresh chile pepper
½	teaspoon salt
¼	teaspoon ground white pepper
2	teaspoons extra-virgin olive oil
1	medium head Boston *or* iceberg lettuce
¼	cup chopped fresh basil *or* Thai basil
1	tablespoon freshly grated lemon zest

1. Combine coconut milk, soy sauce and curry powder in a large saucepan. Set aside.

2. Place pork (or beef), scallions, leek, cornstarch, flour, sesame oil, ginger, chile, salt and pepper in a large mixing bowl. Knead by hand until thoroughly combined and the mixture becomes sticky. Divide into 10 equal portions, about ¼ cup each. Roll each portion into a ball.

3. Heat olive oil in a large nonstick skillet over medium heat, swirling to coat the sides. Add the meatballs and cook, turning occasionally, until browned on all sides, 8 to 10 minutes. Transfer to a plate lined with paper towels.

4. Bring the coconut-milk mixture to a boil over medium-high heat. Add the meatballs; cover, reduce heat to low and cook for 8 minutes.

5. Line a serving bowl with lettuce leaves. Arrange the meatballs on top. Garnish with basil and lemon zest. Serve hot with the coconut-milk sauce drizzled over the top or on the side for dipping.

PER MEATBALL: 116 calories; 7 g fat (3 g sat, 1 g mono); 26 mg cholesterol; 5 g carbohydrate; 0 g added sugars; 10 g protein; 1 g fiber; 261 mg sodium; 174 mg potassium.

EatingWell Tip
Choose "lite" coconut milk over the full-fat version. You'll **save 253 calories and 32 grams of fat** per cup.

Smoky Meatloaf

H✖W

MAKES: 6 servings
ACTIVE TIME: 25 minutes | TOTAL: 1¼ hours

In this lightened-up meatloaf, healthy low-calorie shredded zucchini keeps very lean beef moist but doesn't take away from the meat itself. The flavor gets a boost from a touch of smoked paprika, Worcestershire and a sweet ketchup glaze. We've also included a variation with Italian flavors.

1½	cups shredded zucchini (about 1 small)
½	cup finely diced green bell pepper
1	medium shallot, minced
1	tablespoon water
1	large egg
2	tablespoons tomato paste
4	teaspoons whole-grain mustard
4	teaspoons Worcestershire sauce
2	teaspoons dried marjoram
¾	teaspoon salt
½	teaspoon paprika, preferably smoked (*see Tip, page 486*)
¼	teaspoon freshly ground pepper
¾	cup dry breadcrumbs, preferably whole-wheat (*see Tip, page 481*)
1½	pounds lean (90% or leaner) ground beef
2	tablespoons ketchup *or* barbecue sauce

1. Preheat oven to 375°F. Lightly coat a baking sheet with cooking spray.

2. Place zucchini, bell pepper, shallot and water in a medium microwavable bowl, cover and microwave on High until the vegetables are tender, about 4 minutes. Carefully uncover and drain the vegetables in a sieve, gently pressing out as much moisture as possible; spread out on a large plate to cool slightly.

3. Whisk egg, tomato paste, mustard, Worcestershire, marjoram, salt, paprika and pepper in a large bowl. Add the vegetables and stir to combine. Add breadcrumbs and toss to combine. Add beef and gently knead with clean hands to combine with the vegetable mixture; do not overmix. Form the meat mixture into a loaf shape (approximately 10 by 4 inches) on the prepared baking sheet. Spread ketchup (or barbecue sauce) over the top of the loaf.

4. Bake until an instant-read thermometer inserted in the center registers 160°F, 40 to 45 minutes. Let rest for 10 minutes before slicing.

PER SERVING: 276 calories; 13 g fat (5 g sat, 5 g mono); 109 mg cholesterol; 12 g carbohydrate; 1 g added sugars; 26 g protein; 2 g fiber; 595 mg sodium; 595 mg potassium.
NUTRITION BONUS: Zinc (38% daily value), Vitamin C (30% dv), Iron (21% dv), Potassium (17% dv).

ITALIAN VARIATION:

Substitute ½ cup diced fennel bulb for the bell pepper, 1 teaspoon Italian seasoning for the marjoram, regular paprika instead of smoked and marinara sauce in place of the ketchup (or barbecue sauce).

Classic Beef Chili

H✕W   H⬆F

MAKES: 8 servings, about 1⅓ cups each
ACTIVE TIME: 50 minutes | TOTAL: 50 minutes
TO MAKE AHEAD: Cover and refrigerate for up to 3 days or freeze for up to 1 month.

This classic beef-and-bean chili gets a nutritional boost from shredded sweet potato. We call it a stealth vegetable because it melts into the chili so well that even picky eaters will gobble it up.

- 2 tablespoons canola oil
- 1 large onion, finely chopped
- 4 cloves garlic, minced
- 1 pound lean (90% or leaner) ground beef
- 2 tablespoons chili powder
- 1 tablespoon ground cumin
- ½ teaspoon ground coriander
- ¼ teaspoon salt
- ¼ teaspoon cayenne pepper, or to taste
- 2 cups water
- 1 large sweet potato, peeled and shredded
- 2 15-ounce cans kidney beans, rinsed
- 1 28-ounce can crushed tomatoes
- 1 15-ounce can diced tomatoes, preferably petite diced
- 1 cup shredded extra-sharp Cheddar cheese
- 2 scallions, sliced

Heat oil in a large Dutch oven over medium heat. Add onion and garlic; cook, stirring often, until starting to soften, 3 to 5 minutes. Add beef and cook, breaking it up with a wooden spoon, until no longer pink, about 5 minutes. Stir in chili powder, cumin, coriander, salt and cayenne; cook, stirring, until fragrant, about 1 minute. Stir in water and sweet potato. Bring to a simmer and cook, stirring occasionally and adjusting the heat as necessary to maintain a simmer, until the sweet potato is softened and beginning to break down, 6 to 8 minutes. Add beans, crushed tomatoes and diced tomatoes; return to a simmer and cook, stirring occasionally and adjusting the heat as necessary to maintain a gentle simmer, until the sweet potato starts to melt into the chili, 15 to 20 minutes. Serve topped with cheese and scallions.

PER SERVING: 359 calories; 15 g fat (6 g sat, 6 g mono); 52 mg cholesterol; 35 g carbohydrate; 0 g added sugars; 23 g protein; 11 g fiber; 653 mg sodium; 1,001 mg potassium. NUTRITION BONUS: Vitamin A (148% daily value), Vitamin C (40% dv), Iron (35% dv), Potassium (29% dv), Zinc (28% dv), Calcium (22% dv), Folate & Magnesium (21% dv).

EatingWell Tip

Check the label to be sure you are buying lean ground meat. **Anything labeled 90%-lean or higher is considered a healthy choice.** (*For more on how to choose ground meat, turn to page 215.*)

Quick Pork & Chile Stew

H✖W   H♥H

MAKES: 4 servings, about 1½ cups each
ACTIVE TIME: 25 minutes | TOTAL: 40 minutes

The potatoes in this quick, Tex-Mex-style pork stew are cooked until they are falling apart to add body to the stew. Poblano peppers vary in heat: if you don't like spicy food, use 2 small green bell peppers in place of the poblanos. Serve with warm corn tortillas or cheese quesadillas and a cold India pale ale.

4	teaspoons extra-virgin olive oil, divided
1	pound pork tenderloin, trimmed and cut into 1-inch cubes
1	medium onion, halved and sliced
2	poblano peppers, diced
2	cloves garlic, minced
1	medium russet potato, peeled and cut into ½-inch pieces
1	14-ounce can reduced-sodium chicken broth
1½	teaspoons ground cumin
1	teaspoon dried oregano
½	teaspoon salt
⅛	teaspoon cayenne (optional)
1	tablespoon lime juice

1. Heat 2 teaspoons oil in a large saucepan over medium heat. Add pork; cook, stirring, until no longer pink on the outside, about 4 minutes. Transfer with any juice to a bowl.

2. Add the remaining 2 teaspoons oil, onion and poblanos to the pan. Cook, stirring, until softened, about 3 minutes. Add garlic and cook 1 minute more. Add potato, broth, cumin, oregano, salt and cayenne (if using); bring to a simmer over medium heat. Reduce heat to maintain a low simmer and cook, partially covered and stirring occasionally, until the potato is tender, about 10 minutes. Return the pork and any juice to the pan and cook, partially covered, until the pork is cooked through and the potatoes are fall-apart tender, about 5 minutes more. Stir in lime juice before serving.

PER SERVING: 266 calories; 8 g fat (2 g sat, 5 g mono); 74 mg cholesterol; 22 g carbohydrate; 0 g added sugars; 27 g protein; 4 g fiber; 589 mg sodium; 945 mg potassium.
NUTRITION BONUS: Vitamin C (100% daily value), Potassium (27% dv), Zinc (17% dv), Iron (15% dv).

Middle Eastern Lamb Stew

H✖W   H↑F

MAKES: 8 servings, about 1 cup each
ACTIVE TIME: 40 minutes | SLOW-COOKER TIME: 3-3½ hours
on High or 5½-6 hours on Low | TO MAKE AHEAD: Prepare
the stew, omitting the spinach, cover and refrigerate for
up to 2 days or freeze for up to 4 months. Add spinach
after the stew is reheated. | PREP AHEAD: Trim lamb and
coat with spice mixture. Chop onions. Combine broth,
tomatoes and garlic. Refrigerate in separate covered
containers for up to 1 day. | EQUIPMENT: 4-quart or larger
slow cooker

This brothy stew is boldly flavored with a blend of charac-
teristic Middle Eastern spices and finished with fresh spinach
and fiber-rich chickpeas. Economical lamb shoulder tenderizes
beautifully when leisurely cooked in a slow cooker. If you
can't find boneless shoulder stew meat, do not substitute
more-expensive lamb leg—it tends to dry out during slow
cooking. Instead, purchase lamb shoulder chops and debone
them. Serve over bulgur and accompany with a salad.

1½	pounds boneless lamb stew meat (shoulder cut) *or* 2½ pounds lamb shoulder chops, deboned, trimmed and cut into 1-inch chunks
1	tablespoon extra-virgin olive oil *or* canola oil
4	teaspoons ground cumin
1	tablespoon ground coriander
¼	teaspoon cayenne pepper
¼	teaspoon salt
	Freshly ground pepper to taste
1	large *or* 2 medium onions, chopped
1	28-ounce can diced tomatoes
¾	cup reduced-sodium chicken broth
4	cloves garlic, minced
1	15- *or* 19-ounce can chickpeas, rinsed
6	ounces baby spinach

1. Place lamb in a 4-quart or larger slow cooker. Mix oil, cumin, coriander, cayenne, salt and pepper in a small bowl. Coat the lamb with the spice paste and toss to coat well. Top with onion.

2. Bring tomatoes, broth and garlic to a simmer in a medium saucepan over medium-high heat. Pour over the lamb and onion. Cover and cook until the lamb is very tender, 3 to 3½ hours on High or 5½ to 6 hours on Low.

3. Skim or blot any visible fat from the surface of the stew. Mash ½ cup chickpeas with a fork in a small bowl. Stir the mashed and whole chickpeas into the stew, along with spinach. Cover and cook on High until the spinach is wilted, about 5 minutes.

PER SERVING: 275 calories; 14 g fat (5 g sat, 6 g mono); 61 mg cholesterol; 17 g carbohydrate; 0 g added sugars; 20 g protein; 4 g fiber; 451 mg sodium; 586 mg potassium.
NUTRITION BONUS: Vitamin A (37% daily value), Zinc (26% dv), Vitamin C (24% dv), Iron (22% dv), Folate (19% dv).

EatingWell Tip

Spices are key to healthy cooking because they're a **nearly calorie-free way to make food flavorful and delicious**. Plus many spices have been shown to have health benefits. For example, capsaicin, the active ingredient in cayenne, is an antioxidant and may even boost your metabolism slightly.

Braised Beef & Mushrooms

H✱W H♥H

MAKES: 12 servings, about ¾ cup each
ACTIVE TIME: 1 hour | TOTAL: 3¼ hours
TO MAKE AHEAD: Prepare through Step 4; let cool to room temperature, cover and refrigerate for up to 3 days. Finish with Step 5 just before serving.

Traditional braises usually call for the meat to be browned first, but here that step is skipped to keep it simple. The beef absorbs the wonderful taste of mushrooms, which completely permeates the sauce. If you find them, chanterelle mushrooms can be used in place of the shiitakes. Serve with whole-wheat egg noodles or spaetzle and a mixed green salad.

- **2 tablespoons canola oil**
- **1 tablespoon butter**
- **4 cups finely diced onions**
- **2 large cloves garlic, crushed and peeled**
- **2 tablespoons tomato paste**
- **2 tablespoons sweet paprika**
- **2 teaspoons chopped fresh marjoram *or* 1 teaspoon dried**
- **4 pounds beef chuck, trimmed and cut into 1½-inch pieces**
- **1 teaspoon salt, divided**
- **½ teaspoon freshly ground pepper**
- **2 pounds cremini mushrooms, cut into ½-inch pieces**
- **1 cup reduced-sodium beef broth**
- **8 large shiitake mushroom caps, cut into ½-inch pieces**
- **2-3 teaspoons finely minced fresh tarragon *or* dill for garnish**

1. Preheat oven to 350°F.

2. Heat oil and butter in a large heavy casserole or Dutch oven over medium heat. Add onions and garlic and cook, stirring, until the onions are soft and beginning to brown, 8 to 10 minutes. Stir in tomato paste, paprika and marjoram.

3. Season beef with ½ teaspoon salt and pepper. Add the beef and cremini mushrooms to the pot; gently stir to combine. Add broth and cover the pot with a tight-fitting lid.

4. Transfer the pot to the oven and bake until the beef is very tender, 1¾ to 2½ hours. Stir in shiitake mushrooms and continue baking, covered, for 15 minutes more. Remove from the oven, uncover and let stand, undisturbed, for about 15 minutes.

5. Skim or blot any visible fat from the stew. Transfer the beef and mushrooms to a bowl with a slotted spoon. Return the pot to the stove and bring to a gentle simmer. Cook until the sauce just coats a spoon. Stir the beef, mushrooms and the remaining ½ teaspoon salt into the sauce and heat through, about 1 minute. Serve garnished with tarragon (or dill), if desired.

PER SERVING: 269 calories; 10 g fat (3 g sat, 5 g mono); 66 mg cholesterol; 11 g carbohydrate; 0 g added sugars; 34 g protein; 2 g fiber; 310 mg sodium; 739 mg potassium.
NUTRITION BONUS: Zinc (57% daily value), Potassium (21% dv), Iron (19% dv).

Ragout of Pork & Prunes

H ✖ W

MAKES: 10 servings, about ⅔ cup each
ACTIVE TIME: 1¼ hours | TOTAL: 3 hours
TO MAKE AHEAD: Prepare through Step 5; let cool to room temperature, cover and refrigerate for up to 3 days. Finish with Step 6 just before serving.

Pork shoulder is an inexpensive and juicy cut that lends itself to roasting, grilling and braising. Here it's paired with prunes, which is a natural marriage of flavors, but you can also use butternut squash combined with a few dried apricots. Serve with polenta and roasted carrots. (Photograph: page 350.) **Shopping Tip:** *Port is a sweet fortified wine that provides depth of flavor in cooking. Tawny port is aged in oak, turning it brown (as opposed to dark-red ruby port). Look for it at your wine or liquor store.*

4	**pounds boneless pork shoulder (picnic or Boston-butt), trimmed and cut into 1- to 1½-inch pieces**
1	**teaspoon salt, divided**
½	**teaspoon freshly ground pepper**
2	**tablespoons canola oil, divided**
1	**tablespoon butter**
1	**cup minced shallots (5-6 large)**
2	**teaspoons grated fresh ginger**
1	**tablespoon brown sugar**
¼	**cup sherry vinegar or red-wine vinegar**
1	**teaspoon dried thyme or 1 tablespoon fresh, minced**
1½	**cups reduced-sodium beef broth**
2	**cups large pitted prunes**
1	**cup tawny port (see Shopping Tip)**
2	**tablespoons water**
2	**teaspoons cornstarch**

1. Preheat oven to 350°F.

2. Season pork with ½ teaspoon salt and pepper. Heat 1 tablespoon oil and butter in a large, heavy casserole or Dutch oven over medium heat. Add the pork in batches (do not crowd the pot) and cook until browned on all sides, 3 to 4 minutes per batch. Remove to a large plate.

3. Add the remaining 1 tablespoon oil to the pot. Add shallots and ginger and cook, stirring, until soft and lightly browned, 3 to 5 minutes. Add brown sugar, vinegar and thyme. Bring to a simmer and immediately add broth. Return the pork to the pot and cover with a tight-fitting lid.

4. Transfer the pot to the oven and bake until the pork is very tender, about 1½ hours. Remove from the oven, uncover and let stand for about 15 minutes.

5. While the stew stands, combine prunes and port in a small saucepan. Bring to a simmer and cook for 10 minutes. Skim or blot any visible fat from the stew. Stir in the prunes and port. Return the pot to the stove and bring to a simmer. Reduce heat and simmer over low heat for 10 minutes.

6. Combine water and cornstarch in a small bowl. Transfer the pork and prunes to a bowl with a slotted spoon. Return the sauce to a simmer. Stir in the cornstarch mixture a little at a time, stirring and adding more as needed, until the sauce just coats the spoon. Stir the pork, prunes and the remaining ½ teaspoon salt into the sauce and heat through, about 1 minute.

PER SERVING: 321 calories; 13 g fat (5 g sat, 6 g mono); 56 mg cholesterol; 30 g carbohydrate; 1 g added sugars; 15 g protein; 3 g fiber; 335 mg sodium; 515 mg potassium.
NUTRITION BONUS: Zinc (19% daily value), Potassium (15% dv).

Horseradish-Crusted Beef Tenderloin

H✦W

MAKES: 8 servings
ACTIVE TIME: 15 minutes | TOTAL: 1 hour 10 minutes
EQUIPMENT: Kitchen string

Luxurious beef tenderloin shines when treated to a simple horseradish-mustard rub and roasted for a nicely seared and flavorful crust. Add 5 to 10 minutes to the roasting time if you prefer your meat well done. **Shopping Tip:** *You'll need 2 pounds of trimmed tenderloin for this recipe. Ask your butcher to remove the extra fat, silver skin and the chain (a lumpy, fat-covered piece of meat that runs along the tenderloin). If you buy untrimmed tenderloin, start with about 2½ pounds, then use a sharp knife to trim the silver skin, fat and chain.*

- 2 **tablespoons prepared horseradish**
- 1 **tablespoon extra-virgin olive oil**
- 1 **teaspoon Dijon mustard**
- 2 **pounds trimmed beef tenderloin, preferably center-cut (*see Shopping Tip*)**
- 1 **teaspoon kosher salt**
- 2 **teaspoons freshly ground pepper**
  Creamy Horseradish Sauce (*right*)

1. Preheat oven to 400°F.

2. Combine horseradish, oil and mustard in a small bowl. Rub tenderloin with salt and pepper; coat with the horseradish mixture. Tie with kitchen string in 3 places. Transfer to a small roasting pan.

3. Roast until a thermometer inserted into the thickest part of the tenderloin registers 140°F for medium-rare, 35 to 45 minutes. Transfer to a cutting board; let rest for 5 minutes. Remove the string. Slice and serve with Creamy Horseradish Sauce.

PER SERVING: 211 calories; 11 g fat (4 g sat, 5 g mono); 81 mg cholesterol; 2 g carbohydrate; 0 g added sugars; 26 g protein; 0 g fiber; 286 mg sodium; 435 mg potassium.
NUTRITION BONUS: Zinc (31% daily value).

CREAMY HORSERADISH SAUCE

MAKES: 1½ cups
ACTIVE TIME: 5 minutes | TOTAL: 5 minutes
TO MAKE AHEAD: Cover and refrigerate for up to 3 days.

Horseradish does the talking in this creamy, pungent sauce. Serve with beef tenderloin, Cheddar mashed potatoes or as a sandwich spread.

- 1¼ **cups reduced-fat sour cream**
- ⅓ **cup prepared horseradish**
- 1 **teaspoon kosher salt**
- 1 **teaspoon freshly ground pepper**

Combine sour cream, horseradish, salt and pepper in a medium bowl. Chill until ready to serve.

PER TABLESPOON: 19 calories; 2 g fat (1 g sat, 0 g mono); 5 mg cholesterol; 1 g carbohydrate; 0 g added sugars; 0 g protein; 0 g fiber; 62 mg sodium; 25 mg potassium.

Pork Tenderloin "Rosa di Parma"

H✂W   H♥H

MAKES: 10 servings
ACTIVE TIME: 25 minutes | TOTAL: 55 minutes
EQUIPMENT: Kitchen string

This is a traditional roast from the Italian province of Parma, often served for special family celebrations. "Rosa di Parma" means it's stuffed with Parmigiano-Reggiano and prosciutto. (Photograph: opposite.)

2	teaspoons finely chopped fresh sage
1½	teaspoons minced garlic
1	teaspoon finely chopped fresh rosemary
1	teaspoon kosher salt
1	teaspoon freshly ground pepper
2	pork tenderloins (1-1¼ pounds each), trimmed and double butterflied (*see How To, opposite*)
4	thin slices Italian Parma ham (*prosciutto di Parma*), divided
1	cup freshly grated Parmigiano-Reggiano cheese, divided
3	teaspoons extra-virgin olive oil, divided

1. Combine sage, garlic, rosemary, salt and pepper in a small bowl. Set aside.

2. Preheat oven to 450°F.

3. You're going to double butterfly the tenderloins, so they can be flattened, stuffed and rolled. To do that, you'll make two long horizontal cuts, one on each side, dividing the tenderloin in thirds without cutting all the way through. Working with one tenderloin at a time, lay it on a cutting board. Holding the knife blade flat, so it's parallel to the board, make a lengthwise cut into the side of the tenderloin one-third of the way down from the top, stopping short of the opposite edge so that the flaps remain attached (PHOTO 1). Rotate the tenderloin 180° (PHOTO 2). Still holding the knife parallel to the cutting board, make a lengthwise cut into the side opposite the original cut, starting two-thirds of the way down from the top of the tenderloin and taking care not to cut all the way through (PHOTO 3). Open up the 2 cuts so you have a large rectangle of meat (PHOTO 4). Use the heel of your hand to gently flatten the meat to about ½ inch thick (PHOTO 5).

4. Cover each butterflied tenderloin with 2 of the ham slices, then spread ½ cup Parmigiano-Reggiano over the ham, leaving a 1-inch border. Starting with a long side, roll up each tenderloin so the stuffing is in a spiral pattern; then tie the roasts at 2-inch intervals with kitchen string.

5. Lightly brush the roasts all over with 1½ teaspoons oil then rub with the reserved herb mixture. Heat the remaining 1½ teaspoons oil in a large, heavy, oven-proof skillet over medium-high heat. Add the roasts, bending to fit if necessary, and cook, turning often, until the outsides are browned, 3 to 5 minutes total.

6. Transfer the pan to the oven and roast, checking often, until the internal temperature reaches 145°F, 15 to 20 minutes. Transfer to a cutting board, tent with foil and let rest for 5 minutes. To serve, remove the string and cut the pork into 1-inch-thick slices.

PER SERVING: 175 calories; 7 g fat (3 g sat, 2 g mono); 72 mg cholesterol; 1 g carbohydrate; 0 g added sugars; 26 g protein; 0 g fiber; 539 mg sodium; 367 mg potassium.
NUTRITION BONUS: Calcium (17% dv).

How To: Double Butterfly Pork Tenderloin

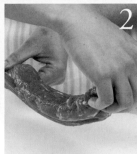

Choosing Pork

Pork is so popular now that it occupies nearly as much space as chicken in grocery stores. Unlike the pork of yore, today's pigs have been bred to be lean, which makes pork a healthy choice—and also makes it trickier to cook. It dries out when overcooked, so make sure to use an instant-read thermometer to cook it just to the right temperature (145°F), and always let the meat rest for 5 to 10 minutes before serving to redistribute its juices. Pork is an excellent source of many nutrients, including thiamin, niacin and riboflavin and vitamin B_6, and a good source of zinc and potassium.

HEALTHY CHOICES: Cuts like tenderloin, loin and sirloin from the middle section of the pig rival skinless chicken breast in percentage of fat, but have a richer flavor. These cuts are tender and delicious when quickly cooked. Tougher cuts, such as pork shoulder (sometimes called pork butt or Boston butt), are a great choice for long, slow cooking. Always trim visible fat from whichever cut of pork you choose.

WHAT TO LOOK FOR: Look for pork that is light red to cherry red, never pale or white. The fat should be white and creamy with no dark spots. Fresh pork should never have any off odors. The best-tasting pork is marbled with flecks of fat interspersed in the lean meat.

Avoid pale, soft pork sitting in liquid in the package. This is called PSE (pale, soft and exudative) and indicates pork that comes from animals mishandled during processing. When you push down on the pork it will not spring back and when you cook it even more juices will flow out. The meat will be dry and tasteless even when cooked to the desired degree of doneness. Alert the store manager that you got bad meat.

CHECK THE LABEL: Because lean pork can dry out so quickly when cooked, many manufacturers sell something called "enhanced" pork. It is injected with a solution of water, salt and phosphates. The percentage of water is usually around 8 to 10 percent. It has a soft, rubbery texture and a slightly acrid or bitter taste. We try to avoid buying pork that has been "enhanced" since it has added sodium.

Apple Cupcakes with Cinnamon-Marshmallow Frosting

Chocolate Tart with Hazelnut Shortbread Crust

Roasted Pear Trifle

Strawberry Rhubarb Pie

Desserts

Individual Cherry-Blueberry Trifles

◀ Individual Cherry-Blueberry Trifles

H ⬆ F

MAKES: 4 servings

ACTIVE TIME: 15 minutes | TOTAL: 1¼ hours

TO MAKE AHEAD: Cover and refrigerate for up to 1 day. Top with almonds just before serving.

Easy as can be, these layered cherry-blueberry trifles are a simple make-ahead dessert. We like to use fresh fruit when in season, but frozen (thawed) fruit is delicious and easy. **Shopping Tip:** *For this recipe, we recommend using ladyfingers with a soft, sponge-cake texture found in the in-store bakery of most supermarkets. The crunchy Italian ladyfingers (sometimes found near specialty cookies) are too big to fit into individual serving dishes and won't soften as well.*

1¼	cups halved pitted fresh cherries *or* thawed and drained frozen cherries
1¼	cups fresh blueberries *or* thawed and drained frozen blueberries
1	tablespoon light brown sugar
16	ladyfingers (*see Shopping Tip*)
1	cup nonfat vanilla Greek yogurt (*see Tip, page 490*)
4	tablespoons sliced almonds, toasted (*see Tip, page 486*)

Toss cherries, blueberries and brown sugar in a medium bowl. Layer 2 ladyfingers, about ¼ cup fruit mixture and 2 tablespoons yogurt in four 10- to 12-ounce tumblers or similar-size glasses. Repeat with another layer of ladyfingers, fruit and yogurt. Refrigerate for at least 1 hour or up to 1 day. Top each serving with 1 tablespoon almonds just before serving.

PER SERVING: 236 calories; 4 g fat (0 g sat, 2 g mono); 14 mg cholesterol; 44 g carbohydrate; 20 g added sugars; 9 g protein; 3 g fiber; 30 mg sodium; 183 mg potassium.

Gingersnap-Banana Frozen Yogurt

Chocolate-Covered Brownie Bites

MAKES: 64 brownie bites
ACTIVE TIME: 15 minutes | TOTAL: 45 minutes
TO MAKE AHEAD: Store airtight in the refrigerator
for up to 1 week.

*Dip bite-size pieces of brownie into melted chocolate
for an easy treat to satisfy your chocolate craving.*

1   **8-inch-square pan chilled brownies, cut into
     1-inch squares**
1   **cup semisweet *or* bittersweet chocolate chips,
     melted (see *How To, page 387*)**

Dip half of each brownie square in melted chocolate,
then place on a baking sheet lined with parchment or
wax paper. (Reheat chocolate, as needed, to keep it
melted.) Refrigerate until the chocolate is set, about
30 minutes.

Per brownie bite: 38 calories; 2 g fat (1 g sat, 0 g mono);
4 mg cholesterol; 6 g carbohydrate; 4 g added sugars;
1 g protein; 0 g fiber; 6 mg sodium; 21 mg potassium.

◀ Gingersnap-Banana Frozen Yogurt

MAKES: 4 servings
ACTIVE TIME: 10 minutes | TOTAL: 20 minutes

*Combine chopped gingersnaps, bananas and toasted
pecans with frozen yogurt for a quick dessert.*

2   **cups vanilla frozen yogurt, softened**
6   **gingersnap cookies, chopped**
2   **bananas, sliced**
¼   **cup chopped toasted pecans**

Layer frozen yogurt, chopped gingersnaps, bananas
and pecans into 4 small dessert cups or glasses. Freeze
until the yogurt is firm, at least 10 minutes.

PER SERVING: 258 calories; 11 g fat (3 g sat, 5 g mono);
1 mg cholesterol; 39 g carbohydrate; 18 g added sugars;
5 g protein; 2 g fiber; 99 mg sodium; 399 mg potassium.

Roasted Pineapple

H✖W   H⬆F   H❤H

MAKES: 6 servings
ACTIVE TIME: 15 minutes | TOTAL: 45 minutes

*Caramelize brown sugar on slices of fresh pineapple
under your broiler for a quick and easy dessert.*

1   **whole pineapple (2½-3 pounds)**
2   **tablespoons brown sugar**

1. Preheat broiler. Trim leaves and bud end from pineapple. Cut into ½-inch-thick slices with a sharp
   knife. Set slices in a single layer on a baking sheet.
   Sprinkle with brown sugar. (Cover the pineapple
   slices only; any sugar on the sheet may burn.)

2. Broil, rearranging slices as needed for even cooking,
   for 10 to 15 minutes. Turn the slices over and continue broiling on the other side until the pineapple
   is tender and golden brown, 5 to 10 minutes.

PER SERVING: 112 calories; 0 g fat (0 g sat, 0 g mono);
0 mg cholesterol; 29 g carbohydrate; 4 g added sugars;
1 g protein; 3 g fiber; 3 mg sodium; 212 mg potassium.
NUTRITION BONUS: Vitamin C (150% daily value).

◄ Cherry Ice Cream Pie with Chocolate Cookie Crust

MAKES: 8 servings

ACTIVE TIME: 15 minutes | TOTAL: 4¼ hours (including 4 hours freezing time) | TO MAKE AHEAD: Cover with foil and freeze for up to 1 week.

This cherry ice cream pie is a simple summertime sweet treat! If you use frozen cherries, the pie will have a fun purple hue.

- 3 cups reduced-fat "light" vanilla ice cream, softened
- 1¼ cups chopped pitted fresh *or* frozen cherries, divided
- 1 9-inch chocolate-cookie pie crust
- 2 tablespoons mini chocolate chips

Gently combine ice cream and 1 cup cherries in a large bowl. Transfer to the crust and garnish with the remaining ¼ cup cherries and chocolate chips. Freeze until firm, at least 4 hours.

PER SERVING: 272 calories; 12 g fat (4 g sat, 5 g mono); 16 mg cholesterol; 38 g carbohydrate; 16 g added sugars; 5 g protein; 1 g fiber; 230 mg sodium; 229 mg potassium.

Frozen Chocolate-Covered Bananas

MAKES: 12 servings

ACTIVE TIME: 15 minutes | TOTAL: 2¼ hours
TO MAKE AHEAD: Store airtight in the freezer for up to 1 week. | EQUIPMENT: 12 wooden popsicle sticks

Kids will love spreading bananas with melted chocolate and rolling them in coconut to make this tasty frozen treat.

- 4 large ripe bananas, peeled and cut into thirds crosswise
- ¾ cup semisweet *or* bittersweet chocolate chips, melted (*see How To*)
- ¼ cup shredded coconut

Line a baking sheet with parchment or wax paper. Insert a popsicle stick into each piece of banana. Cover each piece of banana with melted chocolate using a rubber spatula and sprinkle with coconut. (Reheat chocolate, as needed, to keep it melted.) Place the bananas on the baking sheet and freeze until frozen, about 2 hours.

PER SERVING: 100 calories; 4 g fat (3 g sat, 1 g mono); 0 mg cholesterol; 18 g carbohydrate; 6 g added sugars; 1 g protein; 2 g fiber; 7 mg sodium; 207 mg potassium.

How To

Melt Chocolate | Place chocolate chips (or chopped chocolate) in a bowl and microwave on Medium for 45 seconds. Stir; continue microwaving on Medium, stirring every 20 seconds, until almost melted. Continue stirring until completely melted. Or place in the top of a double boiler over hot, but not boiling, water. Stir until melted.

Vanilla-Orange Freezer Pops

H✂W   H♥H

MAKES: about 10 (3-ounce) freezer pops.
ACTIVE TIME: 10 minutes | TOTAL: 6 hours 10 minutes
TO MAKE AHEAD: Freeze for up to 3 weeks. | EQUIPMENT: Ten 3-ounce (or similar-size) freezer-pop molds

These creamy vanilla-flavored orange juice pops will transport you back to the days of standing in line at the ice cream truck. Add a couple drops each of yellow and red natural food dye to give them a more vivid orange color.

1½   **cups orange juice**
1½   **cups low-fat vanilla yogurt**
1-2   **tablespoons sugar**
½   **teaspoon vanilla extract**

1. Whisk orange juice, yogurt, sugar to taste and vanilla in a medium bowl.

2. Divide the mixture among freezer-pop molds. Insert the sticks and freeze until completely firm, about 6 hours. Dip the molds briefly in hot water before unmolding.

PER SERVING: 53 calories; 1 g fat (0 g sat, 0 g mono); 2 mg cholesterol; 10 g carbohydrate; 4 g added sugars; 2 g protein; 0 g fiber; 25 mg sodium; 155 mg potassium.
NUTRITION BONUS: Vitamin C (32% daily value).

Bourbon Street Sundaes

H♥H

MAKES: 4 servings
ACTIVE TIME: 15 minutes | TOTAL: 15 minutes

Toasted pecans and bourbon flavor this New Orleans-inspired brown sugar sauce.

½   **cup packed dark brown sugar**
1   **tablespoon cornstarch**
¼   **cup nonfat milk**
2   **tablespoons chopped pecans, toasted**
      (*see Tip, page 486*)
1   **tablespoon bourbon**
1   **teaspoon butter**
3   **cups nonfat vanilla frozen yogurt, reduced-fat "light" vanilla ice cream *or* Homemade Vanilla Ice Cream (*page 391*)**

1. Whisk brown sugar and cornstarch in a medium saucepan. Gradually stir in milk; bring to a simmer, stirring, over medium-high heat. Cook, stirring, until thickened, about 1 minute.

2. Remove from the heat and stir in pecans, bourbon and butter. Serve warm over frozen yogurt (or ice cream).

PER SERVING: 301 calories; 4 g fat (1 g sat, 1 g mono); 5 mg cholesterol; 59 g carbohydrate; 52 g added sugars; 8 g protein; 0 g fiber; 111 mg sodium; 396 mg potassium.
NUTRITION BONUS: Calcium (29% daily value).

Sicilian Granita

H✂W

MAKES: 8 servings, ¾ cup each (1½ quarts)
ACTIVE TIME: 2¼ hours | TOTAL: 4¼ hours (including freezing time) | TO MAKE AHEAD: Freeze in a sealable plastic container for up to 1 week.

This is a traditional Sicilian dessert for the hot weather. It starts with an icy espresso granita ("little grains" in Italian). The crystals are scraped up with a fork and served with a dollop of whipped cream. Kitchen Tip: *If you don't have an espresso maker, use instant espresso powder and water; store the powder in your freezer after opening. Instant coffee will also work in a pinch, it just won't be as full-flavored.*

3	**cups freshly brewed espresso (*see Kitchen Tip*)**
⅔	**cup sugar**
½	**cup whipping cream**

1. Stir hot espresso and sugar in a medium bowl until the sugar dissolves. Let the mixture cool to room temperature, then pour into a 9-by-13-inch baking pan. Place on a level surface in your freezer and freeze for 2 hours, stirring and scraping with a fork every 20 minutes to break up the ice crystals. Cover and freeze for at least 1 hour more.

2. Beat cream in a medium bowl with an electric mixer on high speed until medium peaks form, 30 seconds to 1 minute.

3. Scrape the frozen granita into ice crystals using a sturdy fork. To serve, layer the granita with whipped cream in goblets or simply top with a dollop of whipped cream.

PER SERVING: 117 calories; 5 g fat (3 g sat, 1 g mono); 17 mg cholesterol; 19 g carbohydrate; 17 g added sugars; 0 g protein; 0 g fiber; 18 mg sodium; 118 mg potassium.

Instant Frozen Yogurt

H✂W H⬆F H♥H

MAKES: 4 servings, ¾ cup each
ACTIVE TIME: 10 minutes | TOTAL: 10 minutes

We like to use a mixture of raspberries, blueberries and strawberries, but you can use whatever frozen fruit you have on hand in this ultra-quick frozen yogurt that is made without an ice cream maker. Shopping Tip: *Superfine sugar dissolves instantly, preventing a grainy texture in cold desserts and beverages. It is available in the baking section of most supermarkets, but if you can't find it, simply process regular granulated sugar in a food processor or a clean coffee grinder until ground very fine.*

3½	**cups frozen berries *or* other coarsely chopped fruit (about 16 ounces)**
½	**cup sugar, preferably superfine (*see Shopping Tip*)**
½	**cup nonfat plain yogurt**
1	**tablespoon lemon juice**

Combine fruit and sugar in a food processor; pulse until coarsely chopped. Combine yogurt and lemon juice in a measuring cup; with the machine on, gradually pour the mixture through the feed tube. Process until smooth and creamy, scraping down the sides once or twice. Serve immediately.

PER SERVING: 164 calories; 0 g fat (0 g sat, 0 g mono); 1 mg cholesterol; 38 g carbohydrate; 25 g added sugars; 3 g protein; 3 g fiber; 25 mg sodium; 83 mg potassium.
NUTRITION BONUS: Vitamin C (30% daily value).

Homemade Vanilla Ice Cream

H✳W   H♥H

MAKES: 8 servings, ½ cup each (1 quart)
ACTIVE TIME: 15 minutes | TOTAL: 2¾ hours (including 2 hours chilling time) | TO MAKE AHEAD: Store airtight in the freezer for up to 1 week. EQUIPMENT: Ice cream maker

Our simple low-fat vanilla ice cream has all the richness you'll need but about 90 fewer calories than store-bought premium ice cream and a whopping 15 grams less total fat and 10 grams less saturated fat per serving.

1½	teaspoons unflavored gelatin
1	tablespoon water
3	cups low-fat milk, divided
1	vanilla bean
3	large egg yolks
1	14-ounce can nonfat sweetened condensed milk
	Stir-Ins (optional)

1. Sprinkle gelatin over water in a small bowl; let stand, stirring once or twice, while you make the base for the ice cream.

2. Pour 1½ cups milk into a large saucepan. Cut vanilla bean in half lengthwise; scrape the seeds into the milk and add the pod.

3. Heat the milk mixture over medium heat until steaming. Whisk egg yolks and condensed milk in a medium bowl. Gradually pour in the hot milk, whisking until blended. Return the mixture to the pan and cook over medium heat, stirring with a wooden spoon, until the back of the spoon is lightly coated, 3 to 5 minutes. Do not bring to a boil or the custard will curdle.

4. Strain the custard through a fine-mesh sieve into a clean large bowl. Add the softened gelatin and whisk until melted. Whisk in the remaining 1½ cups milk. Cover and refrigerate until chilled, at least 2 hours.

5. Whisk the ice cream mixture and pour into the canister of an ice cream maker. Freeze according to manufacturer's directions. Add Stir-Ins, if desired (*see How To*), during the last 5 minutes of freezing. If necessary, place the ice cream in the freezer to firm up before serving.

PER SERVING: 200 calories; 3 g fat (1 g sat, 1 g mono); 90 mg cholesterol; 35 g carbohydrate; 28 g added sugars; 8 g protein; 0 g fiber; 95 mg sodium; 614 mg potassium.
NUTRITION BONUS: Calcium (25% daily value); Potassium (18% dv).

EatingWell Tip

To **save calories** and still get a smooth, creamy texture in homemade low-fat ice cream, add gelatin. It mimics the texture of fat in full-fat ice cream.

How To

Add Stir-Ins to Homemade Ice Cream | Here are a few tips for successfully adding anything from strawberries to chocolate chips to pretzels to your vanilla ice cream:
1. Stir-ins should be small, about the size of a pea.
2. Cool toasted ingredients completely before adding them to the ice cream maker.
3. Check the ice cream maker's directions when it comes

to judging the volume of your stir-ins. In general, we recommend 1 cup of stir-ins per quart of ice cream.
4. Add stir-ins to the ice cream during the last 5 minutes of freezing. Some of our favorite flavor combinations:
   - Walnut & Chocolate Cookie
   - Strawberry & Chocolate
   - Cherry & White Chocolate
   - Blueberry & Cinnamon
   - Coconut & Almond

Lemon Icebox Pie

H✳W

MAKES: 10 servings
ACTIVE TIME: 40 minutes | TOTAL: 8 hours 40 minutes
(including chilling & freezing time)
TO MAKE AHEAD: Cover and freeze the pie for up to 1 week.

One bite of this bright, lemony pie will have you puckering with delight. Plan ahead so you have time to freeze it.

2	large eggs
1	cup sugar, divided
1	tablespoon freshly grated lemon zest
⅔	cup lemon juice
6	tablespoons warm water
2	tablespoons dried egg whites (*see Tip, page 484*)
	Pinch of cream of tartar
⅓	cup whipping cream
1	9-inch graham cracker crust (*see EatingWell Tip*)
	Lemon slices for garnish

1. Whisk eggs and ⅔ cup sugar in a heavy, nonreactive medium saucepan (*see Tip, page 486*) until smooth. Whisk in lemon juice. Cook over low heat, whisking constantly, until slightly thickened, 7 to 10 minutes. (Do not let the mixture come to a simmer.) Pour through a fine-mesh sieve into a bowl. Stir in lemon zest. Place plastic wrap directly on the surface and refrigerate until thoroughly chilled, about 2 hours.

2. Combine warm water, dried egg whites and cream of tartar in a mixing bowl. Stir gently until egg whites are dissolved, about 2 minutes. Beat with an electric mixer on medium-high speed until soft peaks form. Gradually add the remaining ⅓ cup sugar, beating until stiff and glossy (*see How To*).

3. Whip cream in a small chilled bowl with chilled beaters on medium speed until soft peaks form.

4. Gently fold the chilled lemon mixture into the beaten egg whites with a rubber spatula. Fold in the whipped cream. Pour the filling into the crust and smooth the top. Freeze, uncovered, until firm, about 1 hour. Cover and freeze for at least 6 hours more.

5. Soften the pie in the refrigerator for 20 to 30 minutes before slicing. Garnish with lemon slices, if desired.

PER SERVING: 203 calories; 6 g fat (2 g sat, 1 g mono); 51 mg cholesterol; 34 g carbohydrate; 24 g added sugars; 5 g protein; 0 g fiber; 97 mg sodium; 82 mg potassium.

How To

Identify Soft or Stiff Peaks | When egg whites are beaten to "soft" peaks (PHOTO 1), the whites will still be soft enough to curl over when a beater is turned upside down. The whites are considered "stiff" peaks (PHOTO 2) when they remain stiff and upright.

EatingWell Tip

Beware of hidden sources of heart-damaging trans fats. A label that touts "0 grams trans fats" simply means that a serving has less than 0.5 grams of trans fats (the manufacturer is allowed to round down). If there aren't any partially hydrogenated oils on the ingredients list, you'll know products—from chips to the graham cracker crust we use in this recipe—are actually trans-fat free.

Peach & Blueberry Cobbler

H✳W   H↑F

MAKES: 10 servings
ACTIVE TIME: 20 minutes | TOTAL: 1¼ hours

This is a healthier version of a traditional cobbler, with canola oil in place of some of the butter and whole-wheat flour instead of all-purpose flour. Unlike more classic biscuit-topped cobblers, the peaches and blueberries are nestled into a tender batter that swells around the fruit as it bakes. Other fruits may be substituted. It's especially beautiful when baked in and served right from a cast-iron skillet.

3	**tablespoons unsalted butter**
3	**tablespoons canola oil**
1	**cup whole-wheat flour**
1½	**teaspoons baking powder**
½	**teaspoon salt**
1	**cup reduced-fat milk**
½	**cup sugar**
1	**teaspoon vanilla extract**
3	**ripe but firm peaches (about 1 pound), pitted and sliced into eighths,** *or* **3½ cups frozen slices**
2	**cups blueberries (1 pint), fresh** *or* **frozen**

1. Preheat oven to 350°F.

2. Place butter and oil in a 12-inch cast-iron skillet or a 9-by-13-inch baking pan. Heat in the oven until melted and fragrant, 5 to 7 minutes.

3. Meanwhile, combine flour, baking powder and salt in a large bowl. Add milk, sugar and vanilla; stir to combine.

4. Add the melted butter mixture to the batter and stir to combine. Pour the batter into the hot pan. Spoon peaches and blueberries evenly over the batter.

5. Return the pan to the oven and bake until the top of the cobbler is browned and the batter around the fruit is completely set, 50 minutes to 1 hour. Remove to a wire rack to cool for at least 15 minutes. Serve warm.

PER SERVING: 182 calories; 8 g fat (3 g sat, 3 g mono); 11 mg cholesterol; 26 g carbohydrate; 7 g added sugars; 3 g protein; 3 g fiber; 211 mg sodium; 175 mg potassium.

EatingWell Tip

Try substituting **canola oil** for up to half the butter in baked goods. We cut 2 grams of saturated fat per serving in this recipe by using half butter and half canola oil.

Making Fruit Crisps

A fruit crisp offers the luscious flavor of a fresh fruit pie without the fuss of making a crust. From a nutritional point of view, crisps lend themselves readily to healthful revisions. Most recipes include rolled oats—a fiber-rich, whole-grain food—in the topping. Substituting whole-wheat flour for white is an easy and effective way to boost fiber and nutrients and enhance the nutty taste of the topping. A sprinkling of nuts on the top provides a healthful finish along with a nice crunch, and just a tablespoon of butter provides plenty of the characteristic buttery flavor of typical crisps.

Start by choosing a fruit filling: celebrate the arrival of cherries or midsummer peaches or plums. You can also make any of these with frozen fruit. Serve with reduced-fat vanilla ice cream or frozen yogurt if you'd like.

Master Fruit Crisp Recipe

H✖W   H⬆F   H♥H

MAKES: 8 servings, ½ cup each
ACTIVE TIME: 20-40 minutes
TOTAL: 1 hour-1 hour 20 minutes

    Fruit Filling (*below*)
TOPPING
  ⅔ **cup whole-wheat flour**
  ½ **cup old-fashioned rolled oats (*not* instant)**
  ½ **cup packed light brown sugar**
  1 **teaspoon ground cinnamon**
    Pinch of salt
  1 **tablespoon butter, cut into small pieces**
  1 **tablespoon canola oil**
  3 **tablespoons frozen orange juice concentrate**
  1 **tablespoon chopped almonds *or* walnuts**

1. Preheat oven to 375°F. Coat an 8-inch-square baking dish (or similar 1½- to 2-quart dish) with cooking spray.

2. Combine FRUIT FILLING ingredients in a large bowl; toss to coat. Place the filling in the prepared baking dish. Cover with foil. Bake for 20 minutes.

3. Meanwhile, make TOPPING. Mix flour, oats, brown sugar, cinnamon and salt in a medium bowl with a fork. Add butter and blend with a pastry blender or your fingertips. Add oil and stir to coat. Add orange juice concentrate and blend with your fingertips until the dry ingredients are moistened.

4. After 20 minutes, stir the FRUIT FILLING and sprinkle the TOPPING evenly over it. Sprinkle with almonds (or walnuts). Bake, uncovered, until the fruit is bubbly and tender and the topping is lightly browned, 20 to 25 minutes more. Let cool for at least 10 minutes before serving. Serve warm or at room temperature.

Fruit Fillings

APPLE-CRANBERRY FILLING
 1½ **pounds apples, peeled and sliced (5 cups)**
  1 **cup cranberries, fresh *or* frozen**
  ⅓ **cup sugar**
PER SERVING: 222 calories; 4 g fat (1 g sat, 2 g mono); 4 mg cholesterol; 46 g carbohydrate; 22 g added sugars; 3 g protein; 4 g fiber; 23 mg sodium; 205 mg potassium.
NUTRITION BONUS: Vitamin C (23% daily value).

PLUM FILLING
  2 **pounds plums, pitted and sliced (6 cups)**
  ⅓ **cup sugar**
  2 **teaspoons freshly grated orange zest**
  1 **tablespoon orange juice**
PER SERVING: 232 calories; 4 g fat (1 g sat, 2 g mono); 4 mg cholesterol; 48 g carbohydrate; 22 g added sugars; 3 g protein; 4 g fiber; 23 mg sodium; 301 mg potassium.
NUTRITION BONUS: Vitamin C (35% daily value).

CHERRY FILLING

- 1½   **pounds sweet cherries (5 cups), fresh *or*
         frozen, pitted**
- 1   **cup raspberries, fresh *or* frozen**
- ⅓   **cup sugar**
- 1   **tablespoon cornstarch**
- 1   **tablespoon lemon juice**
- 1   **tablespoon kirsch *or* brandy (optional)**

PER SERVING: 246 calories; 4 g fat (1 g sat, 2 g mono);
4 mg cholesterol; 51 g carbohydrate; 22 g added sugars;
3 g protein; 5 g fiber; 23 mg sodium; 325 mg potassium.
NUTRITION BONUS: Vitamin C (32% daily value).

▲ PEACH-RASPBERRY FILLING

- 2   **pounds peaches, peeled (if desired; *see How To,
         page 416*), pitted and sliced (5 cups),
         or frozen slices**
- 1   **cup raspberries, fresh *or* frozen**
- 2   **tablespoons sugar**
- 1   **tablespoon lemon juice**

PER SERVING: 208 calories; 4 g fat (1 g sat, 2 g mono);
4 mg cholesterol; 42 g carbohydrate; 16 g added sugars;
3 g protein; 4 g fiber; 23 mg sodium; 342 mg potassium.
NUTRITION BONUS: Vitamin C (35% daily value).

Panna Cotta with
Red Wine-Strawberry Compote

H✖W

MAKES: 6 servings

ACTIVE TIME: 30 minutes | TOTAL: 2½ hours

EQUIPMENT: Six 6-ounce (¾-cup) ramekins or molds

Buttermilk gives this silky panna cotta, or "cooked cream,"
a bright, fresh taste. A tart-sweet strawberry sauce is a nice
contrast.

PANNA COTTA

   1   **envelope unflavored gelatin (about 2¼ teaspoons)**
   ¼   **cup water**
   ½   **cup sugar**
   ⅓   **cup whipping cream**
   2⅓ **cups buttermilk (see Tip, page 482)**

COMPOTE

   1   **cup dry red wine**
   ¼   **cup sugar**
   1   **pint strawberries, hulled and sliced (about 2 cups)**

1. **To prepare panna cotta:** Sprinkle gelatin over water
   in a saucepan; let stand for 1 minute. Add ¼ cup
   sugar and cream and heat over low heat until steaming,
   stirring to dissolve the sugar. Remove from heat and
   slowly stir in buttermilk.

2. Divide the custard among six 6-ounce (¾-cup)
   ramekins or molds. Cover and refrigerate the panna
   cottas until firm, about 2 hours.

3. **To prepare compote & serve:** Heat wine and ¼ cup
   sugar in a small nonreactive saucepan over medium
   heat until boiling. Lower heat and simmer until
   reduced to ½ cup, about 15 minutes.

4. Place strawberries in a medium bowl and pour in the
   wine mixture. Let compote cool to room temperature.

5. Dip ramekins or molds into hot water for a few seconds, then invert the panna cottas onto individual
   dessert plates. Shake to loosen, then lift off ramekins
   or molds. Spoon the compote around panna cottas.
   Serve immediately.

PER SERVING: 200 calories; 5 g fat (3 g sat, 1 g mono);
16 mg cholesterol; 32 g carbohydrate; 25 g added sugars;
3 g protein; 1 g fiber; 38 mg sodium; 178 mg potassium.
NUTRITION BONUS: Vitamin C (48% daily value).

EatingWell Tip

Replace almost all the cream in desserts like panna cotta
with buttermilk or low-fat milk to **reduce calories and fat**.

Strawberry-Rhubarb Bread Pudding

H⬆F   H❤H

MAKES: 8 servings

ACTIVE TIME: 30 minutes | TOTAL: 1¾ hours

TO MAKE AHEAD: Prepare the pudding through Step 3; refrigerate overnight. Let stand at room temperature while the oven preheats. Bake as directed in Step 4.

Gingersnaps add a sublime note to the classic spring combination of strawberries and rhubarb. This recipe is a great way to use up bread that's a little past its peak.

4	large egg whites
4	large eggs
1	cup nonfat milk
½	cup sugar
1	tablespoon vanilla extract
1	teaspoon freshly grated orange zest
4	cups whole-grain bread, crusts removed if desired, cut into 1-inch cubes (about 8 ounces, 4-6 slices)
2	cups roughly broken gingersnaps
2	cups quartered strawberries, fresh *or* frozen (thawed)
1	cup diced rhubarb
¼	cup chopped walnuts, lightly toasted (*see Tip, page 486*)

TOPPING

¼	cup chopped walnuts, lightly toasted, *or* Streusel Topping (*see Variation*)

1. Preheat oven to 375°F. Coat an 11-by-7-inch glass baking dish or a 2-quart casserole with cooking spray.

2. Whisk egg whites, eggs and milk in a medium bowl. Add sugar, vanilla and orange zest; whisk to combine.

3. Toss bread, gingersnaps, strawberries, rhubarb and ¼ cup walnuts in a large bowl. Add the custard and toss well to coat. Transfer to the prepared baking dish and push down to compact. Cover with foil.

4. Bake until the custard has set, 40 to 45 minutes. Uncover, sprinkle with ¼ cup walnuts (or Streusel Topping) and continue baking until the pudding is puffed and golden on top, 15 to 20 minutes more. Transfer to a wire rack and cool for 15 to 20 minutes before serving.

PER SERVING: 321 calories; 10 g fat (2 g sat, 3 g mono); 106 mg cholesterol; 45 g carbohydrate; 17 g added sugars; 12 g protein; 4 g fiber; 312 mg sodium; 377 mg potassium.
NUTRITION BONUS: Vitamin C (43% daily value), Folate (20% dv), Iron (15% dv).

STREUSEL TOPPING VARIATION:

Combine ⅓ cup flour, ¼ cup oats (preferably old-fashioned), 2 tablespoons brown sugar and 2 tablespoons canola oil in a small bowl. Sprinkle the mixture on the pudding in Step 4 in place of the walnuts.

EatingWell Tip

Add walnuts to desserts or salads. They **provide omega-3s**, which have anti-inflammatory properties and may benefit heart health.

Maple-Walnut Tapioca Pudding

H ♥ H

MAKES: 2 servings, about ⅔ cup each
ACTIVE TIME: 20 minutes | TOTAL: 45 minutes
TO MAKE AHEAD: Cover and refrigerate the pudding for up to 3 days. Prepare the walnut topping (Step 4) 15 minutes before serving.

Turn comforting tapioca pudding into a special dessert by spiking it with pure maple syrup and finishing it with a simple spiced maple-nut topping. You can easily double the recipe if necessary—it just may take a little longer to cook in Step 2.

1   cup low-fat milk
1   large egg, well beaten
4   teaspoons quick-cooking tapioca
⅛   teaspoon salt
¼   cup plus 1 tablespoon pure maple syrup, divided
½   teaspoon vanilla extract
2   tablespoons chopped walnuts
    Pinch of ground cinnamon
    Pinch of ground nutmeg

1. Combine milk, egg, tapioca and salt in a medium saucepan. Let stand for 5 minutes.

2. Place the saucepan over medium-low heat and cook, stirring constantly, until the mixture comes to a boil, 6 to 18 minutes (depending on your stove). Remove from the heat; stir in ¼ cup syrup and vanilla.

3. Divide the pudding between 2 ramekins or custard cups. Let cool for at least 30 minutes or refrigerate until chilled.

4. Meanwhile, line a small plate with parchment or wax paper. Coat the paper with cooking spray. Combine walnuts, the remaining 1 tablespoon syrup, cinnamon and nutmeg in a small saucepan or skillet. Heat over medium-low heat, stirring, until most of the syrup has evaporated, 1 to 4 minutes. Spread the nuts out onto the prepared paper and place in the freezer until cool, about 10 minutes.

5. Crumble the chilled walnut topping into pieces. Serve the pudding topped with the maple walnuts.

PER SERVING: 296 calories; 9 g fat (2 g sat, 2 g mono); 112 mg cholesterol; 48 g carbohydrate; 30 g added sugars; 8 g protein; 1 g fiber; 239 mg sodium; 353 mg potassium.
NUTRITION BONUS: Calcium & Zinc (21% daily value).

Grilled Pineapple with Coconut Black Sticky Rice

H↑F

MAKES: 6 servings, generous ⅓ cup rice & ½ cup pineapple each
ACTIVE TIME: 30 minutes | **TOTAL:** 45 minutes

A take on the classic Southeast Asian dessert of fresh mango with coconut white sticky rice, this version has grilled pineapple served over cardamom-infused coconut black sticky rice. The consistency should be that of a loose rice pudding. White sticky rice can be substituted for the black sticky rice, but the cooking time in Step 1 will be 12 to 15 minutes and, in Step 2, 10 to 15 minutes. Check the rice while it's cooking to prevent scorching.

1½	**cups water**
1	**cup black sticky rice (*see Tip, page 488*)**
1	**14-ounce can "lite" coconut milk**
½	**teaspoon ground cardamom**
3	**tablespoons finely chopped palm sugar (*see Tip, page 489*) *or* packed brown sugar**
½	**teaspoon salt**
1	**small ripe pineapple, peeled, cored and cut into ½-inch-thick slices (*see How To*)**

1. Combine water and rice in a medium saucepan. Bring to a boil, reduce heat to maintain a gentle simmer, cover and cook until the rice has absorbed all the water, about 20 minutes. The rice should be cooked yet still somewhat firm.

2. Bring the coconut milk to a boil in another medium saucepan. Reduce heat to medium-low, add cardamom, sugar and salt. Stir until the sugar and salt are dissolved. Set aside ¾ cup of the seasoned coconut milk. Add the rice to the pan with the remaining seasoned coconut milk, return to a gentle simmer, cover and cook until the rice softens and absorbs almost all the liquid, about 15 minutes.

3. Meanwhile, preheat grill to high. Oil the grill rack (*see Tip, page 485*). Grill the pineapple slices until slightly charred and softened, 1 to 2 minutes per side. Transfer to a cutting board; let stand until cool enough to handle. Chop the pineapple.

4. Serve rice and pineapple with the reserved coconut milk drizzled on top. Serve hot or at room temperature.

PER SERVING: 237 calories; 6 g fat (3 g sat, 0 g mono); 0 mg cholesterol; 45 g carbohydrate; 8 g added sugars; 5 g protein; 3 g fiber; 215 mg sodium; 121 mg potassium.
NUTRITION BONUS: Vitamin C (80% daily value).

How To

Prepare a Pineapple:
1. Cut off the top and bottom of the pineapple with a sharp knife, making a stable flat base.
2. Stand the pineapple upright and remove the skin.
3. Use a paring knife to remove any remaining eyes.
4. Slice the fruit away from the core. Discard core. Cut the fruit into the desired shape or size.

Roasted Pear Trifle

H✖W   H⬆F   H♥H

MAKES: 20 servings, about ⅔ cup each
ACTIVE TIME: 1½ hours | TOTAL: 4 hours (including chilling time) | TO MAKE AHEAD: Refrigerate, without Vanilla Cream, for up to 2 days. | EQUIPMENT: 8-inch trifle bowl

Trifle, the quintessential British dessert, can be made in endless variations. This crowd-pleasing version is perfect for entertaining—you assemble it in advance and it actually gets better as it sits. The results never fail to impress.
Shopping Tip: Look for amaretto at the liquor store or replace it with 4 tablespoons orange juice mixed with ¼ teaspoon almond extract.

CUSTARD
- 2 **large eggs**
- ½ **cup sugar**
- 6 **tablespoons cornstarch**
- ¼ **teaspoon salt**
- 3½ **cups low-fat milk, divided**
- 2 **teaspoons vanilla extract**

ROASTED PEARS & TRIFLE
- 8 **firm, ripe Bosc pears (about 3¼ pounds), peeled and diced**
- 2 **tablespoons sugar**
- 2 **tablespoons lemon juice**
- ¼ **cup sliced almonds (optional)**
- ¾ **cup apricot fruit spread *or* preserves**
- 3 **3-ounce packages soft ladyfingers (see *Tip*, *page 485*)**
- 4 **tablespoons amaretto, divided (see *Shopping Tip*)**
- 1 **pint fresh raspberries**
- 1¾ **cups Vanilla Cream (*page 404*; optional)**

1. **To prepare custard:** Whisk eggs, ½ cup sugar, cornstarch, salt and ½ cup milk in a medium bowl until smooth. Heat the remaining 3 cups milk in a large heavy saucepan over medium heat until steaming. Gradually pour the hot milk into the egg mixture, whisking constantly. Return this mixture to the pan and cook over medium heat, whisking constantly, until the custard bubbles and thickens. (Use caution, as hot custard will sputter.) Remove from the heat and stir in vanilla. Transfer the custard to a shallow glass dish. Press plastic wrap directly onto the surface and refrigerate until chilled, at least 1 hour or overnight.

2. **To roast pears:** Preheat oven to 400°F. Coat a rimmed baking sheet with cooking spray. Toss pears, 2 tablespoons sugar and lemon juice in a large bowl. Spread the pears on the prepared baking sheet. Roast the pears until tender and golden brown in spots, turning occasionally, 45 to 50 minutes.

3. While the pears are roasting, toast almonds, if using, in a small baking pan until fragrant, 4 to 5 minutes. Set aside.

4. **To assemble trifle:** Melt apricot preserves in a small saucepan over low heat. Arrange 14 to 15 ladyfingers in the bottom of a trifle bowl (8-inch diameter), trimming them if necessary to fit tightly. Drizzle 1 tablespoon amaretto over the ladyfingers and dot with 3 tablespoons of the preserves. Top with one-third of the roasted pears (about 1⅓ cups) and a scant ½ cup raspberries. Spread ¾ cup custard over. Repeat layering 2 more times with ladyfingers, amaretto, preserves, fruit and custard. Top with 13 to 15 ladyfingers (you may have leftovers); drizzle with remaining amaretto. Spread remaining custard over the top. Cover and refrigerate until cold, at least 1 hour.

5. Shortly before serving, spread Vanilla Cream on top of the trifle, if desired, and garnish with toasted almonds, if desired, and the remaining raspberries.

PER SERVING: 192 calories; 1 g fat (1 g sat, 0 g mono); 31 mg cholesterol; 41 g carbohydrate; 19 g added sugars; 3 g protein; 3 g fiber; 61 mg sodium; 173 mg potassium.

Vanilla Cream

MAKES: about 1 cup
ACTIVE TIME: 15 minutes | TOTAL: 1¼ hours (including 1 hour to drain yogurt) | TO MAKE AHEAD: Cover and refrigerate for up to 2 days.

Use this creamy topping in place of regular whipped cream.

1	cup low-fat *or* nonfat vanilla yogurt
¼	cup whipping cream
2½	teaspoons confectioners' sugar (optional)

1. Line a sieve or colander with cheesecloth and set over a bowl, leaving at least ½-inch clearance from the bottom. (*Alternatively, use a coffee filter lined with filter paper.*) Spoon in yogurt, cover and let drain in the refrigerator for 1 hour. Discard whey.

2. Whip cream in a small bowl until soft peaks form. Add sugar, if using, and continue whipping until firm peaks form. Fold in the drained yogurt.

PER TABLESPOON: 24 calories; 1 g fat (1 g sat, 0 g mono); 5 mg cholesterol; 2 g carbohydrate; 1 g added sugars; 1 g protein; 0 g fiber; 11 mg sodium; 37 mg potassium.

▶ Rhubarb Fool

H✖W

MAKES: 8 servings
ACTIVE TIME: 30 minutes | TOTAL: 2½ hours (including 2 hours chilling time) | TO MAKE AHEAD: Cover and refrigerate for up to 6 hours.

Fool is a great easy dessert to make for a party—you make the pudding ahead and serve it chilled when you're ready. Choose the reddest rhubarb stalks you can find to give this fool a pretty pink swirl.

1	cinnamon stick
3	whole cloves
1	2-inch-long strip lemon zest
2¼	pounds rhubarb, trimmed and cut into ½-inch pieces (8 cups)
1¼	cups sugar
1½	cups nonfat vanilla Greek yogurt (*see Tip, page 490*)
½	cup whipping cream

1. Tie cinnamon stick, cloves and lemon zest together in a cheesecloth bag. Combine rhubarb, sugar and the spice bag in a large saucepan and bring to a boil over medium-high heat, stirring occasionally. Cook, stirring frequently, until the mixture has the consistency of applesauce, 6 to 8 minutes. Discard the spice bag. Chill the rhubarb mixture for about 1 hour.

2. Whisk yogurt in a medium bowl until smooth. Fold in the rhubarb mixture lightly, leaving some swirls.

3. Whip cream in a chilled bowl with an electric mixer on medium speed until soft peaks form. Swirl the whipped cream into the fool. Spoon into individual dishes. Cover and refrigerate for at least 1 hour or up to 6 hours.

PER SERVING: 223 calories; 5 g fat (3 g sat, 1 g mono); 17 mg cholesterol; 41 g carbohydrate; 31 g added sugars; 5 g protein; 2 g fiber; 27 mg sodium; 383 mg potassium.
NUTRITION BONUS: Calcium & Vitamin C (17% daily value).

Sunny Citrus Chiffon Cake

H ❤ H

MAKES: 12 servings
ACTIVE TIME: 1¼ hours | **TOTAL:** 3¾ hours (including cooling & glaze-setting time) | **EQUIPMENT:** 10-inch angel food cake pan with removable bottom

Flavored with orange, lemon and lime, this big, beautiful cake is a fitting ending to a celebration.

CAKE
- 1½ **cups cake flour**
- 1½ **cups granulated sugar, divided**
- 1 **teaspoon baking powder**
- ¼ **teaspoon salt**
- 2 **oranges**
- 1 **lemon**
- 1 **lime**
- 10 **large egg whites, at room temperature (*see Tip, page 484*)**
- ½ **teaspoon cream of tartar**
- 3 **large egg yolks**
- 2 **tablespoons Grand Marnier *or* other orange liqueur**
- 1 **teaspoon vanilla extract**

CITRUS GLAZE
- 1 **large orange**
- 1 **lemon**
- 1 **lime**
- 2 **cups confectioners' sugar**

1. Preheat oven to 350°F.

2. **To prepare cake:** Sift flour, ¾ cup granulated sugar, baking powder and salt into a small bowl; set aside. Using a microplane grater or the smallest hole of a box grater, grate oranges to get 2 tablespoons zest. Grate lemon and lime to get 2 teaspoons zest from each. Squeeze 1 tablespoon juice each from the lemon and lime.

3. Beat egg whites and cream of tartar with an electric mixer just until soft peaks form. Beat in the remaining ¾ cup granulated sugar, 2 tablespoons at a time, until the whites are shiny and form soft peaks (*see How To, page 392*).

4. Whisk egg yolks, orange liqueur, vanilla, the orange, lemon and lime zests and the lemon and lime juices in a small bowl. Pour over the egg whites and fold together with a rubber spatula.

5. Resift the reserved dry ingredients over the egg whites in four additions, folding in gently after each. Spoon the batter into an ungreased 10-inch angel food cake pan with a removable bottom. Smooth the top and run a knife or spatula through the batter to remove any air bubbles.

6. Bake the cake until the top is golden and a long skewer inserted into the cake comes out clean, 45 to 50 minutes. Invert the pan over the neck of a bottle and let cool completely, about 2 hours.

7. **To prepare citrus glaze:** Use a citrus zester to remove long threads of zest from orange, lemon and lime (*see How To*). Squeeze 4 teaspoons juice from each fruit. Whisk the juices into confectioners' sugar in a small bowl to make a smooth glaze.

8. Run a knife around the sides and center tube of the pan; lift out the cake and pan bottom. Invert the cake onto a serving plate; use the knife to loosen the pan bottom, then lift it off. Spoon the glaze over the cake, allowing it to drip down the sides. Sprinkle the zest threads on top. Let the cake stand for at least 30 minutes to let the glaze set.

PER SERVING: 286 calories; 1 g fat (0 g sat, 1 g mono); 52 mg cholesterol; 64 mg carbohydrate; 45 g added sugars; 5 g protein; 1 g fiber; 144 mg sodium; 143 mg potassium.
NUTRITION BONUS: Vitamin C (33% daily value), Folate (16% dv).

How To
Make Long Strips of Citrus Zest | Remove threads of zest using a citrus zester (**PHOTO 1**). Or remove long strips with a vegetable peeler, then cut into very thin strips (**PHOTO 2**).

Dark Cherry Bundt Cake

H ❤ H

MAKES: 12 servings
ACTIVE TIME: 45 minutes | TOTAL: 3 hours (including 1½ hours cooling time) | EQUIPMENT: 10-inch Bundt pan

Cherries and almond extract pair beautifully in this delectable cake. Yogurt adds subtle flavor and helps keep the cake moist. **Kitchen Tip:** *Be sure to measure frozen cherries while still frozen, then thaw. (Drain juice before using.)* **Shopping Tip:** *Kirsch (also called kirschwasser) is clear cherry brandy, commonly used as a flavor enhancer in fondue and cherries jubilee. Find it at liquor stores.*

CHERRY FILLING
¼	cup granulated sugar
1½	teaspoons cornstarch
3	cups dark sweet cherries, fresh *or* frozen (thawed), pitted and coarsely chopped (*see Kitchen Tip*)
2	tablespoons kirsch (*see Shopping Tip*) or orange juice
1	teaspoon freshly grated lemon zest
¼	teaspoon almond extract

CAKE
1⅔	cups cake flour
1	cup whole-wheat pastry flour (*see Tip, page 485*)
2½	teaspoons baking powder
½	teaspoon baking soda
½	teaspoon salt
1	cup granulated sugar
3	tablespoons butter, slightly softened
3	tablespoons canola oil
1¼	cups nonfat vanilla *or* lemon yogurt
2	large eggs
2½	teaspoons vanilla extract
1	teaspoon almond extract
2	teaspoons confectioners' sugar, for garnish

1. Preheat oven to 350°F. Very generously coat a 10-inch Bundt with cooking spray. Dust the pan with flour, tapping out the excess.

2. **To prepare cherry filling:** Combine sugar and cornstarch in a medium nonreactive saucepan (*see Tip, page 486*). Stir in cherries, kirsch (or orange juice), lemon zest and almond extract. Bring to a boil over medium-high heat and cook, stirring occasionally, until the mixture looks like very thick jam and has reduced to about 1 cup, 5 to 7 minutes.

3. **To prepare cake:** Sift cake flour, whole-wheat flour, baking powder, baking soda and salt into a medium bowl. Beat sugar, butter and oil in a large bowl with an electric mixer on low, then medium speed, until very light and fluffy, about 1½ minutes, scraping the sides as needed. Add half the yogurt and beat until very smooth. With the mixer on low speed, beat in half the dry ingredients until incorporated. Beat in the remaining yogurt, eggs, vanilla and almond extract until combined, scraping the sides as needed. Stir in the remaining dry ingredients just until incorporated.

4. Spoon a generous half of the batter into the prepared pan, spreading to the edges. Spoon the cherry mixture over the batter. Top with the remaining batter. Grease a butter knife and swirl it vertically through the batter and cherries.

5. Bake the cake until a toothpick inserted in the thickest part comes out with no crumbs clinging to it and the top springs back when lightly pressed, 50 to 65 minutes. (Cakes in dark-colored metal pans usually bake faster than cakes in light-colored or shiny metal pans.) Transfer the pan to a wire rack and let stand until the cake is completely cooled, about 1½ hours.

6. Very carefully run a knife around the edges and center tube to loosen the cake from sides and bottom. Rap the pan sharply against the counter several times to loosen completely. Invert the pan onto a serving plate and slide the cake out. Dust the top with confectioners' sugar before serving.

PER SERVING: 313 calories; 8 g fat (2 g sat, 3 g mono); 43 mg cholesterol; 56 g carbohydrate; 24 g added sugars; 5 g protein; 2 g fiber; 294 mg sodium; 183 mg potassium.
NUTRITION BONUS: Folate (16% daily value).

Raspberry-Swirl Cupcakes

MAKES: 12 cupcakes

ACTIVE TIME: 40 minutes | TOTAL: 3 hours (including cooling and chilling time) | TO MAKE AHEAD: Cover and refrigerate the frosting (Step 7) for up to 3 days. Store cooled cupcakes airtight at room temperature for up to 1 day.

EQUIPMENT: Muffin tin with 12 (½-cup) cups, paper liners

These raspberry-lemon cupcakes are topped with an easy cream cheese frosting tinted pink with a little raspberry puree. For those unaccustomed to the mildly nutty flavor of whole-wheat flour, the flavor of the raspberry puree swirled into the lemony cake makes the wheat flavor undetectable.

CUPCAKES

2	cups raspberries, fresh *or* frozen (thawed and drained), plus 12 fresh berries for garnish (about 12 ounces total)
1	tablespoon plus ¾ cup granulated sugar, divided
¾	cup whole-wheat pastry flour (*see Tip, page 485*)
¾	cup cake flour
1½	teaspoons baking powder
½	teaspoon baking soda
½	teaspoon salt
¼	cup canola oil
2	large eggs
1	teaspoon vanilla extract
1	teaspoon freshly grated lemon zest
½	cup nonfat buttermilk (*see Tip, page 482*)

FROSTING

8	ounces reduced-fat cream cheese (Neufchâtel), at room temperature
1	cup packed confectioners' sugar
½	teaspoon freshly grated lemon zest

1. **To prepare cupcakes:** Preheat oven to 350°F. Line 12 (½-cup) muffin cups with paper liners; coat the liners with cooking spray.

2. Puree 2 cups raspberries and 1 tablespoon granulated sugar in a blender or food processor until smooth. Strain through a fine-mesh sieve into a small bowl, pressing with a rubber spatula to extract all the puree; discard seeds. Reserve 4 teaspoons of the puree for the frosting.

3. Whisk whole-wheat flour, cake flour, baking powder, baking soda and salt in a medium bowl.

4. Beat ¾ cup granulated sugar and oil in a large mixing bowl with an electric mixer on medium speed until combined. Beat in eggs, vanilla and 1 teaspoon lemon zest until well combined. With the mixer on low, alternately mix in the dry ingredients and buttermilk, starting and ending with dry ingredients and scraping the sides of the bowl as needed, until just combined.

5. Fill the prepared cups half full of batter. Place a scant tablespoon of raspberry puree on each cup (you may have some left over). Divide the remaining batter evenly among the cups. Use a wooden skewer or toothpick to swirl and fold the puree into the batter.

6. Bake the cupcakes until a toothpick inserted into the center comes out clean, 22 to 24 minutes. Transfer to a wire rack and let cool completely.

7. **To prepare frosting:** Meanwhile, beat cream cheese, confectioners' sugar, ½ teaspoon lemon zest and the reserved 4 teaspoons raspberry puree with an electric mixer until smooth. Refrigerate the frosting until very cold, at least 2 hours. Spread the frosting on the cooled cupcakes and decorate with a raspberry on top, if desired.

PER CUPCAKE: 272 calories; 10 g fat (3 g sat, 4 g mono); 49 mg cholesterol; 41 g carbohydrate; 24 g added sugars; 5 g protein; 2 g fiber; 486 mg sodium; 85 mg potassium.

EatingWell Tip

Use reduced-fat cream cheese in place of full-fat for cream-cheese frosting to **save about 17 calories and 2 grams fat** per 2-tablespoon serving.

Apple Cupcakes with Cinnamon-Marshmallow Frosting

H ♥ H

MAKES: 12 cupcakes

ACTIVE TIME: 1 hour | TOTAL: 2½ hours (including cooling time) | TO MAKE AHEAD: Store unfrosted cupcakes airtight at room temperature for up to 1 day. | EQUIPMENT: Muffin tin with 12 (½-cup) cups, paper liners

Shredded apple replaces some of the oil and keeps the cake moist in these cinnamon-spiked cupcakes. There is a generous amount of fluffy marshmallow frosting to mound or pipe on top for a festive look. Be sure to frost them right after you make the frosting—it stiffens as it stands and becomes more difficult to spread.

CUPCAKES

- 1½ cups shredded peeled apples
- ½ cup diced dried apples
- 3 tablespoons packed light brown sugar, plus ¾ cup, divided
- 1 teaspoon ground cinnamon, divided
- ⅓ cup canola oil
- 2 large eggs
- 1 teaspoon vanilla extract
- ¾ cup whole-wheat pastry flour (*see Tip, page 485*)
- ¾ cup cake flour
- ¾ teaspoon baking soda
- ¼ teaspoon salt
- ½ cup nonfat buttermilk (*see Tip, page 482*)

FROSTING

- 1 cup light brown sugar
- ¼ cup water
- 4 teaspoons dried egg whites (*see Tip, page 484*), reconstituted according to package directions (equivalent to 2 egg whites)
- ¼ teaspoon cream of tartar
  Pinch of salt
- 1 teaspoon vanilla extract
- ½ teaspoon ground cinnamon, plus more for garnish

1. **To prepare cupcakes:** Preheat oven to 350°F. Line 12 (½-cup) muffin cups with paper liners or coat with cooking spray.

2. Combine shredded and dried apples in a bowl with 3 tablespoons brown sugar and ¼ teaspoon cinnamon. Set aside. Beat oil and the remaining ¾ cup brown sugar in a large mixing bowl with an electric mixer on medium speed until well combined. Beat in eggs one at a time until combined. Add vanilla, increase speed to high and beat for 1 minute.

3. Whisk whole-wheat flour, cake flour, baking soda, salt and the remaining ¾ teaspoon cinnamon in a bowl.

4. With the mixer on low speed, alternately add the dry ingredients and buttermilk to the batter, starting and ending with dry ingredients and scraping the sides of the bowl as needed, until just combined. Stir in the reserved apple mixture until just combined. Divide the batter among the prepared muffin cups. (The cups will be full.)

5. Bake the cupcakes until a toothpick inserted into the center of a cake comes out clean, 20 to 22 minutes. Let cool on a wire rack for at least 1 hour before frosting.

6. **To prepare frosting:** Bring 2 inches of water to a simmer in the bottom of a double boiler (*see How To*). Combine 1 cup brown sugar and ¼ cup water in the top of the double boiler. Heat over the simmering water, stirring, until the sugar has dissolved, 2 to 3 minutes. Add reconstituted egg whites, cream of tartar and pinch of salt. Beat with an electric mixer on high speed until the mixture is glossy and thick, 5 to 7 minutes. Remove the top pan from the heat and continue beating for 1 minute more to cool. Add vanilla and ½ teaspoon cinnamon and beat on low just to combine. Spread or pipe with a pastry bag (*see Tip, page 487*) the frosting onto the cooled cupcakes and sprinkle cinnamon on top, if desired.

PER CUPCAKE: 264 calories; 7 g fat (1 g sat, 4 g mono); 35 mg cholesterol; 47 g carbohydrate; 29 g added sugars; 4 g protein; 2 g fiber; 182 mg sodium; 116 mg potassium.

How To

Improvise a Double Boiler | Set a medium metal bowl over 2 inches of simmering water in a large saucepan.

Peach & Tart Cherry Shortcakes

H↑F

MAKES: 6 servings
ACTIVE TIME: 45 minutes | TOTAL: 1 hour
TO MAKE AHEAD: Prepare the filling (Steps 1 & 2), place plastic wrap directly on the surface and refrigerate for up to 4 hours.

Tender, not-too-sweet biscuits spill over with a luscious mixture of almond-scented peaches and cherries.

FRUIT FILLING

- 1 **pound tart cherries, fresh *or* frozen (*not* thawed), pitted (2 cups)**
- ¼ **cup sugar**
- 1 **teaspoon freshly grated lemon zest**
- 1 **tablespoon lemon juice**
- 1 **teaspoon cornstarch**
- 1 **tablespoon amaretto *or* 1 tablespoon water mixed with ⅛ teaspoon almond extract**
- 4 **medium peaches (about 1½ pounds), peeled (*see How To*) and sliced ¼ inch thick**

BISCUITS:

- 1¼ **cups all-purpose flour**
- 1 **cup whole-wheat pastry flour (*see Tip, page 485*)**
- ⅓ **cup plus 1 tablespoon sugar, divided**
- 1½ **teaspoons baking powder**
- 1 **teaspoon baking soda**
- ¼ **teaspoon salt**
- 2 **tablespoons cold unsalted butter, cut into small pieces**
- ¾-1 **cup buttermilk (*see Tip, page 482*)**
- 1 **tablespoon canola oil**
- ½ **teaspoon vanilla extract**
- ⅛ **teaspoon almond extract**
- 1 **tablespoon nonfat milk**
- ¼ **cup sliced almonds**

1. **To prepare fruit filling:** Combine cherries, ¼ cup sugar and lemon juice in a saucepan. Bring to a simmer over low heat, stirring occasionally, 5 to 10 minutes (depending on whether fruit is fresh or frozen).

2. Stir together cornstarch and amaretto (or water plus extract) in a small bowl. Stir the mixture into the cherries and cook, stirring, just until thickened. Remove from the heat and stir in peaches and lemon zest. Let cool.

3. **To prepare biscuits:** Preheat oven to 425°F. Coat a baking sheet with cooking spray.

4. Stir together all-purpose flour, whole-wheat flour, ⅓ cup sugar, baking powder, baking soda and salt in a mixing bowl. Cut butter into the dry ingredients with a pastry cutter or your fingertips until crumbly. Combine ¾ cup buttermilk, oil, vanilla and almond extracts in a small bowl. Make a well in the center of the dry ingredients and add the buttermilk mixture. Stir with a fork just until combined, adding buttermilk as needed to form a slightly sticky dough. Do not overmix.

5. Place the dough on a lightly floured surface and sprinkle with a little more flour. Gently pat the dough into a 1-inch-thick round. Cut out biscuits with a 3- or 3½-inch round cutter and transfer them to the prepared baking sheet. Press together the scraps of dough and cut out additional biscuits to make 6 total. Brush the tops with milk. Scatter almonds over the tops and sprinkle with the remaining 1 tablespoon sugar.

6. Bake the biscuits until golden, 10 to 15 minutes. Transfer them to a wire rack and let cool slightly. Split the biscuits with a serrated knife. Set the bottoms on dessert plates; spoon on the fruit mixture, if desired, and crown with the biscuit tops. Serve immediately.

PER SERVING: 434 calories; 10 g fat (3 g sat, 4 g mono); 11 mg cholesterol; 78 g carbohydrate; 22 g added sugars; 9 g protein; 6 g fiber; 493 mg sodium; 406 mg potassium.
NUTRITION BONUS: Folate (21% daily value), Vitamin A & Vitamin C (17% dv).

How To

Peel Peaches | Dip peaches in boiling water for 30 or 40 seconds to loosen their skins. Let cool slightly, then slip off skins with a paring knife.

Pecan-Cranberry Tart

H ♥ H

MAKES: 10 servings
ACTIVE TIME: 45 minutes | TOTAL: 3 hours (including cooling time) | EQUIPMENT: 9-inch tart pan with removable bottom

Too often pecan pie is overly sweet and laden with fat. We lightened it up and turned it into a tart to save you over 100 calories and 7 grams of fat compared with a traditional version.

CRUST

½	cup old-fashioned rolled oats
½	cup whole-wheat pastry flour (*see Tip, page 485*)
2	tablespoons granulated sugar
¾	teaspoon baking powder
¼	teaspoon salt
2	tablespoons canola oil
3	tablespoons water

FILLING

1	cup pecan halves, divided
2	large eggs
2	large egg whites
⅔	cup packed dark brown sugar
⅓	cup light corn syrup
1½	tablespoons cider vinegar
1	tablespoon butter, melted
2	teaspoons vanilla extract
	Pinch of salt
⅓	cup coarsely chopped dried cranberries

1. Preheat oven to 375°F. Coat a 9-inch tart pan with a removable bottom with cooking spray.

2. **To prepare crust:** Spread oats in another pie pan and bake, stirring occasionally, until toasted, 6 to 12 minutes. Let cool. Process the oats in a food processor until coarsely ground.

3. Stir together the oats, flour, sugar, baking powder and salt in a large bowl. Drizzle oil onto the dry ingredients and use a fork or your fingers to blend until crumbly. Using a fork, stir in water, 1 tablespoon at a time, until the dough just comes together.

4. Turn the dough out onto a floured surface and knead 7 to 8 times. Overlap 2 sheets of plastic wrap on the work surface, place the dough in the center and cover with 2 more overlapping sheets of plastic wrap. Roll the dough into an 11-inch circle. Remove the top sheets and invert the dough into the prepared pan. Press the dough into the bottom and up the sides of the pan. Remove the remaining plastic wrap. Trim the edges of the dough. (If necessary, use scraps to patch any holes.)

5. **To prepare filling & assemble pie:** Spread ½ cup pecans on a baking sheet and bake until fragrant, 5 to 10 minutes. Let cool and coarsely chop.

6. Whisk eggs, egg whites, brown sugar, corn syrup, vinegar, butter, vanilla and salt in a medium bowl until smooth. Stir in dried cranberries and the chopped pecans. Spoon the filling into the crust. Arrange the remaining ½ cup pecans on top.

7. Bake the tart until the filling is set and the crust is golden, 20 to 25 minutes. Let cool completely on a wire rack before serving.

PER SERVING: 274 calories; 13 g fat (2 g sat, 7 g mono); 45 mg cholesterol; 38 g carbohydrate; 23 g added sugars; 4 g protein; 2 g fiber; 151 mg sodium; 89 mg potassium.

EatingWell Tip
Add **fiber and boost flavor** by toasting oats and grinding them in a food processor to replace some of the flour in pie or tart crusts.

Raspberry-Almond Crumb Tart

H↑F

MAKES: 8 servings
ACTIVE TIME: 20 minutes | **TOTAL:** 2 hours (including cooling time) | **EQUIPMENT:** 9-inch tart pan with removable bottom

You can quickly make the crust for this tart in the food processor and then press it into the pan—no need to dig out a rolling pin and struggle to transfer a tender pastry dough from pin to pan. Extra crust dough doubles as a crumbly topping.

½	**cup sliced almonds**
6	**tablespoons granulated sugar**
1⅓	**cups plus 2 tablespoons all-purpose flour, divided**
½	**teaspoon salt**
6	**tablespoons cold unsalted butter, cut into ¼-inch pieces**
1	**large egg yolk**
1	**teaspoon vanilla extract**
¼	**teaspoon almond extract**
4½	**cups raspberries, fresh *or* frozen (*not* thawed)**
1	**teaspoon confectioners' sugar**

1. Preheat oven to 400°F. Lightly coat a 9-inch removable-bottom tart pan with cooking spray.

2. Combine almonds and sugar in a food processor; pulse until the almonds are finely ground and incorporated with the sugar. Set aside ½ cup of the mixture.

3. Add 1⅓ cups flour and salt to the remaining sugar mixture and pulse briefly to blend. With the motor running, add butter a few pieces at a time until well incorporated.

4. Stir egg yolk, vanilla and almond extracts together in a small bowl until blended. With the motor running, add to the processor and pulse until the mixture begins to clump and form a dough, about 1 minute (the mixture will look like crumbly sand). Set aside ⅓ cup of the mixture for the topping.

5. Transfer the remaining dough to the prepared tart pan; spread evenly and press firmly into the bottom and up the sides to form a crust.

6. Add the remaining 2 tablespoons flour to the reserved almond mixture; stir to blend. Gently toss raspberries with 2 tablespoons of this mixture in a medium bowl until coated. Spread the berries evenly in the tart pan. Sprinkle the remaining almond mixture over the berries. Pinch the reserved dough into small clumps to make crumbs and sprinkle the crumbs on top of the berries.

7. Bake the tart for 15 minutes. Reduce the oven temperature to 350° and bake until the crust and crumbs are golden brown, about 45 minutes more. Let cool on a wire rack for about 30 minutes. Serve warm or at room temperature. Remove the pan sides; place confectioners' sugar in a fine sieve and dust the tart just before serving.

PER SERVING: 275 calories; 13 g fat (6 g sat, 4 g mono); 49 mg cholesterol; 47 g carbohydrate; 10 g added sugars; 5 g protein; 6 g fiber; 149 mg sodium; 175 mg potassium.
NUTRITION BONUS: Vitamin C (30% daily value); Folate (22% dv).

Chocolate Tart with Hazelnut Shortbread Crust

H ⬆ F

MAKES: 10 servings
ACTIVE TIME: 45 minutes | TOTAL: 1¾ hours
TO MAKE AHEAD: Loosely cover and refrigerate the tart for up to 1 day. | EQUIPMENT: 9-inch tart pan (with or without removable bottom)

A sublime silky chocolate custard fills this simple hazelnut shortbread crust. Serve garnished with whipped cream and toasted hazelnuts for a special touch.

CRUST

1	cup whole-wheat pastry flour (*see Tip, page 485*)
¼	cup all-purpose flour
½	cup hazelnuts
¼	cup sugar
½	teaspoon salt
4	tablespoons cold unsalted butter, cut into small pieces
2	tablespoons hazelnut oil *or* canola oil
1	tablespoon ice water

FILLING

1½	teaspoons unflavored gelatin
1	tablespoon water
¾	cup low-fat milk
2	large egg yolks
2½	tablespoons plus ¼ cup sugar, divided
1	tablespoon all-purpose flour
2	ounces unsweetened chocolate, finely chopped
1	tablespoon coffee liqueur, such as Kahlua (optional)
4	teaspoons dried egg whites (*see Tip, page 484*), reconstituted according to package directions (equivalent to 2 egg whites)
⅛	teaspoon cream of tartar

1. Preheat oven to 400°F.

2. **To prepare crust:** Coat a 9-inch tart pan with cooking spray. Combine whole-wheat pastry flour, ¼ cup all-purpose flour, hazelnuts, ¼ cup sugar and salt in a food processor; process until the nuts are finely ground. Add butter one piece at a time, pulsing once or twice after each addition, until incorporated. Add oil and ice water and pulse just until incorporated. Turn the dough out into the prepared pan (it will be crumbly), spread evenly and press firmly into the bottom and all the way up the sides to form a crust.

3. Bake the crust until set and the edges are beginning to brown, about 15 minutes. Let cool on a wire rack.

4. **To prepare filling:** Sprinkle gelatin over water in a small bowl; let stand, stirring once or twice, while you prepare the rest of the filling.

5. Heat milk in a medium saucepan over medium heat until steaming (but not boiling); remove from the heat to cool slightly.

6. Whisk egg yolks, 2½ tablespoons sugar and 1 tablespoon flour in a medium bowl until combined. Gradually whisk in ½ cup of the hot milk. Whisk the egg yolk mixture into the pan with the remaining hot milk. Return to the heat and cook, stirring constantly, until the mixture thickens enough to coat the back of a spoon (do not boil), about 1 minute. Remove from the heat; whisk in chocolate until completely melted. Whisk in the softened gelatin and coffee liqueur (if using) until smooth.

7. Beat reconstituted egg whites and cream of tartar in a large bowl with an electric mixer on low speed until frothy. Increase speed to high and beat until soft peaks form. Gradually add the remaining ¼ cup sugar and beat until stiff peaks form, 3 to 5 minutes. Gently fold the chocolate custard into the egg whites until blended. Spoon the filling into the crust; smooth the top with the back of a spoon and chill, uncovered, until set, about 1 hour.

PER SERVING: 268 calories; 16 g fat (6 g sat, 8 g mono); 55 mg cholesterol; 29 g carbohydrate; 13 g added sugars; 6 g protein; 3 g fiber; 140 mg sodium; 146 mg potassium.

Deep-Dish Apple-Blackberry Pie

H ⬆ F

MAKES: 8 servings

ACTIVE TIME: 30 minutes | TOTAL: 3½ hours (including cooling time) | EQUIPMENT: 9-inch deep-dish pie pan

Late summer, when the first apples of the season are ripe and the blackberry bushes are loaded with fruit, is the perfect time for this pie. See the variations below if you don't happen to have blackberries at the moment.

	Walnut Pastry Dough (*right*)
1½	tablespoons lemon juice
1	teaspoon vanilla extract
1½	pounds tart apples
⅔	cup plus 1 tablespoon granulated sugar, divided
¼	cup cornstarch
2	cups blackberries, fresh *or* frozen (*not* thawed)

1. Preheat oven to 350°F. Coat a 9-inch deep-dish pie pan with cooking spray.

2. Prepare Walnut Pastry Dough.

3. Combine lemon juice and vanilla in a large bowl. Peel apples and cut into ¾-inch chunks, tossing them in the lemon juice mixture as you work. Mix ⅔ cup sugar and cornstarch and toss with the apples. Add blackberries.

4. Overlap 2 sheets of plastic wrap on a work surface. Set the larger disk of dough in the center and cover with 2 more sheets of plastic wrap. Roll the dough into a 13- to 14-inch circle. Remove the top sheets and invert the dough into the prepared pan, letting excess dough hang over the side. Gently press the dough into the bottom and sides of the pan. Remove the remaining plastic wrap. Scrape the filling into the crust.

5. Roll out the smaller disk of dough into an 11- to 12-inch circle. Remove the top sheets of plastic wrap and invert the dough over the filling. Remove the remaining plastic wrap. Press the edges of the dough together to seal. With the tip of a sharp knife, cut 3 or 4 short slashes to vent steam. Moisten a pastry brush with water and lightly brush the top of the pie. Sprinkle with the remaining 1 tablespoon sugar. Place the pie on a rimmed baking sheet.

6. Bake the pie until the crust is golden and the filling is bubbling, 1 to 1¼ hours. Let cool on a wire rack for at least 2 hours before serving.

PER SERVING: 381 calories; 13 g fat (3 g sat, 3 g mono); 8 mg cholesterol; 62 g carbohydrate; 18 g added sugars; 5 g protein; 5 g fiber; 148 mg sodium; 178 mg potassium. NUTRITION BONUS: Vitamin C (20% daily value).

WALNUT PASTRY DOUGH

MAKES: enough for 1 double-crust pie (8 servings)

ACTIVE TIME: 10 minutes | TOTAL: 15 minutes

TO MAKE AHEAD: Wrap in plastic wrap and refrigerate for up to 2 days or freeze for up to 6 months. Return the dough to room temperature before rolling.

1	cup whole-wheat pastry flour (*see Tip, page 485*)
1	cup all-purpose flour
½	cup walnuts, toasted (*see Tip, page 486*)
2	tablespoons granulated sugar
½	teaspoon salt
2	tablespoons cold unsalted butter, cut into pieces
3	tablespoons walnut oil
6-7	tablespoons cold water

1. Combine whole-wheat flour, all-purpose flour, toasted walnuts, sugar and salt in a food processor; process until the walnuts are finely chopped. Add butter and process until incorporated. Transfer to a large bowl.

2. Drizzle oil over the flour mixture. Use your fingertips to rub the oil into the mixture. Add water 1 tablespoon at a time and mix with a fork until the dough is crumbly and holds together when pressed.

3. Divide dough into 2 pieces, 1 slightly larger than the other, and form each into a disk.

VARIATIONS:

To make **Deep-Dish Apple Pie**, omit blackberries and increase tart apples to 2 pounds. To make **Deep-Dish Apple-Cranberry Pie**, omit blackberries and add 1 cup dried cranberries to the filling in Step 3.

Holiday Pumpkin Pie

H ⬆ F

MAKES: 10 servings

ACTIVE TIME: 30 minutes | TOTAL: 4 hours (includes cooling time) | EQUIPMENT: 9-inch pie pan

This lighter pumpkin pie has the rich, subtle spices of the classic and a delicate, faintly sweet crust.

CRUST

- ¾ cup whole-wheat pastry flour (*see Tip, page 485*)
- ¾ cup all-purpose flour
- 1 tablespoon sugar
- ¼ teaspoon salt
- 2 tablespoons unsalted butter
- 3 tablespoons canola oil
- 3-4 tablespoons ice water

FILLING

- 1 15-ounce can unseasoned pumpkin puree (about 2 cups)
- 1 teaspoon ground cinnamon
- ½ teaspoon ground nutmeg
- ¼ teaspoon ground ginger
- ¼ teaspoon ground cloves
- ¼ teaspoon salt
- 1 14-ounce can low-fat sweetened condensed milk
- 2 large eggs, lightly beaten

1. **To prepare crust:** Whisk whole-wheat flour, all-purpose flour, sugar and salt in a medium bowl. Melt butter in a small saucepan over low heat. Cook, swirling the pan, until the butter is light brown, 30 seconds to 1 minute. Transfer to a small bowl to cool. Stir in oil. Slowly stir the butter-oil mixture into the dry ingredients with a fork until the dough is crumbly. Gradually stir in ice water, adding enough so the dough holds together and feels moist. Press the dough into a flattened disk.

2. Overlap 2 sheets of plastic wrap on a work surface, place the dough in the center and cover with 2 more overlapping sheets of plastic wrap. Roll the dough into an 12-inch circle. Remove the top sheets and invert the dough into a 9-inch pie pan. Press the dough into the bottom and up the sides of the pan. Remove the remaining plastic wrap. Fold the dough under at the rim and crimp or flute the edge (*see How To*).

3. Position rack in lower third of oven; preheat to 425°F.

4. **To prepare filling & assemble pie:** Whisk pumpkin, cinnamon, nutmeg, ginger, cloves and salt in a medium bowl until well combined. Add condensed milk and eggs and whisk until smooth. Pour the filling into the prepared crust.

5. Bake the pie for 15 minutes. Reduce the oven temperature to 350° and bake until the filling is set and a knife inserted in the center comes out clean, 35 to 40 minutes more. During baking, cover the crust edges with foil if they are browning too quickly. Let cool completely on a wire rack before serving.

PER SERVING: 292 calories; 9 g fat (3 g sat, 5 g mono); 53 mg cholesterol; 42 g carbohydrate; 22 g added sugars; 7 g protein; 3 g fiber; 174 mg sodium; 482 mg potassium.
NUTRITION BONUS: Vitamin A (137% daily value).

How To

Crimp or Flute Pie Crust | Use a fork to crimp the edge (PHOTO 1). Or use two hands to pinch ("flute") the edge of the crust: push your thumb from one hand in between the thumb and index finger of the opposite (PHOTO 2). Or use one hand to pinch ("flute") the edge of the crust between your thumb and the side of your index finger (PHOTO 3).

Strawberry Rhubarb Pie

H ⬆ F

MAKES: 10 servings

ACTIVE TIME: 1 hour | TOTAL: 4½ hours (including chilling and cooling) | TO MAKE AHEAD: Refrigerate dough for up to 2 days or freeze for up to 6 months. | EQUIPMENT: 9-inch pie pan

Rhubarb and strawberries go hand in hand, and what better way to honor the combination than in this classic summer pie. The lattice top looks fancy but the technique is super-easy to master. (Photograph: page 382.)

CRUST

- 1¼ **cups whole-wheat pastry flour (see Tip, page 485)**
- 1¼ **cups all-purpose flour**
- 2 **tablespoons sugar, plus 1 teaspoon for sprinkling (optional)**
- ½ **teaspoon salt**
- 4 **tablespoons cold unsalted butter**
- ¼ **cup reduced-fat sour cream**
- 3 **tablespoons canola oil**
- 4 **tablespoons ice water**
- 1 **large egg white, beaten, for brushing**

FILLING

- 2½ **tablespoons instant tapioca**
- 4 **cups sliced strawberries (about 1¼ pounds), fresh *or* frozen (*not* thawed)**
- 1 **cup sliced rhubarb, fresh *or* frozen (*not* thawed)**
- ⅔ **cup sugar**
- 1 **tablespoon lemon juice**
  Pinch of ground nutmeg
  Pinch of salt

1. **To prepare crust:** Whisk whole-wheat flour, all-purpose flour, 2 tablespoons sugar and salt in a large bowl. Cut butter into small pieces and, with your fingers, quickly rub them into the dry ingredients until smaller but still visible. Add sour cream and oil; toss with a fork to combine with the dry ingredients. Sprinkle water over the mixture. Toss with a fork until evenly moist. Knead the dough with your hands in the bowl a few times—the mixture will still be a little crumbly. Turn out onto a clean surface and knead a few more times, until the dough just holds together. Divide the dough in half and shape into 5-inch-wide disks. Wrap each in plastic and refrigerate for at least 1 hour.

2. **To prepare filling:** Just before you're ready to roll out the dough, process tapioca in a spice grinder, mini food processor or blender until finely ground. Combine with strawberries, rhubarb, sugar, lemon juice, nutmeg and salt in a large bowl; toss well to combine.

3. Position a rack in the center of the oven and place a foil-lined baking sheet on the rack below; preheat to 425°F.

4. Remove the dough from the refrigerator; let stand for 5 minutes to warm slightly. Roll one portion between sheets of parchment or wax paper into a 12-inch circle. Peel off the top sheet and invert the dough into a 9-inch pie pan. Peel off the remaining paper. Moisten the outer edge of the dough with water. Scrape the filling and any accumulated juices into the crust.

5. **To prepare lattice top:** Roll the remaining dough between sheets of parchment or wax paper into a 12-inch circle. Peel off the top sheet. Cut the dough into 1-inch strips using a pastry wheel or a knife. Lift off every other strip (PHOTO 1) and lay them on top of

the pie, leaving about a 1-inch gap between strips (PHOTO 2). Use the shorter strips for the edges and the longer ones for the middle of the pie. (You may not need to use the outermost strips.) Fold back the first, third and fifth strips of dough to the edge of the pie. Place a shorter strip of dough across the second and fourth strips, about 1 inch from the edge. Unfold the folded strips over the crosswise strip (PHOTO 3). Fold back the second and fourth strips over the first crosswise strip (PHOTO 4). Place another strip crosswise, about 1 inch from the first. Unfold the strips over the second crosswise strip. Continue folding back alternating strips and placing crosswise strips until the top is covered with woven strips. Trim any overhanging crust (PHOTO 5). Crimp the outer edge with a fork (PHOTO 6). Brush the dough with egg white; sprinkle 1 teaspoon sugar (if using) over just the lattice top, not the outer edge.

6. Bake the pie for 20 minutes. Then rotate the pie 180 degrees and lower the oven temperature to 325°. Continue baking until the crust is golden and the filling is beginning to bubble, 30 to 35 minutes more. Cool on a wire rack for at least 2 hours before serving.

PER SERVING: 295 calories; 10 g fat (4 g sat, 4 g mono); 15 mg cholesterol; 47 g carbohydrate; 16 g added sugars; 4 g protein; 3 g fiber; 83 mg sodium; 170 mg potassium.
NUTRITION BONUS: Vitamin C (70% daily value), Folate (16% dv).

EatingWell Tip

Use whole-wheat pastry flour to replace some of the all-purpose flour in delicate baked goods like this pie crust. It has less protein and therefore less gluten-forming potential so it stays tender. Plus it **adds fiber**.

How To: Make a Lattice Top

Almond & Honey-Butter Cookies

Raspberry-Chocolate Thumbprint Cookies

Rosemary-Pine Nut Biscotti

Yummy Molasses Crackles

Cookies & Bars

EatingWell Chocolate Chip Cookies

MAKES: 2 dozen cookies

ACTIVE TIME: 35 minutes | TOTAL: 2 hours (including 1 hour chilling time) | TO MAKE AHEAD: Refrigerate the dough for up to 1 day. Store the baked cookies in an airtight container for up to 2 days.

This awesome lacy chocolate chip cookie is based on a recipe sent to us by one of our readers, Jessie Grearson. We already knew she was a great baker because she'd won our annual cookie contest in the past. This cookie is given a healthful makeover with oats and whole-wheat flour, and canola oil to replace some of the butter.

½	cup instant oats
½	cup whole-wheat pastry flour (*see Tip, page 485*)
½	teaspoon baking powder
¼	teaspoon baking soda
¼	teaspoon salt
⅓	cup light brown sugar
¼	cup honey
3	tablespoons unsalted butter, softened (*see How To*)
3	tablespoons canola oil
1¼	teaspoons vanilla extract
1	large egg
¾	cup pecans, coarsely chopped
1	cup bittersweet chocolate chips *or* chunks

1. Grind or process oats in a blender or food processor to a fine powder, scraping down the sides as necessary. Whisk the oats, flour, baking powder, baking soda and salt in a medium bowl until well combined.

2. Beat brown sugar, honey, butter, oil and vanilla in a large bowl with an electric mixer until well combined. Beat in egg until combined. Add the dry ingredients and beat on low speed until combined. Stir in pecans and chocolate chips (or chunks). Refrigerate the dough for at least 1 hour or overnight.

3. Preheat oven to 375°F. Line a large baking sheet with parchment paper or a nonstick baking mat.

4. Drop level tablespoons of chilled dough onto the prepared baking sheet, at least 2 inches apart, to make 8 cookies at a time. Bake the cookies, in batches, until just golden, 7 to 9 minutes. Cool on the baking sheet for 5 minutes before transferring to a wire rack to cool.

PER COOKIE: 124 calories; 9 g fat (3 g sat, 3 g mono); 13 mg cholesterol; 12 g carbohydrate; 7 g added sugars; 2 g protein; 1 g fiber; 51 mg sodium; 28 mg potassium.

How To

Soften Butter | Let butter stand at room temperature for about 1 hour before using. Warm room temperatures may soften butter more quickly. If you're in a hurry, cut the butter into small pieces and let soften for about 15 minutes. (Softening butter in the microwave is not recommended; microwaves heat unevenly and may melt, instead of soften, butter quickly.)

Peanut Butter Cookies

MAKES: about 4½ dozen cookies
ACTIVE TIME: 30 minutes | TOTAL: 45 minutes
TO MAKE AHEAD: Store in an airtight container for up to 3 days.

A healthier version of an old favorite, these peanut butter cookies have much less saturated fat than traditional recipes.

  2 **cups all-purpose flour**
  ⅔ **cup whole-wheat flour**
  1 **teaspoon baking powder**
  1 **teaspoon baking soda**
  ½ **teaspoon salt**
  2 **cups packed light brown sugar**
  ½ **cup natural peanut butter**
  ¼ **cup canola oil**
  2 **large eggs**
  2 **teaspoons vanilla extract**
  5 **teaspoons water**
  ⅓ **cup chopped unsalted peanuts**

1. Preheat oven to 350°F. Coat 3 baking sheets with cooking spray.

2. Whisk all-purpose flour, whole-wheat flour, baking powder, baking soda and salt in a medium bowl. Combine brown sugar, peanut butter, oil, eggs and vanilla in a large bowl; add water and beat with an electric mixer until smooth. Stir in the dry ingredients just until combined.

3. Roll the dough between your palms into 1-inch balls. Place 2 inches apart on the prepared baking sheets. Flatten the cookies with a fork, dipping it into flour if it begins to stick to the dough. Sprinkle with peanuts, pressing them lightly into the dough with your fingers.

4. Bake the cookies, one sheet at a time, until golden, 8 to 10 minutes. Transfer to a wire rack to cool.

PER COOKIE: 96 calories; 3 g fat (0 g sat, 1 g mono); 9 mg cholesterol; 15 g carbohydrate; 9 g added sugars; 2 g protein; 1 g fiber; 76 mg sodium; 34 mg potassium.

Lemon Thins

MAKES: 3 dozen cookies
ACTIVE TIME: 30 minutes | TOTAL: 45 minutes
TO MAKE AHEAD: Store in an airtight container for up to 3 days.

Light and citrusy, these crisp lemon cookies pair perfectly with sorbets or summery fruit compotes.

  1¼ **cups all-purpose flour**
  ⅓ **cup cornstarch**
  1½ **teaspoons baking powder**
  ¼ **teaspoon salt**
  ¾ **cup sugar, divided**
  2 **tablespoons unsalted butter, softened**
      (*see How To, page 429*)
  2 **tablespoons canola oil**
  1 **large egg white**
  1½ **teaspoons freshly grated lemon zest**
  1 **teaspoon vanilla extract**
  3 **tablespoons lemon juice**

1. Preheat oven to 350°F. Coat 2 baking sheets with cooking spray.

2. Whisk flour, cornstarch, baking powder and salt in a medium bowl. Beat ½ cup sugar, butter and oil in another bowl with an electric mixer on medium speed until fluffy. Add egg white, lemon zest and vanilla; beat until smooth. Beat in lemon juice. Fold in the dry ingredients with a rubber spatula just until combined.

3. Drop slightly rounded teaspoonfuls of dough onto the prepared baking sheets, 2 inches apart. Place the remaining ¼ cup sugar on a small plate. Coat the bottom of a glass with cooking spray and dip it in the sugar. Flatten the cookies with the glass into 2½-inch circles, dipping the glass in the sugar each time.

4. Bake the cookies until just starting to brown around the edges, 8 to 10 minutes. Immediately transfer the cookies to a flat surface (not a rack) to crisp.

PER COOKIE: 60 calories; 2 g fat (1 g sat, 1 g mono); 2 mg cholesterol; 11 g carbohydrate; 5 g added sugars; 1 g protein; 0 g fiber; 46 mg sodium; 10 mg potassium.

Chewy Oatmeal Raisin Cookies

MAKES: about 4 dozen cookies

ACTIVE TIME: 30 minutes | TOTAL: 1 hour

Full of oats, nuts and raisins, these chewy oatmeal raisin cookies can be enjoyed any day of the week. **Shopping Tip:** *Look for apple butter near other fruit spreads and jams at most large supermarkets.*

3	**cups rolled oats**
⅓	**cup chopped walnuts** *or* **pecans**
1	**cup raisins**
1	**cup water**
2	**cups all-purpose flour**
1	**teaspoon baking soda**
½	**teaspoon baking powder**
½	**teaspoon salt**
½	**teaspoon ground cinnamon**
½	**teaspoon ground cloves**
1½	**cups sugar**
½	**cup apple butter (see Shopping Tip)**
¼	**cup canola oil**
2	**large eggs**
1	**teaspoon vanilla extract**

1. Preheat oven to 375°F. Line 2 baking sheets with parchment paper or coat with cooking spray.

2. Spread rolled oats and nuts on an ungreased baking sheet and toast until lightly browned, 5 to 7 minutes; set aside.

3. Combine raisins and water in a small saucepan. Bring to a simmer over low heat and cook until the raisins are plumped, about 10 minutes. Drain, discarding liquid, and set aside.

4. Sift flour, baking soda, baking powder, salt, cinnamon and cloves into a medium bowl. Beat sugar, apple butter, oil, eggs and vanilla in a large bowl with an electric mixer until light and fluffy, about 5 minutes. Stir in the flour mixture with a spoon. Stir in the reserved oats, nuts and raisins; mix well.

5. Drop the dough by rounded teaspoonfuls onto the prepared baking sheets, about 2 inches apart. Bake the cookies, one sheet at a time, until lightly browned, 8 to 10 minutes. Transfer cookies to a wire rack to cool.

PER COOKIE: 96 calories; 2 g fat (0 g sat, 1 g mono); 9 mg cholesterol; 17 g carbohydrate; 6 g added sugars; 2 g protein; 1 g fiber; 46 mg sodium; 38 mg potassium.

EatingWell Tip
Replace some of the fat in cookies like this one with apple butter. The cookies will still be moist, but have a fraction of the calories of traditional cookies.

Yummy Molasses Crackles

MAKES: about 3 dozen cookies
ACTIVE TIME: 15 minutes | TOTAL: 1½ hours
TO MAKE AHEAD: Store in an airtight container for up to 5 days or freeze for up to 3 months.

An old-fashioned ginger molasses cookie gets a little makeover by reducing the butter and adding crystallized ginger for a spicy jolt. (Photograph: page 426.)

- ¼ cup unsalted butter, softened (*see How To, page 429*)
- 1 cup plus ⅓ cup sugar, divided
- 1 large egg, beaten
- ¼ cup molasses
- 2 cups all-purpose flour
- 2 teaspoons baking soda
- 1 teaspoon ground cinnamon
- ½ teaspoon salt
- ¼ teaspoon ground cloves
- ⅛ teaspoon ground ginger
- ⅓ cup crystallized ginger, finely chopped

1. Beat butter and 1 cup sugar in a large bowl with an electric mixer until creamy. Add egg and molasses. Mix well. Whisk flour, baking soda, cinnamon, salt, cloves and ground ginger in another large bowl until well blended. Stir in crystallized ginger. Blend the flour mixture into the butter mixture a cup at a time, mixing well, until it is all incorporated. Chill the dough in the refrigerator until firm, 30 minutes to 1 hour.

2. Preheat oven to 375°F. Lightly coat 2 baking sheets with cooking spray.

3. Place the remaining ⅓ cup sugar in a shallow dish. Roll the dough into 1-inch balls and then roll in the sugar. Place 1½ inches apart on the prepared baking sheet.

4. Bake the cookies, in batches, until they crackle on top, 8 to 10 minutes. Transfer to a wire rack to cool.

PER COOKIE: 79 calories; 1 g fat (1 g sat, 0 g mono); 9 mg cholesterol; 16 g carbohydrate; 9 g added sugars; 1 g protein; 0 g fiber; 106 mg sodium; 43 mg potassium.

► Festive Fruit & Nut Balls

MAKES: about 3 dozen cookies
ACTIVE TIME: 45 minutes | TOTAL: 1½ hours
TO MAKE AHEAD: Place on wax paper; store in an airtight container in the refrigerator for up to 5 days or freeze for up to 1 month.

A no-bake, make-ahead treat, this perfect combination of fruit and nuts is a nutritious, delicious mouthful. Rolling them in shredded coconut gives them their festive look.

- ¾ cup sugar
- ½ cup dried cranberries
- ½ cup pitted and snipped dates
- 2 large eggs, beaten
- ⅓ cup chopped pistachios, preferably unsalted
- ⅓ cup chopped walnuts
- ⅓ cup chopped pecans
- 1 teaspoon rum extract
- ¾ cup shredded coconut

1. Combine sugar, cranberries, dates and eggs in a medium saucepan. Cook over medium-low heat, stirring constantly, until the mixture thickens, is pale yellow in color, registers at least 170°F on an instant-read thermometer and when a spoon is pulled through it, it leaves a clear trail. This will take 6 to 14 minutes, depending on how hot your stove's "medium-low" setting is.

2. Remove from the heat; stir in pistachios, walnuts, pecans and rum extract. Let stand until cool enough to handle, about 45 minutes.

3. With damp or lightly oiled hands, form the mixture into 1-inch balls (about 1 generous teaspoon each). Roll each ball in coconut. Place the finished balls on a baking sheet lined with wax paper and store in the refrigerator.

PER COOKIE: 62 calories; 3 g fat (1 g sat, 1 g mono); 12 mg cholesterol; 9 g carbohydrate; 7 g added sugars; 1 g protein; 1 g fiber; 9 mg sodium; 45 mg potassium.

Lava Rocks

MAKES: 2 dozen cookies

ACTIVE TIME: 25 minutes | TOTAL: 50 minutes

TO MAKE AHEAD: Store in an airtight container at room temperature for up to 3 days or freeze for up to 1 month.

This cookie has three layers of chocolate flavor with cocoa powder, grated bittersweet chocolate and cocoa nibs. Shopping Tips: *One tablespoon of* **vanilla paste** *is equivalent to 1 whole vanilla bean. Find it at specialty baking shops or online at* thespicehouse.com. *You can find* **cocoa nibs** *(bits of roasted and hulled cocoa beans) at large grocery stores, gourmet retailers or online at* chocosphere.com.

2¼ **cups sifted confectioners' sugar**

6 **tablespoons unsweetened cocoa powder**

2 **tablespoons all-purpose flour**
   Generous pinch of sea salt

3 **large egg whites**

¾ **teaspoon vanilla paste (*see Shopping Tips*)**
   ***or* 1 teaspoon vanilla extract**

7 **ounces (about 2 cups) pecans, chopped and toasted (*see Tip, page 486*)**

1½ **ounces bittersweet chocolate, grated**

4 **teaspoons cocoa nibs (*see Shopping Tips*)**

1. Preheat oven to 325°F. Line 2 baking sheets with parchment paper or nonstick baking mats.

2. Thoroughly stir together confectioners' sugar, cocoa, flour and salt in a large bowl. Beat in egg whites, one at a time, with an electric mixer on low speed. Add vanilla paste (or extract) and beat for 1½ minutes on high speed, scraping down the sides of the bowl several times. Fold in pecans, chocolate and cocoa nibs until evenly incorporated.

3. Spoon the dough by heaping tablespoonfuls onto the prepared baking sheets, about 2 inches apart.

4. Bake the cookies, in batches, in the center of the oven, until dry and glossy on the surface but soft in the centers when pressed, 15 to 17 minutes. Let cool on the pan for 5 to 10 minutes. Carefully transfer the cookies, on the paper or mats, to a wire rack to cool completely.

PER COOKIE: 119 calories; 7 g fat (1 g sat, 3 g mono); 0 mg cholesterol; 15 g carbohydrate; 12 g added sugars; 2 g protein; 1 g fiber; 13 mg sodium; 62 mg potassium.

EatingWell Tip

Use dark chocolate, such as bittersweet and semisweet, in baking. It has a stronger flavor than milk chocolate so a little goes a long way. It also contains **flavanols, antioxidants that may benefit cardiovascular health**.

Raspberry-Chocolate Thumbprint Cookies

MAKES: about 2 dozen cookies
ACTIVE TIME: 30 minutes | TOTAL: 1 hour | TO MAKE AHEAD: Store in an airtight container for up to 2 days.

These cookies taste decadent, yet are made with ingredients that have healthful benefits: oats, almonds, fruit and chocolate. The thumbprints are versatile—use a different type of filling or different extracts to create a completely different cookie. This recipe calls for whole almonds and then we grind them in a blender. You can make the cookies with already ground almond flour—you'll need 1¼ cups. (Photograph: page 426.) **Shopping Tip:** *Oat flour, made from finely milled whole oats, is a good source of dietary fiber and whole grains. It can replace some of the all-purpose flour in many baking recipes and adds an oat flavor and texture.*

  1 **cup whole almonds**
 1½ **cups whole-wheat pastry flour (*see Tip, page 485*)**
  ½ **cup oat flour (*see Shopping Tip*)**
  2 **teaspoons baking powder**
  ¼ **teaspoon salt**
  ⅓ **cup light oil, such as safflower *or* canola**
  ⅓ **cup maple syrup**
  ¼ **cup apple juice**
  1 **teaspoon almond extract**
  1 **teaspoon vanilla extract**
  ⅓ **cup chocolate chips, preferably bittersweet**
  2 **tablespoons raspberry preserves**

1. Position rack in center of oven; preheat to 350°F. Coat a baking sheet with cooking spray or line with parchment paper or a nonstick baking mat.

2. Process almonds in a blender in 2 batches until finely ground. Transfer to a large bowl and add whole-wheat flour, oat flour, baking powder and salt. Whisk oil, maple syrup, apple juice, almond and vanilla extracts in a medium bowl. Add the wet ingredients to the dry ingredients; stir to combine. Use your hands to knead the dough together; add 1 to 2 tablespoons additional apple juice if the mixture is too crumbly.

3. Form level tablespoonfuls of dough into balls and place on the prepared baking sheet about 2 inches apart. Gently flatten each ball into a disk, then make an indentation in the center using your thumb or a small spoon. Place a few chocolate chips in each indentation, then cover with ¼ teaspoon preserves.

4. Bake the cookies, one batch at a time, until golden around the edges, 15 to 17 minutes. Transfer to a wire rack to cool completely.

PER COOKIE: 126 calories; 7 g fat (1 g sat, 2 g mono); 0 mg cholesterol; 14 g carbohydrate; 6 g added sugars; 2 g protein; 2 g fiber; 68 mg sodium; 67 mg potassium.

Outrageous Macaroons

MAKES: about 55 cookies
ACTIVE TIME: 50 minutes | TOTAL: 1 hour 50 minutes
TO MAKE AHEAD: These macaroons are best eaten fresh,
but will keep for up to 5 days at room temperature.

*These luxurious macaroons studded with pistachios
and dried cranberries hail from food stylist Katie Webster.
She made them when she was a personal chef for a gluten-
intolerant client. Although you can concoct them with
either sweetened or unsweetened coconut, we find that the
unsweetened packs a more coconutty wallop. For a variation,
substitute chopped crystallized ginger and mini chocolate
chips for the pistachios and cranberries.*

1	**14-ounce can nonfat sweetened condensed milk**
1	**teaspoon almond extract**
2	**cups sliced almonds**
2	**cups coconut flakes, preferably unsweetened**
½	**cup dried cranberries**
½	**cup chopped shelled pistachios**
2	**large egg whites**
¼	**teaspoon salt**

GARNISH (OPTIONAL)

¾	**cup bittersweet *or* semisweet chocolate chips, melted (*see How To*)**
¼	**cup dried cranberries**
¼	**cup chopped pistachios**

1. Position racks in upper and lower thirds of oven; preheat to 325°F. Line 2 large baking sheets with parchment paper or nonstick baking mats.

2. Whisk condensed milk and almond extract in a large bowl until combined. Pulse almonds in a food processor (about 10 quick pulses) until broken unto small pieces. Stir the almonds, coconut, ½ cup cranberries and ½ cup pistachios into the condensed milk mixture.

3. Beat egg whites and salt in a medium bowl with an electric mixer on medium-high speed until soft peaks form, about 1 minute. Fold ½ cup of the egg whites into the coconut mixture. Add the remaining egg whites, gently folding into the mixture until just combined. Drop 1 teaspoon of dough onto a prepared baking sheet and top with another teaspoon of dough, making a double-tall macaroon. Repeat with the remaining batter, spacing the macaroons 1 inch apart.

4. Bake the macaroons, switching the pans back to front and top to bottom halfway through, until the coconut is lightly golden, 18 to 22 minutes (sweetened coconut will brown faster than unsweetened). Let cool on the pans on a wire rack until cool to the touch, 30 minutes.

5. **Optional garnish:** Drizzle or spoon melted chocolate over the top of each cooled macaroon; sprinkle with cranberries and pistachios. Let the chocolate dry completely before storing or packing.

PER COOKIE WITH GARNISH: 85 calories; 5 g fat (2 g sat, 2 g mono); 0 mg cholesterol; 9 g carbohydrate; 7 g added sugars; 2 g protein; 1 g fiber; 22 mg sodium; 134 mg potassium. PER COOKIE WITHOUT GARNISH: 69 calories; 4 g fat (2 g sat, 1 g mono); 1 mg cholesterol; 7 g carbohydrate; 5 g added sugars; 2 g protein; 1 g fiber; 21 mg sodium; 122 mg potassium.

How To

Melt Chocolate | Place chocolate chips (or chopped chocolate) in a bowl and microwave on Medium for 45 seconds. Stir; continue microwaving on Medium, stirring every 20 seconds, until almost melted. Continue stirring until completely melted. Or place in the top of a double boiler over hot, but not boiling, water. Stir until melted.

Almond & Honey-Butter Cookies

MAKES: about 3½ dozen cookies
ACTIVE TIME: 40 minutes | TOTAL: 2 ½ hours
TO MAKE AHEAD: Store in a single layer in an airtight
container for up to 2 days.

*This thumbprint cookie uses honey as the only sweetener
and tender ground almonds to replace much of the butter
found in similar cookies. Just a touch of butter mixed with
honey in the filling gives it a rich flavor without too much
saturated fat.* **Shopping Tip:** *Look for whole-wheat pastry
flour in the natural-foods section of large supermarkets and
natural-foods stores.*

1	cup whole almonds, toasted (*see Tip, page 486*)
1¼	cups whole-wheat pastry flour (*see Shopping Tip*)
1	cup all-purpose flour
1	teaspoon baking powder
½	teaspoon salt
⅔	cup plus ¼ cup honey, divided
⅓	cup canola oil
4	tablespoons unsalted butter, softened (*see How To, page 429*), divided
1	large egg
1	teaspoon vanilla extract
3	tablespoons toasted sliced almonds (*see Tip, page 486*) for garnish

1. Process whole almonds in a food processor or blender until finely ground (you will have about 1¼ cups ground). Transfer to a large bowl and add whole-wheat flour, all-purpose flour, baking powder and salt; stir until just combined. Beat ⅔ cup honey, oil and 3 tablespoons butter in a mixing bowl with an electric mixer on medium speed until well combined. Add egg and vanilla and beat until blended. Add the wet ingredients to the dry ingredients; stir to combine. Refrigerate the dough for 1 hour.

2. Preheat oven to 350°F. Coat 2 baking sheets with cooking spray or line with parchment paper or non-stick baking mats.

3. Roll tablespoons of dough into 1-inch balls and place on the prepared baking sheets about 2 inches apart. Press the tip of your index finger in the center of each cookie to make an indentation. Bake the cookies, in batches, until set and barely golden on the bottom, 13 to 15 minutes. Transfer to a wire rack; let cool for 30 minutes.

4. Combine the remaining ¼ cup honey and 1 table-spoon butter in a small bowl until creamy. Use about ¼ teaspoon to fill each cookie and top with 2 sliced almonds, if desired.

PER COOKIE: 94 calories; 5 g fat (1 g sat, 3 g mono);
8 mg cholesterol; 12 g carbohydrate; 6 g added sugars;
2 g protein; 1 g fiber; 42 mg sodium; 33 mg potassium.

Princess Tea Cakes

MAKES: 3 dozen cookies

ACTIVE TIME: 40 minutes | TOTAL: 2 hours

TO MAKE AHEAD: Prepare the dough (Steps 2 and 3), cover and refrigerate for up to 1 day. Store the cookies in an airtight container at room temperature for up to 3 days. Roll in the second coating of confectioners' sugar just before serving.

Here's a makeover of a classic Russian Tea Cake. Traditionally these are made with butter—but this amazing version uses canola oil instead, so the saturated fat is cut to 0 grams per cookie. **Shopping Tip:** *White whole-wheat flour, made from a special variety of white wheat, is light in color and flavor but has the same nutritional properties as regular whole-wheat flour. Find it at large supermarkets and natural-foods stores and online at* bobsredmill.com *or* kingarthurflour.com. *Store it in the freezer.*

¾	**cup canola oil**
1½	**cups all-purpose flour**
¾	**cup white whole-wheat flour (*see Shopping Tip*)**
2	**cups confectioners' sugar, divided**
3	**tablespoons cornstarch**
⅛	**teaspoon salt**
1	**teaspoon vanilla extract**
¾	**cup very finely chopped nuts, such as pecans, walnuts *or* hazelnuts**

1. Preheat oven to 400°F.

2. Pour oil into a medium bowl. Whisk all-purpose flour, white whole-wheat flour, ¼ cup confectioners' sugar, cornstarch and salt in another bowl.

3. Mix half the dry ingredients into the oil by spoonfuls. Scrape down the sides of the bowl and add vanilla. Mix in the remaining dry ingredients by spoonfuls until thoroughly combined. (The mixture will resemble creamed butter and brown sugar.) Stir in nuts.

4. Roll the dough into 1-inch balls; place about 1 inch apart on an ungreased baking sheet.

5. Bake the cookies until just set, being careful not to let the bottoms get too brown, 10 to 12 minutes. Cool on the pan for 2 minutes; transfer to a wire rack to cool slightly.

6. When the cookies are still warm, but no longer hot, roll them in the remaining 1¾ cups confectioners' sugar and place them back on the rack to continue cooling. (Reserve the sugar.) When the cookies are completely cool, roll them in the sugar again.

PER COOKIE: 103 calories; 6 g fat (0 g sat, 4 g mono); 0 mg cholesterol; 11 g carbohydrate; 4 g added sugars; 1 g protein; 1 g fiber; 8 mg sodium; 18 mg potassium.

Chocolate-Hazelnut Truffles

MAKES: about 32 truffles
ACTIVE TIME: 1 hour | TOTAL: 1 hour
TO MAKE AHEAD: Refrigerate airtight for up to 2 weeks.

Chopped pitted dates are the secret ingredient in these healthy chocolate-hazelnut truffles. Shopping Tip: *Be sure to use chopped pitted dates rather than whole dates, which are too sticky for the food processor.*

- 3 ounces bittersweet *or* semisweet chocolate, divided
- ½ cup chopped hazelnuts, toasted (*see Tip, page 486*)
- 2 cups chopped pitted dates (about 10 ounces; *see Shopping Tip*)
- 1 teaspoon freshly grated orange zest
- 2 tablespoons dark corn syrup
- 1 tablespoon orange juice
- 1 tablespoon Grand Marnier *or* other orange liqueur
- ¼ cup unsweetened cocoa powder

1. Place 2 ounces chocolate in a small bowl. Set bowl in a small skillet of barely simmering water until the chocolate melts. (*To melt chocolate in the microwave, see How To, page 437.*)

2. Combine hazelnuts, dates and orange zest in a food processor; pulse until very finely chopped. Add the melted chocolate, corn syrup, orange juice and orange liqueur; pulse until mixture clumps together.

3. Line a baking sheet with wax paper. Sift cocoa into a pie pan or shallow dish. Coat hands with cooking spray. Pinch off pieces of date mixture and form into 1-inch balls. Roll truffles in cocoa to coat lightly and place on prepared baking sheet.

4. Melt remaining 1 ounce chocolate. Spoon into a paper cone or small plastic bag. Cut a tiny hole in the tip of the cone or corner of the bag. Pipe chocolate decoratively over truffles. Refrigerate, uncovered, until the chocolate has hardened, about 10 minutes.

PER TRUFFLE: 56 calories; 2 g fat (1 g sat, 1 g mono); 0 mg cholesterol; 10 g carbohydrate; 2 g added sugars; 1 g protein; 1 g fiber; 2 mg sodium; 84 mg potassium.

▶ Rosemary-Pine Nut Biscotti

MAKES: about 20 cookies
ACTIVE TIME: 20 minutes | TOTAL: 2¼ hours
TO MAKE AHEAD: Store airtight at room temperature for up to 3 days or freeze for up to 3 months.

These olive oil biscotti are rich with toasty pine nuts. Shopping Tip: *Look for semolina flour, a nutty-tasting coarse flour milled from durum wheat, in natural-foods stores and Italian specialty markets.*

- 1½ cups all-purpose flour
- ⅔ cup semolina flour (*see Shopping Tip*) *or* fine cornmeal
- ⅔ cup pine nuts
- 2 tablespoons fresh rosemary, minced
- 2 teaspoons baking powder
- 2 large eggs, at room temperature
- ⅔ cup sugar
- ⅓ cup extra-virgin olive oil
- ½ teaspoon salt

1. Preheat oven to 350°F. Coat a large baking sheet with cooking spray.

2. Mix all-purpose flour, semolina flour (or cornmeal), pine nuts, rosemary and baking powder in a large bowl to evenly distribute the rosemary. Whisk eggs, sugar, oil and salt in a medium bowl just until combined (but not until the sugar dissolves). Stir the wet ingredients into the dry ingredients. On a lightly floured surface, shape the dough into a 12-by-2½-inch log. Transfer to the prepared baking sheet.

3. Bake for 30 minutes. Let cool on the baking sheet for 15 to 20 minutes. Reduce oven temperature to 325°F. Slice the log crosswise into ½-inch-thick slices. Place the slices cut-side down on the baking sheet. Bake for 10 minutes. Turn over and continue baking for 10 minutes more. Cool on the baking sheet for 5 minutes, then transfer to a wire rack.

PER BISCOTTI: 153 calories; 7 g fat (1 g sat, 4 g mono); 21 mg cholesterol; 19 g carbohydrate; 7 g added sugars; 3 g protein; 1 g fiber; 121 mg sodium; 56 mg potassium.

Marbled Cheesecake Brownies

MAKES: 16 brownies

ACTIVE TIME: 30 minutes | **TOTAL:** 3 hours (including cooling time)

Using reduced-fat cream cheese substantially reduces the fat in these marbled cheesecake brownies. You can use instant coffee mixed into the batter to give them a bold "mocha" flavor. Or omit the coffee if you prefer.

CHEESECAKE TOPPING

8	ounces reduced-fat cream cheese (Neufchâtel)
⅔	cup granulated sugar
½	teaspoon vanilla extract
1	large egg
1	large egg white
1	tablespoon cake flour

BROWNIE BATTER

1	cup sifted cake flour
½	cup Dutch-process cocoa powder
½	teaspoon salt
1½	cups packed light brown sugar
¼	cup canola oil
¼	cup buttermilk (*see Tip, page 482*)
1	large egg
2	large egg whites
1	tablespoon instant coffee granules (optional)
2	teaspoons vanilla extract

1. Preheat oven to 350°F. Coat a 7-by-11-inch baking pan with cooking spray. Dust with flour, tapping out the excess.

2. **To prepare cheesecake topping:** Beat cream cheese in a medium bowl with an electric mixer on medium speed until smooth and creamy, about 1 minute. Beat in granulated sugar and ½ teaspoon vanilla until very smooth, 2 to 3 minutes. Beat in egg, followed by egg white; beat 2 to 3 minutes to thoroughly blend. Add 1 tablespoon flour and, with the mixer on low speed, beat just until blended.

3. **To prepare brownie batter:** Whisk 1 cup flour, cocoa and salt in a small bowl. Beat brown sugar, oil, buttermilk, egg, egg whites, coffee granules, if using, and 2 teaspoons vanilla in a large bowl on high speed until smooth, making sure no lumps of brown sugar remain. Add the dry ingredients and beat on low speed just until blended.

4. Measure out ½ cup of the brownie batter. Transfer the remaining brownie batter to the prepared pan, spreading it into the corners and smoothing the surface. Carefully pour the cheesecake topping onto the brownie batter and spread it evenly to the edges. Dot the cheesecake layer with the reserved brownie batter and swirl it in with a table knife for a marbled effect, without disturbing the bottom brownie layer.

5. Bake the brownies just until the top is set, 40 to 50 minutes. Let cool completely in the pan on a wire rack before cutting.

PER SERVING: 229 calories; 7 g fat (2 g sat, 3 g mono); 34 mg cholesterol; 39 g carbohydrate; 28 g added sugars; 4 g protein; 1 g fiber; 168 mg sodium; 97 mg potassium.

Dark Fudgy Brownies

MAKES: 20 brownies

ACTIVE TIME: 30 minutes | **TOTAL:** 3 hours 20 minutes (including cooling time) | **TO MAKE AHEAD:** Store in an airtight container for up to 3 days or in the freezer for up to 2 weeks.

We like to use chocolate with 60-72% cacao content in these rich, fudgelike brownies, as it imparts a deeper, fuller flavor than less-chocolaty choices. These brownies are small, but they're incredibly intense and fudgy, so you should be able to satisfy a chocolate craving with just one.

- ¾ **cup all-purpose flour**
- ⅔ **cup confectioners' sugar**
- 3 **tablespoons unsweetened cocoa powder**
- 3 **ounces semisweet *or* bittersweet chocolate, coarsely chopped, plus 2½ ounces chopped into mini chip-size pieces, divided**
- 1½ **tablespoons canola oil**
- ¼ **cup granulated sugar**
- 1½ **tablespoons light corn syrup blended with 3 tablespoons lukewarm water**
- 2 **teaspoons vanilla extract**
- ⅛ **teaspoon salt**
- 1 **large egg**
- ⅓ **cup chopped toasted walnuts (*see Tip, page 486*), optional**

1. Position rack in center of oven; preheat to 350°F. Line an 8-inch-square baking pan with foil, letting it overhang on two opposing sides. Coat with cooking spray.

2. Sift flour, confectioners' sugar and cocoa together into a small bowl. Combine 3 ounces coarsely chopped chocolate and oil in a heavy medium saucepan; place over the lowest heat, stirring, until just melted and smooth, being very careful the chocolate does not overheat. Remove from the heat and stir in granulated sugar, corn syrup mixture, vanilla and salt until the sugar dissolves. Vigorously stir in egg until smoothly incorporated. Gently stir in the dry ingredients. Fold in the walnuts (if using) and the remaining 2½ ounces chopped chocolate just until well blended. Transfer the batter to the pan, spreading evenly.

3. Bake the brownies until almost firm in the center and a toothpick inserted comes out with some moist batter clinging to it, 20 to 24 minutes. Let cool completely on a wire rack, about 2½ hours.

4. Using the overhanging foil as handles, carefully lift the brownie slab from the pan. Peel the foil from the bottom; set the slab right-side up on a cutting board. Using a large, sharp knife, trim off any dry edges. Mark and then cut the slab crosswise into fifths and lengthwise into fourths. Wipe the blade with a damp cloth between cuts.

PER BROWNIE: 102 calories; 4 g fat (2 g sat, 2 g mono); 11 mg cholesterol; 17 g carbohydrate; 11 g added sugars; 1 g protein; 1 g fiber; 20 mg sodium; 38 mg potassium.

Making Fruit Bars

These fruit bars are super-easy—the crust comes together in minutes, then you top it with one of these fruit combinations. Bring them to a potluck or pack them in your kids' lunchboxes. For a nut-free version, use oats instead of nuts.

Master Fruit Bar Recipe

MAKES: 18 bars
ACTIVE TIME: 40 minutes | TOTAL: 2¾ hours (including 1½ hours cooling time) | TO MAKE AHEAD: Cover and refrigerate the crust and topping (Steps 1-2) for up to 1 day. Cover or individually wrap and refrigerate the cooled bars for up to 5 days.

CRUST

1	cup chopped nuts (walnuts, pecans, almonds *or* hazelnuts) *or* old-fashioned rolled oats, divided
¾	cup whole-wheat pastry flour (*see Tip, page 485*)
¾	cup all-purpose flour
½	cup sugar
½	teaspoon salt
4	tablespoons cold unsalted butter, cut into small pieces
1	large egg
2	tablespoons canola oil
1	teaspoon vanilla extract
¼	teaspoon almond extract

FRUIT FILLING

see Variations (*opposite*)

1. **To prepare crust:** Combine ¾ cup nuts (or oats), whole-wheat flour, all-purpose flour, sugar and salt in a food processor; pulse until the nuts are finely ground. Add butter; pulse until well incorporated.

2. Whisk egg, oil, vanilla and almond extracts in a small bowl. With the motor running, add the mixture to the food processor. Process, then pulse, scraping down the sides, if necessary, until the mixture begins to clump, 30 to 45 seconds (it will look crumbly; PHOTO 1). Measure out ½ cup of the mixture and combine in a bowl with the remaining ¼ cup chopped nuts (or oats). Set aside for the TOPPING.

3. Preheat oven to 400°F. Generously coat a 9-by-13-inch baking dish with cooking spray.

4. **To prepare fruit filling & assemble bars:** Combine COOKING FRUIT, JUICE, SUGAR & CORNSTARCH in a large saucepan. Bring to a simmer over medium heat, stirring constantly, until the mixture is very thick, 4 to 5 minutes (PHOTO 2). (It may take up to 10 minutes to get a thick result if you start with frozen fruit.) Stir in UNCOOKED FRUIT and FLAVORING.

5. Transfer the dough to the prepared baking dish. Spread evenly and press firmly into the bottom to form a crust (PHOTO 3). Spread the fruit filling over the crust (PHOTO 4). Sprinkle the reserved TOPPING over the filling (PHOTO 5).

6. Bake the bars for 15 minutes. Reduce oven temperature to 350° and bake until the crust and topping are lightly brown, 25 to 30 minutes more. Let cool completely before cutting into bars, at least 1½ hours.

How To: Make Fruit Bars

Variations

DRIED-FRUIT BARS
COOKING FRUIT: 2 cups diced mixed soft dried fruit (about 10½ ounces)
JUICE: 1½ cups apple cider
SUGAR & CORNSTARCH: ½ cup sugar, ¼ cup cornstarch
UNCOOKED FRUIT: 1¼ cups diced mixed soft dried fruit (about 5½ ounces)
FLAVORING: 1 teaspoon vanilla extract
PER BAR: 243 calories; 9 g fat (2 g sat, 2 g mono); 19 mg cholesterol; 40 g carbohydrate; 11 g added sugars; 3 g protein; 3 g fiber; 74 mg sodium; 240 mg potassium.

STRAWBERRY-RHUBARB FRUIT BARS
COOKING FRUIT: 2 cups diced strawberries (fresh *or* frozen) plus 2 cups diced fresh rhubarb
JUICE: ¼ cup orange juice
SUGAR & CORNSTARCH: ½ cup plus 2 tablespoons sugar, ¼ cup cornstarch
UNCOOKED FRUIT: 1 cup diced strawberries (fresh *or* frozen) plus 1 cup diced fresh rhubarb
FLAVORING: 1 teaspoon vanilla extract
PER BAR: 192 calories; 9 g fat (2 g sat, 2 g mono); 19 mg cholesterol; 26 g carbohydrate; 13 g added sugars; 3 g protein; 2 g fiber; 71 mg sodium; 148 mg potassium.

APPLE-CINNAMON FRUIT BARS
COOKING FRUIT: 4 cups diced peeled apples
JUICE: ½ cup apple cider (or orange juice)
SUGAR & CORNSTARCH: ½ cup sugar, ¼ cup cornstarch
UNCOOKED FRUIT: 2 cups diced peeled apples
FLAVORING: 1½ teaspoons ground cinnamon plus 1 teaspoon vanilla extract
PER BAR: 193 calories; 9 g fat (2 g sat, 2 g mono); 19 mg cholesterol; 27 g carbohydrate; 11 g added sugars; 3 g protein; 2 g fiber; 69 mg sodium; 74 mg potassium.

CRANBERRY-ORANGE FRUIT BARS
COOKING FRUIT: 3 cups cranberries (fresh *or* frozen)
JUICE: ½ cup orange juice
SUGAR & CORNSTARCH: ¾ cup sugar, ¼ cup cornstarch
UNCOOKED FRUIT: 2 cups cranberries (fresh *or* frozen) plus 1 cup orange segments
FLAVORING: 1½ teaspoons freshly grated orange zest plus 1 teaspoon vanilla extract
PER BAR: 205 calories; 9 g fat (2 g sat, 2 g mono); 19 mg cholesterol; 30 g carbohydrate; 14 g added sugars; 3 g protein; 3 g fiber; 70 mg sodium; 104 mg potassium. **NUTRITION BONUS:** Vitamin C (25% dv).

STONE-FRUIT BARS
COOKING FRUIT: 4 cups chopped peaches, nectarines, plums *and/or* cherries (any combination, fresh *or* frozen)
JUICE: ½ cup orange juice
SUGAR & CORNSTARCH: ½ cup sugar, ¼ cup cornstarch
UNCOOKED FRUIT: 2 cups chopped peaches, nectarines, plums *and/or* cherries (any combination, fresh *or* frozen)
FLAVORING: 1 teaspoon vanilla extract
PER BAR: 197 calories; 9 g fat (2 g sat, 2 g mono); 19 mg cholesterol; 28 g carbohydrate; 11 g added sugars; 3 g protein; 2 g fiber; 69 mg sodium; 147 mg potassium.

Orange Polentina

Cardamom-Crumb Coffee Cake

Whole-Grain Waffles with Cherry Sauce

Breakfast & Brunch

Cooking Oatmeal

Oatmeal is a fabulously healthy morning meal. It's high in soluble fiber, which may help to lower "bad" LDL cholesterol. Plus oatmeal is a low-glycemic-index (GI) food—and research suggests that eating a low-GI meal before you exercise may help you burn more fat. For a boost of calcium, make oatmeal with low-fat milk instead of water. Then top it with your favorite fruit to add more fiber and nuts for (filling) healthy fats. Here are cooking instructions for the most common types of oatmeal plus some of our favorite toppings.

Use these instructions to prepare 1 serving of oatmeal, or follow package directions. One serving of each type of oatmeal below is about 150 calories and 4 grams of fiber.

QUICK-COOKING OATS have been precooked then dried and rolled. They are sometimes labeled instant oats.

STOVETOP: Bring 1 cup water (or nonfat or low-fat milk) and a pinch of salt (if desired) to a boil in a small saucepan. Stir in ½ cup oats and reduce heat to medium; cook for 1 minute. Remove from the heat, cover and let stand for 2 to 3 minutes.

MICROWAVE: Combine 1 cup water (or nonfat or low-fat milk), ½ cup oats and a pinch of salt (if desired) in a 2-cup microwavable bowl. Microwave on High for 1½ to 2 minutes. Stir before serving.

OLD-FASHIONED OATS have been steamed and then rolled. They are sometimes labeled "rolled oats."

STOVETOP: Bring 1 cup water (or nonfat or low-fat milk) and a pinch of salt (if desired) to a boil in a small saucepan. Stir in ½ cup oats and reduce heat to medium; cook, stirring occasionally, for 5 minutes. Remove from the heat, cover and let stand for 2 to 3 minutes.

MICROWAVE: Combine 1 cup water (or nonfat or low-fat milk), ½ cup oats and a pinch of salt (if desired) in a 2-cup microwavable bowl. Microwave on High for 2½ to 3 minutes. Stir before serving.

STEEL-CUT OATS are toasted and cut oat groats—the oat kernel that has been removed from the husk. They are sometimes labeled "Irish oatmeal."

STOVETOP: Bring 1 cup water (or nonfat or low-fat milk) and a pinch of salt (if desired) to a boil in a small saucepan. Stir in ¼ cup oats and reduce heat to low; cook, stirring occasionally, until the oats are the desired texture, 20 to 30 minutes.

Topping Ideas
• Dried fruit, such as raisins, cranberries, cherries or chopped apricots or dates
• Ground cinnamon or ginger
• Chopped toasted nuts, such as almonds, pecans or walnuts
• Chopped or sliced fresh fruit, such as bananas or apples
• Fresh or frozen berries
• Low-fat (or nonfat) milk or plain yogurt
• Jams, preserves, maple syrup, brown sugar or honey
• Applesauce
• Ground flaxseed

Citrus Berry Smoothie

H↑F H♥H

MAKES: 1 smoothie, about 2 cups
ACTIVE TIME: 5 minutes | TOTAL: 5 minutes

This meal-in-a-glass smoothie is bursting with berries and orange juice, healthful sources of carbohydrate and powerful antioxidants.

1¼	cups fresh berries
¾	cup low-fat plain yogurt
½	cup orange juice
2	tablespoons nonfat dry milk
1	tablespoon toasted wheat germ
1	tablespoon honey
½	teaspoon vanilla extract

Place berries, yogurt, orange juice, dry milk, wheat germ, honey and vanilla in a blender and blend until smooth.

PER SERVING: 376 calories; 4 g fat (2 g sat, 1 g mono); 13 mg cholesterol; 70 g carbohydrate; 17 g added sugars; 17 g protein; 5 g fiber; 180 mg sodium; 1,126 mg potassium. NUTRITION BONUS: Vitamin C (225% daily value), Calcium (48% dv), Potassium (32% dv), Folate (29% dv), Magnesium & Zinc (24% dv).

Overnight Muesli

H⧓W H♥H

MAKES: 6 servings, ½ cup each
ACTIVE TIME: 5 minutes | TOTAL: 8 hours (including chilling time) | TO MAKE AHEAD: Cover and refrigerate for up to 4 days.

Soaking oats and fruit in yogurt is how muesli is traditionally made. A great make-ahead breakfast if you're pressed for time in the morning but still want a healthy start to your day. Serve with sliced fruit and top with toasted nuts.

2	cups nonfat plain yogurt
1	8-ounce can crushed pineapple (undrained)
1	cup uncooked oats (quick *or* old-fashioned)
3	tablespoons honey
1	teaspoon vanilla extract

Stir yogurt, pineapple, oats, honey and vanilla in a medium bowl until blended. Cover and refrigerate overnight or for up to 4 days.

PER SERVING: 152 calories; 1 g fat (0 g sat, 0 g mono); 2 mg cholesterol; 30 g carbohydrate; 9 g added sugars; 7 g protein; 2 g fiber; 64 mg sodium; 309 mg potassium. NUTRITION BONUS: Calcium (18% daily value).

EatingWell Tip
Get oats into your diet. They offer lots of **cholesterol-lowering fiber**, about 4 grams per ½-cup serving.

Orange Polentina

MAKES: 4 servings, about ¾ cup each
ACTIVE TIME: 20 minutes | TOTAL: 20 minutes
TO MAKE AHEAD: Cover and refrigerate the topping (Step 3) for up to 2 days.

🕐 *Italians enjoy cornmeal or polenta in countless prepara-tions. Polentina is a creamier, porridge-like version, often served for breakfast. An orange-infused dollop of tangy mascarpone cheese and yogurt is a rich, delicious topping. But feel free to skip the mascarpone and double the yogurt to save calories. To keep it quick, we use instant polenta or regular fine cornmeal. If you have time, the recipe will work with stone-ground cornmeal. It will take longer to cook, 15 to 20 minutes, but will reward you with rich texture.*

1	**medium orange**
2	**cups water**
1½	**cups low-fat milk**
¼	**teaspoon salt**
¾	**cup instant polenta *or* fine cornmeal**
¼	**cup mascarpone (Italian cream cheese)**
¼	**cup nonfat Greek yogurt (*see Tip, page 490*)**
4	**tablespoons honey, divided**
1	**teaspoon finely chopped fresh tarragon (optional)**

1. Zest the orange to get 1½ teaspoons; set the zest aside. Slice both ends off the orange. Remove the peel and white pith with a sharp knife. Working over a bowl, cut the segments from their surrounding membranes (*see How To*). Set aside for garnish.

2. Combine water, milk and salt in a large heavy saucepan and bring to a boil. Gradually whisk in polenta (or cornmeal) and return to a boil. Reduce heat to medium-low to maintain an even bubble and whisk until the polentina thickens, 1 to 5 minutes (depending on what type you're using). Remove from the heat, cover and let stand for 5 minutes.

3. Combine mascarpone, yogurt, 1 tablespoon honey and ½ teaspoon of the orange zest in a small bowl.

4. Whisk the remaining 3 tablespoons honey and the remaining 1 teaspoon zest into the polentina. Divide among 4 bowls and top with a dollop of the mascar-pone topping. Garnish with the reserved orange segments and sprinkle with tarragon, if desired. Serve immediately.

PER SERVING: 350 calories; 14 g fat (8 g sat, 0 g mono); 40 mg cholesterol; 50 g carbohydrate; 17 g added sugars; 9 g protein; 4 g fiber; 210 mg sodium; 209 mg potassium.
NUTRITION BONUS: Vitamin C (30% daily value), Calcium (18% dv).

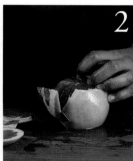

How To
Segment Citrus
1. Slice both ends off the fruit.
2. With a sharp knife, remove the peel and white pith; discard.
3. Working over a bowl, cut the segments from their surround-ing membranes. Squeeze juice into the bowl before discard-ing membrane, if desired.

Apple & Oat Granola

H✂W H♥H

MAKES: about 6 cups
ACTIVE TIME: 20 minutes | TOTAL: 1¼ hours
TO MAKE AHEAD: Store in an airtight container in the refrigerator for up to 1 week or freezer for two months.

Dried apples, cranberries and raisins are a tangy combination in this crunchy oat granola.

- 4 cups old-fashioned oats
- ½ cup sunflower seeds
- ¼ teaspoon salt
- 1 cup apple juice concentrate, thawed
- ¼ cup pure maple syrup
- 1 tablespoon canola oil
- ¼ cup diced dried apples
- ¼ cup dark *or* golden raisins
- ¼ cup dried cranberries

1. Preheat oven to 350°F. Coat a rimmed baking sheet with cooking spray.

2. Combine oats, sunflower seeds and salt in a large bowl. Drizzle with apple juice concentrate, maple syrup and oil; toss until evenly moistened. Spread on prepared baking sheet.

3. Bake the granola until light golden and crisp, 30 to 35 minutes, stirring every 5 minutes. Remove from oven and transfer to a bowl. Toss with dried apples, raisins and dried cranberries. Let cool completely.

PER 1/2-CUP SERVING: 218 calories; 6 g fat (1 g sat, 2 g mono); 0 mg cholesterol; 39 g carbohydrate; 6 g added sugars; 5 g protein; 4 g fiber; 58 mg sodium; 291 mg potassium.
NUTRITION BONUS: Magnesium (21% dv).

Herb & Onion Egg-White Frittata

H✂W H♥H

MAKES: 1 serving
ACTIVE TIME: 10 minutes | TOTAL: 10 minutes

This frittata is loaded with onions and flavored with herbs; try parsley, dill, chervil or marjoram.

- 1 cup diced onion
- ¼ cup plus 1 tablespoon water, divided
- 1 teaspoon extra-virgin olive oil
- 4 egg whites, beaten
- 2 teaspoons chopped fresh herbs *or*
   ½ teaspoon dried
- ⅛ teaspoon salt
- ⅛ teaspoon freshly ground pepper
- 2 tablespoons part-skim ricotta *or* farmer's cheese

1. Bring onion and ¼ cup water to a boil in a small nonstick skillet over medium-high heat. Cover and cook until the onion is slightly softened, about 2 minutes. Uncover and continue cooking until the water has evaporated, 1 to 2 minutes. Drizzle in oil and stir until coated. Continue cooking, stirring often, until the onion is beginning to brown, 1 to 2 minutes more.

2. Pour in egg whites, reduce heat to medium-low and continue cooking, stirring constantly with a heat-proof rubber spatula, until the egg is starting to set, about 20 seconds. Continue cooking, lifting the edges so the uncooked egg will flow underneath, until mostly set, about 30 seconds more.

3. Reduce heat to low. Sprinkle herbs, salt and pepper over the frittata. Spoon cheese on top. Lift up an edge of the frittata and drizzle the remaining 1 tablespoon water under it. Cover and cook until the egg is completely set and the cheese is hot, about 2 minutes. Slide the frittata out of the pan using the spatula and serve.

PER SERVING: 215 calories; 8 g fat (2 g sat, 4 g mono); 10 mg cholesterol; 18 g carbohydrate; 0 g added sugars; 20 g protein; 3 g fiber; 558 mg sodium; 503 mg potassium.
NUTRITION BONUS: Vitamin C (20% daily value).

A Perfect Omelet

One of the fastest meals on the planet is a simple omelet, and it's equally satisfying for breakfast, lunch or dinner. If you have a few eggs on hand, all you need to do is come up with a filling based on what's in your refrigerator. Follow these 3 simple steps and you'll have a perfect omelet in minutes.

Here are the basics:

TOOLS: A medium nonstick skillet and a flexible, heat-resistant spatula.

EGGS: Use 2 eggs to make an omelet for one serving, 4 eggs to make an omelet for two. It's hard to make an omelet with more than 4 eggs in one pan. If you are serving four people, make two omelets back to back. They're that fast.

FILLING: Have the filling (*see below*) prepared and warmed, if it was refrigerated. Don't overstuff: figure about ¼ cup filling for a 2-egg omelet.

How To: Make an Omelet

1. Gently whisk the **eggs** just until blended. Add about 1½ teaspoons **water** per egg, if desired: the water will turn to steam as the eggs heat and make the omelet a little fluffier.

2. Heat 1 teaspoon extra-virgin **olive oil** (or canola oil) in a medium nonstick skillet over medium-high heat until hot. Tilt to coat the pan with oil. Pour the eggs into the pan and immediately stir with a heat-resistant rubber spatula for 5 to 10 seconds. Then push the cooked portions at the edge toward the center (PHOTO 1), tilting the pan to allow uncooked egg to fill in around the edges. When no more egg runs to the sides, continue to cook until almost set and the bottom is light golden. (The omelet will continue to cook as it is filled and folded.) This whole step takes about 1 minute.

3. Remove the pan from the heat and spoon FILLING onto the center third of the omelet perpendicular to the handle. Use the spatula to fold the third of the omelet closest to the handle over the filling (PHOTO 2). Then, grasping the handle from underneath and using the spatula as a guide, tip the omelet onto a plate so that it lands folded in thirds, seam-side down (PHOTO 3).

Filling Ideas

• Sautéed spinach, red bell pepper, red onion, feta cheese
• Leftover mashed potatoes, crumbled cooked bacon, sliced scallions, Cheddar cheese
• Thinly sliced apples, brie cheese
• Leftover roasted vegetables, sautéed onions, Gouda cheese
• Fresh corn kernels, diced tomato, chopped fresh parsley, goat cheese
• Leftover seasoned taco meat, diced pickled jalapeños, sautéed onions, Jack cheese
• Steamed asparagus, Gruyère cheese
• Tomato, basil, smoked mozzarella
• Smoked salmon, cream cheese, red onion, dill, capers

Mini Mushroom-&-Sausage Quiches

H✕W   H♥H

MAKES: 1 dozen mini quiches
ACTIVE TIME: 30 minutes | TOTAL: 1 hour
TO MAKE AHEAD: Individually wrap and refrigerate for up to 3 days or freeze for up to 1 month. To reheat, unwrap, wrap in a paper towel and microwave on High for 30 to 60 seconds.

These crustless mini quiches are like portable omelets. Turkey sausage and sautéed mushrooms keep them light and savory. **Kitchen Tip:** *A good-quality nonstick muffin tin works best for this recipe. If you don't have one, line a regular muffin tin with foil baking cups.*

8	ounces turkey breakfast sausage, removed from casing and crumbled into small pieces
1	teaspoon extra-virgin olive oil
8	ounces mushrooms, sliced
¼	cup sliced scallions
¼	cup shredded Swiss cheese
1	teaspoon freshly ground pepper
5	large eggs
3	large egg whites
1	cup low-fat milk

1. Position rack in center of oven; preheat to 325°F. Coat a nonstick muffin tin generously with cooking spray (*see Kitchen Tip*).

2. Cook sausage in a large nonstick skillet over medium-high heat until golden brown, 6 to 10 minutes. Transfer to a bowl to cool. Add oil to the pan. Add mushrooms and cook, stirring often, until golden brown, 5 to 7 minutes. Transfer the mushrooms to the bowl with the sausage. Let cool for 5 minutes. Stir in scallions, cheese and pepper.

3. Whisk eggs, egg whites and milk in a medium bowl. Divide the egg mixture evenly among the prepared muffin cups. Sprinkle a heaping tablespoon of the sausage mixture into each cup.

4. Bake until the tops are just beginning to brown, 25 minutes. Let cool on a wire rack for 5 minutes. Place a rack on top of the pan, flip it over and turn the quiches out onto the rack. Turn upright and let cool completely.

PER QUICHE: 104 calories; 7 g fat (2 g sat, 2 g mono); 121 mg cholesterol; 3 g carbohydrate; 0 g added sugars; 8 g protein; 0 g fiber; 168 mg sodium; 185 mg potassium.

EatingWell Tip

Use your muffin tin for more than just muffins. You get **perfect portion-controlled servings** and cut down on baking time.

Mushroom & Wild Rice Frittata

H✖W   H♥H

MAKES: 6 servings
ACTIVE TIME: 45 minutes | TOTAL: 1 hour
TO MAKE AHEAD: Prepare the rice (Step 1), cool and store airtight in the refrigerator for up to 3 days.

Packed with a flavorful medley of chewy wild rice and three kinds of mushrooms, this satisfying frittata is perfect for Sunday brunch. Don't worry if you can only find one kind of mushroom—the richly aromatic top of baked Parmesan and crisp prosciutto will make up for it. **Shopping** Tip: *Regular wild rice takes 40 to 50 minutes to cook. To save time, look for a quick-cooking variety that is ready in less than 30 minutes or instant wild rice, which is done in 10 minutes or less.*

WILD RICE

- 2 cups water
- ½ cup wild rice (*see Shopping Tip*), rinsed
- ⅛ teaspoon salt

FRITTATA

- 5 large eggs
- 2 large egg whites
- 2 tablespoons chopped fresh parsley
- ½ teaspoon salt, divided
- ½ teaspoon freshly ground pepper, divided
- ¼ teaspoon ground nutmeg
- 2 teaspoons extra-virgin olive oil
- 1 cup chopped red onion
- 1 tablespoon minced fresh rosemary *or* 1 teaspoon dried
- 1 pound mixed mushrooms (cremini, white button, shiitake), sliced
- ½ cup finely shredded Parmesan cheese
- 4 thin slices prosciutto (about 2 ounces), chopped

1. **To prepare wild rice:** Combine water, rice and salt in a small heavy saucepan; bring to a boil. Cover, reduce heat to maintain a simmer and cook until the rice is tender with a slight bite, 40 to 50 minutes. Drain; you'll have about 1½ cups cooked rice.

2. **To prepare frittata:** About 30 minutes after you start cooking the rice, beat eggs and egg whites in a large bowl with parsley, ¼ teaspoon salt, ¼ teaspoon pepper and nutmeg.

3. Position rack in upper third of oven; preheat broiler.

4. Heat oil in a 10-inch ovenproof skillet, preferably cast-iron, over medium heat. Add onion and the remaining ¼ teaspoon each salt and pepper; cook, stirring, until softened, about 3 minutes. Stir in rosemary, then add mushrooms and cook, stirring frequently, until they release their liquid and the pan is dry, 6 to 8 minutes. Reduce heat to medium-low; stir in the rice.

5. Pour the reserved egg mixture evenly over the rice and vegetables. Partially cover and cook until set around the edges, about 5 minutes. Sprinkle with Parmesan and prosciutto. Place the pan under broiler and broil until the eggs are set and the top is nicely browned, about 2 minutes. Let stand for 5 minutes before serving.

PER SERVING: 210 calories; 9 g fat (3 g sat, 3 g mono); 190 mg cholesterol; 18 g carbohydrate; 0 g added sugars; 17 g protein; 2 g fiber; 681 mg sodium; 426 mg potassium.

EatingWell Tip

Try prosciutto in place of bacon. It adds a bold pork flavor like bacon but with about **3 grams less saturated fat** per ounce.

Whole-Grain Waffles with Cherry Sauce

H⬆F   H♥H

MAKES: 6 servings, one 6-inch Belgian waffle & ¼ cup sauce each

ACTIVE TIME: 1 hour | TOTAL: 1 hour | TO MAKE AHEAD: Prepare the sauce (Step 1), cover and refrigerate for up to 3 days. To serve, gently reheat. Tightly wrap the waffles and refrigerate for up to 3 days or freeze for up to 3 months. Reheat in the toaster. | EQUIPMENT: Belgian-style waffle iron

Cornmeal adds appealing texture to these waffles and hot cherry sauce is a tasty, nutrient-rich alternative to maple syrup. (Photograph: page 448.) **Shopping Tips: White whole-wheat flour**, *made from a special variety of white wheat, is light in color and flavor but has the same nutritional properties as regular whole-wheat flour. Any fine* **cornmeal** *works in this recipe. If you want to use whole-grain cornmeal, look for finely ground cornmeal labeled "whole-grain" or "stone-ground." The flour and cornmeal are available at large supermarkets and at natural-foods stores. Store them in the freezer.*

CHERRY SAUCE

- **2 cups fresh *or* frozen (*not* thawed) pitted cherries (10-ounce package)**
- **¼ cup water**
- **¼ cup honey**
- **2 teaspoons cornstarch**
- **1 teaspoon lemon juice**
- **1 teaspoon vanilla extract**

WAFFLES

- **2 cups white whole-wheat flour (*see Shopping Tips*)**
- **½ cup fine cornmeal (*see Shopping Tips*)**
- **1½ teaspoons baking powder**
- **½ teaspoon baking soda**
- **¼ teaspoon salt**
- **2 large eggs**
- **¼ cup packed light brown sugar**
- **2 cups buttermilk (*see Tip, page 482*)**
- **1 tablespoon extra-virgin olive oil *or* canola oil**
- **2 teaspoons vanilla extract**

1. **To prepare cherry sauce:** Combine cherries, water, honey, cornstarch, lemon juice and vanilla extract in a small saucepan. Bring to a boil over medium heat and cook, stirring occasionally, until the mixture thickens, about 1 minute. Set aside.

2. **To prepare waffles:** Preheat oven to 200°F; place a large baking sheet on the center rack.

3. Whisk whole-wheat flour (*see How To*), cornmeal, baking powder, baking soda and salt in a large bowl. Lightly beat eggs and brown sugar in a medium bowl. Add buttermilk, oil and vanilla; whisk until well blended. Add the wet ingredients to the dry ingredients, stirring until just combined.

4. Preheat a Belgian-style waffle iron. Lightly coat it with cooking spray. Add enough batter to cover about two-thirds of the surface (about ⅔ cup); distribute evenly with a spatula. Close and cook until golden brown, 4 to 5 minutes. Transfer the waffles to the baking sheet to keep warm until ready to serve; do not stack. Repeat with the remaining batter, using more cooking spray as needed. Warm the cherry sauce over medium heat until hot and bubbling; serve with the waffles.

PER SERVING: 380 calories; 5 g fat (1 g sat, 3 g mono); 74 mg cholesterol; 74 g carbohydrate; 20 g added sugars; 12 g protein; 6 g fiber; 456 mg sodium; 346 mg potassium.
NUTRITION BONUS: Iron (35% daily value).

How To

Measure Flour | We use the "spoon and level" method to measure flours. Here's how it is done: Use a spoon to lightly scoop flour from its container into a measuring cup. Use a knife or other straight edge to level the flour with the top of the measuring cup.

EatingWell Tip

Try swapping out regular flour for white whole-wheat. It tastes similar to all-purpose flour, with the benefit of **additional fiber** that helps with digestion.

Banana-Raisin French Toast

H✖W   H⬆F   H♥H

MAKES: 2 servings
ACTIVE TIME: 30 minutes | TOTAL: 30 minutes

This is a fun take on French toast that kids love. We make a creamy banana filling, sandwich it between raisin bread, dip it in egg and cook it. It turns out as a French toast sandwich stuffed with banana.

1	ripe banana, peeled
2	teaspoons frozen orange juice concentrate
4	slices cinnamon-raisin bread
2	large egg whites
¼	cup nonfat milk
¼	cup nonfat *or* low-fat plain yogurt
1½	tablespoons pure maple syrup *or* honey
1	teaspoon butter, divided

1. Mash banana coarsely with a fork in a small, shallow bowl. Stir in orange juice concentrate. Spread the banana mixture over 2 slices of bread and top with the remaining 2 slices of bread, forming 2 sandwiches.

2. Whisk egg whites and milk in a shallow dish; add the sandwiches and soak for about 20 seconds. Turn the sandwiches over and soak for 20 seconds longer. Transfer the sandwiches to a plate.

3. Stir together yogurt and maple syrup (or honey) in a small bowl. Set aside.

4. Melt ½ teaspoon butter in a large nonstick skillet over low heat. Tilt the pan to swirl the butter around the pan. Place the sandwiches in the pan and cook until the undersides are browned, 5 to 7 minutes. Lift the sandwiches and add the remaining ½ teaspoon butter. Turn over and cook until browned on the other side, 5 to 7 minutes longer. Serve with the sweetened yogurt.

PER SERVING: 304 calories; 4 g fat (2 g sat, 1 g mono); 6 mg cholesterol; 57 g carbohydrate; 12 g added sugars; 11 g protein; 4 g fiber; 296 mg sodium; 579 mg potassium.
NUTRITION BONUS: Folate (27% daily value), Vitamin C (23% dv), Potassium (17% dv), Calcium (15% dv).

EatingWell Tip

Don't drench your French toast in syrup. Sugars of any kind add calories without any nutritional value. Try mixing syrup with nonfat or low-fat yogurt. It will still be sweet and creamy, but **less caloric and with the added benefit of a little protein and calcium**.

Chicken-Apple Sausage

MAKES: 8 patties

ACTIVE TIME: 45 minutes | TOTAL: 45 minutes

TO MAKE AHEAD: Freeze the cooked sausage in an airtight container for up to 3 months.

It's easy to make your own patty sausage with just a few healthy ingredients like ground chicken, apples, onion and savory spices like sage and fennel. You can use ground turkey instead of ground chicken if you prefer.

2 teaspoons canola oil

1 small onion, diced

1 medium sweet apple, such as Gala *or* Honeycrisp, peeled and diced

1 pound ground chicken

1 tablespoon finely chopped fresh sage

1 tablespoon packed light brown sugar

½ teaspoon fennel seeds, chopped

¾ teaspoon salt

¼ teaspoon freshly ground pepper

1. Heat oil in a large nonstick skillet over medium heat. Add onion and cook, stirring, until beginning to soften, about 2 minutes. Add apples and cook, stirring, 2 more minutes. Transfer to a large bowl and cool for 5 minutes. Wipe out the pan.

2. Add chicken, sage, sugar, fennel seeds, salt and pepper to the bowl with the apples and onions. Gently mix to combine.

3. Generously coat the pan with cooking spray and heat over medium. Using a ⅓-cup measure, scoop 4 portions of the sausage mixture into pan, flattening each into a 3-inch patty. Cook until the patties are browned and cooked through, about 3 minutes per side, adjusting the heat as necessary to prevent burning. Coat the pan with cooking spray again and repeat with remaining sausage mixture.

PER PATTY: 112 calories; 6 g fat (1 g sat, 3 g mono); 49 mg cholesterol; 5 g carbohydrate; 2 g added sugars; 10 g protein; 0 g fiber; 253 mg sodium; 333 mg potassium.

EatingWell Tip

Try ground chicken instead of regular ground pork. In this recipe you **save 68 calories and 7 grams** of fat per patty.

Cardamom-Crumb Coffee Cake

H⬆F

MAKES: 12 servings
ACTIVE TIME: 30 minutes | TOTAL: 1¼ hours
TO MAKE AHEAD: Prepare through Step 4, cover and refrigerate for up to 1 day; add about 10 minutes to the baking time.

Cardamom's distinctive floral and spice aroma makes for a delicious and unique coffee cake. A member of the ginger family, it is widely used in the baking of Scandinavia and the dishes of Eastern India. If you prefer to go more traditional, cinnamon also works wonderfully in this cake. (Photograph: page 448.)

OATMEAL CRUMB

- 6 tablespoons cold unsalted butter, cut into small pieces
- ½ cup packed light brown sugar
- 1 cup old-fashioned rolled oats, divided
- ¼ cup white whole-wheat flour *or* whole-wheat pastry flour (*see Tip, page 484*)
- ½ teaspoon ground cardamom *or* cinnamon
- ¼ cup chopped walnuts

CAKE

- 2 cups white whole-wheat flour *or* whole-wheat pastry flour (*see Tip, page 484*)
- 2 teaspoons baking powder
- 1 teaspoon ground cardamom *or* cinnamon
- ½ teaspoon baking soda
- ¼ teaspoon salt
- 2 large eggs
- ½ cup packed light brown sugar
- 1 cup buttermilk (*see How To*)
- ¼ cup canola oil
- 1 teaspoon vanilla extract

1. **To prepare oatmeal crumb:** Combine butter, ½ cup brown sugar, ½ cup oats, ¼ cup flour and ½ teaspoon cardamom (or cinnamon) in a food processor. Process until the mixture is crumbly. Turn out into a bowl and add the remaining ½ cup oats and walnuts. Combine with fingertips or a fork until blended.

2. **To prepare cake:** Preheat oven to 350°F. Coat an 8-inch-square pan with cooking spray.

3. Sift 2 cups flour, baking powder, 1 teaspoon cardamom (or cinnamon), baking soda and salt together in a large bowl. Whisk eggs and ½ cup brown sugar in a medium bowl until well blended; gradually whisk in buttermilk, oil and vanilla. Add the wet ingredients to the dry ingredients in 2 additions, stirring each time to thoroughly blend the ingredients together.

4. Spread half the batter in the prepared pan. Sprinkle half the oatmeal crumb evenly on top. Spoon the remaining batter over the crumbs and gently spread in an even layer. Top with the remaining oatmeal crumb.

5. Bake the coffee cake until browned and a toothpick inserted in the center comes out clean, 35 to 40 minutes. Let cool for 10 minutes. Serve warm.

PER SERVING: 300 calories; 14 g fat (5 g sat, 5 g mono); 51 mg cholesterol; 41 g carbohydrate; 18 g added sugars; 6 g protein; 3 g fiber; 228 mg sodium; 136 mg potassium.
NUTRITION BONUS: Iron (21% daily value).

How To

Make Your Own "Buttermilk" | You can replace buttermilk in any recipe with an equal amount of "sour milk." Add 1 tablespoon lemon juice or vinegar to 1 cup low-fat or nonfat milk. Or use buttermilk powder (found in the baking section), prepared according to package directions.

Almond-Honey Power Bar

H✕W H↑F H♥H

MAKES: 8 bars

ACTIVE TIME: 30 minutes | TOTAL: 1 hour (including chilling)

TO MAKE AHEAD: Store in an airtight container at room temperature or in the refrigerator for up to 1 week or freeze for up to 1 month; thaw at room temperature.

Great for breakfast on the go! Golden roasted nuts, seeds and oats are enveloped by flavorful almond butter in these delectably chewy, no-fuss energy bars. Unrefined turbinado sugar adds a deep caramelly undertone. Feel free to use light brown sugar instead. Bars stored at room temperature will be softer than those that are refrigerated. **Shopping Tips:** *For this recipe, we like unsweetened* **multi-grain puffed cereal,** *such as Kashi's 7 Whole Grain Puffs.* **Almond butter** *can be found at natural-foods stores and large supermarkets, near the peanut butter.* **Turbinado sugar** *is steam-cleaned raw cane sugar. It's coarse-grained and light brown in color, with a slight molasses flavor. Find it in the natural-foods section of large supermarkets or at natural-foods stores.*

- 1   **cup old-fashioned rolled oats**
- ¼   **cup slivered almonds**
- ¼   **cup sunflower seeds**
- 1   **tablespoon flaxseeds, preferably golden**
- 1   **tablespoon sesame seeds**
- 1   **cup unsweetened multi-grain puffed cereal (see *Shopping Tips*)**
- ⅓   **cup currants**
- ⅓   **cup chopped dried apricots**
- ⅓   **cup chopped golden raisins**
- ¼   **cup creamy almond butter (see *Shopping Tips*)**
- ¼   **cup turbinado sugar (see *Shopping Tips*)**
- ¼   **cup honey**
- ½   **teaspoon vanilla extract**
- ⅛   **teaspoon salt**

1. Preheat oven to 350°F. Coat an 8-inch-square pan with cooking spray.

2. Spread oats, almonds, sunflower seeds, flaxseeds and sesame seeds on a large, rimmed baking sheet. Bake until the oats are lightly toasted and the nuts are fragrant, shaking the pan halfway through, about 10 minutes. Transfer to a large bowl. Add cereal, currants, apricots and raisins; toss to combine.

3. Combine almond butter, sugar, honey, vanilla and salt in a small saucepan. Heat over medium-low, stirring frequently, until the mixture bubbles lightly, 2 to 5 minutes.

4. Immediately pour the almond butter mixture over the dry ingredients and mix with a spoon or spatula until no dry spots remain. Transfer to the prepared pan. Lightly coat your hands with cooking spray and press the mixture down firmly to make an even layer (wait until the mixture cools slightly if necessary). Refrigerate until firm, about 30 minutes; cut into 8 bars.

PER SERVING: 244 calories; 10 g fat (1 g sat, 5 g mono); 0 mg cholesterol; 38 g carbohydrate; 15 g added sugars; 5 g protein; 3 g fiber; 74 mg sodium; 313 mg potassium.
NUTRITION BONUS: Magnesium (19% daily value).

Baking Muffins & Quick Breads

Muffins are the ultimate grab-and-go breakfast and loaves of fruit-studded quick breads are a welcome addition to a brunch or afternoon tea. Pick one of the 5 following flavor variations to make a batch of muffins or bread, or experiment with your favorite ingredients. Muffins freeze well, so you can keep them on hand for a quick breakfast.

Master Quick Bread Recipe

MAKES: 12 servings

ACTIVE TIME: 25 minutes | **TOTAL:** 1¼-2¼ hours, including cooling times, depending on pan size

TO MAKE AHEAD: Store, individually wrapped, at room temperature for up to 2 days or in the freezer for up to 1 month. Freeze Quick-Bread Dry Mix in a freezer bag for up to 6 months.

Follow these easy steps to make different quick breads (loaf, muffins, mini Bundts, mini loaves) from one master recipe.

QUICK-BREAD DRY MIX

1½	**cups whole-wheat pastry flour (*see Tip, page 485*)** *or* **whole-wheat flour**
1	**cup all-purpose flour**
1½	**teaspoons baking powder**
1	**teaspoon ground cinnamon**
½	**teaspoon baking soda**
¼	**teaspoon salt**

QUICK-BREAD WET MIX

2	**large eggs**
1	**cup buttermilk (*see Tip, page 482*)**
⅔	**cup packed brown sugar**
2	**tablespoons butter, melted**
2	**tablespoons canola oil**
1	**teaspoon vanilla extract**

ADD-INS

| 2 | **cups diced fruit (*see Add-In Variations, opposite*)** |
| ½ | **cup chopped nuts (*see Add-In Variations*), plus more for topping (optional)** |

1. Choose a pan option and preheat oven (*see chart, opposite*). Coat pan(s) with cooking spray.

2. Whisk QUICK-BREAD DRY MIX ingredients in a large bowl.

3. Whisk QUICK-BREAD WET MIX ingredients in another bowl until well combined.

4. Make a well in the center of the DRY MIX, pour in the WET MIX and stir until just combined. Stir in ADD-INS just until combined; do not overmix. Transfer batter to the prepared pan(s). Top with additional nuts, if desired.

5. Bake until golden brown and a wooden skewer inserted in the center comes out clean (*see chart for baking times*). Let cool in the pan(s) for 10 minutes, then turn out onto a wire rack. (*See chart for cooling times.*)

Add-In Variations:

CRANBERRY-WALNUT
- 2   cups chopped cranberries (*see How To*), fresh *or* frozen, thawed
- ½   cup chopped toasted walnuts (*see Tip, page 486*)
- 1   teaspoon freshly grated orange zest

PER SERVING: 239 calories; 9 g fat (2 g sat, 3 g mono); 41 mg cholesterol; 35 g carbohydrate; 12 g added sugars; 5 g protein; 3 g fiber; 199 mg sodium; 108 mg potassium.

PINEAPPLE-PECAN
- 2   cups diced pineapple, fresh *or* canned, drained
- ½   cup chopped toasted pecans (*see Tip, page 486*)

PER SERVING: 244 calories; 9 g fat (2 g sat, 4 g mono); 41 mg cholesterol; 37 g carbohydrate; 12 g added sugars; 5 g protein; 3 g fiber; 199 mg sodium; 120 mg potassium.

PEAR-HAZELNUT
- 2   cups diced peeled pears
- ½   cup chopped toasted hazelnuts (*see Tip, page 486*)
- ½   teaspoon ground allspice

PER SERVING: 243 calories; 9 g fat (2 g sat, 5 g mono); 41 mg cholesterol; 37 g carbohydrate; 12 g added sugars; 5 g protein; 3 g fiber; 199 mg sodium; 133 mg potassium.

MANGO-PECAN
- 2   cups diced mango (*see Tip, page 486*), fresh *or* frozen, thawed
- ½   cup chopped toasted pecans (*see Tip, page 486*)

PER SERVING: 248 calories; 9 g fat (2 g sat, 4 g mono); 41 mg cholesterol; 38 g carbohydrate; 12 g added sugars; 5 g protein; 3 g fiber; 199 mg sodium; 133 mg potassium.

BANANA-BLUEBERRY-ALMOND (*Photograph: page 13.*)
- 1   cup diced banana
- 1   cup blueberries, fresh *or* frozen, thawed
- ½   cup chopped toasted almonds (*see Tip, page 486*)

PER SERVING: 243 calories; 8 g fat (2 g sat, 4 g mono); 41 mg cholesterol; 38 g carbohydrate; 12 g added sugars; 6 g protein; 3 g fiber; 199 mg sodium; 158 mg potassium.

How To

Chop Cranberries | Pulse whole cranberries in a food processor until they are coarsely chopped.

TO STORE MUFFINS FOR LONGER THAN 2 DAYS, wrap individually, place in a storage container or sealable plastic bag and freeze for up to 1 month. To thaw and reheat, unwrap a muffin, wrap it in a paper towel and microwave on High for 30 to 60 seconds.

PAN OPTIONS	OVEN TEMPERATURE	BAKING TIME	COOL ON RACK
12 muffins (standard 12-cup muffin tin, ½-cup capacity per muffin)	400°F	22-25 minutes	5 minutes
1 large loaf (9-by-5-inch pan)	375°F	1 hour 10 minutes	40 minutes
3 mini loaves (6-by-3-inch pan, 2-cup capacity)	400°F	35 minutes	30 minutes
6 mini Bundt cakes (6-cup mini Bundt pan, scant 1-cup capacity per cake)	400°F	22-25 minutes	5 minutes

Resources

How to Follow an EATINGWELL Recipe

Our goal is to provide healthy, delicious recipes that are easy for anyone to cook at home. To make sure you have success when you try our recipes, we test each recipe thoroughly in the EATINGWELL Test Kitchen. Once we're sure the recipe works well, it's up to you to follow the recipe. To that end, it's important to keep in mind a few simple guidelines and tips for how to read our recipes.

How to read an ingredient list

THE COMMA MATTERS: When we call for ingredients, pay attention to where the comma is, as it can have a significant effect on what we're calling for. Here are some examples:

• **1 pound chicken, trimmed** means we are calling for 1 pound purchased chicken and then you trim it.

• **1 cup pecans, chopped** means we are calling for 1 cup of pecans and then you chop them. **1 cup chopped pecans**, on the other hand, means you should chop your pecans and then measure out 1 cup of the chopped nuts.

• **1 cup frozen raspberries, thawed** means we are calling for 1 cup of frozen raspberries and then you thaw them. **1 cup thawed frozen raspberries**, on the other hand, means that you thaw and then measure your berries.

• **1 cup sifted flour** means sift the flour first and then measure it. Alternately, **1 cup flour, sifted** means first measure your flour and then sift it.

MARKET QUANTITIES VERSUS MEASURES: We aim to make shopping as easy as possible, so we usually call for market quantities of ingredients rather than measures. For example, a market quantity would be 1 small onion, while a measure would be ¾ cup diced onion. When we call for a measure it is typically because we think that using the specified amount of the ingredient is important to the outcome of the recipe.

Tips for measuring

TOOLS

Measuring accurately when cooking and baking is one of the best ways to guarantee successful results in the kitchen. In the EATINGWELL Test Kitchen, we use four types of standard, U.S. measuring tools:

DRY MEASURING CUPS: Metal or plastic measuring cups, usually sold in a set, that are available in ¼-, ⅓-, ½-, ¾- and 1-cup sizes. Dry ingredients, such as flour and grains, should be measured in dry measuring cups.

LIQUID MEASURING CUPS: Clear glass or plastic cups with pour spouts that are available in 1-, 2-, 4- and 8-cup sizes that have measurements marked on the side of the cup. When measuring liquids, place a clear liquid measuring cup on a level surface. Pour in the liquid, then verify the measure by looking at it from eye level, not from above.

MEASURING SPOONS: Small spoons in ¼-, ½-, 1-teaspoon and 1-tablespoon sizes designed to measure small quantities of dry or liquid ingredients. When a teaspoon or tablespoon measure is called for in a recipe, we don't mean the regular silverware spoons you eat with.

KITCHEN SCALE: Although it is not necessary to have a kitchen scale to make our recipes, a small digital scale that can measure up to at least 5 pounds is a handy tool to have in the kitchen to ensure accuracy.

INGREDIENTS

FLOUR: We use the "spoon and level" method to measure flours. To properly measure flour this way, use a spoon to lightly scoop flour from its container into a measuring cup. (There's no need to stir up the flour before you scoop it into the cup.) Use a knife or other straight edge to level the flour with the top of the cup. If the measuring cup is dipped directly into the container—a common mistake—the flour will be packed into the cup and result in extra flour being added to the recipe, yielding tough, dense baked goods.

GRANULATED SUGAR should be spooned into the measuring cup. Use a knife or other straight edge to level the sugar with the top of the cup.

BROWN SUGAR should be firmly packed into the measuring cup and leveled by pressing it with your hand or a spoon.

CONFECTIONERS' SUGAR should be measured in the same way as granulated sugar or flour, unless the recipe calls for it to be "packed"—in those recipes, it should be packed as you would brown sugar.

Cooking terms to know

KNIFE SKILLS

The way you cut ingredients is important; it helps distribute the ingredient throughout the dish (mincing or finely chopping garlic, for example), ensure that ingredients cook at the same time (like cutting your carrots and potatoes into 1-inch dice) or improve texture (a thinly sliced piece of smoked salmon, for example, is more tempting on your bagel than a fat chunk). Pay attention to, but don't stress about these terms: your common sense will go a long way in helping you as you cook.

MINCE AND FINELY CHOP: "Mincing" is the finest chop of all, less than ⅛ inch, achieved by cutting, then rocking the knife back and forth across the ingredients, while rotating the blade around on the cutting board. "Finely chop" is a little larger than mince.

CHOP AND COARSELY CHOP: You want to wind up with about a ¼-inch piece when you chop, a bit larger (about ½ inch) when you "coarsely chop." The idea of chopping (unlike dicing) is that the ingredients don't have to be uniform in size.

DICE AND CUBE: You're aiming for uniformity of size here. Most recipes that call for a "dice" or "cube" will indicate the preferred size for cooking in the time allotted (e.g., "cut into 1-inch cubes"). Ignore these measurements and you will alter the cooking time.

SLICE AND THINLY SLICE: "Slice" is a judgment call, but if you insist on a rule of thumb, think of a slice no thinner than ¼ inch. "Thinly slice," however, means you will want to cut the food as thinly as possible. This will vary by ingredient: you can slice an apple to near-transparent thinness, which is hard to do with steak.

SLICE DIAGONALLY: Also known as slicing "on the bias," this is just like slicing, but instead of making a perpendicular cut you cut on an angle. It's an attractive way to cut long vegetables, such as scallions, celery or zucchini. To slice diagonally, hold the knife at a 45-degree angle to the vegetable and then cut it.

CUT INTO MATCHSTICKS: Also known as julienne cut: food is cut into long thin strips. To get a matchstick, first slice the vegetable and then trim the edges to get even rectangles (about 1 to 2 inches long). Then stack the rectangles and slice lengthwise into matchsticks.

Mince

Coarsely chop

¼-inch dice

Slice diagonally

HEATING & COOKING

We try to use terms that are as clear as possible in recipes. But of course how you interpret those words can have an impact on how a dish turns out. Here are some of the words we use and what we mean.

SIMMER: This is low steady cooking in which the liquid in the pan should be steaming and gently bubbling. Usually you can maintain a simmer over low or medium-low heat, depending on your stove. Often we instruct you to bring something to a boil and then reduce to a simmer. When you do this you will probably need to bring it to a boil over higher heat, and then reduce the heat.

BRAISE, STEW: These two terms (you can use them interchangeably) are a subset of "simmer," and involve cooking something in liquid over low heat. Braising is often used for tough cuts of meat, as in pot roast.

SAUTÉ: Usually in a skillet over relatively high heat, sautéing is a quick method of cooking food in a little bit of fat. The food is stirred or moved around occasionally.

STIR-FRY: A high-heat method of searing meats, poultry, fish and vegetables, usually associated with Asian cooking. You must use oil for stir-frying, otherwise the high temperature will cause the natural sugars to burn and foods to stick to the pan—even a nonstick one.

STEAM: Food is cooked by steam rather than by direct contact with a pan or a liquid. Usually we steam using a steamer basket. To steam, you need a pot large enough to hold both the steamer basket and 1 inch of water with plenty of airflow all around the basket. The food should not sit in the water. Check the water level from time to time to make sure the pan isn't dry.

ROAST: Whether at a high or low heat, roasting involves a steady, even, dry heat that cooks from the outside in. Air (and thus heat) should circulate freely around whatever's being roasted; the oven rack should be placed in the center of the oven unless otherwise stated in the recipe.

BROIL: This is an indoor cousin of grilling and sears food with high, direct heat. A broiler should always be preheated for at least 5 minutes; food should be placed so that it (not the broiler pan) is 4 to 6 inches from the heat source. Foods blotted dry broil with less mess.

The EATINGWELL Test Kitchen

Each of our recipes is thoroughly tested in the EATINGWELL Test Kitchen. Why test recipes? With testing, we ensure recipes are great-tasting, but we also make sure they're streamlined, simple and easy to follow.

Our Test Kitchen team cooks and tastes recipes all day long. Fun, yes. But testing is also serious business. They're responsible for making sure EATINGWELL recipes really work when you cook them at home. The team (left to right): Katie Webster, Stacy Fraser, Jessie Price, Hilary Meyer, Carolyn Malcoun and Carolyn Casner.

Here's how our testing process works:

- Recipes are tested on average seven times each.
- Each recipe is tested by multiple testers.
- Both home cooks and culinary school graduates test our recipes.
- We test on both gas and electric stoves.
- We use a variety of ingredients, tools and techniques.
- Testers shop major supermarkets to research availability of ingredients.
- Testers measure active and total time to prepare each recipe.

Key to EATINGWELL Recipes and Nutritional Analysis

WHAT THESE ICONS MEAN

Icons identify recipes that are most appropriate for certain eating goals. Recipes with small serving sizes (e.g., salad dressings, cookies) don't qualify for icons. (For more on our nutritional analysis process and our complete guidelines on how we define each icon, visit *eatingwell.com/go/guidelines*.) A recipe marked…

H✖W **[Healthy Weight]** has reduced calories and limited saturated fat:

	CALORIES	SAT FAT
ENTREES	≤350	≤5g
SIDE DISHES, MUFFINS, BREADS	≤250	≤3g
DESSERTS	≤250	≤5g
DIPS, SALSAS (1/4- TO 1/3-CUP SERVING)	≤100	≤2g
COMBINATION MEALS*	≤420	≤7g
COMPLETE MEALS**	≤500	≤7g

H⬆F **[High Fiber]** provides significant total fiber: entrees/combination meals*/complete meals** have ≥5 grams of fiber per serving. All other recipes have ≥3 grams.

H♥H **[Healthy Heart]** has limited saturated fat:

	SAT FAT
ENTREES	≤3g
SEAFOOD ENTREES	≤5g
SIDE DISHES, MUFFINS, BREADS, DESSERTS	≤2g
DIPS, SALSAS (1/4- TO 1/3-CUP SERVING)	≤1g
COMBINATION MEALS*	≤5g
SEAFOOD COMBINATION MEALS	≤7g
COMPLETE MEALS**	≤7g

*Combination Meal: A serving of protein plus a starch **or** vegetable serving.

Complete Meal: A serving of protein plus a starch **and a vegetable.

 is ready to eat in **45 minutes or less**.

WHAT THESE TERMS MEAN

ACTIVE TIME includes prep time (the time it takes to chop, dice, puree, mix, combine, etc. before cooking begins). It also includes the time spent tending something on the stovetop, in the oven or on the grill—and getting it to the table. If you can't walk away from it for more than 10 minutes, we consider it active time.

TOTAL includes both active and inactive time and indicates the entire amount of time required for each recipe, start to finish.

TO MAKE AHEAD tells when a recipe or part of a recipe can be made in advance and gives storage instructions. If special EQUIPMENT is needed to prepare a recipe, we tell you that too.

HOW WE DO NUTRITIONAL ANALYSIS OF RECIPES

- All recipes are analyzed for nutrition content by a Registered Dietitian.
- We analyze for calories, total fat, saturated (sat) fat, monounsaturated (mono) fat, cholesterol, carbohydrate, added sugars, protein, fiber, sodium and potassium, using The Food Processor SQL© Nutrition Analysis Software from ESHA Research, Salem, Oregon. (Note: Nutrition information is updated regularly. The current analyses appear with the recipes on *eatingwell.com*.)
- When a recipe provides 15 percent or more of the Daily Value (dv) of a nutrient, it is listed as a nutrition bonus. These values are FDA benchmarks for adults eating 2,000 calories a day.
- Recipes are tested and analyzed with iodized table salt unless otherwise indicated.
- We estimate that rinsing with water reduces the sodium in some canned foods, such as beans, by 35 percent. (People on sodium-restricted diets can reduce or eliminate the salt in a recipe.)
- Garnishes and optional ingredients are not included in analyses.
- When a recipe gives a measurement range of an ingredient, we analyze the first amount.
- When alternative ingredients are listed, we analyze the first one suggested.
- We do not include trimmings or marinade that is not absorbed in analyses.

What to Look for on Nutrition Labels

By law, packaged foods sold in the U.S. have a standardized Nutrition Facts Panel, which gives a lot of helpful information—if you focus on these key areas.

SERVING SIZE: To make comparing foods easier, similar foods must have similar serving sizes—but "one serving" might not be what you consume in one sitting. Always check serving size and adjust accordingly.

CALORIES: Again, these just reflect a count for a single serving, and you'll need to adjust if you eat more or less.

TOTAL FAT: Reflects the total grams of fat per serving and the calories coming from fat. This information is less useful than the breakdown of the type of fat in the foods.

SATURATED FAT: Look for as low as possible. Current dietary recommendations say that people should eat 7 percent or less calories from saturated fat. For 2,000-calorie intake, this translates into a total of 16 grams per day.

TRANS FAT: Look for "0." But keep in mind that food with less than 0.5 gram of trans fat per serving can be labeled as "0." Instead look on the ingredient list for any "partially hydrogenated" or "hydrogenated" ingredients, which are sources of trans fats.

CHOLESTEROL: As low as possible (aim for 300 mg or less daily).

SODIUM: As low as possible (USDA Dietary Guidelines recommend 2,300 mg/day or less).

DIETARY FIBER: As high as possible (aim for 25 grams for women or 38 grams for men daily).

SUGARS: Interesting but not always useful, since labels don't discriminate between naturally occurring sugars (such as in milk or fruit) and added sugars.

VITAMINS AND MINERALS: Vitamins A and C, calcium and iron are required to be listed on labels since consuming enough of these nutrients can improve your health and reduce your risk of some diseases. They're shown in the form of Daily Values.

PERCENT DAILY VALUES (DV): These are reference amounts set by the Food and Drug Administration (FDA). You can use Daily Values to help you track how much of your nutrient needs a food fills. But take note: the DVs are set according to how many calories you eat—and labels usually use 2,000 calories as a reference for the vitamin and mineral recommendations and 2,500 calories as the reference for other nutrients. If you're only eating 1,500 calories daily, for example, your DV goals will be approximately one-fourth to one-third lower than what's on the label.

Nutrition Facts

Serving Size	4 Crackers (14g)
Servings Per Container	About 32

Amount per serving

Calories 70	Calories from Fat 25

% Daily Value *

Total Fat 3g	5%
Saturated Fat 1g	5%
Trans Fat 0g	
Polyunsaturated Fat 1g	
Monounsaturated Fat 1g	
Cholesterol 0mg	0%
Sodium 150mg	6%
Total Carbohydrate 9g	3%
Dietary Fiber less than 1g	1%
Sugars 1g	
Protein 1g	

Vitamin A	0%	•	Vitamin C	0%
Calcium	0%	•	Iron	2%

* Percent Daily Values are based on a 2,000 calorie diet. Your daily values may be higher or lower depending on your calorie needs:

	Calories	2,000	2,500
Total Fat	Less than	65g	80g
Sat. Fat	Less than	20g	25g
Cholesterol	Less than	300mg	300mg
Sodium	Less than	2,400mg	2,400mg
Total Carbohydrate		300g	375g
Dietary Fiber		25g	30g

Ingredients: Enriched flour (wheat flour, niacin, reduced iron . . .

Food-Safety Basics

When you cook at home it's important to keep food safety in mind. The basic idea is to keep foods at the right temperature (for example, keep perishables properly chilled in your refrigerator) and avoid cross-contamination. Here are a few simple rules to follow.

Shopping

KEEP FOODS COOL WHEN YOU'RE SHOPPING: If possible, go grocery shopping as your last errand before heading home. If you must run other errands, put a cooler in the car and buy a bag of ice to keep the perishables cold.

WATCH OUT FOR DRIPPING MEATS OR FISH: Put meats or fish in plastic bags before you stick them in your cart so they don't drip on the produce or pantry items.

Storage

REFRIGERATOR: Never store eggs, milk or meat on your refrigerator door, which is the part of the fridge with the greatest temperature fluctuations. We recommend setting your refrigerator temperature control for 40°F, and using the door for storing ketchup, mustard and other condiments that are not so easily subject to spoilage.

FREEZER: Keep your freezer at 2°F for safe frozen-food storage.

Cooking

DEFROST FOOD SAFELY: Defrost food in the refrigerator or the microwave to deter bacterial growth. Leaving it out at room temperature to defrost does the opposite.

WASH YOUR HANDS: Before you begin cooking, wash your hands with soap under warm water for at least 20 seconds (about as long as it takes to sing the chorus of "Jingle Bells").

WASH FRUITS AND VEGETABLES: Rinse off fruits and vegetables under cool running water.

DON'T WASH MEATS: Unwrap meats and fish in the sink and leave them in their container or paper until you're ready to use them. Immediately throw out the container or paper; never reuse it. Despite what your mother may have taught you, it's not wise to rinse off poultry, meat or fish. The bacterial contaminants can only be killed at temperatures above 160°F, far hotter than the hot water in our homes. Rinsing also allows for random splashes—and thus cross-contamination of counters and cabinets.

KEEP CUTTING BOARDS SAFE: Avoid cross-contamination by having at least two cutting boards (*left*), one for meat or fish and another for fresh produce.

Leftovers

FOLLOW THE 2:2:4 RULE: Refrigerate or freeze leftovers within 2 hours of cooking the food. Otherwise throw it away—it may not be safe to eat. Store leftovers in the refrigerator in shallow containers (about 2 inches deep) and use them (or freeze them) within 4 days.

Cleaning Up

Wash plastic cutting boards in the dishwasher. Wash your knives in hot, soapy water. And wash your counters with hot, soapy water. An occasional thorough once-over with a kitchen disinfectant spray is a good idea.

Tools & Equipment

To make your kitchen an enjoyable, easy place to work, make sure your tools and ingredients are handy, your sink is cleared out and your work surfaces are clean. Like any good workspace, your kitchen needs good tools. The following recommendations include what you'll need to cook the recipes in this book, as well as a few other useful items.

BAKEWARE: A 9-by-13-inch baking pan, roasting pan and rack, baking sheets, 3-quart rectangular and 8-inch-square glass baking dishes, muffin tin and loaf pan.

BLENDER & FOOD PROCESSOR: Handy for blending smoothies and salad dressings, chopping vegetables and pureeing soups.

BOWLS: A set of 3 stainless-steel mixing bowls that fit inside one another is a space saver. They are inexpensive, versatile and will last a lifetime.

COLANDER: One that has feet and is the right size for your family (think about how much pasta you need to drain at once). Also make sure it will fit in your sink.

COOKWARE: Nonstick skillets are great tools for all cooks but remember never to use them over high heat or use metal utensils on nonstick pans—scratched surfaces negatively affect their nonstick surface. You'll want both small and large nonstick skillets. You'll also want small and large stainless-steel skillets, as well as small and large saucepans and a stockpot.

CUTTING BOARDS: Two cutting boards are ideal—one for raw proteins and one for cooked foods and produce—to avoid cross-contamination when cooking. Cutting boards made of polyethylene plastic are inexpensive, durable and easy to clean. Look for ones that are dishwasher-safe.

DUTCH OVEN: Many of our recipes call for this double-handled, large, high-sided pot (typically smaller than a stockpot). The Dutch oven is great for soups, stews and braises.

ELECTRIC HAND MIXER: Baked goods are so much easier to make with a hand mixer. You can get one for as little as $15.

INSTANT-READ THERMOMETER: Found in nearly every supermarket meat section or with other kitchen gadgets, an instant-read thermometer is essential for making sure meat and poultry are safely cooked and done to your preference.

KNIVES: You really only need three knives: a serrated knife, a 9- to 10-inch-long chef's knife and a paring knife. Make sure you hold a knife before you buy it; it should feel natural in your hand. Buy the best knives you can afford—they will last for many years.

MEASURING SPOONS & CUPS: One full set of measuring spoons and two sets of measuring cups. One set should be for measuring liquids—those measuring cups usually have handles and pour spouts—and one set for measuring dry ingredients that can be leveled off.

SLOW COOKER: Buy one that's the right size for your family. A great tool for people on the go: a lot of recipes can be made in minutes before work and be ready to eat for dinner.

STORAGE CONTAINERS: Storage containers aren't just for storing leftovers, but can also hold any unused ingredients that come from making dinner.

UTENSILS: Heat-resistant nonstick spatulas, vegetable peeler, rolling pin, meat mallet, a slotted spoon for draining, a wire whisk, tongs, a few wooden spoons, ladle, a microplane grater for zesting citrus.

Meat & Poultry Cooking Guide

The best way to make sure meat and poultry are juicy and delicious is to cook them to the proper doneness. When you overcook meat and poultry they dry out and become tough—but you don't want to undercook them either. The most foolproof way to tell when meat is done, whether you're roasting, grilling or sautéing, is to use an instant-read thermometer. Insert the thermometer about 2 inches into the thickest part of the meat without touching bone. The temperature should register within about 15 seconds (the thermometers are not designed to stay in the food while it's cooking). Look for them at supermarkets or kitchenware shops.

GIVE IT A REST The purpose of allowing meat to rest (sit off the heat after cooking) is to let the juices inside redistribute before you cut into it. This makes the meat more juicy and tender when you eat it. The other thing that happens during resting is that the internal temperature of the cooked meat rises as it rests. How much depends on the size of the meat, how long it rests and the temperature at which it was cooked. One rule of thumb is that the temperature will rise 5 to 10 degrees per 10 minutes of resting. We recommend that larger roasts or whole birds should rest longer than smaller pieces of meat. For example a whole turkey should rest for about a half an hour, while a grilled steak should rest for 5 or 10 minutes.

EATINGWELL Recommended Internal Temperatures* (before resting)		
	Rare	130°F
Beef & Lamb	Medium-rare	140°F
	Medium	145°F
	Well-done	160°F
Bison (steak)	Medium-rare	125°F
Pork	Medium	145°F
	Well-done	160°F
Chicken & Turkey	Well-done	165°F
Duck Breast	Medium	150°F

*The USDA conservatively recommends cooking beef, pork and lamb to higher temperatures; we find this usually yields overdone results, so we offer a lower target. Whole poultry should cook to 165°F. We make an exception for boneless duck breast, which tastes better cooked to medium (150°F). People who are very young, very old or who have compromised immune systems should stick to the USDA recommendations (for more information call the USDA Meat & Poultry hotline, 1-888-674-6854).

Hot Tips for Better Grilling

GAS VS. CHARCOAL? While no studies prove that either is healthier, gas does burn cleaner. Charcoal grills emit more carbon monoxide, particulate matter and soot into the atmosphere, contributing to increased pollution and higher concentrations of ground-level ozone. From a taste perspective, on the other hand, many people prefer the smokier, richer taste of food cooked on a charcoal grill.

IF YOU DO CHOOSE CHARCOAL GRILLING, we recommend additive-free lump charcoal, which is just charred wood. Conventional briquettes may contain wood scraps and sawdust as well as coal dust, sodium nitrate, borax and additives like paraffin or lighter fluid. As for lighter fluid, avoid it altogether. Lighter fluid can release volatile organic compounds (VOCs) into the air and leave an unpleasant residue on food.

USE A CHIMNEY STARTER TO GET CHARCOAL BURNING. They're inexpensive and you can pick them up at a local hardware store. All you have to do is put a piece of crumpled newspaper in the bottom of it, fill the top with charcoal and light the paper. The coals will be ready in about 20 minutes.

GET IT HOT! Preheat your grill 15 to 25 minutes before you start cooking to make sure it reaches the right temperature (and to kill any bacteria). Your grill should be 400-450°F for high, 350-400°F for medium-high, 300-350°F for medium and 250-300°F for low heat. A properly heated grill sears foods on contact, keeps the insides moist and helps prevent sticking. While searing doesn't "seal in" the juices (contrary to popular belief), it does create improved flavors through caramelization.

THE HAND TEST. To gauge the temperature of a grill without a thermometer, place your open palm about 5 inches above the grill rack; the fire is high if you have to move your hand in 2 seconds, medium if you have to move your hand in 5 seconds and low if you have to move your hand in 10 seconds.

BRUSH IT OFF. After preheating, use a long-handled wire grill brush on your grill rack to clean off charred debris from prior meals. Scrape again immediately after use.

OIL IT UP. Reduce sticking by oiling your hot grill rack with a canola oil-soaked paper towel: hold it with tongs and rub it over the rack. (Do not use cooking spray on a hot grill.)

SAFETY FIRST. Never baste with the marinade. (Make extra marinade just for basting or boil your marinating liquid first.)

IS IT DONE? The best way to know if protein is fully cooked is to check its internal temperature with an instant-read thermometer. For cooking times and temperatures, see chart, *opposite*.

USE A GRILL BASKET for foods that might fall through the grill rack or are too cumbersome to turn over one by one. If you don't have one, fold a 24-inch-long piece of heavy-duty foil in half and crimp up the edges to create a lip. Place foil on the grill and cook food directly on foil.

TAME THE FLAMES. Flare-ups happen when fat drips onto the heat source and catches fire. This causes carcinogenic PAHs (polycyclic aromatic hydrocarbons) to form and accumulate on your food. Meat licked by flames also tastes "off" and flames may char the outside of food before the inside has cooked. To reduce flare-ups, select lean meat, trim excess fat and remove poultry skin. And, keep a squirt bottle of water nearby to quickly douse any flare-ups.

KEEP THE LID CLOSED. Unless specified, close the lid while grilling. This traps in the heat and cooks food more quickly.

Grilling Times

Pick one of these lean, quick-cooking proteins—plan on 4 ounces per person. Pair with one of our rubs or marinades (page 352). Follow the marinating times, cooking times and temperatures for juicy, perfect grilling results.

	MARINATING TIME	COOKING TIME* & DONENESS TEMPERATURE	NUTRITION INFORMATION**
Extra-Firm Tofu	30 minutes to overnight	2-3 minutes per side	90 calories; 6 g fat (1 g sat, 4g mono); 0 mg cholesterol; 10 g protein; 8 mg sodium.
Shrimp	15 to 30 minutes	2-3 minutes per side	85 calories; 1 g fat (0 g sat, 0 g mono); 168 mg cholesterol; 18 g protein; 193 mg sodium.
Scallops	5 minutes	3-4 minutes per side	100 calories; 1 g fat (0 g sat, 0 g mono); 37 mg cholesterol; 19 g protein; 183 mg sodium.
Salmon Fillet	30 minutes	3-5 minutes per side	134 calories; 4 g fat (1 g sat, 2g mono); 53 mg cholesterol; 23 g protein; 56 mg sodium.
Mahi-Mahi	30 minutes to 1 hour	5-6 minutes per side	96 calories; 1 g fat (0 g sat, 0 g mono); 83 mg cholesterol; 21 g protein; 100 mg sodium.
Chicken Breast boneless, skinless	2 hours to overnight	6-8 minutes per side; 165°F	122 calories; 3 g fat (1 g sat, 1 g mono); 63 mg cholesterol; 23 g protein; 55 mg sodium.
Chicken Thighs boneless, skinless	2 hours to overnight	6-8 minutes per side; 165°F	164 calories; 9 g fat (2 g sat, 3 g mono); 74 mg cholesterol; 20 g protein; 69 mg sodium.
Chicken Thighs bone-in, skinless	2 hours to overnight	15-25 minutes, turning occasionally; 165°F	178 calories; 9 g fat (3 g sat, 4 g mono); 81 mg cholesterol; 22 g protein; 75 mg sodium.
Duck Breast boneless, skinless	2 hours to overnight	4-8 minutes per side; 150°F	141 calories; 8 g fat (3 g sat, 3 g mono); 63 mg cholesterol; 17 g protein; 46 mg sodium.
Pork Chops bone-in, ¾" thick	2 hours to overnight	3-4 minutes per side; 145°F for medium	142 calories; 6 g fat (2 g sat, 2 g mono); 66 mg cholesterol; 21 g protein; 44 mg sodium.
Pork Tenderloin	2 hours to overnight	14-16 minutes, turning occasionally; 145°F	124 calories; 2 g fat (1 g sat, 1 g mono); 74 mg cholesterol; 24 g protein; 60 mg sodium.
Flank Steak	2 hours to overnight	6-8 minutes per side; 140°F for medium-rare	160 calories; 6 g fat (2 g sat, 2 g mono); 37 mg cholesterol; 24 g protein; 62 mg sodium.
Strip Steak bone-in, ¾"-1" thick	2 hours to overnight	4-5 minutes per side; 140°F for medium-rare	142 calories; 5 g fat (2 g sat, 2 g mono); 49 mg cholesterol; 22 g protein; 46 mg sodium.
Lamb Loin Chops	2 hours to overnight	5-6 minutes per side; 145°F for medium	174 calories; 12 g fat (6 g sat, 5 g mono); 66 mg cholesterol; 14 g protein; 29 mg sodium.

*All cooking times based on medium-high grill temperature and cooking with the grill lid closed.

**Nutritional analysis is for the standard 3-ounce "cooked" portion of meat, fish, tofu or poultry listed as a typical serving in *MyPyramid.gov*. Although our recipes call for 4 ounces per serving uncooked, 1 ounce of water weight is generally lost during cooking.

The Healthy Pantry

While a good shopping list is the key to a quick and painless trip to the supermarket, a well-stocked pantry is the best way to ensure you'll have everything you need to cook once you get home. Our Healthy Pantry includes many of the items you need to prepare the recipes in this book plus a few other ingredients that will make impromptu meals easier.

OILS, VINEGARS & CONDIMENTS
Oils: extra-virgin olive, canola
Vinegars: balsamic, red-wine, white-wine, rice, cider
Asian condiments: reduced-sodium soy sauce, fish sauce, hoisin sauce, oyster sauce, chile-garlic sauce, toasted sesame oil
Barbecue sauce
Hot sauce
Worcestershire sauce
Mustard: Dijon, whole-grain
Ketchup
Mayonnaise, low-fat

FLAVORINGS
Salt: kosher, iodized table
Black peppercorns
Herbs and spices, assorted dried
Onions
Garlic, fresh
Ginger, fresh
Olives: Kalamata, green
Capers
Anchovies or anchovy paste
Lemons, limes, oranges

DRY GOODS
Pasta, whole-wheat (assorted shapes)
Barley: pearl, quick-cooking
Bulgur
Couscous, whole-wheat
Quinoa
Rice: brown, instant brown, wild
Dried beans and lentils
Flour: whole-wheat, whole-wheat pastry (*store opened packages in the refrigerator or freezer*), all-purpose
Rolled oats
Cornmeal
Breadcrumbs: plain dry, coarse whole-wheat
Crackers, whole-grain
Unsweetened cocoa powder
Bittersweet chocolate
Sweeteners: granulated sugar, brown sugar, honey, pure maple syrup

NUTS, SEEDS & FRUITS
(*Store opened packages of nuts and seeds in the refrigerator or freezer.*)
Nuts: walnuts, pecans, almonds, hazelnuts, peanuts, pine nuts
Natural peanut butter
Seeds: pepitas, sesame seeds, sunflower seeds
Tahini (sesame paste)
Dried fruits: apricots, prunes, cherries, cranberries, dates, figs, raisins

CANNED & BOTTLED GOODS
Broth: reduced-sodium beef, chicken and/or vegetable (*or see page 78 for broth recipes*)
Clam juice
"Lite" coconut milk
Tomatoes, tomato paste
Beans: black, cannellini, kidney, pinto, great northern, chickpeas, lentils
Chunk light tuna
Wild Pacific salmon
Wine: red, white or nonalcoholic
Madeira
Sherry, dry

REFRIGERATOR ITEMS
Milk, low-fat or nonfat
Buttermilk or buttermilk powder
Yogurt, plain and/or vanilla, low-fat or nonfat
Sour cream, reduced-fat or nonfat
Parmesan cheese, good-quality
Cheddar cheese, sharp
Eggs (large) or egg substitute, such as Egg Beaters
Orange juice
Tofu, water-packed
Tortillas: corn, whole-wheat

FREEZER BASICS
Fruit: berries, other fruit
Vegetables: peas, spinach, broccoli, corn

Glossary

In 2008, the average U.S. supermarket carried over 45,000 different items, with new items being added all the time. With that sort of variety, it's no wonder you may sometimes be confused by all the choices. Here's a listing of some of the ingredients we call for in this book, what they are, helpful hints about what to look for, where to find them and how to use them. This glossary also includes some of the techniques that we use throughout the book. For more information on cooking terms we use, see page 471.

ALMOND BUTTER: Almond butter can be found at natural-foods stores and large supermarkets, near the peanut butter.

AMARETTO: Amaretto is an almond-flavored liqueur. Look for it at the liquor store or replace it with 4 tablespoons orange juice mixed with ¼ teaspoon almond extract.

ANDOUILLE SAUSAGE: Andouille sausage is a smoky, mildly spicy pork sausage commonly used in Cajun cooking. Look for it near other smoked sausages in large supermarkets or specialty food stores.

APPLE BUTTER: Apple butter is made by cooking down apple sauce until the sugars in the apples caramelize. Look for it near other fruit spreads and jams at most large supermarkets.

ARTICHOKE, HOW TO TRIM: Using a sharp knife, remove ½ inch of leaves from the cone-shaped artichoke top. Trim ½ to 1 inch off the stem end. Remove the small, tough outer layer(s) of leaves from the stem end and snip all remaining spiky tips from the rest of the outer leaves using a pair of kitchen shears. Rub the whole artichoke, especially the cut portions, with the cut side of a lemon half. (*Photographs: page 109.*)

BEAN THREAD NOODLES: Sometimes labeled mung bean, glass or cellophane noodles, bean thread noodles can be found in the Asian section of most large supermarkets or at Asian markets.

BEEF TENDERLOIN: When you purchase beef tenderloin, ask your butcher to remove the extra fat, silver skin and the chain (a lumpy, fat-covered piece of meat that runs along the tender-

loin). If you buy untrimmed tenderloin (purchase more than the recipe calls for), use a sharp knife to trim the silver skin, fat and chain.

BLACK BEAN-GARLIC SAUCE: Black bean-garlic sauce is a savory sauce used in Chinese cooking, made from fermented black soybeans, garlic and rice wine. Find it in the Asian-foods section of most supermarkets or at Asian markets. Refrigerate for up to 1 year.

BREADCRUMBS, HOW TO MAKE: To make your own **fresh breadcrumbs**, trim crusts from whole-wheat bread. Tear bread into pieces and process in a food processor until coarse crumbs form. To make **fine breadcrumbs**, process until very fine. To make **dry breadcrumbs**, spread coarse or fine breadcrumbs on a baking sheet and bake at 250°F until dry, about 10 to 15 minutes. One slice of bread makes about ½ cup fresh breadcrumbs or about ⅓ cup dry breadcrumbs. For store-bought coarse dry breadcrumbs we like Ian's brand, labeled "Panko breadcrumbs." Find them at well-stocked supermarkets.

BREAD, RISING: Cooler temperatures will slow the rising time. If your room is cool or you want to try to speed up the rising process, create a warm environment by microwaving ½ cup water in a 1-cup glass measure just to boiling. Set the water in one corner of the microwave, place the covered dough on the other side of the turned-off microwave and close the door.

BROILER-SAFE BAKING DISH: A broiler-safe baking dish is one that is made of metal or earthenware. Glass baking dishes, such as Pyrex, may shatter under the broiler.

BROTH, HOW TO COOL QUICKLY: *See page 79.*

BROTH, MUSHROOM: Mushroom broth is a savory vegetarian broth made from mushrooms. Look for it in aseptic containers at well-stocked supermarkets or natural-foods stores.

BROTH, NO-CHICKEN: We prefer "no-chicken broth," a vegetarian chicken-flavored broth, to vegetable broth in some recipes for its hearty, rich flavor. Look for it at well-stocked supermarkets.

BULGUR: Bulgur is made by parboiling, drying and coarsely grinding or cracking wheat berries. Don't confuse bulgur with cracked wheat, which is simply that—cracked wheat. Since the parboiling step is skipped, cracked wheat must be cooked for up to an hour whereas bulgur simply needs a quick soak in hot water for most uses. Look for it in the natural-foods section of large supermarkets, near other grains, or online at *kalustyans.com* or *buylebanese.com*.

BUTTERMILK: Buttermilk is a thick, tangy cow's-milk dairy product. Find both low-fat and nonfat versions in the dairy section of the supermarket. You can replace buttermilk in any recipe with an equal amount of "sour milk." Mix 1 tablespoon lemon juice or vinegar to 1 cup low-fat or nonfat milk. Or use buttermilk powder (found in the baking section) prepared according to package directions.

CALAMARI: Also known as squid, calamari is sold frozen or fresh in the seafood department of the grocery store. Look for cleaned calamari, with its cartilage and ink removed; otherwise ask at the fish counter to have it cleaned.

CALLALOO: Callaloo is commonly referred to as amaranth in the U.S. and some farmers consider it to be simply a weed. It has a texture somewhere between that of collard greens and spinach, both of which are fine substitutes. Look for it in bunches at farmers' market or Caribbean markets.

CAULIFLOWER, HOW TO PREP: To prepare florets from a whole head of cauliflower, remove outer leaves. Slice off the thick stem. With the head upside down and holding a knife at a 45° angle, slice into the smaller stems with a circular motion—removing a "plug" from the center of the head. Break or cut florets into the desired size. (*Photograph: page 121.*)

CAVIAR: Caviar (salted sturgeon eggs) from U.S. farmed sturgeon is considered the best choice for the environment. Most imported caviar comes from overfished wild sturgeon.

CELERY ROOT, HOW TO PEEL: *See* Root Vegetables.

CHEESE, HOW TO MAKE CURLS: Use a vegetable peeler to shave curls off blocks of hard cheeses, like Parmigiano-Reggiano or Pecorino Romano.

CHESTNUTS: Chestnuts are available cooked and peeled in jars in the baking aisle or with seasonal foods at many supermarkets. They can also be purchased whole and prepared at home. **To prepare fresh chestnuts:** Using a small knife, score a cross on the flat side of each chestnut. Using a slotted spoon, dip chestnuts, 4 or 5 at a time, into a saucepan of boiling water. Peel away shells and inner brown skins. If chestnuts are difficult to peel, return them to boiling water for a few seconds. Place peeled chestnuts in a large saucepan and add enough water to cover. Simmer, covered, until tender, 30 to 45 minutes. Drain and refresh with cold water. Eight ounces of fresh chestnuts yields about 1 cup peeled and cooked.

CHICKEN, BREAST & TENDERS: It's difficult to find an individual chicken breast small enough for one portion. Removing the thin strip of meat from the underside of a 5-ounce breast—the tender—removes about 1 ounce of meat and yields a perfect 4-ounce portion. (Wrap and freeze tenders for another meal.) If you can only find chicken breasts closer to 8 or 9 ounces each, you'll just need 2 breasts for 4 servings—cut each in half before cooking. Chicken tenders can also be purchased separately. Four 1-ounce tenders yield a 3-ounce cooked portion. Use tenders for stir-fries, chicken satay or kid-friendly chicken "fingers" or "nuggets."

CHICKEN, HOW TO BUTTERFLY WHOLE: *See page 349.*
CHICKEN, HOW TO CARVE ROAST: *See page 345.*
CHICKEN, HOW TO CUT UP WHOLE: *See page 329.*

CHICKEN, HOW TO POACH: If you want cooked chicken in a hurry, the easiest way to cook it is to poach it. Place boneless, skinless chicken breasts in a skillet or saucepan. Add lightly salted water (or chicken broth) to cover and bring to a boil. Cover, reduce heat to low and simmer gently until the chicken is cooked through and no longer pink in the middle, 10 to 15 minutes. (1 pound raw boneless, skinless chicken breasts = about 2½ cups chopped or shredded cooked chicken)

CHILE-GARLIC SAUCE: A blend of ground chiles, garlic and vinegar, chile-garlic sauce is commonly used to add heat and flavor to Asian soups, sauces and stir-fries. It can be found in the Asian section of large supermarkets (sometimes labeled as chili-garlic sauce or paste) and keeps up to 1 year in the refrigerator.

CHILES: *See* Peppers.

CHINKIANG: Chinkiang is a dark vinegar with a smoky flavor. It is available in many Asian specialty markets. If unavailable, white or sherry vinegar are acceptable substitutes.

CHOCOLATE, HOW TO MELT: Place chocolate chips (or chopped chocolate) in a bowl and microwave on Medium for 45 seconds. Stir; continue microwaving on Medium, stirring every 20 seconds, until almost melted. Continue stirring until completely melted. Or place in the top of a double boiler over hot, but not boiling, water. Stir until melted.

CHORIZO: Chorizo, a spicy pork sausage seasoned with paprika and chile, is originally from Spain and is often used in Mexican cooking. Chorizo can be made with raw or smoked, ground or chopped pork. Chorizo is available at well-stocked supermarkets, specialty food stores or online at *tienda.com*.

CITRUS, HOW TO SEGMENT: Slice both ends off the fruit. With a sharp knife, remove the peel and white pith; discard. Working over a bowl, cut the segments from their surrounding membranes. Squeeze juice into the bowl before discarding membrane, if desired. (*Photographs: page 452.*)

CITRUS ZEST: When we call for citrus zest (i.e., ½ teaspoon lemon zest) we are referring to the finely grated outer rind (not including the white pith) of the citrus fruit. Use a microplane grater or the smallest holes of a box grater to grate the zest. In some cases we call for long strips or threads of zest. To get long strips, peel the citrus with a vegetable peeler. To remove long threads, use a 5-hole citrus zester or remove long strips of zest with a vegetable peeler, then use a knife to cut into very thin strips. (*Photographs: page 408.*)

CLAM JUICE: Bottled clam juice can be very high in sodium. We like Bar Harbor brand, which has 120 mg sodium per 2-ounce serving. Look for it in the canned-fish section or the seafood department of your supermarket.

COCOA NIBS: You can find cocoa nibs (also called cacao nibs)—bits of roasted and hulled cocoa beans—at well-stocked grocery stores, gourmet retailers or online at *chocosphere.com*.

COCONUT MILK, LEFTOVER: Refrigerate leftover coconut milk for up to 1 week or freeze for up to 2 months. It will appear separated when thawed; simply mix until smooth.

COD: For sustainably fished cod, choose U.S. Pacific cod or Atlantic cod from Iceland and the northeast Arctic. For more information, visit Monterey Bay Aquarium Seafood Watch at *seafoodwatch.org*.

COLESLAW MIX: Look for preshredded cabbage-and-carrot "coleslaw mix" in the produce section. Or make your own by tossing together very thinly sliced cabbage and grated carrots.

CORN, HOW TO REMOVE KERNELS: Stand an ear of corn on one end and slice the kernels off with a sharp knife. (*Photograph: page 125.*) One ear will yield about ½ cup kernels.

CORNMEAL: If you want to use whole-grain cornmeal, look for finely ground cornmeal labeled "whole-grain" or "stone-ground" at the supermarket or at natural-foods stores. Avoid ones labeled "degerminated." Store it in the freezer.

COTIJA CHEESE: Cotija cheese, also called *queso añejo* or *queso añejado*, is a salty aged Mexican cheese with a crumbly texture. Find it near other specialty cheeses or at Mexican grocery stores.

CRABMEAT: Crabmeat (already removed from the shell) can be purchased canned, in shelf-stable pouches, frozen or pasteurized. Pasteurized usually has the best flavor; look for it in the fresh seafood section of the market. Crab from the U.S. and Canada are both considered good choices for the environment.

CRANBERRIES, HOW TO CHOP: To make quick work of chopping cranberries, place whole berries in a food processor and pulse a few times until the berries are coarsely chopped.

CRÈME FRAÎCHE: Crème fraîche is a tangy, thick, rich cultured cream. Find it in the dairy section of large supermarkets, usually near other specialty cheeses. Sour cream or a combination of equal parts reduced-fat sour cream and nonfat plain yogurt can be substituted.

CROUTONS, HOW TO MAKE: Tear or dice 3 slices of whole-grain bread into ½- to 1-inch pieces. Place on a large baking sheet and toss with 1 tablespoon olive oil. Season with pepper. Bake in a 400°F oven until golden brown and crisp, 10 to 12 minutes. Makes about 2 cups. Store airtight at room temperature for up to 3 days.

DOLMAS: Dolmas are stuffed grape leaves that are traditionally filled with chopped vegetables, grains and sometimes ground meat. Find prepared dolmas in cans or jars near other Middle Eastern ingredients and at some supermarket salad bars.

DRIED CHINESE NOODLES: Dried Chinese noodles, often used in Chinese soups and lo mein, cook quickly and can be found at well-stocked supermarkets or at Asian markets.

DUCK BREAST: Boneless duck breasts range widely in weight, from about ½ to 1 pound, depending on the breed of duck. We prefer the milder flavor of smaller (about ½-pound) breasts. Look for them near other poultry in the fresh or frozen specialty-meat section of well-stocked supermarkets or online at *mapleleaffarms.com* or *dartagnan.com*.

EGGS, HOW TO HARD-BOIL: Place eggs in a single layer in a saucepan; cover with water. Bring to a simmer over medium-high heat. Reduce heat to low and cook at the barest simmer for 10 minutes. Remove from heat, pour out hot water and cover the eggs with ice-cold water. Let stand until cool enough to handle before peeling.

EGGS, HOW TO POACH: Fill a large, straight-sided skillet or Dutch oven with 2 inches of water; bring to a boil. Add ¼ cup distilled white vinegar. Reduce to a gentle simmer: the water should be steaming and small bubbles should come up from the bottom of the pan. Working with one at a time, break an egg into a small bowl, submerge the lip of the bowl into the simmering water and gently add the egg. (Don't poach more than 4 at a time in a large skillet or pot.) Cook for 4 minutes for soft set, 5 minutes for medium set and 8 minutes for hard set. Using a slotted spoon, transfer the eggs to a clean dish towel to drain for a minute before serving. (*Photographs: page 287.*)

EGGS, ROOM TEMPERATURE: To bring an egg to room temperature, either set it out on the counter for 15 minutes or submerge it (in the shell) in a bowl of lukewarm (not hot) water for 5 minutes.

EGGS, SOFT OR STIFF PEAKS: When egg whites are beaten to "soft" peaks, the whites will still be soft enough to curl over when a beater is turned upside down. The whites are considered "stiff" peaks when they remain stiff and upright. (*Photographs: page 392.*)

EGG WHITES, DRIED: Pasteurized dried egg whites are a wise choice in recipes that call for uncooked egg whites. Look for brands like Just Whites in the baking or natural-foods section of most supermarkets. Reconstitute according to package directions or the recipe.

ESPRESSO: If you don't have an espresso maker, use instant espresso powder and water; store the powder in your freezer after opening. Strong brewed coffee or instant coffee will also work in a pinch, it just won't be as full-flavored.

FARRO: Farro is a type of whole-grain wheat used in Italian cooking. Barley or wheat berries can often be substituted if you cannot find farro. Find it at natural-foods stores and at *amazon.com*.

FENNEL, HOW TO PREP: Cut off the stalks and fronds where they meet the bulb, remove any damaged outer layers and cut ¼ inch off the bottom. Quarter the bulb lengthwise and cut out the core. The edible fronds are a delicious garnish for any dish containing the bulb. (*Photograph: page 129.*)

FISH SAUCE: Fish sauce is a pungent Southeast Asian condiment made from salted, fermented fish. Find it in the Asian-food section of well-stocked supermarkets and at Asian specialty markets. We use Thai Kitchen fish sauce, lower in sodium than other brands (1,190 mg per tablespoon), in our recipe testing and nutritional analyses.

FLOUR, BREAD: Milled from high-protein wheat, bread flour develops strong gluten, resulting in well-risen loaves. It helps give breads with a high percentage of whole grains better structure and a lighter texture. Find it near other flours at most supermarkets.

FLOUR, HOW TO MEASURE: *See page 471.*

FLOUR, OAT: Oat flour, made from finely milled whole oats, is a good source of dietary fiber and whole grains. It can replace some of the all-purpose flour in many baking recipes and adds an oat flavor and texture. Find it at large supermarkets and natural-foods stores and at *bobsredmill.com*.

FLOUR, SEMOLINA: Look for semolina flour, a nutty-tasting, coarse flour milled from durum wheat, at natural-foods stores and Italian specialty markets.

FLOUR, WHITE WHOLE-WHEAT: White whole-wheat flour, made from a special variety of white wheat, is light in color and flavor but has the same nutritional properties as regular whole-wheat flour. It is available at large supermarkets and natural-foods stores and online at *bobsredmill.com* or *kingarthurflour.com*. Store it in the freezer.

FLOUR, WHOLE-WHEAT PASTRY: Whole-wheat pastry flour is milled from soft wheat. It contains less gluten than regular whole-wheat flour and helps ensure a tender result in delicate baked goods while providing the nutritional benefits of whole grains. Find it at large supermarkets and natural-foods stores. Store in an airtight container in the freezer.

GARLIC, HOW TO ROAST: Rub off the excess papery skin from 1 large head of garlic without separating the cloves. Slice the tip off the head, exposing the ends of the cloves. Place the garlic on a piece of foil, drizzle with 1 tablespoon extra-virgin olive oil and wrap into a package. Bake at 400°F in a small baking dish until the garlic is very soft, 40 minutes to 1 hour. Unwrap and let cool slightly before squeezing the cloves out.

GINGER JUICE: Bottled ginger juice is made from pressed gingerroot. You can use it to add the taste of fresh ginger without the work of mincing or grating. Use it to flavor drinks, stir-fries, marinades or anywhere you'd use fresh ginger. Find it at specialty food stores or online at *gingerpeople.com*.

GNOCCHI: We like the texture of "shelf-stable" prepared gnocchi found near pasta in many supermarkets. To make your own, see page 248.

GRILL BASKET, HOW TO IMPROVISE: Fold a 24-inch-long piece of heavy-duty foil in half; crimp edges to create a lip. This "basket" will keep small items from falling through the grill rack.

GRILL RACK, HOW TO OIL: Oiling a grill rack before you grill foods helps ensure that the food won't stick. Oil a folded paper towel, hold it with tongs and rub it over the rack. (Do not use cooking spray on a hot grill.) When grilling delicate foods like tofu and fish, it is helpful to coat the food with cooking spray.

GRITS: Look for quick grits (ready in 5 minutes) near other hot cereals or near cornmeal in the baking aisle.

HADDOCK: Atlantic haddock (sometimes labeled scrod) populations are making a comeback after years of overfishing. Avoid haddock caught using bottom trawl gear which can damage the seafloor and also causes a lot of wasted bycatch. Hook-and-line-caught Atlantic haddock is considered a "good alternative" by Monterey Bay Aquarium Seafood Watch.

HALIBUT: Wild-caught halibut from the Pacific is sustainably fished and has a larger, more stable population, according to Monterey Bay Aquarium Seafood Watch (*seafoodwatch.org*).

HARICOTS VERTS: Haricots verts is simply French for "green beans." However, the term is often used for the very slender beans, also called French beans, found at large supermarkets.

HARISSA: Harissa, a fiery North African chile paste, is available at specialty-food stores or at *amazon.com*. Harissa in a tube will be much hotter than that in a jar. You can use Chinese or Thai chile-garlic sauce instead.

HOISIN: Hoisin sauce is a thick, dark brown, spicy-sweet sauce made from soybeans and a complex mix of spices. Look for it in the Asian section of your supermarket.

HOT SESAME OIL: This spicy oil is made from pressed, toasted sesame seeds infused with hot chile peppers. Look for it at Asian markets or in the Asian-foods section of well-stocked supermarkets.

KIRSCH: Kirsch (a.k.a. kirschwasser) is clear cherry brandy, commonly used as a flavor enhancer in fondue and cherries jubilee. Find it at liquor stores.

LADYFINGERS: These small cookies come in two different styles—one has a soft, sponge-cake texture and is found in the in-store bakery of most supermarkets. The other is crunchy, usually imported from Italy and found near specialty cookies at the supermarket or specialty food stores. Use the soft ladyfingers for the trifle recipes in this book.

LAVASH: Lavash is thin, Middle Eastern bread found near other wraps and tortillas. It's a great alternative to flour tortillas for rolling sandwich ingredients into a wrap.

LINGUIÇA: This cured sausage from Portugal is seasoned with garlic and paprika. It's commonly used in Portuguese and Brazilian cooking. Look for it at specialty food stores and well-stocked supermarkets.

MÂCHE: Mâche (pronounced "mosh"), also known as lamb's lettuce or corn salad, is a tangy green that resembles watercress. Popular in Europe, it is enjoyed in the first salads of spring. Look for it at specialty food stores, large supermarkets and farmers' markets.

MADEIRA: Madeira, a fortified wine from the Portuguese island of Madeira, has a sweet, mellow flavor somewhat like sherry. Find it at liquor stores or in the wine section of the supermarket.

MAHI-MAHI: Mahi-mahi (also called dorado) is a firm, meaty fish with a mild flavor. Look for mahi-mahi that was caught with a pole and line or trawl caught. Avoid imported longline-caught mahi. For more information, go to *seafoodwatch.org*.

MANGO CHUTNEY: Look for prepared mango chutney—a sweet, tangy and spicy condiment—near other Indian ingredients in the international aisle at most supermarkets.

MANGO, HOW TO CUT: Slice both ends off the mango, revealing the long, slender seed inside. Set the fruit upright on a work surface and remove the skin with a sharp knife. With the seed perpendicular to you, slice the fruit from both sides of the seed, yielding two large pieces. Turn the seed parallel to you and slice the two smaller pieces of fruit from each side. Cut into desired size. (*Photographs: page 263.*)

MARCONA ALMONDS: Spanish Marcona almonds are flatter than ordinary almonds, with a richer flavor. Always skinned, most have been sautéed in oil and lightly salted when you get them. Find them at specialty food stores or online at *tienda.com*.

MEYER LEMONS: Meyer lemons have a distinct sweet, tart, floral taste. Look for them in late winter and early spring at well-stocked supermarkets and specialty food stores. If you can't find them, use a combination of regular lemons and oranges (juice and/or zest depending on the recipe) instead.

MIRIN: Mirin is a low-alcohol rice wine essential to Japanese cooking. Look for it in the Asian section of the supermarket or at Asian markets. An equal portion of dry sherry or white wine with a pinch of sugar may be substituted.

MISO, WHITE AND RED: Miso is fermented soybean paste made by inoculating a mixture of soybeans, salt and grains (usually barley or rice) with koji, a beneficial mold. Miso is undeniably salty, so a little goes a long way. White or sweet miso (Shiromiso), made with soy and rice, is yellow and milder in flavor; use for soup, salad dressings and sauces for fish or chicken. Red miso (Akamiso), made from barley or rice and soy, is salty and tangy, and the most commonly used miso in Japan. Use in marinades for meat and oily fish, and in long-simmered dishes. Look for it near tofu at well-stocked supermarkets.

MUSSELS, HOW TO CLEAN: Discard mussels with broken shells or whose shell remains open after you tap it. Hold mussels under running water and use a stiff brush to remove any barnacles; pull off any black fibrous "beards" (*photograph: page 304*).

(Some mussels may not have a beard.) Mussels should be "debearded" no more than 30 minutes before cooking.

NONREACTIVE PAN, BOWL OR BAKING DISH: A nonreactive bowl, pan or baking dish—stainless-steel, enamel-coated or glass—is necessary when cooking with acidic foods, such as lemon, to prevent the food from reacting with the pan. Reactive pans, such as aluminum and cast-iron, can impart off colors and/or flavors.

NORI: Toasted nori sheets are thin, dried seaweed wrappers used for sushi maki rolls. Be sure to choose nori that is labeled "toasted" when making maki—untoasted nori is too chewy. Look for them in the Asian section of the supermarket or at Asian markets.

NUTS, HOW TO TOAST: To toast **whole nuts**, spread on a baking sheet and bake at 350°F, stirring once, until fragrant, 7 to 9 minutes. To toast **chopped, small or sliced nuts**, cook in a small dry skillet over medium-low heat, stirring constantly, until fragrant and lightly browned, 2 to 4 minutes.

ONIONS, HOW TO CHOP WITHOUT CRYING: Onions contain a volatile compound called a lachrymator that reacts with the fluid in your eyes and makes them water. To chop them without crying, try wearing goggles or burning a candle nearby.

OREGANO, MEXICAN: This herb tastes similar to Mediterranean oregano but comes from a different plant. The Mexican variety has a stronger flavor and is native to the American Southwest and Mexico. Look for it at well-stocked supermarkets or online at *penzeys.com*.

OYSTER SAUCE: Oyster sauce is a richly flavored Chinese condiment made from oysters and brine. Vegetarian oyster sauces substitute mushrooms for the oysters. Both can be found in the Asian section of large supermarkets or at Asian markets.

PAPRIKA: Paprika is a spice made from grinding dried red peppers. Paprika specifically labeled **Hungarian** delivers a fuller, richer flavor than regular paprika. **Smoked paprika** is made from smoke-dried red peppers and adds earthy, smoky flavor. It can be used in many types of savory dishes. Look for different types of paprika at some large supermarkets or at *tienda.com* or *penzeys.com*.

PARSNIPS, HOW TO PREP: Remove the peel with a vegetable peeler, then quarter the parsnip lengthwise and cut out the fibrous, woody core with a paring knife.

PASTRY BAG, HOW TO IMPROVISE: Fill a 1-quart sealable plastic bag with whatever you want to pipe. Seal the bag almost completely, leaving a small opening for air to escape from the top as you squeeze. Snip off one corner of the bag with scissors, making an opening the size you desire. Fold the top of the bag over a few times, then gently push whatever you're piping down to the snipped corner and proceed with piping in whatever pattern you desire or according to the recipe. (*Photographs: page 154.*)

PEACH, HOW TO PEEL: Dip peaches in boiling water for 30 or 40 seconds to loosen their skins. Let cool slightly, then slip off skins with a paring knife.

PEPPERS, ANCHO: Ancho peppers are dried poblano peppers. They add a not-too-hot, rich flavor to dishes. Look for whole dried anchos in the produce section and **ancho chile powder** in the spice section of well-stocked supermarkets.

PEPPERS, CASCABEL: Cascabels are small, reddish-brown, bell-shaped, medium-hot chile peppers with a rich flavor. Find them with other dried chiles in the produce section or ethnic section of well-stocked supermarkets or online at *melissas.com*.

PEPPERS, CHERRY: Look for red and/or green, jarred, mild (or sweet) cherry peppers near pickles and olives or in the "olive bar" at well-stocked supermarkets and specialty-food stores.

PEPPERS, CHIPOTLE: Chipotle peppers are dried, smoked jalapeños. Look for **ground chipotle** in the spice section of most supermarkets or online at *penzeys.com*.

PEPPERS, CHIPOTLE, IN ADOBO SAUCE: Chipotle chiles in adobo sauce are smoked jalapeños packed in a flavorful sauce. Look for the small cans with Mexican foods at large supermarkets. Once opened, they'll keep up to 2 weeks in the refrigerator or 6 months in the freezer.

PEPPERS, HOW TO ROAST TWO WAYS: 1. OVEN-ROASTING: Place on a baking sheet and bake at 450°F, turning occasionally, until soft, wrinkled and blackened in spots, 20 to 30 minutes. 2. GRILL-ROASTING: Preheat grill to high or prepare a hot charcoal fire. Grill peppers, turning frequently, until the skin is blistered on all sides and blackened in spots, about 10 minutes. 3. Transfer the roasted peppers to a large bowl and cover with plastic wrap. Let steam for 10 minutes to loosen the skins. Uncover and let cool. 4. Peel off the skin with your hands or a paring knife. Remove the stems and seeds. (*Photographs: page 54.*)

PEPPERS, NEW MEXICO: Anaheim chiles (a.k.a. New Mexico chiles) are 7 to 10 inches long, ripen from green to red and are mildly spicy. Look for them in the produce section at Latin markets or well-stocked supermarkets.

PEPPERS, PIQUILLO: These intensely flavored, spicy-sweet peppers from Spain are sold jarred or canned. Look for them at well-stocked supermarkets and gourmet-food shops or online at *spanishtable.com* or *tienda.com*.

PEPPERS, POBLANO: Poblano peppers (sometimes called pasilla peppers) are dark green, about 6 inches long and can be fiery or relatively mild; there's no way to tell until you taste them.

PEPPERS, SCOTCH BONNET: One of the hottest chile peppers, Scotch bonnets come in red, orange and green. They look similar to habaneros, but have a citrus note that makes them undeniably different. Control the heat of a dish a little by discarding the membranes that hold the seeds, which are the spiciest part of chile peppers, along with the seeds themselves. Wash your hands thoroughly after handling hot peppers or wear rubber gloves. Habaneros can be substituted.

PIE CRUST, HOW TO CRIMP OR FLUTE: Use a fork to crimp the edge. Or use two hands to pinch ("flute") the edge of the crust: push your thumb from one hand in between the thumb and index finger of the opposite. Or use one hand to pinch ("flute") the edge of the crust between your thumb and the side of your index finger. (*Photographs: page 423.*)

PIE CRUST, HOW TO MAKE A LATTICE TOP: *See page 425.*

PIMENTÓN DE LA VERA: Spain is known for its superb paprika called *Pimentón de la Vera*, which has a smoky flavor. Look for it at well-stocked supermarkets and gourmet-food shops or online at *spanishtable.com* or *tienda.com*.

PINEAPPLE, HOW TO PREPARE: Cut off the top and bottom of the pineapple with a sharp knife, making a stable flat base. Stand the pineapple upright and remove the skin. Use a paring knife to remove any remaining eyes. Slice the fruit away from the core. Discard core. Cut the fruit into the desired shape or size. (*Photographs: page 401.*)

PIZZA DOUGH: Look for fresh or frozen balls of whole-wheat pizza dough at your supermarket. Check the ingredient list to make sure the dough doesn't contain any hydrogenated oils. To make your own, see page 226.

PIZZA DOUGH, HOW TO ROLL OUT: Turn the dough out onto a lightly floured surface. Dust the top with flour; dimple with your fingertips to shape into a thick, flattened circle—don't worry if it's not perfectly symmetrical. Then use a rolling pin to roll into the desired size. If your dough "resists" being rolled out, let it rest for about 15 minutes, then try rolling it out again.

PORK TENDERLOIN, HOW TO DOUBLE BUTTERFLY: *See page 381.*

PORT: Port is a sweet fortified wine that provides depth of flavor in cooking. Tawny port is aged in oak, turning it brown (as opposed to dark-red ruby port). Look for it at your wine or liquor store.

PORTOBELLO MUSHROOM, HOW TO REMOVE GILLS: The dark gills found on the underside of a portobello mushroom cap are edible, but can turn a dish an unappealing gray color. If you like, gently scrape the gills off with a spoon.

POTATOES, PARTIALLY COOKED AND SHREDDED: Fresh, partially cooked, shredded potatoes for hash browns can be found in the refrigerated produce section or the dairy section of most supermarkets. Alternatively, boil potatoes until they can just be pierced with a fork but are not completely tender. Let cool slightly, then shred.

QUESO FRESCO: *Queso fresco*, also known as *queso blanco*, is a soft, slightly salty fresh Mexican cheese. You can find it at Latin markets and many supermarkets.

QUINOA: Quinoa is a delicately flavored, protein-rich grain. Rinsing removes any residue of saponin, quinoa's natural, bitter protective covering. Find it at natural-foods stores and well-stocked supermarkets.

RICE, BLACK STICKY: Black sticky rice, often called Forbidden rice, has a sweet, nutty taste and is high in fiber and rich in iron. When cooked, the brown-black rice turns a shade of purple-black. It may also be labeled "black glutinous rice" or "black sweet rice." Sushi rice, brown rice or regular white rice cannot be substituted for black sticky rice.

RICE, HOW TO COOK: Perfectly cooked rice can be tricky. To cook whole-grain rice, we recommend a pan with a tight-fitting lid, cooking on your coolest (or simmer) burner and making sure the rice is simmering at the "lowest bubble."

RICE-PAPER WRAPPERS: Rice-paper wrappers are translucent, round sheets made from rice flour. They need to briefly soak in warm water to make them soft and pliable before using. Find them in the Asian section of large supermarkets or at Asian food stores.

RICE, VALENCIA: Valencia rice (sometimes called paella rice) is Spanish-grown, short-grain rice used to make paella. It differs from other short-grain rice because it absorbs moisture without breaking down. When fully cooked, the individual grains remain whole. 'Bomba' is the best variety. Find it at specialty markets or online at *tienda.com*. Arborio rice can be used as a substitute, but yields a creamier dish.

RICE, WILD: Regular wild rice takes 40 to 50 minutes to cook. To save time, look for a quick-cooking variety that is ready in less than 30 minutes or instant wild rice, which is done in 10 minutes or less.

ROOT VEGETABLES, HOW TO PEEL: Beets, carrots and parsnips are easily peeled with a vegetable peeler, but for tougher-skinned roots like celery root, rutabaga and turnips, removing the peel with a knife can be easier. Cut off one end of the root to create a flat surface to keep it steady on the cutting board. Follow the contour of the vegetable with your knife. If you use a peeler on the tougher roots, peel around each vegetable at least three times to ensure all the fibrous skin has been removed.

SAFFRON: The dried stigma from the *Crocus sativus* flower, saffron is the world's most expensive spice. Each crocus produces only 3 stigma, requiring over 75,000 flowers for each pound of saffron. It's used sparingly to add golden yellow color and flavor to a wide variety of Middle Eastern, African and European dishes. Find it in the specialty-herb section of large supermarkets and gourmet-food shops and online at *tienda.com*. Wrapped in foil and placed in an airtight container, it will keep in a cool, dry place for several years.

SALMON: Wild-caught salmon from the Pacific (Alaska and Washington) is considered the best choice for the environment because it is more sustainably fished and has a larger, more stable population. Farmed salmon, including Atlantic, should be avoided, as it endangers the wild salmon population.

SALMON, CANNED: Both wild-caught red salmon, also called sockeye, and pink salmon are available in cans. Red salmon has a richer color and meatier texture, while pink salmon is more pale and tender. Look for "wild Alaskan" on the label.

SALMON, HOW TO SKIN: Place the salmon fillet on a clean cutting board, skin side down. Starting at the tail end, slip the blade of a long, sharp knife between the fish flesh and the skin, holding the skin down firmly with your other hand. Gently push the blade along at a 30° angle, separating the fillet from the skin without cutting through either. (*Photograph: page 295.*)

SCALLOPS, DRY: Be sure to buy "dry" sea scallops. "Wet" scallops, which have been treated with sodium tripolyphosphate (STP), are not only mushy and less flavorful, but will not brown properly. Some scallops have a small white muscle on the side; remove it before cooking (*photograph: page 468*).

SEEDS, HOW TO TOAST: To toast pumpkin seeds (pepitas), poppy seeds, sunflower seeds or sesame seeds, place in a small dry skillet and cook over medium-low heat, stirring constantly, until fragrant and lightly browned, 2 to 4 minutes.

SHAO HSING: Shao Hsing (or Shaoxing) is a seasoned rice wine. It is available at most Asian specialty markets and in the Asian section of some larger supermarkets. If unavailable, dry sherry is the best substitute.

SHERRY: Sherry is a fortified wine originally from southern Spain. Don't use "cooking sherry" sold in many supermarkets—it can be high in sodium. Instead, look for dry sherry with other fortified wines at your wine or liquor store.

SHRIMP: Shrimp is usually sold by the number needed to make one pound. For example, "21-25 count" means there will be 21 to 25 shrimp in a pound. Size names, such as "large" or "extra large," are not standardized, so to get the size you want, order by the count per pound. Both wild-caught and farm-raised shrimp can damage the surrounding ecosystems when not managed properly. Fortunately, it is possible to buy shrimp that have been raised or caught with sound environmental practices. Look for fresh or frozen shrimp certified by an independent agency, such as the Marine Stewardship Council. If you can't find certified shrimp, choose wild-caught shrimp from North America—it's more likely to be sustainably caught.

SHRIMP, DRIED: Dried shrimp are tiny dried crustaceans used in Asian and Latin American cooking. They have a distinctive, pungent, fishy flavor. Look for them at Asian markets or online at *amazon.com*.

SHRIMP, HOW TO PEEL AND DEVEIN: To peel, grasp the legs and hold onto the tail while you twist off the shell. To devein, use a paring knife to make a slit along the length of the shrimp. Remove the dark digestive tract (or "vein") with the knife tip. (*Photographs: page 310.*)

SOLE: The term "sole" is used for many types of flatfish including flounder, sand dab and halibut. Choose sole caught in the Pacific, where these fish have not been overfished and are considered a good alternative to their Atlantic counterparts, according to the Monterey Bay Aquarium Seafood Watch.

SPINACH: Baby spinach is immature or young spinach—it's harvested earlier than large-leaved mature spinach. We like the sturdy texture of mature spinach in cooked dishes and serve tender, mild-flavored baby spinach raw or lightly wilted. Baby and mature spinach can be used interchangeably in many recipes (yields may vary slightly); be sure to remove the tough stems from mature spinach before using.

SPINACH, HOW TO WILT: Rinse thoroughly with cool water. Transfer to a large microwavable bowl. Cover with plastic wrap and poke several holes in it. Microwave on High until wilted, 2 to 3 minutes. Squeeze out excess moisture before using the spinach in a recipe.

SQUASH, BUTTERNUT: For convenience, look for already peeled, seeded and quartered butternut squash in the produce department.

SQUASH, SUMMER, HOW TO SHRED: Cut squash in half lengthwise and scrape out seeds with a spoon. To shred, use the large-holed side of a box grater.

STERILIZE JARS: Steam jars upside down, with their lids alongside, in a closed steamer for 10 minutes. Or place lids and jars in a large pot, add water to cover by 1 inch and boil for 10 minutes.

SUGAR, PALM: Palm sugar, an unrefined sweetener similar in flavor to brown sugar, is used in sweet and savory Asian dishes. Commonly available in podlike cakes, but is also sold in paste form at Asian markets. Store as you would other sugar.

SUGAR, SUPERFINE: Superfine sugar dissolves instantly, preventing a grainy texture in cold desserts and beverages. It is available in the baking section of most supermarkets, but if you can't find it, simply process regular granulated sugar in a food processor or a clean coffee grinder until ground very fine.

SUGAR, TURBINADO: Turbinado sugar is steam-cleaned raw cane sugar. It's coarse-grained and light brown in color, with a slight molasses flavor. Find it in the natural-foods section of large supermarkets or at natural-foods stores.

TAHINI: Tahini is a thick paste of ground sesame seeds. Look for it in large supermarkets in the Middle Eastern section or near other nut butters.

TAMARIND FRUIT: Highly acidic, tart and complex-tasting tamarind fruit is used in southern Indian, African, Caribbean and Mexican cooking. The pulp is extracted and stored in paste form as tamarind concentrate. It is widely available at Indian grocery stores and other ethnic supermarkets. It will keep in a covered container in the refrigerator for up to 1 year. Lime juice is an acceptable substitute.

TILAPIA: U.S. and Central American farm-raised tilapia are both considered good choices for the environment because they are raised in closed farming systems that limit pollution.

TOAST, HOW TO: *See* Nuts, How to Toast; Seeds, How to Toast.

TOMATILLOS: Tomatillos are tart, plum-size fruits that look like small, husk-covered green tomatoes. Find them in the produce section near the tomatoes. Remove outer husks and rinse well before using.

TOMATOES, HOW TO PEEL AND SEED: Bring a large pot of water to a boil. Place a large bowl of ice water next to the stove. Using a sharp paring knife, core the tomatoes and score a small X into the flesh on the bottom. Place the tomatoes in the boiling water, in batches, until the skins are slightly loosened, 30 seconds to 2 minutes. Using a slotted spoon, transfer the tomatoes to the ice water and let sit for 1 minute before removing. Place a sieve over a bowl; working over it, peel the tomatoes using a paring knife, and let the skins fall into the sieve. Halve the tomatoes crosswise and scoop out the seeds with a hooked finger, letting the sieve catch the seeds. Press on the seeds and skins to extract any extra juice. Coarsely chop the peeled tomatoes. (*Photographs: page 252.*)

TOMATOES, ROTEL: We like the flavor of Rotel brand diced tomatoes with green chiles when you're looking for a little kick in your dish. They come in different levels of spiciness.

TORTILLAS, HOW TO WARM TWO WAYS: 1. MICROWAVE: Wrap stacks of up to 12 tortillas in barely damp paper towels; microwave on High for 30 to 45 seconds. Wrap tortillas in a clean towel to keep warm. 2. OVEN: Wrap stacks of 6 tortillas in foil; place in a 375°F oven for 10 to 15 minutes. Wrap tortillas in a clean towel to keep warm.

TUNA, CANNED: Chunk light tuna, which comes from the smaller skipjack or yellowfin, has less mercury than canned white albacore tuna. FDA/EPA advice recommends no more than 6 ounces of albacore a week; up to 12 ounces canned light tuna is considered safe.

TUNA, FRESH OR FROZEN: While the issues around tuna are complex, a good rule of thumb is that most U.S.-caught tuna, including Hawaiian, is considered a good or best choice for the environment because it is more sustainably fished. Look for tuna that was caught with a pole, called "troll," "pole" or "hook & line" caught. If the method of catch is not on the label, ask your fishmonger how it was caught and tell him you want to know in the future. Avoid all bluefin and any species of imported longline tuna. For more information, visit *seafoodwatch.org*.

TURKEY, HOW TO CARVE ROAST: *See page 345.*

VANILLA PASTE: Vanilla paste is made from vanilla beans and vanilla extract; it is used as a convenient replacement for the beans, which dry out as they're stored. One tablespoon of vanilla paste is equivalent to 1 whole vanilla bean. Find it at specialty baking shops or online at *thespicehouse.com*.

VINEGAR, WHITE BALSAMIC: White balsamic vinegar is unaged balsamic vinegar made from Italian white wine grapes and grape musts (unfermented crushed grapes). Its mild flavor and clear color make it ideal for salad dressing.

YOGURT, GREEK: Thick and creamy Greek-style yogurt is made by removing the whey from cultured milk. Because the whey has been removed, you can cook with Greek yogurt without the normal separation that occurs when cooking with regular yogurt. You can strain regular yogurt to make it thick like Greek yogurt. Line a sieve with cheesecloth and set it over a bowl. (*Alternatively, use a coffee filter lined with filter paper.*) Spoon in 1 cup nonfat plain yogurt and let it drain in the refrigerator until reduced to ¾ cup, about 2 hours.

Substitutions & Equivalents

Don't stress if you're cooking a meal and realize you don't have an ingredient you need. Use this chart to make easy swaps for some common ingredients.

DAIRY & EGGS

Buttermilk, nonfat or low-fat, 1 cup	1 cup nonfat (or low-fat) milk plus 1 tablespoon lemon juice (or vinegar) *or* 4 tablespoons buttermilk powder mixed with 1 cup water *or* 1 cup plain yogurt
Cheese, goat	Feta cheese
Cheese, Cheddar	Monterey Jack cheese *or* Colby Jack cheese *or* Colby cheese
Cheese, Parmesan	Romano cheese *or* Asiago cheese *or* Pecorino cheese
Cheese, ricotta, part-skim	Low-fat cottage cheese *or* crumbled tofu [in baked dishes, such as lasagna]
Cottage cheese, low-fat	Part-skim ricotta cheese *or* farmer's cheese
Cream cheese, reduced-fat	Part-skim ricotta (or low-fat cottage cheese) pureed until smooth *or* low-fat Greek yogurt
Cream, half-and-half, ½ cup	½ cup reduced-fat milk plus ¾ teaspoon melted butter *or* ½ cup nonfat (or low-fat) evaporated milk
Cream, heavy, ½ cup	1 teaspoon cornstarch (or all-purpose flour) whisked into ½ cup reduced-fat milk [as a sauce thickener, not as whipped cream]
Cream, sour, reduced-fat	Nonfat sour cream *or* low-fat plain yogurt
Cream, whipped, sweetened	[As a dessert topping: *see* Vanilla Cream, *page 404*]
Eggs	[*See* Baking, *page 492*]
Milk, 1 cup	½ cup evaporated milk plus ½ cup water *or* ¼ cup dry milk powder plus 1 cup water *or* 1 cup soymilk or rice milk or nut milk
Yogurt, low-fat or nonfat	Reduced-fat sour cream *or* nonfat (or low-fat) buttermilk *or* low-fat cottage cheese pureed until smooth

BAKING	
Baking powder, 1 teaspoon	½ teaspoon cream of tartar plus ¼ teaspoon baking soda
Chocolate, bittersweet, 1 ounce	1 ounce unsweetened chocolate plus 2 teaspoons sugar
Chocolate, semisweet, 1 ounce	1 ounce unsweetened chocolate plus 1 tablespoon sugar
Chocolate, unsweetened, 1 ounce	3 tablespoons unsweetened cocoa powder plus 1 tablespoon canola oil (or melted butter)
Cocoa powder, Dutch-processed, 3 tablespoons	3 tablespoons unsweetened cocoa powder plus ⅛ teaspoon baking soda
Cocoa powder, unsweetened, 1 ounce	1 ounce unsweetened chocolate and decrease oil, butter or other fat in the recipe by 1½ teaspoons
Cornstarch, 1 teaspoon (as a thickener)	1 tablespoon all-purpose flour *or* 1½ teaspoons arrowroot
Corn syrup, dark	Light corn syrup
Corn syrup, light, ½ cup	½ cup granulated sugar plus 2 tablespoons water
Eggs, 1 large	2 large egg whites *or* 1½ teaspoons dried egg whites combined with 2 tablespoons water *or* 3 tablespoons liquid egg replacer (or liquid egg whites) *or* ½ mashed banana plus ½ teaspoon baking powder [for baking]
Egg, white, 1 large	2 tablespoons liquid egg whites
Flour, all-purpose (as a thickener), 1 tablespoon	1 teaspoon cornstarch *or* 1½ teaspoons arrowroot
Flour, all-purpose (for baking), 1 cup	½ cup all-purpose flour plus ½ cup whole-wheat *or* ½ cup all-purpose flour plus ½ cup whole-wheat pastry flour *or* 1 cup white whole-wheat flour
Flour, all-purpose (to eliminate gluten), 1 cup	1 cup store-bought gluten-free baking mix *or* 1 cup minus 2 tablespoons rice flour
Flour, bread, 1 cup	1 cup all-purpose flour plus 1 tablespoon wheat gluten
Flour, cake, 1 cup sifted	¾ cup plus 2 tablespoons sifted all-purpose flour
Flour, whole-wheat, white whole-wheat or whole-wheat pastry, 1 cup	1 cup all-purpose flour
Gelatin	1¼-ounce envelope = about 2¼ teaspoons
Sugar, brown, 1 cup	1 cup granulated sugar plus 2 tablespoons molasses
Sugar, granulated, 1 cup	1 cup brown sugar *or* ½-⅔ cup honey* *or* ¾ cup maple syrup* *or* ⅔ cup agave nectar* *or* 1 cup Splenda, granulated *or* 18-24 SteviaPlus Fiber packets
Vanilla bean, 1 whole	2 teaspoons vanilla extract
Yeast, regular or quick/instant active dry	1¼-ounce envelope = about 2¼ teaspoons

Using honey, maple syrup or agave nectar in place of granulated sugar in baking may cause baked goods to brown faster. Oven temperatures may need to be reduced.

HERBS & SPICES	
HERBS	
1 tablespoon fresh chopped herbs	1 teaspoon dried
Basil	Oregano *or* thyme
Chervil	Parsley *or* dill
Chives	Chopped scallion greens
Cilantro	Parsley
Garlic, 1 clove	⅛ teaspoon garlic powder *or* minced dried garlic
Ginger, fresh minced (or grated), 1 tablespoon	⅛ teaspoon ground ginger *or* 1 tablespoon bottled ginger juice
Italian seasoning, 1 tablespoon	½ teaspoon each dried basil, oregano, marjoram, rosemary, sage & thyme
Marjoram	Basil, thyme *or* savory
Oregano	Thyme, basil *or* marjoram
Parsley	Chervil
Poultry seasoning, 1 teaspoon	¼ teaspoon dried thyme plus ¾ teaspoon ground sage
Rosemary	Thyme, tarragon *or* savory
Sage	Savory, marjoram *or* rosemary
Savory	Thyme, marjoram *or* sage
Tarragon	Chervil
Thyme	Basil, marjoram, oregano *or* savory
SPICES	
Allspice, ground, 1 teaspoon	½ teaspoon ground cinnamon plus ¼ teaspoon each ground cloves & nutmeg
Cardamom, ground	Ground ginger *or* cinnamon
Chili powder, ground chipotle, 1 teaspoon	1 teaspoon chili powder plus a pinch of cayenne pepper *or* 1 teaspoon minced canned chipotle in adobo
Cinnamon, ground, 1 teaspoon	¼ teaspoon ground nutmeg *or* allspice
Cloves, ground	Ground allspice, cinnamon *or* nutmeg
Cumin, ground	Chili powder
Curry powder, 1 tablespoon	½ teaspoon each ground cardamom, cayenne, coriander, cumin, ginger & turmeric
Curry powder, Madras, 1 teaspoon	1 teaspoon regular curry powder plus a pinch of cayenne pepper
Five-spice powder, 5 teaspoons	1 teaspoon each ground anise, fennel, cloves, cinnamon & black pepper
Garam masala, 2 tablespoons	Grind in a spice grinder or coffee mill: 1 teaspoon each cardamom seeds, fennel seeds and cumin seeds, 10 whole cloves, ½ each teaspoon black peppercorns and coriander seeds and ¼ teaspoon nutmeg
Mustard, dried, 1 teaspoon	1 tablespoon prepared Dijon mustard
Nutmeg, 1 teaspoon	1 teaspoon ground cinnamon *or* ¼ teaspoon ground ginger
Paprika, smoked, 1 teaspoon	1 teaspoon regular paprika
Pumpkin pie spice, 1 teaspoon	½ teaspoon ground cinnamon, ¼ teaspoon ground ginger, ⅛ teaspoon each ground allspice & nutmeg
Vanilla bean	[*See* Baking, *opposite*]

CONDIMENTS, OILS, VINEGARS & SEASONINGS

Fish sauce, 1 tablespoon	[Also called *nam pla* in Thai and *nuoc mam* in Vietnamese] 1 tablespoon soy sauce plus ½ teaspoon anchovy paste
Hot sauce, 1 teaspoon	½–¾ teaspoon cayenne pepper plus 1 teaspoon vinegar
Ketchup, 1 cup	1 cup tomato sauce plus ½ cup sugar and 2 tablespoons white vinegar
Mayonnaise, low-fat	Reduced-fat sour cream *or* nonfat (or low-fat) plain yogurt
Mustard, prepared, 1 tablespoon	1 tablespoon dry mustard plus 1 teaspoon each vinegar, water and sugar
Oil, canola	Light olive oil
Oil, extra-virgin olive	Canola oil
Oil, sesame, 1 tablespoon	1½ teaspoons sesame seeds sautéed in ½ teaspoon canola oil
Shao Hsing rice wine	Dry sherry
Soy sauce, 2 tablespoons	2 tablespoons tamari *or* 1 tablespoon Worcestershire sauce mixed with ¾ teaspoon water
Vinegar, balsamic	sherry vinegar *or* cider vinegar *or* rice vinegar
Vinegar, red-wine, 4 tablespoons	3 tablespoons cider vinegar plus 1 tablespoon red wine *or* 4 tablespoons white-wine vinegar
Vinegar, sherry	Red-wine vinegar *or* Chinese black vinegar *or* balsamic vinegar
Vinegar, white distilled	Lemon juice *or* apple cider vinegar
Vinegar, white-wine	Lemon juice *or* lime juice *or* red-wine vinegar
Worcestershire sauce	Bottled steak sauce, such as A1 or HP
Zest, citrus, 1 teaspoon	1 teaspoon citrus juice

ALCOHOL-FREE SUBSTITUTIONS FOR ALCOHOL

Beer	Nonalcoholic beer *or* chicken broth *or* apple cider *or* beef broth
Marsala	White grape juice
Port, 1 cup	1 cup Concord grape juice with a pinch of lime zest *or* 1 cup cranberry juice with a dash of lemon juice *or* 1 cup Concord grape juice concentrate
Sherry, 1 cup	1 cup unsweetened apple juice (or orange or pineapple juice) plus 1 teaspoon vanilla extract
Vermouth, dry, 1 cup	1 cup white grape juice *or* ¼ cup white-wine vinegar*
Vermouth, sweet, 1 cup	1 cup apple juice *or* 1 cup white grape juice *or* ¼ cup balsamic vinegar*
Wine, red	Concord grape juice *or* cranberry juice *or* reduced-sodium beef broth
Wine, white	White grape juice *or* apple juice *or* reduced-sodium chicken broth

When substituting with vinegar, if the liquid called for in a recipe is more than ¼ cup, use ¼ cup vinegar and add water, white grape juice or apple juice to get the total amount of liquid specified in the recipe.

Special Indexes

Recipe Index

(Page numbers in italics indicate photographs.)

broccoli
  Best Veggie Burgers, 223
  Broccoli & Tomatoes with Rice Wine-Oyster
    Sauce, 113
  Broccoli-Ricotta Pizza, 227
  Broccoli Salad with Creamy Feta Dressing,
    114, 115
  Broccoli Soup, 52, *52*
  Thai Chicken & Mango Stir-Fry, *322*, 323
  Tofu & Broccoli Stir-Fry, *258*, 259
  Tortellini Primavera, *236*, 237
  Vegetable Satay, 38
broccoli rabe, in Mashed Potatoes & Turnips
  with Greens, 160
Broccoli Rabe with Garlic & Anchovies, *106*,
  115
broth
  Chicken Stock, 338
  Rich Homemade Chicken Broth, 79
  Roasted Vegetable Broth, 78
  Turkey Giblet Stock, 344
Brothy Chinese Noodles, 232, *233*
brownies. *See* cookies and bars; desserts
Brown Rice & Tofu Maki, *272*, 273
Bruschetta, Caramelized Onion & Shrimp, 23
Brussels Sprouts, Shredded, with Bacon &
  Onions, 116
Brussels Sprouts & Chestnuts, Game Hens
  with, 346, *347*
Brussels Sprouts with Hazelnut Brown Butter,
  Roasted, *106*, 116
bulgur, in Apricot-Bulgur Pudding Cake with
  Custard Sauce, 406
Bulgur Pilaf, Fresh Herb & Lemon, *170*, 172
burgers
  Best Veggie Burgers, 223
  "Fajita" Burgers, 222
  Lamb Burgers Topped with Mâche Salad,
    218, *219*
  Spanish Pork Burgers, *216*, 217
  Turkey Burgers with Mango Chutney, 215
  Turkish Lamb Pita Burgers, *220*, 221
Burritos, Shredded Chicken & Pinto Bean,
  340, 341
Butterflied Grilled Chicken with a Chile-Lime
  Rub, *348*, 349
buttermilk
  Apple Cupcakes with Cinnamon-
    Marshmallow Frosting, *414*, 415
  Cardamom-Crumb Coffee Cake, *448*, 464
  Cold Cucumber Soup, 53
  Country Potato Salad, 148, *149*
  Creamy Garlic Dressing, 83
  EatingWell's Died-and-Went-to-Heaven
    Chocolate Cake, 407
  Fried Green Tomato Sandwiches with
    Rémoulade Sauce, 204
  Mashed Potatoes, 150
  Master Quick Bread Recipe, 466
  Panna Cotta with Red Wine-Strawberry
    Compote, 396
  Peach & Tart Cherry Shortcakes, 416
  Picnic Oven-Fried Chicken, *13*, 331
  Poppy Seed Dressing, 83

Ranch Dressing, 83
Raspberry-Swirl Cupcakes, 412, *413*
Real Cornbread, *14*, 190
Spicy Stewed Potatoes & Spinach with
  Buttermilk, *152*, 153
Whole-Grain Waffles with Cherry Sauce,
  448, 460
Butternut Tacos with Green Salsa, Bean &,
  256, 268

C

cabbage
  BBQ Tofu Sandwich, 202, *203*
  Black Bean & Salmon Tostadas, *278*, 280
  Cabbage Slaw, 117
  Coconut-Lime Chicken & Snow Peas, *80*, 99
  "Fajita" Burgers, 222
  Grilled Fish Tacos, 302, *303*
  Shredded Chicken & Pinto Bean Burritos,
    340, 341
  Shrimp Po' Boy, *206*, 207
  Warm Red Cabbage Salad, 117
Caesar Salad Dressing, 260
cakes and cupcakes. *See* desserts
calamari, in Bouillabaisse with Spicy Rouille,
  76, *77*
callaloo, in Quick Pepperpot Soup, 72, *73*
cannellini beans. *See under* beans and legumes
Caper & Parsley seasoned vegetables, 169
Capers, Fish Packets with Potatoes, Lemon &,
  298
Capers, Vermicelli with Tomatoes, Olives &,
  240
Caprese Salad, 86, *87*
Caramelized Onion & Shrimp Bruschetta, 23
Caramelized Onion Lasagna, 255
Cardamom-Crumb Coffee Cake, *448*, 464
carrots
  Carrot & Celery Root Salad with Honey-
    Lemon Dressing, 118, *119*
  Carrot Soup, 52, *52*
  Crunchy Bok Choy Slaw, 112
  Fresh Herb & Lemon Bulgur Pilaf, *170*, 172
  Greek Chicken & Vegetable Ragout, 336,
    337
  Marinated Carrots, 118
  Roasted Squash & Root Vegetables with
    Chermoula, 161
  Roasted Vegetable Broth, 78
  Savory Carrot & Tarragon Tart, 275
  Vietnamese Steak Sandwich, *198*, 214
Casablancaise, Ratatouille à la, 128
cashews. *See under* nuts
catfish. *See under* fish
cauliflower, in Vegetable Satay, 38
Cauliflower Gratin, Skillet, *120*, 121
Cauliflower Soup, Cheddar, *60*, 61
Caviar, New Potatoes with, 25
Celery Root & Parsnip Mash, 144
Celery Root Salad, Carrot &, with Honey-
  Lemon Dressing, 118, *119*
Chard, Chipotle Cheddar, 122
Chard, Garlic Creamed, 122, *123*
chard, in Beets & Greens Salad with Cannellini
  Beans, 111

Cheddar cheese. *See under* cheese
cheese
  Asiago, in Southwest Grilled Chicken Caesar,
    104
  blue cheese
    Blue Cheese Vinaigrette, 83
    Creamy Blue Cheese-Tarragon Dressing,
      100, *101*
    Spring Chicken & Blue Cheese Salad,
      100, *101*
  Cheddar
    Broccoli-Ricotta Pizza, 227
    Cheddar Cauliflower Soup, *60*, 61
    Cheddar-Chive seasoned potatoes, 150
    Cheddar Cornmeal Biscuits with Chives,
      188, 189
    Chicken, Tomato & Jalapeño Pizza, 227,
      227
    Chile con Queso, 34
    Chipotle Cheddar Chard, 122
    Classic Beef Chili, 371
    Macaroni & Cheese, 232
    Savory Carrot & Tarragon Tart, 275
    Shrimp & Cheddar Grits, 299
    Skillet Cauliflower Gratin, *120*, 121
    Southwestern Layered Bean Dip, 32
    Sweet Potato, Red Onion & Fontina Tart
      (option), 276, *277*
  Comte, in Skillet-Seared Tomatoes with
    Melted Gruyère (option), *158*, 159
  Cotija, in Mexican Grilled Corn, *124*, 125
  cottage cheese
    Macaroni & Cheese, 232
    Twice-Baked Goat Cheese Potatoes, 146
  cream cheese (Neufchâtel)
    Marbled Cheesecake Brownies, 444
    Raspberry-Swirl Cupcakes, 412, *413*
  feta
    Bean & Butternut Tacos with Green Salsa,
      256, 268
    Blueberry, Steak & Walnut Salad, 104, *105*
    Broccoli Salad with Creamy Feta
      Dressing, *114*, 115
    Dolmas Wrap, *210*, 211
    Feta & Olive seasoned potatoes, 150
    Greek Salad with Sardines, 96, *97*
    Mint & Feta seasoned grains, 185
    Roasted Garlic Guacamole with Help-
      Yourself Garnishes, *30*, 31
    Spinach-Feta Rolls, 39
  fontina
    Pesto & Spinach Pizza, 227
    Rustic Pesto Tart, 38
    Skillet-Seared Tomatoes with Melted
      Gruyère (option), *158*, 159
    Sweet Potato, Red Onion & Fontina Tart,
      276, *277*
    Tortellini Primavera, *236*, 237
    Turkey Sausage, Fennel & Fontina Pizza,
      227
  goat cheese
    Goat Cheese Sandwiches with Roasted
      Peppers & Onion Jam, 211
    Goat Cheese seasoned potatoes, 150

Creamed Spinach Gratin, 151
Inside-Out Lasagna, *224*, 237
Middle Eastern Lamb Stew, *374*, 375
Pesto & Spinach Pizza, 227
Quick Pepperpot Soup, 72, *73*
Spicy Stewed Potatoes & Spinach with
  Buttermilk, *152*, 153
Spinach-Feta Rolls, 39
Spinach Gnocchi (variation), 248, *249*
Spinach seasoned grains, 185
Spring Green Salad with Rouille Dressing, 85
Warm Dandelion Greens with Roasted
  Garlic Dressing (option), *88*, 89
Spring Chicken & Blue Cheese Salad, 100, *101*
Spring Green Salad with Rouille Dressing, 85
sprouts, in Shrimp Summer Rolls, 40, *41*
squash, summer. *See also* zucchini
  Braised Green Beans & Summer Vegetables,
    130, *131*
  Grilled Salmon & Zucchini with Red Pepper
    Sauce (option), *294*, 295
  Parmesan-Squash Cakes, 164
  Pesto-Topped Grilled Zucchini (option), 164
  Ratatouille à la Casablancaise, 128
  Roasted Vegetable Sandwiches, 208, *209*
  Shrimp & Summer Squash with Saffron
    Rice, 310, *311*
squash, winter
  Bean & Butternut Tacos with Green Salsa,
    256, 268
  Delicata Squash with Orange & Pistachios,
    163
  Holiday Pumpkin Pie, 423
  Pumpkin-Apple Soup, Roasted, 59
  Roasted Acorn Squash with Cider Drizzle,
    162, 163
  Roasted Pumpkin-Apple Soup, 58, *59*
  Roasted Squash & Root Vegetables with
    Chermoula, 161
squid, in Bouillabaisse with Spicy Rouille, 76,
  77
Steak & Potato Kebabs with Creamy Cilantro
  Sauce, 364, *365*
Steak Diane, 350, 353
Stewed Okra & Tomatoes, 138
stews. *See* soups and stews
stock. *See* broth
Stone-Fruit Bars, 447
strawberries
  Grilled Duck with Strawberry-Fig Sauce,
    342, 343
  Instant Frozen Yogurt, 389
  Panna Cotta with Red Wine-Strawberry
    Compote, 396
  Strawberry-Rhubarb Bread Pudding, 397
  Strawberry-Rhubarb Fruit Bars, 447
  Strawberry Rhubarb Pie, *382*, 424
Stuffed Onions, Baked, 139
Stuffing, Sausage, 178
substitutions and equivalents, 491–494
Sugar Snap Pea & Shrimp Curry, *278*, 280
Summer Paella, 313
summer squash. *See* squash, summer; zucchini
Sundaes, Bourbon Street, 388

Sun-Dried Tomato Gnocchi (variation), 248,
  249
sunflower seeds
  Almond-Honey Power Bar, 465
  Apple & Oat Granola, 454
Sunny Citrus Chiffon Cake, 408, *409*
Sweet Pea Mash, 145
sweet potatoes
  Classic Beef Chili, 371
  Curried Sweet Potatoes, 155
  Meringue-Topped Sweet Potato Casserole,
    154
  Quick Pepperpot Soup, 72, *73*
  Roasted Squash & Root Vegetables with
    Chermoula, 161
  Sweet Potato, Corn & Black Bean Hash, 264
  Sweet Potato, Red Onion & Fontina Tart,
    276, *277*
Swiss cheese. *See under* cheese

T

tahini
  Classic Hummus, 27
  Mâche & Chicken Salad with Honey-Tahini
    Dressing, *102*, 103
  Shish Kebab with Tahini Sauce, *366*, 367
Tandoori Tofu, 260, *261*
Tapenade with Crostini, 24
Tapioca Pudding, Maple-Walnut, 398, *399*
Tart, Rustic Pesto, 38
Tart, Savory Carrot & Tarragon, 275
Tart, Sweet Potato, Red Onion & Fontina,
  276, *277*
tarts, dessert. *See* desserts
tatsoi, in Spicy Green Salad with Soy &
  Roasted Garlic Dressing, *14*, 94
Thai Chicken & Mango Stir-Fry, *322*, 323
Thin-Crust Whole-Wheat Pizza Dough, 226
Thumbprint Cookies, Raspberry-Chocolate,
  426, 436
tilapia. *See under* fish
tofu
  BBQ Tofu Sandwich, 202, *203*
  Best Veggie Burgers, 223
  Brown Rice & Tofu Maki, *272*, 273
  Caesar salad dressing, 260
  egg-free tofu mayonnaise, 260
  Tandoori Tofu, 260, *261*
  Tofu & Broccoli Stir-Fry, *258*, 259
  tofu-fruit smoothie, 260
  ways to try, 260
Tomatillo Salsa, 155
tomatillos, in Bean & Butternut Tacos with
  Green Salsa, *256*, 268
tomatoes
  Basque Vegetable Rice, *170*, 179
  Bouillabaisse with Spicy Rouille, 76, *77*
  Braised Fennel with Tomatoes & Potatoes,
    130
  Braised Green Beans & Summer Vegetables,
    130, *131*
  Broccoli & Tomatoes with Rice Wine-Oyster
    Sauce, 113
  Catfish Etouffée, 288, *289*

Chicken, Tomato & Jalapeño Pizza, 227, *227*
Chile con Queso, 34
Classic Beef Chili, 371
Eggplant Pomodoro Pasta, 240
Fresh Tomato & Black Olive Pizza, 227
Fresh Tomato & Shallot seasoned vegetables,
  169
Fresh Tomato Salsa, 35
Fresh Tomato Sauce, 252, *253*
Fried Green Tomato Sandwiches with
  Rémoulade Sauce, 204
Fusilli with Roasted Tomatoes, Asparagus &
  Shrimp, 241
Gnocchi with Tomatoes, Pancetta & Wilted
  Watercress, 238, *239*
Golden Gazpacho, 54, *55*
Green Tomato Chutney, 156
Grilled Garden Pizza, 228, *229*
Grilled Halibut Salad Niçoise, 98
Iberian-Style Sausage & Chicken Ragù,
  246, *247*
Inside-Out Lasagna, *224*, 237
Louisiana Gumbo, 71
Middle Eastern Lamb Stew, *374*, 375
Minestrone with Endive & Pepperoni, 67
Multi-Bean Chili, 269
Mussels with Saffron Cream Sauce, 305
Mussels with Tomatoes & White Wine, 305
Neapolitan Meatballs, *250*, 251
Puerto Rican Fish Stew, *300*, 301
Quick Tomato Soup, 63
Ratatouille à la Casablancaise, 128
Roasted Cod, Tomatoes, Orange & Onions,
  299
Sausage & Vegetable Soup, *50*, 70
Seafood Linguine, *244*, 245
Shredded Chicken & Pinto Bean Burritos,
  340, 341
Skillet-Seared Tomatoes with Melted
  Gruyère, *158*, 159
Southeast Asian-Inspired Salmon Soup, 66
Southwestern Layered Bean Dip, 32, *33*
Spicy Lamb Meatballs in Tomato Sauce, *14*,
  43
Stewed Okra & Tomatoes, 138
Sun-Dried Tomato Gnocchi, 248, *249*
Tomato & Fennel Salad, 156, *157*
Tomato Gratin, 159
Tomato-Herb Marinated Flank Steak, *362*,
  363
Tomato-Jalapeño Bloody Mary, 46
Tomato-Pesto seasoned potatoes, 150
Tomato-Tarragon seasoned grains, 185
Tomato Toast with Sardines & Mint, 20, *21*
Vermicelli with Tomatoes, Olives & Capers,
  240
Tortellini Primavera, *236*, 237
Tortilla Chips, Chile-Lime, 35
Trifle, Roasted Pear, *402*, 403
Trifles, Individual Cherry-Blueberry, *384*, *384*
Tropical Cucumber Salad, 126
trout, smoked. *See under* fish
Truffles, Chocolate-Hazelnut, 443
tuna. *See under* fish

Contributors

Our thanks to these fine food writers whose work was previously published in EATINGWELL Magazine.

BRUCE AIDELLS | Country-Style Chicken Liver Mousse, 45; Guinness-Marinated Bison Steak Sandwiches, 212; Spanish Pork Burgers, 217; Turkish Lamb Pita Burgers, 221; "Fajita" Burgers, 222; Iberian-Style Sausage & Chicken Ragù, 246; Grilled Fish Tacos, 302; Baked Chicken with Onions & Leeks, 331; Butterflied Grilled Chicken with a Chile-Lime Rub, 349; Pork Medallions with Fig & Port Wine Sauce, 356; Cider-Brined Pork Chops, 357; Pork Tenderloin "Rosa di Parma," 380

JOHN ASH | Southeast Asian-Inspired Salmon Soup, 66; Cabbage Slaw, 117; Green Goddess Sauce, 285

NANCY BAGGETT | Minestrone with Endive & Pepperoni, 67; Chicken & Spinach Soup with Fresh Pesto, 69; Grilled Halibut Salad Niçoise, 98; Jeweled Golden Rice, 174; Honey Oat Quick Bread, 186; Crunchy-Munchy Corn & Millet Bread, 191; Parmesan-Herb Focaccia, 192; Black Olive & Herb Yeast Loaves, 195; Dark Cherry Bundt Cake, 411; Dark Fudgy Brownies, 445

MELANIE BARNARD & ELINOR KLIVANS | Sunny Citrus Chiffon Cake, 408

VANESSA BARRINGTON | Bean & Butternut Tacos with Green Salsa, 268

RICK BAYLESS | Roasted Garlic Guacamole with Help-Yourself Garnishes (Guacamole de Ajo Asado con Sabores a Escoger), 31

MARK BITTMAN | Scallop Salad with Mirin-Soy Vinaigrette, 99

MARIALISA CALTA | Tuna-Stuffed Peppers, 27; Broccoli Rabe with Garlic & Anchovies, 115; Red-Wine Risotto, 183

NORA CAREY | Festive Olives, 24

NANCY CAVERLY | Yummy Molasses Crackles, 433

ROXANNE CHAN | Festive Fruit & Nut Balls, 432

LISA CHERKASKY | Rhubarb Fool, 404

YING CHANG COMPESTINE | Scallop & Shrimp Dumplings, 42; Lion's Head Meatballs, 368

NATALIE DANFORD | Korean Chicken Soup, 340

KATHY FARRELL-KINGSLEY | Roasted Pear Trifle, 403

SARAH FRITSCHNER | Soup Beans, 70; Old Corn, 126; Stewed Okra & Tomatoes, 138; Real Cornbread, 190

JOSH GITLIN | Lava Rocks, 434

JOYCE HENDLEY | Green Salad with Asparagus & Peas, 90

SUSAN HERR | Parmesan Skillet Flatbreads, 190; Risotto with Edamame, Arugula & Porcini, 267; Rice & Corn Cakes with Spicy Black Beans, 270

RAGHAVAN IYER | Indian Eggplant-Shallot Stew, 127; Spicy Stewed Potatoes & Spinach with Buttermilk (Aloo chaas), 153

PATSY JAMIESON | Wild Rice with Dried Apricots & Pistachios, 177; Whole-Wheat Couscous with Parmesan & Peas, 177; Neapolitan Meatballs, 251; Picnic Oven-Fried Chicken, 331; Greek Chicken & Vegetable Ragout, 336; Middle Eastern Lamb Stew, 375

CHERYL & BILL JAMISON | Summer Paella, 313

MATTHEW G. KADEY | Salmon & Escarole Packets with Lemon-Tarragon Butter, 296

BARBARA KAFKA | Golden Gazpacho, 54; Cool Fresh Corn Relish, 125; Sugar Snap Pea & Shrimp Curry, 280; Shrimp & Summer Squash with Saffron Rice, 310

KATY KECK | Black-Eyed Pea Spread, 28

BRIDGET KLEIN | Princess Tea Cakes, 441

PEGGY KNICKERBOCKER | Green & Yellow Beans with Wild Mushrooms, 133; Farro with Pistachios & Herbs, 173

DEBORAH MADISON | Mashed Potatoes & Turnips with Greens, 160

PERLA MEYERS | Braised Fennel with Tomatoes & Potatoes, 130; Basque Vegetable Rice, 179; Seared Scallops with Sautéed Cucumbers, 306; Braised Beef & Mushrooms, 376; Ragout of Pork & Prunes, 378

ALYSSA MOREAU | Raspberry-Chocolate Thumbprint Cookies, 436

KITTY MORSE | Ratatouille à la Casablancaise, 128; Roasted Root Vegetables with Chermoula, 161

ELLEN ECKER OGDEN | Garlic-Dijon Vinaigrette, 83; Warm Dandelion Greens with Roasted Garlic Dressing, 89; Spicy Green Salad with Soy & Roasted Garlic Dressing, 94; Smoked Trout Salad with Herb & Horseradish Dressing, 96; Spring Chicken & Blue Cheese Salad, 100; Mâche & Chicken Salad with Honey-Tahini Dressing, 103; Savory Carrot & Tarragon Tart, 275; Chocolate Tart with Hazelnut Shortbread Crust, 421

CHARLES PIERCE | Curried Sweet Potatoes, 155

VICTORIA ABBOTT RICCARDI | Spiced Spanish Almonds, 19; Spicy Lamb Meatballs in Tomato Sauce, 43; Creamy Garlic Dressing, 83; Tomato-Herb Dressing, 83; Warm Green Bean Salad with Toasted Walnuts, 95; Sizzled Green Beans with Crispy Prosciutto & Pine Nuts, 135; Turkish Chicken Thighs, 320; Brazilian Chicken & Peanut Stew, 332

G. FRANCO ROMAGNOLI | Pasta & Chickpea Soup, 63; Baked Stuffed Onions, 139; Penne with Artichoke Hearts (Penne al carciofi), 235; Vermicelli with Tomatoes, Olives & Capers (Vermicelli alla puttanesca), 240

JIM ROMANOFF | Meringue-Topped Sweet Potato Casserole, 154; Roasted Garlic & Meyer Lemon-Rubbed Turkey, 344; Turkey Giblet Stock, 344; Citrus Gravy, 345

SCOTT ROSENBAUM | Puerto Rican Fish Stew (Bacalao), 301

BARTON SEAVER | Tomato Toast with Sardines & Mint, 20

MARIE SIMMONS | Raspberry, Avocado & Mango Salad, 90; Melon Panzanella, 93; Beets & Greens Salad with Cannellini Beans, 111; Skillet-Seared Tomatoes with Melted Gruyère, 159; Fresh Herb & Lemon Bulgur Pilaf, 172; Easy Sautéed Fish Fillets, 284; Roasted Cod, Tomatoes, Orange & Onions, 299; Barbecued Raspberry-Hoisin Chicken, 327; Raspberry-Almond Crumb Tart, 418; Cardamom-Crumb Coffee Cake, 464

MARIA SPECK | Orange Polentina, 452; Mushroom & Wild Rice Frittata, 458; Whole-Grain Waffles with Cherry Sauce, 460; Almond-Honey Power Bar, 465

MOLLY STEVENS | Country Potato Salad, 148; Cheddar Cornmeal Biscuits with Chives, 189

CORINNE TRANG | Grilled Sea Scallops with Cilantro & Black Bean Sauce, 309; Five-Spice Marinade, 352; Grilled Pineapple with Coconut Black Sticky Rice, 401

BRUCE WEINSTEIN & MARK SCARBROUGH | Caramelized Onion & Shrimp Bruschetta, 23; Vegetable Satay, 38; Rustic Pesto Tart, 38; Raspberry Vinaigrette, 83; Spring Green Salad with Rouille Dressing, 85; Celery Root & Parsnip Mash, 144; Grilled Garden Pizza, 228; Eggplant Parmesan Pizza, 231; Brown Rice & Tofu Maki, 273; Mexican-Inspired Mussels, 305; Chicken Breasts with Mushroom Cream Sauce, 318; Barbecue Pulled Chicken, 335; Game Hens with Brussels Sprouts & Chestnuts, 346; Sicilian Granita, 389; Maple-Walnut Tapioca Pudding, 398; Rosemary-Pine Nut Biscotti, 442

VIRGINIA WILLIS | Pork Chops with Peach Barbecue Sauce, 360; Peach & Blueberry Cobbler, 393

JOHN WILLOUGHBY | Tapenade with Crostini, 24

GRACE YOUNG | Broccoli & Tomatoes with Rice Wine-Oyster Sauce, 113

Special Thanks

John Boos & Co., johnboos.com

Vermont Butcher Block & Board Company, vermontbutcherblock.com

Monterey Bay Aquarium Seafood Watch

ADDITIONAL PHOTOGRAPHY:
Jeb Wallace-Brodeur, 11, 256 (bottom left); Foodcollection/Getty Images, 215

ILLUSTRATION: Michael J. Balzano, 185

Acknowledgments

Serendipity brought me to work at EATINGWELL and I've felt lucky ever since. And it's working with the team who put this book together that makes me feel that way. Thank you to all on the EATINGWELL food team who tirelessly cook, taste, edit, write and read to produce recipes that we're proud of, that taste great and really work. Carolyn Malcoun is the master of guides and has an eagle eye for consistency. Just a day after Stacy Fraser's second child was born, she was e-mailing us the "everything you need to know about breadcrumbs" tip. Hilary Meyer's EATINGWELL tips are one of the defining ingredients in the secret sauce that makes this a great book. Carolyn Casner is a ray of sunshine in our Test Kitchen. My sister, Katie Webster, is a true pro, whether developing recipes, styling food or writing the most detailed recipe test reports ever.

This book also reflects the work of all the editors, testers and developers who have worked on EATING WELL recipes in the past. I especially want to thank former EATINGWELL food editors Patsy Jamieson and Jim Romanoff, whom I was lucky enough to work with and who still contribute to EATINGWELL. And of course, thank you to the inspiring recipe developers from around the world whose work appears in this book.

Pretty much everything we produce at EATING WELL would be impossible without Wendy Ruopp. But more importantly, she gets it done with a sense of humor—who else could make rearranging recipes in a chapter so much fun? I hope Alesia Depot can some-day forgive me for all the nutritional analysis (and late nights) she did for this book. This is our best-looking book yet thanks to Amanda Coyle. Really, it's amazing that she can smile and laugh no matter what we throw at her. Thanks to Mike Balzano for overseeing the de-sign, directing photo shoots and saying yes to so many of our whims. We keep upping the number of Ken Burris's mouthwatering photos in each book, and the books keep getting prettier. No coincidence there.

This wouldn't be an EATINGWELL book without some serious nutrition brains at work—thank you to Sylvia Geiger, Brierley Wright and Nicci Micco. Anne Bliss's ability to scrutinize every word and fact is awe-inspiring. Thanks to Jennifer Brown for the thankless job of taskmaster. Lisa Gosselin captains our editorial sailboat, asks the tough questions and always pushes us to be better. Tom Witschi and our whole manage-ment team make this business work, and without that, we'd never get to do what we love. Kermit Hummel, Fred Lee, Lisa Sacks, Tom Haushalter and everyone else at Countryman Press and W.W. Norton have made this an enjoyable and fruitful working relationship. Here's to good luck, hard work and great food. —*Jessie Price*

Other EATINGWELL Books

Available at *eatingwell.com/shop*

EatingWell on a Budget
(The Countryman Press, 2010)
ISBN: 978-0-88150-913-7 (softcover)

EatingWell 500-Calorie Dinners:
Easy, Delicious Recipes & Menus
(The Countryman Press, 2010)
ISBN: 978-0-88150-846-8 (hardcover)

EatingWell in Season: The Farmers' Market Cookbook
(The Countryman Press, 2009)
ISBN: 978-0-88150-856-7 (hardcover)

EatingWell Comfort Foods Made Healthy:
The Classic Makeover Cookbook
(The Countryman Press, 2009)
ISBN: 978-0-88150-829-1 (hardcover)
ISBN: 978-0-88150-887-1 (softcover, 2009)

EatingWell for a Healthy Heart Cookbook:
A Cardiologist's Guide to Adding Years to Your Life
(The Countryman Press, 2008)
ISBN: 978-0-88150-724-9 (hardcover)

The EatingWell Diet: 7 Steps to a Healthy, Trimmer You
150+ Delicious, Healthy Recipes with Proven Results
(The Countryman Press, 2007)
ISBN: 978-0-88150-722-5 (hardcover)
ISBN: 978-0-88150-822-2 (softcover, 2008)

EatingWell Serves Two: 150 Healthy in a Hurry Suppers
(The Countryman Press, 2006)
ISBN: 978-0-88150-723-2 (hardcover)

The EatingWell Healthy in a Hurry Cookbook:
150 Delicious Recipes for Simple, Everyday Suppers
in 45 Minutes or Less
(The Countryman Press, 2006)
ISBN: 978-0-88150-687-7 (hardcover)

The EatingWell Diabetes Cookbook: 275 Delicious
Recipes and 100+ Tips for Simple, Everyday
Carbohydrate Control
(The Countryman Press, 2005)
ISBN: 978-0-88150-633-4 (hardcover)
ISBN: 978-0-88150-778-2 (softcover, 2007)

The Essential EatingWell Cookbook: Good Carbs,
Good Fats, Great Flavors
(The Countryman Press, 2004)
ISBN: 978-0-88150-630-3 (hardcover)
ISBN: 978-0-88150-701-0 (softcover, 2005)